POWER&RESISTANCE

7TH EDITION

SOC 101 Perspectives Canadian Society

5

POWER & RESISTANCE

CRITICAL THINKING ABOUT CANADIAN SOCIAL ISSUES

EDITED BY

JESSICA ANTONY
WAYNE ANTONY
LES SAMUELSON

7TH EDITION

Fernwood Publishing
Halifax & Winnipeg

Copyediting: Jenn Harris
Cover design: Evan Marnoch
Type setting: Jessica Herdman

Printed and bound in Canada

Published by Fernwood Publishing
32 Oceanvista Lane, Black Point, Nova Scotia, B0J 1B0
and 748 Broadway Avenue, Winnipeg, Manitoba, R3G 0X3

fernwoodpublishing.ca

Fernwood Publishing Company Limited gratefully acknowledges the financial support of the Government of Canada, the Canada Council for the Arts, the Manitoba Department of Culture, Heritage and Tourism under the Manitoba Publishers Marketing Assistance Program and the Province of Manitoba, through the Book Publishing Tax Credit, for our publishing program. We are pleased to work in partnership with the Province of Nova Scotia to develop and promote our creative industries for the benefit of all Nova Scotians.

Library and Archives Canada Cataloguing in Publication

Title: Power & resistance : critical thinking about Canadian social issues edited by Jessica Antony, Wayne Antony, Les Samuelson.
Other titles: Power and resistance
Names: Antony, Jessica, editor. | Antony, Wayne Andrew, 1950- editor.
Samuelson, Leslie, 1953-editor.
Description: 7th edition. | Previous editions published under title: Power and resistance.
Fourth edition published under title: Power & resistance.

Includes bibliographical references and index.
Identifiers: Canadiana (print) 20220215146 | Canadiana (ebook) 20220215162
ISBN 9781773635187 (softcover) | ISBN 9781773635392 (PDF)

Subjects: LCSH: Social problems—Canada. | LCSH: Canada—Social conditions.
Classification: LCC HN103.5 .P68 2022 | DDC 305.0971—dc23

CONTENTS

1

SOCIAL PROBLEMS AND SOCIAL POWER
Individual Dysfunction or Social Injustice?

Jessica Antony and Wayne Antony

YOU SHOULD KNOW THIS

- Indigenous resistance against fossil fuel infrastructure projects has stopped or delayed 28 percent of the annual greenhouse gas emissions from the US and Canada.

- Annual greenhouse gas emissions increased by 60 percent between 1990 and 2015, and the richest 10 percent of the global population accounted for 52 percent of those emissions.

- Thirty-six percent of Canada's top-paid CEOs in 2019 ran organizations that received payroll support in 2020 through the Canada Emergency Wage Subsidy.

- In Toronto, 48 percent of the population is white but had only 17 percent of COVID infections; 9 percent of the population is Black and had 21 percent of infections; 3 percent of the population is Latinx and had 10 percent of infections. In Winnipeg, the highest rates of infection were in neighbourhoods with the highest rates of poverty.

- In 2011, annual capital expenditures of First Nations reserves in Canada were estimated to be underfunded by between $169 million and $189 million, leading to a massive infrastructure deficit that is around $8 billion in Manitoba alone.

- Over 500,000 women were victims of sexual assault in Canada between 2011 and 2016, and over 300,000 women were victims of domestic violence during that time.

- By 11:17 a.m. on the first working day of 2019, the average highest-paid CEO was paid as much as the average Canadian worker for the whole year. By lunchtime, the average top-paid CEO was paid $53,482.

- In 2020, 50 percent of families who rented their homes (2.4 million people) were in core housing need — spending more than 30 percent of their income on housing.

- To rent an average-priced two-bedroom apartment — that is, to be adequately housed — a full-time worker would need to make $35.43/hr in Vancouver, $33.70/hr in Toronto, $28.47/hr in Victoria, $26.97/hr in Calgary and $26.08/hr in Ottawa.

- In 2017–18, one in eight households in Canada was food insecure, amounting to 4.4 million people, including more than 1.2 million children. Indigenous (28.2%) and Black (28.9%) households are the most food insecure.

- The average gig worker in Canada is paid $465 for forty-three hours, which is about $10.80/hr. The lowest minimum wage in Canada is $11.81/hr. The average transport/package-delivery gig worker earns $762 per month, a 50 percent decrease since 2012.

Sources: CCPPP 2016; CCPA 2021a, 2021b; CCPA Monitor 2019; Clarke, Mullings and Giwa 2021; Goldtooth and Saldamando 2021; Macdonald 2019; OXFAM International 2020; Tarasuk and Mitchell 2020

WHAT ARE WE TO MAKE OF these things you should know? Pollution of our air, water and soil; poverty that is increasingly widespread and persistent; the epidemic of sexual violence; the housing crisis; the racialized impacts of COVID-19. This book is about exploring the who, what, when, where, how and why of the conflicts, imbalances and oppressions that confront us in Canada.

In a simple but absolutely crucial sense, how we think about social issues depends on how we approach thinking about social life in general. At the risk of oversimplification, we can say that there are two basic approaches to getting below the surface of our social lives. There is what we will call the neoliberal approach — some might see this as a "traditional" or individualist way of looking at social problems — and there is what we will call the critical approach. Many other books on social issues tend to describe three approaches based on traditional divisions in sociology: functionalist,

> How we think about social issues depends on how we approach thinking about social life in general.

interactionist and conflict theories. In Chapter 2, Murray Knuttila describes in more detail some of the sociopolitical theories that make up these two approaches: the traditional includes pluralism and the neoliberal state, while the critical includes neo-Marxism, feminism and corporate colonialism. One way of describing these different ways of understanding social life is to go back to a classic statement on the nature and value of the "sociological imagination" made over sixty years ago. In 1959, US sociologist C. Wright Mills distinguished between "private troubles" and "public issues" as the key way to understanding the sociological imagination. Using the gendered language that was typical in his day, Mills wrote:

> [Private] troubles occur within the character of the individual and within the range of his immediate relations with others; they have to do with his self and with those limited areas of social life of which he is directly and personally aware. [Public] issues have to do with matters that transcend these local environments of the individual and the range of his inner life. They have to do with the organization of many such milieux into the institutions of [a] historical society as a whole, with the ways in which various milieux overlap and interpenetrate to form the larger structure of social and historical life. (Mills 1959: 8)

For some analysts, again at the risk of a little oversimplification, social problems are mainly about private troubles; for others, social problems are the product of public issues.

THE NEOLIBERAL APPROACH: INDIVIDUALS AND FREEDOM

Within the neoliberal approach, society is essentially a bundle of private troubles. In his distinction between troubles and issues, Mills was pointing to a profound bias in North American (actually, specifically US or maybe Anglo-American) thinking: the tendency to see society in individualistic terms. In this individualist way of thinking, the understanding or explanation of how society works really comes down to the choices that individual people make. As human beings, we decide what we will eat, where we will live, what work we will do, how we will treat others, whether or not we

> In this individualist neoliberal way of thinking, the understanding of how society works really comes down to the choices that individual people make.

will go to university or community college, what music we will listen to, who or if we will marry and so on. Almost always, it is assumed, we choose to do what is best for us as individuals. If we need to, we may decide to cooperate with others, like our families or close friends, to achieve some of our goals, but fundamentally and ultimately, we act for ourselves. Even so, these choices are and should be constrained, but only within very wide boundaries. We cannot act in ways that threaten others — their lives, their freedoms or their rights. For instance, we cannot take our neighbour's new car just because driving around in it will make us feel good or because we need a car.

These constraints on individual choice, the traditional approach argues, tend to have two bases: obvious and natural boundaries, and those on which everyone (or at least a majority) agrees. We know, even without there being laws against it, that we cannot take someone else's car just because it may be good for us. We also agree with laws that protect our property, like our cars, and our lives. But according to neoliberals, the legal constraints on freedom must be kept to a bare minimum.

This perspective is also preoccupied with social order and social stability — that is, the social imperative for individuals and the parts of a social system to be working together. The individualists do see that we achieve our goals in the context of others; for example, in the above sense that we all agree on the minimal constraints on our freedom. Achieving this ability to effectively work together — what many neoliberals call "social equilibrium" — comes from a set of beliefs, values and morals that are widely shared and accepted and that hold the system together. In other words, there is an assumption that a consensus exists among the members of society that freedom is paramount, individual merit and responsibility are important and family values, hard work and respecting others' property are what society and life are all about. More than that, neoliberals contend that the social system does generally fit together and function effectively and that it is generally, and must be, in a long-term state of equilibrium. For some (probably most) traditional social analysts, the democratic capitalism that currently dominates and characterizes the societies of the developed industrial world epitomizes just such a free, prosperous and stable social world (see Klein 2007).

Social theorists who call themselves pluralists share this emphasis on freedom (see Chapter 2 for details about pluralism). Pluralists argue that capitalist, liberal democracies are free because there are no groups or individuals that dominate society, at least not for long periods of time or over many sectors of a society. These societies have a free press, and most people have access to the information that they need to know what is going on. Everyone is free to vote and to try to influence social and political processes. For pluralists, elections are the great political equalizer, as one person/one vote makes us all the same. Everyone is free to pursue any form of education and work, and the accompanying lifestyle, they desire. Without these kinds of individual freedoms, society would break down.

Pluralists note that there are powerful people and groups in a society, but that power is always restricted and tempered by the power held by other individuals and groups. As Murray Knuttila (Chapter 2) says, "complex industrial societies are composed of citizens and groups characterized by different religious, class, occupational, ethnic and national backgrounds and interests ... individuals with common characteristics and interests tend to coalesce into groups or organizations to represent their opinions and interests." So many different groups make it at least difficult for one group to exercise power and authority over all of society for long periods of time — for example, the power of corporations is limited by the rights of unions and consumer groups. For pluralists, "no centre of power is dominant or able to consistently get its way, at least over the long term. 'You win some, you lose some' characterizes how different interest groups fare in the political process" (Knuttila, Chapter 2).

In its most radical form, this traditional, individualistic approach can lead to the claim — made by Margaret Thatcher, prime minister of Britain from 1979 to 1990 — that there is no such thing as a society, there are only individuals. Thatcher went on to say that the quality of our lives rests on "how much each of us is prepared to take responsibility for ourselves" (Thatcher 1987: n.p.). This sense of radical individualism underlies the neoliberal revolution, of which Thatcher was the political architect in England (in the US it was Ronald Reagan, who was president from 1980 to 1989). Neoliberalism developed out of the classic liberalism of the late seventeenth and eighteenth centuries, when the ideas of freedom — life, liberty and property — took hold. Developing into a political movement, liberalism was meant to undo the grasp that aristocracy, hereditary privilege and the divine right of kings had over societies, particularly in governing them, especially in Western Europe and the US. For the emerging powerful class of entrepreneurs and businesspeople, hereditary aristocracy (and conservatism) kept them from having much political influence in their society. "By the late eighteenth and early nineteenth centuries the necessary infrastructure was in place ...[so] a new economically dominant class took control of the state, often relegating monarchs to figureheads" (Knuttila, Chapter 2).

Neoliberalism has taken up the essential core of liberalism in its focus on individual freedom, liberty and personal responsibility. This new form of liberalism is used mostly in a political economy sense, proclaiming that the competitive, free market has become the moral and economic guide for everything social. The free market is seen to be "an ethic unto itself, capable of acting as a guide to all human action ... to bring all human action into the domain of the market" (Harvey 2005: 3). In a broad political sense, neoliberalism rests on a holy trinity: eliminating the public sector, liberating corporations from government regulation and bare-bones social spending (Klein 2007). The public sector is held with much suspicion, viewed as inherently inefficient, costly and a waste of taxpayers' money (Knuttila, Chapter 2). Thus, where markets for the things we need to exist are not in place — such as healthcare, social security, water, education and so on — they must be created (Harvey 2005). In strictly economic terms, this means that it is the state's responsibility to ensure the conditions of profitability for private corporations, the economic equivalent of individuals.

In more general social terms, neoliberals see society as made up of freely interacting individuals — the basic unit of society — who are responsible and held accountable for the choices they make (Harvey 2005). What happens to you in your life is the result of choices you make, no one else is responsible or accountable nor obliged to sympathize with your fate in life. If there is even such a thing as the common good, it is produced when these freely interacting individuals are not restricted in the pursuit of their own best interests. For neoliberals, most restrictions on individual freedom, especially in the form of government regulation, are counterproductive to a prosperous and harmonious society.

THE CRITICAL APPROACH:
SOCIAL STRUCTURE, POWER AND SOCIAL JUSTICE

In this book we approach social issues in a different way. We look at society through a critical lens. Keeping in mind Mills' distinction between public issues and private troubles, this approach begins with the observation that to understand our lives we need to examine the institutions — the public issues, the social structure — of our community and society. As Mills (1959) argues, what we experience in our lives is both caused and constrained by the various and specific social settings that we are part of. As such, "to understand the changes of many personal milieux we are required to look beyond them.... To be aware of the idea of social structure and to use it with sensibility is to be capable of tracing [the] linkages among a great variety of milieux. To be able to do that is to possess the sociological imagination." In other words, to fully understand our lives and the society in which we live involves using a structural or institutional — not an individualistic — framework. The inadequacy of an individualistic approach has been made clear by the COVID-19 pandemic. Who has become infected and who has died from the disease has depended on where we live and how easy it has been to stay home (whether sick or not). Equally, how we have coped with COVID-19 and how we will come out of it is based on our connections to others, from the essential workers who've kept our lives going to the vaccination process that rests on taking precautions so that we don't infect others.

This is not to say that as individuals we have no power over the decisions we make in our lives — we do — but that power is constrained and not equally distributed. One way of getting at what this means is to return to the idea of the individual choices that we can and do make. If we think, even for just a minute, about how our choices — clothes, food, jobs, partners, education — play out in everyday life, one of the first things we recognize is that the choices we are presented with are not unlimited. Our choices, for example, are largely influenced by where and when we live, who we are, if we have children, go to school, work part-time or full-time and so forth.

As soon as we give this reality some thought, we will also notice that some people have a wider range of choices than others. For instance, while we do not choose to become ill, the choice to be healthy is not equally distributed. Yet, as Elizabeth McGibbon (Chapter 15) says, "an individualistic, largely apolitical stance about health and illness persists." That is, a neoliberal approach to illness sees it as the consequences of our individual lifestyle choices — whether or not we smoke, if and how we exercise, our eating habits. While these choices do have some bearing on the odds of becoming sick, they are not (easily) available to those who can afford them. As McGibbon demonstrates, "it has been proven time and time again that one of the most accurate predictors of health outcomes is socio-economic status, [access to] food and housing security, the neighbourhoods we live in, our access to health and social care and education, and other forces and systems shaping the conditions of daily life." That is, not everyone is free to make any choice — there are barriers; there are inequalities between individuals.

> If we think about how our choices play out in everyday life, one of the first things we recognize is that some people have a wider range of choices than others.

For critical thinkers, a key feature of our social structure, and the second main component of a critical approach, is social inequality. Inequalities are not just about individual lifestyle choices. It is true that some people may want faster cars, designer clothing, to dine at the most expensive restaurants or to live in luxurious houses while others may not want any of these things. And social structure and inequality do not mean that we do not make choices about our behaviour — we do have what sociologists call "agency" (see Knuttila 2016). The point, however, is that the existence of social inequality means a narrowing of life choices for many people, not just in what they may want but also in what they can do and become. That is, inequality is actually about power differences, not merely lifestyle differences. Or, as Sarah Jaffe puts it in *Work Won't Love You Back,* "the ideals of freedom and choice that neoliberalism claims to embrace, function … as a mechanism for justifying inequality" (2021: 8).

Power resides in social relationships, and it can take many forms. Power can be exercised by virtually anyone, almost anywhere. A CEO tells the executive committee that they must devise plans to increase profits by 20 percent over the next four fiscal quarters. The commissioner of the WNBA fines players for wearing Black Lives Matter

T-shirts on the court. The big kid in Grade 6 forces a smaller kid to give up a place in the cafeteria queue. In other words, there are many possible bases of power, especially when it comes to one individual pitted against another.

But even in these examples, the people acting are not just individuals. That is, power is not randomly distributed; it has a social basis and social patterns. Power, in the social sense, involves the ways in which people in particular social groups can influence, force, coerce and direct people in other social groups to act in certain ways, narrowing their choices in life. These powerful social groups tend to coalesce around race, gender, class and sexuality:

- white people expropriate land from Indigenous people, who are labelled "Indians" by Canadian legislation and then find that they cannot live their lives according to their own views of who they want to be and what kind of direction they want to pursue as individuals, communities and nations (Pamela Palmater, Chapter 3);

- a few large multinational corporations — actually, the capitalists who own them — control how food is produced, how and when it is processed and where it is distributed, and they do so in ways that increase their profits rather than ensuring that everyone has enough to eat (Sarah-Louise Ruder, Dana James, Evan Bowness, Tabitha Robin and Bryan Dale, Chapter 8);

- men use their physical strength and capacity for violence to control women, while the surrounding culture encourages such behaviour and society as a whole overlooks this reality, providing many women with little choice but to cope with the fallout (Elizabeth Sheehy and Lindsey Ostridge, Chapter 11);

- heterosexual people decide that their sexual choices are "normal," thus complicating and denigrating the lives of and experiences of 2SLGBTQ+ people (Chris Campbell, Tracey Peter and Catherine Taylor, Chapter 13).

Power can be enacted through the state or government. For example, James Popham, Anna Johnson and Les Samuelson (Chapter 14) show that what the state legislates as criminal offences in Canada are not always the most harmful or dangerous behaviours. Most of us, at one time or another, will have money unwillingly taken from us by corporations, through everything from misleading advertising to predatory pricing to violations of labour standards regulations. In the eyes of the state, these unethical and harmful corporate acts are far less likely to be seen as needing to be included in the Criminal Code. They are often seen as part of doing business. Or, because corporate decisions are hidden in complex internal structures, the government cannot find the person who acted for a corporation. Thus, it is not surprising that 80 percent of welfare fraud convictions lead to imprisonment while a conviction for tax evasion (which causes far more financial harm to Canadians than so-called welfare cheaters) ends up with a prison sentence in only 4 percent of cases.

Relations of power also occur in other contexts. As Sarah-Louise Ruder, Dana James, Evan Bowness, Tabitha Robin and Bryan Dale demonstrate in Chapter 8, "Food is political. Power permeates the structures that determine how food is 'produced,' who decides what happens to it, who benefits from these decisions and, ultimately, who gets to eat." What we eat, what it will cost and who among us will eat exists, they say, within a "corporate food regime." For Canadians (and most people around the world), food choice is determined by a few very large corporations. Much food is produced by independent farmers in Canada, but they are sorely dependent on the few multinationals who control all the "inputs" — seeds, fertilizers, weed and pest controls — necessary for growing food. A few other companies have significant control over collecting the food grown by farmers and distributing it to food processors. Then a few more corporations have significant control over the consumer market — what will be available, what it will cost, where it can be found — for food that we ultimately eat. So, it is relations of power, not poor food skills or shopping behaviour, that produce the over four million Canadians (Tarasuk and Mitchell 2020) who don't have enough to eat and the actually decreasing level of diversity of food available to us.

The COVID-19 pandemic has also laid bare the power dynamics of our society — it's had a devastating effect on both the health and wealth of some Canadians. A report by CIBC Economics found that in 2020, those hardest hit with job losses were making an hourly wage of $13.91 or less (Bundale 2021). However, the report notes, "not only did high-wage earners not experience job loss, but in fact they have gained almost 350,000 jobs over the past year" (*Advisor's Edge* 2021: n.p.). In addition to increased jobs, Canada's top executives saw a 17 percent increase in their pay. Even those executives whose salaries were cut in 2020 due to the pandemic saw an overall increase in their earnings due to corporate bonuses, which were largely based on redefined performance measures that overlooked the pandemic's effect on business revenue (CCPA 2021b).

Knowing that our society is characterized by inequality and relations of power does not mean that we can be certain of how power will operate. For example, Murray Knuttila (Chapter 2) sets out a critical theory of how the state acts on behalf of the interests of powerful groups (power that relates to class, gender and race). But as Knuttila argues, while we know that such powerful interests dominate society, we cannot specify the actual mechanisms through which power is exercised in specific historical eras. We can say theoretically or abstractly that power does dominate — Knuttila discusses in general the direct and indirect ways in which the powerful influence the state to do what they want it to do. But an understanding of how power actually operates can come only through careful historical research, by uncovering the ways in which the powerful try to protect their interests, sometimes through the state and sometimes not, and the ways in which they are successful or not.

So, as you can see, there are some basic disagreements about the nature of society — how it is organized and how it operates. These disagreements find their way into thinking about social issues and their causes. In general, thinking about social issues involves trying to understand not only what comes to be seen as a social problem but also how to resolve those problems, both of which are connected to what we think causes social problems and how society is organized.

DEFINING OUR CHANGING PROBLEMS

In thinking about social issues, we must first consider what behaviours and conditions are social problems and/or come to be seen as social problems. We won't get into a long discussion of how to define "social problems." Many social problems textbooks do that, but some sociologists claim it has never really been adequately done (Spector and Kitsuse 2017). It is sufficient to say that social problems are behaviours and conditions that both (objectively) harm a large group of people and are behaviours and conditions that have been (subjectively) defined as harmful to a large group of people. Both elements are part of identifying what is a social problem.

Sean Heir (2021) tells us that how social conditions come to be defined as social problems is generally divided between realists and constructionists, which is similar to Augie Fleras's (2005) identification of conditionalists and constructionists (see also Nelson and Fleras 1995). Realists define social problems as conditions that are harmful to a significant segment of the population. Constructionists, on the other hand, define social problems in terms of people's reactions to conditions that are or are perceived as harmful — such circumstances become social problems because people act together to change them. To put it another way, for constructionists, social problems are about "claims making." They are the result of activities by some people "who try to convince [others] about a real or perceived harm to … human well-being" (Heir 2021: 32). Donileen Loseke (1999) says that social problems involve both the actual harm caused by behaviours and conditions as well as what people worry about. In other words, there are both objective (the conditions) and subjective (how things are seen) elements to social problems.

These definitions, which are representative, are useful (see Eitzen, Zinn and Smith 2011 for a recent but similar discussion). But beyond agreement at a very general level that social problems have objective and subjective elements, what we think of as a social problem is not so simple. Our definitions and conceptions of social problems are tied up with how we see society being organized.

THE THINGS THAT HURT US:
THE OBJECTIVE ELEMENT OF SOCIAL PROBLEMS

In 2020, the Office of the Correctional Investigator of Canada reported that almost 30.4 percent of federal prisoners were Indigenous (a historic high). In the Prairie provinces, it was 48 percent, and more than 42 percent of women in federal jails were Indigenous (which is an 83 percent increase since 2003). Indigenous people are less than 5 percent of the population in Canada. The non-Indigenous prison population, on the other hand, decreased by 13.7 percent from 2010 to 2020 (Chapter 3).

Women students reported 179 sexual assaults to their campus authorities in Canada in 2013, a rate that is 21 percent higher than assaults reported in 2012 and 66 percent higher than 2009. Despite this rise in reports of campus sexual assault, only twenty-four of one hundred post-secondary institutions in Canada had, by 2016, adopted a stand-alone policy for sexual violence on campus (Chapter 11).

The global warming limit of 1.5 degrees Celsius by 2050 will very likely be exceeded, which will mean that the Earth band between 20 degrees north and 20 degrees south, where 40 percent of people live, will be uninhabitable (Chapter 10).

In a national survey, over half of 2SLGBTQ+ high school students reported hearing homophobic comments, and over 60 percent were verbally harassed about their sexual orientation every day. As a result, many live with high levels of emotional stress, leading to their isolation and disengagement at school, feeling schools are unsafe places and even contemplating suicide (Chapter 13).

Living in core housing need means that your housing is either in need of repair, overcrowded or unaffordable (that is, it takes up over 30 percent of your income). In Canada, 12 percent of the population is in core housing need. At the same time, over one third of Indigenous peoples living both on and off reserve are in core housing need (Chapter 7).

These facts all indicate serious circumstances that negatively impact the lives of many. There is no doubt that particular social conditions and behaviours that cause suffering to a significant set of people are problems, both for those people and for society. Equally, there is no doubt that such conditions are objectively real. We can observe and articulate those conditions, even though it may be difficult to define just when a social condition becomes a social problem — what level of harm needs to be done and to how many people before it is a social problem? Yet, in many ways, all that this part of the definition tells us is that we can and must articulate who is being harmed and how in order to call something a social problem (see, for example, Heir 2021).

It is important to note that the conditions that can become a social problem are actually the behaviours of some groups of people. They are not abstract circumstances that exist outside of people's behaviours and relationships to one another. This is often obvious: Rates of incarceration are about what is deemed by the criminal justice system to be criminal, who is pursued by law enforcement and who is not. The violence suffered by women is about the behaviour of, mainly, men. Greenhouse gas emissions are about big business and politicians deciding that the economic value of fossil fuel is more important than keeping the temperature of the Earth from rising. Homophobia and transphobia are about heterosexuals and cisgender people in power determining which identities are considered "normal" and which are considered "abnormal." Poverty is about how income and economic resources are distributed through the labour market, which is really businesses and employers deciding who will get paid what for which kind of work.

All too often, though, neoliberal social analyses accept as self-evident the problematic nature of some set of social conditions. In this view, there are behaviours that obviously disrupt the functioning of society as it exists — that is, there are behaviours that clearly cause harm to the lives of real people. For example, we are so often told that violence is a serious problem in our society. Yet, as James Popham, Anna Johnson and Les Samuelson (Chapter 5), and Elizabeth Sheehy and Lindsay Ostridge (Chapter 11), show us, we are much more likely to encounter violence at work or at the hands of people we know intimately (mostly males) than in those "certain parts of the city." This is not to make light of or dismiss so-called stranger violence, for it does occur. In these terms, the nature of the problem of violence is not self-evident, even though violence is harmful.

> Neoliberal social analyses accept as self-evident that there are behaviours that obviously disrupt the functioning of society as it exists.

To take another example, the increasing preponderance of gig work is seen by some as a positive move away from the doldrums of regular employment — for them, it is the future of work. Gig work, it seems, offers flexibility, variety and autonomy, whereas working for the same boss and same organization your entire life fails to do that. Gig work is seen as providing, for example, the flexibility that women, who often have disproportionately more family responsibilities, need. It's seen as an opportunity to make use of an "unused asset," like an Uber driver would make use of their car. But there is little new about gig work — the type of labour gig workers do (cleaning, childcare, delivery) and the casual or on-call nature of that labour has historically been the case under capitalism. Additionally, the fact that gig work is supervised, paid and disciplined through a digital platform means that gig workers are reliant on customer ratings, which can ultimately lower professional standards and deskill their labour. This platform reliance also means that gig workers are more isolated and alienated and can be easily punished or fired because of the lack of employment regulation and unions. As Paul Gray, Stephanie Ross and Larry Savage explain, "By making the employment relationship more impersonal, platforms allow employers to evade responsibility by claiming that the algorithms make managerial decisions" (Chapter 9). Gig work, then, does not offer workers more choice and autonomy, but it is instead an increasingly precarious form of employment that removes even more responsibility for workers from employers, allowing the latter to maximize their bottom line. Very quickly, what was initially called the "sharing economy" has become a "playground of billionaires and exploited workers" and is really just a typical capitalist marketing scheme (Slee 2015: 163). In ways not immediately obvious, some conditions, like gig work, can actually be a social problem.

Thus, we do have to ask about and determine the objective contours of the conditions we call social problems. But when we talk about social conditions, we are actually talking about people's needs. So — to think this through critically and as the above examples illustrate — we also have to ask *whose needs are being met by the existing social setup*. And, on the other side of that coin, we have to ask about *whose needs might be better met by disrupting the functioning of society as it exists*. Taking some social conditions as self-evidently problematic ignores who is raising the question. Some social actors — businesspeople, academics, cishet people, politicians, white people, among others — are positioned so that society functions well for them. As such, they often characterize social conditions from their standpoint and

> We have to ask whose needs are being met by the existing social set-up and whose needs might be better met by disrupting the functioning of society as it exists.

in their interests. This difference of standpoint at times manifests itself in disputes about the facts. For example, there is a long-standing dispute over how many people are poor in Canada, a dispute about how to measure poverty (A.J. Withers, Chapter 7). The Canadian government uses the Market Basket Measure, which is an absolute measure of poverty — that is, it measures whether or not an individual or family make enough income to afford the "cost of a basket of goods and services" that is necessary to meet essential daily needs. If a person doesn't make enough money to afford the basket of goods and services, they are considered poor. If they do, they're not considered poor. But as A.J. Withers explains, "What gets put in the 'basket' is arbitrary and leaving some things out (like childcare) means lots of people aren't considered poor but they would be if those things were in the 'basket.'" Another means of measuring poverty is the Low-Income Measure, which determines whether an individual or family is considered poor based on whether they fall below or above the median income of all Canadians. The LIM thus measures inequality — poverty in relation to others — instead of simply measuring the ability to pay for an arbitrary basket of goods and services. However, by using the MBM, the Canadian government has been able to declare that poverty is declining more steeply than it is (4.4 percent versus 2.1 percent over five years). As Withers puts it, "the fastest and easiest way for a government to reduce poverty is simply to change the definition." So, by this official measurement of it, poverty really isn't a problem, a characterization that is clearly in the interests of some people in our society.

Relatedly, there is also a world food crisis, given the large numbers of starving and hungry people around the world, and its magnitude is not really disputed. Yet this hunger becomes a particular kind of problem depending on how it is discussed and framed and from whose standpoint it is viewed. Sarah-Louise Ruder, Dana James, Evan Bowness, Tabitha Robin and Bryan Dale (Chapter 8) tell us that the Food and Agriculture Organization of the United Nations knows, and tells the world through its reports, that there is actually more than enough food to feed everyone in the world. Yet the food crisis is mostly presented as one in which more food production is necessary. The underlying problem, according to Ruder et al., is that land and food have been transformed into capitalist commodities. Food as a commodity produces dysfunction in the ways it is distributed by a system largely controlled by multi-national agribusiness and governments in Global North countries. So, for example, this system that focuses on producing food for export has meant that 15 percent of all food, and the resources that go into producing it, are wasted. This system is not dysfunctional for agribusiness, as it has made the owners of a few large corporations very wealthy. Framing hunger as a worldwide lack of food, though, serves the needs of these powerful interests rather than the needs of the starving people in the world. Thus, how we think and talk about a particular social condition — how it is framed — is important to defining it as a social problem.

STORIES THAT ARE TOLD:
THE SUBJECTIVE ELEMENT OF SOCIAL PROBLEMS

Framing is about the stories we tell ourselves as societies. Social conditions that are objectively harmful may not be called a social problem and, at times, social problems may not have an objective harm basis (Hier 2021). To demonstrate this complication: there was a lot of awareness of the harm of tobacco before it came to be treated as a social problem; between 1995 and 2014, there were 2,300 traffic deaths, but mass driving has not been called a social problem (Hier 2021); and Mark Hudson (Chapter 10) shows that oil corporations and governments knew long ago that burning fossil fuel causes global warming — some scientists warned of this as early as 1896 (Hier 2021). On the other side of this coin, the fear of razor blades in Halloween apples ran wild for years even though there are no recorded cases of it actually happening (*You're Wrong About* 2018).

So, critical analysts, and some traditional analysts, take a step beyond seeing a social situation as self-evidently, or objectively, a problem. They go on to argue that social conditions can become problems or issues when "some value cherished by publics is felt to be threatened" (Mills 1959: 8). That is, it is not "just the facts" and social harm that cause a social condition to become a social problem. A condition or behaviour can become a social problem if it threatens an important social value or if it is perceived by the public or by a critical mass of people as being such a threat (see Nelson and Fleras 1995; Loseke 1999; Fleras 2005). As already noted, the process from values to problems has been called "claims making" — referring to the ways various groups try to convince others that a social condition is a problem (Hier 2021).

Values are certainly not irrelevant in building an understanding of why some behaviours or conditions are deemed to be social problems. In this regard, both neoliberal and critical social scholars agree that values (and perceptions) are an important part of the social problem process. There is, however, a tendency among neoliberals to define problems as arising from a violation of an assumed value consensus within society. When we conceptualize and study social issues, we must ask and be clear about the cherished values that are being threatened. It is on the issues of what values and whose values that neoliberal and critical scholars part company.

The case of immigration into Canada is very much about values but, as we say, there needs to be clarity on what and whose values. Wendy Chan (Chapter 4) maintains that it is the feelings of insecurity that makes immigration a problem for many Canadians. It is true that immigration has increased in recent decades. Immigrants accounted for half the population growth from 1980 to 2000 and for 80 percent of Canada's population increase in 2017 and 2018. Immigrants are expected to be almost the entire source of population growth by 2030. Yet the people who see immigration as a problem tend to call for strict regulations and law enforcement to deal with the "maladaptation" of immigrants (seeing them as not assimilating enough, taking jobs from Canadians and creating social problems) as well as those they imagine to be criminals and terrorists who enter Canada as refugees. For them, it is not just too many immigrants, but not enough "good" immigrants that threaten the safety, prosperity and harmony of Canada. For example, a 2018 Angus Reid poll found that two thirds of Canadians think there is a crisis of "irregular" and illegitimate refugees coming to Canada. In truth, though, while there were over 54,000 refugee claims in Canada from 2017 to 2020, that amounts to less than 0.3 percent of global refugees. As well, less than 0.5 percent of the refugees coming to Canada have criminal records. But as Chan demonstrates, it is difficult to establish that there is lax enforcement of immigration law or that immigrants are actually an economic drain. Lurking behind the transformation of Canadian immigration law and enforcement and the idea that immigration is a problem is racism. When we drill down into the actual practices of immigration policy and enforcement, the matter of "good" immigrants is not really about skills and adaptation. The new immigrants — who, for the past four decades, have come mainly from China, India, Pakistan, the Philippines and Iran — actually threaten to upset a decades-old policy aimed at "keeping Canada white." Thus, in analyzing social problems we need not only to clearly identify the values that are at risk, but also, more importantly, to ask about *whose* values are at risk.

We also cannot assume that public perceptions are freely formed. Some scholars within the traditional neoliberal framework do suggest that "a problem exists when an influential group defines a social condition as threatening to its values" (Sullivan and Thompson 1988: 3) or when there is a "critical mass" of the general public who see a behaviour or condition as problematic (Fleras 2005: 7). Janet Mosher (2014) refers to the ability of claims makers to convince the rest of us that some condition or group is a problem and to define the problem in ways that suit their interests. She shows us that so-called welfare fraud is treated in public discourse, legislation and enforcement as a crime, while tax evasion (which robs us of much more money) is not treated as a crime and is controlled by much less stringent civil regulation. This has happened, in part, because wealthy tax evaders have convinced government and the public that their behaviour is not really as bad as welfare cheats.

In a different context but illustrating the same process, there is what might be called "oppression framing" regarding Black students do not achieve the same school outcomes as white students. There is, as with many social problems, not much dispute that for Black students proportionately fewer graduate, proportionately fewer go on to post-secondary education, proportionately more are unengaged with school. Typically, this problem is seen as the result of a lack of student aptitude or lack of parental motivation and expectation or a result of living in poverty. But as Robyn Maynard (Chapter 5) demonstrates, Black students are consciously and unconsciously "streamed" into non-post-secondary programs. Black students regularly report that they feel or are made to feel invisible in school, reducing their engagement with education. Moreover, Black students tend be victims of an expectation gap — too many teachers expect that Black students will not and/or do not want to go on to post-secondary education, so they encourage them toward vocational and adult education streams or actively discourage them from post-secondary streams. With lower expectations, other systemic factors come into play: "When they are being streamed into lower-track education programs, Black students are disproportionately assigned to learning platforms that have inadequate resources" (Maynard, Chapter 5). Moreover, school is a dangerous place for many Black students: They experience bullying and harassment in ways never encountered by white students. With the issue framed as one of low motivation in Black students and parents, solutions will be sought in them rather than the systemic racism in education.

The people who have access to the means of public debate and discourse can dominate the public agenda not only by defining what will be seen as social problems but also by framing how certain issues or conditions will be seen as problems. Powerful and socially privileged groups tend to have more access to the means of public discourse. Corporations and the wealthy people who own and control the mass media do not force all of us to think in particular ways, but they have more influence than others regarding what social issues will get into the public domain, and they are more likely than not to frame these issues in ways that support the status quo. A good example

> The people who have access to the means of public debate and discourse can dominate the public agenda not only by defining what will be seen as social problems but also by framing how certain issues or conditions will be seen as problems.

of this is how illness is understood. As Elizabeth McGibbon (Chapter 7) shows us, the main causes of illness are the "social determinants of health" — income, housing, racism, access to good food — rather than lifestyle choices or "genes and germs." When people live in a constant state of stress about affording food and rent, finding a job or being ignored, devalued and dismissed, they have what she calls "oppression stress." Under those conditions, the body's "adrenal system becomes fatigued, which contributes to immunosuppression, diabetes, heart disease and depression." In other words, the body's stress-handling system becomes chronically over-burdened, and "no amount of lifestyle coaching, anti-smoking conversations and comprehensive tips about thrifty shopping will be of any value whatsoever [in the] day-to-day struggle to stay alive." Indigenous peoples in Canada, for example, are much more prone to diabetes, respiratory illness, heart disease, suicide and depression than non-Indigenous Canadians. But the dominant "biomedical gaze" championed by the media, the medical establishment and healthcare corporations frames illness almost exclusively in terms of genetics and lifestyle rather than in the unhealthy (for some) social structure of privilege and power — in this case, racism and colonialism.

Corporations and the wealthy also have privileged access to think tanks and policy networks, which play a role in public discourse (and policy influence). Organizations such as the Canadian Council of Chief Executives and policy research bodies such as the Fraser Institute, the Conference Board of Canada and CD Howe Institute were organized precisely to produce statistics and analyses that shape the social-issues and public-policy agendas in Canada. These organizations have multi-million-dollar budgets financed by donations from corporations and wealthy Canadians (most of whom are also male and white) (Brownlee 2005). For example, statistics show that disabled people have higher rates of poverty than non-disabled people (14 percent versus 10 percent). However, those statistics don't account for the fact that this poverty is largely due to underemployment because most workplaces do not accommodate or prioritize adaptations for disabled employees. As Withers explains in Chapter 7, "The lack of accommodations is not about the shortcomings of individual disabled people to meet societal norms. Rather, it is about social relations being organized to purposefully exclude many disabled people." When organizations and research institutes that have influence over the public discourse around social problems talk about poverty as it relates to disabled people — if they even do — these realities are largely absent from the discussion, and the focus instead is on individual characteristics like job readiness and skills training. Disabled people are made invisible in this context.

For critical analysts, then, the focus is on social power and not merely social values and perceptions. C.W. Mills, so many years ago, highlighted the tendencies in sociology that led to what he terms the "cultural and political abdication" of classical (in our terms, neoliberal) social analysis. He admonished value-oriented theories and analyses (like those of his influential contemporary, Talcott Parsons) that were obsessed with the concept of the normative order, which posited that norms and values are the most important element of social analysis. Such an approach, said Mills, absolves the analyst from any concern with power and political relations, thereby legitimating the existing structures and social arrangements that produce major inequalities in our society. Failing to put "norms and values" into the context of social inequality means that the experiences, values and norms of society's dominant groups are conflated as those of every group in society. The Calgary Stampede, for example, illustrates this process. Kimberly Williams (2021) demonstrates that this annual "celebration," whose mantra is "we're greatest together," is really about justifying the violent, colonial theft of Indigenous land that is the basis of the Alberta-dominant oil industry. It also exemplifies the degraded place of women in Alberta — Calgary is the second worst city in Canada in which to be a woman (McInturff 2016). White wealthy men benefit most from the oil industry, but the Stampede is glorified as benefiting everyone in Alberta — literally connecting oil to and turning elite values into "community spirit" (Williams 2021: 37–38). It turns out that the "we" of the Stampede mantra is a small, privileged group. The problem is that what is good for those in power isn't necessarily good for everyone.

RESOLVING OUR PROBLEMS: CHANGING INDIVIDUALS?

The other key aspect in thinking about social issues is figuring out how to resolve them. We can think and talk about social problems endlessly, but to follow the lead of Karl Marx: "The philosophers have only interpreted the world, in various ways; the point is to change it" (Marx 1888). Proposing solutions to social problems is really extrapolating from what causes them. Even more obvious than the link between our understanding of society and what gets defined as a social problem is the connection between that understanding and the kinds of solutions proposed to resolve social problems.

Given its general social outlook, the traditional neoliberal approach, not surprisingly, tends to see social problems in individual — that is, in pathological — terms. If you see the current society as fundamentally good and sound, then its problems must be due to some "bad apples." In other words, these analyses usually see social problems as emanating from the personal inadequacies of individuals, from their "private troubles." These personal inadequacies are, in turn, often seen as deriving from inappropriate socialization and dysfunctional behaviour choices. For example, the predominant view of violence between men and women is just such an individualistic approach. In this view, women, it is argued, are just as violent as the men with whom they have intimate relationships. The power dynamics present in, for example, cases of domestic violence or rape are left out of the equation, effectively silencing women who are the victims of such sexual and interpersonal vio-

> If you see the current society as fundamentally good and sound, then its problems must be the results of the personal inadequacies of individuals.

lence. If rape and sexual assault are individual problems, then authorities often turn to women to ask what they did wrong or what they failed to do to protect themselves. In fact, the "unfounding rate" — that is, the rate at which police disbelieve complainants — for sexual assault is higher than that of any other crime in Canada (Elizabeth Sheehy and Lindsay Ostridge, Chapter 11). Given this individualistic frame, it is not really surprising, say Elizabeth Sheehy and Lindsay Ostridge, that "men who rape count on the silencing effect of this crime." This silencing effect is aided by the ways in which our knowledge about violence against women at the hands of men is constructed socially. As Sheehy and Ostridge argue, "Police data has been recognized as incomplete both because so few women choose to report to police but also because police recording practices for this category of crime are deeply problematic given the documented biases that infect them." In addition to the inadequacies of police data, crime victimization surveys are also often inaccurate "because they are not specifically tailored to identify for women the range of behaviours that constitute 'sexual assault' in legal terms, nor are the interviewers trained to spend time gaining the confidence of interviewees and responding with empathy." In this way, seeing the solution to sexual assault in the individual behaviours of women (and some men) completely ignores the realities of rape culture and police data inefficiencies, which have a real and harmful effect on the rate of rape and sexual assault.

A focus on individual change can and does take on a broader, more community-oriented approach. It is often argued by neoliberals that whole groups of people need to adjust and change their behaviour to solve social problems. For example, from the time of Confederation, the assimilation of Indigenous peoples has been viewed and enacted as the dominant "solution" to the problems within and of their communities. At the time of the *Indian Act*, the goal of assimilation was blatantly overt, almost taken for granted at the time. "Indian" policy at the time of the Act was designed to "fix" the "Indian problem" by essentially getting rid of Indigenous people as Indigenous. Former deputy superintendent of Indian Affairs Duncan Campbell Scott was very blunt in 1918 when he responded to reports of deaths of children at residential schools: "Indian children … die at a much higher rate [in residential schools] than in their villages. But this alone does not justify a change in the policy of this Department, which is geared towards a final solution of our Indian problem" (Pamela Palmater, Chapter 3; Palmater 2020). The 1969 federal White Paper advocated for the end of special recognition for Indians, of the Department of Indian Affairs and the *Indian Act*. To this day, the Act is still predicated on a "disappearing Indian formula." The Truth and Reconciliation Commission says this assimilative policy is actually "cultural, physical and biological genocide" (Palmater, Chapter 3; Palmater 2020). One specific element of this approach, for example, is to give Indigenous peoples individual rather than band title to treaty and reserve land so it can be bought and sold just like any other piece of property. This is a plan touted often by political scientist Tom Flanagan to end Indigenous poverty. He explains in no uncertain terms the overall objective of the land proposal, like the *Indian Act* and the White Paper before it: "Call it assimilation, call it integration, call it adaptation, call it whatever you want: it has to happen" (Flanagan 2000: 196, cited in Palmater 2017: 67). In other words, if Indigenous peoples became and acted more like non-Indigenous people, their problems (of poverty) would come to an end (see also Vowel 2016).

In recent years, the focus on individualism has taken a new twist, as many within the neoliberal model call for using the competitive market as a model in all our social undertakings. In this view, the market or business way of doing things is seen as the solution for our economic woes and for a host of other social and political problems. Neoliberalism calls for not only deregulating our economy but it also applies business principles to schooling, cultural production, assistance to the destitute, prisons, environmental protection and so on. In a nutshell, the market is seen as being based on and promoting the individual freedom that will pave the way to a prosperous and harmonious society. In healthcare and education, for example, this push has taken the form of privatization — the various ways of shifting authority, ownership, ideology, production and/or delivery of public services from state-controlled to private, market-oriented organizations and frameworks (see Antony et al. 2007; Harvey 2005). While most perceptions of privatization involve selling public resources to for-profit companies, it also occurs when management of public social programs is turned over to corporations or when managers of public institutions, whose goals are far broader than profit making, take up or are forced to take up corporate models as if public services are profit-making businesses.

The privatization of university education in Canada illustrates this form of corporatization (Brownlee 2015). As of 2020, over 50 percent of funding for post-secondary education (PSE) in Canada came from non-government (that is, private) sources (CAUT n.d.). With the switch to a corporate structure, universities are more and more at the whim of their private funders, and this occurs at the cost of academic freedom. In addition, the focus on private funders and their interests has led to a change in curricula and academic programs, and universities are devoting more resources to STEM and business programs while downgrading arts and basic science. Despite the fact that humanities, liberal arts and basic science programs have produced graduates who have succeeded in the Canadian job market, the need to satisfy corporate and private funders has led to this major change in the academic focus of many universities.

Two key examples of the consequences of privatizing PSE are the insolvency crisis at Laurentian University and the CAUT censure of the University of Toronto. Laurentian University became so dependent on tuition fees, especially from foreign students, that it essentially declared bankruptcy in 2021, leading its administration to fire over one hundred faculty and cut sixty-nine programs, mostly in the arts and sciences (CBC News 2021). On April 22, 2021, CAUT voted to censure the University of Toronto after one of its big donors objected to the proposed hiring of an internationally renowned human rights scholar. Dr. Valentina Azarova was the three-person hiring committee's unanimous choice out of 140 applicants (CAUT 2021). Her appointment was overturned by senior U of T administration when the donor objected to her views on Palestine and Israel.

What the reserve land solution and education examples show is that privatization, far from resolving problems of healthcare and education, has all kinds of negative consequences. Put simply, these examples of market-based solutions do not solve our problems because they do not address the abiding inequalities that are at their root.

RESOLVING OUR PROBLEMS: RESISTANCE AND SOCIAL JUSTICE

Seeing social inequality as underlying the problems we face changes the focus of proposed solutions. Social harm, and thus social problems, arise from excesses of private power and are exacerbated when public resources are shifted to the control of elites so that benefits go to the privileged (Barlow 2005). For example, the critical perspective shifts our view and understanding of poverty from looking at what poor people do to seeing wealth as a social problem or, to paraphrase Linda McQuaig and Neil Brooks (2010), "the trouble [is] with billionaires." Seen in this way, the search for solutions takes a different tack: "Critical perspectives ask not only whether individual people have maintained their responsibility to the community, but also whether the community has maintained its responsibility to individuals. The approach does not focus on individual flaws; rather, it questions societal structures ... inequality and disenfranchisement, abuse and victimization, classism, racism, and sexism" (Brooks 2002: 47). The neoliberal approach all too often blames the victim of social problems.

In a sense, for critical observers, social problems are partly the result of choices — the choices of powerful groups in society. As Karl Gardner and Jeffrey Ansloos (Chapter 6) explain, in the case of Indigenous peoples, it is not their failure to assimilate into Canadian society that explains their various dire circumstances, but rather Canada neglecting to live up to its treaty obligations. Through its policies and practices, the Canadian state aimed "to replace Indigenous peoples through a process of elimination or disappearance of Indigenous nations as distinct peoples with distinct relationships and claims to their lands." But settler colonialism — the actions and choices of non-Indigenous settlers — is not historical. As they say, "settler colonialism does not just form Canada's past: it is a living and enduring structure built by settlers to benefit settlers, and it continues to this day." It includes reducing funding for Indigenous education by a third (or more) versus non-Indigenous education, an *Indian Act* that attempted to "thin blood lines" by denying status to Indigenous women who married non-Indigenous men and taking Indigenous children from their communities through residential schools and the Sixties Scoop. There is ongoing colonialism in the child welfare system: Indigenous children, less than 4 percent of the population, make up almost half (up to 90 percent in Manitoba) of the children and youth "in care." In January 2016, the Canadian Human Rights Tribunal ruled that Indigenous children are discriminated against because the federal government has systematically underfunded First Nations child welfare. Yet the Canadian government continues to appeal that decision, leaving those children in need for, now, another five years. For Pamela Palmater (Chapter 3), the issue is not a lack of assimilation into dominant society (the choices and actions of Indigenous peoples) but coercive attempted assimilation (the choices and actions of powerful non-Indigenous people).

> For critical observers, social problems are partly the result of choices – the choices of powerful groups in society.

Thus, for a critical approach to social problems, solutions lie in resistance and social justice action — in working to overturn the basic social inequalities of our unjust social structure. One aspect of being human is "an instinct for freedom ... to control [our] own affairs ... [not] to be pushed around, ordered, oppressed and ... [have] a chance to do things that make sense" (Chomsky 1988: 756). What we also see when we look carefully is that Canadians do act to resist inequality, and we do this in a variety of ways. We do it as individuals and as collectivities; we do it through the state and in non-state organizations. We do not always do it intentionally, and some resistance may be more symbolic than material. But the logic of inequality and oppression forces us to reject and try to change fundamental elements of our society.

> For a critical approach to social problems, solutions lie in resistance and social justice action — in working to overturn the basic social inequalities of our unjust social structure.

Individually, we engage in numerous day-to-day, small activities that are part of the long-term process of changing society. For instance, we buy what we need (as opposed to what we are told we want) from local producers and worker cooperatives; we refuse to be silent when we hear people using racial slurs; and we show our children that men must be involved in caring for them and cleaning our houses. In this vein, Jessica Antony (Chapter 12) shows us, in the context of tattooing, that women, as individuals, do not necessarily consume the commodification agenda of capitalism. It has been profitable for a burgeoning tattooing industry to distance itself from the "deviants" associated with tattoos in the past, thereby stripping permanent body art of any meaning other than as a new form of fashion. What she found in talking to tattooed women is that while many do not see their tattoos as "political" in a very strict sense, neither do they see them as being simply an effort to be seen as trendy. Tattoos have meaning — from spiritual to familial to feminist — because people want and need meaning in what they do. They do resist the tendency in capitalism to make consumption — the market — the only meaningful activity and to promote the idea that everything, including solving social problems, should be about consumption.

We also join with others in resisting inequality and pursuing social justice. The most obvious of these collective actions are the social movements that have already changed our world — the movements we are familiar with, including feminist organizations, labour unions, anti-racist groups, queer rights organizations and environmentalists. The democracy that we probably take for granted did not arrive full blown but rather exists because of the collective action of non-elite Canadians. As Karl Gardner and Jeffrey Ansloos (Chapter 6) explain, Canada was built on a desire to "secure ongoing, uncontested access to Indigenous lands for the purpose of profit ...

[and] erode and depoliticize Indigenous cultures, identities and self-determination." Indigenous peoples have been resisting colonization for generations, both "within and against settler-colonial contexts." And despite the recognition of Indigenous rights by the Canadian state as early as 1950, its relationship with Indigenous peoples remains unchanged. It is through Indigenous efforts like the resistance to the 1969 White Paper or the land defenders at Oka in 1990 or currently at Wet'suwet'en and Fairy Creek that Canada's colonial past — and present — has been undeniably laid bare on a national level with, for example, the 2015 Truth and Reconciliation Commission and the resultant ninety-four Calls to Action. Indigenous resistance and self-determination, then, as Karl and Jeffrey argue, put the onus on settlers to repair their relationship with Indigenous peoples but are also clear examples of collective action against oppression and inequality.

Despite the demands and desires of some neoliberals that government disappear from the social scene, it is clear that we cannot, at this point, live in a society without some form of state. It is through the state, albeit a more participatory and fully democratic one, that we can make the kinds of collective decisions we must make if we are to live together and realize our collective responsibility to each other. Government is a key part of our social lives. Thus, it is no surprise that collective resistance can and does also take place through the state. Christopher Campbell, Tracey Peter and Catherine Taylor (Chapter 13) discuss some of the ways that homophobia and transphobia can be overturned in schools and in society generally. While they recognize the limits of a declaration like the *Charter of Rights and Freedoms* in producing a discrimination-free society, for example, and do see the important place of Gender and Sexuality Alliances for creating safe spaces for 2SLGBTQ+ students, they are optimistic that lobbying governments can result in positive social change. They tell us that schools have become safer for 2SLGBTQ+ students where boards have mandated a "whole-system approach" to include gender and sexual minority content in policies, programs and curricula.

Still, collective action against inequality does not necessarily take place through the state, nor does it have to. At the very least, given the scale of state activities, these institutions can be insensitive to the needs of some people and, in some cases, oppressive. A.J. Withers (Chapter 7) shows that while many of the programs to reduce poverty in Canada came about because of poor people's organizing and resistance, they have been designed in ways that continue to exert control over people living in poverty. Social assistance, for example, serves two purposes: to provide income supports to those living below a certain income level and to regulate the people who receive such assistance. Doing this, the state shows it is "responsive" to the needs of poor people, thus discouraging them from forming unions, as well as attempting to "instill a work ethic unto the poor," given that these income supports are usually insufficient to live on. As Withers explains, "policies like these are designed to push workers into menial, potentially dangerous, work at the first opportunity." It is through a combination of direct action, on-the-ground resistance and mass mobilizing that poor people have made change. For example, the Ontario Coalition Against Poverty works toward short-term and long-term change goals simultaneously. On one hand, they inform people living on assistance of additional supports for food that are available to them (the information about which is kept quiet by the government), connect them with necessary healthcare and advocate for them in their dealings with bureaucracy. And on the other hand, through mass organizing actions they have also been able to win social assistance increases in the province. As Withers says, "winning incremental victories can help reduce the harms of poverty and grow the movement against it."

Agroecology, one of the key paths forward to food security and justice, recognizes the need for state action. As Sarah Ruder et al. (Chapter 8) point out, a just transition to an agriculture that is healthy and socially equitable will require governments to not subsidize corporate agriculture (as they do now to a considerable extent). Governments will have to provide incentives to use ecological farming methods, support research into ongoing organic and ecologically sound farming practices and set up credit-lending programs so farms can transition to agroecology. They also point out that while "small-scale family farmers ... have been leading the fight for food sovereignty [and agroecology] for over twenty-five years," this has occurred, more importantly, through "horizontal knowledge-sharing and decision-making practices, [as] agroecology empowers people to articulate and resolve problems." This means that an ecological and healthy food system has to be decentralized; food production and distribution in agroecology are and will be relocalized. Some examples are "community supported agriculture (CSA) programs that allow people to buy food directly from farmers, the re-establishment of small-scale abattoirs and food processing facilities, and the expansion of community-run cooperatives in food marketing and distribution." It is these ways that change happens by small groups of people acting in ways that challenge current food regime inequalities.

POWER AND RESISTANCE

At their core, social problems are about inequality — they are about power and resistance. The chapters in this book emphasize that — depending on class, race, gender and sexual orientation — people face inequalities of treatment and life chances. Emphasizing power means first recognizing that some groups have privileged access to the resources that make life viable in our society. More importantly, a critical emphasis means revealing how those groups act to maintain and enhance their privilege, thereby creating problems for other groups of people. These inequalities — inherent in an unjust social structure — are the social problems in and of Canadian society. Our focus is not just on documenting existing conditions but also on ways of generating emancipatory resistance and socially just change.

DISCUSSION QUESTIONS

1. Take an issue in the neighbourhood or city you live in or the university you go to. What are the "facts" about it? Where do you get information about those facts? Who provides that information? Is there a debate about the facts? What individuals, groups and organizations represent the various elements of the issue and its debate? What resources do they have to make their case known to other people and groups and/or to government?
2. Does a focus on structure and inequality mean that individuals bear no responsibility for social problems and their solutions? Give examples.
3. Consider the issues of youth gangs, online bullying and equal pay for equal work. How is each issue a private trouble and a public issue?
4. For the issue you thought about in Question 1, think about possible solutions. What government policies are involved? What changes might help? What community organizations and resources are there to help resolve the issue? What new community resources could be developed?

GLOSSARY OF KEY TERMS

Agency: The ability of individuals to make choices in their behaviour and about their lives. Social inequality means that some people have a wider band of choices in their lives.

Claims making: Efforts by various groups to convince others in a community or society that a certain set of social conditions is a problem for everyone; that those conditions are a social problem.

Inequality: The more or less narrow life choices and life chances for individuals and groups of people. Inequality refers not just to what people have; it is not only differences in lifestyle, but also what they can do and what they can become.

Neoliberal(ism): A theory and ideology about political economy that claims human well-being is maximized by liberating individual entrepreneurs within social and political institutions that enhance property rights and the free market. Public goods and community should be replaced with private property and individual responsibility. Where there are not markets, such as in education, healthcare and social security, they must be created.

Objective element of social problems (realism): The basis in reality for whether a social condition or behaviour pattern is a problem or not. This basis involves identifying who is harmed and who benefits, and in what ways, from a social condition or behaviour pattern.

Power: The ability to set limits on the behavioural choices for ourselves and for others. Power is clearly in play when individuals and groups act in ways that achieve their desires, needs and interests against those of others. Power has many bases and faces, from the schoolyard bully to influence over public discourse.

Private troubles: Occur within the character of the individual and within the range of immediate relations with others; they have to do with the self and with those limited areas of social life of which we are directly and personally aware.

Public issues: Matters that transcend the local environments of the individual and the range of inner life. They have to do with the organization of many such milieux into the institutions of a historical society, with the ways in which various milieux overlap and interpenetrate to form the larger structure of social and historical life.

Resistance: Acting to change the basic social inequalities of society. Resistance can be an individual act and can occur in collectivities; it happens through the state and in non-state organizations. It is not always intentional, and some resistance is more symbolic than material. But the logic of inequality forces us to reject and try to change fundamental elements of our society.

Social equilibrium: A traditional, neoliberal sociological concept referring to the claim that, in the long run, the social system does generally fit together and function effectively. Moreover, traditional social analysts see social equilibrium emanating from a set of beliefs, values and morals that are widely shared and accepted, so that they hold the system together.

Social justice: An ideology and activist goal focused on realizing equality in society. Rather than an "equality of sameness" (treating un-alikes as if they were alike) the focus is on achieving an "equality of difference" to ensure that all social groups have access to social, political and economic resources in society and that there are no constraints on life choices based on social group differences.

Structure: Social and political structures are the patterns of behavioural relationships between groups of people in society. They include how men and women, racialized people, young and old, wealthy and poor, governments and citizens relate to one another.

Subjective element of social problems (constructionism): In regard to social issues, this is often called public perception. What people perceive as real will guide their actions and their understanding of society. This refers to the process through which a social condition or pattern of behaviour comes to be called a social problem because of what people think are the consequences of it — who is harmed and who benefits.

RESOURCES FOR ACTIVISTS

Websites

Briarpatch: briarpatchmagazine.com
Canadian Centre for Policy Alternatives: policyalternatives.ca
Democracy Now!: democracynow.org
Herizons: herizons.ca
Rabble: rabble.ca
This Magazine: this.org

Social Media

@decolonizemyself
@smogelgem
@westsuweten_checkpoint
@oncanadaproject
@blmcanada
@theindigenousfoundation

Podcasts

Canadaland
Sandy and Nora
Maintenance Phase
White Hot Hate
Finding Cleo
The White Saviors
Telling Our Twisted Histories

REFERENCES

Advisor's Edge. 2021. "Income Gap Widening Dramatically: Report." *Advisor's Edge*, January 19. <advisor.ca/news/economic/income-gap-widening-dramatically-cibc-report/>.

Antony, W., E. Black, S. Frankel et al. 2007. *The State of Public Services in Manitoba*. Winnipeg: Canadian Centre for Policy Alternatives–Manitoba.

Barlow, M. 2005. *Too Close for Comfort: Canada's Future Within Fortress North America*. Toronto: McClelland and Stewart.

Brooks, C. 2002. "New Directions in Critical Criminology." In B. Schissel and C. Brooks (eds.), *Marginality and Condemnation: An Introduction to Critical Criminology*. Winnipeg and Black Point, NS: Fernwood Publishing.

Brownlee, J. 2015. *Academia, Inc.: How Corporatization Is Transforming Canadian Universities*. Winnipeg and Black Point, NS: Fernwood Publishing.

___. 2005. *Ruling Canada: Corporate Cohesion and Democracy*. Winnipeg and Black Point, NS: Fernwood Publishing.

Bundale, B. 2021. "All the Jobs Lost in 2020 Among Workers with Wages Below Canadian Average: Report." CTV News, February 20. <ctvnews.ca/business/all-the-jobs-lost-in-2020-among-workers-with-wages-below-canadian-average-report-1.5317194>.

CAUT (Canadian Association of University Teachers). n.d. "Canada and the Provinces." In Almanac of Post-Secondary Education. <caut.ca/resources/almanac/2-canada-provinces>.

___. 2021. "University of Toronto Under Censure." <caut.ca/bulletin/2021/05/university-toronto-under-censure>.

CBC News. 2021. "Laurentian University Students and Graduates, Politicians Condemn 'Devastating' Cuts." April 14. <cbc.ca/news/canada/sudbury/laurentian-university-reaction-april-14-1.5985632>.

CCPA (Canadian Centre for Policy Alternatives). 2021a. "Corporate Executive Pay Rose an Average of $171K in 2020 Despite Pandemic: Report." Ottawa: CCPA, August 18. <policyalternatives.ca/newsroom/news-releases/corporate-executive-pay-rose-average-171k-2020-despite-pandemic-report>.

___. 2021b. "Heading into the Pandemic, Canada's Highest Paid CEOs Made 202 Times More Than Average Worker Pay in 2019." Ottawa: CCPA, January 4. <policyalternatives.ca/newsroom/news-releases/heading-pandemic-canada%E2%80%99s-highest-paid-ceos-made-202-times-more-average>.

CCPA *Monitor*. 2019. "Index." Ottawa: CCPA.

CCPPP (Canadian Council on Private-Public Partnerships). 2016. "P3's: Bridging the First Nations Infrastructure Gap." Toronto: CCPPP. <pppcouncil.ca/web/pdf/first_nations_p3_report.pdf>.

Chomsky, N. 1988. *Language and Politics*. Montreal: Black Rose Books.

Clarke, J., D. Mullings and S. Giwa. 2021. "Black Lives Under Lockdown: COVID-19 and Racial Injustice Converge." In *Africentric Social Work*, edited by D.V. Mullings et al. Winnipeg and Black Point, NS: Fernwood Publishing.

Eitzen, D.S., M. Zinn and K. Smith. 2011. *Social Problems*, 12th edition. New York: Pearson.

Fleras, A. 2005. *Social Problems in Canada: Conditions, Constructions and Challenges*. Toronto: Pearson Education.

Goldtooth, D., and A. Saldamando. 2021. *Indigenous Resistance Against Carbon*. Washington, DC: Oil Change International. <ienearth.org/indigenous-resistance-against-carbon/>.

Harvey, D. 2005. *A Brief History of Neoliberalism*. Oxford: Oxford University Press.

Hier, S. 2021. "Beyond Harm: Conditions, Claims and Social Problems Frames." In C. Brooks, J. Popham and M. Daschuk (eds.), *Critical Perspectives on Social Control*. Winnipeg and Black Point, NS: Fernwood Publishing.

Jaffe, Sarah. 2021. *Work Won't Love You Back: How Devotion to Our Jobs Keeps Us Exploited, Exhausted and Alone*. New York: Bold Type Books.

Klein, N. 2007. *The Shock Doctrine: The Rise of Disaster Capitalism*. Toronto: Knopf Canada

Knuttila, M. 2016. *Paying for Masculinity: Men, Boys and the Patriarchal Dividend.* Winnipeg and Black Point, NS: Fernwood Publishing.

Loseke, D. 1999. *Thinking About Social Problems.* New York: Aldine de Gruyter.

Macdonald, D. 2019. *Unaccommodating: Rental Housing Wage in Canada.* Ottawa: CCPA. <policyalternatives.ca/unaccommodating>.

Marx, K. 1888. "Theses on Feuerbach." <marxists.org/archive/marx/works/1845/theses/theses.pdf>.

McInturff, K. 2016. "The Best and Worst Places to be a Woman in Canada 2016: The Gender Gap in Canada's 25 Biggest Cities." Ottawa: CCPA. <policyalternatives.ca/sites/default/files/uploads/publications/National%20Office/2016/10/Best_and_Worst_Places_to_Be_a_Woman2016.pdf>.

McQuaig, L., and N. Brooks. 2010. *The Trouble with Billionaires: How the Super-Rich Hijacked the World and How We Can Take It Back.* Toronto: Penguin Canada.

Mills, C. Wright. 1959. *The Sociological Imagination.* New York: Oxford University Press.

Mosher, J. 2014. "Welfare Fraudsters and Tax Evaders: The State's Selective Invocation of Criminality." In C. Brooks and B. Schissel (eds.), *Marginality and Condemnation,* 3rd edition. Winnipeg and Black Point, NS: Fernwood Publishing.

Nelson, E., and A. Fleras. 1995. *Canadian Social Problems.* Englewood Cliffs, NJ: Prentice Hall.

OXFAM International. 2020. "Carbon Emissions of Richest 1 Percent More than Double the Emissions of the Poorest Half of Humanity." September 21. <oxfam.org/en/press-releases/carbon-emissions-richest-1-percent-more-double-emissions-poorest-half-humanity>.

Palmater, Pamela. 2020. *Warrior Life: Indigenous Resistance and Resurgence.* Winnipeg and Black Point, NS: Fernwood Publishing.

____. 2017. "Death by Poverty: The Lethal Consequences of Colonialism." In W. Antony, J. Antony and L. Samuelson (eds.), *Power and Resistance: Critical Thinking About Canadian Social Issues,* 6th edition. Winnipeg and Black Point, NS: Fernwood Publishing.

Slee, T. 2015. *What's Yours Is Mine: Against the Sharing Economy.* Toronto: Between the Lines.

Spector, M., and R. Kitsuse. 2017. *Constructing Social Problems.* New York: Routledge.

Sullivan, T., and K. Thompson. 1988. *Introduction to Social Problems.* New York: Macmillan.

Tarasuk, V., and A. Mitchell. 2020. *Household Food Insecurity in Canada, 2017–18.* Toronto: PROOF (Research to Identify Policy Options to Reduce Food Insecurity). <proof.utoronto.ca/>.

Thatcher, M., with Douglas Keay. 1987. "Interview for *Women's Own.*" <margaretthatcher.org/document/106689>.

Vowel, C. 2016. *Indigenous Writes: A Guide to First Nations and Métis and Inuit Issues in Canada.* Winnipeg: Highwater Press.

Williams, K. 2021. *Stampede: Misogyny, White Supremacy, and Settler Colonialism.* Winnipeg and Black Point, NS: Fernwood Publishing.

Winseck, D. 2016. "Modular Media." CCPA *Monitor* July.

You're Wrong About (podcast). 2018. "Urban Legends Spectacular." October 24. <podtail.com/en/podcast/you-re-wrong-about/urban-legends-spectacular/>.

2

MECHANISMS OF POWER
Class and the State

Murray Knuttila

YOU SHOULD KNOW THIS

- Canada is a federation, meaning political power is divided among and between a federal, or national, legislature located in Ottawa and provincial or territorial legislatures located in provincial and territorial capitals. In addition, there are smaller local or regional city, town and other municipal councils and assemblies.

- While the distribution of political powers was originally specified in the 1867 *British North America Act* and the 1982 *Constitution Act*, there have been constant debates and shifts involving different political ideologies and positions about their precise distribution between the various levels.

- Democracy did not come easily to all Canadians. In 1916, Saskatchewan, Manitoba and Alberta granted women the right to vote, but it was not until 1920 that women could vote in federal elections. Indigenous persons could not vote until 1960. People in jail could not vote until the Supreme Court ruled in 2002 that preventing them from voting was unconstitutional.

- Pharmaceutical and health product companies in the United States spent 4.7 billion (US) on lobbying US governments between 1999 and 2018.

- Canada's one hundred highest paid CEOs made 227 times more than the average worker made in 2018, surpassing all previous records … that's up from 197 times average worker pay in 2017.

Sources: Wouters 2020; MacDonald 2020.

THIS CHAPTER HAS TWO ESSENTIAL OBJECTIVES: (1) to encourage you to think systematically and theoretically about the about the importance of the state and political power in your society and life; (2) to provide a theory or theoretical perspective to assist in your understanding of the state and its actions particularly as they relate to social problems.

What is the state? The state (also referred to as the polity) is the social institution primarily concerned with the organization of political power, ensuring social order and making decisions ostensibly in the interests of all members of a society. The state is often confused and conflated with the government; however, there is a subtle distinction. *State* refers to the overall institutional and organizational apparatus through which political power is exercised, and decisions impacting society are made on behalf the population of a defined territory. Western liberal democracies are characterized by a variety of different state forms, including republican, parliamentary, parliamentary monarchies and so on. Whatever their form, liberal democracies are typically composed of legislatures or assemblies, cabinets, executive branches, bureaucratic and regulatory organizations, a judiciary and systems of law and regulatory enforcement. The nature and operation of the formal decision-making apparatus of states are typically articulated in a formal constitution. *Government*, on the other hand, refers to a particular assemblage of people who are formally in control of the apparatus of the state for a limited period of time and are subject to renewal or replacement through periodic elections.

Regarding the second objective, theory is often misunderstood as something abstract and difficult or, worse, as dry and irrelevant. Fear not, though: a theory is simply a set of ideas, concepts and propositions that purports to explain some phenomenon. Social or political theories are sets of ideas, propositions, definitions and concepts that attempt to explain phenomenon relating to dynamics and processes of human society, such as social inequality, sexual and gender oppression or how the state works. Various theories have been developed in order to understand how the state operates in liberal capitalist societies and how political decisions are made, by whom and why.

THE STATE AND POLITICAL POWER IN OUR DAILY LIVES

Whether or not we realize it, the policies, actions, programs, regulations and sometimes inaction of the state matter to every day of our lives. Since the British Parliament created Canada through the *British North America Act* in 1867, the Canadian state has passed and implemented innumerable legislative acts, laws, orders-in-council, and regulations. Many chapters of this book address issues that are impacted by the policies and actions of states at some level, be that federal, provincial or local. In North

America, colonial and national states have impacted the lives of Indigenous people from the moment of contact through military conquest, the imposition of alien sovereigns (such as the Hudson's Bay Company), the theft and appropriation of land by treaty and the formal imposition of legislative genocide and colonialism through the *Indian Act* and the residential school system. Non-Indigenous Canadians have been impacted by centuries of immigration laws that sometimes openly invited people to come to New France, British North America and then Canada, while at other times laws and regulations restricted entry, often discriminating on the basis of nationality, ethnicity, religion and class. Canada has a complex system of criminal and civil law that structures and influences many of our daily actions and interactions, such as driving our cars, using cannabis or even going fishing. States and governments make decisions regarding the availability of social, economic and other forms of support for those rendered redundant by the inherent inequalities of the market system or who are subject to economic exclusion by sexism, racism, ageism and other forms of oppression. State and government policies are fundamental in determining the nature and quality of healthcare, how we address climate change, sexual assault, human rights or food availability and safety.

Historical Note on the Context of the Canadian State

For millennia philosophers, theologians, intellectuals, elders and scholars have pontificated, debated and theorized about the nature of political power, who should hold it, the role of force, how to achieve the consent of the governed and so on. The type of state found in Canada, a liberal democracy, emerged from centuries of conflict and war among barons, nobles and lords in England that eventually produced a formally organized national state. As Western European capitalism emerged in the late 1500s and 1600s, all major social institutions, including the state, underwent revolutionary changes. As Karl Polanyi demonstrated in *The Great Transformation,* an active state was necessary for the emergence of capitalism by establishing preconditions like uniform currency, standardized weights and measures, legal codes, enforceable contracts, and permanent police and military forces. By the late eighteenth and early nineteenth centuries, the necessary infrastructure was in place, allowing industrial capitalism to bloom. The activist state of the 1500s and 1600s was no longer required, as a new economically dominant class took control of it, often relegating monarchs to figureheads. The new dominance of a laissez-faire ideology significantly limited the role of the state, particularly when it came to economic regulation.

While we use the language of "liberal democratic" to describe the states that emerged in the eighteenth and nineteenth century in England and Canada, these states were liberal first (fostering and protecting the core economic and property institutions of a capitalist market-based society) but only later democratic. As capitalist societies with inherent class inequalities, neither the United States nor Canada were ever egalitarian societies; however, as their economies developed, the inherent structural inequalities increased. In the period between the end of American Civil War and the early 1900s, the concentration and centralization of economic power resulted in ever larger but fewer corporations controlling major sectors of the economy. At the same time, the size of the wage-earning working class increased. In Britain, the US and Canada, the economically dominant class who controlled the state was literally forced — by protests and social activism among the working classes and, later, by the organized efforts of women — to gradually extend the right to vote. The transition to a liberal democratic state was anything but smooth and automatic.

The emergence of capitalism in England and Western Europe between the sixteenth and eighteenth centuries marked a momentous moment in human history — the advent of the first truly global economic and political system. Within a relatively short period of time, virtually every part of the globe was impacted by colonialism as Western Europeans extracted wealth from around the world through conquest, plunder, trade, raw material extraction and the systematically unequal exchange of commodities. The British invaded, acquired, and assumed control of geographic regions, nations and peoples across the globe, making the British state, virtually from its inception, a colonial state. As capitalism developed, the forms of British domination and control also evolved. In some cases this involved maintaining direct colonial control, while in other circumstances the creation of nominally independent nation-states facilitated the protection and enhancement of British interests while ensuring political stability by allowing some emerging local interests to flourish. Such was the Canadian case.

Canada was created by the British Parliament in 1867 through the *British North America Act*. Canada's colonial status was enshrined in the first paragraph of the BNA *Act*, which states that four provinces will be "federally united into One Dominion under the Crown of the United Kingdom of Great Britain and Ireland, with a Constitution similar in Principle to that of the United Kingdom" (Government of Canada, Department of Justice). Furthermore, measures such as the *Colonial Laws Validity Act* (1865) specified that no colonial law passed in Canada could conflict with imperial statutes. This Act was in place until the *Statute of Westminster* was passed in 1931 (*Canadian Encyclopedia* 2013). It may seem ironic that the English would grant independence to one of its colonies during the late nineteenth century era of renewed colonialism; however, the English were confident that Canada would continue to be a reliable source of raw materials, a market for British manufacturers and offer profitable investment opportunities. The 1837–1838 Rebellions also indicated the presence of a nascent local commercial and industrial class that, after the bitter experience of the American Revolution, might require placation.

The post-Confederation industrial development plan that Canadian capitalists and their British backers developed was itself a colonial project, albeit with an internal focus. The national policy was based on promoting Canadian industry, the settlement of the West and railroad construction, but it required the acquisition of huge tracts of land in the West that were already occupied. Two centuries earlier, the British Crown had created the Hudson's Bay Company (HBC) and essentially granted it sovereignty that was typical of nation-states over much of the Western world. Without even the pretense of consultation or negotiation, the Indigenous population of the entire watershed of Hudson's Bay was essentially handed over to a private company. After Confederation, the Canadian state, in fine colonial fashion, stepped in and purchased the land of the HBC, thus claiming its own sovereignty over the land and its people. Subsequently, through legislation, violence, disease, and negotiation, the Canadian state displaced all the Indigenous people who occupied the land in order to integrate the region into its industrialization strategy.

In the span of a few short years after Confederation, the Canadian state undertook treaty negotiations, quashed two Metis Resistances, passed the *Dominion Lands Act* and funnelled millions of dollars of private capital to build a transcontinental railroad, all in the interest of creating a white-settler society in the West. Even as Indigenous people were being forcibly removed from the land, the *Indian Act* of 1876 was passed in an attempt to further subjugate and control them. It would produce the genocide of residential schools and decades of control and denial of basic human rights for First Nations, Inuit and Métis people. Canada's internal colonial legacy is often ignored and denied as when, speaking to an American audience in 2009, former prime minister Steven Harper quipped, "We also have no history of colonialism. So we have all of the things that many people admire about the great powers but none of the things that threaten or bother them" (quoted in Drohan, 2011). Others, like Justice Mary Ellen Turpel-Lafond, however, know the truth: "The Canadian state is the master's house for us, with all the demeaning slavery connotations of that expression intact. It is not yet our house." She adds, "We do not see the master's house as our only support source nor can we see it at this point as a source of meaningful change" (1997: 77).

The main political decision-making body of the Canadian state system was never a House of Indigenous people. In June 2021, Mumilaaq Qaqqaq, an Indigenous member of Parliament from Nunavut, announced she would not seek re-election after having experienced various indignities in Parliament. Of the House of Commons, she said: "it's a very uneasy place. It's a place where they make laws that result in Indigenous death and resulting turmoil for a lot of our communities. I feel that."

Further, she noted, "The systems are built to work for certain people. It's middle-aged white men. It's a weird thing to realize your lack of privilege, even though you're in a position so full of privileges" (quoted in Raman-Wilms 2021).

The question before us remains: how do we understand how a state such as this works, and in whose interests does it operate? To answer these questions, we need to understand some of the theories put forward to explain the operations of the state in capitalist societies.

Pluralism

In the US, a perennial question has been: how can the state develop goals, priorities and social policies acceptable to the public as a whole in a society composed of individuals, classes and groups with different interests and perspectives? In 1908, Arthur Bentley addressed and summarized the issues in his treatise on government, *The Process of Government*, but it was Charles Merriam (1964) and Robert Dahl (1967, 1972) that systematically articulated the pluralist approach. According to Dahl, complex industrial societies are composed of citizens and groups characterized by different religious, class, occupational, ethnic and national backgrounds and interests. As society evolves and becomes more complex, individuals with common characteristics and interests tend to coalesce into groups or organizations to represent their motivations and interests. The problem faced by states and governments is how to govern in the interests of the whole of society when it is heterogenous and divided. A related problem is how to prevent individuals or particular interest groups from achieving undue influence or control over the state.

Pluralists argue that Western democracies such as the US or Canada have developed political structures and processes that best fulfil the possibilities for democracy in a complex advanced industrial society. The foundation of such a political system is elections based on as broad a franchise as possible and "one person, one vote." Regardless of an individual's income, social status, religion, ethnicity and so on, on election day, every person is deemed to be equal because everyone has the right to vote once. The fact that everyone is entitled to one vote and can organize political parties means, pluralists argue, that all citizens potentially have the same power and opportunity to make an impact on the political process.

> On election day, every person is deemed to be equal because everyone has the right to vote.

The political process is not, however, just about elections and choosing who will make decisions on behalf of the entire society. After and between elections, individuals, groups, associations, and classes have other opportunities to influence government policies and actions. Assuming that liberal-democratic systems are open societies with a free press and multiple modes of communication, citizens have access to information about the activities of the state and government. When the government is deciding on an issue, interested individuals and groups will be aware and have the opportunity to present their views to the government. They can lobby decision makers by meeting with them, writing letters, organizing delegations and communicating in any number of ways to make their case. Lobbying is a process that is available to everyone, whether or not they supported the particular party that was victorious in the electoral process.

As a result, pluralists argue, political power in Western democracies is dispersed across a multitude of individuals, classes, associations and interests that compete through the electoral and lobbying processes to influence government. The existence of plural centres of power means that in the long term no one centre, group or interest is able to dominate. The government must be willing to accommodate a variety of demands and interests or else it runs the risk of becoming viewed as corrupt or undemocratic by being tied to one group or class and incapable of acting as a neutral mediator or arbitrator of disputes or conflicts. If this happens, the government will face certain electoral defeat once it becomes apparent to all the other interests that they are excluded from the political process. Assuming that the various excluded interests comprise the majority, they will be in a position to develop a coalition and work together to remove the offending government from power.

In summary, pluralists claim that liberal-democratic states have developed processes and structures that facilitate social decision-making in a complex and stratified society. The state is the site of mediation and "trade-offs," as the government seeks to balance competing interests and establish policies and priorities that ostensibly represent the interests of the majority (Dahl 1967: 24). No centre of power is dominant or able to consistently get its way, at least over the long term. "You win some, you lose some" characterizes how different interest groups fare in the political process. However, as capitalism developed, some pluralists, such as Charles Lindblom (1977), understood that the concentration of economic power in capitalist society means that business occupies a privileged position.

Economic Crisis and a New State Form

We know that capitalist societies and their associated state structures and processes are constantly changing; therefore, the theories and perspectives we use to understand them must also change. The Great Depression and World War II resulted in a fundamental shift in the role of the state in capitalist societies. The near collapse of the Western capitalist order resulted in a revolution of economic thought based on the work of John Maynard Keynes, a British economist. The Keynesian revolution produced a shift in how the role and function of the state was understood. Simply put, Keynes understood it was possible for capitalist economies to stagnate and experience economic depression if the overall demand for goods and services was insufficient to maintain investment and employment. Under such circumstances, in the interests of keeping capitalist economies functioning, states should spend money (perhaps on social programs or building social infrastructure such as schools and transportation systems) to stimulate demand and regulate economic activity as required. During the early 1940s, massive state spending in the US and Canada on the war effort ended the depression; however, after the war, continued spending and an activist state became understood as a way of maintaining economic growth and prosperity. The late 1940s through to the 1960s was the heyday of what is called the Keynesian welfare state, which was marked by expanded spending on a range of social programs (health insurance, medicare, old age pensions, unemployment insurance, family allowances, child protection legislation and increased forms of social assistance). Additionally, the state oversaw a period of cooperation between labour and capital. The era is often referred to as Fordism because it was in part based on the notion of social stability and progress facilitated by mass production and consumption of a wide range of consumer durables, the vision of Henry Ford for the automotive industry in the 1920s. In return for good wages that allowed high levels of consumption, workers allowed business owners to make major economic decisions while the state regulated industry, expanded the necessary infrastructure and encouraged consumption through social programs. Amid these "happy days," however, class structures in most Western societies grew more complex

> In return for good wages that allowed high levels of consumption, workers allowed business owners to make major economic decisions while the state regulated industry.

while the enormous resources controlled by the corporate sector increased. By the late 1960s, cracks in the system were appearing as social protest against systematic racism and sexism emerged and the growing power of a military-industrial complex highlighted the issues of social inequality and injustice. The inability of the pluralist model to explain the growing power of giant multinational corporations became apparent. The search for alternative explanations of political power led some to the work of Karl Marx.

Marxist Perspectives:
The State and Class in Capitalist Society

It turned out that Marx and his collaborator, Friedrich Engels, did not offer a systematic and well-developed theory of the state. As early as 1845, they suggested that the state in capitalist society must be understood within the context of its inevitable class divisions: "The State is the form in which the individuals of a ruling [capitalist] class assert their common interests" (1970: 80). A few years later, they stated, "the executive of the modern state is but a committee for managing the common affairs of the whole [capitalist class]" (1952: 44). In other works, they present more complex pictures of the state (Marx 1972a, 1972b), but despite the constant theme that the state is central to the process of capitalist-class domination, they presented few concrete ideas about how class and the state were actually connected. Others whose work was informed by Marx, neo-Marxists, took up the task of developing a more systematic approach.

Early Neo-Marxist Perspectives

Among the first systematic neo-Marxist treatment of the state was Ralph Miliband's *The State in Capitalist Society*. In an attempt to expose the inadequacies of the pluralist model, Miliband demonstrated that the dominant economic class in a capitalist society (those who own and control the means of producing goods and services — that is, capitalists) overwhelmingly hold and control economic power (1973: 6). Miliband argued that as a result, the state in capitalist society tends to act in the interests of the capitalist class. In an important sense, he showed that pluralists were wrong — there is a dominant set of interests in a capitalist society.

To illustrate how the capitalist class controls of the operation of the state, Miliband studied its various components: the elected government, the bureaucracy and administrative apparatus and the military. He demonstrated that representatives of the capitalist class or people sympathetic to the interests of the capitalist class tend to control the primary decision-making positions in all major branches of the state. The upper levels or the "officialdom" of the state apparatus are overwhelming occupied by individuals with business connections or who are pro-business, sharing the lifestyles, educational background, networks and value systems of the capitalist class. Miliband (1973: 50–58) rejects the notion that the state establishes social policies and priorities for "the nation" or in "the national interest." Indeed, notions such

> What is claimed to be the national interest often just represents the interests of the dominant class.

as the "national interest" must be approached with a critical and wary eye because what is claimed to be the national interest often just represents the interests of the dominant class. Miliband's approach became known as the "instrumental" approach since the focus was on how, through personal and personnel connections, the state was made an instrument of the dominant class.

For some, Miliband's instrumental focus on personal and personnel connections between members of dominant classes and the state failed to explain instances in which those connections were absent but state actions and policies still favoured the dominant class. In *Political Power and Social Classes* (1968), French neo-Marxist Nicos Poulantzas took up this issue.

Poulantzas argued that it is a mistake to simply examine the personnel and personal connections between the capitalist class and the state. Because capitalism is inherently a class-based system characterized by relations of exploitation, domination and inequalities of power and wealth, it is prone to instability, conflict and crisis. If capitalism is to survive, it requires an institution to stabilize the overall system. This is precisely the function and role of the state, and these functions are more important than the particular individuals who staff the state. Through his "structuralist" approach, Poulantzas directs our attention to the structures, roles, and functions of the state by examining the overall structures, dynamic and logic of capitalism. He locates the need for the state as a stabilizing institution in the context of the inevitable class conflict that often threatens the very existence of the system and the need for the state to undertake certain actions in order to facilitate the interests of the ruling classes that are dominant in capitalism.

In summary, Poulantzas understood the state largely in terms of the functions it performed for the capitalist class by stabilizing the system and allowing capitalists to accumulate wealth. In essence, he uses a functional explanation, explaining the role of the state in terms of its apparent necessary function for the whole system. Miliband examined more direct connections between the capitalist class and the state by looking at state personnel: the personal, lifestyle, interactive and ideological similarities between the capitalist class and those in charge of the state. Miliband and Poulantzas understood that in acting to preserve the total capitalist system, the state is also acting in the interests of the class that benefits most from the maintenance of the status quo. In the early 1970s, as Miliband and Poulantzas were engaging in a spirited debate over the issue of the state, capitalism was entering another period of radical change (Knuttila and Kubik 2000).

Another New State Form: The Neoliberal State

Miliband and Poulantzas were attempting to explain the state at a particular period. After the global devastation of World War II, as a Keynesian state, the US led the successful reconstruction of many Western capitalist economies that was designed to ensure that they remained in the capitalist world system. An unintended result was the emergence of growing economic rivalry between the US and Japan and Western Europe that now had new and more efficient technologies. In many cases, new products produced with more advanced technologies posed a serious threat to North American manufacturing, as consumers switched from Chevys to Toyotas or BMWs and from General Electric to Sony. Globalization added to these problems, as some businesses sought to improve profits by moving to nations in the Global South that had lower labour costs and less regulation. An added crisis was the growth of state deficits and debts from the expenditures associated with the expansion of public services, the space race, and an ongoing war in Indochina.

The 1970s thus marked the emergence of a series of crises for the Keynesian welfare state. The watershed events were the elections of conservatives Ronald Reagan in the US, Margaret Thatcher in Britain and Brian Mulroney in Canada. Driven by "deficit hysteria," these governments began to implement widespread and deep cuts to a range of social programs, including medicare, education, family support, while deregulating the economy and privatizing the functions of the state. "Neoliberalism" describes this shift away from the Keynesian welfare state (Harvey 2005). For neoliberals, the welfare state was the root of all social and economic evils: sapping the work ethic, costing hard-working taxpayers and empowering the state and bureaucracies with counterproductive state regulation. The market was deemed to be the best decision maker for economic matters. David Harvey argues that there was more going on: "[neoliberalism] refers to a class project that coalesced in the crisis of the mid 1970s. Masked by a lot of rhetoric about individual freedom, liberty, personal responsibility and the virtues of privatisation, the free market and free trade, it legitimised draconian policies designed to restore and consolidate capitalist class power" (2010: 10).

The neoliberal revolution brought many changes, but two stand out. First, market ideology was increasingly used to direct the operations of many social institutions, including education, social services and healthcare, valuing cost cutting and so-called efficiencies above human service even as many state functions were taken over by non-government private organizations and corporations. Second, the nation-state itself lost significant power, as multinational organizations such as the World Trade Organization and trade deals such as the North American Free Trade Agreement, which eventually became the United States–Mexico–Canada Agreement (USMCA), increasingly constrained the operations and options of nation-states.

As it turned out, an unregulated and unfettered market economy was not viable. Corruption and mismanagement resulted in a housing crisis and the stock market collapse in 2008–2009, threatening the global capitalist system. Western states were forced to rush in with gargantuan bailout packages for banks and financial, insurance and auto companies. In the United States, an initial bailout was worth more than $700 billion, although the final amount may have been in the trillions of dollars (Collins 2015). In Canada, the Conservative government of Steven Harper provided stimulus spending for some infrastructure projects, to try to create jobs, as well as bailouts to major international corporations while continuing to cut funding to many social programs that benefited marginalized people.

So, there have been many changes to the structures and activities of the Canadian state since Confederation alongside attempts by pluralists and early neo-Marxists to understand how the state works. Yet there is a crucial fact that both pluralists and Marxists have missed — historically, virtually all states in most Western societies have been controlled and dominated by men. This fact must address the interrelatedness of capitalism, patriarchy and the state.

Beyond Class Politics: Feminism and the Capitalist State

Capitalism is an economic order based on the private ownership of society's productive resources and the deployment of those resources to produce profits for the owners. Patriarchy refers to a particular type of sex and gender order characterized by certain social, economic and cultural institutions, ideologies and relationships based on sex and gender. Sex refers to the multiplicity of different physiological characteristics (e.g., chromosomal, cellular, genital, hormonal) that are expressed in a variety of human bodies with, among other characteristics, differing reproductive apparatuses. Concepts such as female, intersex, and male typically refer to different sexes. As opposed to physiological characteristics, the concept of gender refers to the variable historical, cultural and social practices, values, norms, institutional structures and ideological frameworks that have arisen in human societies resulting from, but not determined by, sex differences. Masculinity can be understood as the behaviours, social practices, beliefs and ideological frameworks typically associated with males in a gender order and femininity with female behaviours, social practices, beliefs and ideological frameworks. In many societies, certain types of gendered social practices, institutional behaviours, sets of beliefs and ideologies become dominant or hegemonic (Connell 1995). In addition to this limited and narrow binary perspective, there are alternative, mixed and complex gender practices, values, norms and institutionalized behaviours among groups and individuals who are lesbian, gay, bisexual, transgender, questioning, queer, intersex, pansexual, Two-Spirit, androgynous, and asexual. Bringing these concepts together, patriarchy is "a gender order in which men are dominant and masculinity tends to be esteemed, and in which major social institutions, practices and ideological frameworks tend to support, legitimize and facilitate male and masculine domination and the oppression and exploitation of many women and the concomitant devaluation of femininity" (Knuttila 2016: 31). Understood in these terms, patriarchy does not include or preclude other forms of domination or oppression based on class, ethnicity, race or age.

Despite their many differences, pluralism and much Marxian theory have shared a common shortcoming — they all ignore the importance of sex and gender relations and oppression in society and in the state. In short, they have ignored the potential role of the state in fostering, maintaining and supporting systems of inequality other than class, such as those found in patriarchal gender orders. The most important and systematic critique of this lacuna has come from various schools of feminist thought. Feminists have posed new questions about the state, arguing that in the West, the state plays a central role in maintaining and supporting patriarchy.

> Feminists have posed new questions about the state, arguing that in the West, the state plays a central role in maintaining and supporting patriarchy.

Many feminist scholars have documented the myriad ways the state in Canada has promoted and reinforced unequal sex and gender relations. Jane Ursel (1986) demonstrated that the state is implicated in facilitating both economic production (capitalism) and biological reproduction (patriarchy) (see also Pupo 1988; Brodie 1996). The history of access — actually, lack of access for many decades — to abortion in Canada is one of repression, causing suffering and death as decades of criminalizing a medical procedure denied the simple right of people to control their own bodies (Dubinsky 1985; McDaniel 1985; Gavigan 1987). Barbara Cameron (1996) illustrates the negative impact of trade deals in the arena of new reproductive technologies. Pat Armstrong has demonstrated how the neoliberal erosion of the healthcare system reduces "the capacity of women to remain healthy by dismantling social-security programs, by deregulating industries, and by moving away from an equity agenda" (1996: 45). Varda Burstyn (1985) has described a number of ways the state has played a central role in both economic-class domination and gender-class domination

Catharine MacKinnon put it this way: "The state ... institutionalizes male power over women through institutionalizing the male point of view in law. Its first state act is to see women from the standpoint of male dominance; its next act is to treat them that way" (1989: 169). A theme of much feminist thought is the omnipresence of patriarchal ideologies that simply take for granted male dominance, control, strength and power, along with the oppositional views of women and girls. MacKinnon concludes: "However autonomous of class the liberal state may appear, it is not autonomous of sex. Male power is systemic. Coercive, legitimized and epistemic, it *is* the regime" (emphasis in original, 1989: 170). A 2017 symposium marking the twenty-fifth anniversary of MacKinnon's *Toward a Feminist Theory of the State*. MacKinnon explained her original intention in the context of the time it was written: "*Toward a Feminist Theory of the State* was … to theoretically reframe the perceivable realities of women's lives according to women's own experiences so they could be seen for the first time, in order to change the politics and laws that construct that reality" (MacKinnon 2017: 2). Carole Pateman (1989) provided a key critique of the inherent logic of most political theorizing, arguing that the basic concepts of all Western political discourse and theory are founded on a set of assumptions and arguments that are patriarchal and thus exclusionary for women. The core language, concepts and discourse assume political actors are heterosexual men.

Among the important developments in feminist theory are the criticisms of postmodernists and third-wave feminists. Third-wave feminists call for an explicit acknowledgement of the varied lived experiences of women. Nelson and Robinson (2002: 96) note that "inclusive feminism" is critical of the apparent search by earlier feminists "for the essential experience of generic 'woman.'" Patricia Elliot and Nancy Mandell refer to the new approach as "postmodern feminism," emphasizing the need to include the voices and perspectives of "women of color and women from developing countries" as well as "lesbian, disabled and working-class women" (1995: 24).In her review of some feminist scholarship relating to jurisprudence, criminology and the welfare state, Lynne Haney notes that "feminists have eschewed such conspiratorial notions of state patriarchy to take up the more complicated task of illuminating the ways states shape, and are shaped by, gender relations" (2000: 641). R.W. Connell (2002) demonstrates the complexities and ubiquitous nature of power in a patriarchal gender order. Through her concept of the "patriarchal dividend," defined as the multiple benefits that accrue to males in patriarchal systems, Connell's work offers a clue as to why men in control of the state might be wont to reinforce a patriarchal gender order (Knuttila 2016) — they accrue a dividend (benefits) from doing so. It is clear that political power in patriarchal society is complicated; however, we need an approach to understanding the state that allows deeper explanatory capacity as to how political power in actually exercised.

BEYOND CLASS POLITICS II:
RACIAL CAPITALISM AND CORPORATE COLONIALISM[1]

Similar to feminists who call attention to gender inequality, anti-racist political theorizers show us that capitalism also has a distinctly racist element. According to such theorists, capitalists and capitalism have benefited from various forms of racism. For example, some years ago, economists developed the notion of a dual or split labour market to expose the ways in which racialized people are paid less for the same work done by white people and are pushed into the kinds of work that have low levels of pay and other precarious working conditions (Bonacich 1972). This segmentation is functional for capitalists for several reasons, the key one being that it helps to keep the working class divided, inhibiting their organizing efforts against corporations. The COVID-19 pandemic has made this labour force segmentation clear in that so much essential work, like long-term care, is poorly paid and done mostly by racialized women (Ivanova 2021; Scott 2021). For those who espouse the idea of "racial capitalism," however, the connection goes much deeper.

The concept of "racial capitalism" was first coined by Cedric Robinson (2005) in his book *Black Marxism*. For him, capitalism is inherently racist in its history, its structure and its outcomes. Like classic and neo-Marxists, racial capitalism scholars posit that capitalism requires socio-economic inequality. However, this inequality is based not only on relations to the means of production but also on other worker characteristics such as racialization. Robinson built on the work of earlier Black historians, who showed that the development of industrial capitalism relied on colonialism and slavery. In a historical sense, Robinson argued that capitalism, which in part arose as a challenge to European feudal oppression, was predicated on other oppressions, including racialism. For him, capitalism didn't rid the world of oppression and discrimination; rather, it birthed a new world order that extended oppression and discrimination. He pointed out that capitalism and racial exploitation were inextricably linked during the economic development and expansion of seventeenth-century Western Europe. The growth of capitalism depended on imperialism, genocide and violence against racialized people. David McNally (2020) argues similarly in *Blood and Money* that money as a form of exchange, like capitalism, was born of violence and human bondage.

A prime example is the enslavement of Black people in the foundation of capitalism in the Americas. The transatlantic slave trade saw over twelve million African men, women and children brutally captured, transported and forced to work. Some five million enslaved people were taken to sugar plantations in Brazil. Black slaves were also the foundation of the US cotton plantation economy, which supplied the British textile industry and, by 1860, resulted in "more millionaires in the lower

Mississippi Valley than anywhere else in the US." In 1860, "the 4 million slaves were worth $3.5 billion [about $108 billion in 2020 dollars] ... the largest single financial asset in the entire US economy, worth more than all manufacturing and railroads combined" (McPherson cited in Coates 2014). In 1860, in eleven Confederate states, four of ten people were slaves (Ransom n.d.). Without slaves, the fledgling US capitalist economy simply would not have existed.

In Canada, racial capitalism in the form of slavery existed for over two hundred years, until it was formally abolished in 1834 with the passage of Britain's *Slavery Abolition Act* (Maynard 2017). Canada has a long history of anti-Black racism that continues into the present, but racial capitalism in Canada has mainly taken the form of settler colonialism (see the earlier Historical Note). Settler colonialism is the process whereby one people claim sovereignty over another, particularly their land, to extract resources and accumulate profits at the expense of those colonized (Monchalin 2016). It differs from other forms of colonialism in that the colonizers come to stay rather than taking what they want and leaving. To facilitate the process of extinguishing Indigenous peoples from their land, the Canadian state has claimed control over large swaths of territory, despite signing treaties with the original inhabitants — these have been either ignored or violated with impunity over many decades (RCAP 1996; Palmater 2015, 2020; Craft 2013). White settler society was thereby imposed on Indigenous people, disrupting their own systems of governance and ways of being.

The settler-colonial process shares similarities with the development of capitalism in Western Europe. In that historical process, peasants were forced off their land to make way for the new industrial economy, which denied them of their traditional means of livelihood. Losing their link to the land was a key part of forcing peasants to take up wage labour in the factories of the new capitalist economy. So, the foundation of modern capitalism was itself violent dispossession: stealing land was essential to transforming non-capitalist societies into capitalist ones (Coulthard 2014).

Certainly, all white setters have benefited from colonialism, but corporate capitalist resource extractors have benefited most of all. In Canada, settler colonialism has had a distinct corporate capitalist element from the start. It was and remains a "corporate colonialism" (Palmater 2015). Beginning with the Hudson's Bay Company, corporate colonialism proceeded to build transnational railroads, then moved to fossil fuel, lumber, other resource extraction and agriculture (see prior Historical Note). This kind of colonialism "requires private companies and public agencies to work together to secure access to land and resources" (Preston 2013: 45). The various kinds of raw materials in the land that was essentially stolen from its original inhabitants became the property of mining, lumber, railway and fossil fuel companies.

All this happened through and with the power and authority of the Canadian state, which "redistributed wealth upwards from Indigenous nations and workers to capitalists" (Carroll and Sapinski 2018: 28). Indigenous people had to be cleared from the land to make way for a transcontinental railroad, which was, essentially a private money-making scheme and was promoted by members of the government at the time. Through cash grants, loans, subsidies, land grants, bond guarantees and the like, the Canadian state guaranteed the profitability of the late-1800s railroad-building venture. According to historian Gustavus Myers, writing in 1914, "the totals amounted to 56 million acres of land, $244 million in cash subventions (mostly outright donations) and $245 million in bond guarantees" (Myers 1914 cited in Carroll and Sapinski 2018: 28).

In all of this, the Canadian state relied heavily on militarized force — both its military and its police force, the North-West Mounted Police (which later became the Royal Canadian Mounted Police). In recent years, these private-public partnerships (to use the current term) have been with the oil and gas companies, whereby the Canadian state has used its security forces to try to guarantee big fossil fuel projects. It has had to do that because Indigenous resistance to the projects is a significant barrier and "the nagging issue of Indigenous sovereignty ... won't allow the 'Indian problem' to disappear" (Preston 2013: 44; see also Palmater 2015, 2020).

So, it is clear that capitalism is racial, but its specific logic depends on time and place (Wolfe 2006; Smith 2010; Preston 2013). In these terms, just like the importance of understanding how patriarchy works within and through the state, we need to approach racial capitalism in a way that reveals how political power is actually exercised in specific historical circumstances, an issue we will take up below.

Case Study
Wet'suwet'en and the Coastal Gaslink Pipeline: Corporate Capitalism

In June 2012, it was announced that TransCanada Pipeline (now TC Energy) — one of the largest energy companies in North America — would build a 670-kilometre gas pipeline from Dawson Creek, BC, to Kitimat, BC. The Coastal GasLink Pipeline Project was officially confirmed in October 2018 for completion by 2024–2025. To reach Kitimat, the pipeline had to go through Indigenous territories.

TC Energy obtained consent from all twenty First Nations along the pipeline's path during 2012–2014. These band-run First Nations are governed by elected councils defined in the *Indian Act* and have legal jurisdiction only over the land within their reserves.

However, the pipeline's path also crosses 22,000 square kilometres of Wet'suwet'en land that is unceded territory governed by a system of hereditary chiefs. Wet'suwet'en law existed long before the Canadian state and they never abandoned their form of governance. A majority of the hereditary chiefs oppose the pipeline, holding that development cannot happen without their consent. The 1997 Supreme Court decision in Delgamuukw affirms that position. The Court held that Aboriginal Title is a right to the land itself, for their exclusive use and occupation, and that no other laws override Wet'suwet'en rights with regard to their territory.

To protect their land and uphold their law, Wet'suwet'en chiefs have sanctioned efforts to block building the pipeline — including camps, checkpoints and blockades — and they have issued orders evicting pipeline workers from the territory. TC Energy and Canadian governments (both federal and provincial) see these land defenders as merely "protestors" or even "terrorists."

Since late 2018, BC courts have upheld injunctions against the land defenders, allowing work on the pipeline to continue. The RCMP has enforced the injunctions by arresting and forcibly removing Wet'suwet'en members, their allies, and even reporters (despite the courts upholding the right of the media to observe and report on "protests" without any interference). Photos of RCMP raids in Wet'suwet'en show them entering this unceded territory as a military force — automatic weapons, military garb, helicopters, dogs. Arrests in 2020 sparked widespread solidarity protests across Canada, including a blockade of the main CNR line in eastern Ontario.

As Mi'kmaw lawyer, activist and scholar Pamela Palmater says, "this was never about a protest. This was always about occupying and protecting their lands — something they have the legal right to do ... Canada's invasion of Wet'suwet'en territory through its national police force is [a] blatant violation of the rule of law in favour of non-Indigenous corporate interests" (Palmater 2020: ch 39).

Sources: Yinta Access n.d.; Palmater 2015, 2020; Canadaland 2021; Narwhal n.d.; Martin 2021; Wikipedia n.d.a, n.d.b.)

WHAT DOES THE STATE ACTUALLY DO AND WHY DOES IT MATTER?

Over forty years ago, Göran Therborn published *What Does the Ruling Class Do When It Rules?* Based on the summaries presented above, it is not yet clear that we can answer this question in a concrete and historical manner. A pluralist would argue that the democratic state in capitalist society is the site of competition by basically balanced forces and interests, all equally capable of influencing its direction, priorities and policies. Marx saw the state in capitalist society as tending to serve the long-term interests of the capitalist class, although he was not clear on the mechanisms by which capitalists actually managed this. Subsequent Marxist scholars suggested relatively straightforward linkages (instrumentalism), while others looked to the structural dynamics of a capitalist mode of production (structuralism). Finally, there were those who pointed out that this entire debate about the state in capitalist society bears the hallmark of the society within which it occurred — capitalist patriarchy — and thus, like most discourse, it either ignores issues of sex and gender or uses malestream thought. It is not clear that any of these approaches on their own answer Therborn's question.

Over three-plus decades, Bob Jessop (2010) has made important contributions in analyzing the state in capitalist society. Two aspects of his work stand out. Jessop adopts an approach called "critical realism," which focuses on the mechanisms that actually cause events to occur. Explanation over description. The second notable element of Jessop's work relates to his contribution to developing a systematic theory of the state in capitalist society. Jessop employs a "strategic-relational approach." He argues that in a capitalist society, the opportunities to activate and utilize the power of state institutions and structures are unequally distributed across a number of dimensions of inequality, including class and gender. By noting that the actual decisions and actions of the state are made by politicians and state officials, he brings humans, decision-making actors and groups back in the picture without losing sight of state and other social structures. What is missing in his account is the articulation of just how agents activate or exercise political power; however, there is a way to understand the precise mechanisms that are in play in politics.

Mechanisms of Power

Nearly fifty years ago, Albert Szymanski (1978) outlined the elements of mechanisms of power to actually link individuals, classes and groups to the state. Borrowing from Szymanski, examining and analyzing the use of direct and indirect mechanisms of power, it is possible to understand how classes, individuals, groups and organizations are able to impact, if not control, the policies, actions and decisions of the state.

> Analyzing the use of direct and indirect mechanisms of power, it is possible to understand how classes, individuals, groups and organizations are able to impact, if not control, the state.

Direct Mechanisms of Power

In a liberal democracy, an obvious direct mechanism of power is the electoral process. Elections offer a number of opportunities to influence those who actually makes state decisions by organizing and funding political parties, actively supporting candidates and political parties, facilitating social movements in support of (or in opposition to) parties and policies, or actually seeking office. The precise available options will vary depending on the nature of the political system (parliamentary, republican, etc.), the voting methods (preferential or "first past the post," etc.) and and the legislative apparatus itself (bicameral, single assembly, etc.). In engaging these direct mechanisms, the old adage "those who pay the piper call the tune" is an apt summary.

A second direct mechanism of power is lobbying government and state officials. Lobbying and pressure group tactics can include letter writing, emailing, phone and social media campaigns, individual visitations, group or delegation meetings and staging public demonstrations and protests. Such activities can be directed at political leaders, cabinet members, backbenches or even influential bureaucrats.

A third direct mechanism of power relates to the policy formation process. The development of public policy and legislation requires extensive amounts of research and information. To meet this need, governments often use a variety of means: Royal Commissions, task forces, special committees, as well as seeking advice from experts. In Canada, formal organizations and networks of "experts," specialist advisors and "think tanks" include organizations such as the Fraser Institute, the Canadian Centre for Policy Alternatives and the C.D. Howe Institute. These policy and advocacy institutes are active in research, advising governments, engaging with traditional and social media and publishing papers and reports, all purporting to offer sound, fact-based public policy advice. The coverage that such reports and events receive in the mass media makes it difficult for governments and state personnel to simply ignore them.

Indirect Mechanisms of Power

There are structural or indirect mechanisms related to the larger social and economic environment within which the state operates. The state is merely not separate and isolated from society at large; rather, is it a complex set of relationships and interactions indelibly and intimately intertwined with other institutions. A key component of human societies are ideological or belief systems composed of values, norms and moral codes. Whether described as ideological systems, value orientations or normative prescriptions or public opinion, they are an important element of the wider social structure in which states and governments operate and are an important indirect mechanism of power — ideological power.

The capacity to influence the ideology, beliefs and value system of society as a whole can be a mechanism of power. It can involve the dissemination of the ideologies and worldviews of a dominant class through the education system, religious institutions and the mass and social media. Individuals, classes and groups often attempt to convince other members of society that their interests represent the "national interest," the "public good" or the "natural order" of things. When a group, individual or class is able to establish this equivalency, it becomes more difficult for the state to manoeuvre because certain actions or policies can be perceived as being against the "national interest," "freedom" or the "public good." Sexism, racism and classism represent systems of belief that, once established as part of the value system of a society, are powerful mechanisms for determining state policy and actions. These established belief systems can define the bounds of what is acceptable or not for state policymakers. In North America, particularly in the US, in the aftermath of McCarthyism and the Cold War, the very words socialist and liberal were enough to discredit an opponent for a policy suggestion.

Another indirect mechanism of power is economic. Just as governments and states exist and act in the context of public opinion, they also exist and act in the context of an economic order — in liberal democratic society, typically a capitalist, market-based order. Governments and states rely on a stable and growing economy not just for tax revenue, but also because social stability is dependent on a "healthy" economy in which there is "business confidence," continuing investment, stable and increasing employment and general prosperity. US president Calvin Coolidge understood this when he observed, "After all, the chief business of the American people is business" (Terrell 2019). Former prime minister Steven Harper stated his government's main interests even more directly: "Mr. Speaker, as I have already said many times, the economy remains our focus. This government is determined to continue to increase our international trade, promote opportunities for business owners and industries, and lower taxes" (Hansard, September 17, 2012). The extent to which a class or group is capable of influencing the larger economic environment in a capitalist society will be a central determinant of its capacity to translate its economic power into political power. Given that social stability tends to depend on economic stability, at least in capitalist societies, control over economic resources and power can thus be considered a mechanism of power.

So, how do these mechanisms work in Canada, now and historically?

Decision Makers

At its founding, a very small, select group made political decisions in Canada. The very first Parliament reflected limited voting rights, restricted to male British subjects over twenty-one years of age who met certain property and income requirements. In 1867, businessmen were the largest group among the 206 parliamentarians (eighty-three merchants, businessmen, lumber merchants, contractors and millers), followed by fifty-eight lawyers, twenty-five writers and journalists, twenty-four farmers and seventeen physicians. The first post-Confederation Canadian cabinet was composed entirely of lawyers, businessmen and a newspaper editor (Canada, Elections Canada website 2020). If we look at the forty-third Parliament, elected in 2019, not much has really changed. There is no list of the specific occupations of Canadian parliamentarians in 2021; however, it is possible to search their self-attributed occupations. While some members do not provide this information and others indicate several occupations, a word search of all occupations listed does produce a definite pattern.

MECHANISMS OF POWER IN CANADA

Occupations of MPs, 2019

Self-description/ occupation	Number of members using occupational descriptions	Percent of members using descriptor (duplications result in total not = 100)
Business	71	30
Lawyer	60	25
Consultant	48	20
Political	48	20
Manager	35	15
Executive	35	15
Owner	29	12
Entrepreneur	28	12
Teacher	24	10
Journalist	20	8
Administrator	18	8
Professor	18	8
Public servant	15	6
Military	12	5
Instructor	8	3
Mayor	8	3
Social work	8	3
Athlete	8	3
Police	6	3
Physician	6	3

Community activist	6	3
Advisor	6	3
Unionist	4	2
Nurse	3	1
Community development	3	1

Only twelve of the 338 (5 percent) of members indicate Indigenous origins, the same number with some military service experience. A significant number of members have municipal government experience (sixty-seven) and twenty-six had previously served in provincial governments. A total of fifteen had previous family members serve in Parliament.

Election Funding in Canada

In Canada, there are limits on the amount of money that individuals can contribute to candidates and parties, and corporations and unions are not allowed to donate; however, such limits do not mean that the political parties are equal in terms of the resources they have to run campaigns and conduct their political operations. A party whose ideologies, platforms, policies and proclivities are in the interests of those who control of significant wealth do have more resources. Elections Canada also allows so-called third parties to engage in a number of partisan activities that clearly benefit those capable of funding partisan activities, surveys and advertising (Elections Canada 2019). While everyone faces similar limits, well-off individuals find it easier to meet that limit and the proportion donating and receiving a tax benefit will be higher than lower classes or marginalized groups. The Conservative Party spent $28.9 million on the 2019 election compared to $26.1 million for the Liberals and $10.3 million for the New Democratic Party (Grenier 2020). In the United States, the stakes are much higher. Before the 2020 elections, it was estimated that the total spending by congressional and presidential candidates would be more than US $14 billion (Schwartz 2020). It is not hard to see that the electoral mechanism of power is actually not available to all citizens.

Lobbying

One dimension of the operations and activities of government and the state that typically escapes much public attention are the activities of the various lobbyists. Lobbying does not just involve the "gentle art" of persuasion — lobbyists try to set the terms of a policy debate by identifying what they see as the relevant issues, influencing the media coverage, mobilizing support outside a legislature, anticipating criticism and opposition and offering "answers," impacting social media and motivating supporters (Cave and Rowell 2014). Additionally, lobbyists work through and with think tanks to "write research papers and Op-Ed pieces and participate in countless open panel discussions" (Madrick 2016: 51). Lobbyists can also "develop talking points and explanations of why legislation makes sense, write speeches and letters of support of it, seek out co-sponsors and supporters both within and outside government, and generally see a bill through from start to finish" (Drutman 2016: 51, cited in Madrick 2016). The number of lobbyists in Canada will vary somewhat, because sometimes a group will emerge around a single issue, register as a lobbyist and then become inactive, while other lobbyists are long-standing professional organizations. According to the Office of the Commissioner of Lobbying, in January 2021 there were 1,062 consulting lobbyists, 2,122 corporate lobbyists and 3,085 organizational lobbyists, for a total of 6,269 (Office of the Commissioner of Lobbying n.d.). This does not include the lobbying efforts directed at provincial and municipal governments. But lobbyists do not represent everyone, all interests. For example, in 2020–2021, oil/gas lobbyists met with government officials in Canada 1,224 times — that is, 4.5 times per day (see Mark Hudson, Chapter 10 in this book).

Policy Formation

We have noted the growing importance of organizations offering policy advice and information to "assist" government decision making — the think tanks. The table below uses the annual budgets and the number of television, newspaper and radio references to rank a selection of institutes in Canada (Cardwell 2019). There are stark differences, with two much better financed than all others. But what sort of advice do these institutes offer governments? Most such institutes claim non-partisanship, political neutrality, non-ideological and researched-based analysis, advice and reports. Such claims need to be treated with some skepticism. Steven Tapp (2015) used Twitter followers to identify political leanings, placing a variety of institutes on a left-right continuum. He places the Manning Centre, the Frontier Centre for Public Policy, the Canadian Taxpayers Federation, the Macdonald Laurier Institute, the C.D. Howe Institute and the School of Public Policy at the University of Calgary on the furthest right. On the furthest left, he placed the Caledon Institute, the Broadbent Institute, the Council of Canadians, Democracy Watch, the Parkland Institute, the Mowat Centre, the Ecofiscal Commission and Sustainable Prosperity. In the centre, he located Canada 2020, the Martin Prosperity Institute, the Institute for Research on Public Policy (IRPP), the Public Policy Forum (PPF), the International Development

Research Centre (IDRC), the Centre for International Governance Innovation (CIGI) and the Canadian International Council (CIC). Adding this ideological info to the media reference and budget data shows that conservative (right) leaning think tanks are able to get their messages out quite effectively.

Canadian Think Tanks, Budgets, Media Presence, Ideology

Institute	Annual budget	TV, newspaper and radio references (#)	Political orientation
Fraser Institute	10.0 M	6,022	Right
Conference Board of Canada	40.0 M	5,789	Right
C.D. Howe Institute	3.5 M	4,792	Right
Canada West Foundation	3.0 M	3,897	Right
Canadian Centre for Policy Alternatives	5.0 M	3,185	Left
Pembina Institute	4.0 M	2,319	Left
Public Policy Forum	3.5 M	1,457	Centre
Montreal Economic Institute	2.25 M	517	Right

Looking at two important Canadian institutes, we see the difference that corporate-sector affiliation makes. The Fraser Institute (FI) claims that it "is an independent, non-partisan research and educational organization based in Canada." Its mission statement professes that it works to help Canadians "by studying, measuring, and broadly communicating the effects of government policies, entrepreneurship, and choice on their well-being" (Fraser Institute n.d.). It brings huge resources to its right-wing agenda, including more than 350 authors, academics and researchers from twenty-two countries, including six Nobel laureates. Its research agenda is comprehensive: Aboriginal policy, competitiveness, COVID-19, democracy and governance, economic freedom, educational policy, education, government spending and taxation, healthcare, labour policy, municipal policy, natural resources, pensions and retirement, poverty and inequality, provincial prosperity, school report cards, essential scholars and other research topics. The FI also offers "educational programs" for students, teachers and journalists.

The Canadian Centre for Policy Alternatives' (CCPA's) self-description explicitly includes the word justice: "The Canadian Centre for Policy Alternatives (CCPA) is an independent, non-partisan research institute concerned with issues of social, economic and environmental justice" (CCPA n.d.). A much smaller operation than the FI, the CCPA is overseen by a members' council composed of thirty-two representatives of various unions, academics, and community groups. It has just thirty-seven research associates and a budget that is half of FI's and one fifth of the C.D. Howe Institute's.

Ideological and Economic Mechanisms

Noted US economist Robert Heilbroner describes the complex and close relationship between the economy and the state:

> We have only to pose the respective imperatives of the two realms to see that strong affinities exist despite their dual missions. The [corporate world] cannot perform its [profit] accumulative function without the complementary support of the state.... As the other side of the coin, government is dependent on a healthy condition of the economy for the revenues it needs for its own goals, virtually all of which are expensive. (1992: 55)

He goes on to note, "In this mutual dependency the [corporate world] normally holds the upper hand." Holding the economic upper hand is an economic mechanism of power. If the economy is healthy and growing, if unemployment is low and jobs plentiful, if citizens and consumers are secure and relatively prosperous then it is much easier to operate the state and, if you are the government, to get elected or re-elected. Economic disruptions are undesirable for both corporations (capital) and the population at large. Economic disruptions can have many causes — war, disease, pestilence and natural disasters; however, sometimes they are the result of deliberate action. For workers, the only action that can cause significant economic disruption is a strike.

While it is true that, in some circumstances, workers can shut production in a specific enterprise by withdrawing their labour power, capital, the owners of corporations, can also go on strike. A capital strike looks different because there is no picket line but rather closed and shuttered plants, mines, stores or mills. A strike by capital may not be visible at all because it might take the form of a refusal to invest, resulting in no job creation, unemployment, recession or depression. If the workers in a particular enterprise informed the government that they will go on strike unless the state takes a particular action, the outcome is rarely in the workers' favour. On the other hand, if capital indicates they are going to withdraw investment, refuse to invest or relocate investment, it creates a situation in which governments are often forced to act. The case of the National Energy Program illustrates the power of capital to go on "strike" and to use that ability as a mechanism of power to get policy changes. The 1988 Canadian "Free Trade" election illustrates how a variety of mechanisms of power can be brought to bear on an important policy direction — free trade.

Case Study
The National Energy Program: Ideological and Economic Power

Amid rising world oil prices in the early 1980s, the Liberal government announced the National Energy Program (NEP) to enhance oil security through increased Canadian ownership along with price controls. The fossil fuel sector, controlled by some of the world's largest multinationals, and the Alberta government immediately responded negatively with a massive ideological campaign, court actions, production cuts, layoffs and an investment strike. The ideological or public relations campaign against the NEP included full page anti-NEP advertisements in major newspapers such as one featuring a large maple leaf and, in bold print: "MR. LALONDE PLEASE LISTEN. THE NATIONAL ENERGY PROGRAM IN HURTING *ALL* CANADIANS" (*Financial Post*, April 18, 1981). Various national and regional newspapers carried stories about the loss of jobs due to the exodus of oil drilling companies from Canada, cancelled pipeline projects, Canadian oil capital leaving for Australia, refinery closures, and the collapse of oil company stocks. Headlines such as "NEP Blamed for Stagnant Economy" (*Leader Post*, August 12, 1981), "Gasoline Prices Keep Going Up" (*Leader Post*, October 31, 1981) and "We've Seen the Future — and Its Costly" (*Financial Post*, September 12, 1981) carried the same negative message. There were claims of international opposition: "Reagan Takes Careful Aim at Canada" (*Financial Post*, November 4, 1981) and "Congress to Battle NEP on Oil Sands" (*Financial Post*, May 2, 1981). The Canadian Association of Petroleum Producers stated that the NEP cost fifteen thousand jobs, a 22 percent drop in drilling activity, and a 25 percent reduction in exploration (Corbella 2020). A prerogative of capital in a capitalist economy is to not invest, or to disinvest (close plants and productive enterprises), and this is precisely what happened. Under such relentless economic pressure and a successful conservative ideological campaign, the federal government was forced to entered into negotiations with Alberta to modify parts of the NEP. The federal Progressive Conservatives were always opposed and, after assuming power, they destroyed the remnants of the NEP, including privatizing Petro-Canada, a Crown-owned company whose had profits benefited Canadians.

Case Study
1988 Free Trade Election: Ideology and Economics

In 1988, a Canadian election was fought on a single issue — free trade with the US. Decades of Canadian and American economic integration came to a head in 1986, when Prime Minister Brian Mulroney and his friend, US president Ronald Regan, spearheaded trade negotiations. A deal was reached in the fall of 1987 and became the major issue in the subsequent election. Mulroney, who had opposed free trade in the early 1980s, flipped, arguing that the proposed agreement would herald a new era of prosperity while the Liberals and the NDP campaigned against the deal. During the campaign, the ideological weapons included both sides hauling out the patriotism trope. This was illustrated during a leaders' debate, when Liberal leader John Turner claimed Mulroney had "sold us out." Mulroney angrily replied, "You do not have a monopoly on patriotism … and I resent your implication that only you are a Canadian. I want to tell you that I come from a Canadian family and I love Canada, and that is why I did it, to promote prosperity" (Great Canadian Speeches 1988). The Progressive Conservatives engaged in negative advertising and, with help from "outside groups, financed heavily by the business community, mounted an enormous advertising campaign to save the Free Trade Agreement" (Leduc 1989: 166). The Canadian Alliance for Trade and Job Opportunities "launched a $1.3 million blitz that placed multi-page ads in thirty-five newspapers across the country, predicting severe economic consequences for Canada if it rejected the deal." The pro-free traders spent between $4 million and $5 million, compared to about $750,000 by opponents (Litt 2012: 76). The Mulroney Conservatives won the election and passed the free trade deal with the US that eventually became the North American Free Trade Agreement; it was revised to become the United States–Mexico–Canada Agreement (usmca) in 2020.

The Patriarchal State and Multiple Mechanisms of Power

It is generally the case that several different mechanisms of power are at work to influence political actions and policies. We know that Canada is a patriarchal society in which the state very often acts not just as a capitalist state, but as a patriarchal state. Among the reasons for this is the cast of characters or the personnel who occupy key decision-making positions within governments. At the simple level of legislative personnel, Roselie LeBlanc (LeBlanc and Anderson 2020) notes the overwhelming dominance of males: "In total, Canada has only ever had 12 female premiers, the first being Rita Johnston of BC in 1991. In that same time frame, since the first female premier, there have been more than 75 male premiers." In 2021, only 29 percent of members of Parliament are women (Statistics Canada 2021a).

We know that economic power can be translated into political power through the various mechanisms we've discussed. In Canada, economic power and wealth are also concentrated in the hands of men. In 2019, the pay ratio of annual wages, salaries and commissions paid to women as compared to men was 0.71, meaning for every dollar men earned, women earned 71 cents (Statistics Canada 2021b). In terms of business property ownership, in 2013, of the 1,413,350 business firms in Canada, 78.2 percent were male owned and just 21.8 percent female owned (Statistics Canada 2019). When it comes to employment in the most powerful positions, women again are underrepresented.

Gender of Corporate Management and Directors

Corporate positions	Male (%)	Female (%)
Management—all occupations, 2020	52.9	47.1
Senior management, 2020	71.2	28.6
All corporate boards, 2018	81.7	18.3
Corporate boards, private enterprises, 2018	82.0	18.0

Sources: Statistics Canada 2021c; Statistics Canada 2021d

It is clear that many sexist ideologies are firmly entrenched in Canada. In the fall of 2018 Girl Guides Canada conducted a survey of girls and boys ages twelve to seventeen. The results documented in *Sexism, Feminism & Equality: What Teens in Canada Really Think* should be astonishing, but maybe they are not: "Girls are more likely than boys to report feeling the impact of gender inequality: girls are twice as likely as boys (43% vs. 21%) to report experiencing sexism, and to say that gender inequality has impacted their life (35% vs. 20%)" (Girl Guides Canada 2018). These results are unfortunately in line with other data on the sexist attitudes within the broader Canadian population; a March 2020 survey reported that over 80 percent of survey respondents indicated than women should be primarily responsible for cooking, cleaning and childcare (Plan Canada 2020). While the magazine is not necessarily associated with social activism, *Elle Canada* published an account of the horrendous sexism, harassment, threats and abuse many women active in politics face at all levels — from US vice-president Kamala Harris to Canadian cabinet minister Catherine McKenna and city councillors — two decades into the twenty-first century (Kaur 2021). A post-election analysis of the 2019 Canadian election presents a litany of abuses and threats received by many women running for Parliament, including having vile names painted on their offices and some requiring police protection.

Unlike the employment of mechanisms of power in other, quite specific examples, this overview paints a picture of the larger context within which state decision makers and political actors move. Addressing issues of systemic sexism and male domination requires action to address the overall institutional matrix that is dominated by males. Additionally, social change must address the fact that in a capitalist economic order and a patriarchal gender order, economic power and wealth are male controlled and the overall ideological environment is patriarchal and sexist. While individual males often resist the role of protagonist, the existence of a patriarchal dividend heightens the challenge to equality and equity (Knuttila 2016).

STATE AUTONOMY

While analyzing mechanisms of power is clearly a productive approach, it is important to add a word of caution. Those who run state organizations and institutions can, and often do, have their own interests. An institutionalist perspective recognizes this fact and "emphasizes the relative autonomy of political institutions from other institutions, classes and social interests, the possibilities for inefficiency in history, and the importance of symbolic action to an understanding of politics" (March and Olsen 1984: 734; see also 1989). The role and internal interests of state agencies and the bureaucratic apparatus might be particularly important when there is a change in government, and changes to established institutional priorities, cultures and interests become a potential concern. An example emerged in 2017 when, as the Harper Conservatives prepared to privatize the Canadian Wheat Board, the board leadership actively defended itself, working with and supporting the majority of farmers in favour of keeping the agency (Magnan 2016).

The question of what degree of autonomy a liberal democratic state has from various social classes, groups and interests also becomes more important during times of political or social crisis. In 1970, following years of political, social and cultural nationalist turmoil and protest in Quebec, a militant political organization called the Front de libération du Québec (FLQ) kidnapped an international political figure and a Quebec cabinet minister. While many of the demands of the FLQ and other left-wing political organizations were distinctively anti-capitalist, the speed with which the federal government took matters into its own hands was surprising.

Prime Minister Pierre Trudeau imposed the *War Measures Act* and deployed the Canadian military, mainly in Quebec. Imposed for the first time ever during peace time, the *War Measures Act* removed all basic human rights and constitutional freedoms in Canada, including search and seizure of personal property without warrants and arrest and detention without cause. As Lorne Brown (1987) has demonstrated, throughout Canadian history, governments have demonstrated a willingness to use force and violence to ensure "social order": in the military defeat of the Métis and the execution of Louis Riel; the suppression of the Winnipeg General Strike in 1919; the Regina Riot, when hundreds of unemployed workers were, under the prime minister's orders, forced off a train in Regina, resulting bloody violence. All of these events represent suspensions of the normal operation of political decision making.

The actions of the federal government and of various provinces in response to the 2020 outbreak of the COVID-19 virus is a more contemporary instance of states' relatively high degree of autonomy. Acting on the basis of expert health and epidemiological advice but often without public debate, never mind formal legislative approval, federal and provincial governments imposed strict behavioural and mobility regulations on Canadians. Mandated under the authority of health officials, closures, lockdowns and curfews temporarily shuttered many major social institutions, including schools, businesses and churches. Despite what we think are the heuristic values of a mechanisms-of-power approach, sometimes an understanding of the actions, decisions and policies enacted during such times, when "all rules are off," requires an appreciation of the notion of state autonomy.

THE STATE, POWER AND SOCIAL ISSUES

The central message of this chapter is that understanding and explaining the actions, policies and decisions of liberal democratic states and governments is a difficult task. It should be noted that important theoretical streams, including elite theory, rational choice theory and American functionalist theory, have been ignored here, as have the important critiques of state activities associated with various streams of anarchist thought. What the chapter has offered is an outline of an approach that has the potential to uncover and understand some of the complexities of political decision making and how it is possible to connect social classes, groups and interests empirically and historically to liberal democratic states.

In a liberal-democratic system, all citizens, individuals, associations, groups and parties have the formal legal right to engage the mechanisms of power discussed above. All citizens can run for office, support parties financially and otherwise, lobby governments and officials, attempt to influence public opinion, make decisions regarding economic activities and so on. What emerges, however, when we analyze the actual capacity and ability of various interests and actors to engage these mechanisms are patterns of inequality. One only need ask the somewhat rhetorical question, "What does it take to run for office, fund political activities, engage in lobbying, undertake public relations and ideological campaigns, and make important economic decisions?" The answer is, of course, access to and control of economic and ideological resources. In a class-based society, those who control the major economic institutions make the major economic decisions and reap the overwhelming economic benefits of global capitalism. Having said this, it is important to remember that conceptualizing struggles over political power in a liberal-democratic society within the context of the mechanisms of power noted previously does leave room for various social and economic interests to attempt to engage those mechanisms. This is why, as the title of this chapter indicates, matters of the state *do* matter! In the chapters that follow, you will learn more about the extent to which such access and control is equally or unequally distributed in contemporary Canada.

DISCUSSION QUESTIONS

1. What are the core tenets of the pluralist understanding of political power? Do these assumptions stand up to critical scrutiny given the inequality of incomes that typically characterize market-based societies?
2. Which theory discussed in the chapter might best explain why labour or social-democratic governments often align themselves with dominant economic interests?
3. Feminists have demonstrated that capitalist states typically fail to address patriarchal domination. Explain why you think this is the case.
4. What are the essential elements of a mechanisms-of-power approach?
5. Compare how two different theories or approaches to understanding the state would explain the decline of the welfare state over the past three decades.

GLOSSARY OF KEY TERMS

Corporate colonialism: A form of colonialism whereby various kinds of raw materials in the land (and often the land itself) are essentially stolen from the original inhabitants and made the property of mining, lumber, railway and fossil fuel companies.

Feminism: A diverse set of beliefs, political practices, social practices, social movements and sociological theories predicated on a set of underlying assumptions and principles that recognize the historical subordination and oppression of women.

Feminists not only commit to explaining this phenomenon, but they also seek alternative non-oppressive modes of social organization.

Fordism: An economic and political system in which the state provides a social safety net and uses its resources to direct investment and economic activity. But business makes most of the economic decisions here, especially in key industrial sectors where it is given a free hand to introduce technological change and other labour-saving innovations. Workers, through their unions, get wage increases in line with productivity gains plus inflation.

Government: Refers to a particular assemblage of people, generally organized into a political party or social movement, who are formally in control of the apparatus of the state for a limited period of time and, in a liberal-democratic system, are subject to renewal or replacement through periodic elections.

Instrumentalist Marxism: A neo-Marxist view, this approach emphasizes personal and personnel connections between representatives of the capitalist class and the state. Instrumentalists maintain that the capitalist class is able to control and direct the activities of the state because the people operating the state either come directly from the capitalist class or share the values, ideologies and objectives of the capitalist class.

Mechanisms of power: An approach to the state stressing that there are a number of different means that can be employed to influence the state in capitalist society. This includes both direct (personnel and personal connections, lobbying and impacting policy formation) and indirect (using economic power, ideological power and political funding) mechanisms of power. All classes and individuals are able to use these mechanisms; however, the class and groups with overwhelming economic power are better able to exercise them.

Pluralism: Pluralists recognize that individuals will differ in terms of their income, social status or authority but assert that liberal-democratic systems prevent these from becoming entrenched social inequalities. Pluralists maintain that in democratic electoral systems, an open process of decision making and group lobbying ensures a democratic process because all groups and interests in society have a more or less equal opportunity to influence the government through electoral and lobbying activities.

Racial capitalism: Capitalism requires socio-economic inequality based not only on relations to the means of production but also on other worker characteristics such as racialization. Black historians have shown that the development of industrial capitalism relied on colonialism and slavery.

Settler colonialism: The process whereby one people claim sovereignty over another, particularly their land, to extract resources and accumulate profits at the expense of those colonized. It differs from other forms of colonialism in that the colonizers come to stay and dispossess Indigenous peoples from their territories versus taking what they want and leaving. Settler society is imposed on Indigenous people, disrupting their own systems of governance and ways of being.

State system/polity: All of the institutions, organizations and agencies connected with the political processes in societies, including formally organized political institutions. In Western liberal democracies, the state system or polity includes the formally elected apparatus of government, appointed officials, the state bureaucracy, the judiciary, police, military, and national and international agencies.

Structuralist Marxism: A version of neo-Marxist theory that sees the state's major role as attempting to prevent inherent conflicts and contradictions, related to fundamental class inequality, from destroying the capitalist system. It is the needs and logic of the system that determine the role and function of the state and not the connections of state personnel to the capitalist class.

Third-wave feminism: Emphasizes the necessity of recognizing the complexities of women's situations and experiences by rejecting any simple notion of "women" as a homogeneous category or group. Third-wave feminists draw attention to issues of class, race, ethnicity, age, geographic location, national identity and a host of other differences and divisions that combine to oppress women. Thus, there cannot be a singular, totalizing or universal feminist theory.

RESOURCES FOR ACTIVISTS

Alternative Federal Budget: policyalternatives.ca/projects/alternative-federal-budget
United Food and Commercial Workers union (UFCW Canada) "UFCW Canada Political Action": ufcw.ca/index.php?option=com_content&view=article&id=60:political-action&catid=22:political-action&Itemid=352&lang=en
Democracy Watch: democracywatch.ca/
Canadian Research Institute for the Advancement of Women: criaw-icref.ca
Food Tank: foodtank.com/

NOTE

1 Thanks to Wayne Antony for authoring racial capitalism and the Wet'suwet'en case study.

REFERENCES

Armstrong, P. 1996. "Unravelling the Safety Net: Transformations in Health Care and their Impact on Women." In J. Brodie (ed.), *Women and Canadian Public Policy*. Toronto: Harcourt Brace.

Bentley, A.F. [1908] 1995. *The Process of Government: A Study of Social Pressures*. New Brunswick, NJ: Transaction Publishers.

Bonacich, E. 1972. "A Theory of Ethnic Antagonisms: The Split Labor Market." *American Sociological Review* 37.

Brodie, J. (ed.). 1996. *Women and Canadian Public Policy*. Toronto: Harcourt Brace.

Brown, L. 1987. *When Freedom Was Lost*. Montreal: Black Rose Books.

Burstyn, V. 1985. "Masculine Domination and the State." In D.E. Smith and V. Burstyn (eds.), *Women, Class, Family and the State*. Toronto: Garamond.

Cameron, B. 1996. "Brave New Worlds for Women: NAFTA and New Reproductive Technologies." In J. Brodie (ed.), *Women and Canadian Public Policy*. Toronto: Harcourt Brace & Company.

Canada, Elections Canada website. 2020. "A History of the Vote in Canada." <elections.ca/content.aspx-?section=res&dir=his&document=index&lang=e>.

Canadaland. 2021. "Jailed for Journalism: Amber and Michael Speak Out." #735.

Canadian Encyclopedia. 2013. "Statute of Westminster, 1931: Document." <thecanadianencyclopedia.ca/en/article/statute-of-westminster-1931-document>.

Cardwell, M. 2019. "Think Tanks Fill an Important Niche Within Canada's Public Policy Landscape." *University Affairs*, April 10. <universityaffairs.ca/features/feature-article/think-tanks-fill-an-impor-tant-niche-within-canadas-public-policy-landscape/>.

Carroll, W., and J.P. Sapinski. 2018. *Organizing the 1%: How Corporate Power Works*. Winnipeg and Black Point, NS: Fernwood Publishing.

Cave, T., and A. Rowell. 2014. "The Truth about Lobbying: 10 Ways Big Business Controls Government." *Guardian*, March 12. <theguardian.com/politics/2014/mar/12/lobbying-10-ways-corprations-influ-ence-government>.

CCPA (Centre for Policy Alternatives). n.d. "About Us." <policyalternatives.ca/>.

Coates, T. 2014. "Slavery Made America." *The Atlantic*, June 24.

Collins, M. 2015. "The Big Bank Bailout." *Forbes*, July 14. <forbes.com/sites/mikecollins/2015/07/14/the-big-bank-bailout/#6d5594483723>.

Connell, R.W. 2002. *Gender*. Cambridge, Polity Press.

___. 1995. *Masculinities*. Berkley: University of California Press.

Corbella, L. 2020. "40 Years Later, National Energy Program Has Lessons to Teach Today." *Calgary Herald*, October 20. <calgaryherald.com/news/local-news/corbella-nep>.

Coulthard, G. 2014. *Red Skins, White Masks: Rejecting the Colonial Politics of Recognition*. Minneapolis: University of Minnesota Press.

Craft. A. 2013. *Breathing Life into the Stone Fort Treaty: An Anishnabe Understanding of Treaty One*. Vancouver: UBC Press.

Dahl, R. 1972. *Democracy in the United States*. Chicago: Rand.

___. 1967. *Pluralist Democracy in the United States*. Chicago: Rand.

Drohan M. 2011. "Canada as Colonial Power: A Review of Todd Gordon's *Imperialist Canada*." *Literary Review of Canada*, January–February. <reviewcanada.ca/magazine/2011/01/canada-as-coloni-al-power/>.

Dubinsky, K. 1985. *Lament for a "Patriarchy Lost?" Anti-Feminism, Anti-Abortion and R.E.A.L. Women in Canada*. Ottawa: CRIAW.

Elections Canada. 2019. "Political Financing Handbook for Third Parties, Financial Agents and Auditors (EC 20227) — August 2019." <elections.ca/content.aspx?section=pol&dir=thi/ec20227_old&docu-ment=index&lang=e>.

Elliot, P., and N. Mandell. 1995. "Feminist Theories." In N. Mandell (ed.), *Feminist Issues*. Scarborough,

ON: Prentice-Hall.

Fraser Institute. n.d. "Welcome to the Fraser Institute." <fraserinstitute.org/about>.

Gavigan, S.A.M.1987. "Women and Abortion in Canada: What's Law Got to Do With It?" In H.J. Maroney and M. Luxton (eds.), *Feminism and Political Economy: Women's Work, Women's Struggles.* Toronto: Methuen.

Girl Guides Canada. 2018. *Sexism, Feminism & Equality: What Teens in Canada Really Think* <girl-guides.ca/WEB/Documents/GGC/media/thought-leadership/201SexismFeminismEquality-What-TeensinCanadaReallyThink.pdf>.

Government of Canada, Department of Justice. 1867. *British North America Act, 1867 — Enactment no. 1.* <justice.gc.ca/eng/rp-pr/csj-sjc/constitution/lawreg-loireg/p1t11.html>.

Great Canadian Speeches. 1988. "John Turner, Brian Mulroney Debate Free Trade, Oct. 1988." <greatca-nadianspeeches.ca/2019/09/18/john-turner-brian-mulroney-debate-free-trade-oct-1988/>.

Grenier, É. 2020. "Conservative Election Spending Outpaced Liberals by a Little and the NDP by a Lot." CBC News, June 23. <cbc.ca/news/politics/grenier-election-spending-1.5622721>.

Haney, L.A. 2000. "Feminist State Theory: Applications to Jurisprudence, Criminology, and the Welfare State." *Annual Review of Sociology* 26.

Hansard, Canada. 2012. House of Commons Debates. September 17.

Harvey, D. 2010. *The Enigma of Capital and the Crisis of Capitalism.* New York: Oxford University Press.

___. 2005. *A Brief History of Neoliberalism.* Oxford: Oxford University Press.

Heilbroner, R. 1992. *Twenty-first Century Capitalism.* Toronto: House of Anansi.

Ivanova, I. 2021. *Inequality, Employment and COVID-19.* Vancouver: CCPA-BC. <policyalternatives.ca/sites/default/files/uploads/publications/BC%20Office/2021/07/ccpa-bc_Inequality-Employment-COVID_full.pdf>.

Jessop, B. 2010. "Redesigning the State, Reorienting State Power, and Rethinking State Theory." In C. Jenkins and K. Leicht (eds.), *Handbook of Politics: State and Society in Global Perspective.* New York: Springer.

Kaur, W. 2021. "Prominent Women in Public Office Say that Systemic Sexism Needs a Political Shakedown." *Elle Canada,* January 5. <ellecanada.com/culture/society/prominent-women-in-pub-lic-office-say-that-systemic-sexism-needs-a-political-shakedown>.

Knuttila, M. 2016. *Paying for Masculinity: Boys, Men and the Patriarchal Dividend.* Halifax: Fernwood Publishing.

Knuttila, M., and W. Kubik. 2000. *State Theories: Classical, Global and Feminist Perspectives.* Halifax, NS: Fernwood Publishing and Zed Books.

LeBlanc, R., and B. Anderson. 2020. "Canadians Mostly Believe We've Achieved Gender Equality. But It's Not True." *Canada's National Observer*, June 18. <nationalobserver.com/2020/06/18/opinion/ca-nadians-mostly-believe-weve-achieved-gender-equality-its-not-true>.

Leduc, L. 1989. "The Canadian Federal Election of 1988." *Electoral Studies* 8, 2.

Lindblom, C.E. 1977. *Politics and Markets.* New York: Basic Books.

Litt, P. 2012. "The Fight of His Life: John Turner and the Free Trade Election." *Policy Options*, December–January. <irpp.org/wp-content/uploads/assets/po/the-year-in-review/litt.pdf>.

Macdonald, D. 2020. "Fail Safe: CEO Compensation in Canada." *Canadian Centre for Policy Alternatives*, January. <policyalternatives.ca/publications/reports/fail-safe>.

MacKinnon, C. 2017. "Response to Five Philosophers: Toward a Feminist Theory of the State Some Decades Later." *Feminist Philosophy Quarterly* 3, 2.

___. 1989. *Toward a Feminist Theory of the State.* Cambridge, MA: Harvard University Press.

Madrick, J. 2016. "How the Lobbyist Marxists Win in Washington." *New York Review of Books,* April 7.

Magnan, A. 2016. *When Wheat Was King: The Rise and Fall of the Canada–UK Grain Trade.* Vancouver: UBC Press.

March, J.G., and J.P. Olsen. 1989. *Rediscovering Institutions: The Organizational Basis of Politics.* New York: Free Press.

___. 1984. "The New Institutionalism: Organizational Factors in Political Life." *American Political*

Science Review 78, 3.

Martin, M. 2021. "Out of Focus at Wet'suwet'en." *Winnipeg Free Press*, December 3. <winnipegfreepress.com/local/out-of-focus-at-wetsuweten-575856532.html>.

Marx, K.[1850] 1972a. *The Class Struggles in France*. Moscow: International.

___. [1852] 1972b. "The Eighteenth Brumaire of Louis Bonaparte." In R. Tucker (ed.), *The Marx–Engels Reader*. New York: Norton.

Marx, K., and F. Engels.[1848] 1952. *Manifesto of the Communist Party*. New York: International.

___. [1845] 1970. *The German Ideology*. New York: International.

Maynard, R. 2017. *Policing Black Lives: State Violence in Canada From Slavery to the Present*. Black Point, NS, and Winnipeg: Fernwood Publishing.

McDaniel S.A. 1985. "Implementation of Abortion Policy in Canada as a Women's Issue." *Atlantis* 10, 2.

McNally. D. 2020. *Blood and Money: War, Slavery, Finance and Empire*. Winnipeg and Black Point, NS: Fernwood Publishing.

Merriam, C.E. 1964. *Political Power*. New York: Free Press.

Miliband, R. 1973. *The State in Capitalist Society*. London: Quartet.

Monchalin. L. 2016. *The Colonial Problem: An Indigenous Perspective on Crime and Justice in Canada*. Toronto: University of Toronto Press.

Narwhal. n.d. "Wet'suwet'en."<thenarwhal.ca/?s=Wet'suwet'en+>.

Nelson, A., and B. Robinson. 2002. *Gender in Canada,* 2nd edition. Toronto: Prentice-Hall.

Office of the Commissioner of Lobbying. n.d. "The Registry of Lobbyists. Active Lobbyists and Registration by Types." <lobbycanada.gc.ca/app/secure/ocl/lrs/do/guest>.

Palmater, P. 2015. *Indigenous Nationhood: Empowering Grassroots Citizens*. Winnipeg and Black Point, NS: Fernwood Publishing.

___. 2020. *Warrior Life: Indigenous Resistance and Resurgence*. Winnipeg and Black Point, NS: Fernwood Publishing.

Pateman, C. 1989. *The Disorder of Women*. Stanford, CA: Stanford University Press.

Plan International Canada. 2020. "A Woman's Place in Canada Is in the Kitchen?" March 2. <newswire.ca/news-releases/a-woman-s-place-in-canada-is-in-the-kitchen--850577384.html>.

Polanyi, K. 1944. *The Great Transformation*. New York: Farrar and Rinehart.

Poulantzas, N. 1968. *Political Power and Social Classes*. New York: New Left Books.

Preston, J. 2013. "Neoliberal Settler Colonialism, Canada and the Tar Sands." *Race and Class* 55, 2.

Pupo, N. 1988. "Preserving Patriarchy: Women, the Family and the State." In N. Mandell and A. Duffy (eds.), *Reconstructing the Canadian Family: Feminist Perspectives*. Toronto: Butterworths.

Raman-Wilms, M. 2021. "MP Says She Found House an 'Uneasy Place.'" *Globe and Mail,* June 17.

Ransom, R. n.d. "The Economics of the Civil War." *EH.net*. <eh.net/encyclopedia/the-economics-of-the-civil-war/>.

RCAP (Royal Commission on Aboriginal Peoples). 1996. "Report of the Royal Commission on Aboriginal Peoples, Vols. 1–5." Ottawa: Minister of Supply and Services Canada.

Robinson. C. 2005. *Black Marxism: The Making of the Black Radical Tradition*. U of North Carolina Press. [1983, Zed Books].

Schwartz, Brian. 2020. "Total 2020 Election Spending to Hit Nearly $14 Billion, More than Double 2016's Sum." CNBC, October 28. <cnbc.com/2020/10/28/2020-election-spending-to-hit-nearly-14-billion-a-record.html>.

Scott. K. 2021. *Women, Work and COVID-19*. Ottawa: Canadian Centre for Policy Alternatives.

Smith, A. 2010. "Indigeneity, Settler Colonialism, White Supremacy." *Global Dialogues* 12, 2.

Statistics Canada. 2021a. "Representation of Women and Men Elected to National Parliament and of Ministers Appointed to Federal Cabinet." Table 10-10-0137-01. <open.canada.ca/data/en/dataset/052d45dd-9fc3-4063-b2cc-979e3e7d0d7a>.

___. 2021b. "Average and Median Gender Pay Ratio in Annual Wages, Salaries and Commissions." Table 14-10-0324-01. <www150.statcan.gc.ca/n1/en/catalogue/1410032401>.

___. 2021c. "Proportion of Women and Men Employed in Management Positions, Annual." Table 14-

10-0335-03. <www150.statcan.gc.ca/t1/tbl1/en/tv.action?pid=1410033503>.

___. 2021d. "Representation of Men And Women on Boards Of Directors." Table 33-10-0218-01. <www150.statcan.gc.ca/t1/tbl1/en/tv.action?pid=3310021801>.

___. 2019. "Private Enterprises by Ownership Gender, Age Group of Primary Owner and Enterprise Size." Table 33-10-0192-01. <www150.statcan.gc.ca/t1/tbl1/en/tv.action?pid=3310019201>.

___. 2004. "A Profile of Canada's North American Indian Population with Legal Indian Status." Ottawa: Statistics Canada.

Szymanski, A. 1978. *The Capitalist State and the Politics of Class*. Cambridge: Winthrop.

Tapp, S. 2015. "This Simple Measure for Think Tank Ideology Uses Social Media Data from Twitter and the Natural Tendency for Like-Minded People to Associate." *Policy Options*, January 5. <policyoptions.irpp.org/magazines/environmental-faith/tapp/>.

Terrell, E. 2019. "When a Quote Is Not (Exactly) a Quote: The Business of America Is Business Edition." *Library of Congress*, January 17. <blogs.loc.gov/inside_adams/2019/01/when-a-quote-is-not-exactly-a-quote-the-business-of-america-is-business-edition/>.

Therborn, G. 1978. *What Does the Ruling Class Do When It Rules?* New York: Schocken Books.

Turpel-Lafond, M.E. 1997. "Patriarchy and Paternalism; The Legacy of the Canadian State for First Nations Women." In C. Andrew and S. Rodgers (eds.), *Women and the Canadian State/Les femmes et l'Etat canadien*. Montreal: McGill-Queen's University Press.

Ursel. J. 1986. "The State and the Maintenance of Patriarchy: A Case Study of Family, Labour and Welfare Legislation in Canada." In J. Dickinson and B. Russell (eds.), *Family, Economy and State*. Toronto: Garamond Press.

Wikipedia. n.d.a. "Coastal GasLink Pipeline." <en.wikipedia.org/wiki/Coastal_GasLink>.

___. n.d.b. "TC Energy." <en.wikipedia.org/wiki/TC_Energy>.

Wolfe. P. 2006. "Settler Colonialism and the Elimination of the Native." *Journal of Genocide Research* 8, 4.

Wouters, O. 2020. "Lobbying Expenditures and Campaign Contributions by the Pharmaceutical and Health Product Industry in the United States, 1999–2018." *JAMA Internal Medicine* 180, 5. <doi.org/10.1001/jamainternmed.2020.0146> <ncbi.nlm.nih.gov/pmc/articles/PMC7054854/>.

Yinta Access. n.d. "No Access Without Consent: History and Timeline." <yintaaccess.com/history-andtimeline>.

3

DEATH BY POVERTY
The Lethal Impacts of Colonialism

Pamela D. Palmater

YOU SHOULD KNOW THIS

- Despite a Liberal promise to fix the crisis, thirty-eight First Nations still have long-term water advisories and 73 percent of First Nations water systems are at high or medium risk of contamination.

- Fifty-two percent of all children in foster care are Indigenous.

- Forty-seven percent of First Nations children live in poverty.

- Since 2010, the Indigenous population in prisons has increased by 43.4 percent, while the non-Indigenous prison population has declined by 13.7 percent.

- In 2016, Indigenous people were 5 percent of Canada's population but were 3 percent of undergrad students, 0.9 percent of doctorates and 1.3 percent of full-time faculty.

- If nothing changes, it will take sixty-three years to close the income gap between First Nations and Canadians.

Sources: ISC 2020b; AFN 2019; Council of Canadians n.d.; UC 2019; OCI 2020; Lorraine 2016; OAG 2004.

THE THEMES THAT EMERGED FROM A review of the circumstances of the deaths and lives of the youth, was not a story of capitulation to death, but rather, a story of stamina, endurance, tolerance, and resiliency stretched beyond human limits until finally, they simply could take no more (Office of the Chief Coroner for Ontario 2012: 99).[1]

From time immemorial, the sovereign Indigenous nations[2] of what is now known as Canada have thrived in their rich, vibrant cultures with their own languages, customs and traditions, developing complex governments, laws and political structures. They prospered from their vast territories, careful management of the natural resources and strategic use of intertribal trading networks. While disputes did occur, their military strategies and treaty negotiating skills always served them well. Post-contact, these Nations fought to maintain their way of life despite the diseases, colonial violence, land theft and manufactured poverty that ravaged their peoples. With the future of their peoples in the balance, Indigenous nations risked all to assert, live and defend their sovereignty and governance over their territories. Land was not only central to their identities, but they knew then, as they do now, that the gifts from the lands, waters, plants and animals are what sustains their Nations. The colonization of Indigenous peoples and territories by foreign countries targeted Indigenous lands and trading networks, literally stealing the lifeblood of Indigenous peoples. It should be no surprise, then, that First Nations in Canada, have gone from the richest peoples in the world to the most impoverished, as their lands, resources and ways of being were stolen from them through the violent process of colonization.

> First Nations in Canada, have gone from the richest peoples in the world to the most impoverished, as their lands, resources, and ways of being were stolen from them through the violent process of colonization.

Today, Canada may be full of political apologies, but it is not a post-colonial country. In fact, federal, provincial and territorial laws and policies not only put First Nations in their current state of extreme poverty, they also keep Indigenous communities in this state. Federal laws assume jurisdiction over First Nations and every aspect of their lives, yet the corresponding policies fail to live up to those constitutional responsibilities. Provincial and territorial laws don't fare much better, as they run roughshod over Aboriginal and treaty rights, including Aboriginal title (constitutionally protected rights to their lands) (see, for example, *Haida Nation v. BC* 2004: 513). The resulting dispossession and oppression of Indigenous peoples has left many of those who have survived injured, impoverished and impacted by intergenerational trauma.

While the focus here is the ongoing colonization and dispossession of Indigenous peoples through government policies and funding mechanisms, it would be incomplete without an acknowledgement of the equally lethal damage done by corporate colonization and dispossession of Indigenous peoples. The violence and lethal nature of colonization hasn't changed much since contact — except for the colonizers themselves. Some argue that we have entered a second phase of colonization, or "re-colonization," of Indigenous peoples, which has the possibility of being just as lethal (Banerjee 1999: 7). Large domestic and multinational corporations can be as politically powerful as governments, and their false promise of corporate social responsibility has wreaked havoc on Indigenous lands, waters and resources for decades (Frynas 2005). It only follows that so many uninformed commentators sought to blame First Nations for their current state of affairs when the previous Conservative government, led by former prime minister Stephen Harper, publicly blamed the victims and portrayed them as threats to national security for trying to defend their lands and waters. After Justin Trudeau's Liberal government took power in 2015, he made promises to reject the "'adversarial,' 'ineffective' and 'profoundly damaging' approaches of the past" (Forester 2020). However, Trudeau's government spent $3.5 million more than the Conservative government on litigation against First Nations, totalling $95.9 million between 2015 and 2018. Trudeau, like so many before him, resorts to the colonial "rule of law" when Indigenous peoples defend their lands. Most Canadians would like to think they can move forward with reconciliation, believing that atrocities against First Nations are in the past — but they continue. Further, they fail to see that the second phase of colonization is equally as lethal — and it is delivered through corporations empowered by governments. It is true that all Canadians benefit from the dispossession of Indigenous peoples — but corporations reap the biggest profits. The "new corporate colonialism" (Vidal 2013) — that is, the corporate quest for minerals, trees, oil, and gas — amounts to blood money and has its origins in pre-Confederation colonization, where large companies worked with colonial governments to help clear the lands for development and settlement (Hall 2010). The result, then, is the same as now: First Nations die premature deaths from the resulting extreme poverty, violent extractive activities and ongoing genocidal laws, policies and practices by the state. There is no more denying this stark reality — Canada has been found guilty of both

> The corporate quest for minerals, trees, oil, and gas amounts to blood money and has its origins in pre-confederation colonization, where large companies worked with colonial governments to help clear the lands for development and settlement.

historic and ongoing genocide by the National Inquiry into Missing and Murdered Indigenous Women and Girls (National Inquiry 2019a).

Corporate colonization of Indigenous lands and resources, taken together with ongoing government colonization and genocidal practices, creates significant barriers for Indigenous peoples and makes efforts at resistance and protection of lands and peoples very difficult. Governments have maintained their vise-like grip on First

Nations through literally thousands of racist laws and regulations, in addition to tightly managed and chronically underfunded government programs. Just consider the plight of Pikangikum First Nation in Ontario: Despite all the natural wealth and beauty that surrounds the community, they have been living under a dark cloud for many years because their children are taking their own lives. This has attracted the attention of the Ontario Chief Coroner (2012: 99):

> Pikangikum is an impoverished, isolated First Nations community where basic necessities of life are absent. Running water and indoor plumbing do not exist for most residents. Poverty, crowded substandard housing, gainful employment, food and water security are daily challenges. A lack of an integrated health care system, poor education by provincial standards and a largely absent community infrastructure are uniquely positioned against a backdrop of colonialism, racism, lack of implementation of self-determination and social exclusion. They all contribute to the troubled youth.

The healthcare residents do receive is "fragmented, chaotic and uncoordinated" with "clear gaps in service." Pikangikum First Nation's school burnt down in 2007 and wasn't replaced for over a decade, despite empty promises by Indian and Northern Affairs Canada (now Indigenous Services Canada, ISC) to do so. Construction for a new school was finally completed in 2016. Yet the chronic underfunding of Pikangikum students as compared to Canadian students means that the students who are the most disadvantaged and have the greatest needs receive the least assistance. While the education funding gap can range from 20 to 50 percent, on average, First Nations receive 30 percent less than their provincial counterparts (Porter 2016; Drummond and Rosenbluth 2013). In 2016, a community of only 2,400 people had two hundred child welfare files open and eighty children in care. Due to the lack of housing and the high levels of overcrowding, when children are apprehended from their parents, they are sent to foster homes far away from their First Nation. Should anyone be surprised by the fact that sixteen children between the ages of ten and nineteen took their own lives in Pikangikum between 2006 and 2008, living under these conditions? The suicide crisis did not abate with the submission of the coroner's report. In 2011 alone, two sixteen-year-old girls committed suicide within twenty days of one another (Patriquin 2012). The following six weeks saw two men and two women commit suicide. In fact, Pikangikum had the highest suicide rate in the world and held that record for over twenty years. In 2021, the community of nearly 3,600 people continued to see high rates of youth suicide (*Globe and Mail* 2021). This is what it means to be a First Nation person living under federal jurisdiction in Canada today. While the conditions vary on the 634+ First Nations in Canada, a significant number suffer similar socio-economic circumstances. Few realize the true extent of First Nation poverty, its root causes or why it is getting worse. Nor do they understand that the high suicide rates, like poverty, are of Canada's own making (Palmater 2020: Ch. 16).

THE REALITY OF FIRST NATION POVERTY

First Nation poverty is not a new phenomenon, nor is it so hidden as to be unknown to either the public or our policymakers. Doctors, academics and other experts have tried to bring First Nation poverty and its devastating social effects to the forefront for many years. In countless reports and studies, the extreme poverty in First Nations has been described by researchers as "pervasive," a "national disgrace," a "national shame," "unacceptable" and an "emergency" situation of "intolerable" conditions (National Council on Welfare 2007; OCI 2000–2010; Eggerton 2007; OAG 2000–2010; RCAP 1996). Political leaders, organizations and commentators have described the extreme poverty in First Nations as a "crisis," an "epidemic" and a matter of "life or death" (Mary Simon, president of Inuit Tapiriit Kanatami, and the former Ontario lieutenant governor, James Bartleman, quoted in Eggerton 2007: 1). The former lieutenant governor, James Bartleman, called the situation a "national shame" (APTN 2011). Even a former prime minister referred to the underfunding of First Nation education as "immoral discrimination" (Talaga 2011). While historical colonial laws and policies created the dependency relationship, current federal laws and policies maintain the national crisis of poverty in First Nations, which in turn results in the premature deaths of First Nations peoples.[3] This is why the National Inquiry concluded that "Canada's colonial history provides ample evidence of the existence of a genocidal policy, a 'manifest pattern of similar conduct,' which reflects an intention to destroy Indigenous Peoples." They concluded that "Canada has displayed a continuous policy, with shifting expressed motives but an ultimately steady intention, to destroy Indigenous peoples physically, biologically, and as social units" (National Inquiry 2019b: 24).

Incredibly, politicians have turned a blind eye to the problem while conditions in First Nations have worsened. Although Canada has publicly denounced the attitudes of superiority upon which assimilatory laws and policies were previously based, the majority of these laws and policies remain unchanged (CBC News 2016; Harper 2008; Venne 1981; Wilson 1993; *Indian Act* 1985). Trudeau was originally elected on a campaign promise to amend or repeal all the laws imposed on First Nations by the former Harper government — but he has failed to do so seven years later. He campaigned on a promise to have a National Inquiry but has failed to act on its Calls for Justice. How can Canada in one instance defend the assimilatory registration provisions of the *Indian Act* (Palmater 2010) while at the same time claim to support self-government? How can Canada promote economic self-sufficiency yet criminalize or otherwise restrict the economic activities of Indigenous peoples (Palmater 2020: Chs. 32, 40)? These underlying conflicts in policy objectives act as significant impediments to progress. Policymakers will not be able to move forward in addressing the crisis of poverty in First Nations until these conflicting policy objectives are finally resolved.

The large national and multinational corporations involved in extractive industries like mining, forestry, fracking, and oil and gas have added another layer to the ongoing colonization of Indigenous peoples and lands (Alfred 2009). These corporations have been authorized, subsidized and protected by federal and provincial governments to carry out their extractive activities on Indigenous lands. The free, informed and prior consent of Indigenous peoples is rarely obtained, nor is due consideration given to the actual costs of extraction, such as violence to Indigenous women and girls, environmental damage, water contamination, air pollution and the destruction of plant, fish and animal habitat. Governments and industry have worked together to literally blockade Indigenous peoples from accessing their own economies, which are based on their lands, waters, trading routes and resources. Governments have also created legal and economic blockades through laws and policies that have excluded Indigenous peoples, while at the same time creating, maintaining and defending a system of forced dependence on government programs and services (Palmater 2015). In refusing to address chronic underfunding of essential social services like food, water, housing and health, governments have told Indigenous peoples to work with corporations to address their conditions of poverty (Lukas 2015; Penner 2014).

However, there is no relief to be found with corporations — they offer mere beads and trinkets in exchange for the mass exploitation of Indigenous lands and bodies. For those corporations that offer anything at all, the most typical form of compensation is a promise for a few jobs or some business contracts. Often these jobs never appear, and any discussions about Indigenous ownership and control over the impacted lands or resources ends with Indigenous peoples being sent back to government, facing heavily armed law enforcement or expensive litigation. Environmental racism results in Indigenous peoples bearing the disproportionate burden of environmental destruction left behind by these corporations and makes this crisis of poverty even worse (Jacobs 2010). UN rapporteur James Anaya noted the dramatic contradiction of Indigenous poverty in the face of so many corporations making profits from Indigenous lands with government backing:

> One of the most dramatic contradictions indigenous peoples in Canada face
> is that so many live in abysmal conditions on traditional territories that are

full of valuable and plentiful natural resources. These resources are in many cases targeted for extraction and development by non-indigenous interests. While indigenous peoples potentially have much to gain from resource development within their territories, they also face the highest risks to their health, economy, and cultural identity from any associated environmental degradation. Perhaps more importantly, indigenous nations' efforts to protect their long-term interests in lands and resources often fit uneasily into the efforts by private non-indigenous companies, with the backing of the federal and provincial governments, to move forward with natural resource projects. (UNHRC 2014: par. 69)

In 2019, the province of British Columbia passed Bill 41, the *Declaration on the Rights of Indigenous Peoples Act* (DRIPA), which was an important step in ensuring the application of international human rights standards to the province in its dealings with Indigenous peoples. To date, many First Nations in BC criticize the province for failing to respect their free, prior and informed consent over developments on their lands. The Trans Mountain pipeline continues without consent on Secwepemc territory, the Coastal Gaslink pipeline continues on Wet'suwet'en territory without consent, as do many other extractive projects in BC. More recently, the Trudeau government passed Bill C-15, *An Act respecting the United Nations Declaration on the Rights of Indigenous Peoples* (UNDRIP) which received royal assent on June 21, 2021. Shortly thereafter, Canada was plunged into an early federal election campaign, so it is too early to know if, and to what extent, Canada's laws and policies will change to end the oppression and dispossession of Indigenous peoples. What we do know is that corporations were concerned about free, prior and informed consent being formally recognized as a human right for Indigenous peoples. The recent RCMP armed invasions in Wet'suwet'en territory to facilitate the construction of the Coastal Gaslink pipeline shows that corporations have little to fear without legal changes (Palmater 2020: Ch. 36; Palmater 2021a).

STARTLING STATISTICS

According to the 2016 census, there are 1,673,780 Indigenous people in Canada.[4] There are approximately 977,235 First Nations individuals, a number that breaks down into 744,855 registered (status) Indians and 232,380 non-registered (non-status) Indians (Statistics Canada 2006).[5] As of 2016, there were over 630 First Nations representing more than fifty Nations (CIRNAC 2021). BC has the largest number of First Nations (198), while Ontario has the second highest (133). In the period from 2001 to 2016, the gap in educational attainment (completion of high school) between the non-Indigenous population and the status Indian population increased from a twenty-point difference (77 percent versus 57 percent) to a thirty-three-point difference (89 percent versus 66 percent) (ISC 2020a). The gap for university education has also not seen significant progress as it went from 20 percent versus 5 percent to 29 percent versus 8 percent. These numbers should be taken with great caution, though, given the trend of fraudulent claims to Indigenous identity that would skew these numbers, especially in the Métis category (see Leroux 2019; Nagle 2019; Andersen 2021).

Employment between 2001 to 2011 also showed a widening gap between status Indians and the non-Indigenous population: rates went from 58 percent and 80 percent, respectively, to 57.1 percent and 75.8 percent (Statistics Canada 2015). This means the gap remained relatively the same over ten years. It is important to note here that future statistics will have to take into account the impact of the COVID-19 pandemic. In 2010, the median total income of status Indians on and off reserve was reported at $16,905 and $30,021, respectively, compared to $41,225 for the non-Indigenous population. In 2015, there was no substantial change, as the median income for First Nations on reserve was still under $20,000 while for the non-Indigenous population it was over $40,000 (ISC 2020a). The situation is worse for status Indian women, too, whose average total income is $1,013 lower compared to status Indian men and $10,548 lower compared to non-Indigenous women. A statistical report comparing Indigenous people with so-called ethnic minorities said the income disparity is "very large," making Indigenous peoples the most disadvantaged group in Canada. Income gaps for Indigenous people range from 10 to 20 percent for women and 20 to 50 percent for men, whereas for ethnic minorities it is 0 to 10 percent for women and 20 to 50 percent for men. Even "a little 'Aboriginality' is associated with very poor labour market outcomes" (Statistics Canada 2004: 17, 18, 19; Pendakur and Pendakur 2011: 72).

> When compared to so-called ethnic minorities, the Indigenous income disparity gap is "very large," making Indigenous peoples the most disadvantaged group in Canada.

First Nation governments also face significant funding inequities on essential social services when compared to funding provided for provincial services:

> The reality behind the myths is that the money provided by the Federal Government to First Nations is insufficient rather than excessive, well-accounted for rather than misused, and almost all goes to pay debts and obligations to First Nations rather than the generous hand-out it is most often portrayed to be. Only $7,200 is spent on each First Nation individual in com-

parison to $14,900 per non-Aboriginal person who has the added benefit of provincial funding. (AFN n.d.: 3–5)

Less than two thirds of the INAC[6] budget makes it past Canada's large Indian Affairs bureaucracy down to First Nations (see Barnsley 2002; AFN n.d.). While the objective of federal policy was to use a funding formula that would provide "equity, predictability and flexibility" in the funding of services like First Nations child and family services, just the opposite has occurred (McDonald, Ladd et al. 2000: 10).[7] Even INAC's own internal documents have admitted that "the lack of in-home family support for children at risk and inequitable access to services have been identified … by INAC as important contributing factors to the overrepresentation of Aboriginal children in the Canadian child welfare system" (INAC 2004). More recently, the Canadian Human Rights Tribunal found that Canada had knowingly discriminated against First Nation children in care by providing less funding to those children because they are First Nations (FNCFCSC *v. Canada* 2016). Since this original decision, the federal government continues to litigate against the First Nations Child and Family Caring Society, challenging orders of the Tribunal and recently appealing a federal court decision upholding those orders (*Guardian* 2021). Canada would still rather spend millions to fight than end the racial discrimination against First Nations children in foster care (Stefanovich and Boisvert 2021).

An independent national assessment of First Nation water and sewer systems released in July 2011 was conducted with 571 of 587 First Nations. It found that 73 percent of all water systems and 65 percent of all wastewater systems in First Nations are characterized as medium to high risk.

> Nationally, based on the 10-year projected populations, the combined water and wastewater servicing needs are estimated to be $4.7 billion plus a projected operating and maintenance budget of $419 million per year. The projected future servicing cost per dwelling unit is estimated to average $29,600 per unit with an annual operating and maintenance cost of $2,700 per unit. (Neegan Burnside Ltd 2011: I, 34)

Despite many political promises, First Nations in Canada do not all have access to clean running water and in some cases no access to sewer and sanitation. This is yet another crisis of Canada's own making (Palmater 2020: Ch. 11). Moreover, a 2003 report of the Office of the Auditor General (OAG) of Canada found that First Nations were also facing a "critical shortage of housing" — more specifically, "a shortage of 8,500 houses, which is forecasted to increase by about 2,000 units per year over the next 10 years." The OAG report also revealed that "44 percent of the 89,000 existing houses require renovations" (Barrados 2003; OAG 2003: 12).[8] AFN research shows that the housing need is far more than the 8,500 referred to by the Auditor General and is much closer to 85,000 homes for over 615 First Nations (AFN 2011b). The housing crisis continues to such an extent that several First Nations over the past few years have declared states of emergency (Turner 2021). Funding inequities and states of crisis exist in all social program areas, and these poor living conditions have led to predictable and preventable harmful health and social outcomes.

PREDICTABLE OUTCOMES

In August 2011, the *American Journal of Public Health* published an article highlighting the associated persistence of poverty and inequality to mortality, arguing that "there is strong evidence for the negative, nonlinear association between income and mortality in the United States." They found that "decades of research have shown that low-income people have poorer self-reported health and higher rates of communicable and noncommunicable diseases and injuries because of a constellation of risk factors, such as smoking, unhealthy diet associated with food poverty and insecurity, stress and anxiety, and unemployment and job insecurity, among others." In 2000, at least of 874,000 deaths in the United States were attributable to social factors like low education and poverty (Galea et al. 2011: e7).[9] Indigenous populations in Canada, Australia and New Zealand all face higher mortality rates, higher rates of chronic and infectious diseases and poorer overall health, leading to decreased life expectancies ranging from five to fifteen years less than non-Indigenous populations (Hayman, Reid and King 2015). Socio-economic factors are now widely acknowledged to be determinants of both health and life expectancy, and this is especially true for marginalized groups like Indigenous peoples (Raphael 2016). Canadian studies also show that thousands of preventable deaths occur in Canada every year, and First Nations are overrepresented in those numbers. In 2018, federal documents showed that the lifespan of Indigenous peoples is fifteen years less than Canadians (Canadian Press 2018).

Those same federal documents found that diabetes is four times higher in Indigenous peoples than Canadians — a finding consistent with previous studies. A study conducted on the prevalence of type 2 diabetes in Indigenous communities showed that globally, Indigenous peoples are disproportionately affected by the disease and its associated effects. According to the study, Indigenous peoples are diagnosed at an increasingly younger age and develop higher rates of complications. Indigenous children suffer higher rates of microvascular disease, including chronic kidney disease (CKD), lower limb amputation, foot abnormalities, higher rates of cardiovascular disease and more severe retinopathy (Crowshoe et al. 2018).

The largest gaps found between Indigenous and non-Indigenous children related to the prevalence of type 2 diabetes; approximately 50 percent of all youth-onset type 2 diabetes occurs in Indigenous children (Crawford et al. 2019: 1). Another study noted that diabetes was prevalent in marginalized communities that struggle with socio-economic disadvantages, substance abuse and stress. Suicide, depression and addictions are also overrepresented in young Indigenous people; these phenomena all have roots in colonialism and are greatly exacerbated by poverty and social marginalization (Campbell 2002). In fact, Health Canada reports from 2011 and 2016 noted that suicide was the highest among First Nations peoples ages fifteen to twenty-four and accounts for 48.7 percent of all deaths of First Nations youth in that age range (Statistics Canada 2019). To put this in context, the First Nations suicide rate between 2011 and 2016 was more than three times the national rate — significant levels of "premature mortality." It is clear that Indigenous status and poverty are

> Suicide accounts for 48.7 percent of all deaths in First Nation youth ages fifteen to twenty-four, a rate that was more than three times the national rate.

linked to the overall poor health and premature deaths of First Nations in Canada (National Collaborating Centre for Aboriginal Health 2020).

The *Canadian Medical Association Journal*, in noting that "Nunavut has recorded the largest tuberculosis outbreak in the territory's 10-year history," specifically pointed to social factors like poverty and overcrowded housing as the primary causes (MacDonald et al. 2011). Today, TB rates in First Nations (23.8 per 100,000) and Inuit (170.1 per 100,000) far exceed rates in the Canadian population (0.6 per 100,000) (CPS 2020). Across the country, 23.1 percent of First Nation homes reported overcrowding, and although occupant density has decreased in the non-Indigenous population, it has actually increased in First Nations (Statistics Canada 2016). Waterborne diseases from contaminated drinking water are also widespread on reserves, which can cause severe illness (NCCIH 2018). On any given day, there can be one hundred or more First Nations in Canada with short-term boil-water advisories, long-term advisories or no access to clean running water at all (OAG cited in Palmater 2021b). Given the extremely high numbers of First Nations who have unsafe drinking water and are under boil-water advisories, First Nations have an increased risk of death and disease from contaminated water. These are all preventable situations (Neegan Burnside Ltd. 2011: *cf* 17).

Winnipeg has some of the best drinking water in the world. But Indigenous peoples were literally kicked off their traditional lands so that the city could access a lake to provide clean water to its residents (Puxley 2015). Moreover, the Indigenous community — specifically Shoal Lake Reserve 40 — was not just relocated away from the water source, but it was moved to an island that was created by the construction of an aqueduct to transfer water to the city. Ironically, Shoal Lake First Nation didn't have clean drinking water and was under a boil-water advisory for twenty-four years. Their long-standing water crisis is a prime example of the social impacts of blatant racism, discrimination and colonialism in Canada (Lorraine 2016). In 2021, a water treatment plant was finally built (Peters and Reimer 2021) and will hopefully end their decades-long battle for clean water, assuming appropriate resources are provided for hiring, training, and operation and maintenance of water systems — a common failure of federal funding formulas.

There can be no greater evidence of ongoing racism and colonialism in Canada than the gross overrepresentation of Indigenous peoples in Canada's prisons and jails. Under former prime minister Stephen Harper, the number of racialized people in Canadian prisons increased by 75 percent, while the numbers of white prisoners reduced significantly (Brosnahan 2013). This trend continued in the Trudeau era, where incarceration rates skyrocketed for Indigenous peoples. According to the Office of the Correctional Investigator (OCI), "since April 2010 the Indigenous inmate population has increased by 43.4% (or 1,265), whereas the non-Indigenous incarcerated population has declined over the same period by 13.7% (or 1,549)" (OCI 2020). Today more than 30 percent of all prisoners in federal corrections are Indigenous and that number is even higher for Indigenous women (42 percent and growing). In a statement issued December 17, 2021, the OCI (2021) said that Indigenous women now represent nearly 50 percent of those in federal prisons. The problem of overrepresentation of Indigenous people in federal jails is actually getting worse, as the number of Indigenous prisoners increased by 9.6 percent in the period from 2009 to 2019 — and the increase of Indigenous women in prisons was an incredible 131 percent (OCI 2020). It is also worthy to note that over 28 percent of Indigenous prisoners in federal institutions were raised in the child welfare system, and another 15 percent were raised in residential schools (OCI 2013). An earlier study, undertaken by the AFN in 2001, showed that about two thirds (63 percent) of Indigenous prisoners in federal institutions in the Prairies had previously been involved in child welfare. While Indigenous children make up less than 8 percent of the total population, they represent over 52.2 percent of the 29,000 children and youth in foster care (ISC 2020b). The OCI found

> Indigenous children make up less than 8 percent of the total population, yet they are over 52.2 percent of the 29,000 children and youth in foster care.

the path to jail for First Nation people is directly linked to federal policies and the poverty crisis in First Nations (Mann 2009: 4). The Investigator also emphasized the fact that the increase in prison populations is not crime driven, but instead due to government policies (see also Brosnahan 2013). The evidence showing the direct causal link between Canada's history of colonization, its modern-day discriminatory policies and poverty in First Nations is overwhelming, yet Canada continues to ignore this growing problem.

IGNORING THE PROBLEM

Canada controls the lives of First Nations peoples and provides inequitable funding that results in conditions of extreme poverty. Research has shown that poverty leads to many premature deaths. The ongoing funding inequities for basic social services have resulted in Third-World living conditions, poor health, barriers to education and employment, social dysfunction, overrepresentation in jails and children in care, and premature death in First Nations. For example, at current rates, it will take at least twenty-eight years to close the education gap (OAG 2004) and sixty-three years to close the income gap (Wilson and Macdonald 2010: 3). Surely reconciliation cannot mean that Indigenous peoples must wait many more generations before substantive change occurs.

Canada seems to put more energy into protecting its reputation than into fulfilling its mandate to Indigenous peoples. For example, governments frequently skew the public's perception of Indigenous people in the wording used around funds that flow to First Nations. Instead of acknowledging that these funds represent legal obligations through treaties and other agreements, the government often portrays the funds as handouts. Much of Canada's lands and resources are unceded and still legally belong to First Nations. Yet, most First Nations do not reap the benefits of the trillions of dollars that have been made on their lands. Canadians, governments and large corporations accrue the majority of the benefits, leaving Indigenous peoples in poverty. Former Aboriginal Affairs minister John Duncan said that poverty is a local issue and not one the government can fix with more government money. He explained that the government purposely keeps the funding low to act as an incentive for Indigenous people to get off welfare (Macleod 2015). These kinds of statements lead the general public to believe that it is their tax money going to First Nations, when in fact Canadians don't pay enough taxes for their own social programs, let alone constitutionally protected First Nation programs. About one third of Canadian workers and many (large) corporations don't pay taxes at all (Moretti 2011; Deneault 2018). Moreover, "funding" First Nations programs is actually inexpensive rent for the land on which Canada stands and from which Canada derives huge economic benefits. Framing such funding as "taxpayer" money misses the point that the money is derived from the land and its resources.

The debate over the nature of the funding aside, it is painfully clear from most research that the federal government chronically underfunds all First Nation social programs. If we take former minister Duncan at his word, it does so purposely. The crisis in poverty continues to get worse without corresponding action to address it. The federal government has been in a holding pattern on this issue, perhaps as a means of trying to determine the true extent of their legal obligations and potential liabilities. Many court cases have not gone in Canada's favour on key issues like Aboriginal and treaty rights. The recent Canadian Human Rights Tribunal (CHRT) case brought by Dr. Cindy Blackstock on behalf of the First Nations Child and Family Caring Society highlights, in great detail and with much clarity, both the extent of underfunded social programs and the devastating impacts that this kind of blatant racial discrimination has on First Nations. The Tribunal ruled that Canada's chronic underfunding of First Nations child and family services programs, which led to higher rates of child apprehension into foster care and the denial of social programs, was racial discrimination. This, together with their failure to end this racial discrimination after the CHRT order, resulted in an award of $40,000 per child — something Canada could have avoided. The government appealed the decision to the federal court, which upheld the Tribunal's ruling. The government has filed for a third review of the Tribunal decision (Forester 2021).

Even the United Nations has taken notice of the "abysmal poverty" created and maintained in First Nations by Canada. The former special rapporteur for Indigenous peoples, James Anaya, explained in his report on Canada, "The most jarring manifestation of these human rights problems is the distressing socio-economic conditions of indigenous peoples in a highly developed country" (UNHRC 2014: par. 15). He went on to conclude: "One of the most dramatic contradictions indigenous peoples in Canada face is that so many live in abysmal conditions on traditional territories that are full of valuable and plentiful natural resources" (par. 69). Perhaps Canada is holding out on the FNCFCS case for a more favourable decision from the Supreme Court of Canada? Whatever the reason, Canada's blatant pattern of ignoring First Nation poverty has made a crisis situation even worse.

DEFER, DEFLECT, DENY

The Canadian government has taken what appears to be a three-step approach to avoid dealing with what has become one of the most significant policy issues facing Canada today. First, the federal government has become extremely adept at deferring significant and even crisis issues by calling for additional studies or research to examine the problem. Take the crisis in First Nation education, for example. The Assembly of First Nation's (AFN's) website contains over thirty major reports addressing issue of the education gap between First Nations and Canadians, and many contain substantial and achievable recommendations. Yet when the issue gained attention under Harper's term, the Aboriginal Affairs minister announced that the federal government would spend over $600,000 to create a national expert panel on First Nation education to once again study the issue. It is as if the minister had forgotten that in 2002 the federal government had created the National Working Group on Education, which provided recommendations regarding "strategies and measures required to foster excellence in First Nation elementary and secondary education" and to "reduce the gap in academic results between First Nations and other Canadians." Referring to a "multitude of reports and studies" that have been consistent in their recommendations, the group concluded, "First Nations must have the resources and the means to design, develop and deliver life-long education, on- and off-reserve" (Minister's National Working Group on Education 2002: t51, 2). Fifteen years later, a very similar conclusion was reached in a report done for the federal government by Hill & Knowlton Strategies Canada — a "new partnership" needs to be established between First Nations and Canada to ensure First Nation students receive a high-quality education (ISC 2017). Nothing seems to change.

Some thought that a change in government from Conservative to Liberal would be the answer to the First Nation education underfunding issue — yet many forget that it was the Liberals who originally imposed a 2 percent funding cap. That being said, Justin Trudeau campaigned on a platform that included a promise to add an extra $2.6 billion to First Nation education as well as to lift the 2 percent funding cap. Since being elected, Trudeau has broken both promises (Parkin 2016; Smith 2016). His first federal budget only offered a little over $1 billion during the four-year mandate (Palmater 2020: 36), and the release of government documents proved Trudeau did not lift the 2 percent funding cap (Smith 2016). The recommendations to increase First Nations' control over their lives and to provide them with equitable funding are consistent throughout other reports across every sector, yet INAC continues to defer the problem through new studies, perhaps in hopes of different results (Palmater 2015).

There are times when deferring a crisis issue does not satisfy the media, and INAC is forced to publicly address the issue. When this happens, deflection seems to be Canada's backup plan to detract attention from responsibility. INAC appears to strategically use the media by making announcements about unrelated projects it recently or previously funded, or by offering commentary that indirectly blames or vilifies First Nations in another part of the country about completely unrelated matters. For example, the Auditor General's report for spring 2011 contained damning findings in relation to INAC and its failure to address issues like the gap in education, overcrowded housing and unsafe drinking water in First Nations (OAG 2011). Within minutes, INAC made an announcement about the Joint Action Plan with the AFN that would deal with issues like education and economic development and spoke of the "long-term prosperity of First Nation people" (INAC 2011b). Upon a closer reading, it was obvious that nothing new was contained in the announcement, as it simply highlighted initiatives that were already ongoing. A promise to set up a joint engagement process on an education framework (legislation) was old news, as were the promises to remove the residential school provisions from the *Indian Act* and to increase government transparency of First Nations. The Joint Action Plan was successful, however, in deflecting attention from the Auditor General's scathing report and INAC's continued failure to address its legislative responsibilities with regard to First Nations (see also Warry 2008).

Canada also denies the problem of First Nation poverty directly via its litigation and political positions and indirectly by simply failing to act and/or consistently ignoring alarms raised by its own federal officials. For example, Canada's litigation position in many court cases deny any responsibility for a wide variety of problems it has created, like sex discrimination in the *Indian Act*, despite parliamentary reports that clearly confirm otherwise (Palmater 2011). The OCI and the OAG have consistently tried to raise the alarm about First Nation poverty and discrimination, demanding that Canada take action — all to no avail. In 2002, the OCI was alarmed that the over-incarceration situation was worsening for Aboriginal people (OCI 2002); in 2006, the OCI explained that Canada's lack of an action plan meant that the situation was as bad as it was twenty years ago (OCI 2006); and in 2010, the OCI found that "inequitable and differential outcomes for Aboriginal offenders" are the direct result of "federal correctional policies and practices" (OCI 2010: 43; see also Sapers 2009).[10] The OCI recently confirmed that increasing prison rates are due to federal policy and not to increasing crime rates (Sapers 2015; Brosnahan 2013). Here we are today, with Indigenous women representing nearly 50 percent of federal prison inmates (OCI 2020). Incredibly, the OAG reports document Canada's similar track record for ignoring the crisis of poverty that is created and maintained largely by Canada's discriminatory laws and policies. According to the OAG, continued denial of the problem (and failure to act) will have disastrous results:

> The Office of the Correctional Investigator found that "inequitable and differential outcomes for Aboriginal offenders" are the direct result of "federal correctional policies and practices."

The education gap between First Nations living on reserves and the general Canadian population has widened, the shortage of adequate housing on reserves has increased, comparability of child and family services is not ensured, and the reporting requirements on First Nations remain burdensome.... There is a risk that living conditions on many First Nations reserves will remain significantly below national averages, with little prospect of a brighter future, until these concerns are addressed. (OCI 2010: 8)

In 2008, the Auditor General concluded, "current funding practices do not lead to equitable funding among Aboriginal and First Nation communities," which results in an inability for First Nations to provide adequate service to their communities. In fact, the inequities are such that when INAC adjusts the funding formula in Alberta, they will have increased the funding by 74 percent just to keep up with the province (OAG 2008: 1, 2). While Crown–Indigenous Relations and Northern Affairs Canada (CIRNAC) has acted on a few of the OAG's recommendations over the years, the OAG found that overall, CIRNAC has consistently failed to implement those recommendations that "are most important to the lives and well-being of First Nations people" (OAG 2008: 1). These are clear policy choices being made by Canada with the full knowledge of the devastating impacts these choices will have on the lives of First Nations. The CHRT's decision related to the discriminatory underfunding of First Nations child and family services referred to the federal government's own internal documents, which showed that the government knew that chronic underfunding led to an increase in child apprehension but did it anyway (*First Nations Child and Family Caring Society of Canada et al. v. Canada* 2016). The FNCFCS's Spirit Bear Plan has long called on Canada to do a complete analysis of funding failure across all social programs for First Nations — something that goes beyond child welfare services and represents a call to end all racial discrimination and inequalities in all public services, including housing, education, and healthcare (FNCFCS n.d.).

Canada has shown a tendency to avoid addressing crises by engaging in endless studies but avoids the collection of critical data that would support different policy choices. An example of this is the replacement of the mandatory long-form census with a voluntary one, which resulted in the chief statistician, Munir Sheikh, resigning his post (*Globe and Mail* 2010a, 2010b).[11] Even the provinces publicly denounced the move, explaining that it "will undermine the accuracy of budget decisions and erode the ability to direct social programs to the most vulnerable" (*Globe and Mail* 2010c). Aboriginal groups also took issue with the move, and an internal memo at Statistics Canada came to a similar conclusion:

Indian and Northern Affairs Canada's objectives are to improve the social and economic outcomes and well-being of Aboriginal peoples. Absence of reliable long-form data will not allow them to effectively manage, evaluate and measure performance of their programs in areas of Aboriginal health, housing, education and economic development. (Kumagai 2011)

In 2010, the federal government stopped counting the number of fires on First Nations reserves, claiming it was too much of a reporting burden on First Nations (Roman 2016), but given that First Nations are ten times more likely to die in house fires than Canadians (Canadian Press 2015), it looks more like a shirking of federal responsibility or perhaps liability. Regarding over-incarceration, in 2008, the OCI concluded that there was no evidence of improved data collection or analysis and "therefore, parliamentarians and Canadians have no way of evaluating the Correctional Service's progress, or lack thereof, in this priority area of concern. The lack of openness and the refusal to engage in full reporting on this critical file remain a serious concern to this office" (OCI 2008: 34–35). In 2003, the OAG (2008: 30) found that CIRNAC "did not have a plan in place to ensure the fulfillment of their obligations under the agreements, and it had not monitored whether the departments had fulfilled their obligations." As the OAG put it:

> We found that INAC has little information on the outcomes of its funding on the safety, protection, or well-being of children living on reserves. As a result, it is unaware of whether or to what extent its program makes a positive difference in the lives of the children it funds. In our view, the information INAC collects falls far short of the child welfare program and policy requirements. (2008: 28)

By not sharing the data collected, it is impossible to monitor or analyze compliance. The OAG also found that CIRNAC lacked data related to actual education costs, cost comparisons for different delivery methods or appropriate performance and results indicators (OAG 2002). This refusal to collect or share relevant data presents one of the most significant challenges for policymakers in moving to address First Nation poverty. In 2014, the OAG could only assess the food subsidy program for northern Indigenous communities based on comparable data from 2009. Canada had failed to conduct annual reviews or to verify that subsidies even reach these Indigenous populations. Even on that limited data, the Auditor General found that CIRNAC did not identify communities based on need or establish criteria for food subsidies that are "fair or accessible" (OAG 2014: Ch. 6). The problem of data collection seems to be across all sectors — even police forces — making the accurate and timely tracking and identification of other crisis issues, like murdered and missing Indigenous women and girls and those who committed these offences, difficult (Palmater 2015). Though the United Nations human rights treaty bodies have long called on Canada to collect disaggregated race-based data, it continues to shirk its responsibilities and hamper monitoring and compliance with basic human rights.

BLAMING THE VICTIM

The public at large is relatively uneducated about First Nation poverty and its historical roots. As a result, they can be easily swayed by the media and other commentators who blame First Nations for the current situation. Explanations for poverty in society are often divided into two main categories: blaming the victims as the authors of their own circumstances or, alternately, looking to societal factors that create, contribute to or exaggerate the disadvantages faced by the impoverished (see Chapter 7, Withers; also see Varcoe n.d.; Centre for Research on Inner City Health 2009; Steckley and Cummins 2008). According to the US-based Institute of Medicine, standardized data collection is critical in understanding and eliminating racial and ethnic disparities in healthcare. A critical barrier to eliminating disparities and improving the quality of patient care within healthcare organizations is the frequent lack of even the most basic data on race, ethnicity and primary language of patients (Hasnain-Wynia, Pierce and Pittman 2004; see also Percival 2011). While the focus here is on societal factors that have created the situation, one cannot ignore the real role that blaming the victim has on society's reactions to people living in poverty, their lack of empathy and their failure to demand that their governments address the situation. Some have argued that poor people are "genetically inferior," resulting in a lower IQ, for example (Varcoe n.d: 5). These types of arguments were once very common among those who looked to race to explain poverty. Other explanations are that certain groups of people have a "culture of poverty," so their specific attitudes or cultural values keep them in poverty (Varcoe n.d.). While these explanations do not hold up against close and informed scrutiny, they have allowed Canada's relatively privileged society to justify their ongoing advantage:

> Blaming the poor for their poverty remains a popular way of understanding poverty in part because this provides explanations which do not threaten those with privilege.... The most painless way to do this is to believe, if only vaguely, that the poor are somehow unworthy. While this is never fully convincing, especially because of the problem of children who cannot be seen as deserving to be poor, nevertheless it reduces the moral pressure on the middle class and the wealthy to take seriously the problem of changing institutions to eliminate poverty. (Varcoe 2009: 6)

This makes it far easier to blame First Nations' cultures, attitudes, values or perceived race for the crisis of poverty in which they currently live than it is to acknowledge the hard truth. The mainstream belief is that current generations did not personally steal the land or create the discriminatory laws and barriers, but in fact the recent finding by the National Inquiry that Canada is guilty of both historic and ongoing genocide means everyone is implicated in both perpetuating the situation and remedying it. Canadians also benefit handsomely from the cheap "rent" from stolen lands and social programs funded in large part from the resources and wealth stolen from Indigenous lands. One need only refer back to the Winnipeg water issue as an example. Settlers not only benefit from historical Indigenous dispossession, but they also have a role in perpetuating the crisis of poverty today through their own (in)action.

> Settlers not only benefit from historical Indigenous dispossession, but also have a role in perpetuating the crisis of poverty today through their own actions and inactions — by not assuming personal and collective responsibility for change.

While the prevalent attitude of blaming the victim can be explained, in part, by governments' negative public statements about First Nations, one cannot overlook the epic failures of federal, provincial and territorial governments in educating Canadians and their own bureaucrats about the real histories, laws and rights of Indigenous peoples and Canada's role in creating the current crisis situation. "Canadians remain remarkably insulated from the misery of the world.… We know that we are privileged.… Yet there remains within Canada an almost unspeakable reality, which, like a cancer, slowly sickens the body politic. This is the reality of life for Aboriginal peoples … who live in Third World conditions" (Warry 2008: 13).

While the media cannot shoulder all the blame for the current public attitude towards First Nations, it plays a significant role in helping to foster a societal attitude of blaming the victim:

> The mainstream media play a pre-eminent role in shaping the view Canadians and the world have of the history and contemporary circumstances of First Nations people.… The violence of Oka, the blocked logging roads of British Columbia, casinos and cigarettes in Ontario and Quebec, skid row everywhere, and substance abuse are the topics profiled and the images fed to a mainstream public which, with no knowledge of history or contemporary community life, responds with a mixture of pity, distaste, and a way of thinking that lays blame on the victims rather than the perpetrators. (Benyon 1994)

By way of example, in 2005, CBC News reported on the evacuation of Kashechewan due to contaminated drinking water, yet followed it up with a story about alleged corruption in Natuashish.[12] Even if the leaders in Natuashish in Newfoundland had been corrupt (and the resulting INAC report said they were not), what would that have to do with the members of Kashechewan in northern Ontario? These are two different First Nations from two different provinces. "In short, such editorial decisions blame the victim and create the impression that Aboriginal peoples are responsible for their ill health, rather than decades of government inaction and centuries of colonialism. Is it a surprise then, that many Canadians blame Aboriginal people for their problems?" (Warry 2008, 69–70). The ways in which society seeks to blame First Nations for their impoverished situation does not reflect historical or present reality but acts as a justification for governments' failure to act. Similarly, the CBC article "$1.2-million price tag for wildfire evacuations of First Nations in Ontario over last five years" discusses the price of evacuations (Turner 2019). Given that the article does not discuss the connection between colonialism, resource extraction industries and climate change, the leap to implicitly blaming First Nations for the cost of evacuations is an easy one. In contrast, media coverage of the recent flooding crisis in BC, did not focus on the costs of rescuing stranded BC residents.

Perhaps the most significant factor in the blame-the-victim attitude is one that government has refused to confront head on: blatant, overt anti-Indigenous racism. Just as there is no excuse on the part of governments for failing to address racism against Indigenous peoples in Canada, there is no excuse on the part of settlers for failing to push their governments to address racism or for taking individual steps to end racism in their own settler communities. The Truth and Reconciliation Commission report, which released details about the atrocities committed in residential schools and their enduring intergenerational impacts, made the point that everyone is responsible to make change and lists recommendations involving more than just governmental changes (TRC 2015a). While it is true that not all Canadians know all the legal, political and historical complexities around the crisis, the public cannot say they are not aware of the problem. There have been many commissions, inquiries and investigations into racism in Canada's justice system, all of which were not only made public but also turned into books, movies and widely covered in the media — let alone university and college courses that cover racism and the justice system. The Royal Commission on Donald Marshall's wrongful prosecution, the Ipperwash Inquiry on the police shooting of unarmed land defender Dudley George, the Manitoba Aboriginal Justice Inquiry and many other investigations have all pointed to overt and systemic racism in policing and the justice system (Palmater 2016). Racism is not just offensive; racism is literally killing Indigenous peoples (Palmater 2015). This crisis of poverty is a matter of life and death. Anti-Indigenous racism and misogyny is at the heart of abused, exploited, disappeared and murdered Indigenous women and girls, high rates of foster care, increasing incarceration rates, high rates of police killings of Indigenous peoples and even the denial of access to healthcare (Ministry of Health BC 2020).

A MATTER OF LIFE AND DEATH

The ISC's Community Well-Being (CWB) Index — based on education, labour force activity, income and housing — shows that there remains a significant gap in the overall standard of living between First Nations and Canadians, and there has been little improvement since the turn of the century. ISC found that over one third of all First Nations and Inuit communities showed a marked decline in CWB scores between 2001 and 2006 (INAC 2010: 11, 24). A recent ISC evaluation of the CWB shows a continued downward slide. While there has been improvement in some First Nations and Inuit communities, "there continues to be a substantial CWB gap between Indigenous and non-Indigenous communities." The gap did start to narrow up to 2001, but since then it has returned to its historic difference. Put simply, Indigenous communities are doing worse compared to non-Indigenous communities (ISC 2019b).

By way of comparison, the United Nations also collects data related to well-being, through the Human Development Index (HDI). In 2019, Canada ranked sixteenth in the world (United Nations Development Programme 2020). However, if the data is adjusted to consider only the conditions on First Nations, then Canada would rank fifty-second, below countries like Chile and Argentina (ISC 2019a: 26). According to the Yellowhead Institute, there are persistent deficits: "Indigenous communities are receiving well-being scores equivalent to those that non-Indigenous communities received in 1981" (Guthro 2021).

There is no doubt that society at large plays a role in pressuring governments; however, the need to end the current poverty crisis in First Nations is not a matter of good will or charity by the public. As Nelson Mandela put it, "Overcoming poverty is not a task of charity, it is an act of justice. Like Slavery and Apartheid, poverty is not natural. It is man-made and it can be overcome and eradicated by the actions of human beings. Sometimes it falls on a generation to be great" (Make Poverty History n.d.). UN rapporteur James Anaya urged Canada to take action:

Indigenous peoples' concerns merit higher priority at all levels and within all branches of government, and across all departments. Concerted measures, based on mutual understanding and real partnership with aboriginal peoples, through their own representative institutions, are vital to establishing long-term solutions. (UNHRC 2014: 2)

The barrier for developing just policy is contained in the fundamental settler/federal government's conflicting policy objectives: the assimilation (and elimination) of First Nations versus the rebuilding (and returning the lands and resources) of First Nations.

RESOLVING THE POLICY CONFLICT

Historically, Indian policy in Canada changed quickly from one based on nation-to-nation treaty making and recognition of Indigenous sovereignty (Moss and Gardner-O'Toole 1991) to one of domination and aggressive assimilation (Long et al. 1982: 190; CBC News 2008; see also RCAP 1996). For the most part, Indigenous peoples have had very little input, if any, into the policymaking process and even less input on the laws that pertain to them (Gibbons 1984; Long et al. 1982). The policies and laws created to deal with Indians and the reserve lands to which they were relocated were based on several problematic assumptions about Indigenous peoples that have led to ineffective and even harmful results. The first assumption was that Indigenous peoples were inferior to Europeans, and the second was that Indigenous peoples were slowly dying off. When diseases, like smallpox, starvation and scalping bounties did not kill Indigenous peoples fast enough, the former deputy superintendent of Indian Affairs, Duncan Campbell Scott, led an aggressive policy of assimilation. His characterization of the *Indian Act* said it all: "I want to get rid of the Indian problem.... *Our objective is to continue until there is not a single Indian in Canada* that has not been absorbed into the body politic and there is no Indian question, and no Indian Department, that is the whole object of this Bill" (cited in RCAP (Volume 1) 1996: 183, emphasis added). Getting rid of Indians has been the cornerstone of Canada's Indian policy ever since — something that is very much in line with Sir John A MacDonald's vision of Canada as an "Aryan" nation focused on "Aryan race" and "Aryan principles" (Wherry 2012). Despite political apologies to the contrary, various provisions in the *Indian Act*, originally intended to speed up assimilation, are still in effect and, in fact, are vigorously defended by Canada.

> Former deputy superintendent of Indian Affairs, Duncan Campbell Scott's characterization of the *Indian Act*: "Our objective is to continue until there is not a single Indian in Canada that has not been absorbed into the body politic and there is no Indian question, and no Indian Department, that is the whole object of this Bill."

For Canada, it was thought that thinning the blood lines of Indians through intermarriage with whites could help speed up assimilation and thus the land acquisition process. This was to be accomplished in two ways: first, to "bleed off" Indian women and their children from their communities and, second, to "transfuse" the communities by incorporating into them non-Indian women and their children (Palmater 2011). Statistics show that this amounted to an almost complete blood transfusion, as 16,800 Indian women lost their Indian status and 16,000 non-Indian women gained their status (Harper 2008; Access to Information and Privacy Request to Indian and Northern Affairs Canada dated April 1, 2011). In addition to excluding Indian women and children from membership in their communities, these assimilatory laws also impacted the ability of men to provide for their families, as engaging in colonial occupations required a significant sacrifice: to give up one's Indian identity (RCAP 1996; Palmater 2011; Venne 1981). If an Indigenous man wanted to get a university degree or become a doctor or lawyer, he was required to give up his status as an Indian, which meant that his Indian wife and children were automatically disenfranchised as well. The loss of one's status as an Indian meant that they were no longer entitled to live in their community, have a voice in the affairs of their Nation or access rights under the various treaties signed with the Crown. Treaty rights, which often protected the traditional means of providing for the community and Nation, like the right to hunt, fish and gather, or the right to trade, would also be inaccessible to anyone who received an education.

Over the years, there has been some movement by the federal government to amend political positions, but modern legislation is still firmly rooted in the historical core objectives of Indian policy. "Because of the intensity of genocidal policies that Indigenous people have faced and continue to face, a common error on the part of anti-racist and post-colonial theorists is to assume that genocide is virtually complete, that Indigenous peoples, however unfortunately, have been 'consigned to the dustbin of history' … and no longer need to be taken into account" (Lawrence and Dua 2005: 123).

Although assimilation as a formal policy objective became less palatable politically, it nevertheless resurfaced in 1969 when Prime Minister Pierre Trudeau and the minister of Indian Affairs, Jean Chretien, presented the White Paper on Indian policy. The White Paper advocated abolishing all special recognition for Indians, CIRNAC and the *Indian Act*, as well as the transfer of reserve lands to individual Indians (Indian Affairs and Northern Development 1969). The reaction to this policy by First Nation leaders was so swift and so fierce that the plan was eventually abandoned, but the goal of the White Paper was not. Tom Flanagan, an outspoken academic against First Nations Rights, explains the overall policy objective: "Call it assimilation, call it integration, call it adaptation, call it whatever you want: it has to happen" (Flanagan 2000: 196; see also Flanagan et al. 2010; Cairns 1999; Widdowson and Howard 2008; Helin 2008; Gibson 2009). Flanagan agrees with this long-held view and suggests that the solution to finally rid Canada of the burden of First Nations and their impoverished communities is for them to be assimilated into the general population. He views this process as being "historically inevitable" and largely complete and says it will remain the basis of Canadian society (Cairns and Flanagan 2001: 51). The government trend now is to promote individual initiatives that look beneficial on the surface but will result in the eventual assimilation of First Nations. For example, getting rid of the *Indian Act* and giving Indians individual interests in reserve lands is an idea currently being sold as a positive solution to poverty, but such notions are also the original keys to Canada's assimilation policy (Flanagan 2000; Flanagan, Alcantra and Le Dressey 2010; see also Palmater 2010). Getting rid of the *Indian Act* might clear the path for more formal recognition of First Nation jurisdiction or — more likely — it may be used to do away with all recognition and federal obligations, as proposed in the White Paper. The government's view of treaties was that they contained "limited and minimal promises" and their significance "will continue to decline" until they are finally "ended" (Canada 1969: Section 5). Despite the subsequent constitutional protection afforded treaties in Section 35 of the Constitution, Canadian governments still minimize their relevance.

In essence, this "policy" blames the victim, but in a larger, nation-based, not individual, sense. It is the racist idea that First Nations' sovereignty and independence is somehow "backwards" or "primitive" and that is the cause of their poverty and troubles, not colonialism. Critics like Flanagan suggest that if First Nations would just become like settler capitalist societies, they would be just fine. The urge to assimilate Indigenous peoples has not lessened over time and remains a powerful force against which Indigenous peoples strenuously resist (Simpson 2017; Starblanket and Hunt 2020). In order to move forward, Canada will have to decide what its underlying policy objective is with regard to Indigenous peoples. Will reconciliation be centred on assimilation and integration or self-determination and reparation? This policy decision will determine whether future initiatives will rid Canada of the problem of poverty in First Nations or rid Canada of the "problem" of First Nations.

The proposed solutions that fall into the other category of rebuilding and supporting First Nations tend to be more comprehensive in nature. This is why the Royal Commission on Aboriginal Peoples (RCAP) was such an important report. The commissioners not only envisioned healthy, prosperous, self-governing First Nations that would take them from poverty to prosperity, but actually had a detailed plan and budget on how to get there. The report called for "sweeping changes" to the current relationship with the federal government that would be founded on the recognition of Aboriginal Peoples as self-governing Nations.

Recommendations made by the RCAP related to the recognition of First Nation jurisdiction, equitable funding for core programs like education, child welfare and housing, and the resolution of long-outstanding land claims and treaties. The

Commission's implementation strategy proposed that governments increase spending to reach $1.5 billion by year five of the strategy and $2 billion in the subsequent fifteen years. This would include new legislation that would clearly outline treaty recognition and processes as well as specifically recognize Aboriginal Nations as a third order of government. Aboriginal lands and resources would be expanded to support their governments and a new Aboriginal parliament would be created. The central theme was First Nation jurisdiction over every aspect of their lives, from education to health to governance.

The more recent Truth and Reconciliation Commission Report echoed many of the same sentiments and issued Calls to Action that focused on addressing the crisis in First Nations with proper funding, legal recognition of rights and Indigenous-led solutions (TRC 2015b). For example, the first Call to Action calls on governments to ensure proper funding so that Indigenous governments can run child and family services. Calls to Action seven through ten call on governments to work with Indigenous peoples to address education and employment, which includes proper funding of First Nation education and First Nation consent to any legislation developed as a part of that strategy. Other recommendations include providing adequate funding for health, the preservation of Indigenous languages, the elimination of the overrepresentation of Indigenous peoples in jail and taking action on murdered and missing Indigenous women and girls (TRC 2015b). The National Inquiry made many similar observations and calls for action on a wide variety of Indigenous rights centred on self-determination.

> The TRC Report issued Calls to Action that focused on addressing the crisis in First Nations with proper funding, legal recognition of rights and Indigenous-led solutions.

Part of the problem policymakers have and will continue to face is that they require clear, consistent direction from politicians on how to move forward on First Nation issues. That is, what is required is a policy objective that transcends the inevitable changes in government every four years, changes in political parties and the changes in ideological slants of academics, the media and the public. If Canada cannot decide whether it wants to eliminate First Nations or empower them, then we will continue to see social programs and policies that do more harm than good. Although the law has advanced Aboriginal and treaty rights somewhat, this should not be seen as a replacement for sound policymaking. As James Anaya noted, all the legal protections in Canada have not abated the human rights violations and extreme poverty in First Nations: "It is difficult to reconcile Canada's well-developed legal framework and general prosperity with the human rights problems faced by indigenous peoples in Canada that have reached crisis proportions in many respects" (UNHRC 2014: par. 14). While jurisprudence may help guide policymakers on the higher-level core matters, it is simply not feasible to address issues of poverty in the courts on a case-by-case basis. Incremental legislative or policy changes are not enough to combat the crisis of poverty in First Nations. Canada must finally reconcile itself to the fact that Indigenous peoples in Canada are here to stay and act on that constitutional and political reality.

SIGNS OF HOPE

However, despite the very slow progress to date and the lack of attention that the crisis of First Nation poverty has been given, there are signs of hope that come from the most unexpected places. Take, for example, the situation at Attawapiskat First Nation in Ontario. This Cree community has been fighting for a new elementary school for decades (Wawatay News online 2015). So, their youngest members travelled all the way to Ottawa to bring the issue to the attention of the minister, who, sitting in his lush office, told thirteen-year-old Shannen Koostachin that he did not have the funds to build them a new school. CIRNAC had promised them a new school four times previously because their current school was full of mould, mice, cracked walls and reeked of diesel fuel (Goyette 2010). After Shannen passed away unexpectedly, those she inspired launched the "Shannen's Dream" campaign to end the discrimination in funding for First Nation education across the country. All of the subsequent pressure and publicity seemed to work in Attawapiskat's favour (NDP 2011). The United Nations Committee on the Rights of the Child decided to investigate Canada's failure to protect the rights of First Nations children (Provincial Advocate for Children and Youth 2011). The public pressure and international spotlight on Canada essentially shamed CIRNAC into announcing funding for a new school to be built in 2013 (INAC 2011a, 2011b). It was finally built and opened in late 2014 (CBC News 2014). None of this would even have been possible but for the courage of Cree youth to exercise their voices and stand up for their community (Provincial Advocate for Children and Youth 2011).

There are also signs of hope that come from the very act of nation building and cultural revitalization in First Nation communities. Take, for example, the changes to educational programming in Nunavut noted by the Standing Committee on Indigenous Affairs and Northern Development in 2007 (Canadian Council on Learning 2007). Since 1985, the Nunavut Sivuniksavut Program has offered Nunavut high school graduates culturally appropriate transitional programming. This program not only had an 80 percent completion rate but also resulted in a very high employment record for its students. Similarly, cultural revitalization goes hand in hand with traditional governance practices and the assertion of jurisdiction over their own affairs. In fact, research has shown that acts of self-determination and cultural revitalization can even reduce the number of suicides in communities (Chandler and Lalonde 2008, 1998).[13] This is due to the presence of "cultural continuity factors," which include the achievement of at least some measure of self-government and control over key services like health, education and policing and community facilities to preserve culture (Chandler and Lalonde 2008: 6). There is still a long way to go before all First Nations enjoy this kind of success in all aspects of their lives, but the formula for success is backed up by research. Policymakers need to focus on (1) the redistribution (return) of Indigenous lands and resources; (2) the recognition of First Nation jurisdictions, laws and governance systems; (3) the provision of needs-based funding to critical First Nation social programs to address long-standing inequities created by discriminatory laws and policies; and (4) the implementation of fully supported cultural revitalization policies to achieve healthy, sustainable and self-determining Indigenous nations.

> Acts of self-determination and cultural revitalization can reduce the number of suicides due to the presence of "cultural continuity factors" — the achievement of at least some measure of self-government and control over key services like health, education and policing and community facilities to preserve culture.

Conversely, it is clear without doubt that the long-term costs of doing nothing far outweigh the immediate investment required to eliminate the gaps in health, education and income between First Nations and Canadians (Coffey 1997). For example, the cost of incarcerating one Indigenous person for one year is $116,070 (for females, it is $175,000 per year), which far outweighs the $13,200 it costs to send one Indigenous person to university for one year (Elizabeth Fry Northern Alberta n.d.; John Howard Society 2018). Yet, First Nation post-secondary education funds have been capped since 1996. If these funds were raised to the more equitable level of $20,000 per person per year, even a four-year degree would still be cheaper than one year of prison. Educating First Nations "would add $179 billion to Canada's GDP by 2026 through employment and by reducing government expenditures on income support, social services, health care, and security" (AFN 2011a: 4). Even the initial costs of resolving treaties and land claims are far outweighed by long-term financial and other benefits. One study found that the benefits of settling treaties earlier resulted in greater benefits being delivered sooner (Price Waterhouse Coopers 2009). Conversely, the longer it takes to settle treaties, the overall net benefit to Canadians and First Nations is reduced. Thus, the quicker we address poverty in First Nations, the more we will all benefit.

SOVEREIGNTY AND LIVING A GOOD LIFE

The colonization and aggressive assimilation policies of the past have turned thriving Indigenous nations into small communities of people who are barely surviving. Understanding the historical context and root causes of the current crisis of poverty in First Nations is absolutely essential to developing policy solutions that can turn this trend around. Past laws and policies were explicitly designed to impoverish First Nations — current laws and policies maintain their impoverishment. Canada controls the lives of First Nations and provides them with inequitable funding that results in conditions of extreme poverty, leading them to their premature deaths. The startling statistics illustrate the true extent of the chronic underfunding of essential social services, the cap on education funding, the lack of basic infrastructure and maintenance support and the discrimination experienced in health and justice services. This has led to predictable results — namely, lower educational achievement, poor health outcomes and high unemployment and suicide rates. There is a direct causal link between premature deaths in First Nations and the chronic poverty originally created and now sustained by federal policy. Justice Murray Sinclair did not mince words in the TRC report when he said that Canada has engaged in all forms of genocide in its dealings with Indigenous people — cultural, biological and physical genocide (TRC 2015a: 1). It is long past time that we confronted the lethal nature of racism.

However, instead of acting on the current medical, legal and social science research, Canada's tendency appears to be to ignore the problem. Canada's ability to defer, deflect and deny the problem is bolstered by the blame-the-victim mentality of many right-wing commentators, media outlets, policymakers and politicians. Policies have waivered back and forth between assimilation and promotion of self-government. Yet, the two objectives cannot both underpin future policy. Canada has used the impoverished condition of First Nations in the last 250-plus years as justification for both the assumption of jurisdiction over them and the paternalistic management of Indian affairs. This has led to the current crisis of poverty and premature death in First Nations.

Yet First Nations have had far more experience in governing themselves and creating strong, prosperous, thriving Nations than Canada has had tearing them down. Despite all the challenges, there are signs of hope in First Nations that offer small glimpses into what is possible. Increased employment rates, reduced suicide rates and improved educational rates are all possible with access to equitable funding and First Nation jurisdiction over key areas like health, education, justice and child welfare. The resolution of land claims and treaties not only benefit First Nations, but all Canadians. First Nations can create success in their communities by addressing federal control, inequitable funding and discrimination prevalent in federal policies. The well-being of future generations can be assured through cultural revitalization in First Nations. First Nation youth need to know that there is nothing wrong with them — it is the system under which they are controlled that needs to be addressed. They have no less of a desire to live and experience the world than anyone else. The deprivation associated with extreme poverty stretches them "beyond all human limits" until they simply can't take it anymore. Decades ago, anthropologists, sociologists and other researchers used to study First Nations and write reports documenting their cultures; today, coroners study First Nations and write death reports. Indigenous peoples deserve the same rights as other peoples to enjoy their sovereignty and have a fair chance to live the lives they believe in. They deserve a chance to live the "good life" that everyone else gets to take for granted.

DISCUSSION QUESTIONS

1. How much of a factor is racism in the decisions made by federal and provincial governments in relation to First Nations?
2. Do Canadians, individually or collectively, share in any of the responsibility for the socio-economic conditions of First Nations today?
3. How will we know when the colonization of Indigenous peoples has ended?

GLOSSARY OF KEY TERMS

Assimilation: The process by which Indigenous peoples were expected, or forced, to conform to the ideas, values, cultures, and beliefs of the settler populations.

Blaming the victim: A devaluing act through which the victims of a crime, accident, hardship or wrongful act are held to be entirely or partially responsible for the harm committed against them, and which is often associated with negative, stereotypical and/or racist and sexist views about them.

Colonialism: The state practice of taking full or partial control over another territory and its inhabitants with a view to exploiting the lands, waters, peoples, and resources for economic profit.

First Nation: Replaces the term "Indian band," which refers to a specific Indigenous community that occupies land set aside under the *Indian Act* for their use and benefit. In some circumstances, First Nations are one of several smaller communities that form part of larger traditional Indigenous nations such as the Mi'kmaq or Cree.

Poverty: Often defined as a lack of money or financial wealth relative to others. In an Indigenous context, poverty specifically includes a lack of the basic necessities of life, including food, water, sanitation, shelter, heat and access to medical care.

Self-determination: An internationally recognized right of peoples to freely determine their own political status and economic, social and cultural development as well as control and benefit from their traditional lands, waters and natural resources.

Treaty: A sacred agreement between individual First Nations and/or larger Indigenous nations and the Crown as represented by Her Majesty the Queen (in the case of historic treaties) or the Crown as represented by Canada and/or the provinces (in the case of modern treaties) and may protect hunting and fishing rights, set apart lands for First Nations and/or implement First Nation governments and related powers that are now constitutionally protected.

RESOURCES FOR ACTIVISTS

350: 350.org
Amnesty International–Canada: amnesty.ca
Council of Canadians: canadians.org
David Suzuki Foundation: davidsuzuki.org
Defenders of the Land: defendersoftheland.org
First Nations Child and Family Caring Society of Canada: fncaringsociety.com
Indigenous Nationhood: indigenousnationhood.blogspot.com
MiningWatch Canada: miningwatch.ca
Pam Palmater website: pampalmater.com

NOTES

1   This report included a special chapter related to the deaths by suicide in Pikangikum First Nation between the years of 2006 and 2008, where sixteen children between the ages of ten and nineteen took their own lives.
2   The term "Indigenous Nation(s)" is used to refer to the original sovereign Nations on Turtle Island, like the Mi'kmaq, Wolastoqey or Wet'suwet'en. The term "First Nation" will be used to refer to *Indian Act* bands. The term "Aboriginal" which is defined in Section 35 as including Indians, Inuit and Métis, will only be used in the context of Section 35 Aboriginal Rights or as quoted from other sources. The term "Indigenous" will be used to refer to First Nations, Inuit, and Métis generally.
3   *Constitution Act, 1867* (UK), 30 and 31 Vict., c.3 [*Constitution Act, 1867*]. I have focused my research on First Nations, which at times includes data related to the Inuit as well. Both groups are subject to federal jurisdiction as per Section 91(24) of the *Constitution Act, 1867*. The Métis are a newer social phenomenon, having only existed 250-plus years. As they are under provincial jurisdiction and have

very different histories and social conditions, they were not included in this research except where specifically noted.

4   The census includes North American Indians or First Nations (both registered and unregistered), Métis and Inuit in that definition. It is also important to note that this report focuses on the Aboriginal identity statistics. Statistics Canada makes a distinction between those with Aboriginal identity and those who report Aboriginal ancestry: "Aboriginal identity refers to those persons who reported identifying with at least one Aboriginal group, that is, North American Indian, Métis or Inuit, and/or those who reported being a Treaty Indian or a Registered Indian, as defined by the Indian Act of Canada, and/or those who reported they were members of an Indian band or First Nation." Aboriginal ancestry, on the other hand, is defined as referring to "the ethnic or cultural origin of a person's ancestors, an ancestor being usually more distant than a grandparent. In the census, if a person reports at least one Aboriginal ancestry response, the person is counted in the Aboriginal ancestry population."

5   The non-registered Indian population increased 53 percent, more than twice that of the registered population (24 percent). "This growth may be in part related to provisions of the Indian Act governing the transmission of registered status to children."

6   INAC is now known as Indigenous Services Canada (ISC). Throughout the chapter, it is called by its name at the time.

7   There are no routine price adjustments incorporated in the operations formula. There appears to have been no price adjustments to the formula since the 1994–1995 fiscal year. FNCFS agencies indicated that they all thought that an adjustment for remoteness was necessary. DIAND has been limited to 2 percent budgetary increases for the department while expenditures for FNCFS agencies have been rising annually at an average rate of 6.2 percent. The average per-capita per-child in care expenditure of the DIAND-funded system is 22 percent lower than the average of the selected provinces.

8   INAC and CMHC have not been able to demonstrate that all reserve homes meet the national building code, and "although mould contamination has been identified as a serious and growing health and safety problem for several years, a comprehensive strategy and action plan has not yet been developed." Further, on pages 21–22, the Auditor General also criticized INAC for failing to give Parliament a complete picture — that instead of housing stock increasing, "the average number of homes constructed since the adoption of the policy in 1996 actually declined by 30 percent."

9   The breakdown was as follows: "245,000 deaths in the United States in 2000 were attributable to low education, 133,000 to poverty, 162,000 to low social support, 39,000 to area-level poverty, 119,000 to income inequality, and 176,000 to racial segregation." They also found: "These mortality estimates are comparable to deaths from the leading pathophysiological causes. For example, the number of deaths we calculated as attributable to low education is comparable to the number caused by acute myocardial infarction (192 898), a subset of heart disease, which was the leading cause of death in the United States in 2000. The number of deaths attributable to racial segregation is comparable to the number from cerebrovascular disease (167 661), the third leading cause of death in 2000, and the number attributable to low social support is comparable to deaths from lung cancer (155 521)."

10 "I would be the first to acknowledge that many of the factors contributing to the excessively high rates of aboriginal incarceration — poverty, social exclusion, substance abuse, discrimination — go well beyond the capacity of the correctional service to address in isolation. I am well aware that the federal correctional authority does not have control over the number of federally sentenced offenders. Nevertheless, the report states that the Correctional Service of Canada has the jurisdiction and the obligation, statutory and constitutional, to manage sentences in a culturally responsive manner. On this point the federal correctional service has fallen short, with negative consequences for aboriginal offenders and their communities." See also page 2: "Over the years, my office has issued a series of reports and recommendations regarding the treatment of aboriginal offenders under federal sentence. In fact, the very first annual report released by the Office of the Correctional Investigator more than 35 years ago documented instances of systemic discrimination against federally sentenced aboriginal offenders. Unfortunately, many of our recommendations made since then have

gone unheeded or only partially addressed, or the response to them has not yielded the intended result" (OCI 2010).

11 It was also reported by Statistics Canada employees that the Conservative government was moving away from social statistics to those that focus exclusively on economic issues.

12 "On 26 October 2005, the CBC National News reported on the evacuation of the Kashechewan Reserve in Northern Ontario due to the failure of its water treatment system, which led to the contamination of drinking water. This was an important story that potentially could have been used to educate viewers about the poor water quality and other environmental health problems on hundreds of reserves. But the CBC chose to follow the evacuation story immediately with a feature on mismanagement by, and potential corruption in, the Natuashish Band Council" (Warry 2008: 69–70).

13 See page 4: "If instead, one's culture is marginalized, or vandalized, or turned into a laughingstock; and if (because of colonization or decolonization or globalization) the familiar and trustworthy ways of one's community are criminalized, legislated out of existence, or otherwise assimilated beyond easy recognition, then woe be upon those transiting toward maturity, and for whom otherwise customary ways and means of warranting one's personal persistence often no longer suffice. The predictable consequence of such personal and cultural losses is often disillusionment, lassitude, substance abuse, self-injury and self-appointed death at an early age" (Chandler and Lalonde 1998).

REFERENCES

AFN (Assembly of First Nations). n.d. "Federal Government Funding to First Nations: The Facts, the Myths, and the Way Forward." Ottawa. <turtleisland.org/news/funding.pdf>.

____. 2019. *Towards Justice: Tackling Indigenous Child Poverty in Canada.* <afn.ca/wp-content/uploads/2019/07/Upstream_report_final_English_June-24-2019.pdf>.

____. 2011a. "It's Our Time: A Call to Action on Education." <afn.ca/uploads/files/11-06-11_a_call_to_action_year_in_review.pdf>.

____. 2011b. "Fact Sheet: Quality of Life of First Nations." Ottawa. <afn.ca/uploads/files/factsheets/quality_of_life_final_fe.pdf>.

Alfred. T. 2009. "Colonialism and State Dependency." *Journal of Aboriginal Health* 42.

Andersen, C. 2021. "Indigenous Identity Fraud is Encouraged in Academia. Here's How to Change That." CBC News, November 4. <cbc.ca/news/canada/saskatchewan/opinion-chris-andersen-indigenous-identity-fraud-1.6236018>.

APTN (Aboriginal Peoples Television Network). 2011. "First Nations Face 'Life or Death' Struggle: Atleo." Moncton, NB, July 12. <aptnnews.ca/national-news/first-nations-face-life-or-death-struggle-atleo/>.

Banerjee, S. 1999. "Whose Mine Is It Anyway? National Interest, Indigenous Stakeholders and Colonial Discourses: The Case of the Jabiluka Uranium Mine." Presented at the Critical Management Studies Conference (Postcolonial Stream), Manchester, UK, July 14–16. <mngt.waikato.ac.nz/ejrot/cmsconference/1999/documents/PostColonialism/postcolonial.pdf>.

Barnsley, P. 2002. "How Much Goes to Indians? Not as Much as You Think!" *Windspeaker* 19, 11. <ammsa.com/node/25042>.

Barrados, M. (Assistant Auditor General of Canada). 2003. "Opening Statement to the Standing Committee on Public Accounts — Federal Government Support to First Nations — Housing on Reserve." May 5. <oag-bvg.gc.ca/internet/English/osh_20030505_e_23387.html>.

Benyon, J. 1994. "First Nations: The Circle Unbroken, Review." *Canadian Journal of Education* 19, 2.

Brosnahan, M. 2013. "Canada's Prison Population at All-Time High." CBC News, November 25. <cbc.ca/news/canada-s-prison-population-at-all-time-high-1.2440039>.

Cairns, A. 1999. *Citizens Plus: Aboriginal Peoples and The Canadian State.* Vancouver: UBC Press.

Cairns, A., and T. Flanagan. 2001. "Flanagan and Cairns on Aboriginal Policy." *Policy Options* 43 (September).

Campbell, A. 2002. "Type 2 Diabetes and Children in Aboriginal Communities: The Array of Factors that Shape Health and Access to Health Care." *Health Law Journal* 10.

Canada, Government of. 1969. *Statement of the Government of Canada on Indian Policy.* <publications. gc.ca/site/eng/9.700112/publication.html>.

Canadian Council on Learning. 2007. "Redefining How Success Is Measured in First Nations, Inuit and Métis Learning: Report on Learning in Canada 2007." Ottawa.

Canadian Press. 2018. "Lifespan of Indigenous People 15 Years Shorter Than That of Other Canadians, Federal Documents Say." CBC News, January 23.

___. 2015. "First Nations 10 Times More Likely To Die in House Fires: Report." CBC News, December 21.

CBC News. 2008. "Residential Schools: A History of Residential Schools in Canada." May 16. <cbc. ca/news/canada/story/2008/05/16/f-faqs-residential-schools.html?sms_ss=facebook&at_xt=4d-8618622dc81306%2C0>.

___. 2014. "New Attawapiskat School Opens Today." August 14. <cbc.ca/news/canada/sudbury/new-at-tawapiskat-school-opens-today-1.2750480>.

___. 2016. "What did Justin Trudeau say about Canada's history of colonialism?" April 22. <cbc.ca/news/indigenous/trudeau-colonialism-comments-1.3549405>.

Centre for Research on Inner City Health. 2009. "Measuring Equity of Care in Hospital Settings: From Concepts to Indicators: 2009." <stmichaelshospital.com/crich/reports/measuring-equi-ty-of-care-in-hospital-settings/>.

Chandler, M., and C. Lalonde. 2008. "Cultural Continuity as a Protective Factor Against Suicide in First Nations Youth." *Horizons — A Special Issue on Aboriginal Youth, Hope or Heartbreak: Aboriginal Youth and Canada's Future* 10, 1.

___. 1998. "Cultural Continuity as a Hedge Against Suicide in Canada's First Nations." *Transcultural Psychiatry* 35, 2. <web.uvic.ca/~lalonde/manuscripts/1998TransCultural.pdf>.<psych.ubc.ca/~chandlerlab/Chandler%20&%20Lalonde%20(2008).pdf>.

CIRNAC (Crown-Indigenous Relations and Northern Affairs Canada. 2021. "First Nations." <rcaanc-cirnac.gc.ca/eng/1100100013791/1535470872302>.

Coffey, C. 1997. "The Cost of Doing Nothing: A Call to Action." Royal Bank of Canada. <rbcroyalbank.com/aboriginal/r_speech.html>.

Constitution Act, 1867 (UK), 30 & 31 Vict., c.3.

CPS (Canadian Paediatric Society). 2020. "Tuberculosis among First Nations, Inuit and Métis Children and Youth in Canada: Beyond Medical Management." January 14. <cps.ca/documents/position/tu-berculosis-among-first-nations-inuit-and-metis-children-and-youth>.

Crawford, R., et al. 2019. "Traditional Knowledge-Based Lifestyle Interventions in the Prevention of Obesity and Type 2 Diabetes in Indigenous Children in Canada: A Systematic Review Protocol." *Systemic Reviews* 69, 8.

Crowshoe, L., et al. 2018. "Type 2 Diabetes and Indigenous Peoples." *Canadian Journal of Diabetes* 42.

Deneault, A. 2018. *Legalizing Theft: A Short Guide to Tax Havens.* Black Point/Winnipeg: Fernwood Publishing.

Drummond, D., and E. Rosenbluth. 2013. "The Debate on First Nations Education Funding: Mind the Gap." Working Paper 49. Queen's University, Kingston, ON.

Eggerton, L. 2007. "Physicians Challenge Canada to Make Children, Youth a Priority." *Canadian Medical Association Journal* 176, 12.

Elizabeth Fry Northern Alberta. n.d. "The Cost of Incarceration." <efrynorthernalberta.com/cost-of-in-carceration>.

First Nations Child and Family Caring Society of Canada et al. v. Canada. 2016. Canadian Human Rights Tribunal 11, File No.: T1340/7008.

Flanagan, T. 2000. *First Nations? Second Thoughts.* Montreal: McGill-Queen's University Press.

Flanagan, T., C. Alcantra, and A. Le Dressey. 2010. *Beyond the Indian Act: Restoring Aboriginal Property Rights.* Montreal: McGill-Queen's University Press.

FNCFCS (First Nations Child and Family Caring Society). n.d. "Spirit Bear Plan." Ottawa. <fncaringso-

ciety.com/spirit-bear-plan>.

Forester, Brett. 2021. "Canada Files 3rd Judicial Review of Canadian Human Rights Tribunal Ruling." APTN National News, September 24. <aptnnews.ca/national-news/canada-files-3rd-judicial-review-canadian-human-rights-tribunal/>.

___. 2020. "Despite Promise of Reconciliation, Trudeau Spent Nearly $100M Fighting First Nations in Court during First Years in Power." APTN News, December 18. <aptnnews.ca/national-news/trudeau-spent-nearly-100m-fighting-first-nations-in-court-during-first-years-in-power/>.

Frynas. J. 2005. "The False Developmental Promise of Corporate Social Responsibility: Evidence from Multinational Oil Companies." *International Affairs* 81, 3.

Galea, S., M. Tracy, K. Hoggatt, C. Dimaggio, and A. Karpati. 2011. "Estimated Deaths Attributable to Social Factors in the United States." *American Journal of Public Health* 101, 8.

Gibbons, R. 1984. "Canadian Indian Policy: The Constitutional Trap." *Canadian Journal of Native Studies* 1.

Gibson, G. 2009. *A New Look at Canadian Indian Policy: Respect the Collective — Promote the Individual.* Vancouver: Fraser Institute.

Globe and Mail. 2010a. "Canada's Long-Form Census Debate." July 21. <theglobeandmail.com/news/politics/canadas-long-form-census-debate/article1387599/>.

___. 2010b. "Statistics Canada Chief Falls on Sword over Census." July 21. <theglobeandmail.com/news/politics/statistics-canada-chief-falls-on-sword-over-census/article1320915/>.

___. 2010c. "Provinces Rally against Ottawa as Anger Over Census Mounts." July 21. <theglobeandmail.com/news/politics/provinces-rally-against-ottawa-as-anger-over-census-mounts/article1368555/>.

___. 2021. "It's Time to Treat Pikangikum as a Nation." <theglobeandmail.com/opinion/article-its-time-to-treat-pikangikum-as-a-nation/>.

Goyette, L. 2010. "Still Waiting in Attawapiskat." *Canadian Geographic.* December 1. <canadiangeographic.ca/magazine/dec10/attawapiskat.asp>.

Guardian. 2021. "Trudeau Files Last-Ditch Appeal Against Billions for Indigenous Children." <theguardian.com/global-development/2021/oct/29/trudeau-government-canada-indigenous-children>.

Guthro, Ethan. 2021. "Measuring Indigenous Well-Being: What is Indigenous Services Missing?" *Yellowhead Institute* 101.

Haida Nation v. BC (Minister of Forests). 2004. 3 S.C.R

Hall, A. 2010. *Earth into Property: Colonization, Decolonization, and Capitalism.* Montreal: McGill-Queen's University Press.

Harper, S. 2008. "Statement of Apology to Former Students of Indian Residential Schools." June 11. Ottawa: Government of Canada.

Hasnain-Wynia, R., D. Pierce, and M.A. Pittman. 2004. "Who, When, and How: The Current State of Race, Ethnicity, and Primary Language Data Collection in Hospitals." Health Research and Educational Trust, American Hospital Association.<aapcho.dreamhosters.com/download/PDF/HasnianWynia_WhoWhenHow.pdf>.

Hayman, N., P.M.J. Reid and M. King. 2015. "Improving Health Outcomes for Indigenous Peoples: What Are the Challenges?" *Cochane Library*, August 6.

Helin, C. 2008. *Dances with Dependency: Out of Poverty Through Self-Reliance*, 2nd edition. California: Ravencrest Publishing.

Indian Act, R.S.C. 1985, c. I-5.

Indian Affairs and Northern Development. 1969. "Statement of the Government of Canada on Indian Policy Presented to the First Session of the Twenty-Eighth Parliament by the Honourable Jean Chretien, Minister of Indian Affairs and Northern Development." Ottawa.

INAC (Indian and Northern Affairs Canada). 2011a. "Minister Duncan Announces Funding for a New School at Attawapiskat First Nation." May 19.

___. 2011b. "Minister Duncan and AFN National Chief Atleo Announce Joint Action Plan." June 9.

___. 2010. "First Nation and Inuit Community Well-Being: Describing Historical Trends (1981–2006)." Ottawa.

___. 2004. "Speaking Points: Domestic Affairs Committee." December 13.

ISC (Indigenous Services Canada). 2020a. "Annual Report to Parliament." <sac-isc.gc.ca/eng/16020106 09492/1602010631711>.

___. 2020b. "Reducing the Number of Indigenous Children in Care." <sac-isc.gc.ca/eng/15411873522 97/1541187392851>.

___. 2019a. "Application of the United Nations Human Development Index to Registered Indians in Canada, 2006–2016." <publications.gc.ca/collections/collection_2021/sac-isc/R2-345-2019-eng.pdf>.

___. 2019b. "National Overview of the Community Well-Being index, 1981 to 2016." <sac-isc.gc.ca/en g/1419864229405/1557324163264>.

___. 2017. "Let's Talk On-Reserve Education: Survey Report." December 18. <sac-isc.gc.ca/eng/150901 9844067/1531399883352>.

Jacobs, B. 2010. "Environmental Racism on Indigenous Lands and Territories." Canadian Political Science Association. <cpsa-acsp.ca/papers-2010/Jacobs.pdf>.

John Howard Society of Canada. 2018. "Financial Facts on Canadian Prisons." August 23. <johnhoward. ca/blog/financial-facts-canadian-prisons/>.

Kumagai, D. 2011. "Native Groups Fight Feds in Court." <longformcensus.kingsjournalism. com/2011/03/aboriginal-groups-challenge-census-in-court/>.

Lawrence, B., and E. Dua. 2005. "Decolonizing Antiracism." *Social Justice* 32, 4.

Leroux, D. 2019. "How Some North Americans Claim a False Indigenous Identity." *The Conversation*, September 22. <theconversation.com/how-some-north-americans-claim-a-false-indigenous-iden-tity-121599>.

Long, A., et al. 1982. "Federal Indian Policy and Indian Self-Government in Canada: An Analysis of a Current Proposal." *Canadian Public Policy* 8, 2.

Lorraine, B. 2016. "Shoal Lake 40 Water Crisis an Ugly Reminder of Canadian Colonialism." *Ricochet*, June 22. <ricochet.media/en/1239/shoal-lake-40-water-crisis-an-ugly-reminder-of-canadian-co-lonialism>.

Lukas, M. 2015. "Canadian Government Pushing First Nations to Give Up Land Rights for Oil and Gas Profits." *Guardian*, March 3. <theguardian.com/environment/true-north/2015/mar/03/documents-harper-pushing-first-nations-to-shelve-rights-buy-into-resource-rush>.

MacDonald, N., et al. 2011. "Tuberculosis in Nunavut: A Century of Failure." *Canadian Medical Association Journal* 183, 7.

Macleod, A. 2015. "Aboriginal Peoples Responsible to Raise Selves Out of Poverty, Conservatives Say." *The Tyee*, September 29. <thetyee.ca/News/2015/09/29/John-Duncan-Aboriginal-Poverty-Debate/>.

Make Poverty History. n.d. "Mandela's Speech: Extracts." <makepovertyhistory.org/extras/mandela. shtml>.

Mann, M. 2009. "Good Intentions, Disappointing Results: A Progress Report on Federal Aboriginal Corrections." Ottawa: Office of the Correctional Investigator.

McDonald, R., P. Ladd, et al. 2000. "First Nations Child and Family Services: Joint National Policy Review: Final Report." Ottawa: AFN. <afn.ca/uploads/Social_Development/National Policy Review 2000_en only.pdf>.

Minister's National Working Group on Education. 2002. "Our Children — Keepers of the Sacred Knowledge: Final Report." AFN. <afn.ca/uploads/files/education/23._2002_dec_jeffrey_and_jette_ final_report_to_min_national_working_group_ourchildrenkeepersofthesacredknowledge.pdf>.

Ministry of Health BC. 2020. *In Plain Sight: Addressing Indigenous-Specific Racism and Discrimination in BC Health Care.* <engage.gov.bc.ca/app/uploads/sites/613/2020/11/In-Plain-Sight-Summary-Report.pdf>.

Moretti, S. 2011. "One-third of Canadian Adults Pay No Income Taxes." *Toronto Sun*, April 30. <to-rontosun.com/2011/04/30/onethird-of-canadian-adults-pay-no-income-taxes>.

Moss, W., and E. Gardner-O'Toole. 1991. "Aboriginal People: History of Discriminatory Laws." Ottawa:

Library of Parliament. <publications.gc.ca/Collection-R/LoPBdP/BP/bp175-e.htm>.

Nagle, R. 2019. "How 'Pretendians' Undermine the Rights of Indigenous People." *High Country News*, April 2.

National Collaborating Centre for Indigenous Health (NCCIH). 2020. "Poverty as a Social Determinant of First Nations, Inuit, and Métis Health." <nccih.ca/docs/determinants/FS-Poverty-SDOH-FNMI-2020-EN.pdf>.

___. 2018. "The Built Environment: Understanding How Physical Environments Influence the Health and Well-Being of First Nations Peoples Living On-Reserve." <nccih.ca/docs/emerging/RPT-Built-Environment-Stout-EN.pdf>.

National Council on Welfare. 2007. "First Nations, Métis and Inuit Children and Youth: Time to Act." Ottawa: National Council of Welfare. <publications.gc.ca/collections/collection_2007/hrsdc-rhdsc/HS54-1-2007E.pdf>.

National Inquiry (National Inquiry into Missing and Murdered Indigenous Women and Girls). 2019a. *Reclaiming Power and Place: The Final Report of the National Inquiry into Missing and Murdered Indigenous Women and Girls*. Ottawa.

___. 2019b. *A Legal Analysis of Genocide: A Supplementary Report of the National Inquiry into Missing and Murdered Indigenous Women and Girls*. Ottawa. <mmiwg-ffada.ca/wp-content/uploads/2019/06/Supplementary-Report_Genocide.pdf>.

NDP. 2011. "Attawapiskat School a Victory for Northern Kids: Fight Continues for Equal Rights for First Nations Students across Canada." <ndp.ca/news/attawapiskat-school-victory-northern-kids-ndp>.

Neegan Burnside Ltd. 2011. "National Assessment of First Nations Water and Wastewater Systems: National Roll-up Report — Final." Ottawa: INAC. <sac-isc.gc.ca/eng/1100100034982/1584021932182>.

OAG (Office of the Auditor General of Canada). 2014. "2014 Fall Report of the Auditor General of Canada." <oag-bvg.gc.ca/internet/English/parl_oag_201411_e_39950.html>.

___. 2011. "Interim Auditor General's Opening Statement." June 9. <oag-bvg.gc.ca/internet/English/osm_20110609_e_35409.html>.

___. 2000–2010. "Status Report of the Auditor General of Canada to the House of Commons." <publications.gc.ca/site/eng/search/search.html?st=1&e=0&f=0&ssti=on&ast=Status+Report+of+the+Auditor+General+of+Canada+to+the+House+of+Commons&cnst=&adof=on>.

___. 2004. "Report of the Auditor General: Chapter 5 — Education Program and Post-Secondary Student Support." <oag-bvg.gc.ca/internet/English/parl_oag_200411_05_e_14909.html>.

___. 2003. "Federal Government Support to First Nations—Housing on Reserves." <oag-bvg.gc.ca/internet/docs/20030406ce.pdf>.

OCI (Office of the Correctional Investigator). 2021. "Proportion of Indigenous Women in Federal Custody Nears 50%." December 17. <oci-bec.gc.ca/cnt/comm/press/press20211217-eng.aspx>.

___. 2020. "Indigenous People in Federal Custody Surpasses 30% Correctional Investigator Issues Statement and Challenge." <oci-bec.gc.ca/cnt/comm/press/press20200121-eng.aspx>.

___. 2013. "Backgrounder: Aboriginal Inmates." <oci-bec.gc.ca/cnt/rpt/oth-aut/oth-aut20121022info-eng.aspx>.

___. 2000–2010. "Annual Report of the Office of the Correctional Investigator." <oci-bec.gc.ca/rpt/index-eng.aspx>.

Office of the Chief Coroner for Ontario. 2012. "Report of the Paediatric Death Review Committee and Deaths Under Five Committee, Annual Report, 2012." Ontario. <ncfrp.org/wp-content/uploads/Publications/PDRC_Annual_Report_2012>.

Palmater, P. 2021a. "RCMP Still Clearing Indigenous Lands for Corporate Interests." *The Breach*. November 26.

___. 2021b. "Canada Still Failing to Fix Water Crisis in First Nations Communities, Says AG." *Rabble.ca*, March 4. <rabble.ca/anti-racism/canada-still-failing-address-water-crisis-first-nations/>.

___. 2020. *Warrior Life: Indigenous Resistance and Resurgence*. Black Point and Winnipeg: Fernwood Publishing.

___. 2016. "Shining Light on the Dark Places: Addressing Police Racism and Sexualized Violence Against Indigenous Women and Girls in the National Inquiry." *Canadian Journal of Women and the Law* 28, 2.

___. 2015. *Indigenous Nationhood: Empowering Grassroots Citizens*. Winnipeg and Halifax: Fernwood Publishing.

___. 2011. *Beyond Blood: Rethinking Indigenous Identity*. Saskatoon: Purich Publishing.

___. 2010. "Opportunity or Temptation: Plans for Private Property on Reserves Could Cost First Nations Their Independence." *Literary Review of Canada*, April. <reviewcanada.ca/reviews/2010/04/01/opportunity-or-temptation/>.

Parkin, T. 2016. "Trudeau's Confused Reconciliation Agenda." *Toronto Sun*, August 14. <torontosun.com/2016/08/14/trudeaus-confused-reconciliation-agenda>.

Patriquin, M. 2012. "Canada, Home to the Suicide Capital of the World." *Maclean's*, March 30.

Pendakur, K., and R. Pendakur. 2011. Aboriginal Income Disparity in Canada. Canadian Public Policy 37, 1. <sfu.ca/~pendakur/aboriginal_incomes_CPP.pdf>.

Penner, D. 2014. "'Unprecedented Opportunity' in Resource Development, Prime Minister Tells First Nations." *Vancouver Sun*, June 1. <vancouversun.com/business/resources/unprecedented+opportunity+resource+development+prime/9356519/story.html>.

Percival, T. 2011. "Political Governance and Health." July 6 presentation at Samoa Conference II: New Zealand Collects Heath Data at Hospitals by Ethnicity.

Peters, S, and W. Reimer. 2021. "New Treatment Plant Ends Shoal Lake 40 First Nation's 24-Year Boil Water Advisory." *Global News*, September 10. <globalnews.ca/news/8180664/shoal-lake-40-water-treatment-plant/>.

Porter, J. 2016. "First Nations Students Get 30 Per Cent Less Funding than Other Children, Economist Says." CBC News, March 14. <cbc.ca/news/canada/thunder-bay/first-nations-education-funding-gap-1.3487822>.

Price Waterhouse Coopers. 2009. "Financial and Economic Impacts of Treaty Settlements in BC." Executive Summary. <statcan.ca/census-recensement/2006/as-sa/97-558/p1-eng.cfm>.

Provincial Advocate for Children and Youth. 2011. "Our Dreams Matter Too: First Nations Children's Rights, Lives, and Education: An Alternate Report from the Shannen's Dream Campaign to the United Nations Committee on the Rights of the Child on the Occasion of Canada's 3rd and 4th periodic reviews." <uvic.ca/icwr/docs/research/OurDreams-LoRes.pdf>.

Puxley, C. 2015. "The Price of Winnipeg's Water: Man-Made Misery for a Native Community." *Globe and Mail*, March 12. <theglobeandmail.com/news/national/the-price-of-winnipegs-water-man-made-misery-for-a-native-community/article23417422/>.

Raphael, D. 2016. *About Canada: Health and Illness*, 2nd edition. Halifax and Winnipeg: Fernwood Publishing.

RCAP (Royal Commission on Aboriginal Peoples). 1996. "Report of the Royal Commission on Aboriginal Peoples, Vols. 1–5." Ottawa: Minister of Supply and Services Canada.

Roman, K. 2016. "Ottawa Stopped Counting Fires on First Nation Reserves in 2010." CBC News, September 23.

Sapers, H. 2015. "Annual Report of the Office of the Correctional Investigator: 2014–15." <oci-bec.gc.ca/cnt/rpt/pdf/annrpt/annrpt20142015-eng.pdf>.

___. 2009. "Evidence to Standing Committee on Aboriginal Affairs and Northern Development." November 26. <parl.gc.ca/content/hoc/Committee/402/AANO/Evidence/EV4268865/AANOEV40-E.PDF>.

Simpson, L.B. 2017. *As We Have Always Done: Indigenous Freedom through Radical Resistance*. Minnesota and London: University of Minnesota Press.

Smith, J. 2016. "First Nations Funding Cap Is Still There Despite Trudeau's Promise." *Huffington Post*, June 16. <huffingtonpost.ca/2016/06/16/political-will-to-lift-first-nations-funding-cap-is-there-needs-time-chief_n_10515960.html>.

Starblanket, G., and D. Hunt. 2020. *Storying Violence: Unravelling Colonial Narratives in the Stanley*

Trial. Winnipeg: ARP Books.

Statistics Canada. 2019. "Suicide among First Nations People, Métis and Inuit (2011–2016): Findings from the 2011 Canadian Census Health and Environment Cohort (CanCHEC)." <statcan.gc.ca/n1/pub/99-011-x/99-011-x2019001-eng.htm>.

___. 2016. "Census in Brief: The Housing Conditions of Aboriginal People in Canada." <statcan.gc.ca/census-recensement/2016/as-sa/98-200-x/2016021/98-200-x2016021-eng.cfm>.

___. 2015. "Aboriginal Statistics at a Glance: Employment." <statcan.gc.ca/n1/pub/89-645-x/2015001/employment-emploi-eng.htm#a1>.

___. 2006. "2006 Census: Aboriginal Peoples in Canada in 2006: Inuit, Métis and First Nations, 2006 Census: Highlights." Ottawa. <statcan.ca/census-recensement/2006/as-sa/97-558/p1-eng.cfm>.

Steckley, J., and B. Cummins. 2008. "The Story of Minnie Sutherland: Death by Stereotype?" In J. Steckley and B. Cummins (eds.), *Full Circle: Canada's First Nations*, 2nd edition. Toronto: Pearson Education Canada.

Stefanovich, O. and N. Boisvert. 2021. "Ottawa Will Appeal Court Ruling on Indigenous Child Welfare but Says It's Pursuing a Compensation Deal." cbc News, October 29. <cbc.ca/news/politics/ottawa-federal-court-ruling-appeal-decision-child-welfare-1.6229567>.

Talaga, T. 2011. "Lack of Proper Schools for Natives is 'Immoral Discrimination,' Martin Says." *Toronto Star*, May 18. <thestar.com/news/canada/2011/05/18/lack_of_proper_schools_for_natives_is_immoral_discrimination_martin_says.html>.

TRC (Truth and Reconciliation Commission of Canada). 2015a. *Honouring the Truth, Reconciling the Future: Summary of the Final Report of the Truth and Reconciliation Commission of Canada.* <trc.ca/websites/trcinstitution/File/2015/Honouring_the_Truth_Reconciling_for_the_Future_July_23_2015.pdf>.

___. 2015b. *Calls to Action*. <trc.ca/websites/trcinstitution/File/2015/Findings/Calls_to_Action_English2.pdf>.

Turner, L. 2019. "$1.2-Million Price Tag for Wildfire Evacuations of First Nations in Ontario Over Last Five Years." cbc News, August 6. <cbc.ca/news/canada/thunder-bay/cost-wildfire-evacs-first-nation-communities-ontario-1.5234882>.

___. 2021. "First Nations Leaders Say Next Government Must Consider On-Reserve Housing for '7 Generations Down the Line.'" cbc News, September 19. <cbc.ca/news/canada/thunder-bay/fn-reserve-housing-election-issue-1.6180068>.

UC (Universities Canada). 2019. "Equity, Diversity and Inclusion at Canadian Universities." <univcan.ca/wp-content/uploads/2019/11/Equity-diversity-and-inclusion-at-Canadian-universities-report-on-the-2019-national-survey-Nov-2019-1.pdf>.

UNHRC (United Nations Human Rights Council). 2014. Report of the Special Rapporteur on the Rights of Indigenous Peoples — The Situation of Indigenous Peoples in Canada. <ohchr.org/Documents/Issues/IPeoples/SR/A.HRC.27.52.Add.2-MissionCanada_AUV.pdf>.

United Nations Development Programme. 2020. "Human Development Report 2020 — The Next Frontier: Human Development and the Anthropocene." <hdr.undp.org/sites/all/themes/hdr_theme/country-notes/CAN.pdf>.

Varcoe, C. n.d. "Harms and Benefits: Collecting Ethnicity Data in a Clinical Context." Prepared for the Michael Smith Foundation for Health Research. <ciqss.umontreal.ca/Docs/SSDE/pdf/Varcoe.pdf>.

___. 2009. "Harms and Benefits: Collecting Ethnicity Data in a Clinical Context." <ciqss.umontreal.ca/Docs/SSDE/pdf/Varcoe.pdf>.

Venne, S. 1981. *Indian Acts and Amendments 1868–1975: An Indexed Collection*. Saskatoon: University of Saskatchewan Native Law Centre.

Vidal, J. 2013. "Indonesia is Seeing a New Corporate Colonialism." *Guardian*, May 25. <theguardian.com/world/2013/may/25/indonesia-new-corporate-colonialism>.

Warry, W. 2008. *Ending Denial: Understanding Aboriginal Issues*. Toronto: University of Toronto Press.

Wawatay News online. 2015. "Attawapiskat Students Back to School." February 7. <wawataynews.ca/30-editions-30-years/attawapiskat-students-back-school>.

Wherry. A. 2012. "Was John A. Macdonald a White Supremacist?" *MacLean's*, August 21. macleans.ca/politics/ottawa/was-john-a-macdonald-a-white-supremacist/.

Widdowson, F., and A. Howard. 2008. *Disrobing the Aboriginal Industry: The Deception Behind Indigenous Cultural Preservation*. Montreal: McGill-Queen's University Press.

Wilson, Z. (ed.). 1993. *The Indian Acts and Amendments 1970–1993: An Indexed Collection*. Saskatoon: University of Saskatchewan Native Law Centre.

Wilson, D., and D. Macdonald. 2010. *The Income Gap Between Aboriginal Peoples and the Rest of Canada*. Ottawa: Canadian Centre for Policy Alternatives. <policyalternatives.ca/sites/default/files/uploads/publications/reports/docs/Aboriginal Income Gap.pdf>.

4

KEEPING CANADA WHITE
Immigration Enforcement in Canada

Wendy Chan

YOU SHOULD KNOW THIS

- In 2019, a total of 341,180 immigrants were admitted to Canada as permanent residents.

- Between 2017 and 2018, net immigration accounted for 80 percent of Canada's population increase.

- In 2019, the top source countries for immigrants to Canada were India, China, the Philippines and Nigeria. India made up 25 percent (85,592) of all permanent residents coming to Canada that year.

- In 2019, there were over 64,000 asylum claims in Canada, the highest yearly number ever recorded. The top source countries for asylum seekers were India, Mexico, Iran and Nigeria.

- Between April 2017 and December 2020, there were 58,506 refugee claims made by irregular border crossers. The bulk of these claims, 36,761, were made in 2018 and 2019.

- In 2018–2019, 9,500 individuals were removed from Canada. There were 15,300 individuals waiting to be removed and 34,700 individuals who had enforceable removal orders but their whereabouts were unknown.

- Individuals ordered removed from Canada can only be removed once all available legal recourses have been waived or exhausted. Sometimes this can take many years to finalize.

- In 2019–2020, there were 8,825 individuals under immigration detention in Canada. The average length of detention was 13.9 days while the median length of detention was one day. Sixty-eight percent of detainees were held in immigration holding centres (IHCs) across the country while 32 percent of detainees were held in non-IHC centres.

Sources: IRCC 2020; Auditor General of Canada 2020; CBSA 2020; Immigration and Refugee Board of Canada 2021

AT THE HEIGHT OF THE CONTROVERSY in 2018 surrounding asylum seekers walking across into Canada from the United States at an unofficial border point, questions were raised about whether these asylum seekers were "irregular" border crossers or "illegal" border crossers (Hill 2018a). Even though it is not illegal to cross an international border to claim asylum, nonetheless, this question captured the political and public divide about refugees and asylum seekers in Canada. Characterizing asylum seekers as illegitimate and criminalizing their behaviour has been popular with politicians and members of the public who would like to see Canada reduce its support for refugees on the grounds that too many asylum seekers are not genuinely in need of protection and are simply trying to bypass the immigration system. Refugee advocates and supporters point out that globally, the number of refugees worldwide continues to increase dramatically due to conflict and natural disasters, and they assert that Canada should continue to support the international effort to provide protection to those who need it.

The influx of irregular border crossers seeking asylum, primarily in Quebec, and more recently, the closing of Canada's borders to international travellers as a result of the pandemic are two key events that have shaped Canada's immigration enforcement system in recent years. In both cases, the government sought to balance the safety and security of Canadians with the needs of asylum seekers and those of the economy. These two critical moments highlight the importance of having a fair, equitable and robust immigration enforcement system in place since both events escalated quickly and forced the federal government to respond immediately. Yet, while there was strong political and public consensus for significant border restrictions during the pandemic, there was much less agreement, both politically and publicly, on how to manage asylum seekers entering Canada from the United States outside of official border entry points (Harris 2019).

Immigration enforcement, particularly when it comes to refugees and asylum seekers, continues to be a hotly contested and often polarizing topic. An op-ed in the *Montreal Gazette* called on the government to be more humane in its practices of immigration detention and to apply greater compassion, justice and respect for human rights in its enforcement practices (Jeanes and Clarke 2020). However, while the Liberal government, compared to the previous Conservative government, has softened its approach to enforcement in some areas (CBSA 2018), overall, immigration enforcement has not changed significantly since the Conservative government overhauled enforcement policies over a decade ago. The transformation of the immigration system by Harper's Conservative government into a system that is "faster, more flexible and responsive" (CIC 2014) continues to shape enforcement practices today. They implemented a broad range of reforms and legislation within the immigration system, citing the need to enhance enforcement measures, improve administrative efficiency and boost Canada's economy (Alboim and Cohl 2012). Today, many critics argue that the Liberal government's approach is more of the same. As ongoing examples of the misery created by Canada's immigration enforcement policies, they cite Canada's policy blocking child refugees from reuniting with their parents (Hill 2018b), the significant backlog of unprocessed refugee claims due to deliberate underfunding of the Immigration and Refugee Board (Canadian Press 2018) and the expansion of the Safe Third Country Agreement with the US, which allows Canada to reject asylum seekers from the US (Carbert and Morrow 2019).

It is not surprising that public support for restrictive immigration policies continues unabated after two decades of heightened fears around terrorism, a Trump government that stoked anxieties on both sides of the border about undocumented immigrants, and constant media stories that our borders are too porous and the wrong types of people are entering the country. However, these concerns have to be balanced by the recognition that in order to keep Canada's economy competitive globally, there is a continued need for more immigrants in order to address the shifting demographics and the global war for talent (Nixon 2014). Critics argue that the economic consequences of failing to support further immigration would result in slower economic development and growth for Canada, particularly in a post-pandemic world. Yet the process of determining how to select the "best" immigrants continues to fuel debate and controversy. Canada wants to attract "good" immigrants while ensuring that "undesirable" immigrants are not allowed in.

What are we to think about Canada's approach to immigration enforcement? Is it too harsh and racist, as many immigrants argue? Or is it not harsh enough because it permits immigrants and refugees who arrive through irregular channels to enter Canada?

Many immigration scholars agree that successive reforms to immigration policies in Canada have resulted in increasingly harsh and punitive measures, particularly with regard to the enforcement provisions of the *Immigration Act*. Both the language used and the substantive changes contained in various amendments to the

Act construct negative images of immigrants as "abusers" of Canada's "generous" immigration system, as "bogus" refugee claimants and as "criminals" who "cheat" their way into Canada. The latest immigration act, the *Immigration and Refugee Protection Act* (IRPA), exemplifies the criminalizing and retributive tone that is now commonplace in immigration policymaking. The convergence of criminal justice strategies with concerns regarding immigration control found in the IRPA, the most comprehensive set of amendments since the introduction of the *Immigration Act* in 1976, marks an important shift in Canadian immigration policymaking.

Yet some immigration critics continue to argue that not enough is being done to ensure that the best immigrants are allowed entry while potential immigrants who pose a threat are screened out. Those same critics also argue that the rules must be the same for everyone, and therefore undocumented immigrants should not be given "special" treatment. Ironically, after being elected in early 2006, Stephen Harper's minority Conservative government — many of whose members were once among Canada's harshest immigration critics — recognized that these issues are more complex and difficult than newspapers/some critics suggest.

Untangling the myths and controversies around immigration enforcement requires a critical examination of enforcement provisions in the IRPA. Taking a critical approach involves asking how immigration laws and policies acknowledge inequities of gender, race and class in the development, interpretation and application of the country's approaches. The allegations of an effort to keep Canada "white" by excluding immigrants of colour call for a close consideration of how well (or not) immigrants of colour fare under the current *Immigration Act*. As we shall see, the trend towards criminalizing and demonizing immigrants is nothing new. Race and racism have played an important role in organizing racial identities and enforcing a specific racial reality in Canada. Then, too, the enforcement provisions of the IRPA seek to address public concerns over "problem" immigrants. Hence, it is important to consider the rationale for these provisions, as well as the responses and criticisms to them. Is there an adequate balance between enforcement and protection for immigrants and refugees? The IRPA appears to mark racialized immigrants as criminals and outsiders, with enforcement provisions driven by the need to scapegoat and punish immigrants for a range of fears and insecurities, an approach legitimized by racist ideologies and practices. Immigrants of colour pay the price for Canadians' need to be reassured that their established way of life will not be lost and that immigrants are not "taking over" their country. The result

> The allegations of an effort to keep Canada "white" call for a close consideration of how well (or not) immigrants of colour fare under the current *Immigration Act*.

is that many immigrants will continue to be marginalized and excluded as full participants in Canadian society.

CANADIAN IMMIGRATION POLICY: RECENT YEARS

Canada, like many Western democratic countries, has experienced a continued decline in births since the 1960s, combined with a relatively low level of immigration. The implications of this demographic trend have raised concerns about whether or not there would be enough people to keep the country afloat. In the 1980s, Brian Mulroney's Progressive Conservative government sought to address these problems, and boost the economy, by increasing levels of immigration, targeting both young people, particularly those of child-bearing age, and skilled immigrant workers. The result was a significant increase in immigration levels during the late 1980s and early 1990s. Between 1980 and 2000, immigration accounted for almost half of the country's population growth, with over 3.7 million immigrants admitted (Li 2003: 32). In comparison, between 1955 and 1970, Canada had admitted just over 1.6 million immigrants, accounting for 30 percent of total population growth. Since 2000, immigration has continued to hold steady, with approximately 250,000 immigrants admitted annually. The key shifts during this period have been a reduction in family (26.6 percent in 2001 to 21.5 percent in 2010) and refugee (11.1 percent in 2001 to 8.8 percent in 2010) class immigrants and an increase in economic class immigrants (from 62.1 percent in 2001 to 66.6 percent in 2010) (Alboim and Cohl 2012: 61). In the last decade, between 2010 and 2020, immigrants made up almost 22 percent of Canada's population. The expectation is that immigration will become the entire source of population growth by the early 2030s, so that immigrants as a share of the total population will increase to 28.2 percent by 2036 (Carey 2018).

The composition of immigrants was also shifting. Whereas in the post-World War II period, immigrants came mainly from Britain and continental Europe (87 percent of immigrants from 1946 to 1955), by the 1980s and 1990s, Asia and the Pacific region had become the key source continent for immigrants (53.8 percent from 1970 to 2000). By 1998–2000, the top four source countries were China, India, Pakistan and the Philippines (CIC 2001a: 8). A decade and a half later, these four countries, along with Iran, continue to be the top five source countries between 2000 and 2014 (CIC 2015: 28). Much of this shift can be attributed to alterations in immigration policies in the 1960s. With the implementation of the point system in 1967 and, subsequently, the *Immigration Act* of 1976, immigrants were assessed on the basis of age, education, language skills and economic characteristics and assigned points for each of these categories. Applicants who have a sufficient number of points are eligible for entry (Boyd and Vickers 2000). The changes allowed Canada to abandon national origin as a selection criterion and admit immigrants from all over the world. Importantly, the explicit racial and ethnic discrimination found in previous policies were removed, with the effect that many more immigrants from non-European countries were now being admitted into Canada (Li 2003).

Throughout the 1980s and 1990s, the public debate about immigration was also heating up. The increasing numbers of non-white immigrants had not gone unnoticed. This change contributed to a backlash that promoted views that Canada could not absorb all this "diversity" (Li 2001) and that the "quality" of immigrants was threatening to destroy the nation (Thobani 2000). While immigration was on the increase, so too were unemployment rates. Public-opinion polls highlighted immigration as a hot-button issue — primarily, many pollsters believed, because the public associated high unemployment rates with too much immigration (Palmer 1996; Economic Council of Canada 1991). Opinion polls recorded between 1988 and 1993 found that 30–45 percent of the Canadian population believed the country had too many immigrants and indicated that hostility towards immigrants was on the rise (Palmer 1996). The polls expressed fears and anxieties about immigrants not assimilating sufficiently, taking jobs from Canadians and creating social problems. Clearly, the issue of immigration had become highly charged, with pro-immigration and anti-immigration sentiments being strongly asserted in all types of public forums.

The issue, however, was not so clear-cut. While immigration was increasing, only certain types of immigrants were gaining access to Canada. The gender, class and race dynamics of the immigration system were not lost on many critics. Although the point system appeared to be neutral in terms of how it evaluated potential immigrants, the resources provided to immigration offices located outside of Canada for processing applications abroad were having an impact on who actually got their applications processed in a timely manner. Canadian immigration offices in the United States, Britain and Western Europe had reasonably adequate immigration services, but in non-traditional source areas, such as Africa and parts of South Asia, immigration services were few and far between, resulting in administrative delays and long waiting periods. As well, the professional qualifications of potential immigrants from countries in the northern hemisphere were given greater weight than the qualifications of immigrants trained in the south (CCR 2000). Wealthier applicants were also given preferential treatment in that they were not assessed on all criteria of the points system if they met the criteria of the investors program. The longest running investor program was the Immigrant Investor Program (IIP), which operated between 1986 and 2014. Applicants who had a net worth of at least $800,000 and who were willing to provide the Canadian government with a five-year interest-free loan of $400,000 were granted permanent residency visas, along with their immediate family members, and would eventually be eligible for citizenship (Ware, Fortin and

Paradis 2010). These hidden biases resulted in continued racial and ethnic as well as class-based discrimination by favouring potential immigrants from countries more similar to Canada than not.

Gender biases also played a role, particularly in the categories that immigrants slotted themselves into when they applied for entry into Canada. Typically, men are the primary or main applicants and women are in the category of dependent spouse. Although many women who come to Canada are skilled, they may not have had access to a traditional education, which is recognized through the point system and which in turn makes it difficult for them to succeed as the main applicant. Abu-Laban and Gabriel (2002) also point out that how skills are constructed relies on a sexual division of labour. Women's work, both paid and unpaid — for example, cleaning, caring, cooking — is devalued in the point system because it is classified as unskilled or semi-skilled, offering few if any points. Furthermore, patriarchal attitudes continue to cast women into the role of being dependent on men, and Canadian immigration policies and practices rely on these assumptions in the processing of applications. The net effect is that potential female immigrants have the best chances of entering into Canada by assuming the role of dependent spouse regardless of whether they fit that category or not. For women who do not have male applicants to support their immigration applications, the chances of successfully immigrating are greatly diminished.

The worry over illegal immigration to Canada and what some people saw as a high number of refugee applications further intensified the debate about the effectiveness of Canada's immigration system. Although the problem of "illegal" entry is an accepted problem in any immigration system, a number of high-profile cases of immigrants and refugees seeking entry led the public to conclude that Canada's immigration system was no longer effective and that more reform was necessary. The public wasn't aware, however, that most "illegal" immigrants were not in fact people seeking entry, but instead people whose visas had expired and who had not yet left the country. Furthermore, governments have never, historically, regarded the problem of "illegal" entry into Canada to be a major immigration issue. Indeed, over the years a number of amnesty programs had been implemented to regularize immigrants who lacked proper documentation (Robinson 1983). If a "crisis" situation did exist, it was more likely the result of the media and political opportunists creating a panic in the public imagination, allowing it to run unchecked. The result: uninformed speculation about Canada's immigration system.

power over the messages sent regarding immigrants

CONTROLLING IMMIGRATION AND IMMIGRANTS

A key element of many Western countries' immigration programs includes determining who is denied access. In Canada, the perceived need to control the flow
of immigrants resulted in a marked resurgence of strictures in Canadian policy in
the 1980s, a trend that peaked in the 1990s and coincided with the politicization of
immigration. Beginning with the *Immigration Act* of 1976, numerous reforms and
amendments led to stricter and more exclusionary requirements. Search-and-seizure
provisions were expanded, and refugee claimants were photographed and finger-
printed upon arrival. Fines and penalties were increased for transportation companies that brought in individuals who lacked appropriate documentation (Kelley and
Trebilcock 1998).

Various explanations have been offered for why these changes occurred. Many
authors cite the breakdown in Canada's refugee system combined with the rise in
requests for asylum as major contributing factors (Creese 1992; Matas 1989). The
backlog of applications, the cumbersome administrative process and allegations that
the refugee system was being abused challenged the legitimacy of the system. Other
explanations included the lack of consensus among the political parties over what
was an acceptable level of immigration, along with the belief that immigrants applying to Canada should be more self-reliant. These conditions paved the way for independent immigrants (typically male, economic class immigrants that held high levels
of education and labour market skills) to be viewed as more desirable than dependent immigrants (often referred to as family class immigrants, composed typically of
women and children who are sponsored by the primary applicant on an economic
class application, a Canadian citizen or permanent resident who agrees to ensure
that their essential needs are met so that the sponsored person(s) will not resort to
social assistance). Racist beliefs — to the effect that racial and ethnic backgrounds
of particular immigrants were eroding Canadian values and traditions — shaped the
contours of the debates around these issues (Frideres 1996).

In 1987, the federal government introduced two major policy reforms, Bill C-55
and Bill C-84, in response to unanticipated levels of refugee claims, which were placing a major strain on the immigration system. The *Refugee Reform Act* (Bill C-55)
created the Immigration and Refugee Board of Canada (previously the Immigration
Appeal Board) and restructured the refugee determination process to respond to
the problem of unfounded refugee claims. Refugees were now required to undergo a
screening hearing to determine the credibility of their claims. The *Refugee Deterrents
and Detention Act* (Bill C-84) gave immigration officers and agents more power to
detain and remove refugee arrivals, particularly those considered criminals or a security threat (Kelley and Trebilcock 1998). Both of these reforms led to heated debates,

with many critics arguing that the changes proposed were not well-thought-out pieces of legislation but, rather, a reactionary and knee-jerk response to an alleged refugee "crisis" that had been created by the media (Creese 1992: 140–41). Interestingly,
the procedure of screening refugees at the beginning of the refugee determination
process was eventually eliminated when it was discovered that 95 percent of refugee
claims were legitimate (Garcia y Griego 1994: 128). In other words, the speculation
that many refugees were "bogus" was unwarranted. The process of forcing refugees
to undergo a screening was eventually removed in 1992.

Attempts to curtail and control immigration continued into the 1990s, when
two more pieces of legislation were introduced to address security concerns and
the growing belief that illegal immigrants, rather than legitimate refugees, were in-
filtrating Canada's borders. Introduced in June 1992, Bill C-86 proposed primarily
restrictive revisions to the refugee determination system. The restrictions included
fingerprinting refugee claimants, harsher detention provisions and making refugee
hearings open to the public. As well, Convention refugees — which is anyone holding
a well-founded fear of persecution based on one or more of five grounds as defined
in the UN Convention Relating to the Status of Refugees — applying for landing in
Canada were required to have a passport, valid travel document or "other satisfacto-
ry identity document" (CCR 2000). In addition, individuals with criminal or terrorist
links would no longer be admissible. In July 1995, the government introduced Bill
C-44, better known as the "Just Desserts" bill, in response to the killing of a Toronto
police officer by a landed immigrant with a long criminal record. Sergio Marchi, the
immigration minister, reminded Canadians that immigration is a privilege and not a
right, and he proposed changes that would "go a long way to stopping the tyranny of
a minority criminal element" (Marchi 1995). Bill C-44 made it easier to remove from
Canada permanent residents who were deemed by the minister to be a "danger to
the public." This would be done by restricting their ability to appeal their deportation
orders or submit a refugee claim.

Like the earlier reforms, these two bills were equally divisive and resulted in intense public and political debates. The most controversial change implemented was
the discretionary power given to the immigration minister to deport a permanent
resident. Widespread academic and public discussions ensued, with legal scholars
arguing that returning discretionary power to the minister was "a throwback to a
less enlightened era" (Haigh and Smith 1998: 291). Advocates for a fairer immigration policy argued that the new provisions were racist and would have the result
of increasing the criminalization of non-European individuals in Canada (Hassan-
Gordon 1996; Noorani and Wright 1995). Yet some critics believed that Bill C-44
had not gone far enough in tightening up the system against false claimants and
criminals. The Reform Party argued that a "criminal is a criminal" and that it was

not sufficient to define "serious criminality" as offences carrying a ten-year sentence or longer (Kelley and Trebilcock 1998: 434). That party's position demonstrates how, despite the lack of research demonstrating any links between immigrants and high crime rates, public fear about crime, based only on several high-profile cases, could be easily manipulated to argue for tighter immigration controls.

These debates highlight how immigration had, by the mid-1990s, become a hot-button issue for politicians and policymakers as the Canadian public became more involved in shaping Canada's immigration system. Teitelbaum and Winter (1998) attribute this change to the presence of the Reform Party and its call in the 1993 election

> By the mid-1990s, immigration had become a hot-button issue for politicians and policymakers as the Canadian public became more involved in shaping Canada's immigration system.

for an abandonment of the policy of multiculturalism and significant reductions in Canada's annual immigration levels. The right-wing populist movement in Canada, as elsewhere, used immigration and immigrants as easy targets in placing blame for the economic troubles of the time:

> The Fraser Institute report says newcomers pay about half as much in income taxes as other Canadians but absorb nearly the same value of government services, costing taxpayers roughly $6,051 per immigrant and amounting to a total annual cost of somewhere between $16.3-billion and $23.6-billion. "It's in the interest of Canada to examine what causes this and to fix it," said Herbert Grubel, co-author of the report *Immigration and the Canadian Welfare State*. "We need a better selection process ... We're not here, as a country, to do charity for the rest of the world." (Carlson 2011)

Such views coincided neatly with the shift to neoliberal approaches in public policy development — approaches that fostered a belief that the vulnerable people of society, such as single mothers and immigrants, were to blame for the lack of jobs or high crime rate (Abu-Laban 1998). Good immigrants, it was understood, were those who could look after themselves and their families. With this came the "common-sense" view that strong immigration controls were a necessary component of any effective immigration system. The harsh government reforms of the 1980s and 1990s delivered the message that security and enforcement were now key priorities in immigration policymaking.

THE *IMMIGRATION AND REFUGEE PROTECTION ACT* OF 2002

Crepeau and Nakache (2006) note that while immigration controls emerged years before 9/11, those attacks gave authorities more incentive to radically overhaul policies and make them harsher towards unwanted migrants. Canada, like many other states affected by aspects of globalization, transformed immigration from an economic and population policy issue into a security issue. The introduction of the *Immigration and Refugee Protection Act* (IRPA) in 2002 thus marks an important shift in Canadian immigration policymaking. As the Standing Committee on Citizenship and Immigration (2001) affirmed, "The *Immigration and Refugee Protection Act* represents a significant step in addressing current security concerns. Even though it was drafted before September 11, the legislation was clearly created with the threat of terrorism in mind." The Canadian government's response in deterring these activities and individuals was to impose tighter sanctions and increase levels of scrutiny and authority for immigration officers.

According to Citizenship and Immigration Canada (CIC), the IRPA is intended to serve a number of different immigration goals, such as attracting skilled workers, protecting refugees, allowing family reunification and deterring traffickers. The aim, according to the Liberal government at the time, was to accomplish these goals by simplifying the legislation and striking the necessary balance between efficiency, fairness and security. CIC asserts that there is a need to "simplify," "strengthen," "modernize" and "streamline" the immigration system. A key priority in this set of policy reforms was to close "the back door to criminals and others who would abuse Canada's openness and generosity." This would be achieved by including in the Act the necessary provisions to "better ensure serious criminals and individuals who are threats to public safety are kept out of Canada, and, if they have entered the country, that they are removed as quickly as possible" (CIC 2001b).

The IRPA did have a significant impact on controlling immigration to Canada. Immigrant support organizations pointed to growing concerns and trepidation about an act that was overly reactive and too obsessed with security issues. As the Maytree Foundation[1] (2001: 3) stated, the IRPA "is much more about who cannot come to Canada and how they will be removed, than it is about who we will welcome, who we will protect, and how we will do that." The addition of several legislative amendments to the IRPA such as the *Protecting Canada's Immigration System Act* in 2012 and the *Faster Removal of Foreign Criminals Act* in 2013 highlight how strong enforcement measures would remain a central feature of controlling immigration. Many organizations expressed an uneasiness that racialized immigrants would suffer the consequences of immigration officers' concerns about the need to maintain border security. Moreover, women refugees and immigrants would be likely to shoulder the burden of the many changes that encompassed racist and sexist practices.

IMMIGRATION DETENTION

With the IRPA, immigration detention and the power to detain have been fortified. Sections 55 and 56 of the new Act state that someone can be detained if there are reasonable grounds to believe that the person would be inadmissible to Canada, a danger to the public or unlikely to appear for future proceedings. Enhanced powers have also been given to immigration officers at ports of entry to detain people on the basis of administrative convenience so that an examination of the person can be completed, on suspicion of inadmissibility on the grounds of security or human rights violations and due to failure to establish identity for any immigration procedure under the Act. Immigration officers also have wider discretion to arrest and detain a foreign national but not a protected person without a warrant, even in cases where they are not being removed (s. 55[2]). The length of detention is not specified for any of these grounds, although periodic reviews are mandatory. Thus, someone who fails to provide adequate identification can be detained for the same length of time as can a person who is considered a danger to the public (s. 58[1]). Children can be detained, but only as a measure of last resort (s. 60).

Many concerns have been raised about the nature of the detention provisions and the manner in which they are or will be executed. The fear among most immigrant and refugee organizations is that conferring greater powers to individual immigration officers will result in racial profiling and that a high proportion of racialized migrants will end up being detained (CCR 2001; Getting Landed Project 2002). Other worries include the broad and arbitrary use of power by immigration officers, the possibility of long-term detention of migrants who fail to establish their identities, the criminalization of trafficked or smuggled migrants who will be detained for the purpose of deterring human traffickers and the use of detention on the basis of group status rather than on the particular circumstances of the person involved.

It has also been revealed that immigrant detainees are not adequately treated while in detention. A Red Cross investigation of detention conditions at Canadian facilities found that detainees were housed in triple-bunked cells and that there was a lack of support for children and inadequate medical care available (Bronskill 2014). More recently, the continued detention and housing of child migrants in Canadian detention facilities, despite a 2017 government directive instructing the Canadian Border Services Agency (CBSA) to limit this practice, has been heavily criticized by refugee advocacy organizations (Gros and Song 2016; CCR 2019).

The United Nations High Commission for Refugees (UNHCR) states that it opposes any detention policy that is fashioned to deter asylum seekers or to discourage them from pursuing their refugee claims. Moreover, it cautions against establishing a policy that detains migrants on the basis of being "unlikely to appear" at an immigration hearing because of their "mode of arrival" to Canada — many refugees are forced to use smugglers in order to reach safety (UNHCR 2001: 29). Finally, it argues that detaining a person for failing to establish their identity, which includes making determinations about the person's level of cooperation with authorities, calls for a recognition of the difference between a wilful intention to deceive and the inability to provide documentation (UNHCR 2001: 30). The UNHCR joins the voices of others (CCR 2001; Maytree Foundation 2001) who recommend that the government needs to establish clear guidelines and criteria as to what constitutes a refusal to cooperate.

The drift towards the use of "preventative detention" to deal with migrants perpetuates the mistaken and prejudiced perceptions that those being detained are a threat to public safety and are behaving illegally rather than being people who actually need safety from danger (CCR 2010b). Indeed, the culture of criminalization within the present immigration system points to disturbing trends. Unlike convicted offenders, migrants can face indefinite lengths of detention as they wait for the arrival of their identity documents, and they can be detained on the basis of suspicion or convenience. As well, the lack of independent oversight of the CBSA, the deaths of migrants in immigration detention and the continued use of prisons to detain migrants are some of the key reasons cited for why there needs to be a fundamental overhaul of immigration detention in Canada. Even though a new National Immigration Detention Framework was implemented in 2017, critics contend that these policy changes are "reactive, incremental and far from transformative" (BCCLA 2017; Ethans 2020). Asylum seekers are increasingly presumed to be acting fraudulently and required to demonstrate their innocence in an immigration system that has become preoccupied with securitization and criminalization.

Ongoing allegations of bias and unfair treatment over the use of immigration detention by the Immigration and Refugee Board led to the first ever independent audit of detention reviews in 2017/2018. The audit sought to determine whether detention hearings in cases where immigration detention exceeded one hundred days met standards of fairness and compliance with the *Charter of Rights and Freedoms* (Immigration and Refugee Board of Canada 2017/2018). The audit identified eleven areas of concern in the adjudication of detention reviews, including making decisions using inaccurate or inconsistent information, relying on inaccurate statements by the CBSA, not allowing the detainee to hear and present evidence and adopting an overly rigid interpretation of the rules while failing to take into account the circumstances of the individual case (Immigration and Refugee Board of Canada 2017/2018). The auditor noted that "at times, it seemed like the immigration division had its own 'dangerous offender designation,' without any of the safeguards of that process in the criminal justice system," and "the assumption seemed to be that any risk was enough risk. As long as there was a chance that the person might not appear, that justified de-tention" (Immigration and Refugee Board of Canada 2017/2018). As Nicholas Keung of the *Toronto Star* observed, this was a "damning" report and "shocked even the most seasoned critics and rights advocates" (Keung 2018). The denial of due process and basic rights of detainees is clearly evident, and the report speculates that many detainees may have been released years earlier if they had been given a fair review. Yet a culture of imprisonment at the Immigration Division combined with the use of stereotypes and prejudices by Immigration Division Members (judges) in the review hearings perpetuated the indefinite detention of many detainees unnecessarily.

LOSS OF APPEAL RIGHTS

The elimination of immigration appeals in Canada, particularly in cases where "se-rious criminality" is involved, is a measure that many other countries have not im-plemented to the same extent. Section 64 of the IRPA states that individuals found to be inadmissible on considerations of security, violating human rights, serious crimi-nality, organized criminality or individuals convicted of a crime and given a term of imprisonment of two years or more may not be allowed to appeal to the Immigration Appeal Division. Although judicial review remains available, applicants who lose their right to appeal can apply to the federal courts but only with leave from the court and only if there is a purely legal issue that needs to be dealt with. Therefore, if a factual mistake is made, or if all the evidence was not reasonably considered by the original decision maker (even if that person reached the wrong conclusion), the federal court will not intervene. The effect of this change is to disallow any of the dis-cretion formerly exercised in determining whether an individual should or should not be removed based on the circumstances of their case. While these changes may make the system more efficient, they do so at the cost of diminishing the rights of immigrants. As one commentator notes, such an approach illustrates a move towards a "mechanical application of the rules," which is the antithesis of the just administra-tion of the law (Dent 2002: 762).

The introduction of the IRPA also included provisions for the establishment of a Refugee Appeal Division, where refugee determinations could be reviewed. However, the number of Immigration and Refugee Board members was reduced from a panel of two to one to balance the right to an appeal for refugees (Crepeau and Nakache 2006: 15). In 2010, the Refugee Appeal Division was finally established, almost eight years after the implementation of IRPA. The provisions for the Refugee Appeal Division were part of the reforms found in the *Balanced Refugee Reform Act*. However, also contained in this Act were less welcoming reforms such as the denial of appeal to refugee claimants arriving from "safe countries of origin" (CCR 2010c). The problem with this country-of-origin criterion is that it is unclear what constitutes a "safe" country, and activists argue that refugee determination should never be based on a blanket judgment such as country of origin. Instead, each case is unique and requires an individual assessment in order to achieve a fair outcome (CCR 2010c). Although the government argued that designating some claims as "safe" will help to streamline the refugee determination process, critics fear that many claimants may fall through the cracks if they do not have access to a full hearing. When refugees and immigrants do have the right to an appeal, their access to the process is made all the more difficult because of reduced funding in legal aid. Depending on the province in which the appeal takes place, some appellants may never see the inside of a hearing room because some provinces do not have any funding available to migrants.

The recent debate over whether or not the United States, under the Trump administration, could still be considered a "safe country" highlights how restrictions on appealing refugee decisions needs to be attuned to the current political context. The Safe Third Country Agreement between Canada and the United States has been in effect since 2004. It is intended to share the burden of refugee protection between the two countries since both countries have similar refugee determination systems in place and both countries are considered safe for refugees (Spade and McDermott 2020). What this means in practice is that a refugee from the United States arriving at a Canada-US land border point cannot, except under limited exceptions, make a refugee claim in Canada. Under the agreement, any refugees from the United States asking for protection from Canada will be turned back to the US and told to apply for protection there. However, under the Trump administration, the US immigration system declared itself openly hostile to immigrants and refugees through an executive order that indefinitely suspends the resettlement of Syrian refugees and pauses the overall refugee resettlement program (Pierce and Meissner 2017). Many refugees who are turned back by Canada find themselves immediately imprisoned and mistreated by US immigration officials (Amnesty International Canada and CCR 2017). The election of Joe Biden as president has not really changed this situation: Biden has wavered on this issue, initially saying he would raise the Trump cap on refugees admitted but is dragging his feet on actually making any changes.

The rapid deterioration of how refugees in the US are treated led to a legal challenge in the Federal Court of Canada in 2017 by the Canadian Council of Refugees, the Canadian Council of Churches and Amnesty International Canada (CCR 2017). They argued that the United States could no longer be considered a "safe third country," given the serious violations of refugees' basic rights, and that this designation should be removed and refugees in the United States should be allowed to apply for refugee protection from Canada or appeal a negative refugee decision (CCR 2017). In July 2020, the Federal Court of Canada determined that the Safe Third Country

Agreement is of no force or effect because it violates refugee claimants' Charter rights to liberty and security of the person (Tunney 2020). The Canadian government disagreed, they appealed the decision, and the Federal Court of Appeal reversed the decision, ruling that the Safe Third Country Agreement is constitutional and does not violate the Charter (*Global News* 2021). This decision is a significant disappointment for refugee advocates and demonstrates not only the difficulties of mounting such a legal challenge, but also the importance of having appeal options for refugee claimants that are not circumscribed by "safe" country designations. As Spade and McDermott (2020) point out, "the notion of 'safety' is a construct unfree of political bias, and long-standing political alliances mean that Canada is not objective when making this determination."

PROTECTING IMMIGRANTS' RIGHTS

Many critics of the IRPA note the erosion of immigrant rights in the legislation. The emphasis on security and terrorism has clearly overshadowed migrants' rights and the need for a more balanced approach. Kent Roach (2005) observes that governments have taken advantage of concerns around security to reconfigure immigration law in ways that bypass the human rights of migrants. He states, "Immigration law has been attractive to the authorities because it allows procedural shortcuts and a degree of secrecy that would not be tolerated under even an expanded criminal law" (Roach 2005: 2).

Critics argue that the IRPA and its subsequent amendments have had a detrimental effect on racialized individuals, groups and communities. For example, the attempts by government to combat human smuggling and trafficking should not occur at the expense of further victimization of the migrants smuggled or trafficked. The National Association of Women and the Law (NAWL) and the United Nations High Commission for Refugees (UNHCR) assert that by failing to include adequate protection for trafficked or smuggled migrants, the Canadian government is reneging on its responsibility to international protocols. The UNHCR notes that many reasons exist as to why migrants resort to smugglers and traffickers. While many migrants are people searching for better economic opportunities, many others are refugees whose only option for escape is with the smugglers or traffickers. NAWL believes that this new category of immigration enforcement will result in smugglers and traffickers charging migrants higher prices to escape. For women and children, who are less likely to have the financial resources to pay, the possibilities of fleeing persecution, conflict and human rights abuses will become even more remote unless they are willing to pay the costs in the form of enforced prostitution and sexual violations (NAWL 2001). It has been strongly recommended that the Canadian government provide protection to migrants by granting them immigration relief, access to permanent residency or the opportunity to submit applications to stay on humanitarian and compassionate grounds (see briefs by NAWL 2001; CCR 2001; and UNHCR 2001). Affording migrants the necessary protection would help to alleviate their vulnerability to the smugglers or traffickers.

Racialized women migrants in particular will experience the impact of the IRPA in harsh and uncompromising terms because they are typically more vulnerable to the effects of migration. For example, a third of all women who immigrate to Canada do so through the family class category (NAWL 2001). In its brief to the Standing Committee on Citizenship and Immigration, NAWL (2001) recommended that family reunification be recognized as a funda-

> Racialized women migrants are typically more vulnerable to the effects of migration.

mental human right and, specifically, that people who are being reunited with their families in Canada be given the right to obtain permanent residence in Canada in order to avoid the development of exploitative or abusive relationships. In its review of the first several years of the IRPA, NAWL points out that neither this recommendation nor any of the others it submitted has been implemented, although cursory attention to the issue of gender in immigration has been paid. It notes, "Almost four years after the adoption of the new legislation, the only tangible result of any gender-based analysis of the legislative commitment to gender-based analysis of the Act is the sex-disaggregated data in the Annual Report 2005" (NAWL 2006).

There is an abundance of evidence for raising concerns about the violation of migrants' civil liberties, particularly when the majority of them are racialized migrants. Indeed, many organizations believe that the increased use of detention is a racist and reactionary response to the arrival of boatloads of Chinese and Tamil migrants to the shores of British Columbia in the late 1990s, many of whom were primarily economic migrants seeking a new life in Canada. That their arrival resulted in their immediate detention without much public outcry highlights how racism, through the practice of racial profiling, was used to gain legitimacy for the government's practices. The public reaction to the Chinese migrants was generally one of hostility; they tended to be regarded as "bogus" refugees. Many of them were detained and eventually deported back to China (see briefs by Coalition for a Just Immigration and Refugee Policy 2001; NAWL 2001; the Getting Landed Project 2002; African Canadian Legal Clinic 2001; UNHCR 2001). The assumption was that if one boatload of migrants were "bogus" refugee claimants, then all migrants would be as well, which justified the government's "tough"[2] stance on "illegal" immigrants (CBC News 1999a, 1999b; CCR 2010a).

Similar logics have been applied to migrants crossing from the United States into Canada at unofficial border points. Claims of "fraudulent" refugees entering Canada once again resurfaced as refugees desperate for protection sought Canada's help when the US suspended its refugee protection program in January 2017. Between February 2017 and March 2021, 59,148 refugee claims were made by irregular border crossers — individuals who entered Canada by land between official ports of entry (Immigration and Refugee Board of Canada 2021). Typically, these individuals walk across the border, many at the Roxham Road crossing in Quebec (Glavin 2019). There was widespread perception that these were "fraudulent" refugee claimants because they were coming from a "safe" country (Spade and McDermott 2020). In an effort to combat myths and misinformation about these individuals, a report by the UNHCR notes that over half of the refugee claimants (55 percent) crossing at an unofficial border point were recognized as refugees, with many fleeing violence and persecution (UNHCR 2019). Furthermore, the report points out that these refugee claimants are not queue-jumping since they are processed in entirely different programs; they are not given priority over other refugee claimants, as everyone is processed on a first-come, first-serve basis; finally, there are no shortcuts for crossing the border irregularly (UNHCR 2019). It's also important to remember that Canada receives less than 0.3 percent of the world's refugee population, there is a rigorous screening process in place and less than 0.5 percent of irregular claimants have a serious criminal background (UNHCR 2019). Yet, despite these statistics, politicians and the media continue to stoke fears about these "queue-jumping" migrants seeking asylum in Canada, leading to high levels of public support for harsher policies against irregularly arrived migrants. An Angus-Reid poll found that two thirds of the Canadian public state that irregular migration by asylum seekers has reached crisis levels, and most Canadians would prefer to direct resources to border surveillance and security rather than accommodating newly arrived migrants because Canada has become "too generous" (Angus Reid Institute 2018). Racism cannot be divorced from these concerns that Canada's generosity has reached its limit. The perceived illegitimate status of irregular border crossers has weakened support for their desperate desire to find safety and it has bolstered the call for denying them entry into Canada. An Ipsos poll found 54 percent of respondents believe Canada is too welcoming to immigrants (Vomiero 2019) while an EKOS poll revealed that more Canadians state there is too much non-white immigration than those stating that the current mix is "just right" or that we need more non-white immigrants (EKOS Politics 2019). These hardened attitudes towards racialized migrants allowed the federal government to enact changes to the IRPA disqualifying refugee claimants from being considered if they had previously made a claim in another country, had their claim previously rejected in Canada or have been granted refugee protection elsewhere. According to the Liberal government, the aim of these amendments to the IRPA, buried deep in an almost four-hundred-page omnibus bill, is "to better manage, discourage and prevent irregular migration" (Coyne 2019). The hypocrisy of these changes was not lost on many critics, who saw the Liberal government praising itself on the one hand for its commitment to refugee rights, while, on the other hand, stealthily limiting the rights of refugees.

For many activists and scholars involved in debating and discussing the IRPA, the government's recognition of the importance of human rights does indeed appear to be either non-existent or timid at best. Crepeau and Nakache (2006) argue that governments need to recognize that the principle of territorial sovereignty is not incompatible with protecting individual rights and freedoms. One way of recognizing this principle is to clearly identify and justify all security exceptions to the recognition of human rights that are normally conferred by the state to migrants. The extent to which Canada and other Western nations will give priority to human rights while pursuing an immigration agenda focused on security and control remains to be seen. Catharine Davergne observes:

> The proliferation of human rights norms over the last half century has not markedly increased rights entitlements at the moment of border crossing, nor has it significantly increased access to human rights for those with no legal status, those "illegals" beyond the reach of the law but at the centre of present rhetoric. (2004: 613)

As a result, the approach taken continues to reinforce the unequal distribution of rights on the basis of birthplace, and it leaves those who are unprotected vulnerable and open to intimidation and exploitation.

RACE AND NATION: NATIONAL FEARS AND IMMIGRANT SCAPEGOATING

As the successor to the 1976 *Immigration Act*, the IRPA represents a different era of immigration policymaking. The 1976 Act was born out of a perceived need for "race-neutral" categories of eligibility and non-discriminatory treatment of immigrants; it is considered to be liberal in its approach. This view of the 1976 *Immigration Act* has been challenged by critical immigration scholars, who contend that while the Act did not directly discriminate against particular racial and ethnic groups, the outcome of the point system nonetheless resulted in differential access to immigration (see Thobani 2000; Jakubowski 1997). The IRPA emerged out of the continuing racialization[3] of immigration, whereby immigrants of colour have come to be viewed not only as threats to the social, cultural and linguistic order of the nation, but also as threats to national security. Martin Rudner (2002: 24), for example, blames Canada's immigration policy for the presence of "large, identifiable homeland communities from societies in conflict," communities that presumably become attractive arenas for fostering international terrorist networks. These anti-immigrant sentiments are not new and were present in various forms during previous immigration debates. However, in recent times they occupy a greater role in framing immigration debates as a result of the negative representation of immigrants of colour by the media in Canada and the realignment of immigration policymaking towards a conservative agenda (Abu-Laban 1998; Teitelbaum and Winter 1998).

It would seem that public concerns and anxiety about immigrants and national security are linked to "perceived immigrant desirability and legitimacy," as Buchignani and Indra (1999: 416) remark, rather than to any real threat to Canada's borders or sovereignty. Garcia y Griego (1994: 120) concurs, "Canada has never lost control over its borders, but it has, on more than one occasion, lost control over its own admission process." This state of affairs has been made possible through the belief that it is the "outsider," the migrant or foreign national, that poses the greatest threat and that this threat can only be contained by retaining tighter control over the criteria for determining who can immigrate to Canada. This view is evident in statements made by Public Safety and Emergency Preparedness Canada (2004), which notes that "many of the real and direct threats to Canada originate from far beyond our borders."

The implication is that problems are imported into the country via immigrants and that only through the adoption of a security-driven, regulatory agenda will those problems be contained. Indeed, the flurry of immigration reforms post-9/11 is perhaps more a reflection of the government of the time demonstrating that it had matters under control than it is a proportionate response to security issues. What this allows for, as Maggie Ibrahim (2005) points out, is the legitimization of new racist fears. Instead of focusing on how to support immigrants who are at risk, a security-driven approach emphasizes the need to protect citizens because the incorporation of immigrants will result in an unstable host state. Of significant concern is that these sentiments are no longer being echoed by conservative, right-wing political parties and organizations only. They are also being legitimized by more liberal, humanitarian-focused groups such as the UN and liberal-minded academics (Ibrahim 2005).

Immigrants who do not fit into the predefined mould of what constitutes a "good immigrant" will increasingly become the targets of the new security-focused state. Hate crimes have risen dramatically since 9/11 (Statistics Canada 2004) and many people of colour speak of experiencing racial profiling on a daily basis at the hands

> Immigrants who do not fit into the predefined mould of a "good immigrant" will become the targets of the new security-focused state.

of various law enforcement agents (Bahdi 2003; Maynard 2017). The public acceptance of racist treatment towards people of colour is evident in the ways in which the Canadian mainstream media described Muslims during the June 2006 arrest of seventeen Muslim men in Canada. The *Globe and Mail*'s (Appleby and Ghandi 2006) front-page story noted, "Parked directly outside his ... office was a large, grey, cube-shaped truck and, on the ground nearby, he recognized one of the two brown-skinned young men who had taken possession of the next door rented unit." As Robert Fisk points out, "What is 'brown-skinned' supposed to mean — if it is not just a revolting attempt to isolate Muslims as the 'Other' in Canada's highly multicultural society?" (Fisk 2006). Backed into a corner, Muslim groups and organizations have no choice but to join this process of "Othering" by distancing themselves from the men arrested and attempting to calm an increasingly hostile public through reinforcing the idea of peace as the centrepiece of their religion (Ghafour 2006). Good Muslims, they argue, are not violent and do not engage in terrorist activities. Within all these discussions, it is clear that in a climate of fear, suspicion and hostility produced by the association between Muslims and terrorist activities, homogeneity becomes the default security blanket, now made all the more possible by the IRPA.

A close look at the enforcement provisions of the IRPA shows that the process of blaming and punishing immigrants allows for a "suitable enemy" to blame for the problems of society (Christie 1986). Few strategies are as effective as processes of criminalization for reinforcing an ideology of "us" and "them," with the immigrant, usually understood as non-white, poor and/or female, occupying the status of the outsider (Bannerji 2000). The racialized, gendered and class-based nature of this marking ensures that in the construction and definition of who is Canadian, access to this identity is far from equal. Casting immigrants into the role of the "Other" has been beneficial in suppressing public fears and insecurities about immigrants "terrorizing" Canadians, taking jobs away from Canadians and overtaxing the welfare system.

As immigration authorities seek to reclaim their ability to secure Canada's borders and to argue that the integrity of the immigration system has not been compromised by "illegal" migrants, an increase in the degree of punishment to offenders allows governments to demonstrate their power through the use of force. Such has been the case in the European Union, where resolutions and legislation were brought in to counter a broad range of terrorist activities (these include not just terrorist organizations, but also anti-globalization protests, animal rights activism and youth subcultures), resulting in the use of deportation and detention without trial against foreign nationals suspected of posing a security risk (Fekete 2004).

KEEPING CANADA WHITE

Historically, notions of immigration control linked the decline of the nation with the sexual excesses and mental and moral degeneration of Indigenous Peoples and people of colour. Racist ideas determined which groups of people would be regarded as having more character and thus be considered more "civilized." People of British descent were viewed as morally superior for their ability to self-regulate and exercise self-control (Valverde 1991: 105). Importantly, this position was not contested, but rather taken for granted by moral reformers at the turn of the century in Canada (Valverde 1991). The historical studies on immigration by Barbara Roberts (1988) and Donald Avery (1995) confirm the presence of these beliefs. The Canadian government sought to attract the most desirable immigrants, which it had identified — not surprisingly — as white, British, English-speaking and Protestant. As Strange and Loo (1997: 117) note, "Determining who could become or remain Canadian was one more way to shape the moral character of the nation." Immigrants identified as "low quality" or morally degenerate would find themselves subjected to various forms of regulation, with deportation being the most drastic measure imposed. Here, gendered and racialized ideologies shaped the circumstances that would be defined as undesirable. For men, unemployment or left-wing affiliation were sufficient to warrant deportation, while for women, having children out of wedlock, carrying venereal disease or tuberculosis or appearing to court more than one man would bring them to the attention of immigration officials (Strange and Loo 1997). In terms of racial exclusions, simply being non-white was sufficient to be classified as undesirable. The exclusion of Black and Chinese people from Canada was made on the belief that they posed a moral threat that could not be overcome by any means, and therefore special measures needed to be taken to ensure that they did not corrupt the moral integrity of the nation (Bashi 2004; Strange and Loo 1997). Examples of measures taken included the *Chinese Immigration Act* in 1923, which excluded anyone of Chinese descent from immigrating to Canada, prohibited the employment of white women by Asian employers and prevented Chinese people from forming families in Canada (Strange and Loo 1997).

> Gendered and racialized ideologies shape the circumstances that define immigrants as undesirable.

An overarching feature of immigration policies in Canada, both historically and at present, is to build a nation of people who fulfill the highest moral standards. As Strange and Loo (1997) observe, ideals of purity, industry, piety and self-discipline were regarded as essential features of Canadianness. Few would argue that these standards continue to characterize and shape present-day immigration policies, often to the detriment of non-white immigrants seeking to come to Canada. Vukov (2003) points out how public articulations about desirable and undesirable immigrants in both the news media and governmental policy with respect to sexuality and security issues reinforce the long-standing fears that sexually deviant immigrants and criminals continue to threaten the process of replenishing and sustaining a secure population base. Likewise, Angel-Ajani (2003) argues that this climate of anti-immigrant rhetoric relies on the dual discourses of criminalization and cultural difference. Within this climate of insecurity, a wide range of screening practices have been enacted to ensure that people belonging to designated groups are properly filtered out. The construction of Middle Eastern, West Asian and Muslim peoples as security threats to the nation since the events of 9/11, and the introduction of new policy measures to secure our border, underscore the ways in which definitions of undesirable immigrants are highly racialized (Vukov 2003).

The narrative that emerges from the IRPA supports this vision of Canada, with the good immigrant reaffirming Canada's essential goodness and "the bad immigrant forcing otherwise generous people into taking stern disciplinary measures" (Razack 1999: 174). A critical component of this ongoing story is that "good" is equated with whiteness and with being Canadian, while "bad" is associated with being an immigrant, an outsider to the nation. Thobani's (2000) study of the Immigration Policy Review in 1994 highlights this most clearly. She found that throughout the public consultation process, Canadians expressed concerns that their national values were being eroded and degraded by immigrants who did not share these values. While Canadians saw themselves as respectful, honest and hard-working, immigrants were consistently represented as criminal, disease-ridden and lazy. Thobani notes that by placing immigrant values in the context of social and cultural diversity, definitions of immigrants and Canadians are reproduced in racialized terms. Audrey Kobayashi (1995: 71) sums up the situation in asserting that immigration law is a central site for articulating how Canada imagines itself:

> people have faith in the law; it establishes a moral landscape and it codifies our myths about ourselves. It is our recourse to defining ourselves and others, as well as a means of systematically reproducing our imagined reality.

These comments highlight why the harsh treatment of immigrants, particularly immigrants of colour, is so uncontroversial. For to question how immigration practices are carried out within Canada would not just be a challenge to the fairness of the system, it would also call into question how Canada envisions itself. Such a challenge would be neither lightly accepted nor welcomed.

SCAPEGOATING IMMIGRANTS

As the boundaries between insider and outsider become more ambivalent and converge with nostalgia for a bygone period of immigration, immigrants of colour are the ones classified and defined as inauthentic, "illegal" or outsiders. Anti-racists allege that racial identity remains a key marker of those who are not perceived as belonging, as "legitimate" immigrants of the nation. Even though Canada moved away from blatant forms of discrimination in its immigration policies in the 1960s and 1970s, racism and patriarchy continued to define spatial and/or social margins in portrayals of the dominant vision of the nation (Pottie-Sherman and Wilkes 2012; Gulliver 2017).

The racialization of immigration, which focuses on the process of constructing racial identities and meanings, enables ideas about "race" to proliferate. Now, cultural differences, rather than racial inferiority, become the distinguishing markers between us and them. Avtar Brah (1996: 165) writes that this is "a racism that combined a disavowal of biological superiority or inferiority with a focus on 'a way of life,' of cultural difference as the 'natural' basis for feelings of antagonism towards outsiders." This tendency has made it possible, for example, for recurring themes to continue to characterize immigration debates — themes alleging that too much racial diversity will lead to conflict, that immigrants have large families that expect to be supported by the welfare state, that immigrants are criminals with no respect for the law or that immigrant workers take jobs away because they are willing to work for low wages (Hintjens 1992). In Canada and other Western nations, immigrants are now required to speak the official languages as proof of their adequate assimilation into mainstream culture (Fekete 2004). As Thobani (2000: 293) observes, such demands elevate Europeanness/whiteness over other cultures and ethnicities and clearly redefine the national Canadian identity as being "white" while seemingly appearing to be race-neutral.

The lack of public outcry over the treatment of immigrants in the new legislation suggests that the public's imagination has been captured in such a way that immigration is understood as a sign of Canada's decline. While Canada cannot do without immigrants, those who are admitted are expected to adhere to Canadian values and adopt a "Canadian" way of life. Two examples of this are the ban on wearing religious symbols by the Quebec government, which many critics contend is really a ban on Muslim women wearing the hijab or niqab, and Hérouxville, Quebec's "Code of Life" document, which is given to immigrant newcomers to inform them of the norms of acceptable behaviour and the types of "immigrant" practices that are outlawed (Pottie-Sherman and Wilkes 2014; Vomiero 2019). Non-compliance is not an option, because failure to assimilate has become a sign of being someone who is a potential contributor to uprisings and terrorist activities. While Canada has always been distrustful of racialized immigrants, the IRPA highlights how we need to find a "suitable enemy" for whom we can blame all our failures and insecurities. Recent amendments to the IRPA suggest that the emphasis on security and enforcement shows no signs of abating.

> While Canada has always been distrustful of racialized immigrants, IRPA highlights how we need to find a "suitable enemy" to blame for our failures and insecurities.

Racialized immigrants have been, and continue to be, the scapegoats for a variety of economic and cultural insecurities (Beisel 1994). The increase in hate crimes against Asian Canadians, who are blamed for causing the COVID pandemic, is one recent example of how a racialized group can be targeted and branded an enemy (Chung 2021). One consequence of this is that any benefits that immigrants provide to host societies like Canada are drowned out by the discourse of exclusion (*Toronto Star* 2006). Yet it would be a mistake to believe that immigrants and those working within the immigrant community are unwittingly accepting the recent immigration reforms that construct refugees and asylum seekers as illegitimate and fraudulent. The raft of punitive amendments in the last two decades has led to immigration advocacy groups developing a strong grassroots movement to challenge these reforms. Although largely hidden from public view, two recent gains made by immigration activists suggest that resistance to the immigration enforcement agenda has not been in vain. First, activists worked tirelessly to defeat efforts to deny healthcare to failed refugee claimants still in Canada. The federal court ruled that lack of access to health coverage while awaiting court processes in Canada was "cruel and unusual" treatment (Chung 2014). Second, a ban on wearing niqabs at citizenship ceremonies was struck down and upheld by the Federal Court of Appeal, which stated that the ban violates the *Citizenship Act* as the greatest possible religious freedom must be allowed when administering the citizenship oath (CBC News 2015). These victories suggest that there is a diverse range of views about immigrants and refugees, and many immigration advocacy groups continue to campaign and educate Canadians about the realities of migration. In addition, with the increasing support of the international community, such as Human Rights Watch[4] and Amnesty International, current immigration and refugee reforms will be even more carefully scrutinized to ensure that Canada does not violate its obligations to the global community. As Audrey Macklin and Sean Rehaag sum it up:

> About 30,000 asylum seekers arrive in Canada each year. In the fall, shortly after the arrival of around 500 Tamils on a boat in British Columbia, some

30,000 Burmese refugees fled into neighbouring Thailand — over a period of 48 hours. Let's get some perspective. (*Toronto Star* 2010)

Although it is an uphill battle, the path towards an inclusive and anti-racist immigration system in Canada continues to be fought on many different levels with numerous campaigns calling on the current Liberal government to take a humanitarian approach to immigrants and refugees. A recent decision by the immigration minister, John McCallum, to reverse the deportation order of a Roma family who had been persecuted in Hungary but whose refugee claim was denied because their Toronto lawyer failed to adequately represent their case (Chung 2016), is one of the many small victories that will shape how Canada treats its newcomers in the twenty-first century.

DISCUSSION QUESTIONS

1. Do you think immigration control is possible without engaging in racist or discriminatory behaviour?
2. How can we balance issues of security and enforcement with a more humanitarian approach? Are the two approaches incompatible?
3. How can we create a more welcoming and inclusive society for immigrants and refugees?
4. Should refugees who arrive in Canada via irregular means (e.g., on a boat with others) be treated differently than refugees who arrive through regular channels (e.g., on a plane)?

GLOSSARY OF KEY TERMS

Criminalize: Turning an activity into a criminal offence by making it illegal.

Deportation: The act of expelling a non-citizen from a country, usually on the grounds of illegal status or for having committed a crime.

Discrimination: The unjust or prejudicial treatment of different categories of people or things.

Immigrant: A person who comes to live permanently in a foreign country.

Point system: Immigrants are assessed on the basis of age, education, language skills and economic characteristics and assigned points for each of these categories. Applicants who have a sufficient number of points are eligible for entry.

Protected person: A person who has been granted refugee protection by the Government of Canada.

Refugee: A person in flight from their home country who seeks to escape conditions or personal circumstances found to be intolerable.

Human smuggling: Consensual transactions where the transporter and the transportee agree to circumvent immigration control for mutually advantageous reasons.

Human trafficking: The recruitment, transportation, transfer, harbouring or receipt of persons by means of the threat or use of force or other forms of coercion.

Irregular border crossers: Individuals who enter a country between official ports of entry seeking to make a refugee claim.

RESOURCES FOR ACTIVISTS

UNHCR, Refugees in Canada: unhcr.ca/in-canada/refugees-in-canada/
International Organization for Migration: iom.int/
Canadian Council for Refugees: ccrweb.ca/
End Immigration Detention Network: endimmigrationdetention.com/
Centre for Refugee Studies, York University: crs.info.yorku.ca/
Mosaic: mosaicbc.com
No One Is Illegal Vancouver: noii-van.resist.ca/

NOTES

1 According to its website, maytree.com, "The Maytree Foundation is a Canadian charitable foundation established in 1982. Maytree believes that there are three fundamental issues that threaten political and social stability: wealth disparities between and within nations; mass migration of people because of war, oppression and environmental disasters, and the degradation of the environment."
2 Supporters of the migrants argued the government had overreacted in this situation, while critics contended that the government needed to take harsher measures.
3 Racialization "refers to the historical emergence of the idea of 'race' and to its subsequent reproduction and application" (Miles 1989: 76). This suggests that the criminalization of certain racialized groups within the Canadian context can be understood, first, in light of the ways in which white, majority groups have been constructed as race-less and, second, within the context of historical relations between First Nations peoples, early settlers and recent immigrants and migrants.
4 Human Rights Watch. 2011. "Open Letter to Canada's Prime Minister Stephen Harper and Federal Party Leaders on Human Rights Priorities," May 9. <hrw.org/en/news/2011/05/09/open-letter-canada-s-prime-minister-stephen-harper-and-federal-party-leaders-human-r>.

REFERENCES

Abu-Laban, Y. 1998. "Welcome/Stay Out: The Contradiction of Canadian Integration and Immigration Policies at the Millennium." *Canadian Ethnic Studies* 30.
Abu-Laban, Y., and C. Gabriel. 2002. *Selling Diversity*. Peterborough: Broadview Press.

African Canadian Legal Clinic. 2001. "Brief to the Legislative Review Secretariat." <aclc.ne>.

Alboim, N., and K. Cohl. 2012. "Shaping the Future: Canada's Rapidly Changing Immigration Policies." *The Maytree Foundation*, October. <maytree.com/wp-content/uploads/2012/10/shaping-the-future.pdf>.

Amnesty International Canada and CCR (Canadian Council for Refugees). 2017. "Contesting the Designation of the US as a Safe Third Country." <ccrweb.ca/en/contesting-designation-us-safe-third-country>.

Angel-Ajani, A. 2003. "A Question of Dangerous Races?" *Punishment and Society* 5.

Angus Reid Institute. 2018. "Two-Thirds Call Irregular Border Crossings a 'Crisis,' More Trust Scheer to Handle Issue than Trudeau." <angusreid.org/safe-third-country-asylum-seekers/>.

Appleby, T. and U. Ghandi. 2006. "The Evening All Hell Broke Loose." *Globe and Mail*, June 6.

Auditor General of Canada. 2020. *Reports of the Auditor General of Canada to the Parliament of Canada. Report 1 — Immigration Removals.* <oag-bvg.gc.ca/internet/english/parl_oag-_202007_01_e_43572.html>.

Avery, D. 1995. *Reluctant Host: Canada's Response to Immigrant Workers 1896–1994.* Toronto: McClelland and Stewart.

Bahdi, R. 2003. "No Exit: Racial Profiling and Canada's War Against Terrorism." *Osgoode Hall Law Journal* 41.

Bannerji, H. 2000. "The Paradox of Diversity: The Construction of a Multicultural Canada and 'Women of Colour.'" *Women's Studies International Forum* 23.

Bashi, V. 2004. "Globalized Anti-Blackness: Transnationalizing Western Immigration Law, Policy and Practice." *Ethnic and Racial Studies* 27.

BCCLA (BC Civil Liberties Association). 2017. "Oversight at the Border: A Model for Independent Accountability at the Canada Border Services Agency." June 14. <bccla.org/news/2017/06/oversight-border-new-bccla-report-proposes-independent-accountability-cbsa/>.

Beisel, D. 1994. "Looking for Enemies, 1990–1994." *Journal of Psychohistory* 22, 1.

Boyd, M., and M. Vickers. 2000. "100 Years of Immigration to Canada." *Canadian Social Trends* 58.

Brah, A. 1996. *Cartographies of Diaspora: Contesting Identities.* New York: Routledge.

Bronskill, Jim. 2014. "Red Cross Uncovers Problems Facing Canadian Immigration Detainees." *Toronto Star*, September 25. <thestar.com/news/canada/2014/09/25/red_cross_uncovers_problems_facing_canadian_immigration_detainees.html>.

Brosnahan, Maureen. 2016. "Deported Roma Refugee Family Receives Permission to Return to Canada." CBC News, February 8. <cbc.ca/news/canada/toronto/roma-refugee-canada-return-1.3437968>.

Buchignani, N., and D. Indra. 1999. "Vanishing Acts: Illegal Immigration in Canada as a Sometimes Social Issue." In D. Haines and K. Rosenblum (eds.), *Illegal Immigration in America.* Westport, CT: Greenwood Press.

Canadian Press. 2018. "Asylum Seekers Will Wait up to Two Years for Refugee Claims to Be Processed." *Globe and Mail,* November 2. <theglobeandmail.com/politics/article-wait-times-for-asylum-claims-at-21-months-despite-infusion-of-federal/>.

Carbert, Michelle, and Adrian Morrow. 2019. "Canada, US Move to Redraft Border Treaty to Cut Flow of Asylum Seekers." *Globe and Mail,* April 1.

Carey, D. 2018. "Making the Most of Immigration in Canada. OECD Economics Department Working Paper No. 1520." *Organisation for Economic Co-operation and Development.* <doi.org/10.1787/6813672e-en>.

Carlson, Kathryn Blaze. 2011. "Immigrants Cost $23B a Year: Fraser Institute Report." *National Post*, May 17. <nationalpost.com/news/canada/immigrants-cost-23b-a-year-fraser-institute-report>.

CBC News. 2015. "Niqab Ban at Citizenship Ceremonies Unlawful, as Ottawa Loses Appeal." September 15. <cbc.ca/news/politics/niqab-ruling-federal-court-government-challenge-citizenship-ceremonies-1.3229206>.

___. 1999a. "Officials Recommend Migrants Remain in Custody." September 2. <cbc.ca/news/canada/officials-recommend-migrants-remain-in-custody-1.182464>.

___. 1999b. "Department Seeks More Teeth to Detain Migrants." September 23. <cbc.ca/news/canada/dept-seeks-more-teeth-to-detain-migrants-1.193774>.

CBSA (Canadian Border Services Agency). 2020. "Annual Detention, fiscal year 2019–2020." <cbsa-asfc.gc.ca/security-securite/detent/stat-2019-2020-eng.html>.

___. 2018. "Minister Goodale Announces Roll-Out of Expanded Alternatives to Detention Program through the National Immigration Detention Framework." July 24. <canada.ca/en/border-services-agency/news/2018/07/minister-goodale-announces-roll-out-of-expanded-alternatives-to-detention-program-through-the-national-immigration-detention-framework.html>.

CCR (Canadian Council for Refugees). 2019. "Immigration Detention and Children: Rights Still Ignored, Two Years Later." <ccrweb.ca/en/immigration-detention-and-children-november-2019>.

___. 2017. "Legal Challenge of Safe Third Country Agreement Launched." <ccrweb.ca/en/media/legal-challenge-safe-third-country>.

___. 2010a. "C-47-Key Concerns." <ccrweb.ca/en/c49-key-concerns>.

___. 2010b. "Some Comments on Bill C-49." <ccrweb.ca/en/comment-c49>.

___. 2010c. "Refugee Reform: Weighing the Proposals." <yumpu.com/en/document/read/31602780/refugee-reform-weighing-the-proposals-canadian-council-for->.

___. 2001. "Bill C-11 Brief." <ccrweb.ca/sites/ccrweb.ca/files/c11submissionmay2010.pdf>.

___. 2000. "A Hundred Years of Immigration to Canada 1900–1999: A Chronology Focusing on Refugees and Discrimination." <ccrweb.ca/history.html>.

Christie, N. 1986. "Suitable Enemies." In H. Bianchi and R. van Swaaningen (eds.), *Abolitionism: Towards a Non-Repressive Approach to Crime.* Amsterdam: Free University Press.

Chung, A. 2021. "In 2021, Asian Canadians Document Hate Crimes to Be Believed." *Huffington Post,* March 1. <huffingtonpost.ca/entry/anti-asian-racism-canada_ca_603d08cdc5b682971502118f>.

CIC (Citizenship and Immigration Canada). 2015. *Canada Facts and Figures 2014: Immigrant Overview — Permanent Residents.* Ottawa: CIC Research and Evaluation Branch.

___. 2014. *Canada Facts and Figures 2013: Immigrant Overview — Temporary Residents.* Ottawa: CIC Research and Evaluation Branch.

___. 2001a. *Facts and Figures 2000: Immigration Overview.* Ottawa: Minister of Public Works and Government Services.

___. 2001b. "Bill C-11 — Immigration and Refugee Protection Act: Overview." <lop.parl.ca/sites/PublicWebsite/default/en_CA/ResearchPublications/LegislativeSummaries/371LS397E>.

Coalition for a Just Immigration and Refugee Policy. 2001 "Position Paper on Bill C-11." Toronto.

Coyne, A. 2019. "In Two Years, Liberals Go from #Welcometocanada to Deportations without Hearings." *National Post,* April 13. <nationalpost.com/opinion/andrew-coyne-in-two-years-liberals-go-from-welcometocanada-to-deportations-without-hearings?video_autoplay=true>.

Creese, G. 1992. "The Politics of Refugees in Canada." In V. Satzewich (ed.), *Deconstructing A Nation.* Halifax: Fernwood Publishing.

Crepeau, F., and D. Nakache. 2006. "Controlling Irregular Migration in Canada." IRPP *Choices* 12, 1.

Davergne, C. 2004. "Sovereignty, Migration and the Rule of Law in Global Times." *Modern Law Review* 67.

Dent, J. 2002. "No Right of Appeal: Bill C-11, Criminality, and the Human Rights of Permanent Residents Facing Deportation." *Queen's Law Journal* 27.

Economic Council of Canada. 1991. *New Faces in the Crowd: Economic and Social Impacts of Immigration.* Ottawa: Economic Council of Canada, Study No. 22-171.

EKOS Politics. 2019. "Increased Polarization on Attitudes to Immigration Reshaping the Political Landscape in Canada." April 15. <ekospolitics.com/index.php/2019/04/increased-polarization-on-attitudes-to-immigration-reshaping-the-political-landscape-in-canada/>.

Elliott, L. 2014. "Refugee Health-Cuts Ruling Appealed by Ottawa." CBC News, October 1. <cbc.ca/news/politics/refugee-health-cuts-ruling-appealed-by-ottawa-1.2783819>.

Ethans, P. 2020. "Canada Has a Dismal Record of Locking up Migrants." *The Tyee,* February 11. <thetyee.ca/Opinion/2020/02/11/Canada-Arbitrarily-Detains-Migrants/>.

Fekete, L. 2004. "Anti-Muslim Racism and the European Security State." *Race and Class* 46.

Fisk, R. 2006. "Has Racism Invaded Canada?" *Counterpunch*, June 12. <counterpunch.org/2006/06/12/has-racism-invaded-canada/>.

Frideres, J. 1996. "Canada's Changing Immigration Policy: Implications for Asian Immigrants." *Asian and Pacific Migration Journal* 5.

Garcia y Griego, M. 1994. "Canada: Flexibility and Control in Immigration and Refugee Policy." In W. Cornelius, P. Martin and J. Hollifield (eds.), *Controlling Immigration: A Global Perspective*. Stanford: Stanford University Press.

Getting Landed Project. 2002. "Protecting the Unprotected: Submission to the House of Commons Standing Committee on Citizenship and Immigration." <cpj.ca/story-getting-landed-project>.

Ghafour, H. 2006. "Terrorism Cases Strikingly Similar." *Globe and Mail,* June 10. <theglobeandmail.com/news/world/terrorism-cases-strikingly-similar/article18165326/>.

Glavin, T. 2019. "Why Race and Immigration Are a Gathering Storm in Canadian Politics." *Maclean's*, April 23. <macleans.ca/news/canada/why-race-and-immigration-are-a-gathering-storm-in-canadian-politics/>.

Global News. 2021. "Safe Third Country Agreement on Returning Asylum Seekers to US Ruled Constitutional." April 15. <globalnews.ca/news/7759738/safe-third-country-agreement-constitutional-federal-court/>.

Gros, H., and Y. Song. 2016. "No Life for a Child: A Roadmap to End Immigration Detention of Children and Family Separation." International Human Rights Program, University of Toronto Faculty of Law.

Gulliver, T. 2017. "Canada the Redeemer and Denials of Racism." *Critical Discourse Studies* 15, 1.

Haigh, R., and J. Smith. 1998. "Return of the Chancellor's Foot? Discretion in Permanent Resident Deportation Appeals under the Immigration Act." *Osgoode Hall Law Journal* 36.

Harris, K. 2019. "Scheer Vows to Stop Illegal Border Crossings, Prioritize Economic Immigrat-ion." CBC News, October 9. <cbc.ca/news/politics/scheer-roxham-road-asylum-seekers-immigration-1.5314527>.

Hassan-Gordon, T. 1996. "Canada's Immigration Policy — Detention and Deportation of Non-Europeans." <hartford-hwp.com/archives/44/032.html>.

Hill, B. 2018a. "'Illegal' or 'Irregular'? Debate about Asylum-Seekers Needs to Stop, Experts Warn." *Global News*, July 26. <globalnews.ca/news/4355394/illegal-or-irregular-asylum-seekers-crossing-canadas-border/>.

____. 2018b. "Former UN Human Rights Chief Calls Canada's Handling of Child Refugees 'Inhumane.'" *Global News*, September 3. <globalnews.ca/news/4421908/former-un-human-rights-expert-criticizes-canada/>.

Hintjens, H.M. 1992. "Immigration and Citizenship Debates: Reflections on Ten Common Themes." *International Migration* 30.

Ibrahim, M. 2005. "The Securitization of Migration: A Racial Discourse." *International Migration* 43.

Immigration and Refugee Board of Canada. 2021. "Irregular Border Crosser Statistics." <irb-cisr.gc.ca/en/statistics/Pages/Irregular-border-crosser-statistics.aspx>.

____. 2017/2018. *Report of the 2017/2018 External Audit (Detention Review)*. <irb.gc.ca/en/transparency/reviews-audit-evaluations/Pages/ID-external-audit-1718.aspx>.

IRCC (Immigration, Refugees and Citizenship Canada). 2020. "2020 Annual Report to Parliament on Immigration." <canada.ca/en/immigration-refugees-citizenship/corporate/publications-manuals/annual-report-parliament-immigration-2020.html>.

Jakubowski, L. 1997. *Immigration and the Legalization of Racism*. Halifax: Fernwood Publishing.

Jeanes, J., and P. Clarke. 2020. "Opinion: Immigration Enforcement Must Be More Humane." *Montreal Gazette*, February 26. <montrealgazette.com/opinion/opinion-immigration-enforcement-must-be-more-humane>.

Kelley, N., and M. Trebilcock. 1998. *The Making of the Mosaic: A History of Canadian Immigration Policy*. Toronto: University of Toronto Press.

Keung, N. 2018. "Audit of Immigration Detention Review System Reveals Culture that Favours

Incarceration." *Toronto Star*, July 20.

Kobayashi, A. 1995. "Challenging the National Dream: Gender Persecution and Canadian Immigration Law." In P. Fitzpatrick (ed.), *Nationalism, Racism and the Rule of Law*. Aldershot: Dartmouth.

Li, P. 2001. "The Racial Subtext in Canada's Immigration Discourse." *Journal of International Migration and Integration* 2, 1.

_____. 2003. *Destination Canada*. Don Mills: Oxford University Press.

Marchi, S. 1995. "Speech: Tougher Tools for Deporting Criminals." *Canadian Speeches* 9 (August/September).

Matas, D. 1989. *Closing the Doors: The Failure of Refugee Protection*. Toronto: Summerhill.

Maynard, R. 2017. *Policing Black Lives*. Halifax: Fernwood Publishing.

Maytree Foundation. 2001. "Brief to the Senate Committee on Social Affairs, Science and Technology regarding Bill C-11, Immigration and Refugee Protection Act." Toronto, October. <maytree.com/wp-content/uploads/summaryc11senatebrief2001.pdf>.

Miles, R. 1989. *Racism*. London: Routledge.

NAWL (National Association of Women and the Law). 2006. "Update on the Immigration and Refugee Protection Act and Women." March 30. <nawl.ca/update-on-the-immigration-and-refugee-protection-act-and-women/>.

_____. 2001. "Brief on the Proposed Immigration and Refugee Protection Act (Bill C-11)." <nawl.ca/brief-on-the-proposed-immigration-and-refugee-protection-act-bill-c-11-memo/>.

Nixon, G. 2014. "Canada Must See Immigration as a Competitive Edge." *Globe and Mail*, May 12. <theglobeandmail.com/opinion/canada-must-see-immigration-as-a-competitive-edge/article18584128/>.

Noorani, A., and C. Wright. 1995. "They Believed the Hype: The Liberals Were Elected as 'the Friend of the Immigrant': A Year Later, They're Fanning the Flames of Crime Hysteria with their New Pals, the Tabloids and Preston Manning." *This Magazine* 28 (December/January).

Palmer, D. 1996. "Determinants of Canadian Attitudes Toward Immigration: More than Just Racism?" *Canadian Journal of Behavioural Science* 28.

Pierce, S., and D. Meissner. 2017. "Trump Executive Order on Refugees and Travel Ban: A Brief Review." *Migration Policy Institute*. <migrationpolicy.org/research/trump-executive-order-refugees-and-travel-ban-brief-review>.

Pottie-Sherman, Y., and R. Wilkes. 2014. "Good Code Bad Code: Exploring the Immigration-Nation Dialectic Through Media Coverages of the Hérouxville 'Code of Life' Document." *Migration Studies* 2, 189.

_____. 2012. "Anti-Immigrant Sentiment in Canada." In M. Verea (ed.), *Anti-Immigrant Sentiments, Actions and Policies in North America and the European Union*. Mexico City: Centro de Investigaciones Sobre America del Norte (CISAN), Universidad Nacional Autonoma de Mexico.

Public Safety and Emergency Preparedness Canada. 2004. "Securing Canada: Laying the Groundwork for Canada's First National Security Policy." <circ.jmellon.com/agencies/psc/>.

Razack, S. 1999. "Law and the Policing of Bodies of Colour in the 1990s." *Canadian Journal of Law and Society* 14.

Roach, K. 2005. "Canada's Response to Terrorism." In V. Ramraj, M. Hor, and K. Roach (eds.), *Global Anti-Terrorism Law and Policy*. Oxford: Cambridge University Press.

Roberts, B. 1988. *Whence They Came: Deportation from Canada, 1900–1935*. Ottawa: University of Ottawa.

Robinson, W.G. 1983. "Illegal Migrants in Canada: A Report to the Honourable Lloyd Axworthy, Minister of Employment and Immigration." Ottawa: Employment and Immigration Canada.

Rudner, M. 2002. "The Globalization of Terrorism: Canada's Intelligence Response to the Post-September 11 Threat Environment." *Canadian Issues* 24 (September).

Spade, C., and T. McDermott. 2020. *"Safe" Countries and "Fraudulent" Refugees: Tools for Narrowing Access to Canada's Refugee System*. Toronto: Ryerson Centre for Immigration and Settlement.

Standing Committee on Citizenship and Immigration. 2001. *Hands Across the Border: Working Together at Our Shared Border and Abroad to Ensure Safety, Security and Efficiency*. Ottawa: Public Works.

Statistics Canada. 2004. "Pilot Survey of Hate Crime." June 1. <statcan.gc.ca/daily-quotidien/040601/dq040601a-eng.htm>.

Strange, C., and T. Loo. 1997. *Making Good: Law and Moral Regulation in Canada, 1867–1939*. Toronto: University of Toronto Press.

Teitelbaum, M., and J. Winter. 1998. *A Question of Numbers: High Migration, Low Fertility and the Politics of National Identity*. New York: Hill and Wang.

Thobani, S. 2000. "Closing Ranks: Racism and Sexism in Canada's Immigration Policy." *Race and Class* 42, 35.

Toronto Star. 2010. "Playing Politics with Refugees." December 3.

____. 2006. "Letter to Editor: 'Afraid Every Morning I Wake Up.'" May 28.

Tunney, C. 2020. "Canada's Asylum Agreement with the US Infringes on Charter, Says Federal Court." cbc News, July 22. <cbc.ca/news/politics/safe-third-country-agreement-court-1.5658785>.

UNHCR (United Nations High Commissioner for Refugees). 2019. "What to Know About Irregular Border Crossings." July. <unhcr.ca/wp-content/uploads/2019/07/Facts-About-Irregular-Border-Crossings.pdf>.

____. 2001. "Comments on Bill C-11: Submission to the House of Commons Standing Committee on Citizenship and Immigration." Ottawa, March. <ccrweb.ca/c11hcr.PDF>.

Valverde, M. 1991. *The Age of Soap, Light and Water: Moral Reform in English Canada, 1885–1925*. Toronto: McClelland & Stewart.

Vomiero, J., and A. Russell. 2019. "Ipsos Poll Shows Canadians Have Concerns about Immigration." *Global News*, January 22. <globalnews.ca/news/4794797/canada-negative-immigration-economy-ipsos/>.

Vukov, T. 2003. "Imagining Communities Through Immigration Policies." *International Journal of Cultural Studies* 6.

Ware, R., P. Fortin, and P. Paradis. 2010. "The Economic Impact of the Immigrant Investor Program in Canada." Montreal: Analysis Group. <analysisgroup.com/Insights/publishing/the-economic-impact-of-the-immigrant-investor-program-in-canada-english/>.

5

THE (MIS)EDUCATION OF BLACK YOUTH
Anti-Blackness in the School System[1]

Robyn Maynard

You Should Know This

- The last segregated school in Canada closed in 1983 in Nova Scotia, several decades after the *Brown v. Board of Education* (1954) decision ended segregated schooling in the United States.

- In Ontario, Black community members have taught young Black people and run their own schools dating back to *at least* the nineteenth century, when schools were often segregated. But the first Black teacher, Wilson Brooks, was only hired by a public school in Toronto in 1952.

- In 2017, Freedom School, BLM-TO, Education Not Incarceration and Latinx, Afro-Latin-America, Abya Yala Education Network (LAEN) made history when they organized the first successful campaign in North America to get police out of schools.

ON SEPTEMBER 30, 2016, THE MOTHER of a Black Grade 1 student missed several calls from her daughter's school in Mississauga, a suburb of Toronto. When she called back, a school official passed the phone to a police officer, who informed her that her six-year-old daughter had been placed in handcuffs. Upon arriving at the school, the mother learned that the police had been called in by school staff because her daughter had been reportedly acting in a violent manner. The two police officers had handcuffed the girl — who weighed a total of forty-eight pounds and was unarmed — by attaching her hands and her feet together at the wrists and ankles. While the girl's mother said that her daughter had been treated like a "dog" or a "monster" and not a human child (*Toronto Star* 2017), Peel Regional Police spokesperson Sergeant Josh Colley defended the fact that a young Black child had been handcuffed by stating that it had been done for "the safety of other students and ultimately the child" (Cheung and Sienkiewicz 2017). School officials issued no immediate apology, and Sgt. Colley told the media that it was "disgusting" that this behaviour could be construed as racist (Cheung and Sienkiewicz 2017). The family's lawyer, however, alongside the African Canadian Legal Clinic, went on to file complaints against both the school and the police for anti-Black racism (Westoll 2017).

It is difficult to imagine how any child weighing forty-eight pounds could be thought to pose such a danger to anyone, let alone in the presence of school officials and two police officers. Only by attending to the ongoing governing power of anti-Blackness can we make sense of how two armed men could decide to handcuff an unarmed child, likely one quarter of their size, in the name of "safety." What this incident illustrates is that, in the eyes of white society and state institutions, Black children are not conceived of as children at all and are attributed with supernatural, dangerous abilities far beyond their age, size and physical capabilities. The way that Black children and youth are treated — and the way that their suffering is largely ignored or unseen — makes clear that anti-Blackness over-determines their experiences within the education system and beyond.

Education is one of the bedrocks of Canadian society. Legislated as "a fundamental social good," it is intended to provide both socialization and opportunities to develop youth's minds and relationships, and to help them build their futures (OHCR 2003: 18). This is largely rhetorical; schools continue to be underfunded and under-resourced, and teachers are widely devalued and poorly compensated. Nonetheless, publicly funded education is generally understood as creating options and facilitating advancement in society. For many Black students, though, schools are places where they experience degradation, harm and psychological violence (Codjoe 2001). Even as education environments continue to under-serve many communities from different backgrounds, there are unique dimensions to the experiences of Black youth, who experience schools as carceral places characterized by neglect, heightened surveillance and arbitrary and often extreme punishment for any perceived disobedience (Wun 2016; Salole and Abdulle 2015). Schools in Canada remain permeated with anti-Blackness. Because Black youth are so often not seen or treated as children, schools too often become their first encounter with the organized and systemic devaluation of Blackness present in society at large.

> For many Black students, though, schools are places where they experience degradation, harm and psychological violence.

THE EVACUATION OF BLACK CHILDREN
FROM THE CONSTRUCTION OF "INNOCENCE"

In order to fully grasp the current treatment of Black youth and children across Canadian institutions, it's necessary to look at how Black childhood has been historically represented (and denied), both by the state and more broadly. The state's negation of Black childhood innocence has been an important part of the maintenance of white supremacy. In Canadian society, and Western society more broadly, since the end of the nineteenth century, children have been construed as innocent, vulnerable and in need of the state's protection. The concern for children's welfare was correlated to the state's focus on building the nation, accompanied by "an emerging belief that children represented the future of the young dominion, and their healthy growth and development became inextricably linked to the welfare of Canadian society" (Schumaker 2012: 26). As the symbol of society's future, young persons were seen as requiring and deserving protection, guidance and societal investment. However, the purported innocence of children, and thus the worthiness of ensuring their security and protection, was largely determined by their race. Youthful innocence, according to historian Robin Bernstein, was raced white (Bernstein 2011). Many children have always been formally or informally excluded from this and have fallen outside of those seen as vulnerable and deserving of safety. While the protection of (white) children was, in many ways, more ideological than actual — many poor white children remained vulnerable to a multiplicity of harms — Black children have, as a group, been excluded from even the very conception of childhood purity or vulnerability. That Black and Indigenous children were considered property in earlier Canadian history testifies to the delineations of sanctified childhood. At the turn of the twentieth century, white toddlers were associated with attributes such as purity, innocence and fragility, qualities denied to Black and Indigenous children (Lafferty 2013). The preservation of white childhood innocence has often taken place at the expense of the safety and security of Black children. In Nova Scotia, the vulnerability of white children was invoked to push forward the exclusion of Black children from many public and church-based institutions: "For members of the white community, segregation of the black child was thus a natural and logical part of child saving, just as was maintaining religious separation" (Lafferty 2013: 72). Innocent (white) childhood could be protected, in part, by maintaining distance from the corrupting force of "uncivilized" and immoral Black children. Their innocence negated, Black children were therefore denied the protections that would safeguard it. The new articulation of (white) childhood innocence meant that while white children were construed as requiring nurturing and protection, Black children were thought to be impervious to suffering:

this thinking was a relic of an era in which enslaved children were not, as a whole, considered "children ... pain, and the alleged ability or inability to feel it, functioned in the mid-nineteenth century as a wedge that split white and black childhood into distinct trajectories." (Bernstein 2011: 20)

This belief has ramifications to this day; though segregation is formally over, the de-sanctification of Black childhood is ongoing.

Today, Black children and youth remain outside the construction of innocence, as well as that of childhood itself, and the suffering that they are exposed to is frequently erased or negated. In a large-scale study of American police officers' perceptions of Black children, psychologists found that racially motivated dehumanization plays a significant role in the designation of innocence. To use their words,

As the perception of innocence is a central protection afforded to children ... it follows that this social consideration may not be given to the children of dehumanized groups ... in equal measure as they are given to their peers ... In this context, dehumanization serves to change the meaning of the category "children." (Goff et al. 2014: 527)

In other words, Black children are still not considered to really be children. The authors found that once Black children reached the age of ten, they were perceived as "significantly older and less innocent than other children of any age group" (Goff et al. 2014: 527). Childhood itself takes on a different meaning depending on race, and the category of "innocent youth" continues to be raced white. This has substantial and harmful effects: "The evidence shows that perceptions of the essential nature of children can be affected by race, and for Black children, this can mean they lose the protection afforded by assumed childhood innocence well before they become adults" (American Psychological Association 2014). Not only are Black children and youth denied the protections that accompany presumptions of innocence and vulnerability, but in the present, they are also still imbued with the quality of danger. Black youth, like Black adults, are frequently attributed with "superhuman" capabilities, believed (by whites) to possess supernatural qualities that transcend the laws of nature and to have a decreased ability to experience pain (Hoffman, Trawalter and Waytz 2015).

There are numerous publicized cases that illustrate the impact that dominant conceptions of Black (non-) children can have. One must only look at the killings of

Tamir Rice in 2014 or Aiyana Jones in 2010, Black children killed by police in the United States. In Canada, a similar picture emerges. The above-cited handcuffing of the six-year-old Black girl in her school is only one example of how Black youth are widely treated as if they are threatening and possibly dangerous even to adults. A staff official working in an Ontario youth penal institution reported that staff members became so concerned when Black youths would socialize together that multiple staff meetings had to be called to address widespread fears that the Black youth were organizing a riot (Commission on Systemic Racism in the Ontario Criminal Justice System 1994). Neither did their youth protect two Black children from having the car they were inside of pepper-sprayed in 2015. In this incident, two girls, aged seven and ten, were treated in the hospital after their father was pepper-sprayed by the police while seated in front of them in a car. He and his wife had described the incident to the press as a traffic stop that was random, non-violent, non-criminal and unwarranted (CTV News 2015). Black children and youth are frequently exposed to traumatic and violent state actions, with little regard to their vulnerability, because their suffering is not conceived of as suffering. Today, it remains the case that Black youth of all genders, sexual identities and abilities are forced to suffer a severe punishment for merely existing in an anti-Black society. Though these examples make visible how police and corrections staff consciously or unconsciously dehumanize Black youth, this fundamental disregard for young Black people's lives is endemic across state institutions. Black children are often the receptacles of the negative projections of a society mired in the fear of Blackness. Societal hostility is often woven into everyday life for young Black persons; everywhere they go, they encounter psychological violence in terms of systemic disregard, surveillance, suspicion and the presumption of guilt. The demonization of Black youth and children is visible in the hostility, surveillance, punishment and neglect in the fabric of the education system.

ABANDONMENT AND CAPTIVITY: EDUCATION POLICY AS A TOOL TOWARD WHITE SUPREMACY

Historically, Canada's public education system has been an explicit tool toward the advancement of white supremacy, and public schools have been a site of both abandonment and captivity for Black youth. The segregated schooling of Black children and the explicit disinvestment in the education of Black youth in most parts of Canada (excluding Quebec) was "a direct by-product of the system of chattel slavery" and was used to strip African people of their humanity and turn them into vehicles of cheap labour (Hamilton 2011: 98). In the nineteenth century, Black children, it was believed, would have a morally corrupting influence on white children (K. McLaren 2008: 7). In the words of an Ontario school trustee, it was better to "cut their children's heads off and throw them into the ditch" than "have them go to school with [*the n word*]" (in Walker 2010: 36). The practice of segregated and unequal schooling, while not practised in all provinces, lasted well into the late twentieth century. Although the Supreme Court in the United States outlawed segregation in schools in 1954, the practice continued in Nova Scotia and Ontario until much later, and the last segregated school in Canada did not close until 1983 (Hamilton 2011: 101). Even in Nova Scotia's "integrated schools," Black students had to use separate entrances, exits and washrooms throughout the 1950s and 1960s (BLAC 1994: 26).

Slavery, followed by centuries of segregation in the school system in many provinces, left an indelible legacy of racism in publicly funded Canadian education institutions, visible in a lasting inequity between Black and white educations in Canada. In Nova Scotia, upon integration, many Black schools were defunded and closed. Black students had to be bussed long distances to attend white schools, thus bearing the entire burden of integration (BLAC 1994: 51). In Nova Scotia in 1969, only 3 percent of Black students graduated from high school and only 1 percent of the graduates attended university (Pratt 1972 in Bombay and Hewitt 2015: 31). A survey conducted in 1962 by the Institute of Public Affairs in Nova Scotia found that most Black adults had education levels between Grades 4 and 9 (in BLAC 1994). The researchers identified several contributing factors to these lower levels of schooling, such as the harassment of Black students, poverty, derogatory comments by teachers affirming that Black students stayed in lower grades and were likely to fail, the low number of Black teachers and the absence of Black history in the curriculum (BLAC 1994: 27).

That education was a tool of white supremacy is visible, as well, in the legacy of settler colonialism. The violent dehumanization, forced assimilation and genocide enacted en masse on Indigenous children by means of residential schools from 1883 until the late 1990s cannot be seen as separate from the development of publicly funded education, and must be understood as foundational toward the development of white supremacy. Though officially called "schools," the Truth and Reconciliation Commission has noted that residential schools were educational in name only and, in truth, functioned as part of a violent, "coherent policy to eliminate Aboriginal people as distinct peoples and to assimilate them into the Canadian mainstream against their will" (TRC 2015: 3). At least 150,000 Indigenous children were forced into these schools, which were rife with state-sanctioned acts of monstrous violence, including continuous sexual, physical and emotional abuse; this abuse was enacted by state agents as cogs in a larger genocidal attempt to eradicate

> That education was a tool of white supremacy is visible, as well, in the legacy of settler colonialism.

Indigenous culture and, indeed, the very survival of Indigenous persons (TRC 2015: 105). Generations of stolen children experienced trauma so severe that it endangered the physical and mental health of not only those who attended residential schools, but their children and grandchildren as well (TRC 2015).

Indigenous children continue to face significant dehumanization, measurable by the particularly acute disinvestment in their success and well-being compared to other children: only one in four graduate high school, and federal funding for on-reserve schools is 40 percent less than for other children and 70 percent less for on-reserve high schools (Matthew 2000 in Blackstock 2011). The living legacies of slavery and colonization persist today in the (mis)education of Black and Indigenous children and youth that continues to expose education institutions as fundamentally white supremacist institutions.

"SECOND GENERATION SEGREGATION": STREAMING BLACK STUDENTS

Though education is seen as a "public good" and is allegedly race-neutral, informal practices throughout the school systems in Canada continue to stream students based on race. Of course, class has also played a significant role in education inequalities for youth of all backgrounds, and wealth disparities reproduce unequal outcomes between children of wealthy and poor families as well (Canadian Council on Learning 2006). However, while race and class are inextricably linked — Black families being among the poorest in Canada — it would be a mistake to reduce the streaming of Black youth and children to an issue of class. While systemic barriers resulting from poverty impact youth of all racial backgrounds, Black youth face unique and acute disadvantages because of long-standing associations linking Blackness to a lack of intelligence and inferiority more generally.

Black youth continue to be disproportionately streamed into lower education tracks as a result of both individual prejudice and systemic factors. Racial stereotypes held by teachers play a significant role in the streaming of Black students (Codjoe 2001; Dei, Mazzuca and McIsaac 1997). Instructors continue to hold racist stereotypes, or "assumptions of separate racialised groups possessing distinct mental and physical abilities," that affect their interactions with Black youth (Small 1994: 105 in Codjoe 2001: 354). For example, Black students in Alberta have expressed that instructors give African-descended students the "silent treatment" or try to dissuade them from higher education by expressing their uncertainty, for example, that "a Black could study to become a doctor" (Codjoe 2001: 350, 354). This treatment, widespread in many Canadian cities, has an important role in the experiences and development of Black students and their education.

According to a survey of Black students' needs, teacher expectations play a significant role in the academic engagement of Black students (Livingstone and Celemencki 2010). Black youth in major cities across the country have consistently named their teachers' low expectations as a major factor when it comes to their overall engagement. They report that they are pressured into vocational training or into adult education, that they are not encouraged to finish on the regular academic track and that they are steered away from challenging courses (Livingstone and Celemencki 2010; BLAC 1994; Dei, Mazzuca and McIsaac 1997). To use the words of a Black student, Black youth often feel their presence is unwanted: "they don't care about Black students. They don't care if you are there or not" (BLAC 1994: 63). In a 2006 census survey, only 54 percent of Black youth reported that they felt supported by teachers (Rankin, Rushowy and Brown 2013). Black students continue to name that teachers assume they are less intelligent, and they report witnessing and experiencing differential treatment based on race, with negative assumptions of their academic abilities being an ongoing issue (James 2019; YRDSB 2020). This lack of support affects more than academic achievement; the Ontario Human Rights Commission states that it is often "in relation to their teachers that children begin to develop a perception of themselves and of the world around them" (OHRC 2003: 18). Discriminatory treatment at this young age, then, can create lasting damage on development.

When they are being streamed into lower-track education programs, Black students are disproportionately assigned to learning platforms that have inadequate resources. In Quebec, students with Caribbean backgrounds are three times more likely to be identified as SHSMLD (students with handicaps, social maladjustments or learning difficulties) and subsequently placed in separate classes for "at-risk" students. This designation is decided by school officials, a practice that has been associated with racial profiling as it gives "substantial discretionary power to school personnel in terms of deciding which students it should be applied to" (CDPDJ 2011: 67). Similarly, Caribbean and other racialized students are frequently placed in closed "welcoming classes" for new immigrants, a practice that the Commission des droits de la personne et des droits des jeunesse (CDPDJ) found to be ill-suited and deficient in meeting their students' needs, causing delays in transitioning students into regular classes. In one instance, a Haitian student in elementary school was placed in a welcoming class solely because he was Haitian, without any other evaluation. A judge found him to have been a victim of racial profiling (*Mondestin v. Commission scolaire de la Pointe-de-l'Île* 2010 in CDPDJ 2011).

Following streaming in high school, Black students are then frequently directed, or pushed, into the adult sector to receive their high school diplomas (CDPDJ 2011). Streaming has been documented in several other Canadian cities. In Halifax, Black students are massively overrepresented in what are called "individual program plans"

(IPPS). In 2015, the results of a random sample taken of students placed in IPPs in the Halifax Regional School Board exposed that almost half of the IPP students were Black (Woodbury 2016). The phenomenon has also been documented in Toronto (Rushowy 2015), where Black students make up 13 percent of the student body but only 3 percent of those labelled "gifted," compared to white students, who are one third of the student population but more than half of those labelled "gifted" (Maharaj 2015). A 2017 report by Carl James and Tana Turner (2017) found that in the ensuing decades and into the present, Black students were twice as likely to be enrolled in applied courses rather than academic courses compared to students of other backgrounds, and only 0.4 percent of Black high school students were identified as gifted and put into the gifted programs. Data released from the Peel District School Board identified streaming of Black students in Grades 9 and 10 (Chadha, Herbert and Richard 2020) with similar issues raised in the York Region District School Board (YRDSB 2020).

The practice, whether formal or informal, of streaming students according to race has been aptly coined "second generation segregation" because of the ongoing inequities that it perpetuates (Mickelson 2007). Streaming students into different tracks is demonstrably inequitable, as students in higher education tracks are generally afforded more resources as well as a wider variety of teaching methods (BLAC 1994).

The harmful impacts of streaming have been widely known for decades, with concerned parents and community members sounding alarms regularly. In 2015, a report from the advocacy group People for Education highlighted that separating Grade 9 students into applied and academic streams severely reduces students' chances of graduating and going on to post-secondary education. The authors highlighted research demonstrating that only 40 percent of students who were streamed into applied courses had graduated after five years (Cameron and Hamlin 2015). In short: the practice cements racial and economic inequalities rather than challenging them (Cameron and Hamlin 2015; Maharaj 2015).

This disinvestment in Black youth has definite effects on their future opportunities as well as on their own sense of self-worth. The privileging of the lives and worthiness of white students demonstrates the ongoing societal devaluation of Black childhood. The racially differential treatment experienced by Black youth also demonstrates a concerted lack of empathy for the feelings and dignity of Black students on the part of instructors. Responding to ongoing pressure from Black community advocacy and long-standing criticisms of endemic anti-Black racism, in 2018 Toronto District School Board director John Mallory pledged to end streaming over a three-year period (Gordon 2018). The Ontario government followed suit: in 2020, Ontario's education minister, Stephen Lecce, pledged to end the practice, describing it as "systemic, racist, discriminatory" (Rushowy 2020). However, Black community advocates such as Leroi Newbold, co-director of

Toronto-based Freedom School, have highlighted that further work is required through French immersion and specialized programs (Newbold 2021).

In addition to experiencing a lack of support and active streaming into lower tracks of education opportunities, Black students contend with "erasure," which is itself arguably a form of violence, in that Black history and Black realities are systemically excluded from curricula across Canada. Both invisibility within curricula and the predominantly white demographic makeup of educators continue to negatively affect Black students. Besides one Africentric school established in Toronto after much community agitating and organizing (Brown 2014) and the newly available African-Canadian studies material in Nova Scotian high schools (Hamilton 2011), most educational institutions lack content highlighting Canada's history of slavery and segregation, and they overlook the history of Black institutions and Black resilience more largely (BLAC 1994; CDPDJ 2011; Livingstone and Celemencki 2010; Henry 1993).

Representation, when available, has often been offensive. The 2020 case of an eleven-year-old Black girl in a Montreal school who was sent home with homework that contained the N-word in it highlights this offensiveness (Canadian Press 2020). Recently, the Ontario Black History Society mounted a campaign urging the Ministry of Education to make curricula changes to offer more comprehensive coverage of Black history in Canada. They also created a video illustrating "what happens when you remove all the non-Black history from a Canadian history textbook" — only thirteen of 255 pages remained (cited in Garel 2020). In Alberta, as of October 2021, over 44,000 people have signed a petition demanding the Alberta Ministry of Education address the "over-looked and under-taught" Black history in the province's schools. The petitioners list the need to teach Canada's involvement in slavery and the transatlantic slave trade, modern impacts of racism, and Black history in Canada and globally (Change.org 2020).

Not only are Black students not seeing themselves reflected and celebrated in curricula, but there is also a dismal lack of racial representation in school staff. Being taught by largely white instructors and, therefore, being denied positive Black role models within institutions of learning only further entrenches the lower status of Black students. Quebec, for example, continuously misses the mark on its already too-low targets for racial diversity in the makeup of educators (CDPDJ 2011). Ontario has recently pledged to address the lack of Black teachers (Rushowy 2020).

SCHOOL DISCIPLINE POLICIES:
RACIALIZED SURVEILLANCE AND PUNISHMENT

Black students are not only treated as if they are inferior, but they are also frequently treated as if they are a threat in educational settings. The presence of Black children and youth remains unwelcome and undesirable in many public schools, and their movements are closely monitored and subject to correction. While racism and harassment from other students has long played a vital role in making Black youth and children feel unwanted in many Canadian public schools (Codjoe 2001), school disciplinary policies have helped to cement the undesirability of Black students that is apparent within the education system. Black youth face heightened surveillance and disciplinary measures at massively disproportionate rates compared to their white peers.

Over the years, schools have become an increasingly carceral experience for Black, Indigenous and other racialized students, in terms of both the general environment and disciplinary practice. In addition to experiencing overtly racist treatment from teachers (Livingstone and Celemencki 2010), Black students have likened their treatment by school officials to their experiences with the police (CDPDJ 2011). Montreal-based Black youth frequently report being treated by teachers as if they are in a gang solely because of their skin colour. School and security staff often dissuade them from gathering in groups and subject them to heightened surveillance and frequent identity checks (Livingstone and Celemencki 2010; CDPDJ 2011). In sum, Black youth are often treated as suspects instead of as the children they are, in the very place where children get socialized and educated. Experiencing this typecasting and demonization is deeply harmful to Black youth, who are still in their formative years. The feelings of exclusion and pain cause emotional harm and limit Black students' ability to thrive in the public education setting (Wong, Eccles and Sameroff 2003 in Livingstone and Celemencki 2010). Formal and informal school discipline policies are forms of policing and criminalizing of Black children and youth that position them as "captive objects" within schools (Wun 2016).

The assumption that Black youth are less innocent than white youth, and that their mere presence harbours danger, colours disciplinary practices in public schools across the country. While repressive school practices affect all youth, racialized youth are most heavily targeted. Handled by school officials as if they are "threatening" (CDPDJ 2011: 59), Black students are subjected to much more extreme disciplinary measures than white students. In a school in Durham, Ontario, an investigation by the provincial Human Rights Commission found that Black students in the Ontario school system were nearly eight times more likely to face discipline than white students (Szekely and Pessian 2015b). Suspension and expulsion play an important role in banishing Black youth from schools, particularly for young Black males. Across many Canadian cities, youth of African descent are suspended or expelled at disproportionately high rates. In schools, as elsewhere in society, race plays an important role in the administration of punishment, even in the case of similar offences (Ferguson 2000, Morris 2005; Skiba et al. 2002 in Morris and Perry 2016). Systemic racism and discrimination, as opposed to a propensity for "bad behaviour," explain the significant differences in the ways that Black and white students are disciplined.

In Toronto, between 2011–2012 and 2015–2016, almost half of the students expelled from the Toronto District School Board (TDSB) were Black, and only 10 percent of those expelled were white students (Naccarato 2017). Similarly, during the 2006–2007 school year, Black students in Toronto were three times more likely to be suspended than white students (Rankin, Rushowy and Brown 2013). A study of the Peel District School Board found that in 2019 Black secondary students, who made up 10.2 percent of the school population, made up 22.5 percent of suspensions (Cadha, Herbert and Richard 2020). Black students and parents highlighted that teachers "use any excuse" to exclude Black students, including wearing hoodies or hoop earrings (Chadha, Herbert and Richard 2020). In the TDSB, nearly 42 percent of all Black students had been suspended at least once, compared to only 18 percent of white students and 18 percent of other racialized students (James and Turner 2017).

Age doesn't seem to be a protective factor when it comes to this trend. Younger Black students have not been exempt from punitive treatment, either — quite the opposite. In 2006–2007, nearly half of all suspensions and 14 percent of expulsions in Toronto were doled out to elementary school students (Rankin and Contenta 2009c). The rates remain particularly high for younger Black students in Toronto. They represented 15 percent of the Grade 7 and 8 student body but nearly 40 percent of suspensions. Among this population, one in seven Black students had been suspended at least once, compared to one in twenty white students (Rankin, Rushowy and Brown 2013).

In Halifax, during the 2015–2016 school year, Black students made up 8 percent of the student body but 22.5 percent of total suspensions (Woodbury 2016). The rate of suspensions has changed little since the 1980s and has been protested as an injustice to the Black community dating back at least decades (BLAC 1994). A similar picture emerges in the province of Quebec, where Black and other racialized students also face disproportionate rates of suspension and expulsion. The CDPDJ found that Black students, particularly Haitians, were frequently suspended and expelled in a discriminatory fashion for minor infractions, such as being late. The commission stated that they were subjected to a "zero tolerance" framework that other students did not face (2011). This exemplifies perfectly the functioning of racialized punishment: actions that result in a minor sanction when committed by a white youth are punished by disproportionately extreme measures when committed by a Black child or youth. Indeed, despite favourable comparisons to the United States that are frequently drawn throughout popular culture, the suspension rates of Black youth in many Canadian schools are comparable to those found in the United States; according to the United States Department of Education, Black students are suspended at a rate three times higher than white students (in Wong 2016). These expulsions fuel a cycle of miseducation and abandonment. Special schools for expelled students are disproportionately attended by Black students (ACLC 2012; Rankin and Contenta 2009a and 2009b; CDPDJ 2011). These schools have been criticized for offering too few hours and classes for students to be able to fulfill the requirements for passing all of their courses (ACLC 2012; Rankin and Contenta 2009b), effectively stunting their ability to further their studies or even stay engaged in the education system.

The heightened discipline directed at Black youth that creates a hostile learning environment extends beyond the treatment of Black students into the entire Black family. Black parents, as well, frequently suffer from discriminatory treatment and from the encroachment of policing in educational institutions. This was seen most recently when Nancy Elgie, an eighty-two-year-old white school board trustee, was forced to resign after calling a Black mother named Charline Grant the N-word at the close of a York school board meeting in November 2016 (Price 2017). A lawyer serving the Black community in Toronto reported that parents, particularly Black women, are often met with hostility and aggression:

> The parents are absolutely targeted. The kids will get slapped with a suspension, but the parents will get do-not-trespass notices and be themselves subject to fairly aggressive measures … [The] underlying racist stereotyping by principals and teachers … crystallizes with the Black mother. All we have is someone trying to talk about what is happening. But it is immediately interpreted as violent, hysterical and threatening. (Bhattacharjee 2003: 41)

Black parents end up on the receiving end of trespassing orders and have been reported to Children's Aid Society for "offences" that have included, for example, challenging school officials on whether a child needs medication for attention deficit disorder (Bhattacharjee 2003).

Even as Black students are targeted with disproportionate disciplinary measures, the same concerted attention is not necessarily granted toward protecting them from the often extreme and daily racism that many Black youth have reported experiencing from their peers (Codjoe 2001). A nine-year-old Nova Scotian Black girl told acclaimed researcher Dr. Wanda Bernard that she often skipped school because of unchecked racism from her peers: "They make me hate myself " (Bernard in Noble-Hearle 2014). In one case in 2017, Adrienne Charles, the mother of two elementary-school-aged Black children in Montreal, was forced to go to the media in addition to filing complaints against the school because school officials refused to take concerted action to address the virulent racism that her sons experienced from white students (Perron 2017). In the York Region District School Board, families described Black children enduring years of racist bullying, with Black students being called the N-word as early as Grade 1. They further identified that when Black children finally responded after long-standing bullying, they were suspended (YRDSB 2020). While Black youth and children face heightened surveillance and extremely limited tolerance for even minor disobedience, the racist hostility of white students appears to be granted far more leniency. School discipline policies both place Black youth under constant surveillance and render "the complexities of their lives, pain, and suffering" — the result of structural, institutional and interpersonal racism — invisible (Wun 2016: 174).

THE SCHOOL-TO-PRISON PIPELINE

While the informal school environment is itself highly carceral for Black youth, formal surveillance and criminalization also occur within public schooling. School disciplinary policies work in conjunction with the racialized surveillance of Black youth across multiple institutions that "begins in school and is directly connected to practices that continue outside of schools" (Meiners 2009 in Salole and Abdulle 2015: 129). Not only do disciplinary policies mimic youth's treatment by law enforcement officers, but schools also expose youth to further encounters with police or security guards. In Quebec, the task of the surveillance and discipline of (disproportionately Black) students is increasingly contracted out to private security firms (CDPDJ 2011). In Toronto, mandated police presence in schools has made Black and other racialized youth increasingly vulnerable to criminalization. Black families in the York Region District School Board reported that when it came to Black children — including those who were very young —schools involved police in minor issues. As a result, Black students were leaving schools because they did not feel safe (Chadha, Herbert and Richard 2020). Further, even in the absence of mandated police presence, police are frequently called into Toronto schools and will often handcuff Black youth for relatively minor infractions (Bhattacharjee 2003). The punitive and carceral atmosphere of schools was cemented in 2008 when, in addition to heightening surveillance policies, including cameras at school, lockdown policies and hall monitors, the School Resource Officer (SRO) program was launched within the Toronto District School Board and twenty-nine uniformed police officers were placed in Toronto schools. This was contested by many parents, teachers and community members as contributing to a hostile environment for marginalized students. Following years of these policies, a survey of largely Black, school-aged youth in Toronto found that youth reported feeling that they were constantly under surveillance while at school (Salole and Abdulle 2015).

Beyond the increasingly prison-like atmosphere of many public schools, disciplinary policies in schools, particularly suspensions and expulsions, contribute directly to the grossly disproportionate number of encounters between Black youth and the criminal justice system. Suspensions and expulsions have extremely damaging effects on all youth and can be life changing. A recent US study found that school discipline, particularly suspension, leads to poorer academic achievement in Black youth and "is a major source of the racial achievement gap and educational reproduction of inequality" (Morris and Perry 2016; CDPDJ 2011). Yet beyond inequality, expulsion and suspension correlates quite directly with their likelihood to end up behind bars. This dynamic has been coined the "school-to-prison pipeline." Black legal scholar Kimberlé Crenshaw (2015: 5) explains: "It is well-established in the research literature and by educational advocates that there is a link between the use of punitive disciplinary measures and subsequent patterns of criminal supervision and incarceration." Though it takes place only in schools, the concept of the school-to-prison pipeline encapsulates the multiple state agencies that lead to students being pushed out of school and into incarceration. This is why Michelle Alexander defines the school-to-prison pipeline as the numerous institutional forces that "collectively under-educate and over-incarcerate students of colour at disparate rates" (2012: 104).

The pipeline is not only a US phenomenon. The link between school discipline, system involvement and incarceration is a Canadian reality as well (Salole and Abdulle 2015). The African Canadian Legal Clinic has found that school officials often contact the police to instigate criminal charges against Black youth for minor infractions and they are then given court conditions that prevent them from coming near their school (ACLC 2012). Students who are suspended and expelled are also more frequently found in public spaces. Black students in public spaces face extremely high rates of police surveillance and harassment, which often leads to arrest. Black students have substantially higher rates of arrests than their white peers (Charest 2009; Bernard and McAll 2010; CDPDJ 2011). In 2009, a *Toronto Star* analysis found that the Toronto schools that had the highest suspension rates tended to be in parts of the city that also had the highest rates of provincial incarceration (*Toronto Star* 2009 in ACLC 2012). It is essential to locate some of the responsibility for the massive incarceration of Black youth within the school system.

PUSHED OUT OF SCHOOL: FUGITIVITY AND RESISTANCE

White-run public schools remain largely a site of racialized violence for many marginalized students. Black youth are exposed to a "hostile environment" in which they undergo "psychological damage, emotional pain, and … personal humiliation" due to racially discriminatory treatment (Codjoe 2001: 349, 351) by those tasked with their education. For this reason, many youth disengage from school entirely. While it is frequently referred to as "dropping out," this language disguises the structural racism both inside and outside of the education system that impacts Black children's ability to remain in school. It presumes an individual problem found in these Black boys and girls, while erasing the contextual factors within school and society that contribute to this phenomenon (Dei, Mazzuca and McIsaac 1997). For this reason, "dropping out" or "low academic achievement" can more accurately be described as the result of a concerted "push-out." The concept of the "push-out" has become an important reframing of the crisis by Black activists and researchers alike: Black youth are pushed out by various school structures and policies that neglect their needs, single them out and cause them to disengage (Dei, Mazzuca and McIsaac 1997; Crenshaw 2015).

Indeed, Black students continue to be pushed out of school at significant rates. While the rate of high school completion rose over the past decade and the racial gap narrowed, Black students continue to have a higher dropout rate than the rest of the population (McAndrew, Ledent and Ait-Said 2005 and Torczyner 2010 in Livingstone 2010; Dei, Mazzuca and McIsaac 1997). Data from the Toronto school board found that, overall, Black students had the lowest graduation rate of any group — 65 percent for the 2006 to 2011 cohort (Szekely and Pessian 2015b). A similar picture emerges in Quebec, where nearly half of the province's Black students continue to drop out of high school. In 2004, a study demonstrated that a group of Black students in Quebec who started high school between 1994 and 1996 had a 51.8 percent graduation rate, compared to 69 percent for the population as a whole (McAndrew and Ledent 2004 in Hampton 2010: 106). The push-out of Black youth, while impacting all youth of African descent in important ways, is nonetheless not experienced identically by all Black students. Public discussions about racial inequality in schools tend to focus more on the experience of Black boys.

Even when gender is not specified, it is the young Black, cisgender boy who is often pictured when the topic of systemic racism in the education system is raised. This attention is warranted because it is true that, empirically, both in the United States and in Canada, Black boys represent the highest percentages of dropouts, suspensions and expulsions (Crenshaw 2015; Woodbury 2016). Yet a more complex story emerges when looking at these trends from an intersectional perspective. The experience of school "push-out" takes different forms for those Black youths who are also marginalized by their gender, sexual minority status, (dis)ability and immigration status. Racist violence directed at Black girls may be less visible, but it is not less harmful. Existing research and data "often fail to address the degree to which girls face risks that are both similar to and different from those faced by boys" (Crenshaw 2015: 8). To leave these experiences out risks insulating or invisibilizing the discrimination experienced by Black girls.

Gender remains "a crucial variable in the construction of inequality for Black youth" in Canadian schools (Dei, Mazzuca and McIsaac 1997: 102). Like boys, Black girls in Canada have also expressed experiencing school "as a system of domination" (Dei and James 1998: 102). Educators in the Greater Toronto Area (GTA), for example, shared concerns that Black girls were frequently "adultified" compared to white children of the same age, being described as "having an attitude" as early as four years old (YRDSB 2020: 18).

Though it appears to be at a lesser rate than Black boys, Black girls are impacted by discriminatory disciplinary practices as well. For example, in 2008, a Black girl attending a Durham area school was arrested in her school by the police and criminally charged for allegedly slapping another student. She denied the allegations and her family subsequently complained to the Ontario Human Rights Tribunal, which found there was indeed a racial disparity in her treatment by the school officials (Szekely and Pessian 2015a and 2015b). In Ontario, two Black female students were suspended from school for "weapon possession" because they had brought nail files to school (Bhattacharjee 2003: 3). A questionnaire given to Black youth of all genders in Calgary, Halifax and Toronto found no difference between them in terms of racialized devaluation experienced by boys and girls. Both reported being treated as if they were "stupid" and identified this as one of their most stressful experiences in the context of their education (James et al. 2010: 94). For Black girls, streaming occurs along the lines of both race and gender: Black girls reported being channelled into both racialized and gendered segments of the labour market and discouraged from taking math and sciences (Dei, Mazzuca and McIsaac 1997: 102). While Black culture and contributions are largely absent from the curriculum, what does exist focuses only on the contributions of Black men (Dei, Mazzuca and McIsaac 1997). Less visible forms of violence experienced by Black girls at school often go unaddressed and unseen by traditional measures. One American study by critical race scholar Connie Wun (2016) found that, while Black girls are subject to comparatively fewer suspensions and expulsions than Black boys, they reported experiencing heightened surveillance and discipline that was more difficult to measure with statistics. They reported that even for the smallest of movements in class, their behaviours were constrained and punished.

Black girls, like Black women, are impacted not only by racialized and gendered criminalization, but also by neglect across state institutions (Ritchie 2012; Wun

2016). Inaction in the case of conflicts between students at school can also be a form of racialized and gendered violence toward Black girls. Though more research is necessary, Black girls report experiencing high levels of sexual harassment at school (Dei, Mazzuca and McIsaac 1997) and, in general, face higher rates of sexual assault than white girls (Tanner and Wortley 2002 in Owusu-Bempah and Wortley 2014). These racialized and gendered experiences create unique barriers for Black girls in completing their education (Crenshaw 2015). Indeed, while Black girls remain vulnerable to both heightened surveillance and punishment as well as sexual harassment and violence, their unique needs within the Canadian education system still go too often unaddressed. Black and other racialized youth who are gender or sexual minorities experience school as a particularly hostile environment.

The combination of the school system's policies and inaction or silence surrounding racism, transphobia and homophobia exacerbates the risks of discrimination, violence and abuse for 2SLGBTQI+ youth. The school system's status quo indeed creates and upholds the conditions that end up fuelling perhaps the most extreme conditions of a structural "push-out." Gender and sexual minority youth of all racial backgrounds are already pushed out of schools at an enormous rate. A large-scale Canadian study found that up to half of students who were sexual minorities reported having experienced sexual harassment at school. Trans students face appallingly high levels of harassment, including bullying, sexual harassment and violence. Over one quarter of transgender students reported hearing teachers make transphobic comments on a daily or weekly basis. Almost half of transgender students have skipped school due to feeling unsafe (Taylor and Peter 2011).

Youth of colour who are gender and sexual minorities face particularly high rates of physical harassment and assault at school because of the multiple layers of stigmatization they face (Taylor and Peter 2011). This push-out is particularly violent and dangerous since youth who are gender and sexual minorities, especially those who are racialized or Indigenous, also face the highest rate of homelessness in Canada (Abramovich 2015). For racialized gender and sexual minorities, homelessness vastly increases their chances of being criminalized and incarcerated. This amounts to an even more direct demonstration of the dynamics of the school-to-prison pipeline. The way the Canadian education system functions is far from the sole factor in the extreme hardship, violence and neglect faced by Black youth who are sexual minorities. Yet exclusion from secure housing and employment, combined with rejection and violence in the education system, puts Black, Indigenous and other racialized sexual minority youth in situations of extreme precarity.

Beyond gender- and sexuality-based oppression, youth with disabilities face enormous challenges in the school system. Youth who are navigating marginalization because of their race while also living with one or many physical or mental disabilities are very vulnerable to multiple forms of systemic discrimination. For one, navigating race and mental health are related in many ways. One reason for this is that racism contributes to mental health issues in racialized communities, particularly the kind of racial discrimination faced by racialized immigrants (Rollock and Gordon 2000 and Ontario Human Rights Commission 2012 in Chan and Chunn 2014). That said, without recognizing this vulnerability, Black youth are disproportionately labelled as "special needs," a term that encompasses students with mental health issues as well as those with linguistic or behavioural challenges (Woodbury 2016; CDPDJ 2011). The intersection of race and disability places Black students labelled as disabled at a heightened risk of being pushed out of school. The Ontario *Safe Schools Act* (2001–2008), which created harsher and more punitive suspension and expulsion policies until it was repealed, resulted in a massive spike of expulsions that impacted Black students and students with disabilities most severely (Bhattacharjee 2003). Though information specifically addressing race, disability and expulsions is not tallied, observers called it "a logical inference" that suspensions and expulsions would "impact even more heavily on Black students in special needs classes" and noted that, "moreover, other factors such as poverty and immigrant/refugee status may further compound the impact" (Bhattacharjee 2003: 50). In one case, it was reported that a fourteen-year-old Black student with an intellectual disability was suspended because his teacher was struck by an object in a classroom that was darkened because of a film screening. The vice-principal questioned the student for over an hour before the police were called. Although all charges were dropped, this student's suspension lasted three months (Bhattacharjee 2003) Once out of school and spending more time in public spaces, both Black persons and persons with mental health issues are more likely to be treated with excessive force by police officers as well as being more likely to be arrested and put behind bars (Chan and Chunn 2014). Despite the recent abolition of the *Safe Schools Act* and "zero tolerance" policies in Ontario, students with disabilities are still vulnerable to being punished for their disability. New "exclusions" permitted by Ontario's *Education Act* allow Ontario principals to remove special needs children from school indefinitely if they do not have the resources to support them. The government has neither set limits nor imposed any tracking of this practice (Robinson 2016).

Black migrant youth who are undocumented continue to be excluded from schools in several Canadian cities. Because of the clandestine nature of living in Canada without papers, it is difficult to examine the experiences of Black and other racialized students who live without legal immigration status and who seek to access the education system. Following years of organizing by migrant justice activists, Vancouver and Toronto have adopted "don't ask, don't tell" policies as part of efforts aimed at ensuring that all city residents, including people without full immigration status, can access essential services (housing, healthcare, education, social services, emergency services) without fear of being detained or deported. In principle, adopting these policies should mean that non-status students are able to go to school. That said, significant barriers remain. Toronto has since seen incidents in which students without papers were apprehended at school and deported, alongside their families (Community Social Planning Council of Toronto 2008). In the province of Quebec, the Ministry of Education has granted some leeway toward allowing non-status students to attend school by adopting non-binding guidelines in the spirit of "don't ask, don't tell." However, since they are non-binding, the ongoing fear of apprehension and deportation means that many non-status children, most of whom are Black and brown, are still unlikely to attend school at all as they continue to be at risk of discovery and removal (Collectif éducation sans frontières 2013).

Despite being exposed to both systemic and individual hostility within the education system as well as violence from their peers, school officials and teachers beginning at a young age, Black youth continue to apply survival strategies and find ways to navigate exceedingly complex situations. Resistance tactics employed by Black students take many forms, both large and small. Widely acclaimed ethnographer George J. Sefa Dei, who, with his assistants, has conducted research with Black students in Ontario, has argued that in the face of acute racial domination, "oppositional behaviours," including adopting unique dress and language styles that conflict with dominant society, are ways in which Black youth subvert the hegemonic norms being imposed upon them in schools. Further, he has argued that given the experiences of Black youth in public schools, "dropping out and the behaviours associated with 'fading out' of school (e.g., 'truancy,' lack of interest and participation in school, etc.) can be seen as forms of resistance" (Dei, Mazzuca and McIsaac 1997: 25). This sentiment is echoed in the work of critical education scholar Damien M. Sojoyner, who has argued against pathologizing Black youth who choose to leave hostile and violent school environments, recasting this as akin to "fugitivity" since, in effect, Black youth are fleeing sites of racial violence (in Allen 2016).

> Despite systemic and individual hostility as well as violence from their peers, school officials and teachers, Black youth continue to apply survival strategies and find ways to navigate exceedingly complex situations.

While disengagement can be a form of resistance amid limited options, engaging within education institutions can also be a form of resisting the racial violence that often dominates the school environment. Black youth also engage in school clubs and activities to try to create social change within educational institutions (Dei, Mazzuca and McIsaac 1997). For example, for decades, Black youth across the province of

Nova Scotia have participated in celebrating Black history and African contributions, countering the too-frequent absence of Black realities found in schools (Oostveen n.d.). In addition, many Black youth who have been pushed out of high school go on to achieve high rates of graduation in adult education settings, GED and trade schools (BLAC 1994; CDPDJ 2011). Despite the conditions of imposed upon them, Black youth continue to resist their denigration in a multitude of ways.

FIGHTING BACK, FIGHTING TO WIN

Decades after the integration of Canada's last segregated school, Black students continue to be pushed out of schools and streamed into poverty, low-waged work and youth correctional facilities. Not only are schools underserving young Black minds, but they are also functioning as one arm of the carceral system that grips entire segments of the Black community. The systemic abandonment felt by so many Black youth is psychologically harmful — a student's school experience can have "a major effect on his or her self-image and self-esteem and on his or her development in later life" (OHRC 2003: 18). The realities facing Black youth in the school system are neither well known outside of the Black community nor widely seen as a crisis, yet they are, to use the words of Afua Cooper, a "national disgrace" (CBC News 2016). It is urgent to counter the devaluation and vilification of Black youth in the school system with a focus away from carceral trends in the education system and toward a system that invests in nurturing, rather than punishing, Black youth.

Deeper institutional transformations that tackle systemic racism from an intersectional framework are required. Those transformations must address the general societal disinvestment in education that affects students of all backgrounds as well as to redress the racism structured into the education system. Yet it is crucial to note that much as substantive and transformative shifts are still required to make schools livable places for young Black people, many of the changes currently being forwarded by school boards and provincial ministries of education across Canada have been developed as a result of collective organizing led by Black communities. It is Black parents, community members and students who have been on the front lines to address and counter the (mis)education of Black youth, often at great personal cost.

> Black families have always, despite enormous obstacles, worked to find ways to educate their children formally or informally, regardless of the abandonment of Black youth by wider society.

Black families have always, despite enormous obstacles, worked to find ways to educate their children formally or informally, regardless of the abandonment of Black youth by wider society (Hamilton 2011; Cooper 1999). Historically, Black communities did not passively accept segregation in schools but actively contested it until it ended. Indeed, Black families and Black educators have played an important role toward redressing the systemic injustices experienced by Black youth and children. Schools founded specifically to address and remedy anti-Blackness, which can be found in Toronto and Halifax, only exist because of decades of concerted organizing (Hampton 2010).

Toronto's Africentric Alternative School, founded in 2009 as a product of Black community mobilizing and developed to counter the erasure of Black realities found in the mainstream school system, has been remarkably successful. Performance in standardized tests is well above average, with students testing above the provincial average in reading, writing and math (CBC News 2010). Toronto Freedom School, an initiative co-founded and co-directed by Leroi Newbold and Naouda Robinson, fights anti-Black racism in the school system and forwards queer, disabled and Afro-Indigenous-centred Black liberatory education, including a Saturday school program, a three-week summer program, and a "Black Liberation Comic Club." Black educators in Nova Scotia, including Rachel Zellars, created Nova Scotia's first African Nova Scotian Freedom School in the summer of 2020. The non-cred school for Black children was built in part to counter a lack of mandatory courses on Black Nova Scotian history in the province's curriculum (Garel 2020). Young Black people have taken enormous risks to resist the racial harms they experience in their schools. In fall of 2020, several hundred Black students walked out of schools in Calgary protesting multiple incidents of teachers using the N-word while talking to students. Some also decried the general erasure of Black history from their schools and many walked from their school to Calgary police headquarters chanting "Black Lives Matter" (Ferguson 2020). In Dartmouth's Prince Andrew High School, dozens of students staged a "Black Minds Matter" walkout in November 2020 to highlight endemic racism from fellow students and demanded expanded commitment on Black culture and history (McSheffrey 2020). That same fall, another walkout, organized in the GTA by Students Speak Up YCDSB, saw students demand hiring more Black teachers, mandatory anti-Black and anti-Indigenous racism training, and a mechanism to allow them to report racism at York's Catholic school board (CBC News 2020).

Black students, Black parents and other racialized community members have also been on the forefront of the now North-America wide movement for police-free schools. While numerous studies have highlighted that the presence of law enforcement in schools has been "disastrous" for Black and racialized youth (Petteruti 2011; Nolan 2011; Madan 2016), police-in-school programs have begun to be terminated en masse after significant organizing by impacted communities. In Toronto, the Toronto Freedom School, Black Lives Matter Toronto, Latinx, Afro-Latin-America, Abya Yala

Education Network (LAEN) and Education Not Incarceration led a successful struggle to remove student resource officers (SROS) from the country's largest school board, the TDSB, in 2017 (Cole 2020). This win was the first of its kind, but it indicates a particular sea change in victories in the wake of the historic Black-led struggles following the police lynching of George Floyd in 2020. After a Black ESL

> Black students, Black parents and other racialized community members have also been on the forefront of the now North-America wide movement for police-free schools.

student was dragged out of a Hamilton-area school in handcuffs, Hamilton Students for Justice staged an eight-hour sit-in, as well as an ongoing campaign, to terminate the police-in-schools programs. In 2020, they were victorious with a school-board vote in their favour. Similar successful efforts have passed across the country since 2020: a successful "Cops Out of Our Schools" campaign led by the Asilu Collective at the Ottawa-Carleton District School Board and a vote to end SRO programs in the Peel Region after a powerful campaign by Parents of Black Children, led by Black mothers Claudette Rutherfod, Kearie Daniel and Charline Grant. Since the uprisings of 2020, school boards have also voted to remove police liaison programs in Vancouver, in both the New Westminster School Board and the Vancouver School Board, where the School Liaison Officer program had been in place since 1972. And the Upper Grand District School Board in Guelph voted to terminate its police liaison program after mobilizing by Black Lives Matter Guelph (see Maynard and Diverlus 2021). Indeed, Toronto's legacy has now been successfully recreated across national borders: in the United States, twenty-five cities have cancelled contracts with police departments and removed SROS from schools (Ritchie 2021). In sum, the intellectual and political labour displayed in the form of Black and Black-led protest has changed the political terrain substantively. Today, the presence of law enforcement officers in places ostensibly geared toward learning is becoming increasingly morally indefensible. And if the broader #PoliceFreeSchools movement is successful, the very notion that schools once intentionally hosted armed and violent agents of the state could be relegated to an embarrassing and shameful chapter in history. Yet there is still much work to undertake before this becomes a reality.

Challenging harms spanning curricula to disciplinary policy to cops in the classroom, Black communities continue to be on the vanguard of life-saving changes in Canadian education, challenging the (mis)education of Black youth at every turn. Children, teenagers, parents, teachers and community members are building more liberatory futures not only for young Black people in schools, but for all young people. It is from these movements that we are able to witness the truth in the maxim "change comes from below." Those in positions of power ought to take note that change is on its way, and whether or not they are ready, it is happening before all of our eyes.

DISCUSSION QUESTIONS

1. Name three things you learned about the history of Black student and parent organizing in Canada.
2. What are some reasons Black history has been written out of so many textbooks and curriculum? Who benefits from the ongoing erasure of Black history, and of Canada's treatment of Black communities, from curricula across the country?
3. Instead of using law enforcement to police children for difficult behaviour at school, what are some other ways you can think about that would keep *all students* (including Black students) safe?

GLOSSARY OF KEY TERMS

Carceral: A term that highlights the prison-like features of a place or a practice, drawing attention to structural forms of surveillance, immobilization and heightened vulnerability to punishment; understood to be features or practices that can exist both within and well beyond jails and prisons.

"Don't ask, don't tell": Under a "don't ask, don't tell" policy, service providers are forbidden from asking service users about their immigration status in Canada and, if services discover the immigration status of a client, they are forbidden from sharing this information with others. This ensures that regardless of immigration status, people are able to access essential services like housing, healthcare and/or education.

ESL: English as a second language.

Freedom schools: Free, alternative schools or schooling programs intended to foster a liberatory education for Black young people in order to counter the harms of white supremacist education practices. Part of and tied to broader Black freedom struggles, including the civil rights movement and the Black Power era.

2SLGBTQI+: Two-Spirit, lesbian, gay, bisexual, trans, queer and intersex.

Streaming: The formal or informal practice of separating students into classes or learning tracks based on their *perceived* intellectual or academic abilities.

"Push-out": A term that draws attention to the practices within schools that cause students to leave before graduating, including a reliance on overly punitive disciplinary measures, a lack of culturally appropriate learning materials, hostility or indifference from teachers and lack of supports more generally, all of which disproportionately impact low-income learners, Black, Indigenous and racialized and/or migrant students. Used to draw attention to the structural factors that cause students to leave school, as differentiated from the term "dropout," which focuses more on individual actions.

School-to-prison pipeline: A term that highlights the continuities between disciplinary practices in schools, disproportionately borne by Black learners, that puts students at risk of further interactions with law enforcement, either in or outside of schools, contributing to the hyper-criminalization of Black and racialized young people.

SRO: Shorthand for "school resource officer," a name often used for the partnerships between police and schools that structure the presence of law enforcement in schools. Many, but not all, all police-school liaison programs in North America use this terminology.

RESOURCES FOR ACTIVISTS

Hamilton Students for Justice: hs4j.ca
Freedom School Toronto: freedomschooltoronto.ca
African Nova Scotia Freedom School: freedomschoolns.wixsite.com/ansfs
"Teaching African Canadian History": Lesson Plans/Teachers Guides by Natasha Henry: teachingafricancanadianhistory.weebly.com/lesson-plans.html
Parents of Black Children: parentsofblackchildren.org

NOTE

1   This is a revised and updated version of the chapter "The (Mis)Education of Black Youth," originally published in *Policing Black Lives: State Violence in Canada from Slavery to the Present*. Special thanks to Leroi Newbold for his feedback on recent shifts in province-wide school policies.

REFERENCES

Abramovich, A. 2015. "It's About Time Canada Stood Up for Homeless LGBT Youth." *Huffington Post*, March 25. <huffpost.com/archive/ca/entry/lbgt-homeless-shelter-toronto_b_6933278>.

ACLC (African Canadian Legal Clinic). 2012. *Canada's Forgotten Children: Written Submissions to the Committee on the Rights of the Child on the Third and Fourth Reports of Canada*. Toronto: African Canadian Legal Clinic. <www2.ohchr.org/english/bodies/crc/docs/ngos/Canada_African_Canadian_Legal_Clinic_CRC61.pdf>.

Alexander, M. 2012. *The New Jim Crow: Mass Incarceration in the Age of Colorblindness*. New York: The

New Press.

Allen, R.M. (host). 2016. "Damien M. Sojoyner, First Strike: Educational Enclosures in Black Los Angeles." New Books Network. <newbooksnetwork.com/search?+q=Damien+M.+Sojoyner%2C+-First+Strike%3A+Educational+Enclosures+in+Black+Los+Angeles/>.

American Psychological Association. 2014. "Black Boys Viewed as Older, Less Innocent than Whites, Research Finds." <apa.org/news/press/releases/2014/03/black-boys-older.aspx>.

Bernard, L., and C. McAll. 2010. "Jeunes Noirs et systeme de justice." *Revue du Cremis* 3, 1.

Bernstein, R. 2011. *Racial Innocence: Performing Childhood and Race from Slavery to Civil Rights*. New York: NYU Press.

Bhattacharjee, K. 2003. *The Ontario Safe Schools Act: School Discipline and Discrimination*. Toronto: Ontario Human Rights Commission.

BLAC (Black Learners Advisory Committee). 1994. BLAC *Report on Education: Redressing Inequity — Empowering Black Learners*. Halifax.

Blackstock, C. 2011. "The Canadian Human Rights Tribunal on First Nations Child Welfare: Why if Canada Wins, Equality and Justice Lose." *Children and Youth Services Review* 33, 1. <cwrp.ca/publica-tions/canadian-human-rights-tribunal-first-nations-child-welfare-why-if-canada-wins-equality>.

Bombay, A., and K. Hewitt. 2015. *A Report from the Committee on Aboriginal and Black/African Canadian Student Access and Retention: A Focus on Financial Support*. Halifax: Dalhousie University. <dal.ca/content/dam/dalhousie/pdf/dept/senior-administration/VPAP/reports/otherreports/Aboriginal%20and%20Black-African%20Canadian%20students%20-%20Final%20report%20Oct%201%202015.pdf>.

Brown, L. 2014. "Africentric High School Students Thrive in Pioneering Program." *Toronto Star*, February 26. <thestar.com/yourtoronto/education/2014/02/26/africentric_high_school_students_thrive_in_pioneering_program.html>.

Cameron, D., and D. Hamlin. 2015. "Applied or Academic: High Impact Decisions for Ontario Students." Toronto: *People for Education*. <peopleforeducation.ca/wp-content/uploads/2017/07/Applied-or-Academic-Report-2015.pdf>.

Canadian Council on Learning. 2006. "The Social Consequences of Economic Inequality for Canadian Children: A Review of the Canadian Literature."

Canadian Press. 2020. "Anti-Black Racism Case against School Board Heading to Quebec Rights Tribunal." *Toronto Star*, December 7. <thestar.com/politics/2020/12/07/anti-black-racism-case-against-school-board-heading-to-quebec-rights-tribunal.html>.

CBC News. 2020. ""We Need a Radical Change': Toronto-Area Students Stage Walkout to Protest Racism." November 20. <cbc.ca/news/canada/york-catholic-school-board-racism-student-walk-out-1.5808243>.

___. 2016. "Black Drop-Out Rate in Canada 'A National Disgrace': Professor Afua Cooper." *Radio Canada International*. <rcinet.ca/bhm-en/2015/01/30/english-black-drop-out-rate-in-canada-a-na-tional-disgrace-professor-afua-cooper/>.

CDPDJ (Commission des droits de la personne et des droits de la jeunesse Québec). 2011. *Profilage racial et discrimination systémique des jeunes racisés*. Bibliothèque et Archives nationales du Québec.

Chadha, E., S. Herbert, and S. Richard. 2020. "Review of the Peel District School Board." Peel District School Board, *Ontario Ministry of Education*. <edu.gov.on.ca/eng/new/review-peel-district-school-board-report-en.pdf>.

Chan, W., and D. Chunn. 2014. *Racialization, Crime, and Criminal Justice in Canada*. Toronto: University of Toronto Press.

Change.org. 2020. "Alberta Schools: Add Black History to Curriculum!" [petition]. <change.org/p/adriana-lagrange-alberta-minister-of-education-alberta-schools-need-black-history-and-its-mod-ern-impacts-to-be-part-of-the-curriculum?utm_source=share_petition&utm_medium=custom_url&recruited_by_id=003490b0-194a-11e9-81c7-1f169237aa22>.

Charest, M. 2009. *Mécontentement populaire et pratiques d'interpellations du SPVM depuis 2005: Doit-on garder le cap après la tempête?* Montreal, Quebec. <securitepublique.gc.ca/cnt/rsrcs/lbrr/ctlg/dtls-en.

aspx?d=PS&i=80747081&wbdisable=true#archived>.

Cheung, A., and A. Sienkiewicz. 2017. "Mississauga Mom Launches Complaint after Police Handcuff Her 6-Year-Old Daughter." CBC News, February 24. <cbc.ca/news/canada/toronto/mississauga-mom-launches-complaint-after-police-handcuff-her-6-year-old-daughter-1.3964827>.

Codjoe, H.M. 2001. "Fighting a 'Public Enemy' of Black Academic Achievement — the Persistence of Racism and the Schooling Experiences of Black Students in Canada." *Race Ethnicity and Education* 4, 4.

Cole, D. 2020. *The Skin We're In: A Year of Black Resistance and Power.* Toronto: Doubleday Canada.

Collectif éducation sans frontières. 2013. "Statement on Quebec Ministry of Education Guidelines by the Collectif éducation sans frontières." December 7. <solidarityacrossborders.org/en/enfants-sans-papiers-declaration-du-collectif-education-sans-frontieres-au-sujet-des-directives-du-ministere-de-leducation>.

Commission on Systemic Racism in the Ontario Criminal Justice System. 1994. Canadian Race Relations Foundation. <crrf-fcrr.ca/en/clearinghouse-search/author/298-c73722>.

Community Social Planning Council of Toronto. 2008. The Right to Learn: Access to Public Education for Non-Status Immigrants, June. <socialplanningtoronto.org/wp-content/uploads/2009/02/right_to_learn.pdf>.

Cooper, A. 1999. "Black Women and Work in Nineteenth-Century Canada West: Black Woman Teacher Mary Bibb." In P. Bristow, D. Brand, L. Carty, et al. (eds.), *"We're Rooted Here and They Can't Pull Us Up": Essays in African Canadian Women's History.* Toronto: University of Toronto Press.

Crenshaw, K.W. 2015. *Black Lives Matter: The Schott 50 State Report on Public Education and Black Males.* Schott Foundation for Public Education. <blackboysreport.org/>.

CTV News. 2015. "Quebec Man Pepper-Sprayed by Police Officer Appealing Traffic Tickets." <ctvnews.ca/quebec/quebec-man-pepper-sprayed-by-police-officer-appealing-traffic-tickets-1.4006680>.

Dei, G. and I-M. James. 1998. "'Becoming Black': African-Canadian Youth and the Politics of Negotiating Racial and Racialised Identities." *Race Ethnicity and Education* 1, 1.

Dei, G.J., J. Mazzuca, and E. McIsaac. 1997. *Reconstructing 'Dropout': A Critical Ethnography of the Dynamics of Black Students' Disengagement from School.* Toronto: University of Toronto Press. <doi.org/10.3138/9781442679078>.

Ferguson, E. 2020. "Hundreds of High School Students Join Walkout in Support of Anti-Racism." *Calgary Herald*, October 8. <calgaryherald.com/news/local-news/hundreds-of-high-school-students-join-walkout-in-support-of-anti-racism>.

Garel, C. 2020. "Black History Is Sorely Lacking in Canada's Curriculum. These Educators Are Fixing That." *Huffington Post*, September 28. <huffpost.com/archive/ca/entry/black-history-nova-scotia-freedom-school_ca_5f6e2494c5b61af20e752bea>.

Goff, P.A., M.C. Jackson, B.A. Di Leone, et al. 2014. "The Essence of Innocence: Consequences of Dehumanizing Black Children." *Journal of Personality and Social Psychology* 106, 4.

Gordon, A. 2018. "TDSB Head Wants to Phase Out Streaming, Expand Access to Specialty Schools." *Toronto Star*, January 28. <thestar.com/yourtoronto/education/2018/01/28/tdsb-head-wants-to-phase-out-streaming-expand-access-to-specialty-schools.html>.

Hamilton, S. 2011. "Stories from the Little Black School House." In A. Mathur, J. Dewar and M. DeGagn (eds.), *Cultivating Canada: A Reconciliation through the Lens of Cultural Diversity.* Ottawa: Aboriginal Healing Foundation.

Hampton, R. 2010. "Black Learners in Canada." *Race & Class* 52, 1. <mcgill.ca/dise/files/dise/hampton_-_black_learners_in_canada.pdf>.

Henry, A. 1993. "Missing: Black Self-Representations in Canadian Educational Research." *Canadian Journal of Education* 18, 3.

Hoffman, K.M., S. Trawalter and A. Waytz. 2015. "A Superhumanization Bias in Whites' Perceptions of Blacks." *Social Psychological and Personality Science* 6, 3.

James, C., D. Este, W.T. Bernard, et al. 2010. *Race & Well-Being : The Lives, Hopes, and Activism of African Canadians.* Black Point, NS and Winnipeg: Fernwood Publishing.

James, C.E. 2019. *We Rise Together*. York University, March 11. <yorku.ca/edu/wp-content/uploads/sites/28/2020/08/We-Rise-Together-report-March-18-002.pdf>.

James, C.E., and T. Turner. 2017. *Toward Race Equity in Education: The Schooling of Black Students in the Greater Toronto Area*. Toronto: York University, April. <edu.yorku.ca/files/2017/04/Towards-Race-Equity-in-Education-April-2017.pdf>.

Lafferty, R.N. 2013. "Race Uplift, Racism, and the Childhood Ideal: Founding and Funding the Nova Scotia Home for Coloured Children, 1850–1960." In *The Guardianship of Best Interests: Institutional Care for the Children of the Poor in Halifax*. Montreal: McGill-Queen's University Press. <jstor.org/stable/j.ctt24hn8q>.

Livingstone, A-M. 2010. *Black Youth's Perspectives on Educational Challenges and Policy*. School of Social Work, McGill University.

Livingstone, A.-M., and J. Celemencki. 2010. "Black Youths' Perspectives on Educational Challenges and Policy." <academia.edu/11447204/BLACK_YOUTHS_PERSPECTIVES_ON_EDUCATION_CHALLENGES_AND_POLICY>.

Madan, G.R. 2016. "Policing in Toronto Schools: Race-ing the Conversation." MA thesis, University of Toronto. <tspace.library.utoronto.ca/bitstream/1807/71685/1/Madan_Gita_R_201603_MA_thesis.pdf>.

Maharaj, S. 2015. "Streaming Students." An excerpt from the 2015 Annual Report on Ontario's Publicly Funded Schools. *People for Education*. <peopleforeducation.ca/wp-content/uploads/2017/10/streaming-students-2015.pdf>.

Maynard, R., and P. Diverlus. 2021. "The Struggle for Police-Free Schools." *Building the World We Want*. <buildingtheworldwewant.com/resources>.

McLaren, K. 2008. "'We Had No Desire to Be Set Apart': Forced Segregation of Black Students in Canada West Public Schools and Myths of British Egalitarianism." In B. Walker (ed.), *The History of Immigration and Racism in Canada: Essential Readings*. Toronto: Canadian Scholars Press.

McSheffrey, E. 2020. "Prince Andrew Students Walk Out of Class to Protest Racism Within Nova Scotia School System." *Global News*, November 30. <globalnews.ca/news/7492638/prince-andrew-students-walk-out-protest-racism/>.

Mickelson, R.A. 2007. "First and Second Generation School Segregation And Maintenance Of Educational Inequality." In R. Teese, Stephen Lamb, and Marie Duru-Bellat (eds.), *International Studies in Educational Inequality, Theory and Policy*. New York: Springer.

Morris, Edward W. 2005, "'Tuck in that Shirt!' Race, Class, Gender, and Discipline in an Urban School." *Sociological Perspectives* 48, 1.

Morris, Edward W., and B.L. Perry. 2016. "The Punishment Gap: School Suspension and Racial Disparities in Achievement." *Social Problems* 63, 1. <doi.org/10.1093/socpro/spv026>.

Naccarato, L. 2017. "Almost Half of TDSB Students Expelled over Last 5 Years Are Black, Report Says." CBC News, April 11. <cbc.ca/news/canada/toronto/almost-half-of-tdsbstudents-expelled-over-last-5-years-are-black-report-says-1.4065088>.

Newbold, L. 2021. Personal communication, October 31.

Noble-Hearle, M. 2014. "Killing Us Softly: Wanda Thomas Bernard on Racism in Nova Scotia." *Dal News*, November 21. <dal.ca/news/2014/11/21/-killing-us-softly---wanda-thomas-bernard-on-racism-in-nova-scot.html>.

Nolan, K. 2011. *Police in the Hallways: Discipline in an Urban High School*. Minneapolis: University of Minnesota Press.

OHRC (Ontario Human Rights Commission). 2003. *Paying the Price: The Human Cost of Racial Profiling*. <ohrc.on.ca/en/paying-price-human-cost-racial-profiling>.

Oostveen, J. n.d. "Began with a Group of Youth." *Chronicle Herald*. <thechronicleherald.ca/community/bedford-sackville/1186550-began-with-a-groupof-youth>.

Owusu-Bempah, A., and S. Wortley. 2014. "Race, Crime, and Criminal Justice in Canada." In S. Bucerius and M. Tonry (eds). *The Oxford Handbook of Ethnicity, Crime and Immigration*. Oxford: Oxford University Press.

Perron, L.-S. 2017. "Cri Du Coeur D'une M.re . Bout De Ressources." *La Presse*, March 3. <plus.lapresse.ca/screens/cb9f1a97-5b50-4152-82b7-7439c81b0768%7C_0.html>.

Petteruti, A. 2011. *Education Under Arrest: The Case Against Police in Schools*. Washington, DC: *Justice Policy Institute*. <justicepolicy.org/wp-content/uploads/justicepolicy/documents/educationunder-arrest_fullreport.pdf>.

Price, N. 2017. "Why Nancy Elgie's Resignation Is No Victory for the Black Community." *Now Toronto*, February 22. <nowtoronto.com/news/nancy-elgie-resignation-no-victory-for-toronto-black-community>.

Rankin, J., and S. Contenta. 2009a. "Are Schools Too Quick to Suspend?" *Toronto Star*, June 8. <thestar.com/news/gta/2009/06/08/are_schools_too_quick_to_suspend.html>.

____. 2009b. "Suspended Sentences: Forging a School-to-Prison Pipeline?" *Toronto Star*, June 6. <thestar.com/news/gta/article/646629>.

____. 2009c. "Expulsion Class Gives Students Another Chance." *Toronto Star*, June 7. <thestar.com/news/gta/2009/06/07/expulsion_class_gives_students_another_chance.html>.

Rankin, J., K. Rushowy, and L. Brown. 2013. "Toronto School Suspension Rates Highest for Black and Aboriginal Students." *Toronto Star*, March 22. <thestar.com/news/gta/2013/03/22/toronto_school_suspension_rates_highest_for_black_and_aboriginal_students.html>.

Ritchie, A.J. 2021. "The Demand Is Still #DefundPolice." *Interrupting Criminalization*, January. <interruptingcriminalization.com/defundpolice-update>.

____. 2012. *Arrested (in)Justice: Black Women, Violence, and America's Prison Nation*. New York: New York University Press.

Robinson, M. 2016. "School Exclusions Can Give Special-Needs Students the Boot — Indefinitely." *Toronto Star*, February 15. <thestar.com/yourtoronto/education/2016/02/15/school-exclusions-can-give-special-needs-students-the-bootindefinitely.html>.

Rushowy, K. 2020. "Ontario to End Streaming in Grade 9 and Change Other 'Racist, Discriminatory' Practices." *Toronto Star*, July 6. <thestar.com/politics/provincial/2020/07/06/ontario-to-end-streaming-in-grade-9-and-change-other-racist-discriminatory-practices.html>.

____. 2015. "End Streaming in Schools, Report to Toronto Trustees Recommends." *Toronto Star*, October 7. <thestar.com/yourtoronto/education/2015/10/07/end-streaming-in-schools-report-to-toronto-trustees-recommends.html>.

Salole, A.T., and Z. Abdulle. 2015. "Quick to Punish: An Examination of the School to Prison Pipeline for Marginalized Youth." *Canadian Review of Social Policy* 72/73.

Schumaker, K. 2012. "An Exploration of the Relationship Between Poverty and Child Neglect in Canadian Child Welfare." PhD thesis, University of Toronto. <tspace.library.utoronto.ca/bitstream/1807/34913/5/Schumaker_Katherine_201209_PhD_thesis.pdf>.

Szekely, R., and P. Pessian. 2015a. "Parents Warn Black Youth Are Being Racially Profiled in Durham Schools." *DurhamRegion.com*, August 6. <durhamregion.com/news-story/5787027-parents-warn-black-youth-are-being-racially-profiled-in-durham-schools/>.

____. 2015b. "Ontario Human Rights Tribunal Finds There Is a 'Racial Disparity' in Durham." *DurhamRegion.com*, August 6 <durhamregion.com/community-story/5787114-ontario-human-rights-tribunal-finds-there-is-a-racial-disparity-in-durham/>.

Taylor, C., and T. Peter. 2011. *Every Class in Every School: The First National Climate Survey on Homophobia, Biphobia, and Transphobia in Canadian School: Executive Summary*. Egale, Toronto. <egale.ca/awareness/every-class/>.

Toronto Star Editorial Board. 2017. "A 6-Year-Old Should Never Be Placed in Handcuffs: Editorial." *Toronto Star*, February 6. <thestar.com/opinion/editorials/2017/02/06/a-6-year-old-should-never-be-placed-in-handcuffs-editorial.html>.

TRC (Truth and Reconciliation Commission). 2015. *Honouring the Truth, Reconciling for the Future: Summary of the Final Report of the Truth and Reconciliation Commission of Canada*. <publications.gc.ca/site/eng/9.800288/publication.html>.

Walker, B. 2010. *Race on Trial: Black Defendants in Ontario's Criminal Courts, 1858–1958*. Toronto:

Published for the Osgoode Society for Canadian Legal History by University of Toronto Press.

Westol, N. 2017. "Mother Upset after 6-Year-Old Daughter Handcuffed by Police at Mississauga School." *Global News,* February 3. <globalnews.ca/news/3224634/mother-upset-after-6-year-old-daughter-handcuffed-by-police-at-mississauga-school/>.

Wong, A. 2016. "How School Suspensions Push Black Students Behind." *The Atlantic*, February 8. <theatlantic.com/education/archive/2016/02/how-school-suspensions-pushblack-students-behind/460305/>.

Woodbury, R. 2016. African-Nova Scotian Students Being Suspended at Disproportionarly Higher Rates." CBC News, December 12. <cbc.ca/news/canada/nova-scotia/african-nova-scotian-students-suspension-numbers-1.3885721>.

Wun, C. 2016. "Against Captivity: Black Girls and School Discipline Policies in the Afterlife of Slavery." *Educational Policy* 30, 1.

YRDSB (York Region District School Board). 2020. *Dismantling Anti-Black Racism Strategy: Creating Anti-Racist and Black Affirming Learning and Working Environments (Part 1: Background Report).* Toronto. <www2.yrdsb.ca/sites/default/files/2021-03/ABR-STRATEGY-Part1.pdf>.

6

SETTLER COLONIALISM AND INDIGENOUS RIGHTS IN CANADA
Thinking With and Beyond a Human Rights Framework

Karl Gardner and Jeffrey Ansloos

YOU SHOULD KNOW THIS

- Canada was one of only four countries to reject the United Nations Declaration on the Rights of Indigenous Peoples and held "permanent objector status" until 2016, before formally adopting the Declaration in 2020.

- Until 1960, Indigenous peoples had to permanently give up their status and associated rights in order to vote and were not allowed to hire legal representation to challenge the Canadian government, giving them virtually no access to political or legal justice.

- In 2019, the United Nations Human Rights Committee found that Canada was discriminating against Indigenous women and their descendants by denying rights through gender-based discrimination within the *Indian Act*.

- Clean water and sanitation are human rights. Canada is one of the most freshwater-abundant countries in the world, yet there remain forty-three long-term boil water advisories in effect in thirty-one First Nations.

- The judicial system is one of the primary contexts where Canada challenges its fiduciary responsibilities to Indigenous peoples. Between 2012 and 2018, the Canadian government spent $188 million fighting Indigenous nations in court.

- In 2016, the Truth and Reconciliation Commission of Canada concluded that Indian residential schools were tantamount to cultural genocide. In 2019, the Inquiry on Missing and Murdered Indigenous Women and Girls concluded that through the residential school system, Canada had deliberately violated human and Indigenous rights, and this amounted to genocide.

- In 2021, more than 1,200 remains from unmarked graves have been recovered from the sites of residential schools across the country, with many sites yet to be searched. Considering these mass unmarked graves, Canada could face international legal consequences if it is found that the country committed crimes against humanity or genocide.

- Between January 2019 and March 2020, the federal government spent over $13 million on RCMP and policing operations deployed against Indigenous land defenders opposing the construction of the Coastal GasLink Pipeline through Wet'suwet'en territories.

- The criminalization and overrepresentation of Indigenous peoples in the correctional system is a major human rights concern in Canada. In 2020, Indigenous peoples, who account for less than 5 percent of the total population of Canada, represented over 30 percent of those who are incarcerated.

Sources: Fontaine 2016; Bill C-15 2021; Canadian Encyclopedia 2020; Deer 2019; Government of Canada 2021; Forester 2020; APTN National News 2015; National Inquiry for Missing and Murdered Indigenous Women and Girls 2019; Al Jazeera 2021; Bellrichard 2020; Government of Canada 2020

INTRODUCTION

FOR INDIGENOUS PEOPLES,[1] TO LIVE IN Canada is to live in a land of contradictions. It is to live in a place where Indigenous rights are acknowledged by the government in public but are treated as a nuisance in private. It is to live in a place where Prime Minister Stephen Harper can apologize to Indigenous peoples for the colonial violence of Indian residential schools but a year later can boast at the international meeting of the G20 that Canada "has no history of colonialism." Where an Inuk woman can be appointed the Governor General of Canada — one of the most prestigious positions in the country — yet thirty-one Indigenous communities still do not have stable access to clean water. It is where Prime Minister Justin Trudeau can declare a National Day of Truth and Reconciliation but spend that day on a vacation with his family while rejecting invitations to mourn and reflect with Indigenous communities in the wake of the discovery of mass graves at residential school sites.

We could fill every page of this textbook and more with Canada's colonial contradictions. One that we will focus on in this chapter is the paradox often posed by Indigenous rights. Canada — through the Crown, as a government, and as a society — has always had a fraught relationship to Indigenous peoples' political, cultural and land rights. Indigenous rights have always been understood as a problem or a puzzle that the Canadian government must "solve." In response, the Government of Canada has variously sought to *remove* rights from Indigenous peoples, *recognize* them in flashy press conferences or legal documents or *reconcile* them with the unbroken and continued sovereignty of the Crown.

Indigenous rights are, of course, human rights. However, beyond the universal human rights we all inherently possess, Indigenous rights seek to account for, and respond to, the unique histories and positionalities of Indigenous peoples vis-à-vis global processes of colonialism, imperialism and genocide. Even though they are increasingly recognized in Canada, Indigenous rights are still contained and curtailed so as to not challenge or undermine the tenuous legitimacy of the Canadian state. Indigenous rights remain important tools in establishing a baseline of Indigenous dignity and well-being within settler-colonial countries like Canada. But the limited scope of Indigenous rights and inclusion within Canadian society has also encouraged Indigenous peoples to take matters into their own hands and assert their presence on their territories, regenerate their cultural practices and reclaim their rights to self-determination, sometimes without the involvement or the permission of the Canadian state.

In this chapter we trace the history of settler colonialism in Canada, paying close attention to the role that Indigenous rights have played in shaping this history. We begin with a brief discussion of "settler colonialism," offering a definition and explanation of its importance in framing Canadian history. We then turn to a discussion of the effects of settler colonialism on Indigenous rights. Here, we describe three broad historical orientations of the Canadian state toward Indigenous rights: removal, recognition and reconciliation. We show how, despite the shifting policies, practices and languages of Canadian approaches to dealing with Indigenous peoples and their rights, the logic of settler colonialism remains the constant foundation upon which the Canadian government continues to operate. We then consider how Indigenous and non-Indigenous people have advanced arguments for "equal" or "enhanced" rights as ways to address the ongoing effects of colonialism in Canada. While there is much to be gained through some rights-based approaches, we ask: what would it mean to move *beyond* rights as the sole framework for thinking about and responding to the injustices endured by Indigenous peoples? Our final section responds to this question by illuminating various approaches that move beyond rights, toward building "right relations" as an effective way to resist colonialism and support the flourishing of Indigenous peoples within, against and beyond the limits imposed by the settler-colonial state.

DEFINING SETTLER COLONIALISM

What is settler colonialism? What do we mean when we say Canada is a settler-colonial state? This term distinguishes countries like Canada, the US, Australia and Israel from other places that have endured colonial occupation and rule. In many other parts of the world, colonialism was imposed by a minority of European colonizers in the name of geopolitical power, enslavement, resource and labour extraction and empire building. Indigenous populations everywhere resisted and revolted against colonial rule, and many places eventually achieved independence and established post-colonial states. Despite generations of Indigenous resistance within and against settler-colonial contexts, however, colonial occupation continues to this day. This is because, as late anthropologist Patrick Wolfe argued, unlike other forms of colonialism, "settler colonizers come to stay." This means that in places like Canada, "invasion is a structure, not an event" (2006: 338). The goal of settler colonialism is distinct in that it seeks to construct an entire political, economic and social order on top of Indigenous lifeways, with the ultimate goals of securing access to land while absorbing Indigenous peoples into settler society. In other words, settler colonialism does not just form Canada's past; it is a living and enduring structure built by settlers to benefit settlers, and it continues to this day.

Two key features of settler colonialism are dispossession and assimilation. Dene scholar Glen Coulthard describes settler colonialism as a "relatively secure or sedimented set of hierarchical social relations that continue to facilitate the dispossession of Indigenous peoples of their lands and self-determining authority" (2014: 7). Dispossession was first justified by the doctrine of discovery, an international law

> Two key features of settler colonialism are dispossession and assimilation.

that justified Christian-European countries to lay claim to lands considered *terra nullius,* meaning "land belonging to nobody." Because Indigenous peoples' use and stewardship of their territories was not perceived by Europeans as "ownership," Turtle Island was said to be "discovered" by European explorers and therefore fell under their respective country's sovereign rule. Consider this perspective by late Secwepemc political leader Arthur Manuel:

> Europeans made their initial land claim on our Secwepemc lands in 1778 when Captain Cook sailed along the British Columbia coast, more than four

hundred kilometres away from our territory. According to the tenets of the doctrine of discovery, all that Europeans had to do to expropriate the lands in a region was to sail past a rover mouth and make a claim to all of the lands in its watershed. Outlands, given to us by our Creator and inhabited by us for thousands of years, were transformed into a British "possession," not only without our consent and without our knowledge, but also without a single European setting foot on our territory. (2015: 4)

Though the Supreme Court of Canada has gradually started to recognize that Indigenous peoples' land and cultural rights exist and pre-date the arrival of European settlers, the legal fiction of *terra nullius* continues to be the basis upon which the Canadian state claims sovereign ownership of Indigenous lands today. At the foundation of this claim is the desire of the Canadian government and corporations to secure ongoing, uncontested access to Indigenous lands for the purpose of profit. Whether it is displacing Indigenous peoples in order to build early settler cities, national railroads, extractive mines or leaky pipelines, this is as true today as it was in the early years of colonization.

Related to dispossession, Indigenous peoples have also been subject to concerted efforts to erode and depoliticize Indigenous cultures, identities and self-determination. Indeed, settler-colonial policies pursued by the Canadian state seek to replace Indigenous peoples through a process of elimination or disappearance of Indigenous nations as distinct peoples with distinct relationships and claims to their lands (Lawrence and Dua 2005). Indigenous peoples have been consistently represented as a "problem" by settler society. Late Stó:lō poet and writer Lee Maracle (1996: 93) noted that "the aims of the colonizer are to break up communities and families, and to destroy the sense of nationhood and the spirit of cooperation among the colonized." Consider the words of the past superintendent of Indian Affairs, Duncan Campbell Scott, who stated:

> Indigenous peoples have been consistently represented as a "problem" by settler society.

I want to get rid of the Indian problem. I do not think as a matter of fact, that the country ought to continuously protect a class of people who are able to stand alone.... Our objective is to continue until there is not a single Indian in Canada that has not been absorbed into the body politic and there is no Indian question, and no Indian Department, that is the whole object of this Bill. (National Archives of Canada)

The desire to erase Indigenous cultural practices and self-governance through government policies, laws and social exclusion is crucial for a settler society intent on settling its claim to uncontested ownership of these lands. And while in contemporary Canadian politics such violent attempts at assimilation have begun to be replaced by more covert efforts while acknowledging and apologizing for past harms, Indigenous peoples remain subject to tokenistic recognition with limited substantive changes. Indeed, recognition is often paired with a desire to eventually "let bygones be bygones" and establish the inevitability of settler society. As conservative political scientist Tom Flanagan (2000: 196) puts so plainly, "Call it assimilation, call it integration, call it adaptation, call it whatever you want: it has to happen." In fact, to say nothing of the unspeakable loss of life suffered by Indigenous peoples resisting settler colonialism, the Truth and Reconciliation Commission of Canada concluded in 2015 that Canada's long pursuit of Indigenous elimination-by-assimilation must be described as "cultural genocide."

THE EFFECTS OF SETTLER COLONIALISM ON THE RIGHTS OF INDIGENOUS PEOPLES

Consistent with the process of settler colonialism, the Canadian Crown, state and society have a long and shameful history of continuous attempts to dispossess Indigenous peoples of their lands, self-determination, culture and basic human rights. To simultaneously demonstrate the core feature of settler colonialism while also revealing its shifts in form and content, in the following section we present a brief summary of some of the effects of settler colonialism on the rights of Indigenous peoples in three broad periods: removal, recognition, and reconciliation. These periods are not meant to convey definitive, air-tight historical phases. There is considerable overlap between them, and the practices that have come to define these periods borrow and build upon previous moments in Canadian history.

Removing Rights

For the sake of brevity, we begin in 1857 with the passage of the *Gradual Civilization Act* by the Province of Canada. This Act represents one of the earliest attempts to legislatively remove any formal distinctions between Indigenous peoples and settlers and facilitate the gradual elimination of Indigeneity within settler society. The Act begins by stating that

> it is desirable to encourage the progress of Civilization among the Indian Tribes in this Province, and the gradual removal of all legal distinctions be-

tween them and Her Majesty's other Canadian Subjects, and to facilitate the acquisition of property and of the rights accompanying it.

Indigenous men considered worthy of enfranchisement by virtue of their assimilation into settler society could be "no longer deemed to be an Indian" and become a British subject. His "wife, widow, and lineal descendants" would also become enfranchised and lose their Indian status. Indigenous peoples were incentivized to accept enfranchisement, with the government offering them in exchange for the right to vote, "a piece of land not exceeding fifty acres," and "a sum of money ... to be ascertained and paid to him by the said Superintendent [General of Indian Affairs]."

Ten years later, the Province of Canada, Nova Scotia and New Brunswick confederated and created what we now know as "Canada" in 1867. Celebrated as a historic joining of "two founding nations" (anglophones and francophones), there was little consideration and no acknowledgement of the hundreds of Indigenous nations across the vast territories now claimed by Canada. The Canadian government also assumed all responsibility for past and future treaties and relationships with Indigenous peoples. Soon after, the *Gradual Enfranchisement Act* was passed in 1869, expanding on the *Gradual Civilization Act* discussed above. Among other things, this act stripped status from Indigenous women (and their children) who married non-Indigenous men and imposed the band council system of governance[2] on all recognized Indigenous nations in Canada, forcefully replacing various existing traditional and established governance systems.

In the same year, the Canadian government was surveying its recently acquired Rupert's Land with the intent of replacing pre-existing land titles of the hunters and farmers situated around the Red River, many of whom were Métis, with standardized English plots. Louis Riel, a Métis leader within the Red River Colony, barred colonial officials from entering their territory and announced the creation of a provisional Métis government. The Red River Colony was interested in negotiating its entry into Canada. But Prime Minister MacDonald, who had a well-documented aversion to Indigenous peoples, did not recognize the legitimacy of the provisional government and created the Province of Manitoba in 1870 instead. Despite armed rebellions in 1870 and 1885 by Métis, other Indigenous nations and settler allies, the government of Canada was prepared to violently oppose attempts to (re-)establish self-determining Indigenous nations. Following violent suppression of the five-month-long Northwest Rebellion in 1885, Canadian troops carried out the largest mass hanging in Canadian history. Louis Riel was captured at this time and was hanged separately shortly thereafter.

In 1876, the *Indian Act* was passed, which combined and extended various acts that had been previously adopted to govern and assimilate Indigenous peoples. The

Indian Act is an invasive piece of legislation that attempts to assert governmental control over every aspect of Indigenous life. To begin, it establishes control over who can be recognized as a "status Indian." As Métis writer Chelsea Vowel (2016: 35) sees it: "The Canadian government basically takes the position that, 'you're an Indian if we *say* you're an Indian.'" The *Indian Act* also created reserves, an apartheid land system that established designated tracts of land held by the Canadian government for the exclusive use of recognized Indian bands. These tracts of land represent tiny fractions of the traditional lands used and claimed by Indigenous peoples (with some entirely outside traditional territories); were established in isolated and remote locations with intentionally little value in terms of agriculture or resource extraction; and were (and continue to be) systematically under-resourced and ignored. Though not formally codified into the *Indian Act*, in practice there was a government policy establishing that, in order to travel outside one's reserve, Indigenous peoples had to ask for a "pass" from the Indian agent in charge of their band. Additionally, cultural and spiritual practices integral to Indigenous community life, like the Potlach and the Sundance, were outlawed. Indigenous peoples were also forbidden from obtaining a lawyer (and raising funds to obtain a lawyer) for the purposes of challenging Canada's discriminatory policies and would face imprisonment if they did. As Prime Minister MacDonald proclaimed, "the great aim of our legislation has been to do away with the tribal system and assimilate the Indian people in all respects with the other inhabitants of the Dominion, as speedily as they are fit for the change" (Beazley 2017: n.p.).

A particularly insidious feature of the *Indian Act* was the establishment of Indian residential schools. These schools were a tool used by the Canadian government to inflict far-reaching harm upon generations of Indigenous young people in the name of "civilizing" them. The goal was to enforce a physical, cultural and spiritual separation between Indigenous young people and their lands, languages, cultures and families — in short, from the very thing that animates nationhood: Indigeneity. Residential schools operated in Canada for 150 years, with the last school only closing its doors in 1996. The Canadian government entrusted the operation of these schools largely to the Roman Catholic Church, with Anglican, United and Presbyterian churches also playing significant, but smaller, roles. Overall, it is estimated that 150,000 Indigenous young people attended these schools. Residential schools were places of routine physical and sexual abuse, and — as the recovering of mass, unmarked graves at residential school sites across the country is emphasizing — all too often proved to be deadly for Indigenous

> Residential schools operated in Canada for 150 years, with the last school only closing its doors in 1996.

young people. The Truth and Reconciliation Commission of Canada (TRC) estimated in 2016 that least six thousand Indigenous young people died in the residential school system. However, the recovery of hundreds of remains from unmarked graves and intentionally poor recordkeeping in schools leads us to believe this number is undoubtedly too low.

As is by now clear, from the early formation of the Canadian state, there have been egregious violations of the basic human rights of Indigenous peoples. Through the denial of basic human rights, or the removal of Indigenous peoples' rights through various colonial policies, the settler-colonial project was furthered. Nonetheless, Indigenous peoples have persisted and demanded reckoning. And as we now turn, for a period, this has taken the shape of recognition.

Recognizing Rights

Beginning in the 1950s, the relationship between Canada and Indigenous peoples began to gradually shift. In 1951, the government proposed a series of amendments that granted Indigenous women the right to vote in band council elections and removed the bans on communal practices like the Sundance and the Potlatch. As well, the ban on organizing a legal challenge to the Canadian state was lifted, opening the door for future legal action. Unfortunately, the amendments did not lift the gendered discrimination within the *Indian Act*, and instead they created more avenues for Indigenous women to lose their Indian status. All Indigenous people were still barred from being able to vote in elections without relinquishing their status first, a profoundly unjust clause that would only be removed in 1960. These amendments also clarified limited provincial jurisdiction over child welfare, which led to the Sixties Scoop — a process whereby provincial officials forcefully removed Indigenous young people from their families to place them for adoption. As Métis writer Chelsea Vowel (2016: 181) argues, "the Sixties Scoop picked up where the residential schools left off," continuing a process of "cultural annihilation." It is estimated that over twenty thousand Indigenous young people were affected by this insidious process (Fournier and Crey 1997), causing irreparable intergenerational trauma.

In 1969, Prime Minister Pierre E. Trudeau and Indian Affairs minister John Chrétien tabled *The Position of the Canadian Government on Indian Policy*, also known as the "White Paper." In the White Paper, it was argued that

> not always, but too often, to be an Indian is to be without — without a job, a good house, or running water, without knowledge, training or technical skill, and above all, without those feelings of dignity and self confidence that a man must have if he is to walk with his head held high…. Special treatment

has made of Indians a community disadvantaged and apart. Obviously, the course of history must be changed. (Government of Canada 1969: 1)

Therefore, the Government of Canada was taking the position that it was Indigenous peoples' specific social and legal status that was disadvantaging and excluding them from the quality of life being enjoyed by the rest of Canada. The solution proposed in the White Paper was, among other things, to abolish the *Indian Act*. This would mean the elimination of Indian status altogether, turning reserves into private property to be owned and/or sold away by band councils, and the dismantling of the Department of Indian Affairs — all in the name of equality for Indigenous peoples. Strangely, the promise of equality for Indigenous peoples was premised on the very erasure of their recognition as Indigenous peoples altogether. The White Paper represented yet another attempt at the total assimilation of Indigenous peoples, this time through the language of multicultural inclusion and individual equality. This misguided attempt at "addition by subtraction" — increasing Indigenous peoples' rights and equality by subtracting their rights and statuses *as Indigenous peoples* — was swiftly and effectively opposed by Indigenous peoples across the country, leading the government to put the White Paper to rest in 1971.

> The White Paper represented yet another attempt at the total assimilation of Indigenous peoples.

Dene scholar Glenn Coulthard argues that settler colonialism in Canada has shifted since the White Paper, "from a more or less unconcealed structure of domination to a form of colonial governance that works through the medium of state recognition and accommodation" (2014: 24). In other words, the Canadian state began to recognize some of the past harms it had inflicted upon Indigenous communities and some of the limited rights that Indigenous peoples were entitled to. As many Indigenous scholars remind us, however, this did not fundamentally change or challenge the settler-colonial relationship between Canada and Indigenous peoples. Instead, this "politics of recognition" continued to facilitate the dispossession of Indigenous peoples from their lands.

Take, for example, the landmark legal recognitions of Indigenous rights that followed closely after the White Paper was summarily defeated. In 1973, the court decision *Calder v. British Columbia* was the first time the Canadian courts recognized that Indigenous peoples had legal title to their lands prior to the arrival of European settlers. The courts argued that "Indian title" was not automatically extinguished with the arrival of settlers or explorers but had to be clearly surrendered to the Crown (Asch 2014). While the definition, extent and implications of "Indian title" were not prescribed, the *Calder* case opened the door for many future court cases.

For example, in 1973 the James Bay Cree organized a significant challenge to a massive hydroelectric dam project that was to be constructed on their lands. Their opposition was premised upon their historical claims and uses of the lands that would be flooded or otherwise transformed by the dam project. In response to this opposition, in 1975 the *James Bay and Northern Quebec Agreement* was signed, which

> stipulated that, in exchange for agreeing to extinguish rights based on the pre-existence of their societies, the Cree and the other Indigenous communities (including the Inuit of the region) would receive both cash compensation and specified rights, including some that provided significant protection for and enhancement of their traditional economy and society in lands not flooded. (Asch 2014: 19)

This agreement was an early example of how Indigenous rights to land were addressed by the Canadian government: a one-time cash payment and a handful of specific rights in exchange for extinguishing all future claims to land and rights. Importantly, the Agreement set a precedent for future disputes over claims to and uses of land by Indigenous nations.

In 1982, the historic signing of the Canadian Constitution and the *Charter of Rights and Freedoms* included references to both "Aboriginal rights" and "Aboriginal title," codifying them in the country's most important legal document. Importantly, the Constitution did not specify the content of these codified rights, leaving their interpretation up to the courts. Soon after, in 1985, many (though not all) of the aspects of the *Indian Act* that were designed to strip Indigenous women of their status were revoked, returning formal recognition of status to thousands of Indigenous women and starting a long process of gradually reinstating status to more and more women (Lawrence 2003). Indigenous peoples welcomed this shift in tone from the federal government but remained skeptical about the possibility of the newfound recognition translating into meaningful shifts in the settler-colonial relationship.

In 1990, there would be a conflict that would lay bare the limit of recognized Indigenous rights. Oka, a town near Kanehsatà:ke, unilaterally approved plans to expand a golf course and build a residential development on traditional Kanehsatà:ke land. This was strongly opposed by members of the Mohawk community, as the development would further encroach on The Pines, a place of great historical significance and a Mohawk burial site. There was little consultation with Kanehsatà:ke and no assessments of the development's environmental or historical impact were conducted. In response, the Mohawk erected barricades to block access to the area. The result was an extraordinary police and military campaign against Kanehsatà:ke land defenders. Initially, the Quebec Provincial Police were sent to use force to break the blockade. The police used tear gas, flash-bang grenades and guns to attempt remove the barricades, but they were unsuccessful. After the police retreated and word got out, Indigenous peoples and their allies from across the country offered their support for the barricades. The Canadian government then assigned 3,700 military troops to remove the blockade. A seventy-eight-day standoff ensued, becoming the largest Canadian military operation since the Korean War ended in 1953. Negotiations between the Mohawks of Kanehsatà:ke and federal and provincial governments did not resolve the dispute. Faced with further military action, the Mohawks chose to leave the barricades peacefully. The police arrested many of the land defenders, but all were eventually acquitted, and the land dispute remains ultimately unresolved (for more information, see Simpson and Ladner 2010).

We share this story to demonstrate what has happened when Indigenous peoples asserted the very rights and land titles that the Canadian government claimed to recognize. The events above are now commonly referred to as the "Oka Crisis," which frames the assertion of Indigenous rights as a "crisis" to be responded to violently by the government. We would contend, however, that the events at Oka reveal a deeper crisis: the foundational conflict between, on the one hand, Indigenous rights and land title, and the Canadian government's claim to unilateral sovereignty on the other. The Kanehsatà:ke land defence represents a turning point for how the Canadian government would approach its relationship with Indigenous peoples. Recognizing the rights of Indigenous peoples had opened the door for a wide variety of claims and conflicts; the Canadian government would now attempt to close that door by trying to "reconcile" these rights with its own claims to sovereignty, with the goal of "settling" the question of Indigenous land claims once and for all.

Reconciling Rights

In the years following the 1990 Oka Crisis and into the 2000s, a period of substantive efforts to reconcile the rights of Indigenous peoples evolved. While this period built on the victories of advocacy in previous decades, particularly in the judicial context, progress was and remains uneven and fraught with imbalances of political power made highly visible through the events of Oka. As we will show, judicial ruling on Aboriginal and treaty rights have consistently stalled, and when they have occurred, they have tended to advance only through processes that advantage the Canadian state. Indigenous governance arrangements and policy frameworks have steadily evolved in ways that are heavily weighted toward protecting the state and that require the reconciling of Indigenous rights claims with the often-unquestioned sovereignty of the Canadian Crown. Importantly, "reconciling rights" as discussed here is not so much a matter of processes that promote ethical relations between Indigenous peoples and settler society, but instead processes that seek to address the incommensurability of inherent Indigenous rights with the goals of the settler state. In addition to these judicial, legislative and policy processes, this era of reconciliation has also seen the expansion of Indigenous rights advocacy through transitional justice processes, such as commissions, inquiries and judicial and non-judicial mechanisms for redress and reform.

Beginning with lawsuits as an example, in the early 1990s, a Stó:lō woman from British Columbia, Dorothy Van der Peet, was charged for selling salmon caught under a non-commercial fishing licence. Provincial legislation prohibited the sale of salmon under this licence to non-Indigenous people. Indigenous fishing rights extended only to the harvesting of fish for food and cultural and ceremonial tradition. Van der Peet challenged the Province of British Columbia in court on the basis that her Aboriginal and treaty rights that were recognized and affirmed by the Constitution were, in this case, contravened. Her appeal ultimately went to the Supreme Court of Canada, which affirmed her rights as a Stó:lō person to fish for personal and ceremonial purposes but ruled that these rights do not include selling fish. The Supreme Court's ruling was not unanimous, and two dissenting judges established a precedent that an Aboriginal right needed to be consistent with customs and land uses that could be proven to pre-date European colonization. It also provided clarity for Indigenous rights advocates on how to demonstrate a right within the Canadian judicial system — for example, based on oral histories, tradition or other non-Western forms of documentation. However, the ruling effectively froze the definition of "Aboriginal rights" in the past and set the legal agenda for "reconciling" this past with the settler-colonial present. Consider this passage: "Aboriginal rights recognized and affirmed by s. 35(1) must be directed towards the *reconciliation* of the pre-existence of aboriginal societies with the sovereignty of the Crown" (*R. v. Van der Peet* 1996).

The uneven process of reconciling rights extended into the Canadian government's dealings with lands, through major land claims settlements like that of the *James Bay and Northern Quebec Agreement* in 1975 and the *Nunavut Land Claims Agreement Act* in 1993. It also extended into the domain of specific claims dating back to the late nineteenth century. Specific claims made by Indigenous nations against Canada dealt primarily with the issue of lands, waterways and other matters of Indigenous rights afforded by treaties in the formation of the settler state. By the early 1990s, there were hundreds of unsettled specific claims. While the comprehensive and specific land claims processes[3] do offer an avenue to partially redress past injustices, their ultimate goal is to "settle" these disputes with one-time deals that preclude any future negotiations on the matters.

In response to the conflict in Oka, in 1991 the Royal Commission on Aboriginal Peoples was established to address the challenges of Indigenous-Canadian relations. As one of the first major transitional justice processes enacted by the Canadian government, this commission was to make concrete recommendations to enhance the quality of relationship of Indigenous peoples with the Crown. In 1996, the Royal Commission on Aboriginal Peoples released a four-thousand-page report with 440 recommendations to facilitate renewed relationships between Indigenous peoples and the state, including ideas like the devolution of the *Indian Act*, frameworks for Indigenous self-governance and the need for an independent tribunal to advance settlement on historic claims. In 1997, in a special report called *Gathering Strength,* the government committed to acting on only a handful of these recommendations, laid out specific recommendations to advance settlement and gestured towards terms of self-government.

While the precedent established in the 1970s made clear that Aboriginal title pre-existed the arrival of Europeans, reconciliation through settlement processes developed with the primary goal of maintaining the authority and protection of the Crown. It also rejected the idea that Aboriginal title exists in perpetuity by enacting a process where the settlement of claims occurs through the extinguishing or modification of rights in a one-time negotiation. Reconciling rights in this period remains contested because, ultimately, "settling" rights claims through government processes serves the interests of the Crown. Colonial infringements on Indigenous peoples' rights — be that through treaty, historical expansion or ongoing treaty violations — would never be overturned, but instead could be settled legally at least one time and remained settled in perpetuity.

> Ultimately, "settling" rights claims through government processes serves the interests of the Crown.

The 2000s have become defined by a new governmental language and posture of reconciliation. While much more austere under Harper's Conservative government, Prime Minister Justin Trudeau's Liberals have fully embraced the term. We are now in a time when the federal and, to a lesser extent, provincial governments will more openly admit their past wrongs, apologize for them and commit to "reconciling" these events while restoring a "nation-to-nation" relationship. Consider prime ministers Harper and Trudeau publicly apologizing for the violence of the residential school system; the rebranding of the Department of Crown-Indigenous Relations; the establishing of a National Day of Truth and Reconciliation; or even Minister Marc Miller appropriating the Indigenous movement demand of #LandBack in a press conference. Reconciliation is the defining term of this phase of settler colonialism, but we must ask: has it resulted in tangible, meaningful and ongoing shifts in the power relations between settler governments and Indigenous peoples?

ADVANCING INDIGENOUS PEOPLES' RIGHTS

As our brief survey of the history of Indigenous peoples' rights in Canada highlights, Indigenous peoples have consistently resisted the imposition of settler colonialism and demanded justice at the level of basic human rights and rights as Indigenous peoples living amid and often in the crosshairs of a settler-colonial society. In reckoning with the history of settler colonialism, this following section highlights two important approaches to Indigenous rights in Canada.

Equal Rights?

What does equality mean under settler colonialism? Are Indigenous peoples' rights special and does that create social inequalities in Canada? The 1969 White Paper, critiqued for its assimilationist agenda, was built on the assumption that Indigenous peoples experienced disadvantage and exclusion in Canada through the presence of legislated distinction in Canadian law. It proposed the abolition of the *Indian Act* and the dissolution of treaties and corresponding rights, along with the devolution of colonial governance as a means of achieving the notion of equality under the law.

The abolition of the *Indian Act* and the devolution of colonial governance structures like the reserve system reveal an important quandary to consider in the context of Indigenous rights advocacy. Given that the *Indian Act* and its associated governance structures such as the reserve system are in fact deeply problematic and oppressive for Indigenous peoples, shouldn't we seek to abolish the Act altogether? The answer is not so simple. Indigenous advocates in the 1960s understood this clearly. Cree lawyer and Chief Harold Cardinal explained:

> We do not want the Indian Act retained because it is a good piece of legislation. It isn't. It is discriminatory from start to finish. But it is a lever in our hands and an embarrassment to the government, as it should be. No just society and no society with even pretensions to being just can long tolerate such a piece of legislation, but we would rather continue to live in bondage under the inequitable Indian Act than surrender our sacred rights. Any time the government wants to honour its obligations to us we are more than happy to help devise new Indian legislation. (1999: 140)

The *Indian Act*, which is at its core an apartheid legislation, results in racial inequities. It is fundamentally a piece of legislation that has been used to racially segregate people and specifies differential treatment for some and not others. For example, it structures inequitable funding for public services for Indigenous children on reserve, who receive much less per-capita funding than non-Indigenous children. Nonetheless, the abolition of the *Indian Act* and the systems of governance that animate its administration is tricky, as it also affords some of the few legislative and legal mechanisms available to make the government accountable for the delivery of treaty and Aboriginal rights.

In 1996, the Royal Commission on Aboriginal People called for a range of reforms to the *Indian Act*, as have subsequent commissions including the Truth and Reconciliation Commission on Indian Residential Schools in 2015. At the time of the first election of Prime Minister Justin Trudeau in 2015, discussion of reforms to the *Indian Act*, its modernization and its potential abolition again gained prominence amid national calls for reconciliation. But this too was widely rejected. As Mi'kmaw legal scholar Dr. Pam Palmater writes:

> Yes, the Indian Act is racist; it was designed with the intention of legislating Indians out of existence.... However, the complexities of the Indian Act [go] beyond racism. It also serves as a legislative tool by which to hold the federal government accountable for their legal responsibilities. (2019: n.p.)

The proposed abolition of the *Indian Act* obscures the ongoing inequalities of human rights experienced by Indigenous peoples as well as the denial of Aboriginal and treaty rights. To erase Indigenous status, even as imperfectly and offensively as it is described in the *Indian Act*, is to erase the evidence of genocidal violence altogether and negates the fiduciary responsibilities of the settler state. What comes to matter is the kind of mechanism that could replace the *Indian Act*, one that ensures equality of human rights for all people in Canada, without negation of special rights afforded to Indigenous peoples living within a settler-colonial society.

> To erase Indigenous status is to erase the evidence of genocidal violence altogether.

Enhanced Rights

Contrary to the proposals noted above, which essentially constitute a modern form of enfranchisement, there have also been attempts to *enhance* the specific and unique rights of Indigenous peoples. We can see evidence of this in the Red Paper, which was the Indigenous response to Prime Minister Pierre Trudeau's White Paper. Delivered to Parliament in 1970 by the Indian Association of Alberta and backed by the Indian Brotherhood, the Red Paper rejected the claim that any legal or legislative differences with respect to Indigenous peoples should be removed in the name of "equal" rights.

Instead, the Red Paper argues:

> We say that the recognition of Indian status is essential for justice. Retaining the legal status of Indians is necessary if Indians are to be treated justly. Justice requires that the special history, rights and circumstances of Indian People be recognized. (Indian Chiefs of Alberta, 1970: 192)

In other words, rather than the elimination of difference between Indigenous and non-Indigenous people as the "solution" to the "Indian problem," the Red Paper claimed the opposite: it is the recognition of the historical, cultural and political uniqueness of Indigenous peoples that will form the basis of justice. We can see in the history we recounted above how this approach eventually becomes the norm and informs the future of Indigenous-Canada relations.

One of the most prominent frameworks that has taken the approach of enhancing Indigenous rights as the pathway toward justice is the United Nations Declaration on the Rights of Indigenous Peoples (UNDRIP). Passed in 2007, UNDRIP is one of the most comprehensive frameworks outlining Indigenous rights. It is therefore somewhat unsurprising that it was four prominent settler-colonial states that opposed its adoption at the United Nations: Canada, the United States, Australia and New Zealand. The Declaration begins with two articles affirming that Indigenous peoples are entitled to enjoy the same rights as everyone else. But the next three articles recognize Indigenous peoples' rights to self-determination (Article 3); to autonomy or self-government in matters related to local affairs and finances (Article 4); and to "maintain and strengthen their distinct political, legal, economic, social, and cultural institutions, while retaining their right to participate fully, if they so choose, in the political, economic, social and cultural life of the State" (Article 5; UNDRIP 2007: 8-9). The Declaration then continues to outline various political, economic, social and cultural rights and protections for Indigenous peoples.

In 2016, Canada removed its permanent objector status to UNDRIP. And in June 2021, Parliament adopted legislation requiring the government to align its laws with the Declaration. At the time of writing, there is little detail about what exactly this will entail. Is this another symbolic manoeuvre in the name of pro-government reconciliation? Maybe. But there is also cautious optimism on behalf of Indigenous communities that this may represent the first step toward establishing a more equal, nation-to-nation relationship that respects and enhances the rights of Indigenous peoples.

Beyond Rights

As we have shown so far, many historical and contemporary discourses, policies and activisms related to Canada's relationship with Indigenous peoples have orbited around the concept and language of rights. Historically, Indigenous peoples have been denied even the most basic human rights. In response, many politicians, policymakers, advocates and Indigenous peoples have demanded not only rights equal to those of Canadian citizens, but enhanced rights that respond to histories of colonialism and protect Indigenous peoples from its ongoing effects.

However, we argue that to resist and eventually transcend colonialism — settler or otherwise — we need more than just rights. We are certainly not the first to argue this. In a now much-quoted passage, Hannah Arendt responded to the 1948 United Nations Declaration of Human Rights by asking who, in fact, possesses "the right to have rights" (1973: 298)? Here, Arendt points toward the gap between the theory and practice of human rights: While they are inherent to each person in theory, they are only effective and enforced through the state in practice. In other words, human rights today only exist insofar as a state is willing to recognize and respect them. Therefore, human rights can be given and taken away at the whim of a government, regardless of their universality in principle. For

> Human rights today only exist insofar as a state is willing to recognize and respect them.

example, consider how the Canadian state choses to enforce the rights of corporations to impose pipelines, strip mines and fracking fields on Indigenous territories at gunpoint but seems to ignore the basic right to clean drinking water on dozens of reserves. Appeals to rights may therefore have the effect of reinforcing the legitimacy and rightful authority of the settler state to adjudicate the nature, scope and application of Indigenous rights. And while there have been important strides made by the federal and provincial governments along with the courts, history teaches us to understand the limitations of leaving the rights of Indigenous peoples in the hands of settler political and legal systems. Indeed, Indigenous scholars have convincingly shown that the limited recognition of Indigenous peoples' rights in the name of reconciliation and affirming a "nation-to-nation" relationship can actually serve to entrench the underlying power of the settler state while reinforcing unequal power relationships between the Canadian government and Indigenous peoples (Ladner 2001; Coulthard 2014).

TOWARD RIGHT RELATIONS

In response to the limits of a human rights approach, we do not advocate a turning away from rights altogether. Rather, we follow many Indigenous scholars and communities in employing a historically informed skepticism toward appeals to human rights. We also acknowledge the possibilities that emerge when Indigenous peoples and settlers turn away from the state and toward each other to build relationships of mutual recognition and solidarity. Below, we sketch some initial directions for action that seek to move past human rights and toward developing right relations with each other. We consider ways to invigorate processes of public education and truth telling about the history of settler colonialism and the rights of Indigenous peoples. We discuss the importance of anti-colonial resistance and collective action for land defence. Finally, we consider what it means to form ethical relations through the practice of resurgence.

Toward Right Relations through Education and Truth Telling

As the history of Canada has unfolded, colonial education in its many forms, such as residential schools, has sought to bring about the type of conformity that further extinguishes Indigenous peoples' presence and claims to self-determinism. If we are to move toward right relations, education for the purpose of Indigenous freedom is urgently needed. Indeed, public education holds great promise to advance Indigenous rights and strengthen Indigenous-Canadian relations, and this can occur in a variety of ways, including through projects of public memory, educational reform and at the level of individual and community learning.

> Education for the purpose of Indigenous freedom is urgently needed.

In terms of public memory, one of the substantive contributions of the Truth and Reconciliation process in Canada was its national engagement in truth telling about the history of residential schools and its effects. As a process, inviting people to share these experiences and convening contexts for people to bear witness to this history highlights the importance of large-scale efforts to bolster public memory of our collective past and present responsibilities. Projects of public memorialization of this history are important and can occur through various practices, including engagement within the cultural sector (museums, broadcasting and days of commemoration). While these things do not in and of themselves materially improve the status of Indigenous peoples or alter the settler-colonial relationship, they do indeed play a role in creating the social conditions for positive engagement and increased public attention on these matters.

Further, major reforms are needed within public education systems to advance better relationships. The TRC envisioned these reforms occurring at every level of public education, with reforms to early childhood education through to university. To achieve this, we need much more dynamic accounts of Canadian and Indigenous histories, treaty education, Indigenous rights education, Indigenous inclusion within social studies and civic education, as well as Indigenous language education. And within university education, knowledge related to ensuring and promoting Indigenous rights needs to be infused within every discipline, with pathways into various social and public sectors. This responsibility extends far beyond surface-level efforts to simply hire more diverse staff and add a handful of courses that focus on Indigenous issues. Commitments to transformative education require comprehensive commitments to integrating not only reconciliation, but stronger workplace protections, anti-racism, gender justice and disability justice into every aspect of educational institutions. It cannot, for example, be solely up to the handful of Indigenous faculty, Elders and student groups to lead an entire university's efforts to engage in reconciliation.

True reconciliation is crucial to building a better future for everyone, and it therefore requires the active participation of Indigenous and non-Indigenous people in creating not only better educational institutions but a more just society. Education is our individual responsibility, and so each person and community can take everyday steps towards learning their own personal histories and intersecting responsibilities to Indigenous peoples. The stakes are high. In the absence of these efforts, negation and denialism can fester, as evidenced recently by prominent Canadian political leaders. For example, former Manitoba premier Brian Pallister recently propagated historical revisionism when he stated that "[t]he people who came to this country before it was a country and since, didn't come to destroy anything. They came here to build" (Stranger 2021: n.p.). Here, Pallister obscures the fact that Indigenous peoples were displaced from their lands and their political, economic and social orders were intentionally *destroyed* in order to *build* a settler-colonial state and society in their place. Moreover, the absence of truth telling and public education about our histories, rights and responsibilities can lead to increased political polarization and the expanding violence of the settler state. If no one knows about our own histories, rights and responsibilities, the burden of holding governments and people accountable is left on the shoulders of those most oppressed by it — Indigenous peoples.

Toward Right Relations through Resistance and Land Defence

We mentioned earlier the need to move from a rights- and responsibilities-based framework to achieve meaningful steps toward justice. If one good thing has come from the chorus of reconciliation talk we're hearing, it is that it reveals the responsibilities of settler society to seriously reckon with and redress the past and ongoing colonial violence against Indigenous peoples. For non-Indigenous people, the TRC's ninety-four Calls to Action all centre upon the responsibilities of the Canadian government and every Canadian to take meaningful action toward reconciliation. We cannot expect the government to take the kind of initiative that is required to engage in true reconciliation. Perhaps more importantly, we cannot expect Indigenous peoples to continue to take on the majority of this work. It is the responsibility of non-Indigenous people and institutions to fully recognize their complicity in ongoing processes of settler colonialism and take tangible steps to divest from these power structures. This means challenging the status quo, opposing corporate encroachments onto Indigenous lands and holding provincial and federal governments accountable to turn their symbolic embrace of reconciliation into tangible legal and legislative reforms. While not explicitly contained within the TRC's Calls to Action, we see participating in social movements and collective acts of resistance as an additional and crucial step toward cultivating right relations.

Social movements and collective actions are necessary when the Canadian government and the status quo inevitably fail to address issues of inequality and injustice in society. Therefore, when Indigenous rights are not recognized or upheld by settler governments or corporations, Indigenous peoples must mobilize outside of traditional political processes like elections or consultations and instead take direct action. For example, in the fall of 2012, the Idle No More movement emerged to challenge the adoption of Bill C-45, inconspicuously named the *Jobs and Growth Act*, by Harper's Conservative government. Bill C-45 was a four-hundred-page omnibus bill that removed environmental protections from hundreds of lakes and rivers across Canada and facilitated resource development projects by limiting the need for environmental impact assessments, among other changes. In response, four women from Saskatchewan started a public campaign called "Idle No More" to educate people about Bill C-45 and organize popular, non-violent actions to oppose it (Kinonda-niimi Collective 2014). A week before the Senate was expected to pass the Bill, Theresa Spence, then the Chief of the Cree Nation of Attawapiskat, declared she would begin a hunger strike near Parliament Hill to bring awareness to Indigenous critiques of Bill C-45 as well as to highlight the housing crisis unfolding in her own community. Idle No More teach-ins, flash mobs, drum circles, public demonstrations and road and railway blockades appeared across the country in December 2012 and January 2013. The movement commanded national attention, shedding a harsh light on the continued inequalities experienced by Indigenous peoples across the country. The mass social mobilization resulted in a sweeping Declaration of Commitment by the Assembly of First Nations, the Native Women's Association of Canada and the federal New Democratic and Liberal parties. While Bill C-45 was ultimately passed without consultation with Indigenous communities or amendments, Idle No More revealed the breadth of support for Indigenous rights across Canada.

Idle No More is just one of countless mobilizations and social movements that have been organized by Indigenous and non-Indigenous people to challenge the continued political, legal, economic and socio-cultural conditions faced by Indigenous peoples in Canada. From Kitchenuhmaykoosib Inninuwug to Gustafsen Lake, Elispogtog to Barriere Lake, Grassy Narrows to Wet'suwet'en, people have taken collective actions that, in some cases, represent a demand to respect Indigenous rights and, other times, respond to the limits of such rights and demand forms of justice that extend beyond state-based rights. These Indigenous struggles are only bolstered by the humble solidarity and participation of non-Indigenous people, who see it as their responsibility to offer their time, resources and sometimes physical bodies in support of Indigenous peoples defending their lands and asserting their rights. Consider the railroad blockades across the country in support of Wet'suwet'en land defenders (CTV 2020), or the bi-annual "River Runs" (Letson and Lannon 2021) and direct actions (Leslie 2016) supporting the people of Grassy Narrows First Nation in their fight against mercury poisoning in their community. Such collective acts are a crucial avenue through which to hold settler governments and corporations accountable. For example, solidarity campaigns with Grassy Narrows First Nation successfully won $85 million from the Ontario government to clean the community's river of the high levels of mercury (Bruser, Benzie and Poisson 2017), and another $69 million to help build a care centre for those in the community suffering from mercury poisoning (CBC 2021). But participation in collective acts of solidarity and in social movements are also generative spaces through which to begin forging decolonial relationships within and across Indigenous and settler positionalities and, in the process, create pathways toward social transformation.

Toward Right Relations through Resurgence

In the face of centuries of colonial genocide, Indigenous scholars and communities have emphasized the importance of protecting, regenerating and critically reconstituting Indigenous traditions. Michi Saagiig Nishnaabeg writer Leanne Betasamosake Simpson explores the need balance "trying to transform the colonial outside" with efforts to promote "the flourishment of the *Indigenous* inside." She continues:

> We need to rebuild our own culturally inherent philosophical context for governance, education, healthcare, and economy. We need to be able to articulate in a clear manner our visions for the future, for living as *Indigenous Peoples* in contemporary times. (2011: 17)

Indigenous scholars have conceptualized this process of regenerating Indigenous laws, languages, cultural practices, political structures and knowledges as *Indigenous resurgence*. The point here is not to literally return to static conceptions of the past, but to "explore the role that critically revitalized traditions might play in the (re)construction of decolonized Indigenous nations" (Coulthard 2014: 148; see also Simpson 2011). Resurgence is therefore not only the critical revitalization of Indigenous traditions themselves, but also found in the *process* of regenerating, reconstructing and living these traditions (Alfred and Corntassel 2005).

Land reclamations in both urban and non-urban spaces also constitute efforts to revitalize Indigenous relationships to land and cultural practices. The Oshkimaadziig Unity Camp, which was in what is now Awenda Provincial Park in southern Ontario, reclaimed a sacred site, council rock, as well as a place traditionally used for treaty-making and communication between Anishinaabe and Haudenosaunee nations. For nearly five years, the land reclamation camp sought to

> reclaim and reignite traditional teachings, ceremonies, and governance structures in order to resist the unbroken legacy of colonialism in Canada. The space is meant to provide an environment within which relations old and new, with First Nations and settlers, may be made and remade through the fundamental principles of peace, co-existence, and non-interference. (Gardner and Giibwanisi 2014: 169)

There are innumerable other examples of land reclamations that resist settler colonialism and seek to regenerate Indigenous traditions. From the Tiny House Warriors in Secwepemc territories to the Kanonhstaton occupation in Six Nations, from the Rooster Town Blockade in Winnipeg (Treaty 1 territory) to the Unist'ot'en camp on Wet'suwet'en territories, Indigenous peoples are asserting their presence on their traditional lands and creating spaces of autonomy and self-governance. Many other forms of resurgence exist, but at their core they share a commitment to taking collective action to revitalize Indigenous traditions and reclaim land with the goal of establishing autonomous and *Indigenous* space within, against and beyond the settler-colonial state.

An important feature of Indigenous resurgence is that it does not depend on the recognition of the state. It is a turning away from appeals for rights and a turning toward the (re)creation of strong Indigenous communities rooted in the very traditions that the Canadian state intended to erase. Indeed, as Lee Maracle (1996: 40) remarks, "before I can understand what independence is, I must break the chains that imprison me in the present, impede my understanding of the past, and blind me to the future." Therefore, Maracle reminds us that it is just as important to

struggle against the colonial state for independence as it is to recover Indigenous traditions that would ground and animate such independence. In a similar vein, Leanne
Betasamosake Simpson notes:

> We do not need funding to do this. We do not need a friendly colonial polit-
> ical climate to do this. We do not need opportunity to do this. We need our
> Elders, our languages, and our lands, along with vision, intent, commitment,
> community, and ultimately, action. We must move ourselves beyond resist-
> ance and survival, to flourishment and mino bimaadiziwin.[4] (2011: 17)

Here we see that Indigenous resurgence involves both a negation — a resistance and
refusal of the settler-colonial present — and an affirmation of Indigenous lifeways. It
is this affirmation and flourishing of Indigeneity in the face of ongoing colonial genocide that arguably makes resurgence such a potent approach to establishing "right
relations" between Indigenous peoples and Canadian society. Indeed, Indigenous resurgence "draw[s] strength and sustenance that is independent of colonial power …
[and] is regenerative of an authentic, autonomous, Indigenous existence" (Alfred and
Corntassel 2005: 613). Rather than reproducing asymmetrical and unequal relations
by depending on government processes of recognition and reconciliation, strategies
of resurgence take the term self-determination literally: it is not a power given to
Indigenous peoples by the government, but a power that comes from within strong
Indigenous communities. By refusing to seek recognition from the settler state and
asserting their rights and self-determination, Indigenous resurgence puts the onus
on settler society to reconcile its relationship with Indigenous nations, not the other
way around. Put another way, when Indigenous peoples reassert their nationhood
through practices of resurgence, it necessitates that the settler state reconcile itself to
Indigenous nations rather than Indigenous nations to the Crown.

Resurgence is a practice that is concerned with enhancing ethical relations and
self-determinism for Indigenous peoples, and this can be actualized in many ways.
It is something that can be understood as our personal and collective responsibility
to oppose colonialism and foster decolonial spaces and relationships at the level of
the everyday. That is, we can learn to align ourselves and our relationships through
the lens of Indigenous ways of being and doing, in the intimate, the proximal and
the everyday spaces of our lives. As Cherokee political scientist Jeff Corntassel (2018:
17) writes, "focusing on everydayness helps make visible the often unseen or unacknowledged actions that embody Indigenous nationhood." As Sarah Hunt and Cindy
Holmes (2015: 157–58) remind us, "while large-scale actions such as rallies, protests
and blockades are frequently acknowledged as sites of resistance, the daily actions
undertaken by individual Indigenous people, families and communities often go

unacknowledged but are no less vital to decolonial process." The everydayness of resurgence looks like the principles of self-de-
terminism and respect for the dignity of all
relations in the most intimate spaces of one's
life: how you treat your friends, partners,
families, animals, land and indeed yourself.

> The everydayness of resurgence is self-determinism in the most intimate spaces of one's life.

Everyday actions are not universal, but
deeply contextual. If you find yourself in the Prairies, perhaps this everydayness begins in learning about the history of numbered treaties or standing with those who
oppose fracking. If you find yourself in the Maritimes, it is in learning about the
history of fishing rights and standing with Mi'kmaq and Maliseet against the rising
encroachment of these rights by boycotting non-Indigenous commercial fisheries.
If you are living on the Great lakes, perhaps your learning is to understand the Dish
With One Spoon treaty and to enact our collective responsibilities to water protection by holding corporations responsible for privatizing clean water and polluting
public water sources, or organizing against the dumping of toxic waste into Ontario's
freshwater channels. If you find yourself on the shores of the Salish Sea, perhaps
your responsibility is to learn about resource extraction and crude oil, and to join
with land defenders not only in opposing pipelines expansion, but in reducing your
carbon footprint. If you find yourself in the North, in Inuit Nunangat, then perhaps
your practice is to learn to speak Inuktitut or Inuinnaqtun, because with each word
spoken you are protecting a language and a way of life.

The rights of Indigenous peoples to land, self-determination and dignity have
always existed. These rights were violently stripped away by European settlers
and then by the Canadian government. Against centuries of genocidal violence,
Indigenous peoples have continued to affirm their Indigeneity, protect their cultures
and assert their rights. The Canadian government has tried strategies of removing,
recognizing and reconciling the rights of Indigenous peoples in ways that protect its
sovereignty and limit Indigenous self-determination. This chapter has illuminated
two perspectives on the past, present and future of Indigenous rights in Canada.
First, there are good reasons to fight for enhanced rights within and against the continued violence wrought by the Canadian state and society. Indeed, there have been
major victories won in this way. However, a rights-based approach is limited insofar
as it depends on colonial governments and courts to award and respect Indigenous
rights. Therefore, the second perspective offered here is one that encourages us to
think beyond human rights and toward establishing right relations. By turning our
focus away from appeals to power and toward taking tangible actions to challenge
colonialism — be it through organizing opposition to unjust government policies,
environmental destruction by corporations, racist policing practices or the kinds of

everyday actions discussed above — we enact new ways of being that are not fundamentally defined by the logics of settler colonialism. Working toward right relations
is an important way to transcend the limits of human rights and foster new relationships based on principles of solidarity, mutual aid and decolonization.

DISCUSSION QUESTIONS

1. How do the practices of removing, recognizing and reconciling Indigenous rights
   overlap? Can you think of other examples of these practices?
2. Are Indigenous rights different from universal human rights? Explain why, along
   with where these rights might intersect.
3. What are some of the challenges involved in abolishing or reforming the *Indian Act*?
4. What are our responsibilities to uphold Indigenous rights? How does where we
   live shape our responsibilities to uphold Indigenous rights?
5. Are social movements and blockades effective ways to defend and uphold
   Indigenous rights?
6. What are some everyday acts that you can take toward establishing right relations?

GLOSSARY OF KEY TERMS

Aboriginal: A legal category defined by the Canadian state that includes First
Nations, Métis and Inuit peoples. There are Indigenous peoples in Canada who
are therefore not recognized as Aboriginal by the Canadian government.

Aboriginal rights: Rights that First Nations, Métis and Inuit peoples in Canada hold
that are based in constitutional recognition and treaty agreements and are interpreted and defined primarily by the judicial system.

Indian Act: A legislative act that governs many aspects of Aboriginal peoples' lives as
subjects of the Canadian state, from the process of registration and management
of lands through to the reserve system.

Indigenous rights: Indigenous rights are the inherent and collective rights to self-determination regarding governance, land, resources and culture of Indigenous nations. They account for, and respond to, the unique histories and positionalities
of Indigenous peoples vis-à-vis global processes of colonialism, imperialism and
genocide.

Resurgence: Resurgence is the process of Indigenous peoples enacting their self-determinism through regenerating Indigenous laws, languages, cultural practices,
political structures and knowledges.

Settler colonialism: A unique form of colonialism that seeks to construct an entire political, economic and social order on top of pre-existing Indigenous orders and lifeways. Settler-colonial societies pursue the dual goals of (1) acquiring sole possession of land for the purpose of profit, and (2) absorbing Indigenous peoples into settler society, thereby erasing histories of genocide.

Terra nullius: The Latin phrase "land belonging to nobody." It is a principle in international law that was used to justify European claims to sovereign control over lands that it occupied, which negated the historical presence of Indigenous nations.

Transitional justice: Processes and mechanisms — such as declarations, commissions, inquiries and judicial and non-judicial forums — for institutional, local and/or national redress and reform.

White Paper (1969): A policy document that proposed abolishing Aboriginal status, the *Indian Act* and all related treaty and Aboriginal law with it, in order to assimilate Indigenous peoples.

United Nations Declaration on the Rights of Indigenous Peoples: A comprehensive document outlining the universal and inexorable rights of Indigenous peoples around the world.

RESOURCES FOR ACTIVISTS

Truth and Reconciliation Commission of Canada Final Report and Calls to Action: nctr.ca/records/reports/
LandBack Movement: landback.org
Wet'suwet'en land defence: unistoten.camp and yintahaccess.com/news/calltoaction
Grassy Narrows Solidarity: freegrassy.net
The Yellowhead Institute: yellowheadinstitute.org
Indigenous Rising: indigenousrising.org
The Raven Trust: raventrust.com

NOTES

1   A note on terminology: "Indigenous peoples" is an expansive term meant to encompass all peoples with long histories of settlement and connection to specific lands, and who have experienced and resisted colonialism. "Aboriginal" is a specific legal category created by the Canadian government that includes First Nations, Métis and Inuit peoples. There are, therefore, Indigenous peoples in Canada who are not recognized as Aboriginal peoples.
    Aboriginal peoples are registered and governed as "status Indians." "Indian" is the legal terminology

used in Canadian legislation, such as the *Indian Act*, which pertains to status Indians in Canada. In this chapter, we primarily use Indigenous for its expansive and political character. Terms such as Aboriginal and Indian are used when we are specifically referring to legislative or legal categories.

2 The contemporary form of governance on most First Nations reserves are band councils, a governance system that was unilaterally imposed on Indigenous nations by the Canadian government. Band councils were created in order to replace traditional forms of Indigenous governance. Métis and Inuit people are not subject to the Band government system, as the courts have specified that laws relating to "Indians" do not apply to them and they are therefore not governed by the *Indian Act*.

3 Specific land claims pertain to agreements made between the Crown (or the Canadian government) and particular Indigenous nations that have not been upheld. This might include a treaty agreement that, for example, promised lands to Indigenous nations but did not follow through such commitments. There are hundreds of such claims, with many still unresolved. Comprehensive land claims cover claims to Indigenous title over lands that have never been ceded to the Crown (or Canadian government). These "modern treaties" stem from the *Calder* decision discussed previously and often result in one-time monetary compensation in exchange for the extinguishing of all Indigenous title over the lands in perpetuity.

4 *mino bimaadziwin* is an Anishinaabe phrase meaning "living a good life" or "living life in a good way."

REFERENCES

Court Cases

Calder v. Attorney-General of British Columbia [1973] S.C.R. 313
R. v. Van der Peet [1996] S.C.R. 507

Government Legislation

An Act respecting the United Nations Declaration on the Rights of Indigenous Peoples Act (Bill C-15), 2021
Gradual Civilization Act, 1857
Gradual Enfranchisement Act, 1869
Indian Act, 1876
Jobs and Growth Act (Bill C-45), 2012

General References

Alfred. T. 2009. "Colonialism and State Dependency." *Journal of Aboriginal Health* 42.
Alfred, T., and J. Corntassel. 2005. "Being Indigenous: Resurgences against Contemporary Colonialism." *Government and Opposition* 40, 4.
Al Jazeera News. 2021. "New Search Begins for Residential School Graves in Canada." *Al Jazeera News Indigenous,* November 9. <aljazeera.com/news/2021/11/9/new-search-begins-for-residential-school-graves-in-canada>.
APTN News. 2015. "Canada Guilty of Cultural Genocide against Indigenous Peoples: TRC." June 2. <aptnnews.ca/national-news/canada-guilty-cultural-genocide-indigenous-peoples-trc-2/>.
Arendt, H. 1973. *The Origins of Totalitarianism*. New York: Harcourt Brace & Company.
Asch, M. 2014. *On Being Here to Stay: Treaties and Aboriginal Rights in Canada*. Toronto: University of Toronto Press.
Beazley, D. 2017. "Decolonizing the Indian Act: No One Likes It, So Why Is It So Hard to Change?"

National Magazine, December 18. <nationalmagazine.ca/en-ca/articles/law/in-depth/2017/decolonizing-the-indian-act>.

Bellrichard, C. 2020. "RCMP Spend More than $13M on Policing Coastal GasLink Conflict on Wet'suwet'en Territory." CBC News, October 21. <cbc.ca/news/indigenous/rcmp-wetsuweten-pipeline-policing-costs-1.5769555>.

Bruser, D., R. Benzie and J. Poisson. 2017. "Ontario Commits $85 Million to Clean Up 'Gross Neglect' at Grassy Narrows." *Toronto Star*, June 27. <thestar.com/news/gta/2017/06/27/ontario-gives-85-million-to-clean-up-gross-neglect-at-grassy-narrows.html>.

Canada. 1997. "Gathering Strength: Canada's Aboriginal Action Plan." Ottawa: Minister of Indian Affairs and Northern Development. <ahf.ca/downloads/gathering-strength.pdf>.

Canadian Encyclopedia. 2020. "Indian Act." December 16. <thecanadianencyclopedia.ca/en/article/indian-act>.

Cardinal, H. 1999. *The Unjust Society*. Vancouver: Douglas & MacIntyre.

CBC. 2021. "Grassy Narrows to Get $68.9M More from Ottawa for Centre to Care for People with Mercury Poisoning." CBC News, July 26. <cbc.ca/news/canada/thunder-bay/grassy-narrows-mercury-care-facility-ottawa-funding-1.6117975>.

Corntassel, J. 2018. *Everyday Acts of Resurgence: People, Places, Practices*. Olympia: Daykeeper Press.

Coulthard, G. 2014. *Red Skin, White Masks: Rejecting the Colonial Politics of Recognition*. Minneapolis: University of Minnesota Press.

CTV. 2020. "Timeline: Rail Disruptions by Wet'suwet'en Supporters across Canada." CTV News, February 17. <bc.ctvnews.ca/timeline-rail-disruptions-by-wet-suwet-en-supporters-across-canada-1.4815263>.

Deer, K. 2019. "Indian Act Still Discriminates against First Nations Women, says UN Human Rights Committee." CBC News, January 17. <cbc.ca/news/indigenous/indian-act-sex-discrimination-un-committee-1.4982330>.

Flanagan, T. 2000. *First Nation? Second Thoughts*. Montreal and Kingston: McGill-Queen's University Press.

Fontaine, T. 2016. "Canada Removing Objector Status to the UN Declaration on the Rights of Indigenous Peoples." CBC News, May 8. <cbc.ca/news/indigenous/canada-position-un-declaration-indigenous-peoples-1.3572777#:~:text=Indigenous-,Canada%20removing%20objector%20status%20to%20UN%20Declaration%20on%20the%20Rights,Affairs%20Minister%20Carolyn%20Bennett%20says>.

Forester, B. 2020. "Despite Promise of Reconciliation, Trudeau Spent Nearly $100 Million Fighting First Nations in Court During First Years in Power." APTN News, December 18. <aptnnews.ca/national-news/trudeau-spent-nearly-100m-fighting-first-nations-in-court-during-first-years-in-power/>.

Fournier, S., and E. Crey. 1997. *Stolen from Our Embrace: The Abduction of First Nations Children and the Restoration of Aboriginal Communities*. Vancouver: Douglas and McIntyre.

Gardner, K., and R. Peters (Giibwanisi). 2014. "Toward the 8th Fire: The View from the Oshkimaadziig Unity Camp." *Decolonization: Indigeneity, Education, Society* 3, 3.

Government of Canada. 2021. "Ending Long-Term Drinking Water Advisories." Ottawa: Government of Canada. <sac-isc.gc.ca/eng/1506514143353/1533317130660>.

___. 2020. "Indigenous People in Federal Custody Surpasses 30%: Correctional Investigator Issues Statement and Challenge." Ottawa: Office of the Correctional Investigator. January 21. <oci-bec.gc.ca/cnt/comm/press/press20200121-eng.aspx>.

___. 1969. *Statement of the Government of Canada on Indian Policy*. Ottawa: Government of Canada.

Hunt, S., and C. Holmes. 2015. "Everyday Decolonization: Living a Decolonizing Queer Politics." *Journal of Lesbian Studies* 19, 2.

Indian Chiefs of Alberta. 1970. *Citizens Plus*. Edmonton: Indian Association of Alberta.

Kino-nda-niimi Collective. 2014. *The Winter We Danced: Voices from the Past, the Future, and the Idle No More Movement*. Winnipeg: ARP Books.

Ladner, K. 2001. "Negotiated Inferiority: The Royal Commission on Aboriginal People's Vision of a

Renewed Relationship." *American Review of Canadian Studies* 31, 1/2.

Lawrence, B. 2003. "Gender, Race, and the Regulation of Native Identity in Canada and the United States: An Overview." *Hypatia* 18.

Lawrence, B., and E. Dua. 2005. "Decolonizing Antiracism." *Social Justice* 32, 4.

Leslie, K. 2016. "Grassy Narrows Protesters Bring Mercury Fears to Legislature." *Toronto Star*, June 23. <thestar.com/news/queenspark/2016/06/23/grassy-narrows-protesters-bring-mercu-ry-fears-to-the-legislature.html>.

Letson, R., and V. Lannon.2021. "Grassy Narrows: The Struggle for Mercury Justice Continues." *Spring Magazine,* March 30. <springmag.ca/grassy-narrows-the-struggle-for-mercury-justice-continues>.

Manuel, A. 2015. *Unsettling Canada: A National Wake-Up Call.* Toronto: Between the Lines.

Maracle, L. 1996. *I Am Woman: A Native Perspective on Sociology and Feminism.* Richmond: Press Gang.

National Archives of Canada. Record Group 10, volume 6810, file 470-2-3, Volume 7, 55 (L-3) and 63 (N-3).

National Inquiry into Missing and Murdered Indigenous Women and Girls. 2019. *Reclaiming Power and Place: The Final Report of the National Inquiry into Missing and Murdered Indigenous Women and Girls.* Ottawa. <mmiwg-ffada.ca/final-report/>.

Palmater, P. 2019. "Abolishing the Indian Act Means Eliminating First Nations' Rights." *Maclean's*, October 10. <macleans.ca/opinion/abolishing-the-indian-act-means-eliminating-first-nations-rights/>.

Royal Commission on Aboriginal Peoples. 1996. Report. <bac-lac.gc.ca/eng/discover/aboriginal-herit-age/royal-commission-aboriginal-peoples/Pages/final-report.aspx>.

Simpson, L. 2011. *Dancing on Our Turtle's Back.* Winnipeg: ARP Books.

Simpson, L.B., and K. Ladner. 2010. *This Is an Honour Song: Twenty Years Since the Blockades.* Winnipeg: ARP Books.

Stranger, D. 2021. "Former Manitoba Indigenous Relations Minister Criticizes Premier after Stepping Down From Post." APTN News, July 21. <aptnnews.ca/national-news/former-manitoba-indige-nous-relations-minister-clarke-criticizes-premier-after-stepping-down-from-post/>.

TRC (Truth and Reconciliation Commission). 2015. *Honouring the Truth, Reconciling for the Future: Summary of the Final Report of the Truth and Reconciliation Commission of Canada.* <publications. gc.ca/site/eng/9.800288/publication.html>.

United Nations. 2007. United Nations Declaration on the Rights of Indigenous Peoples. <un.org/de-velopment/desa/indigenouspeoples/wp-content/uploads/sites/19/2018/11/UNDRIP_E_web.pdf>.

Vowel, C. 2016. *Indigenous Writes: A Guide to First Nations, Métis, and Inuit Issues in Canada.* Winnipeg: Highwater Press.

Wolfe, P. 2006. "Settler Colonialism and the Elimination of the Native." *Journal of Genocide Research* 8, 4.

7

CAPITALISM, POVERTY AND POOR PEOPLE'S RESISTANCE

A.J. Withers

YOU SHOULD KNOW THIS

- First Nations women make 48 percent of what white men make.

- One in ten Canadians fall below Canada's official poverty line.

- One third of all tenants live in unaffordable housing.

- Homelessness can reduce life expectancy by up to 40 percent.

- Half of on-reserve households in the Prairie provinces have inadequate housing.

- Black people have 3.5 times the rate of food insecurity of white people.

- 22.5 percent of households that rely on government benefits for their income do not have food security.

Sources: Claveau 2020; CMHC 2018; Statistics Canada 2018, 2020, 2021b; Webster 2017

POVERTY: THE PROBLEM IS CAPITALISM

CANADA IS ONE OF THE RICHEST countries in the world — yet millions of people here continue to live in poverty. Poverty is a state of material deprivation and poor people experience violence and oppression because of it. There can be serious and lasting consequences of poverty. Poverty is a social determinant of health, which means it influences health outcomes. Poor people are more likely to have shorter lives, HIV/

AIDS, diabetes mellitus and chronic obstructive pulmonary disease (COPD) than people in higher income brackets. Homelessness can reduce life expectancy by up to 40 percent (Webster 2017). Poor kids are more likely to develop asthma (Dorman et al. 2013). It was racialized and poor people, and particularly racialized poor people, that disproportionately caught COVID-19 and got more severe symptoms when they caught it (Bryant, Aquanno and Raphael 2020). Poverty also increases the likelihood of precarity through both housing and food insecurity.

Poor people experience poverty as the social problem in their lives, but the underlying social problem is its cause: capitalism. Capitalism is an economic system based on profit and exploitation. Land, water, labour and knowledge are exploited by some, who then reinvest those profits in order to get more profits. Profits are not invested in the social good or the workers whose labour is exploited in the first place. Capitalism, then, produces tremendous wealth and poverty and, therefore, it creates inequality. The state — which includes the government, bureaucracy, police and military — facilitates the exploitation of people, water, land and knowledge — this is one of the reasons that capitalism and colonialism are interlocked. Because capitalism produces poverty, truly resisting poverty means resisting capitalism.

WHAT IS POVERTY?

Defining poverty can be complex and it is always political. People who "live below the poverty line" have been talked about for decades but that has meant many different things. Poverty is more complex than material deprivation or income. The official definition of poverty is what is called the Market Basket Measure (MBM) and, according to the federal government, it is "based on the cost of a basket of goods and services that individuals and families need in order to meet their basic needs and achieve a modest standard of living" (Employment and Social Development Canada 2018: 6). About 4.1 million Canadians live in poverty according to the MBM (Statistics Canada 2019f, 2021b).[1] The MBM is an absolute measure of poverty, which means a specific dollar amount is established (relative to family size) — those who fall below it are considered poor and those who do not are not poor. What gets put in the "basket" is arbitrary and leaving some things out (like childcare) means lots of people aren't considered poor but they would be if those things were in the "basket." The Liberal government chose this measure over the Low-Income Measure (LIM), which is a relative measure of poverty. Using the LIM, the "poverty line" was "50 percent of median household incomes, accounting for household size" (Employment and Social Development Canada 2018: 71). Median income is the dollar amount that evenly splits the population into those who make more and those who make less than that amount. This measure determines if someone is low income based in relation to what others in the country have. In other words, measuring relative poverty is a way to measure of inequality — how evenly resources are distributed in a society (Block, Galabuzi and Tranjan 2019). Measuring absolute poverty simply measures people's ability to pay for a set of goods and services.

Drop in Poverty Levels Depends on Measure

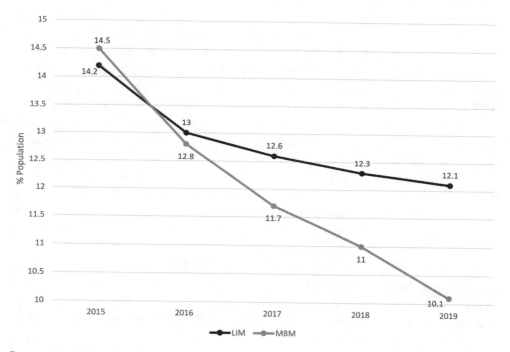

Source: Statistics Canada n.d.b, n.d.c.

The percent of the population that is poor in Canada has been declining. However, it declined more steeply using the government's official MBM poverty line (4.4 percent over five years) than with the LIM (2.1 percent over five years). In 2018, poverty rates increased with the LIM but decreased with the MBM. The difference between the two measures in 2019 is that 700,000 more people are considered poor under the after-tax LIM than the official poverty line. The fastest and easiest way for a government to reduce poverty is simply to change the definition.

> The fastest and easiest way for a government to reduce poverty is simply to change the definition.

Additionally, the poverty line can mean a lot or very little in a person's or family's existence. There may be no difference in the day-to-day life of someone who lives $5 below the official poverty line and someone who lives $5 above it. The person who is not technically poor, whether they are $5 or $500 above the official poverty line, but who is a single parent and must spend half of their income on childcare may be far worse off than someone who is below the poverty line but doesn't pay for childcare. Childcare is not considered part of the "basket" of necessary costs under the MBM. Likewise, debt payments, which many poor people live with, are taken out of "disposable income," although that income is far from disposable. Debt repayments can eat up many items in the "market basket" for those who live near but not below the official poverty line (Djidel et al. 2020). By excluding necessary costs like childcare, tuition and prescription medication in "disposable income," the official poverty line is kept artificially low (Heisz 2019). Of course, there can be a very real difference for a person or a family who lives a few dollars below the MBM cut-off and one who lives on almost no income at all. The distance someone is from the poverty line is called "the poverty gap."

Some people live in "deep poverty." Statistics Canada considers someone living below 75 percent of the official poverty line as living in deep poverty — this is currently 5 percent of Canadians (Statistics Canada 2019h). In most provinces, someone on disability social assistance, for example, lives in deep poverty and someone on welfare lives in even deeper poverty.

Even when established with the most exhaustive and thoughtful methodologies, poverty lines are arbitrary. But they also equate poverty with income (how much money someone makes in any given year). However, income and poverty are not equivalent. Collapsing income and poverty "hides the structural violence of capitalism" (Truscello and Nangwaya 2017: 11). This violence includes, but is far from limited to, hunger, homelessness, police brutality, child apprehension and displacement. Poor people's dispossession and exploitation are not captured in income. Further, it is oppressed groups, as this chapter will show, who disproportionately experience poverty. The environmental devastation, like the climate crisis, that is often caused and driven by capitalism is hidden by the poverty line — even though it is poor people, especially BIPOC people, who are disproportionately impacted by this devastation (Crouse, Ross and Goldberg 2009; Truscello and Nangwaya 2017; Waldron 2018). Conflating income with poverty makes poverty a statistically measurable phenomenon while erasing its true causes. The poverty line, therefore, "legitimates the deprivation and suffering of millions without containing the wealth and power accumulation of the ruling class," argue Truscello and Nangwaya. They say:

the poverty line says, as long as an acceptable number of people are earning an acceptable amount of money — no matter how humiliating and debilitating their work, no matter how their working and living conditions deteriorate from the distribution of resources, no matter how much the economic system deprives them of agency — the system is working. (2017: 11)

This chapter recognizes the multitude of issues with conflating income and poverty and recognizes poverty lines as wholly inadequate to measure and describe the complexities of poverty. Nevertheless, there are few other mechanisms available to understand poverty on a national scale. Therefore, this chapter uses some official poverty lines while being conscious of their ineptitude.

There are some other measures that can be useful to assess poverty, like examining housing and food security. Someone is in core housing need, for example, if their housing is either unaffordable (over 30 percent of their income), inadequate (needs major repair) or unsuitable (overcrowded). In Canada, 12 percent of the population is in core housing need. Tenants have high rates of core housing need, with nearly a quarter of them in this situation (23 percent) (Claveau 2020). Food insecurity is a lack of access to food in quantity or quality because of cost. Nine percent of the population had some level of food insecurity before the COVID-19 pandemic; that had increased to 16 percent by December 2020 (Polsky and Gilmour 2020). Food insecurity and housing precarity can help round out what poverty looks like because these material depravations help to capture some of the negative impacts of poverty. Relative poverty measures, like the LIM, can help capture distributive justice. Societies that have a great deal of wealth and yet choose to maintain high poverty levels impact poor people. Poor people are often aware that the deprivation they experience daily could be ameliorated with social policies if governments choose. Those who are not aware of this can learn from and through poor peoples' organizing.

WHO IS POOR?

Anyone can become poor but not everyone has an equal chance of being poor. Members of oppressed groups are much more likely to be poor because of that oppression. Poor people are also divided into groups of what are perceived to be the "deserving" and "undeserving" poor based on people's social value and the perceived cause of their poverty; this is often directly related

> Who someone is can have a big impact on if they become poor, if they stay poor and their experience of poverty.

to whether or not they are part of an oppressed group. All of this means that who someone is can have a big impact on if they become poor, if they stay poor and their experience of poverty.

This chapter attempts to carefully, however briefly, attend to the different ways that various groups experience poverty. Two things are important to note, though: First, highlighting these experiences does not discount the terrible experiences of poor people who are not part of these groups. Second, oppressions aren't necessarily experienced as separate and distinct by oppressed people. This chapter relies on a lot of statistical data that often negates the reality of interlocked oppression and makes many oppressed people invisible. The Canadian Housing Survey report by Statistics Canada, for example, provides information about gender, Indigeneity, race and sexuality as separate and distinct categories. But each of these groups aren't homogenous and don't experience housing in the same way. For instance, only providing information about the category "women" erases the important and distinct experiences of many oppressed women. Two-Spirit women likely face some of the highest rates of housing precarity, but Two-Spirit women do not exist in the data — only Indigenous peoples, sexual minorities[2] and women exist as separate groups. Because of the unique historical and current circumstances of oppressed groups and because of the way that most of the available data works, varied oppressed groups are discussed separately here. This separation is made for explanatory purposes; please do not lose track of how oppressions are interlocked and intersectional (Fellows and Razack 1997; Crenshaw 1989).

Indigenous Peoples

Canada is a settler-colonial country. That means that the land that is now called Canada has undergone a particular process of colonization in which the original populations of Indigenous peoples were intended to be replaced by settlers (Wolfe 2006). As a result of Canada's colonial policies, past and present, there are profound levels of poverty among Indigenous peoples both on and off reserve (see Palmater, Chapter 3). About a third of people identifying specifically as First Nations people and nearly a quarter of all Indigenous peoples[3] fell below the LIM during the last census (Statistics Canada 2019b). A third of Indigenous households have core housing need, both on and off reserve (Claveau 2020; CMHC 2018). In the Prairie provinces, however, that number jumps to about half of Indigenous households with inadequate housing on reserve: Manitoba at 51 percent, Saskatchewan at 47 percent and Alberta at 49 percent (CMHC 2018).[4] Historic and ongoing Canadian settler colonialism results in significant and

> Historic and ongoing Canadian settler colonialism results in significant and disproportionate levels of poverty in Indigenous communities.

disproportionate levels of poverty in Indigenous communities; the consequences of this translate into not only inadequate housing, but also large numbers of people without access to potable water, high rates of child apprehension and incarceration and negative health outcomes (Palmater, Chapter 3).

Low Income Levels By Race

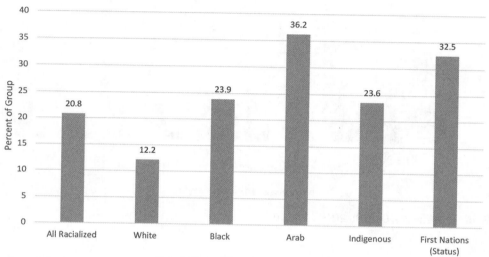

Source: Statistics Canada 2019a, 2019b.

Racialized People

It is often said that Canada is a nation of immigrants. This construction erases the colonial project and Indigenous peoples. It also erases the history of Canadian slavery, constructing many Black people as immigrants rather than the descendants of enslaved people who were forcibly brought to Canada (Mugabo 2014). First slavery and then a series of state policies, including segregation and a lack of equitable access to education and the labour market, have ensured material deprivation in Black communities for hundreds of years (Maynard 2017). Nearly a quarter of Black people live below the poverty line (after-tax LIM) (Statistics Canada 2019a), and over a quarter (29 percent) of Black people are food insecure — this is 3.5 times the rate of food insecurity of white people (PROOF and FoodShare 2019). Black people experience high rates of poverty, much higher rates than white people.

Canada's Racial Income Inequality

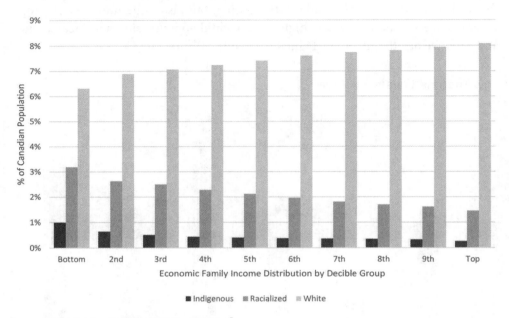

Economic Family Income Distribution by Decible Group

■ Indigenous ■ Racialized ■ White

Source: Statistics Canada 2019c, 2019d.[5]

Racism leads to disproportionate rates of poverty in other racialized groups as well, and this is experienced unevenly depending on the group. Over a third of all Arabs (36 percent) live in poverty and over a fifth of all racialized people live in poverty (21 percent). This is much higher than the rate for white people (12 percent) (Statistics Canada 2019a). White people have the highest portion of their population in the top 10 percent of incomes and the lowest portion of their population in the bottom 10 percent of overall incomes. The exact inverse is true for Indigenous and racialized people — both groups' highest shares of their populations are in the bottom 10 percent and they decline with each decile to the top 10 percent (Statistics Canada 2019c, 2019d). Racialized people (14 percent) are twice as likely to have a core housing need than white people (7 percent) (Claveau 2020). Overall, BIPOC people are much more likely to live below the poverty line, have core housing need and are much less likely to be rich than white people.

Migrants

Intimately related to the racialization of poverty are issues of migration. The majority of immigrants to Canada are now from countries with primarily racialized populations (Statistics Canada 2017a). In addition to facing the difficulties of having to settle in a new country, newcomers to Canada often encounter racism. Anti-immigrant practices, like requiring people to have Canadian experience in order to be hired, have been called "racism without racists" (Bonilla-Silva 2003 in Ku et al. 2019: 294).

The way that people come to Canada can also impact how well they do here. Refugees and people who were sponsored by their families are more likely to live in poverty for five years or longer (Picot and Lu 2017). There are also many migrants in Canada as part of work programs. They are often paid little and live in precarious situations — many care workers reside in their employers' homes, for example. COVID-19 increased the exploitation and vulnerability of many migrant workers (see Bejan and Allain 2021; Faraday 2021). For instance, work conditions for many live-in care workers changed dramatically under COVID-19 lockdowns. The children they cared for no longer went to school while the parent(s) were often at home full-time. These workers were often denied overtime and even forbidden to leave the house, so they couldn't bring the virus into the home (Caregivers' Action Centre et al. 2020; Wadehra 2021). What were often dilapidated and overcrowded living conditions for migrant farm workers before the pandemic became vehicles for COVID-19 transmission (Mojtehedzadeh 2021).

If someone is in Canada without immigration status, they are especially vulnerable and at constant risk of deportation. They also don't have any employment protections, including labour and minimum wage laws, and they cannot access social programs like welfare. Toronto, Hamilton, Edmonton, Vancouver and other cities have adopted sanctuary city policies that are supposed to allow non-status people access to services and supports without risk of deportation; however, considerable barriers exist. In Toronto, for example, the police continue to provide information to immigration officials, which puts people at risk of deportation if they report a crime. Also, most benefits, including social assistance and healthcare, are provincial and not covered by these sanctuary policies (Hershkowitz, Hudson and Bauder 2021; Smee 2018). The immigrant and refugee population in Canada is diverse; the circumstances under which one has left their country of origin and their legal status in Canada can impact the likelihood of being poor and of getting assistance while poor.

Disabled People

Disabled people also have high rates of poverty (14 percent versus 10 percent for non-disabled people (Statistics Canada 2021a). Every province and territory has specific social assistance rates or programs for disabled people, but these programs have low rates that keep disabled people poor (Djidel et al. 2020; Laidley and Aldridge

2020). Many disabled people are on social assistance because of low rates of employment (59 percent for people ages twenty-five to sixty-four); this is much lower than people without disabilities (80 percent) (Statistics Canada, n.d.). Lack of employment accommodations leads to un(der)employment in disabled communities even though there is research from all over the world that demonstrates disability accommodations increase company profits (Lindsay et al. 2018). A US study found that 58 percent of workplace accommodations have no cost; the rest cost less than $500 on average (Solovieva et al. 2009). Disabled people are also much more likely to have core housing need than non-disabled people; here, too, accommodations are a central issue (Claveau 2020). The lack of accommodations is not about the shortcomings of individual disabled people to meet societal norms. Rather, it is about social relations being organized to purposefully exclude many disabled people. These relations are apparent in many ways in everyday life. It is evident in the physical world being built for people who walk rather than wheel around — including the frequency of stairs. It is also evident in the policing of people whose behaviour is outside of the norm — and when that behaviour is exhibited by racialized people, especially Black men, the disproportionate killing by police. This exclusion exists because disabled people are deemed less socially valuable — it is about oppression. Lack of accommodations feeds into high disability poverty rates, which contributes to even more barriers. A million disabled people, 17 percent of all disabled people in Canada, have an unmet disability need because of cost (Morris et al. 2018). Disabled people, then, are more likely to be poor than non-disabled people and are likely to not have accommodations and disability needs being met. There appears to be a relationship between the two in which poverty is, at least partly, caused by disability needs not being met and further causes disabled people to be unable to afford to meet disability needs.

2SLGBTQI+ People

Based on a number of indicators, Two-Spirit, lesbian, gay, bisexual, trans, queer, intersex (2SLGBTQI+)[6] people are more likely to live in poverty. 2SLGBTQI+ youth make up 20 to 40 percent of all homeless youth (Abramovich and Shelton 2017). Straight people are much less likely to have core housing need than people who aren't straight (Claveau 2020).[7] In Ontario, and likely the rest of Canada, the majority of trans people live in poverty, with a fifth of people unemployed or on disability social assistance (Bauer et al. 2011; Transpulse 2010). The 2SLGBTQI+ community makes less employment income than their cis and straight counterparts in what has been called a "'coming out' penalty" (Kia et al. 2020: 14). There is a commonly held misperception that gay men make more money than others and this may contribute to the invisibility and lack of study of 2SLGBTQI+ poverty (Kia et al. 2020; Mulé 2005). Indeed, gay men experience a "sexual minority wage gap," making significantly less than heterosexual men (Waite and Denier 2015). Statistics Canada doesn't measure individual 2SLGBTQI+ income, only that of same-sex couples; this also makes it hard to compare actual income levels and wage disparities. Couples cannot stand in for the entire diverse community and its variety of living situations, especially because lone parents and individuals are those most likely to be poor (Fox and Moyser 2018). There is also strong evidence that Two-Spirit and Indigenous LGBTQI+ people face disproportionate and deep levels of poverty in relation to non-Indigenous LGBTQI+ people and cis, straight Indigenous people (Kia et al. 2020). While there is significant evidence that 2SLGBTQI+ people are disproportionately poor, this poverty is often made invisible because of prejudice and a lack of acknowledgement — including comprehensive study by Statistics Canada.

Women

Women only had slightly higher poverty rates than men overall according to the latest census data. But patriarchy and poverty interlock in many ways in different women's lives. Lone mothers and senior women have disproportionately high rates of poverty. Women over age sixty-five have a poverty rate of 16.3 percent, 4.4 percent higher than senior men. Lone mothers have an overall poverty rate of 34.5 percent, and the average after-tax income for lone mothers is $15,000 a year less than it is for lone fathers (Fox and Moyser 2018). Disabled women are more likely than disabled men to be poor (Morris et al. 2018). Likewise, Indigenous and racialized women are more likely to be poor than Indigenous and racialized men, respectively (Arriagada, Hahmann and O'Donnell 2020; Feng, Frank and Schimmele 2020). More Indigenous and racialized women are in the bottom half of the economic family income distribution and in each of the bottom first through fifth deciles than men for these respective groups; they also have lower median incomes (Statistics Canada 2019c, 2019d). The gender pay gap is something that has been frequently discussed in the media. The most recent study, before COVID-19, put this gap at $0.13, which means that women make $0.87 for every $1 men make (Statistics Canada 2019g). This is a product of sexism and it, too, is experienced unevenly depending on different social stratifications. Part of this gap is what is often called the "motherhood penalty" through which women are disadvantaged for each child they have (Budig, Misra and Boeckmann 2012). Mothers remain "segregate[ed] in low-paying employment" because those jobs offer the flexibility mothers seek (Fuller 2018: 1443). Some of the motherhood penalty is attributable to the persistent and disproportionate burden of domestic labour that women continue to carry — and this intensified during the COVID-19 pandemic. Many women had to take on child-rearing and working at home simultaneously. Twelve times more women left the workforce than men did — primarily to care for children (Nolen 2021). There was such a dramatic impact on women's ability to work and income levels that it was dubbed a "she-cession" (Lum 2021: n.p.).

Gender and Race Employment Income Gap in Canada

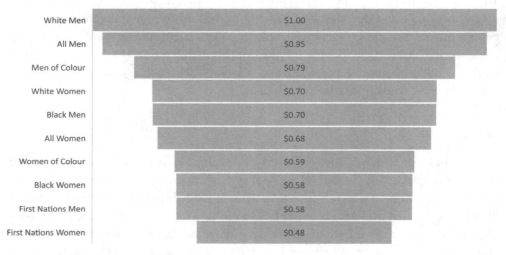

Source: Statistics Canada 2018, 2019e.

In addition to the wage gap — the difference between the hourly wage men and women earn — there is also an employment income gap that factors in employee bonuses, salaries, commissions, tips and other taxable benefits beyond just wages (Statistics Canada 2017c). The employment income gap is much larger, as white men, it appears, are compensated much more readily through non-wage mechanisms than members of oppressed groups. As the Gender and Race Employment Income Gap chart shows, for every dollar in employment income that white men get, white women only make $0.70, $0.11 more than racialized women. All women make $0.27 less on the dollar than all men, $0.14 higher than what the government formally recognizes as the gender pay gap. Women who identify as First Nations make less than half of what white men make. This pay gap is also significant for BIPOC men as well. First Nations men with are paid $0.58 on the dollar. Black women are paid $0.01 less than women of colour ($0.59). Black men, however, are paid $0.09 less than all men of colour ($0.79). The operation of racist and patriarchal relations are evident in how people are paid.[8] While poverty is both more complex and dynamic than income, white men get paid more and this economic advantage means they are less likely to be poor and it is typically easier for them to get out of poverty too.

Household Makeup

The kind of household someone lives in also has an impact on how likely they are to be poor. Lone-parent households with kids under seventeen years old are the most likely to be poor (36.5 percent); over half of these families are poor if they have three or more kids (54.4 percent). Single people also have high rates of poverty (26.8 percent); nearly a third of single people living alone are living in poverty (32.0 percent). Couples who have no children — known as DINKS, for double income, no kids — have very low rates of poverty (9.0 percent) (Statistics Canada 2017b). The Canada Child Benefit has made important gains in reducing poverty for families with kids overall in Canada. The federal government says, for example, that the benefit "helped lift about 300,000 children out of poverty" in 2016–2017 alone (Government of Canada 2018). However, the evidence suggests that racialized families, especially Indigenous families living on reserve, did not benefit as much as white families (Li and Neborak 2018; Macdonald and Wilson 2016). Household makeup, like all of these social factors, does not operate independently of the many forms of oppression.

THE DESERVING AND UNDESERVING POOR

The social stratification of poor people is not new. The social assistance system that exists today originated from the *British Poor Relief Act*, enacted in 1601. This law divided poor people into two groups: those who were considered able to work and those who couldn't. Those classified as unable to work were allotted assistance — or relief, as it was called then — because they were thought to be deserving of it. Those who could work were undeserving of relief and were forcibly confined in workhouses if they were unemployed and needed material aid (Stone 1984; Quigley 1998). These groups are commonly called the "deserving poor" and the "undeserving poor."

Today, who is and is not the deserving poor shifts depending on jurisdiction and which government is in power. The deserving poor — children, disabled people and seniors — are viewed as deserving of social supports, especially income. The undeserving poor are people who need material supports but are not considered "worthy" of them, so they are given low welfare rates. Non-disabled adults who are not yet seniors are typically considered the undeserving poor. Parents are largely part of the undeserving poor although, as will subsequently be shown, this has changed over time. Parents' deservingness is largely determined through their children — by how old they are and how much care they need. The undeserving poor are constructed as social burdens who don't deserve social supports — at least not beyond subsistence levels. Disability social assistance rates are higher in all provinces and territories than welfare rates; in Alberta, welfare payments are less than half of permanent disability payments, and in Saskatchewan, BC and Ontario, they're 56 percent — 65 percent of permanent disability payments (Laidley and Aldridge 2020).[9] This is because people who are considered to be unable to work, like four centuries ago, are viewed as deserving of assistance; the undeserving poor are expected to find jobs (even if none are available).

Deservingness is interpreted through existing oppressions. For example, Black physically disabled men's deservingness is interpreted through racist assumptions about Black criminality, so that they are interpreted to be less deserving than disabled white people or, perhaps, part of the undeserving poor. Deservingness, like oppression, changes over time as social views about various groups change. For example, unwed white women with children were once viewed as "fallen women" whose poverty (and shame) was their own doing. They were not considered deserving of social supports. However, as views about women shifted, largely as a result of middle-class white women's activism, single mothers became eligible for social assistance (Little 1994). For instance, Ontario established its Mothers' Allowance program in 1920. With the rise of neoliberalism — a philosophy that supports individual responsibility, privatization and free markets — however, single mothers were reframed. Premier Mike Harris initially justified cutting a food supplement for pregnant mothers, saying: "What we are making sure is that those dollars don't go to beer, don't go to something else" (Galvin 2018). Harris didn't only cut this benefit, but all of welfare was slashed by 22 percent and he eliminated what was, by that time, called family benefits — a catchall for families with kids and single disabled people (Galvin 2018; Little and Morrison 1999). All parents, which were disproportionately single moms, were shifted onto welfare unless they were disabled. A new, disability-specific social assistance class was created — the Ontario Disability Support Program — and single moms were no longer among the deserving poor. Once their children reached a certain age, there were (and remain) increasingly punitive measures to push these women into the labour market (Little 1994; Little and Morrison 1999).

The divide between the so-called deserving and undeserving poor is used to justify the punitive treatment of those classified as undeserving — which has material implications. In addition to the massive cut to social assistance that happened in Ontario when people lost over a fifth of their incomes overnight, welfare recipients in almost every province and territory experience a spending power cut in social assistance nearly every year.[10] Aside from deep poverty, constructing people on welfare as undeserving also enables them to bring in new policies designed to push people off of social assistance and into the "first available job." This "work first" approach prioritizes availability over everything else (including suitability, conditions and pay) (Graefe 2015: 114). This includes prohibiting childless adults from collecting welfare for periods of time (like BC's short-lived "two years out of five" rule) and making people who qualify for benefits undergo a waiting period before they can collect (Klein 2012). Governments have exaggerated the rates of welfare fraud and encouraged people's neighbours, friends and family to surveil their behaviour and report anything they consider suspicious (White 2018). It also includes attempting to implement workfare programs that require welfare recipients to work a minimum number of unpaid hours to receive their welfare cheques (Graefe 2015; Shragge 1997). All these measures are intended to push poor people into the labour market. "Work first" measures also exist to punish undeserving poor people for being poor in the first place — they are blamed for their own circumstances and expected to act as examples to ensure others do all they can to avoid falling into the social safety net.

Imagine a parking lot. It only has so many parking spaces, and as long as there are more cars than spaces, some cars will not be able to park. This is not a deficiency of the car, but an issue of space. This parking lot metaphor is like the economy if there are more people than jobs — that is a problem with the economy, not the individual people (Mullaly 2010). Having too few spaces in the parking lot is a characteristic of the capitalist system. Karl Marx called all the people who were unemployed and those who might enter the labour market the "reserve army of labour" (Marx 1887, 1991). A large number of unemployed workers who are eager to take any job helps keep wages down. "Less eligibility" is a principle that is evident in Canadian social assistance programs and contributes to the desperation of unemployed workers. This principle was introduced with a British poor law reform in 1834 and it is designed to disincentivize people from collecting benefits by keeping assistance much lower than the lowest paying job (Webb and Webb 1929). The intention is to make people on social assistance desperate, so they will get to work — but, of course, there are never enough jobs for everyone. When there aren't enough workers, they have more power to demand higher pay, but when there is a line of workers down the road looking for spaces, workers have very little power and less capacity to demand good wages.

Even if some governments sometimes raise the minimum wage, they also help keep downward pressure on wages. In addition to less eligibility — which is largely imposed through social assistance at the provincial level but is also evident for many workers in Employment Insurance — the federal government influences interest rates and works with the Bank of Canada to set inflation control targets (Bank of Canada 2021). These have significant impacts on employment levels. The news media often talks about Bank of Canada interest rates in terms of the impact on mortgage rates, but interest rates do a lot more than that. Allan Greenspan, head of the US Federal Reserve, explained: "At some point in the continuous reduction in the number of available workers willing to take jobs, short of the repeal of the law of supply and demand, wage increases must rise above even impressive gains in productivity. This would intensify inflationary pressures or squeeze profit margins, with either outcome capable of bringing our growing prosperity to an end" (Russell 2002: 124). What Greenspan is explaining here is that low unemployment means that workers become pickier about what jobs they take and demand higher pay. So, even with gains in productivity, at some point, worker wage growth would either increase inflation *or owners would lose profit*. The government, therefore, raised interest rates to create unemployment to protect owners' profits from rising workers' wages.

In the construction of the deserving and undeserving poor, those cast as undeserving are often those who are considered able to work. Yet there are factors well beyond their control that determine the availability of jobs. Indeed, it is often the same politicians who blame the so-called undeserving poor for their poverty who are the architects of policies that ensure capitalist relations continue to benefit owners and their profits over workers, both employed and unemployed.

CHILD POVERTY AND THE CYCLE OF POVERTY

Children are among the "deserving poor." In Canada, there is often a great deal of attention paid to child poverty and breaking what is called "the cycle of poverty." We are told children are "innocent victims" (Salvation Army 2014). Their parents — with a few exceptions, like disabled parents — are the "undeserving poor"; they are guilty, they deserve their lot in life. Consequently, reducing child poverty is often set as a key social policy goal. *Pathways to a Better Future: Manitoba's Poverty Reduction Strategy*, for example, set reducing child poverty 25 percent by 2025 as its only independent goal in its entire poverty reduction strategy (Government of Manitoba 2019).

Important research on the social determinants of health shows that there can be life-long negative health implications for children who grow up in poverty (Evans and Kim 2007; Francis 2009; Marmot et al. 2012). Growing up poor also has significant negative educational implications (Ferguson, Bovaird and Mueller 2007; Roos, Wall-Wieler and Lee 2019). The discourse about child poverty, however, pre-dates meaningful concerns about the social determinants of health lasting into adulthood. For example, turn-of-the-twentieth-century social workers expressed concern about the harm of poverty to "innocent" children in multiple ways, from providing charity relief in the form of food and coal to families to campaigning to sterilize women on eugenic grounds to prevent the creation of more poor children (Chapman and Withers 2019). As discussed earlier, at various times, parents (especially mothers) are considered deserving because they are attached to deserving children but, in other periods, they are not. Neoliberalism has resulted in a re-severing of "deserving" children from "undeserving" parents through, for example, policies that require parents to seek work once their children reach a certain age; this has been lowered to three years old in British Columbia and two years old in Manitoba (Government of Manitoba, n.d.; Klein and Pulkingham 2008).

The separation of "deserving" and "undeserving" within families requires some impressive cognitive dissonance because families exist as economic units. Kids don't get to pay a portion of their household rent ensure their individual housing security because their innocence is independent of their parents' ability to make full rent. Nevertheless, some governments create programs to uphold this fictional divide. In Ontario, for example, the provincial government created the Ontario Child Benefit under the guise of alleviating child poverty. With the new benefit, working parents were much better off but parents on social assistance did not gain significantly and in fact lost benefits for winter and school clothes. It also meant that parents with joint custody would only receive the benefit for six months out of the year, an impossible situation for those living in deep poverty trying to raise a child year-round (Income Security Advocacy Centre 2009).

Within this logic, children, not yet contaminated by the poor decisions, values and work ethics that make their parents poor, can be rescued from poverty. This is called "breaking the cycle of poverty." The federal poverty-reduction strategy, for example, says it wants to create "a Canada in which all children can grow up to become all they can be" (Employment and Social Development Canada 2018: 9). Education is frequently a central pillar of these policies: "Supporting children and youth to meet their full potential represents an opportunity to break the cycle of poverty for generations" (Government of Manitoba 2019: 28). The idea is that providing good education to poor people means they can access good jobs and they can climb out of poverty. With the cycle broken, that person who got "to become all they could be" won't have poor kids or grandkids — or, at least, this will be much less likely.

There are significant flaws in this neoliberal logic. First, it individualizes poverty. The problem of poverty, in this view, is poor people and so the solution is to fix poor people. Even when social issues are partially acknowledged, poverty is still individualized. For example, BC's plan says poverty reduction means "making sure that workers of all kinds in BC have fair wages and fair working conditions" and the government has followed through by raising the minimum wage. It also names multiple oppressed groups and tells us discrimination "hurts people and holds them back" (Government of British Columbia 2019: 3). Education targets are specific and come with resources attached. While the government recognizes discrimination, the targets on this matter are all vague and involve no new money; the plan only contains resources that have already been announced. Yet this government also emphasizes that "[b]reaking the cycle of poverty means ensuring that people living in poverty

— and their children and grandchildren — have access to opportunity. That means giving people access to education and skills training so they can reach their potential" (Government of British Columbia 2019: 16). Or, as the Ontario government put it, with the right help, struggling poor kids can "excel in school, get good jobs and become contributing members of society ... the intergenerational cycle of poverty can be broken" (Government of Ontario 2008: 7). This individualizing approach also blames poor people for their poverty even though poverty is an inherent component of the same capitalist economy that these neoliberal governments support. "Cycle of poverty" discourses also erase the many ways that oppressed groups are disproportionately poor. Two of the groups that experience disproportionate poverty rates are Indigenous and Black people. Nearly a third of Black kids (30 percent) and nearly half of status First Nations kids (53 percent on reserve, 47 percent overall) live in poverty, as compared to 14 percent of white kids (Beedie, Macdonald and Wilson 2019; Statistics Canada 2019a).[11] Interventions like education to "break the cycle of poverty" will disproportionately target Black and Indigenous youth. It is essential that the governments work to eliminate anti-Black and anti-Indigenous racism and reconcile colonialism. That may seem like what is happening here, but this particular kind of targeting is problematic.

Education has been used as a tool to attempt to assimilate people and erase their cultures for a very long time in Canada. Canada's Indian residential school system has been formally acknowledged as genocidal (Truth and Reconciliation Commission of Canada 2015).[12] As the Truth and Reconciliation Commission of Canada (2015: 317) concluded: "The way we educate our children and ourselves must change." There has been no transformation of the education systems by the federal and provincial governments that call for education to (help) break the cycle of poverty rather than decolonize schools by adding educational units on residential schools. The Canadian education system continues to be assimilationist; it continues to work to bring students into the dominant white culture. Indigenous scholar Marie Battiste (2013: 87) says, "In forcing assimilation and acculturation to Eurocentric knowledge, modern governments and educational systems have displaced Indigenous knowledge." In addition, Indigenous university students report experiencing microaggressions, overt racism and institutional racism (Canel-Çınarbaş and Yohani 2019). In effect, the government's solution to the disproportionate poverty in Indigenous communities, which is directly tied to colonialism, is further colonialism.

Black youth face high levels of racism in school. As Robyn Maynard (2017: 209) says, "for many Black students, though, schools are places where they experience degradation, harm and psychological violence." Maynard argues that Black youth experience carceral environments at school, both informally and through conventional surveillance, disciplinary policy and procedures and criminalization. Black youth are streamed away from university and face significant barriers entering and staying in university because of systemic racism (Cameron and Jefferies 2021). Here, too, the solution to poverty, which can be directly traced to racism, is a racist system.

However, the problem of education as the solution to "breaking the cycle of poverty" is more than what is described above and analogous to trying to heal a burn with a blowtorch. Cycle of poverty discourse positions poverty at the individual level and travelling along family lines. Inserting education at some point between generations to "break the cycle" is about assimilating BIPOC people, especially Black and Indigenous people, into middle-class white norms. The education system works to, if not eradicate children's accents and non-normative dialects, at least normalize them such that they appropriately code switch (flip between ways of speaking) when they aren't in their communities. School moulds all children's behaviour but it assimilates BIPOC children's behaviour into Canadian white culture. Through education, poor BIPOC people can become what Bhabha (2004: 123, 128) says is "almost the same, but not quite" or "almost the same but not white."[13]

It is true, however, that there are cycles of poverty in Canada. These cycles can't be neatly blamed on poor people because the three cycles of poverty and poverty creation are systemic. Capitalism is a cycle that creates poverty. Simplistically, those with the means of production (land, technology) exploit workers' labour to get money, which they can use to get more means of production and continue the cycle. Another, related cycle is the increasing wealth of the rich. As the rich make

> Capitalism is a cycle that creates poverty.

more money, they can generate even greater wealth (through assets and property, including the means of production) to get even richer. But for poor people, income is consumed by survival needs and they can't generate wealth. Over the past two decades, the top 0.1 percent of earners' incomes[14] have doubled. In 2018, the top 1 percent of earners, or fewer than 300,000 people, made 10 percent of all of the income in Canada; the top 5 percent of earners (1.4 million people) made nearly a quarter (23 percent) of all of the income. The bottom 50 percent, or fourteen million people, only made 18 percent of all of the income (Statistics Canada n.d.a). BIPOC people are especially disadvantaged when it comes to wealth accumulation in Canada (Block, Galabuzi and Tranjan 2019), due to current practices of racist labour discrimination, mass incarceration and immigration fees, as well as historical practices of colonialism, slavery, immigration head taxes, and racist labour discrimination that make accumulating and passing on income and wealth far less likely than for white people. The third cycle is one in which some people get large wealth transfers because they are born lucky and inherit wealth. This creates an intergenerational cycle of wealth accumulation. Breaking these cycles could mean dismantling capitalist relations, interrupting the rich-get-richer cycle by redistributing those resources or banning inheritance. Banning inheritance doesn't mean forbidding the passing on of keepsakes and personal property, but it does mean stopping the transferring of real estate and wealth — largely as a birthright that helps ensure power and wealth remain concentrated in the hands of the few (Burgis 2020). It is through breaking the cycle of wealth accumulation that resources can be more fairly distributed.

Growth in Income Share for Rich Since 1982

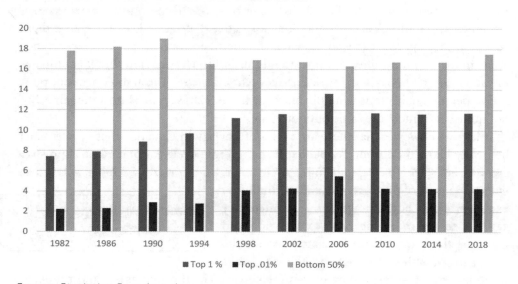

Source: Statistics Canada, n.d.a

REMEDIATING POVERTY

Together, the provinces and federal government administer a series of programs that make up Canada's social safety net. Nets, by definition, have holes. Canada's social safety net has many holes; they vary depending on the jurisdiction and have gotten larger with decades of neoliberal cuts. The social safety net is made up of programs, like social assistance and the guaranteed income supplement, that are directed specifically towards poor people in order to alleviate poverty. These are specific, means-tested interventions, which is to say only those living below a certain means — below set income and asset levels — qualify for these benefits. Some benefits are paid to people with a wider range of incomes, but they decrease as income levels increase. The Alberta Child and Family Benefit is an example of this kind of benefit (Government of Alberta n.d.).

The overt purpose of income supports is to ameliorate the worst effects of poverty. A pluralist — someone who believes governments mediate between competing groups and their interests — would say this is the sole purpose of social assistance. Others argue that there is a covert purpose for these programs: to regulate poor people. Income assistance, according to Piven and Cloward (1993), subdues and controls poor people so that they do not revolt. For example, workers' compensation programs were some of the earliest positive programs implemented for workers. They were first created in Germany in the late 1880s as an attempt to suppress union and socialist organizing (Fay 1950; Stepanov 2008; Weber 2008). When workers' compensation programs were adopted in Canada, there was significant pressure from unions (Guest 1997). Social insurance in the United States was also created to undercut socialist organizing and growing popularity (Weber 2008). Both the Canadian and American governments implemented early forms of social welfare to show workers that the government was responsive to their needs — that they didn't need to become unionists or socialists. Many of the programs that poor people rely on today trace their lineage to protest movements of the past (Palmer and Héroux 2016; Piven and Cloward 1979).

Income assistance can also be operationalized to mould the behaviours of poor people and attempt to make them more beholden to the labour market. Many benefits pay an additional amount if someone in the family works in paid employment. For example, the Alberta government says, for the Alberta Child and Family Benefit, "As families work more they receive more benefits, encouraging them to join or remain in the workforce" (Government of Alberta n.d.: n.p.). The logic here is to instill a work ethic onto the poor, who are constructed as not having initiative themselves. With social assistance rates that are often too low to get by on, policies like these are designed to push workers into menial, potentially dangerous work at the first opportunity. These types of benefits also act as a subsidy for employers who can, therefore, not pay workers sufficiently to support their families.

While there are social policies to soften the blows of poverty, there are other policies that make being poor much harder. For instance, lack of legal representation, which has become increasingly prominent with cuts to legal aid in some jurisdictions (Brewin and Stephens 2004; Hasham 2020), means that poor people are less likely to be represented for eviction hearings and criminal and immigration matters. This means that people can be deported, incarcerated or made homeless because they cannot afford a lawyer. Further, social assistance in many provinces penalizes people for cohabiting with a partner by providing a lower amount of assistance for a couple than two individuals. Further, Ontario considers a couple to be common-law spouses after three years but legally spouses for the purposes of social assistance after three months (Community Legal Education Ontario 2017; Ministry of the Attorney General 2012). This means that if someone moves in with a partner, their already low payments will be reduced. If that partner isn't on social assistance, the person could be cut off and made entirely financially dependent on their partner. This can be especially devastating for someone on disability benefits, for whom it could take many months to requalify if the couple breaks up. Social policy could redistribute income in Canada much more than it does; instead of reducing poverty, many policies make poor people's lives harder and diminish their ability to fight those policies.

Charity is also used to soften the blows of the violence of poverty. Charity, often taking the form of food or survival supplies, can be helpful — even lifesaving. But the social relation of charity is clear: there is a giver (of a donation or paid labour) and a receiver. Charity does not address the causes of poverty. Also, with it, power flows down from the giver to the receiver; the giver decides what is needed, and what is given can be taken away (or stopped). With charity, poor people are passive recipients and the root causes of poverty are not addressed (Chapman and Withers 2019; Withers 2012).

POOR PEOPLE'S RESISTANCE AND SOLVING POVERTY

The cycle of wealth accumulation can be broken, and poverty can be eliminated. Poor people can, have and do resist exploitation, oppression and impoverishment.

> The cycle of wealth accumulation can be broken, and poverty can be eliminated.

The social services that protect so many of us were won through organized resistance that poor people were a part of (Palmer and Héroux 2016; Piven and Cloward 1979). This includes workers' compensation, as discussed above, and access to and funding for social housing (Withers 2020). Further, it was after years of protests by mostly unemployed people, including violent, repressive attacks by the police through the Great Depression, that unemployment insurance (now employment insurance) was won. It was finally granted to workers in 1940, not out of generosity but out of fear — fear that they would continue to protest and possibly force even more radical changes (Manley 1998; Struthers 1983).

As the rich increasingly concentrate their wealth, poor people must mobilize not only to protect what already exists from neoliberal attack but to end the cycle of wealth accumulation. Historically, a major source of power for working poor people has been through organized labour, or unions. Many of the protections that workers enjoy today, like the eight-hour workday, parental leave and equal pay for equal work were fought for and won by unions (Ontario Federation of Labour 2013). Unions bargain collectively for workers and have the power of the strike if they need to use it. This collective power is demonstrated through higher pay rates for workers with union coverage ($32.66/hour), who make higher wages on average than those workers without union coverage ($28.08/hour). This especially impacts temporary workers with union coverage who make, on average, $9/hour more than workers without any union coverage (Statistics Canada 2021c).

However, unions are increasingly under attack. Neoliberal governments have implemented legislation to make it harder for unions to organize in several provinces (Canadian Foundation for Labour Rights n.d.). The business model for much of the gig economy is to combat worker power, especially unionization (Johnston and Land-Kazlauskas 2018). When Foodora workers won the right

> Neoliberal governments have implemented legislation to make it harder for unions to organize.

to unionize in Canada, the company left the country (Edmiston 2020). These things, and the rise in precarious work in general, have led to a decline in the number of people in unions. The private sector union coverage rate dropped 5.5 percent between 1997 and 2020; the overall unionization rate declined 2.4 percent. These may not seem like substantial numbers, but they represent tens of thousands of workers (Statistics Canada n.d.e). Unions have also been criticized for developing their own labour bureaucracy that contains and manages worker resistance rather than developing and building it. Canadian unions continue to win important worker protections; however, they do not organize large-scale resistance to capitalist interests through general strikes and disruptive protests as they have in days gone by. Wide-scale, organized labour resistance movements have the potential to be rekindled.

Union strikes are powerful because "unionized workers can assert their strength by not being where their employer wants them to be." But, collectively, poor unemployed people "can only have power by being where they're not supposed to be" (Clarke 2010: n.p.). It is through disruption — being where they aren't supposed to be, behaving in ways they are not supposed to behave — that poor people can win meaningful gains (Piven and Cloward 1979). Organizing within poor communities, however, can be very difficult. Poor people often have few resources, must spend a lot of time trying to solve their immediate material needs (including trying to exit poverty), are often politically disempowered and are not necessarily living in situations where they can take risks (risks that include opposing the powers that be, investing their time and resources on something that might not work out, confronting multiple forms of oppression) (see, for example, Combahee River Collective 1977; Cress and Snow 1996; Piven and Cloward 1979). In addition to these issues, the divisions between the "deserving" and "undeserving" poor that have been constructed impede class solidarity: working poor people and disabled people are reticent to align themselves with "lazy welfare bums," for example. Poor people also often adopt oppressive attitudes that are designed to pit them against one another. An example of this is when homeless white people blame refugees for their lack of housing rather than capitalist social relations and the governmental withdrawal from sufficient social housing provision.

One of the ways that organizing poor people has been successful has been to organize to address people's immediate needs while fighting for long-term social change. Groups often do different kinds of political education to combat the divide between the "deserving" and "undeserving" poor and unite people across oppressions (Piven and Cloward 1979; Walia 2013; Withers 2021). This is because, as long-time activist Beric German (2009) put it, "It cannot just be pie in the sky, it has to be pie that you can eat." Different communities have had various ways of carrying out this basic strategy of mass mobilizing while meeting immediate need. Perhaps the most well-known group to have done this is the Black Panther Party (BPP), which was founded in Oakland, California, in 1966 (Hassberg 2020). The BPP was a Black Power organization fighting for the implementation of their "Ten-Point Program." This included reparations for slavery, full employment, housing, free healthcare, elimination of police brutality, the decarceration of all Black men,[15] ending the draft for Black men, land, bread, justice and peace. Their first demand stated: "We want freedom. We want power to determine the destiny of our Black community" (Black Panther Party 1968: 16). The Ten-Point Program articulates a long-term struggle calling for radical social transformation. Recognizing the material deprivation in the Black community, it established numerous "survival programs" over its many chapters; these included health clinics, legal aid, services to test for sickle cell anemia, schools, an ambulance program, cop watches and a breakfast program that fed roughly fifteen thousand to thirty thousand children a day (Hassberg 2020). While the long-term struggle that was put forward in the Ten-Point Program continues, the BPP has had a significant influence on generations of community organizers, and it forced the government to implement some programs that helped the Black community. Perhaps the most overt victory for the BPP was that the government of California adopted state-wide breakfast programs in 1975.

> As long-time activist Beric German put it, "It cannot just be pie in the sky, it has to be pie that you can eat."

Many other groups of poor people and their allies organize on a smaller scale and are still impactful in winning change. The Ontario Coalition Against Poverty (OCAP), for example, is a Toronto-based organization that has done direct action casework coupled with mass mobilizing. The Special Diet Campaign it organized was designed to put more money directly into the pockets of those on social assistance while they collectively fought for higher social assistance rates (medium term) and an end to poverty and capitalism (long term). As the group organized towards these larger struggles, it worked to help people get all the benefits they were entitled to through social assistance. One of these benefits was extra money for food. If a social assistance recipient form was filled out by a healthcare provider, they could get up to $250 a month; for a family of five, this was an extra $1,250 a month, or $18,750 a year. OCAP did three things so people could access the benefit. First, it informed poor people about the benefit. Many people on social assistance are living in food and housing insecurity and they could access more funds, but government bureaucracy keeps that information from them. Second, OCAP connected people to healthcare providers so they could access the benefit. This was important because a lot of poor people don't have access to (decent) healthcare providers. Third, OCAP worked with the community to have people's backs if they were denied all or part of the Special Diet Benefit. OCAP would go with groups of people on social assistance who were being denied and their allies to the welfare or disability office and not let business as usual happen until they got a meeting with a supervisor and, ultimately, got people's money. The first year of the campaign, spending on the benefit increased by $71 million. In the second year of the campaign, OCAP held a "Mass Hunger Clinic" on the lawn of the legislative grounds. That single day, over a thousand people were signed up to the Special Diet Benefit. The province repeatedly slashed the benefit to try and keep poor people from accessing funds for food but continued to be met with resistance and growing numbers of people accessing the Special Diet. By 2013, $200 million a year more was going directly to poor people than had been when the campaign had begun nine years earlier (Withers 2019, 2021). Throughout this period, OCAP worked to build poor peoples' resistance, "showed that it is possible to reject the role of the help-less victim and fight back" and was able to help secure small raises in social assistance along the way (Lightman, Mitchell and Wilson 2009; OCAP 2015: 2).

The wealthy continue to consolidate their wealth and neoliberalism has only intensified over the last decades. This, of course, takes place in the context of a growing climate crisis. The casualties of the climate crisis, like the global pandemic, are largely poor people and primarily Indigenous and racialized people — people who do not have the resources to shield themselves from the crises around them. British Columbia experienced a deadly "heat dome" in 2021 that killed eight hundred people. The people who died were largely seniors living alone in inadequately ventilated units — it certainly wasn't largely people who could afford pools and central air (Weichel 2021). Additionally, a Human Rights Watch (2019) report found that climate change means Indigenous peoples' "rights to food, health, and culture are at risk."

However, there is one thing that the greed of the rich has left the poor with: numbers. While Canada is a very wealthy nation, it has large numbers of poor people, which opens the possibility for poor people to build a strong resistance. As this chapter has shown, poverty impacts all demographic groups, but the impact is uneven and oppressed groups are much more likely to be poor. Divisions like "deserving" and "undeserving" poor, as well as prejudice, can divide poor people and keep them from mobilizing together. This is one thing that political organizing can help overcome, especially if it provides political education while working to address immediate material needs as part of the long-term resistance to poverty.

Poor and working-class people's organizing has won important gains that make up the foundation of Canada's social safety net, a safety net that has undergone many neoliberal cuts. Poor people's organizing can defend what currently exists and win new concessions. However, as long as there is capitalism, there will be poverty because capitalism requires a reserve army of labour. The only way to truly abolish poverty is to abolish the capitalist relations that create and benefit from it. Eliminating capitalism is a long-term struggle and there are many things that can be done along the way.

Winning incremental victories can help reduce the harms of poverty and grow the movement against it. The two most pressing needs for people are housing and income. Social assistance raises are needed across the country. People are fighting to protect or improve specific benefits and make sure individuals get what they are entitled to. Some communities have also set up sharing economies so people can trade their time instead of money for what they need. Canada needs hundreds of thousands of units of social housing and only a strong social movement will push the government into building them. In the interim, some communities are organizing eviction defence groups, where neighbours are coming together to help keep people in their homes. Others are working to defend shelter beds and homeless encampments from cutbacks and evictions. Canada has profound wealth and profound inequality. By working together, poor people and their allies can win better resource distribution and social programs now and an end to poverty in the future.

DISCUSSION QUESTIONS

1. What is the relationship between the capitalist economic system and poverty?
2. Why are different social groups more or less likely to be impacted by poverty? What are some policy interventions that could be taken to diminish the disparities between social groups? What are some things that you and your community can do to help change this phenomenon?
3. Why is measuring poverty such a complex undertaking? What are the benefits and drawbacks of using absolute and relative measures of poverty? What do those measures tell us about poor people in a given society? What do they tell us about a given society?
4. Why have governments not introduced more adequate measures to reduce poverty?

What are actions you and your community could take to help change this?

5. Why do you think the Canadian government publicizes the gender wage gap rather than the income gap?

6. What are some organizing projects that you could do or get involved in to help reduce or end poverty?

GLOSSARY OF KEY TERMS

Capitalism: The economic system, driven by profit, in which private owners use the means of production to dispossess and exploit the working class and poor.

Deserving poor: Those considered to be deserving of assistance because the cause of their poverty is deemed no fault of their own.

Cycle of poverty: Poverty that is passed on from one generation to the next.

Food insecurity: Not having access to sufficient quality or quantity of food.

Housing insecurity (core housing need): Lack of proper housing in terms of affordability (costs over 30 percent of income), adequacy (requires major repair) and suitability (it is overcrowded, does not have appropriate rooms and so on).

Low-Income Measure (LIM): A relative poverty measure that sets the poverty line below a percent of median household incomes (i.e., 50 percent), adjusted for family size. After-tax LIM adjusts for tax transfers and redistribution.

Market Basket Measure (MBM): An absolute poverty measure that establishes a necessary "basket" of goods per household; they fall below the poverty line if their income cannot obtain the entire "basket." What gets put in the basket is always somewhat arbitrary and can exclude necessary expenses that make poverty rates look lower than they are.

Poverty: A position of material deprivation that can be relative to others in society (LIM) or absolute, which means one cannot secure a necessary set of goods (MBM).

Poverty line: The arbitrary line that, if one makes a lower amount than others in a set time for a given region, they are considered poor. Canada's poverty line is the MBM.

Undeserving poor: Poor people discursively constructed as not deserving of assistance because they are supposedly responsible for their circumstances, said to be lazy or lacking work ethic and needing to be disciplined to get to work.

RESOURCES FOR ACTIVISTS

Crackdown podcast: crackdownpod.com
Eviction Defence Network: evictiondefencebc.org
le Front d'action populaire en réaménagement urbain (FRAPRU): frapru.qc.ca
Ontario Coalition Against Poverty: ocap.ca
People's Defence Toronto: facebook.com/PeoplesDefenceTO
Redbraid Alliance for Decolonial Socialism: redbraid.org
Shelter and Housing Justice Network: shjn.ca

NOTES

1 Author's calculation.
2 The terms "sexual minority" and "Two-Spirit" cannot be collapsed. Some Two-Spirit people identify as sexual minorities, while some may identify as lesbian, gay, bi, queer or asexual, for example. Others identify as trans (along gender but not sexuality lines) while others identify solely as Two-Spirit, rejecting colonial conceptualizations of sexual and gender identity.
3 Here, Indigenous peoples are people who identified as an "Aboriginal person" in the 2016 census; "this includes those who are First Nations (North American Indian), Métis or Inuk (Inuit) and/or those who are Registered or Treaty Indians (that is, registered under the *Indian Act* of Canada), and/ or those who have membership in a First Nation or Indian band" (Statistics Canada 2015).
4 Statistics Canada includes Indigenous peoples in the category of "non-visible minority," deflating the poverty line for white people. The simple explanation for this is that race and Indigeneity are dealt with in separate questions, so creating a category of "non-visible minority" that excludes people who answer positively to the "visible minority" question is simplistic and expedient. However, in Canada generally, there is an absence of clear and specific race-based data. Including Indigenous peoples in this category makes using the term "white" here problematic. "White" is used here because not using it allows the Canadian settler state to depoliticize this data with the term "non-visible minority" and negate the realities of racism in Canada.
5 Author's tabulation. Adjusted to remove separate Indigenous and white populations.
6 There was no available research on intersex-specific poverty. These two groups, if mentioned at all in the Canadian poverty literature, are simply added to the list of identities under the "rainbow umbrella." Intersex people are included here because the oppression and struggles of this group are documented and similar to, although distinct from, the other groups listed. Additionally, by trans, I mean trans, transgender, transsexual, non-binary, gender variant, bi-gender, cross-gender, gender-queer, MTF, FTM, transwomen, transmen, trans-identifying Two-Spirit and other similarly identified people.
7 This study only reported results for LGB people. Non-binary and other gender-diverse people were permitted to report that they identified as "gender diverse" but their aggregated responses were with-held for confidentiality purposes.
8 No data was available for 2SLGBTQI+ people and disabled people but the employment income pay gap is also likely substantial and higher for people who are also members of other oppressed groups.
9 Percentages calculated by author.
10 Alberta had tied disability benefits to inflation but the United Conservative Party government un-tied them in 2019, ensuring that disability benefits will likely decline in real dollars over time as well (Yousif 2019). However, that same government raised welfare rates well above inflation in 2019 as well. The Yukon ties welfare directly to inflation (Laidley and Aldridge 2020).

11 Additionally, 25 percent of all racialized kids are poor. Because of available Statistics Canada data, Black and racialized kids are categorized as ages zero to seventeen while First Nations kids are ages zero to fifteen.

12 Canada frequently tries to minimize this by calling it "cultural genocide," but Patrick Wolfe (2006: 398) tells us not to confuse "definition with degree."

13 There are some important exceptions to this: there are First Nations-run schools and Indigenous schools as well as Afrocentric schools. These, however, are few and far between. The vast majority of people being educated will be educated under the white, colonial system. Until that system is undone, education will continue to be offered as an assimilative individual solution to eliminate poverty.

14 Incomes here are what were reported in taxes, so they are likely underreported by wealthy people who have greater capacity to evade taxes.

15 The Black Panthers were often progressive in terms of gender; for example, many women had prominent leadership positions. However, their call for the decarceration of all Black *men* either represents the erasure of Black women through the universal use of "men" or of the disproportionate rates of Black women's incarceration. Like everyone, the Black Panthers were imperfect and always ran the risk of reinforcing oppressions as they worked to dismantle them.

REFERENCES

Abramovich, A., and J. Shelton. 2017. "Introduction: Where Are We Now?" In A. Abramovich and J. Shelton (eds.), *Where Am I Going To Go? Intersectional Approaches to Ending* LGBTQ2S *Youth Homelessness in Canada & the US*. Toronto: Canadian Observatory on Homelessness Press.

Arriagada, P., T. Hahmann and V. O'Donnell. 2020. "Indigenous People in Urban Areas: Vulnerabilities to the Socioeconomic Impacts of COVID-19." *StatCan* COVID-19: *Data to Insights for a Better Canada*. <www150.statcan.gc.ca/n1/pub/45-28-0001/2020001/article/00023-eng.htm>.

Bank of Canada. 2021. "Core Functions." *Bank of Canada*. <bankofcanada.ca/core-functions/monetary-policy>.

Battiste, M. 2013. *Decolonizing Education: Nourishing the Learning Spirit*. Saskatoon: Purich Publishing.

Bauer, G., N. Nussbaum, R. Travers et al. 2011. "We've Got Work to Do: Workplace Discrimination and Employment Challenges for Trans People in Ontario." *Trans* PULSE *E-Bulletin* 2, 1. <transpulseproject.ca/wp-content/uploads/2011/05/E3English.pdf>.

Beedie, N., D. Macdonald, and D. Wilson. 2019. "Towards Justice: Tackling Indigenous Child Poverty in Canada." Saskatoon: CCPA *and Upstream*. <afn.ca/wp-content/uploads/2019/07/Upstream_report_final_English_June-24-2019.pdf>.

Bejan, R., and K. Allain. 2021. "Profits Trump COVID-19 Protections for Migrant Seafood Workers in Atlantic Canada." *The Conversation*, March 4. <theconversation.com/profits-trump-COVID-19-protections-for-migrant-seafood-workers-in-atlantic-canada-154920>.

Bhabha, H. 2004. *The Location of Culture*. New York: Routledge.

Black Panther Party. 1968. "The Black Panther Ten-Point Program." *The North American Review* 253, 4.

Block, S., G.-E. Galabuzi, and R. Tranjan. 2019. "Canada's Colour Coded Income Inequality." Canadian Centre for Policy Alternatives, December. <policyalternatives.ca/sites/default/files/uploads/publications/National%20Office/2019/12/Canada%27s%20Colour%20Coded%20Income%20Inequality.pdf>.

Bonilla-Silva, E. 2003. *Racism Without Racists: Color-Blind Racism and the Persistence of Racial Inequality in the United States*. Lanham: Rowman and Littlefield.

Brewin, A., and L. Stephens. 2004. *Legal Aid Denied: Women and the Cuts to Legal Services in BC*. Vancouver: Canadian Centre for Policy Alternatives. <policyalternatives.ca/sites/default/files/uploads/publications/BC_Office_Pubs/legal_services.pdf>.

Bryant, T., S. Aquanno, and D. Raphael. 2020. "Unequal Impact of COVID-19: Emergency Neoliberalism and Welfare Policy in Canada." *Critical Studies: An International & Interdisciplinary Journal* 15, 1. <ojs.scholarsportal.info/ontariotechu/index.php/cs/article/view/108>.

Budig, M.J., J. Misra, and I. Boeckmann. 2012. "The Motherhood Penalty in Cross-National Perspective: The Importance of Work-Family Policies and Cultural Attitudes." *Social Politics: International Studies in Gender, State & Society* 19, 2.

Burgis, B. 2020. "Abolish Inherited Wealth." *Jacobin,* December 31. <jacobinmag.com/2020/12/abolish-inherited-wealth-inequality>.

Cameron, E.S., and K. Jefferies. 2021. "Anti-Black Racism in Canadian Education: A Call to Action to Support the next Generation." *Healthy Populations Journal* 1, 1.

Canadian Foundation for Labour Rights. n.d. "Restrictive Labour Laws: Labour Rights Under Attack 230 Restrictive Labour Laws." <labourrights.ca/restrictive-labour-laws>.

Canel-Çınarbaş, D., and S. Yohani. 2019. "Indigenous Canadian University Students' Experiences of Microaggressions." *International Journal for the Advancement of Counselling* 41, 1. <doi.org/10.1007/s10447-018-9345-z>.

Caregivers' Action Centre, Vancouver Committee for Domestic Workers and Caregivers Rights, Caregiver Connections Education and Support Organization, and The Migrant Workers Alliance for Change. 2020. "Behind Closed Doors: Exposing Migrant Care Worker Exploitation During covid-19." <migrantrights.ca/wp-content/uploads/2020/10/Behind-Closed-Doors_Exposing-Migrant-Care-Worker-Exploitation-During-covid19.pdf>.

Chapman, C., and A.J. Withers. 2019. *A Violent History of Benevolence: Interlocking Oppression in the Moral Economies of Social Working.* Toronto: University of Toronto Press.

Clarke, J. 2010. "ocap Marks Its First Twenty Years." *The Bullet*, November 26. <socialistproject.ca/bullet/432.php>.

Claveau, J. 2020. "The Canadian Housing Survey, 2018: Core Housing Need of Renter Households Living in Social and Affordable Housing." Statistics Canada. <www150.statcan.gc.ca/n1/pub/75f-0002m/75f0002m2020003-eng.htm>.

cmhc (Canada Mortgage and Housing Corporation). 2018. "Housing Conditions of Aboriginal Households Living On-Reserve." <cmhc-schl.gc.ca/en/professionals/housing-markets-data-and-research/housing-data/data-tables/household-characteristics/housing-conditions-aboriginal-households-living-on-reserve>.

Combahee River Collective. 1977. "The Combahee River Collective Statement." <blackpast.org/african-american-history/combahee-river-collective-statement-1977/>.

Community Legal Education Ontario. 2017. "Social Assistance Rules About Couples: What You Need to Know If You Live With Someone." <cleo.on.ca/en/publications/cohab-en>.

Crenshaw, K. 1989. "Demarginalizing the Intersection of Race and Sex: A Black Feminist Critique of Antidiscrimination Doctrine, Feminist Theory and Antiracist Politics." *University of Chicago Legal Forum* 1, 8.

Cress, D.M., and D.A. Snow. 1996. "Mobilization at the Margins: Resources, Benefactors, and the Viability of Homeless Social Movement Organizations." *American Sociological Review* 61, 6.

Crouse, D.L., N.A. Ross, and M.S. Goldberg. 2009. "Double Burden of Deprivation and High Concentrations of Ambient Air Pollution at the Neighbourhood Scale in Montreal, Canada." *Social Science & Medicine* 69, 6.

Djidel, S., B. Gustajtis, A. Heisz et al. 2020. "Report on the Second Comprehensive Review of the Market Basket Measure." *Statistics Canada.* <www150.statcan.gc.ca/n1/pub/75f-0002m/75f0002m2020002-eng.htm>.

Dorman, K., R. Pellizzar, M. Rachlis, and S. Green. 2013. "Why Poverty Is a Medical Problem." *Ontario Medical Review* Part 1. <healthprovidersagainstpoverty.files.wordpress.com/2015/07/part-1-why-poverty-is-a-medical-problem.pdf>.

Edmiston, J. 2020. "Foodora to Close Canadian Operations amid Union Push by Couriers." *Financial Post*, April 27. <financialpost.com/news/retail-marketing/foodora-to-close-canadian-operations-amid-union-push-by-couriers>.

Employment and Social Development Canada. 2018. "Opportunity for All: Canada's First Poverty Reduction Strategy." <publications.gc.ca/site/eng/9.857663/publication.html>.

Evans, G.W., and P. Kim. 2007. "Childhood Poverty and Health." *Psychological Science* 18, 11. <doi.org/10.1111/j.1467-9280.2007.02008.x>.

Faraday, F. 2021. "covid-19's Impact on Migrant Workers Adds Urgency to Calls for Permanent Status." *The Conversation*, February 24. <theconversation.com/covid-19s-impact-on-migrant-workers-adds-urgency-to-calls-for-permanent-status-148237>.

Fay, S.B. 1950. "Bismarck's Welfare State." *Current History* 18, 101.

Fellows, M.L., and S. Razack. 1997. "The Race to Innocence: Confronting Hierarchical Relations among Women." *Journal of Gender, Race and Justice* 1.

Feng, H., K. Frank, and C. Schimmele. 2020. "Economic Impact of covid-19 among Visible Minority Groups." *StatCan covid-19: Data to Insights for a Better Canada. Statistics Canada.* <www150.statcan.gc.ca/n1/pub/45-28-0001/2020001/article/00042-eng.htm>.

Ferguson, H.B., S. Bovaird, and M.P. Mueller. 2007. "The Impact of Poverty on Educational Outcomes for Children." *Paediatrics & Child Health* 12, 8.

Fox, D., and M. Moyser. 2018. "Women in Canada: A Gender-Based Statistical Report The Economic Well-Being of Women in Canada." *Statistics Canada.* <www150.statcan.gc.ca/n1/pub/89-503-x/89-503-x2015001-eng.htm>.

Francis, D.D. 2009. "Conceptualizing Child Health Disparities: A Role for Developmental Neurogenomics." *Pediatrics* 124 (Supplement 3).

Fuller, S. 2018. "Segregation across Workplaces and the Motherhood Wage Gap: Why Do Mothers Work in Low-Wage Establishments?" *Social Forces* 96, 4.

Galvin, D. 2018. "Remembering Kimberly Rogers." *Hamilton Spectator*, August 16.

German, B. 2009. "No Title." *Worker's Assembly Public Meeting*, October 2.

Government of Alberta. n.d. "Alberta Child and Family Benefit." <alberta.ca/alberta-child-and-family-benefit.aspx#jumplinks-1>.

Government of British Columbia. 2019. "Together BC: British Columbia's Poverty Reduction Strategy." Victoria. <www2.gov.bc.ca/assets/gov/british-columbians-our-governments/initiatives-plans-strategies/poverty-reduction-strategy/togetherbc.pdf>.

Government of Canada. 2018. "Backgrounder: Strengthening the Canada Child Benefit." <canada.ca/en/department-finance/news/2018/03/backgrounder-strengthening-the-canada-child-benefit>.

Government of Manitoba. n.d. "Employment and Income Assistance: For Single Parents." <gov.mb.ca/fs/eia/eia_single_parents.html>.

___. 2019. *Pathways to a Better Future: Manitoba's Poverty Reduction Strategy.* Winnipeg. <gov.mb.ca/povertyreduction/pubs/pathways_to_a_better_future.pdf>.

Government of Ontario. 2008. "Breaking the Cycle: Ontario's Poverty Reduction Strategy." Toronto. <docs.ontario.ca/documents/3367/breaking-the-cycle.pdf>.

Graefe, P. 2015. "Social Assistance in Ontario." In D. Béland and P.-M. Daigneault (eds.), *Welfare Reform in Canada: Provincial Social Assistance in Comparative Perspective.* Toronto: University of Toronto Press.

Guest, D. 1997. *The Emergence of Social Security in Canada*, 3rd edition. Vancouver: ubc Press.

Hasham, A. 2020. "Legal Aid Ontario Facing up to $70 Million Funding Drop amid covid-19 'Perfect Storm.'" *Toronto Star*, July 13. <thestar.com/news/canada/2020/07/13/legal-aid-ontario-facing-up-to-70-million-funding-drop-amid-covid-19-perfect-storm.html>.

Hassberg, A.H. 2020. "Nurturing the Revolution: The Black Panther Party and the Early Seeds of the Food Justice Movement." In H. Garth and A.M. Reese (eds.), *Black Food Matters: Racial Justice in the Wake of Food Justice.* Minneapolis: University of Minnesota Press.

Heisz, A. 2019. "An Update on the Market Basket Measure Comprehensive Review." *Income Research Paper Series. Statistics Canada.* <www150.statcan.gc.ca/n1/pub/75f0002m/75f0002m2019009-eng.htm>.

Hershkowitz, M., G. Hudson, and H. Bauder. 2021. "Rescaling the Sanctuary City: Police and Non-Status Migrants in Ontario, Canada." *International Migration* 59, 1.

Human Rights Watch. 2019. "'My Fear Is Losing Everything': The Climate Crisis and First Nations' Right to Food in Canada." <hrw.org/report/2020/10/21/my-fear-losing-everything/climate-crisis-and-first-nations-right-food-canada>.

Income Security Advocacy Centre. 2009. "Social Assistance Rate Restructuring and the Ontario Child Benefit." *Fact Sheet: Update.* <incomesecurity.org/wp-content/uploads/2020/04/Rate_Restructuring_and_the_Ontario_Child_Benefit_-_Fact_Sheet_-_Update_-_2009.doc>.

Johnston, H., and C. Land-Kazlauskas. 2018. "Organizing On-Demand: Representation, Voice, and Collective Bargaining in the Gig Economy." Geneva: International Labour Office. <ilo.org/wcmsp5/groups/public/---ed_protect/---protrav/---travail/documents/publication/wcms_624286.pdf>.

Kia, H., M. Robinson, J. MacKay, and L.E. Ross. 2020. "Poverty in Lesbian, Gay, Bisexual, Transgender, Queer, and Two-Spirit (LGBTQ2S+) Populations in Canada: An Intersectional Review of the Literature." *Journal of Poverty and Social Justice* 28, 1.

Klein, S. 2012. "New BC Welfare Rules: Some Positive Steps Forward (and a Couple Steps Back)." *Policy Note*, June 12. <policynote.ca/new-bc-welfare-rules-some-positive-steps-forward-and-a-couple-steps-back>.

Klein, S, and J. Pulkingham. 2008. *Living on Welfare in BC: Experiences of Longer-Term "Expected to Work" Recipients.* Vancouver: *Canadian Centre for Policy Alternatives — BC Office and Raise the Rate*s. <policyalternatives.ca/sites/default/files/uploads/publications/BC_Office_Pubs/bc_2008/bc_LoW_full_web.pdf>.

Ku, J., R. Bhuyan, I. Sakamoto et al. 2019. "'Canadian Experience' Discourse and Anti-Racialism in a 'Post-Racial' Society." *Ethnic and Racial Studies* 42, 2.

Laidley, J., and H. Aldridge. 2020. "Welfare in Canada, 2019." Toronto: Maytree and Caledon. <maytree.com/wp-content/uploads/Welfare_in_Canada_2019.pdf>.

Li, J., and J. Neborak. 2018. "Tax, Race, and Child Poverty: The Case for Improving the Canada Child Benefit Program." *Journal of Law and Social Policy* 28, 2.

Lightman, E., A. Mitchell, and B. Wilson. 2009. *Sick and Tired: The Compromised Health of Social Assistance Recipients and the Working Poor in Ontario.* Toronto: Community Social Planning Council of Toronto (CSPC-T), University of Toronto's Social Assistance in the New Economy Project (SANE) and the Wellesley Institute. <wellesleyinstitute.com/wp-content/uploads/2011/11/sickand-tiredfinal.pdf>.

Lindsay, S., E. Cagliostro, M. Albarico et al. 2018. "A Systematic Review of the Benefits of Hiring People with Disabilities." *Journal of Occupational Rehabilitation* 28, 4.

Little, M.H. 1994. "'Manhunts and Bingo Blabs': The Moral Regulation of Ontario Single Mothers." *Canadian Journal of Sociology / Cahiers Canadiens de Sociologie* 19, 2. <doi.org/10.2307/3341346>.

Little, M.H., and I. Morrison. 1999. "'The Pecker Detectors Are Back': Regulation of the Family Form in Ontario Welfare Policy." *Journal of Canadian Studies/Revue d'études Canadiennes* 34, 2.

Lum, Z.-A. 2021. "A New Task Force Hopes to Tackle Canada's 'She-Cession.' Here's What They're Up Against." *Chatelaine*, March. <chatelaine.com/news/task-force-women-economy-canada>.

Macdonald, D., and D. Wilson. 2016. "Shameful Neglect: Indigenous Child Poverty in Canada." *Canadian Centre for Policy Alternatives.* <policyalternatives.ca/sites/default/files/uploads/publications/National%20Office/2016/05/Indigenous_Child%20_Poverty.pdf>.

Manley, J. 1998. "'Starve, Be Damned!' Communists and Canada's Urban Unemployed, 1929–39." *Canadian Historical Review* 79, 3. <doi.org/10.3138/CHR.79.3.466>.

Marmot, M., J. Allen, R. Bell et al. 2012. "WHO European Review of Social Determinants of Health and the Health Divide." *The Lancet* 380, 9846.

Marx, K. [1894] 1991. *Capital: A Critique of Political Economy, Volume III*, trans. David Fernbach. London: Penguin Books.

___. 1887. *Capital: A Critical Analysis of Capitalist Production, Volume I*, trans. Samuel Moore and Edward Aveling. New York: International Publishers.

Maynard, R. 2017. *Policing Black Lives: State Violence in Canada from Slavery to the Present.* Halifax and Winnipeg: Fernwood Publishing.

Ministry of the Attorney General. 2012. "What You Should Know About Family Law in Ontario." <attorneygeneral.jus.gov.on.ca/english/family/familyla.html>.

Mojtehedzadeh, S. 2021. "How Crowded Are Migrant Worker Bunkhouses? A Survey Shines a Light on Housing Conditions That 'Cost Lives.'" *Toronto Star*, June 10. <thestar.com/news/canada/2021/06/10/how-crowded-are-migrant-worker-bunkhouses-a-survey-shines-a-light-on-housing-conditions-that-cost-lives.html?rf>.

Morris, S., G. Fawcett, L. Brisebois, and J. Hughes. 2018. "A Demographic, Employment and Income Profile of Canadians with Disabilities Aged 15 Years and Over, 2017." Statistics Canada. <www150.statcan.gc.ca/n1/pub/89-654-x/89-654-x2018002-eng.htm>.

Mugabo, D. 2014. "Race & Intersectionality Panel Presentation." *Study in Action*, March 22.

Mulé, N. 2005. "Beyond Words in Health and Well-Being Policy." *Canadian Review of Social Policy / Revue Canadienne de Politique Sociale* 55.

Mullaly, B. 2010. *Challenging Oppression : A Critical Social Work Approach*, 2nd edition. Don Mills: Oxford University Press.

Nolen, S. 2021. "The Mother Lode: COVID-19 Created a Crisis of Care — and Working Mothers Bore the Burden." *Toronto Star*, July 28. <thestar.com/news/atkinsonseries/2021/COVID-19-working-mothers-child-care.html>.

OCAP (Ontario Coalition Against Poverty). 2015. *25 Years of Fighting to Win: Ontario Coalition Against Poverty Photo Book*. Toronto.

Ontario Federation of Labour. 2013. "The Rising of Us All: Responding to the Attack on Ontario's Unions." Toronto. <ofl.ca/wp-content/uploads/RisingOfUsAll.pdf>.

Palmer, B.D., and G. Héroux. 2016. *Toronto's Poor: A Rebellious History*. Toronto: Between the Lines.

Picot, G., and Y. Lu. 2017. "Chronic Low Income Among Immigrants in Canada and Its Communities." *Statistics Canada*. <www150.statcan.gc.ca/n1/pub/11f0019m/11f0019m2017397-eng.htm>.

Piven, F.F., and R.A. Cloward. 1993. *Regulating the Poor: The Functions of Public Welfare*. Updated. New York: Vintage Books.

____. 1979. *Poor People's Movements: Why They Succeed, How They Fail*. New York: Vintage Books.

Polsky, J.Y., and H. Gilmour. 2020. "Food Insecurity and Mental Health during the COVID-19 Pandemic." *Statistics Canada, Health Reports*. <doi.org/10.25318/82-003-x202001200001-eng>.

PROOF and FoodShare. 2019. "Fact Sheet: Race and Food Insecurity." <foodshare.net/custom/uploads/2019/11/PROOF_factsheet_press_FINAL.6.pdf>.

Quigley, W.P. 1998. "Backwards into the Future: How Welfare Changes in the Millenium Resemble English Poor Law of the Middle Ages." *Stanford Law Review* 9, 1.

Roos, L.L., E. Wall-Wieler, and J.B. Lee. 2019. "Poverty and Early Childhood Outcomes." *Pediatrics* 143, 6. <doi.org/10.1542/peds.2018-3426>.

Russell, M. 2002. "What Disability Civil Rights Cannot Do: Employment and Political Economy." *Disability & Society* 17, 2. <doi.org/10.1080/09687590120122288>.

Salvation Army. 2014. "Child Poverty Rates in Canada Remain High." July 24. <salvationarmy.ca/blog/child-poverty-rates-in-canada-remain-high/>.

Shragge, E. (ed.). 1997. *Workfare: Ideology for a New Under-Class*. Toronto: Garamond Press.

Smee, M. 2018. "Group Claims Police Are Improperly Helping CBSA Round up Undocumented Immigrants." CBC News, December 18. <cbc.ca/news/canada/toronto/group-claims-police-are-improperly-helping-cbsa-round-up-undocumented-immigrants-1.4950177>.

Solovieva, T.I., R.T. Walls, D.J. Hendricks, and D.L. Dowler. 2009. "Cost of Workplace Accommodations for Individuals with Disabilities: With or Without Personal Assistance Services." *Disability and Health Journal* 2, 4.

Statistics Canada. n.d.a. "Table 11-10-0055-01 High Income Tax Filers in Canada." <doi.org/10.25318/1110005501-eng>.

____. n.d.b. "Table 11-10-0135-01." <doi.org/10.25318/1110013501-eng>.

____. n.d.c. "Table 11-10-0135-02." <doi.org/10.25318/1110013501-eng>.

____. n.d.d. "Table 13-10-0377-01 Labour Force Status of Persons with and without Disabilities

Aged 25 to 64 Years, by Age Group and Sex, Canada, Provinces and Territories." <doi. org/10.25318/1310037701-eng>.

____. n.d.e. "Table 14-10-0132-01 Union Status by Industry." <doi.org/10.25318/1410013201-eng>.

____. 2021a. "Canadian Income Survey (5200), Custom Tabulation." <www150.statcan.gc.ca/n1/daily-quotidien/210323/t004a-eng.htm#fn02>.

____. 2021b. "Canada's Official Poverty Dashboard of Indicators: Trends, March 2021." <www150.statcan.gc.ca/n1/pub/11-627-m/11-627-m2021010-eng.htm>.

____. 2021c. "Table 14-10-0066-01 Employee Wages by Job Permanency and Union Coverage, Annual." Ottawa. <doi.org/10.25318/1410006601-eng>.

____. 2020. "Household Food Insecurity, 2017/2018." *Health Fact Sheets.* <www150.statcan.gc.ca/n1/pub/82-625-x/2020001/article/00001-eng.htm>.

____. 2019a. "2016 Census of Population, Statistics Canada Catalogue No. 98-400-X2016211." <www150.statcan.gc.ca/n1/en/catalogue/98-400-X2016211>.

____. 2019b. "Statistics Canada Catalogue No. 98-400-X2016173." *2016 Census of Population.*

____. 2019c. "Statistics Canada Catalogue No. 98-400-X2016174." *2016 Census of Population.*

____. 2019d. "Statistics Canada Catalogue No. 98-400-X2016212." *2016 Census of Population.*

____. 2019e. "Statistics Canada Catalogue No. 98-400-X2016277." *2016 Census of Population.*

____. 2019f. "Table 17-10-0009-01." *Canada at a Glance 2019.*

____. 2019g. "The Gender Wage Gap in 2018." <www150.statcan.gc.ca/n1/pub/11-627-m/11-627-m2019065-eng.htm>.

____. 2019h. "Canada's Official Poverty Rate." *Canada's Official Poverty Dashboard*, July 18. <www150.statcan.gc.ca/n1/pub/11-627-m/11-627-m2019053-eng.htm>.

____. 2018. "Statistics Canada Catalogue No. 98-510-X2016001." *Aboriginal Population Profile.*

____. 2017a. "Immigration and Ethnocultural Diversity: Key Results from the 2016 Census," 2017. <www150.statcan.gc.ca/n1/daily-quotidien/171025/dq171025b-eng.htm?indid=14428-1&indgeo=0>.

____. 2017b. "Tables 98-400-X2016124 Low Income Indicators…" 2016 Census of Population. <www150.statcan.gc.ca/n1/en/catalogue/98-400-X2016124>.

____. 2017c. "Wages, Salaries and Commissions." *Dictionary, Census of Population, 2016.* <www12.statcan.gc.ca/census-recensement/2016/ref/dict/pop128-eng.cfm>.

____. 2015. "Aboriginal Identity of Person." <www23.statcan.gc.ca/imdb/p3Var.pl?Function=DEC&Id=42927>.

Stepanov, V.L. 2008. "The Social Legislation of Otto von Bismarck and Worker Insurance Law in Russia." *Russian Studies in History* 47, 3. <doi.org/10.2753/RSH1061-1983470303>.

Stone, D.A. 1984. *The Disabled State.* Philadelphia: Temple University Press.

Struthers, J. 1983. *No Fault of Their Own: Unemployment and the Canadian Welfare State, 1914–1941.* Toronto: University of Toronto Press.

Transpulse. 2010. "Who Are Trans People in Ontario?" *Trans PULSE E-Bulletin* 1. <transpulseproject.ca/research/who-are-trans-people-in-ontario/>.

Truscello, M., and A. Nangwaya. 2017. "Introduction: Why Don't the Poor Rise Up?" In M. Truscello and A. Nangwaya (eds.), *Why Don't the Poor Rise Up?: Organizing the Twenty-First Century Resistance.* Oakland: AK Press.

Truth and Reconciliation Commission of Canada. 2015. *Honouring the Truth, Reconciling for the Future: Summary of the Final Report of the Truth and Reconciliation Commission of Canada.* Ottawa.

Wadehra, R. 2021. "Equal Rights for Migrant Workers: The Case for Immigration Policy Transformation" CCPA, October 5. <policyalternatives.ca/publications/reports/equal-rights-migrant-care-workers>.

Waite, S., and N. Denier. 2015. "Gay Pay for Straight Work: Mechanisms Generating Disadvantage." *Gender & Society* 29, 4.

Waldron, I.R.G. 2018. *There's Something in The Water: Environmental Racism in Indigenous & Black Communities.* Black Point, NS: Fernwood Publishing.

Walia, H. 2013. *Undoing Border Imperialism.* Oakland: AK Press/Institute for Anarchist Studies.

Webb, S., and B. Webb. 1929. *English Poor Law History: Part 2, The Last Hundred Years*, Vol. 1. London:

Longmans, Green and Co.

Weber, M.C. 2008. "Disability Rights, Disability Discrimination, and Social Insurance." *Georgia State University Law Review* 25.

Webster, P. 2017. "Bringing Homeless Deaths to Light." *Canadian Medical Association Journal* 189, 11. <doi.org/10.1503/cmaj.1095399>.

Weichel, A. 2021 "Number of Deaths Recorded during B.C.'s Heat Wave up to 808, Coroners Say." CTV News, July 16. <bc.ctvnews.ca/number-of-deaths-recorded-during-b-c-s-heat-wave-up-to-808-coroners-say-1.5512723>.

White, A. 2018. "Rampant Welfare Fraud Is a Myth Ontario PCs Have Used to Vilify the Poor." *Huffpost*, November 1. <huffpost.com/archive/ca/entry/welfare-fraud-ontario-conservatives_a_23577276>.

Withers, A.J. 2021. *Fight to Win: Inside Poor Peoples' Organizing*. Black Point, NS: Fernwood Publishing.

___. 2020. "Mapping Ruling Relations through Homelessness Organizing." PhD dissertation, York University. <truthout.org/wp-content/uploads/2020/03/Withers_A_J_2020_PhD.pdf>.

___. 2019. "Fighting to Win: Radical Anti-Poverty Organizing." In *Routledge Handbook of Radical Politics*, edited by U. Gordon and R. Kinna. New York: Routledge.

___. 2012. *Disability Politics and Theory*. Black Point, NS: Fernwood Publishing.

Wolfe, P. 2006. "Settler Colonialism and the Elimination of the Native." *Journal of Genocide Research* 8, 4. <doi.org/10.1080/14623520601056240>.

Yousif, N. 2019. "UCP's New Budget Met with Outrage over the Untying of Disability Benefits to Inflation." *Toronto Star*, October 25. <thestar.com/edmonton/2019/10/25/ucps-new-budget-met-with-outrage-over-the-untying-of-disability-benefits-to-inflation>.

8

CANADA'S CORPORATE FOOD REGIME
Prospects for a Just Transition

Sarah-Louise Ruder, Dana James, Evan Bowness,
Tabitha Robin and Bryan Dale

YOU SHOULD KNOW THIS

- In 2017–2018, 4.4 million Canadians lived in food-insecure households, including more than 1.2 million children under the age of eighteen.

- During the COVID-19 pandemic, the portion of the population experiencing food insecurity increased to 14.6 percent (5.2 million people).

- People racialized as Black or Indigenous are more likely to experience poverty and therefore food insecurity.

- Almost 40 percent of university students report experiencing food insecurity due to the high costs of food, tuition, and housing.

- By 2013, six agricultural input companies — BASF, Bayer, Dow, DuPont, Monsanto, and Syngenta — controlled 75 percent of the global agrochemical market, 63 percent of the commercial seed market and 75 percent of all private sector research in seeds and pesticides.

- Agricultural sectors are even more concentrated and interconnected: In 2015, Dow and DuPont merged, and in 2016 ChemChina acquired Syngenta and Bayer acquired Monsanto.

Sources: Tarasuk and Mitchell 2020; Polsky and Gilmour 2020; Silverthorn 2016; etc 2015, 2019

A CRITICAL APPROACH TO UNDERSTANDING THE FOOD SYSTEM

FOOD IS POLITICAL. POWER PERMEATES THE structures that determine how food is "produced," who decides what happens to it, who benefits from these decisions and, ultimately, who gets to eat.

> Power permeates how food is "produced," who decides what happens to it, who benefits and, ultimately, who gets to eat.

This chapter takes a "critical" approach to understanding food and agricultural issues in the Canadian context. This critical approach means asking questions such as: What "social problems" are present in how we produce, distribute and consume food? Who defines these problems? Who is affected by them? What can be done to change the food system so that it is more ecologically sustainable and socially just? Our approach stems from the interdisciplinary field of Critical Food Studies (CFS), which draws primarily from sociology, anthropology, political economy, political science, and geography. CFS is positioned to examine the social and political structures shaping food — for example, the interlocked nature of the food system with the unsustainable fossil energy system in Canada (asking, for example: what are the ecological impacts of the industrial and corporate food system, and what are the barriers to change?). In addition, CFS analyzes individual and collective experiences of food (in)security (e.g., which groups of people are more likely to experience food insecurity and why?). At the same time, CFS examines the prospects for resistance and social change.

Being critical means more than being skeptical or disapproving. CFS research is also generative — it contributes alternatives to inequitable and unsustainable structures in food and agriculture. In recognizing the forms of power that travel through the food system, we therefore note that "wherever there is power, there is resistance" (Foucault 1979). Resistance across food and energy systems takes many forms, and this resistance seeds the potential for what is increasingly being referred to as a "just transition" (McCauley and Heffron 2018; Newell and Mulvaney 2013; Snell 2018). With roots in the labour movements of North America, the just transition is a social movement and policy framework for protecting workers during sustainability transitions. The just transition framework rejects the "jobs versus environment" binary that is often expressed in public debates. In contrast to this binary, the framework prioritizes justice and equity, and it insists that policies to shift away from fossil fuels need not compromise the livelihoods and well-being of workers who have been caught up in "dirty" industries (Just Transition Research Collaborative 2018). The just transition mobilizing has built momentum as a rallying cry for social movements and political campaigns advocating for both a cleaner economy and more secure green jobs. It has been endorsed by the UN's International Labour Organization and the Framework Convention on Climate Change (ILO 2013; UNFCCC 2016) and has been underscored in Canada's own federal task force to support workers, particularly coal miners, affected by the national climate change plan (Government of Canada 2019).

The just transition framework is relevant to Canada's food and agricultural systems. However, it is essential to consider specifically *how* policies under this framework are developed if they are to be truly just. For example, federal and provincial "just transition" policies in Alberta, designed in consultation with labour organizations, feature plans to phase out coal mines and power plants while making associated infrastructure investments and providing income support and skills (re)training for coal workers. While this seems like a positive step, this approach benefits a relatively high-income group of coal workers and excludes contract workers who already have less job security, those indirectly employed by the sector (e.g., secondary service industries), and other marginalized groups in coal-dependent communities (Mertins-Kirkwood and Deshpande 2019). These same kinds of questions — who is consulted, who benefits and who is excluded? — will need to be considered to ensure a just transition in the food system.

A "food system" refers to the social, ecological and political relationships, processes and networks that are linked to food. Rather than being a rigid structure or linear "food chain," food systems evoke a more holistic, dynamic frame that highlights complexity. Food systems are "constituted by complex and dynamic local-global and global-local flows of seeds, agricultural practices and systems, price signals, social customs, consumer tastes, models of regulation, and perhaps most importantly, forms and sites of political struggles and solidarity" (Clapp, Desmarais and Margulis 2015: 2). Food system(s) approaches emphasize the multidimensional nature of food, interconnections across processes, time and space, as well as dynamic feedbacks across inputs, activities and outputs (Ericksen 2008). CFS researchers in particular often aim to understand how these systems have led to and perpetuate injustice, as well as to identify leverage points for resistance and change.

The dominant food system in Canada, and globally, is often referred to as the "corporate food regime." It is an unsustainable form of social organization based on historical, interrelated and contemporary processes of colonization, industrialization and capitalism. In particular, it is deeply interconnected with the extractive fossil energy sector. In recent years, more ecologically regenerative and equitable food systems based in agroecology and Indigenous food sovereignty have emerged to overcome these forces.

THE CORPORATE FOOD REGIME IN CANADA

One way to identify the important elements of the global food system is through a "food regime" analytic frame (Friedmann 2005; Friedmann and McMichael 1989; McMichael 2009a), which provides a critical, historically informed perspective on the political economy of food. Food regimes are "the economic and political relations through which food is produced and through which capitalism is reproduced" (McMichael 2009b: 218). This approach considers how formal laws, trade relations and governance institutions shape and are shaped by the global food system. Food regimes change over time, and the contemporary regime, called the "corporate food regime," is marked by concentrated corporate power, large-scale and export-oriented production, the tight coupling of food to (fossil) fuel and farmer dependence on commercial seeds, pesticides and fertilizer — also called agrochemicals or "farm inputs" (Holt-Giménez and Wang 2011). Key elements of the corporate food regime include government (de)regulation, multinational agribusiness firms, trade relations, international commodity markets, capital flows, agricultural labour markets and, critically for food systems, land itself.

Canada's Colonial Legacy of Land Dispossession

The corporate food regime framework focuses primarily on how capitalism and the accumulation of capital shape food systems. In particular, the corporate food regime is organized around the transformation of land, as well as farm inputs and outputs, into commodities (a process known as "commodification") for the purpose of creating private profit. A critical examination of the commodification process shows the ways in which this profit for some depends on the exploitation of others — namely, farm labourers, farmers and the land itself. This is especially evident where settler agriculture has dispossessed Indigenous peoples of their territories, transforming land into property to be bought, sold and otherwise used for growing or raising food commodities. Capitalism — or, more specifically, commodification — and colonialism are therefore closely connected social phenomena. One way to view these phenomena is to treat capitalism and colonialism as two fundamentally separate processes that have overlapping impacts that oppress some groups of people (namely, the poor, Indigenous peoples and also other socially marginalized groups). From another, specifically Marxist perspective, colonialism is not a separate process but instead another expression of commodification and the expansion of capitalism, where land is commodified for the benefit of the property-owning class. Regardless of the approach taken, we argue that industrial agriculture and food regimes cannot be discussed in isolation from colonialism.

Colonialism in Canada has sought to control both Indigenous lands and Indigenous bodies, resulting in loss, trauma, dispossession, oppression, marginalization and subjugation (LaRoque 2010; McCallum and McCallum 2017). Though often presented as a historical event in the creation of Canada, colonialism is not over: The bodies and lands of Indigenous peoples continue to be subject to Canada's ongoing colonial project (Monchalin 2016). In the current moment of racial reckoning, it is critical to understand the historical context of the many contemporary and systemic injustices and inequities that Indigenous peoples experience, as they are rooted in a colonial past and present. Much has been written on colonialism and its impacts on Indigenous peoples (for example, see Smith 2005), but colonial realities are complex: colonial discourses and impacts are not homogenous or unitary (Hart 2007).

> Though often presented as a historical event in the creation of Canada, colonialism is not over.

Agriculture has been both a dangerous tool and an outcome of colonization. As a means of clearing and preparing what would become "Canada" for settler agriculture and development, European colonialists saw the "need" to control lands that they viewed as being "squandered" by Indigenous peoples. Arthur Manuel and Grand Chief Ronald M. Derrickson (2015) write of these many mistruths that were perpetuated by the state in order to gain control of lands, such as the idea of *terra nullius* (a colonial concept that treated land as "empty" or unoccupied) and the "doctrine of discovery" (a colonial concept that dictated that these "empty" lands were open for settlement). They state, "We had condemned, as Indigenous Peoples, the innocent-sounding doctrine of discovery, which was the tool — the legal fiction — Europeans used to claim our lands for themselves" (Manuel and Derrickson 2015: 3). European theorist John Locke's concept of "agrarian labour," which argued that if land was not being used agriculturally, it was being wasted and therefore open to claim by Europeans, was another tool used by colonizers to claim "Canada" as their own. As Monchalin writes, "this definition of property effectively dispossessed Indigenous peoples of their land" (2016: 66). Colonizers' early attempts to rid the lands across Turtle Island (North America) of Indigenous bodies came from the desire to be the new "original" inhabitants.

Indigenous populations, specifically in the Prairies, experienced high rates of starvation, disease and malnutrition along with oppression and subjugation as their lands were given away to early settlers. Agriculture was offered as salvation; it was seen as godly, a mechanism to rid Indigenous peoples of their perceived heathenism (Acoose-Miswonigeesikokwe 2016; Carter 1990). Moreover, agriculture was presented to Indigenous peoples as the means to end hunger. However, implementing agricultural practices in Indigenous communities was largely a failure given the lack of government support and the establishment of policies that hindered agricultural development in Indigenous communities (Carter 1990; Vowel 2012). These processes entirely disregarded Indigenous peoples' knowledge around food production. Oppressive policies such as the pass system, which restricted Indigenous peoples' movement, further intensified the colonizer's attempts to separate people from the land. With diminishing natural food stocks, hunger became a significant issue for many Indigenous communities. Today, Indigenous peoples' relationships with the land continue to be eroded through dispossession — Indigenous peoples occupy a mere 0.2-0.35 percent of all land in Canada — and degradation, as they are disproportionately faced with the negative consequences of resource extraction and so-called development. The colonial project continues.

INDUSTRIALIZATION AND THE CORPORATE FOOD REGIME[1]

While colonization was essential to establishing the corporate food regime in Canada, it has been further entrenched through the process of food system "industrialization." The contemporary global food system is often described as industrial because some of its key features emerged during the Industrial Revolution. First, industrialization includes and refers to "specialization" (focusing specifically on doing or producing one thing) and "homogenization" (making elements similar to one another, or standardized and uniform) in production. Specialization and homogenization contribute to achieving "economies of scale" (lowering the cost per unit of production as a result of efficiencies gained through mass production). "Mechanization" (the use of machinery rather than human labour) is also integrally tied to these processes of specialization and homogenization (Weis 2022). As a result of these features, industrialization is very energy-intensive and is particularly dependent on fossil fuels. Today, an enormous amount of energy is used to produce, transport, process and distribute food. For example, the industrial food system heavily relies on agrochemicals like synthetic fertilizers and pesticides. Another large energy cost is long-distance transportation. Following the logic of "comparative advantage," agriculture takes place in locations that are claimed to be best suited to it, and the products are sold on the global market. This means that food that could be grown locally is often shipped from very faraway places where the costs of production are lower and regulatory frameworks (for example, labour and environmental laws) are less developed and/or poorly enforced. Despite all of the resources and energy that go into this system, nearly 15 percent of all food — and therefore the energy and resources that were used to produce it — ends up being lost or wasted (FAO 2019).

The industrial food system is also embedded within the political economy of neoliberal capitalism. Food is treated as a commodity to be produced and exchanged in a "free" global market. "Free" is in quotation marks here as the free market is often assumed to be unhindered by government regulation — however, it is often government interventions that enable the so-called free market. The primary motivation in this market is to maximize private profit. Neoliberalism, the most recent form of capitalism, emphasizes the shift away from state governance and provision of public goods and services (for example, social welfare) to the private sector; deregulation of industry (for example, through the watering down of competition laws); and trade liberalization. In the food system, neoliberalism has resulted in the vast majority of profits being captured by a network of agrifood corporations (farm input suppliers, food manufacturing conglomerates, and retail chains) that increasingly operate across national borders. This corporate network has also grown incredibly concentrated, as noted above, with only four firms — Corteva, Bayer, BASF, and ChemChina-Syngenta — now controlling 65 percent of the global agrochemical market and much of the seed sector (Hendrickson et al. 2020).

In sum, the corporate food regime is made up of highly concentrated and powerful agrifood corporations that facilitate the use of energy-intensive technologies and industrial processes to distribute food commodities at a global scale. This system is dominated by very few companies that wield an incredible amount of power over farmers, workers and eaters. Due to their economic position, these same corporations are able to lobby governments to relax regulations, including those that protect the environment and impose minimum standards for working conditions (Harvey 2005).

> The corporate food regime is made up powerful agrifood corporations, energy-intensive technologies and industrial processes to produce and distribute food at a global scale.

Understanding the corporate food regime is critical for describing the ways in which social problems in food and agriculture are driven by powerful corporate and state actors and their desire for control over land. In Canada, the development of the corporate food regime is integral to the ongoing process of colonization and has driven increased farmland concentration, especially in the prairie provinces (Qualman et al. 2020). The corporate food regime is also highly industrialized and energy intensive, reflecting the interdependence of the agrifood and fossil energy sectors. While these features cause significant ecological and social harm, despite claims otherwise, the corporate food regime is firmly entrenched and difficult to change.

HARMS OF THE CORPORATE FOOD REGIME[2]

What are the major implications of a highly industrialized corporate food regime? On the one hand, it is thanks to industrialization that we see an incredible selection of "cheap" products on the shelves when we go to a grocery store or on the menu at a take-out restaurant. And indeed, we are often told by these very agrifood corporations that they play a key role in "feeding the world," having contributed to the seemingly countless options at grocery outlets. However, this belies the fact that there is currently more than enough food in the world, with the majority of it being produced by peasants and small-scale and family farmers and fishers. The major bottleneck in realizing food security — or regular access to healthy foods — for the approximately two billion food insecure people globally (FAO et al. 2020) is not really about yield and production. People struggle to receive adequate nourishment because of the inequitable distribution of and access to food as a result of inadequate infrastructure and social programming (including safety nets and welfare), along with land and wealth inequality.

As well, supposedly "cheap" foods are not, in fact, cheap. There are many hidden costs to this system that need to be taken into account. At first glance, the relatively low-cost of this bewildering variety of foods seem to benefit us as consumers or eaters. But when you look deeper, it becomes clear that this is only because eaters are not paying for the true cost of our food up front. However, we do pay for it later — "cheap" foods (typically featuring the same roster of corn, wheat, and soy derivatives) have contributed to low-quality, highly processed diets that have made our society's healthcare costs skyrocket, while food and agricultural workers are underpaid and undervalued. Ironically, what appears to be a diversity of options at the grocery store masks the fact that there has been a steep decline in crop and animal diversity in Canada and globally, largely due to industrial food production. In addition to biodiversity loss, other environmental effects of industrial agriculture in Canada include anthropogenic climate change, land degradation, and pollution. Ultimately, the environment and our communities do pay for these costs (otherwise known as "negative externalities") many times over — but the large agrifood companies that are responsible for the risks and damage too often do not (Bowness et al. 2020). In addition, these risks and harms disproportionately fall on specific groups (for example, food workers) and populations (for example, Indigenous and Black communities and other communities of colour). We now turn to exploring how these harms play out in so-called Canada.

Climate Change

It is now widely accepted that anthropogenic climate change poses a serious threat to natural and social systems as we know them. This is a pressing issue for Canadian food systems, where the climate is warming faster than the rest of the world. As stated in the Canada's Changing Climate Report, "both past and future warming in Canada is, on average, about double the magnitude of global warming" (Bush and Lemmen 2019). Given how dependent agriculture is on the weather, climate change has important implications for this sector in Canada. On one hand, rising average temperatures can bring about new possibilities for growing crops in regions that were previously too cold. In other words, climate change may cause a "northward" expansion of agriculture into regions such as the boreal forest, which comprises a significant amount of Canada's land mass (King et al. 2018). For example, aggregated climate models compiled in the Climate Atlas of Canada indicate that parts of the Prairies, where the majority of Canadian agricultural land is located, are projected to resemble northern Texas if greenhouse gas (GHG) emissions continue unchecked (Prairie Climate Centre 2019), and rising temperatures will likely put increased pressure on already depleted water sources. On the other hand, extreme weather events, such as extreme heat and humidity, along with widely varying rainfall patterns, threaten the viability of agriculture and create increased pressure for farmers to adapt their practices to new conditions.

Not only is Canadian agriculture affected by climate change, it is also a contributor to the climate crisis. The Intergovernmental Panel on Climate Change has called for "far-reaching and unprecedented changes in all aspects of society" to bring down GHG emissions to avert global catastrophe (IPCC 2019a; see also the 2021 IPCC report). A key aspect of society in need of transformation is the global food system, which accounts for 21 to 37 percent of anthropogenic GHG emissions (IPCC 2019b). Food production in particular is responsible for emissions in the form of enteric fermentation (which causes livestock burps) and emissions released from agricultural soils and from the production and use of chemical inputs like nitrogen-based fertilizers. As the climate changes, the "northward" expansion of agriculture may increase farm land area and the length of harvest seasons, which could increase the environmental impacts of the food system.

How humans produce food will clearly need to change. Canadian farmers are positioned to contribute to this shift (Qualman and NFU 2019; NFU and Qualman 2021). This can take the form of resisting input suppliers from the corporate food regime, who extract a significant amount from farm revenues, and turning instead to low-input and diversified farming systems that can improve farm resilience in the face of climate and other shocks.

Biodiversity Loss

The ongoing climate crisis also contributes to the biodiversity crisis. Biodiversity is important to the functioning of ecosystems and to human cultures, yet we are currently losing species at a rapid pace. Globally, extinction rates are current- ly a thousand times higher than back- ground rates, or what would be nor- mally expected (Coristine et al. 2018). This has led to predictions that "around one million species already face extinction, many within decades, unless action is taken to reduce the intensity of drivers of biodiversity loss" (IPBES 2019: 12). The main drivers of biodiversity loss around the world include land use change/native habi- tat loss, primarily from agricultural expansion and development; overexploitation of species and resources; climate change; industrial and agricultural pollution; and in- troductions of invasive species to areas with high levels of endemism (geographically specific and unique species) (Coristine and Kerr 2011; IPBES 2019).

> The ongoing climate crisis also con- tributes to the biodiversity crisis.

In Canada, land use change from natural habitats to agriculture and urban areas has contributed greatly to terrestrial species endangerment (Kerr and Cihlar 2004; Venter et al. 2006; Kraus and Hebb 2020). In particular, high biomass, high-intensity agriculture — where there is corn and soy production and converted pasture for livestock — and associated agricultural pollution has a strongly negative effect on native species' abun- dance and distribution (Kerr and Cihlar 2004). In agricultural areas where some native habitat remains, "progressively fewer native species [persist] as pesticide and fertilizer applications in surrounding areas increase" (Kerr and Cihlar 2004: 750). Other stud- ies show that "increased mechanization (number and value of tractors), increased ag- ricultural inputs (inorganic fertilizer and insecticides), and larger farm size and capital," which are generally linked to specialized and industrial crop production, have a negative effect on biodiversity and on a suite of other ecosystem processes (Frei et al. 2018: 2737).

Overfishing and overharvesting are also major threats to biodiversity and are the primary drivers of declining marine species. For endangered fish, "bycatch" (species that are unintentionally caught by the fishers) is the most important cause of over- exploitation. Human disturbance (shipping vessel traffic) also contributes to habitat degradation and species decline (Venter et al. 2006). These forces — overexploitation, habitat loss, pollution, and degradation through conversion to industrial agriculture and other forms of industrial development (e.g., energy projects, including oil sands development) — have major implications not only for biodiversity loss, but also for food security and food sovereignty (or peoples' right to define and control their food systems), including through the erosion of biocultural heritage that has developed around local plant and animal varieties.

Social and Environmental Injustice

The interconnections of industrial agriculture and fossil energy systems also have unequal impacts on people. While Canadian companies are major players in extractive industries abroad, particularly in the Global South, we will focus here on the role of the Canadian state and industries in causing and perpetuating environmental harms within Canada's national borders.

In Canada, large-scale industrial projects and associated waste facilities are more likely to be sited near racialized communities, resulting in communities of colour being exposed to higher rates of land, water and air pollution — conditions that have proven fatal (Waldron 2018a; Tuncak 2020). In a 2020 report based on his visit to Canada, the UN Special Rapporteur, on the "implications for human rights of the environmentally sound management and disposal of hazardous substances and wastes," notes, "the invisible violence inflicted by toxics is an insidious burden disproportionately borne by Indigenous peoples in Canada" (Tuncak 2020: 7). For example, Indigenous communities surrounding the oil sands experience high rates of cancer (McLachlan 2014). Indigenous communities have long been organizing resistance to extractive projects in Canada, including coal mines that threaten endangered populations of caribou, a culturally important food for a number of western and northern First Nations; commercial fishery and forestry operations that have fuelled conflict and disrespected First Nations' fishing and harvesting rights; and numerous oil and gas pipelines that cross Indigenous territories without free, prior and informed consent (see "Canada" at EJAtlas 2021). Scholar-activists have referred to these environmental injustices as "sacrifice zones" (Lerner 2010; Klein 2014), where certain lands and bodies are deemed lesser-than, or even disposable, in the pursuit of "development."

Yet even within communities, it's important to recognize that the burden of risk, disease and harm is not experienced in the same way. For example, women in these communities may experience specific reproductive-related health issues as a result of exposure to pollutants (Waldron 2018b), and Indigenous women in particular are more exposed to sexual assault and violence from industrial camps (National Inquiry into Missing and Murdered Women and Girls 2019). The connections between violence against the land and violence against women have led scholars to declare that "patriarchy is an ecological regime" (Collard and Dempsey 2020).

Workers in the agrifood and fossil energy sectors also face specific social and environmental injustices. At least three million workers in Canada "are exposed to carcinogens and other hazardous substances at work.... The exposures that many workers endure are much higher than the exposure levels of the general population, often to substances with no safe level of exposure" (Tuncak 2020: 12). Farm workers, many of whom are migrant workers, face acute and particular occupational risks and harms including but not limited to pesticide exposure; a lack of appropriate personal protective equipment; inadequate housing and sanitation conditions; and high-pressure, physically tiring and repetitive work (Otero and Preibisch 2015; MWAC 2020). For many, precarious immigration status and language barriers make it hard to report violations and to access healthcare services. Not surprisingly, women farm workers face compounded issues, including discrimination, harassment and sexual abuse; lack of access to reproductive care; and higher rates of loneliness and depression (Edmunds et al. 2011; McLaughlin 2008).

Given the social and environmental injustices described above, among other evidence that demonstrates how the corporate food regime is unjust and unsustainable, why is the regime still in place? Why is it so hard to transform the food system to become more equitable, sustainable and resilient? Scholars describe this intransigence as having to do with the "locked-in" power structures between food and fossil fuels.

LOCK-INS THAT MAINTAIN THE CORPORATE FOOD REGIME

There are similarities across structures and mechanisms of power in "big food" and "big fossil fuel" industries at a global scale. Agriculture and fossil fuel extraction share an ongoing legacy of governments and corporations dispossessing local and Indigenous peoples from their territories to extract "resources" (and capital) from the land (Whyte 2017). Likewise, both agrifood and energy sectors are characterized by corporate concentration that contributes to social inequality and environmental degradation (Clapp and Purugganan 2020).

The agriculture and fossil energy sectors in Canada are not independent of one another. There are important — and often overlooked — connections between food and fossil fuels with respect to social problems, power, and resistance. There are specific interactions that present "lock-ins" (IPES-Food 2016) that make it difficult to change the corporate food regime. Lock-ins in the Canadian context include subsidies and policy instruments, farmland concentration, biofuel production and corporate concentration in agricultural technologies, among others.

Subsidies and Policy Instruments

States play an important role in establishing and maintaining social and political structures, through material, political, cultural and other means. In Canada, government activities create interlocking support for industrial agriculture and fossil fuel development, often based on a narrowly focused goal of increasing economic growth (Qualman 2011, 2019). Take, for instance, the federal government's use of subsidies.

Governments use subsidies to support particular economic sectors, actors or individuals through direct (e.g., grants, loans) or indirect (e.g., tax breaks, exemptions) measures (Corkal and Gass 2020).

In 2020 alone, the Canadian government provided at least $1.91 billion in fossil fuel subsidies — more than 200 percent over 2019 levels (Laan and Corkal 2020). These subsidies buttress the fossil fuel industry and contribute to its resilience. Government supports for renewable energy, on the other hand, are dwarfed in comparison. For example, the Emerging Renewable Power Program (ERPP) offered up to $200 million over four years (2018–2021) to support commercially viable renewable energy ventures (Government of Canada 2021). In addition, supports for renewable energy usually take place in the form of market incentives, which are reduced as the price of the technology decreases, such as the feed-in tariffs for renewable energy in Ontario starting in 2009 (Ontario 2019). With the agricultural sector being so fossil-fuel dependent, the government's strong and ongoing support for fossil fuels also sustains an industrial, corporate food system.

The Canadian government's support for industrial agriculture goes back decades. Specific initiatives and acts of Parliament following the Second World War had the effect of encouraging an increase in the size of farms, along with monoculture crop production, mechanization and chemical use (see Dale 2019: 11–12 for examples). Government responses to the recommendations of the 1969 report of the Federal Task Force on Agriculture furthered these trends to "modernize" agriculture in Canada. As a consequence, smaller farms were pushed out of the sector, while more heavily capitalized farms were able to take advantage of the consolidation. In recent years, provincial and federal expenditures for the agrifood sector have totalled several billion dollars annually, with a substantial portion of these funds going to program payments that favour large-scale, export-oriented farms (AAFC 2016 2017; Wiebe 2017). Examples of programs that tend to support farms with larger volumes of production include AgriInvest, AgriStability, and AgriInsurance, all of which are overseen by Agriculture and Agri-food Canada (AAFC). As noted by Wiebe (2017: 146), "approximately 64 percent of program payments [are going] to the 27 percent of Canadian farms with gross revenues over $250,000 per year."

There are also complex interactions between agriculture and policy instruments to reduce emissions. Despite the agrifood sector's large contribution to Canada's GHG emissions, governments in Canada hold protected channels for agriculture to circumvent policy instruments to lower emissions. For example, carbon pricing and related policy instruments do not include biological emissions (e.g., livestock burps, carbon released from soil) (AAFC 2018). Additionally, the federal *Greenhouse Gas Pollution Pricing Act* (S.C. 2018, c. 12, s. 186) outlines exemptions for fossil fuel use for farm machinery with an amendment in 2021, Bill C-206, to include natural gas and propane in the exemption. There are similar farm exemptions to carbon policies at the provincial level, namely in Alberta (Government of Alberta n.d.), British Columbia (Province of British Columbia n.d.), and Ontario (OFA 2019). While it is indeed important to support farmer livelihoods, unfortunately this approach has solidified the integration of fossil fuels with agricultural practices.

Farmland Concentration

Another major "lock-in" keeping the status quo in place is the concentration of land ownership, which feeds into a concentration of resources, wealth and power. Canada lost 55 percent of its farms between 1966 and 2016 (Qualman et al. 2020), the majority of which were small- to medium-sized operations. These farms have been increasingly consolidated into larger-scale operations. It is estimated that currently, "less than three-tenths-of-one-percent of Canadians own half of this country's (privately-owned) food-producing acreage" (Qualman et al. 2020: 15).

Zooming in to the Prairies — which host 70 percent of Canadian farmland — Qualman et al. (2020: 11) note in their recent report on farmland concentration that over "the past 30 years, farms with more than 5,000 acres have increased the amount of land they operate from 11 percent to 37 percent of the total land farmed [while] those with fewer than 1,000 acres have seen their share of land decline from 32 percent to 13 percent." These five-thousand-acre-plus farms — only 6 percent of Prairie farm operations — take in a third of gross revenues and net income (Qualman et al. 2020).

Why should we care about the consolidation and concentration of land ownership? The development of large-scale agriculture increases farmers' dependence on fossil-fuel-intensive agricultural inputs, such as synthetic fertilizers and pesticides, as well as capital- and energy-intensive infrastructure. This not only shapes the role of agriculture in contributing to climate change, but it also reduces farmers' ability to adapt to biophysical and/or economic changes, while also hindering the transition to more equitable and resilient agroecosystems.

Corporate Concentration in Agricultural Technologies

Mega-mergers and acquisitions in the agricultural input sector over the past decade have concentrated power and wealth among agrochemical corporations, "locking in" the use of fossil fuels in industrial agriculture (Clapp 2018). By 2013, the top six agricultural input companies — BASF, Bayer, Dow, DuPont, Monsanto and Syngenta — controlled 75 percent of the global agrochemical market, 63 percent of the commercial seed market and 75 percent of all private-sector research in seeds and pesticides

(ETC Group 2015). Now the sectors are even more concentrated and interconnected, as Dow and DuPont announced a merger in 2015, and two other major mergers occurred in 2016: ChemChina acquired Syngenta and Bayer acquired Monsanto (ETC Group 2019). The concentration of power represented by these mergers not only reinforces the structures of industrial agriculture and the associated environmental problems, but it also presents a regime of obstruction in agrifood governance through corporations' power to influence policy outcomes and the weak and fragmented mechanisms for government regulation (Clapp 2018).

These same corporations are also gaining increasing ownership and control over other technology — namely, digital tools, and their associated (big) data, and biotechnology such as gene editing (Clapp and Ruder 2020; ETC 2019). Though perspectives and motivations differ, many academic, public and private actors are calling this integration the fourth industrial revolution in agriculture: "Agriculture 4.0" or the digital agricultural revolution (Gibson 2019; Rose and Chilvers 2018). The existing power imbalances between farmers and agricultural input, farm equipment and technology companies mean that an increasingly concentrated group of powerful corporate actors have control over the design of agricultural technologies, the data they collect and the farm practices they enable (Carbonell 2016). The concentration of data is likely to reinforce corporate power in the food system because of what (big) data enables — namely, behaviour prediction and targeted marketing, the ability to charge farmers for access to their own data and the advantages of aggregated data to direct profit-maximizing agri-tech innovation.

Biofuel Production

A discussion of the intersections across the agricultural and energy sectors would be incomplete without mention of the "food versus fuel" debate. In the mid-2000s, there was global enthusiasm for biofuel innovations — using renewable fuels made from biomass feedstocks (e.g., wood, food crops, algae) — to replace fossil fuels and support agricultural producers (FAO 2008). From 2001 to 2011, global biofuel production increased from twenty billion to one hundred billion litres, due in no small part to government subsidies and rising food prices in 2007–2008 (HLPE 2011, 2013).

In an effort to reduce GHG emissions, provincial and federal governments require biofuels to be blended into gasoline and diesel (McKnight et al. 2021). Since 2013, at least 6 percent (by volume) of the Canadian gasoline pool is comprised of biofuels like corn ethanol (Navius Research 2020). In Canada, consumption of biofuels roughly doubled between 2010 and 2017 and increased as a relative share of total fuel consumption from 3 to 5 percent (Wolinetz, Hein and Moawad 2019). Internationally, Canada is a key exporter of biofuel feedstocks, namely corn and wheat (Government of Canada 2017). Although currently the United States, Brazil, and Europe are the most important biofuel producers, there are recent claims that using wheat straw as a cellulosic feedstock could revitalize the Canadian biofuel industry (McKnight et al. 2021).

While proponents argue that biofuels can help the global economy transition away from fossil fuels, there are important ecological trade-offs to consider (Demirbas 2009; Rosillo-Calle 2012). Contentious debates around the environmental, social and economic implications of biofuels quickly followed the expansion of the global biofuel market (Rosillo-Calle 2012). In the context of global food security concerns, biofuels have been critiqued since they divert farmland and food crops away from people (compromising food supply or availability) and make food more expensive (limiting access to food) (FAO 2008). Using crops for food, animal feed, and biofuels presents competition for not only land, but also other ecological and economic resources (Banerjee 2011; Muscat 2020). Critics have also argued that biofuels contribute to the volatility of food prices (McKeon 2015) and that increases in biofuel production led to large-scale land acquisitions by domestic and transnational companies (i.e., "land grabs"), as these companies see an investment opportunity in so-called flex crops, or crops with multiple potential uses (Borras et al. 2016). And importantly, biofuels based on food crops, like corn, lock in industrial agricultural practices, resulting in questionable (if any) gains if one performs a comprehensive analysis of the energy returned on the energy invested. As such, there are good reasons to critique the role that biofuels can play in the shift toward a more sustainable and resilient global food system.

TOWARD A JUST TRANSITION FOR THE CORPORATE FOOD REGIME

To summarize, the colonial and industrial corporate food regime is incredibly harmful. It drives climate change and biodiversity loss and preserves legacies of social inequity. Furthermore, it is fortified through political and economic "lock-ins." The corporate food regime is deeply entrenched in processes of industrialization, with profit-seeking tendencies preventing a meaningful shift away from a dependence on fossil fuels in the agrifood sector. This system cannot continue in its current form, and the radical change needed to transition away from the energy-intensive and harmful system cannot be solely technological in nature. In other words, what is needed is a "just transition" not only in Canada's fossil energy system but also in the food system. Fortunately, over the last several years, scholars and activists have

> Intractable problems in food and agriculture must be approached in holistic, relational ways.

been increasingly discussing the relevance of the just transition framework for agriculture (see Carlisle et al. 2019; Dale 2020; Rossman 2013). However, the concept should in fact be applied to the entire food system. Intractable problems in food and agriculture must be approached in holistic, relational ways if a radical transformation of Canada's food system is to be achieved.

To provide one key example: foods produced through climate-friendly agricultural practices typically require increased labour (to substitute for chemical fertilizers, pesticides and diesel-powered machinery), which increases the price of these foods. Measures to reduce inequality and food insecurity are therefore also relevant to a just transition, to ensure that it is not only the most privileged groups in society who can afford to shift toward more sustainable eating. Many advocates for a transformed food system in Canada are therefore pushing for the adoption of a basic income guarantee, to help reduce poverty by ensuring that all people can afford the necessities of life (Coalition Canada n.d.; OBIN n.d.). Such a program would complement (as opposed to replace) other forms of social assistance, at least until living wages, affordable housing and other social programs and policies can be guaranteed. In terms of how such initiatives could be paid for, many experts argue that it will be important to introduce tax reforms so that Canada's corporations and the ultra-rich pay more through wealth and inheritance taxes, along with the tightening of loopholes that allow for tax avoidance and evasion (Canadian for Tax Fairness n.d.; CCPA 2021). Indeed, a robust vision of a just transition can weave together a wide range of socio-economic issues and proposals.

Food sovereignty is another far-reaching concept that overlaps with struggles for a just transition. It refers to the "right of peoples to healthy and culturally appropriate food produced through ecologically sound and sustainable methods, and their right to define their own food and agriculture systems" (LVC 2007). Small-scale family farmers, who have been leading the fight for food sovereignty for over twenty-five years, have been specifically striving to regain control from the corporate actors who have come to dominate so many aspects of the neoliberal capitalist food system. This is relevant to just transition conversations in that it is essential to democratize governance and ensure the inclusion of equity-seeking groups in developing strategies to transform the food system (Andrée et al. 2019; Desmarais, Claeys and Trauger 2017). In short, corporate lobbying and similar approaches that have captured political processes in recent decades must be reversed in order for a more agroecological food system to be realized. Food sovereignty-oriented governance could include, for example, food policy councils at multiple scales (municipal, provincial/territorial and national), cooperative structures in workplaces and other institutions (allowing for more democratic, horizontal decision making) and a strong public sector that resists corporate capture.

Two specific elements that are key to a just transition in Canadian food systems are agroecology and Indigenous food sovereignty.

Agroecology

Agroecology is typically described as encompassing a science, a social movement and a variety of on-farm practices — three spheres of activity that can take place in parallel but which have the greatest potential impact when they overlap (Méndez, Bacon and Cohen 2013; cf. Gliessman 2015; Rosset and Altieri 2017; Wezel et al. 2009). In essence, agroecology is about trying to encourage ecologically oriented agricultural models that help to foster healthy soils and biodiversity, reduce off-farm inputs and contribute to rural livelihoods. The concept's overlap with just transition is evident, in the sense that agroecology offers a vision of a climate-friendly agricultural system; however, the complementarity between the two frameworks goes further. Although agroecology is not widespread in Canada, overshadowed by the corporate food regime and industrial farming methods (Isaac et al. 2018), it offers a methodology for transitioning to a food system that is both ecologically healthy and socially just.

Agroecology is a central pillar of food sovereignty. As a holistic approach to growing food, agroecology intentionally closes "ecological loops" by recycling local nutrients and resources, as opposed to industrial agriculture's reliance on agrochemical inputs that contribute significant GHG emissions. In much the same way, agroecology closes "socio-economic loops" by circulating economic resources and sharing skills locally, in contrast to how agrifood corporations extract profits from a distance. It foregrounds the expertise of farmers and rural workers, including women and other actors whose voices are often ignored within the corporate food regime (Bezner Kerr et al. 2019; Laforge et al. 2021; LVC 2015; Sachs et al. 2016). Through horizontal knowledge-sharing and decision-making practices, agroecology empowers people to articulate and resolve problems, whether they pertain to immediate matters at the level of farming practices or to broader systems. Tangibly, within the Canadian context, an agroecological approach can be used to advance a just transition in a number of ways. Some of the key examples and considerations are:

> Through horizontal knowledge-sharing and decision-making practices, agroecology empowers people to articulate and resolve problems, whether they pertain to immediate matters at the level of farming practices or to broader systems.

1) Agroecology is a process that includes all farmers.

By encouraging systems thinking, agroecology brings focus to political-economic issues that affect a food system at a given scale, including many of the factors that have led to the industrialization and corporatization of Canada's agrifood sector. As such, a just transition must involve reorienting and reversing policies and economic processes that have for decades pushed farmers to prioritize economies of scale, specialization, homogenization, mechanization and a reliance on off-farm (fossil fuel-dependent) inputs. An agroecological approach recognizes that farming practices exist along a spectrum, rather than a binary such as "conventional" (e.g., pesticides and GMOs) versus "ecological" (e.g., certified organic) practices. Thus, all farmers should be supported and incentivized to farm as ecologically as possible. It is not enough, for example, to suggest that certified organic practices are a perfect end goal. These practices are relatively sustainable, but they can be improved upon through the inclusion of labour justice, animal welfare and more profoundly regenerative practices, all while resisting co-optation from corporations that would pursue "industrial organic" agriculture (Dale 2020; Freyer and Bingen 2015; Guthman 2004). Industrial organic agriculture refers to approaches that may be certified organic but which may still rely on monocultural (specialized) growing, the use of some permitted substances that are still harmful to soil health, exploitative labour regimes and marketing approaches through corporate distribution and retail.

2) Labour justice throughout the food system must be central to a just transition.

Moving away from fossil fuel use in agriculture will likely necessitate increased on-farm labour. In order for an agroecological system to function, fair labour regimes must be guaranteed, featuring living wages, robust and enforceable health and safety standards and the ability for farm workers to unionize. At present, exemptions in agricultural labour laws in Canada mean that none of these conditions are assured. This is especially evident in the case of migrant farm work. With the country relying on the agricultural labour of approximately sixty thousand migrants each year, a transition toward agroecology will mean that new systems and legal structures will need to be in place so that these workers' rights are upheld, with employers held to account for any infractions (McLaughlin and Weiler 2016; Migrant Rights Network n.d.; Weiler, Otero and Wittman 2016). Importantly, migrant farm workers must not have their contracts tied to any single employer, and they must be provided with a route to permanent status in Canada. As agroecology considers analysis and actions beyond the farm level, labour justice must also be part of the transition in areas such as food processing (including, importantly, meat processing), food transportation and delivery, food retail and the restaurant and hospitality sector. Given the fact that people of colour are disproportionately represented in many of the most dangerous, dirty and underpaid jobs in these areas, the struggle for labour justice therefore overlaps significantly with racial justice organizing and movement building.

3) Both governments and communities will be involved in the just transition.

A shift towards agroecology in Canada will require governments at various levels to establish policies, laws and programs that facilitate a rapid increase in climate-friendly farming models while simultaneously reigning in the corporate food regime. This will include, for example: providing incentives for new farmers to use ecological agricultural practices; reinvesting in government programs and research that supports ecological farming; and rebalancing insurance, credit lending and other programs that currently focus on agricultural exports and rewards for volume of production. At the same time, governments must also make way for community innovation. Given agroecology's focus on knowledge sharing and problem solving, food system governance must in many ways be decentralized and devolved. A transition toward relocalized food systems will mean that food infrastructure and institutions must function effectively to meet the needs of local communities. This will look different in different places but could include a replication of community supported agriculture (CSA) programs that allow people to buy food directly from farmers, the re-establishment of small-scale abattoirs and food processing facilities, and the expansion of community-run cooperatives in food marketing and distribution. Furthermore, we also want to stress the importance of addressing the issue of land by calling on governments and communities to work towards land redistribution through establishing alternative land relations that reverse the commodification of land and the ongoing processes of settler colonialism that have devastated many Indigenous food systems.

Indigenous Food Sovereignty

Practised since time immemorial, Indigenous food sovereignty (IFS) describes the practices and processes of upholding Indigenous ancestral responsibilities toward the land. IFS represents a movement, epistemology and way of life for Indigenous peoples in which land-based food systems are cared for and in active relationship with Indigenous bodies (Coté 2016; Morrison 2011). Importantly, IFS lacks a single definition: with diverse contexts, histories and geographies, Indigenous peoples across Turtle Island will experience and express their own forms of food sovereignty in their own ways (Daigle 2019).

Grounded in theories of Indigenism and anti-colonialism, IFS represents a shift away from the colonial food system with which Indigenous peoples have been saddled (Robin, Dennis and Hart 2020). Rather than notions of rights, IFS centres the responsibilities Indigenous peoples have towards Creation. While the language of "sovereignty" is seemingly at odds with the responsibility-based discourse of Indigenous food sovereignty — Indigenous notions of land, for example, are not mired in ownership or control of nature — the word "sovereignty" nonetheless serves as an important marker of the political nature of Indigenous peoples' lands, bodies and spirits. Food, for Indigenous peoples, is political and has been used as a weapon against them through coercion, oppression and starvation. This works against ancestral, traditional and ceremonial understandings of food in Indigenous cultures. From an Indigenous perspective, food contains spirit and is connected intrinsically to lands, waters, culture, ceremonies and languages. Indigenous food sovereignty initiatives vary in scope and scale and range from land-based education programs and community freezers to advocacy for land protection (for examples, see Robin 2019). These initiatives speak to the hope and potential of Indigenous reclamation. According to Potawatomi scholar Kyle Powys Whyte, food injustice for Indigenous peoples can be viewed as a

> violation of their collective self-determination over their food systems.... Some food injustices against Indigenous peoples are best understood ... as violations of Indigenous food sovereignty that colonial societies ... inflict on Indigenous peoples as strategies in the larger project of undermining Indigenous collective self-determination (2018: 346–47).

To this end, a just transition in the food system must prioritize the reclamation of Indigenous lifeways and Indigenous food sovereignty, including through respecting and upholding Indigenous communities' rights to exercise self-governance and determine their present and future land and food systems.

> A just transition must prioritize Indigenous food sovereignty and Indigenous communities' rights to determine their present and future land and food systems.

A Just Transition through Alliances and Decolonization

A CFS lens highlights how the industrial food system in Canada is interconnected with other systems, such as the fossil energy system. A critical approach also allows us to interrogate the socio-ecological problems fuelled by the unsustainable and inequitable corporate food regime: climate change, biodiversity loss, and social and environmental injustices. Yet the corporate food regime is entrenched through lock-ins, including corporate concentration and capture of government subsidies, consolidation of farmland, biotechnology and biofuels. Importantly, a critical approach goes beyond critiques and diagnoses of social and environmental ills to also look toward possible ways to overcome these problems. Therefore, pathways out of the corporate food regime require developing and strengthening alliances across farmer, food, energy and environmental movements in Canada, and food activists, researchers and allies must engage with labour, anti-racist and Indigenous movements in pursuit of a just transition toward more equitable and less harmful land and food systems based on agroecology and Indigenous food sovereignty. Critically, land-based decolonization (or, more specifically, land redistribution to Indigenous communities) and reconciliation are essential if food systems are to become "just."

DISCUSSION QUESTIONS

1. How is the corporate food regime in Canada also a colonial food regime?
2. What are the defining features of industrialization in the food system and what are their social and environmental impacts?
3. In what ways do agroecology, the just transition and Indigenous food sovereignty frameworks present forms of resistance to the corporate food regime?

GLOSSARY OF KEY TERMS

Agroecology: A science, a social movement and a variety of on-farm practices that are geared toward encouraging ecologically oriented agrifood systems that foster healthy soils and biodiversity, reduce off-farm inputs and contribute to human well-being.

Corporate food regime: A cluster of related actors, including food corporations and firms in related sectors such as fossil energy, that dominate the food economy and shape how we grow, transport and consume food. Their main goal is profit maximization rather than food security.

Off-farm inputs: Commercial seeds, pesticides, fertilizer and other resources that are introduced to a farm operation. In industrial agriculture, these inputs are often genetically modified (in the case of seeds) and synthetic (in the case of pesticides and fertilizers).

Food security: At the World Food Summit in 1996, the Food and Agriculture Organization defined food security as the condition where "all people, at all times, have physical and economic access to sufficient, safe and nutritious food to meet their dietary needs and food preferences for an active and healthy life." The four key pillars of food security are food availability (overall food supply), food access (whether or not people can obtain food, either through growing it themselves, trading it or purchasing it), food stability (regular and consistent food access) and food utilization (being able to obtain or prepare nutritious and safe food).

Food sovereignty: La Vía Campesina, the largest transnational food movement, defines food sovereignty as the right of peoples to healthy and culturally appropriate food produced through ecologically sound and sustainable methods, as well as their right to define their own food and agriculture systems.

Food system: All of the institutions and people involved in producing, processing, transporting, selling, consuming, recycling or otherwise managing the food that human societies depend on. Food systems also include the environmental, economic, cultural and political factors that shape these institutions and processes.

Indigenous food sovereignty: Indigenous food sovereignty lacks a singular definition. However, it refers to the land-based movement and practices of Indigenous peoples seeking to uphold their ancestral responsibilities to the land. Expressions of IFS vary from nation to nation.

Industrial agriculture: A form of agriculture that has incorporated processes developed through industrialization and a reliance on fossil fuels: specialization (focusing specifically on doing or producing one thing), homogenization (making elements similar to one another, or standardized and uniform), mechanization (using machinery and other technology to reduce labour) and development and use of energy-intensive external inputs like chemical fertilizers, pesticides and fungicides. These processes contribute to achieving "economies of scale" (lowering the cost per unit of production as a result of efficiencies gained through mass production).

Just transition: A social movement and policy framework for involving and protecting workers during sustainability transitions. Rooted in the 1970s labour movements across North America, the just transition framework rejects the "jobs versus environment" binary, insisting instead that policies to shift away from fossil fuels need not compromise the livelihoods and well-being of workers. The just transition(s) framework gained international traction in the 2015 Paris Agreement.

RESOURCES FOR ACTIVISTS

Working Group on Indigenous Food Sovereignty (WGIFS): indigenousfoodsystems.
   org/about
United Food and Commercial Workers union (UFCW Canada): ufcw.ca/index.
   php?lang=en
National Farmers Union (NFU): nfu.ca/
Union Paysanne: unionpaysanne.com/
Food Secure Canada: foodsecurecanada.org/
Food Policy for Canada: foodpolicyforcanada.info.yorku.ca/
Farmers for Climate Solutions: farmersforclimatesolutions.ca/

ACKNOWLEDGEMENT

We thank Mark Hudson for his help and guidance in the conceptual development of this chapter, as well as Wayne Antony and an anonymous reviewer for their constructive feedback.

AUTHOR ROLES

Sarah-Louise Ruder, Dana James and Evan Bowness contributed equally to this chapter, and Tabitha Robin and Bryan Dale contributed equally to this chapter.

NOTES

1   This section has been adapted from James and Bowness 2021.
2   This section has been adapted from James and Bowness 2021.

REFERENCES

AAFC (Agriculture and Agri-Food Canada). 2018. *Agriculture and Climate Change Policy Financial Impacts of Carbon Pricing on Canadian Farms, 2018*. Government of Canada.
___. 2017. *An Overview of the Canadian Agriculture and Agri-Food System, 2017*. Government of Canada. Ottawa: Agriculture and Agri-Food Canada.
___. 2016. *An Overview of the Canadian Agriculture and Agri-Food System, 2016*. Government of Canada. Ottawa: Agriculture and Agri-Food Canada.
Acoose-Miswonigeesikokwe, J. 2016. *Iskwewak Kah' Ki Yaw Ni Wahkomakanak: Neither Indian Princess nor Easy Squaws*, 2nd edition. Toronto: Women's Press.
Andrée, P., J.K. Clark, C.Z. Levkoe, K. Lowitt (eds.) 2019. *Civil Society and Social Movements in Food System Governance*. London: Routledge.
Banerjee, A. 2011. "Food, Feed, Fuel: Transforming the Competition for Grains." *Development and Change* 42, 2.

Bezner Kerr, R., C. Hickey, E. Lupafya, and L. Dakishoni. 2019. "Repairing Rifts or Reproducing Inequalities? Agroecology, Food Sovereignty, and Gender Justice in Malawi." *Journal of Peasant Studies* 46, 7.

Borras, S.M., J.C. Franco, S.R. Isakson et al. 2016. "The Rise of Flex Crops and Commodities: Implications for Research." *Journal of Peasant Studies* 43, 1.

Bowness, E., D. James, A.A. Desmarais et al. 2020. "Risk and Responsibility in the Corporate Food Regime: Research Pathways Beyond the COVID-19 Crisis." *Studies in Political Economy* 101, 3.

Bush, E., and D.S. Lemmen (eds.). 2019. *Canada's Changing Climate Report*. Government of Canada, Ottawa. <changingclimate.ca/CCCR2019/>.

Canadians for Tax Fairness. n.d. *Canadians for Tax Fairness*. <taxfairness.ca>.

Carbonell, I.M. 2016. "The Ethics of Big Data in Big Agriculture." *Internet Policy Review* 5, 1.

Carlisle, L., M. Montenegro de Wit, M.S. DeLonge et al. 2019. "Transitioning to Sustainable Agriculture Requires Growing and Sustaining an Ecologically Skilled Workforce." *Frontiers in Sustainable Food Systems* 3, 96 (November).

Carter, S.A. 1990. *Lost Harvests: Prairie Indian Reserve Farmers and Government Policy*. Montreal: McGill-Queen's University Press.

CCPA (Canadian Centre for Policy Alternatives). 2021. "One Year into the Pandemic Canadian Billionaire Wealth Up by $78 Billion." <policyalternatives.ca/newsroom/news-releases/one-year-pandemic-canadian-billionaire-wealth-78-billion>.

Clapp, J. 2018. "Mega-Mergers on the Menu: Corporate Concentration and the Politics of Sustainability in the Global Food System." *Global Environmental Politics* 18, 12.

Clapp, J., A. Desmarais, and M. Margulis. 2015. "Mapping the State of Play on the Global Food Landscape." *Canadian Food Studies/La Revue Canadienne Des Études Sur l'Alimentation* 2, 2.

Clapp, J., and J. Purugganan. 2020. "Contextualizing Corporate Control in the Agrifood and Extractive Sectors." *Globalizations* 17, 7.

Clapp, J., and S.-L. Ruder. 2020. "Precision Technologies for Agriculture: Digital Farming, Gene-Edited Crops, and the Politics of Sustainability." *Global Environmental Politics* 20, 3.

Coalition Canada. n.d. *Welcome to Coalition Canada, Basic Income/Revenu de Base*. <basicincomecoalition.ca/en/>.

Collard, R., and J. Dempsey. 2020. "Patriarchy Is an Ecological Regime." *Progressive International*. <progressive.international/blueprint/e7d4b341-d047-4bda-a032-6a3fe3ee36c9-dempsey-collard-patriarchy-is-an-ecological-regime/en>.

Coristine, L.E., A.L. Jacob, R. Schuster et al. 2018. "Informing Canada's Commitment to Biodiversity Conservation: A Science-Based Framework to Help Guide Protected Areas Designation Through Target 1 and Beyond." *Facets* 3, 1.

Coristine, L.E., and J.T. Kerr. 2011. "Habitat Loss, Climate Change, and Emerging Conservation Challenges in Canada." *Canadian Journal of Zoology* 89, 5.

Corkal, V., and P. Gass. 2020. "Unpacking Canada's Fossil Fuel Subsidies." *International Institute for Sustainable Development*. <iisd.org/articles/unpacking-canadas-fossil-fuel-subsidies-faq?q=faq/unpacking-canadas-fossil-fuel-subsidies/#howmuch>.

Coté, C. 2016. "'Indigenizing' Food Sovereignty. Revitalizing Indigenous Food Practices and Ecological Knowledges in Canada and the United States." *Humanities* 5, 3.

Daigle, M. 2019. "Tracing the Terrain of Indigenous Food Sovereignties." *Journal of Peasant Studies* 46, 2. <doi.org/10.1080/03066150.2017.1324423>.

Dale, B. 2020. "Alliances for Agroecology: From Climate Change to Food System Change." *Agroecology and Sustainable Food Systems* 44, 5.

___. 2019. "Farming for System Change: The Politics of Food Sovereignty and Climate Change in Canada." PhD thesis, University of Toronto. <academia.edu/41184251/Farming_for_System_Change_The_Politics_of_Food_Sovereignty_and_Climate_Change_in_Canada>.

Demirbas, A. 2009. "Political, Economic and Environmental Impacts of Biofuels: A Review." *Applied Energy* 86, 1.

Desmarais, A.A., P. Claeys, and A. Trauger. 2017. *Public Policies for Food Sovereignty: Social Movements and the State.* Milton: Routledge Studies in Food, Society and the Environment.

Edmunds, K., H. Berman, T. Basok, et al. 2011. "The Health of Women Temporary Agricultural Workers in Canada: A Critical Review of the Literature." *Canadian Journal of Nursing Research* 43, 4.

EJAtlas. 2021. "The Global Atlas of Environmental Justice." <ejatlas.org>.

Ericksen, P.J. 2008. "Conceptualizing Food Systems for Global Environmental Change Research." *Global Environmental Change* 18.

ETC Group. 2019. *Plate Tech-Tonics: Mapping Corporate Power in Big Food.* <etcgroup.org/sites/www.etcgroup.org/files/files/etc_platetechtonics_a4_nov2019_web.pdf>.

___. 2015. "Breaking Bad: Big Ag Mega-Mergers in Play: Dow + DuPont in the Pocket? Next: Demonsanto?" Communiqué #115. <etcgroup.org/sites/www.etcgroup.org/files/files/etc_break-bad_23dec15.pdf>.

FAO. 2019. *The State of Food and Agriculture 2019: Moving Forward on Food Loss and Waste Reduction.* Rome. <fao.org/3/ca6030en/ca6030en.pdf>.

___. 2008. *The State of Food and Agriculture 2008: Biofuels: Prospects, Risks and Opportunities.* Rome. <fao.org/3/i0100e/i0100e00.htm>.

FAO, IFAD, UNICEF, WFP, and WHO. 2020. *The State of Food Security and Nutrition in the World 2020: Transforming Food Systems for Affordable Healthy Diets.* Rome: FAO. <fao.org/3/ca9692en/online/ca9692en.html>.

Foucault, M. [1976] 1979. *The History of Sexuality Volume 1: An Introduction.* London: Allen Lane.

Frei, B., D. Renard, M.G.E. Mitchell et al. 2018. "Bright Spots in Agricultural Landscapes: Identifying Areas Exceeding Expectations for Multifunctionality and Biodiversity." *Journal of Applied Ecology* 55, 6.

Freyer, B., and J. Bingen (eds.). 2015. *Re-Thinking Organic Food and Farming in a Changing World.* Dordrecht: Springer.

Friedmann, H. 2005. "From Colonialism to Green Capitalism: Social Movements and Emergence of Food Regimes." *New Directions in the Sociology of Global Development* 11.

Friedmann, H., and P. McMichael. 1989. "Agriculture and the State System: The Rise and Decline of National Agricultures, 1870 to the Present." *Sociologia Ruralis* 29, 2.

Gibson, J.W. 2019. "Automating Agriculture: Precision Technologies, Agbots, and the Fourth Industrial Revolution." In J.W. Gibson and S.E. Alexander (eds.), *In Defense of Farmers: The Future of Agriculture in the Shadow of Corporate Power.* Lincoln: University of Nebraska Press.

Gliessman, S.R. 2015. *Agroecology: The Ecology of Sustainable Food Systems,* 3rd edition. New York: CRC Press.

Government of Alberta. n.d. "Alberta Farm Fuel Benefit." Alberta. <open.alberta.ca/dataset/2fac6387-01ba-4999-83dc-9f75efa0885c/resource/bc983a56-9b09-4333-af44-b5b6c5d5bffe/download/affb-factsheet-june2015.pdf>.

Government of Canada. 2021. "Emerging Renewable Power Program." <nrcan.gc.ca/climate-change/green-infrastructure-programs/emerging-renewable-power/20502>.

___. 2019. "Just Transition Task Force." <wd-deo.gc.ca/eng/19814.asp>.

___. 2017. "About Renewable Energy." <nrcan.gc.ca/our-natural-resources/energy-sources-distribution/renewable-energy/about-renewable-energy/7295>.

Guthman, J. 2004. *Agrarian Dreams: The Paradox of Organic Farming in California.* Berkeley: University of California Press.

Hart, M.A. 2007. "Indigenous Knowledge and Research: The Míkiwáhp as a Symbol for Reclaiming Our Knowledge and Ways of Knowing." *First Peoples' Child and Family Review* 3, 1.

Harvey, D. 2005. *A Brief History of Neoliberalism.* New York: Oxford University Press.

Hendrickson, M.K., P.H. Howard, E.M. Miller and D.H. Constance. 2020. "The Food System: Concentration and Its Impacts." *Family Farm Action Alliance.* <farmactionalliance.org/concentrationreport/>.

HLPE (High Level Panel of Experts on Food Security and Nutrition). 2011. *Food Security and Nutrition:*

Building a Global Narrative Towards 2030. Rome: FAO. <fao.org/3/ne664en/NE664EN.pdf>.

___. 2013. Biofuels and Food Security." Rome: FAO. <fao.org/3/i2952e/i2952e.pdf>.

Holt-Giméénez, E., and Y. Wang. 2011. "Reform or Transformation? The Pivotal Role of Food Justice in the US Food Movement." *Race/Ethnicity: Multidisciplinary Global Contexts* 5, 1.

ILO (International Labour Organization). 2013. "Sustainable Development, Decent Work and Green Jobs." <ilo.org/ilc/ILCSessions/previous-sessions/102/on-the-agenda/green-jobs/lang--en/index.htm>.

IPBES (Intergovernmental Science-Policy Platform on Biodiversity and Ecosystem Services). 2019. *Global Assessment Report on Biodiversity and Ecosystem Services: Summary for Policymakers*. Bonn. <ipbes.net/sites/default/files/2020-02/ipbes_global_assessment_report_summary_for_policymakers_en.pdf>.

IPCC (Intergovernmental Panel on Climate Change). 2021. *Climate Change 2021: The Physical Science Basis*. <ipcc.ch/report/sixth-assessment-report-working-group-i/>.

___. 2019a. *Global Warming of 1.5°C: An IPCC Special Report on the Impacts of Global Warming of 1.5°C Above Pre-Industrial Levels and Related Global Greenhouse Gas Emission Pathways, in the Context of Strengthening the Global Response to the Threat of Climate Change, Sustainable Development, and Efforts to Eradicate Poverty*. <ipcc.ch/sr15/download/#full>.

___. 2019b. *Climate Change and Land: An IPCC Special Report on Climate Change, Desertification, Land Degradation, Sustainable Land Management, Food Security, and Greenhouse Gas Fluxes in Terrestrial Ecosystems*. <ipcc.ch/srccl/>.

IPES-Food (International Panel of Experts on Sustainable Food Systems). 2016. *From Uniformity to Diversity: A Paradigm Shift from Industrial Agriculture to Diversified Agroecological Systems*. <ipes-food.org/_img/upload/files/UniformityToDiversity_FULL.pdf>.

Isaac, M.S. Isakson, B. Dale et al. 2018. "Agroecology in Canada: Towards an Integration of Agroecological Practice, Movement, and Science." *Sustainability* 10, 3299.

James, D., and E. Bowness. 2021. *Growing and Eating Sustainably: Agroecology in Action*. Winnipeg and Halifax: Fernwood Publishing.

Just Transition Research Collaborative. 2018. *Mapping Just Transition(s) to a Low-Carbon World*. UNRISD. <unrisd.org/unrisd/website/projects.nsf/(httpProjects)/5A869CB10DDF0AEDC125824F0057605B>.

Kerr, J.T., and J. Cihlar. 2004. "Patterns and Causes of Species Endangerment in Canada." *Ecological Applications* 14, 3.

King, M., D. Altdorff, P. Li et al. 2018. "Northward Shift of the Agricultural Climate Zone Under 21st-Century Global Climate Change." *Scientific Reports* 8, 7904.

Klein, N. 2014. *This Changes Everything: Capitalism vs. the Climate*. New York: Simon & Schuster.

Kraus, D., and A. Hebb. 2020. "Southern Canada's Crisis Ecoregions: Identifying the Most Significant and Threatened Places for Biodiversity Conservation." *Biodiversity and Conservation* 29, 13.

Laan, T., and V. Corkal. 2020. "International Best Practices: Estimating Tax Subsidies for Fossil Fuels in Canada." *International Institute for Sustainable Development*. <iisd.org/system/files/2020-12/tax-subsidies-fossil-fuels-canada.pdf>.

Laforge, J., B. Dale, C.Z. Levkoe, and F. Ahmed. 2021. "The Future of Agroecology in Canada: Embracing the Politics of Food Sovereignty." *Journal of Rural Studies* 81.

LaRocque, E. 2010. *When the Other Is Me: Native Resistance Discourse, 1850–1990*. Winnipeg: University of Manitoba Press.

Lerner, S. 2010. *Sacrifice Zones*. Cambridge and London: MIT Press.

LVC (La Vía Campesina). 2015. "Declaration of the International Forum for Agroecology." <viacampesina.org/en/declaration-of-the-international-forum-for-agroecology/>.

___. 2007. "Declaration of Nyéléni." <viacampesina.org/en/declaration-of-nyi/>.

Manuel, A., and R.M. Derrickson. 2015. *Unsettling Canada: A National Wake-Up Call*. Toronto: Between the Lines.

McCallum, M.J., and L. McCallum. 2017. "Starvation, Experimentation, Segregation, and Trauma: Words for Reading Indigenous Health History." *Canadian Historical Review* 98. <doi.org/10.3138/chr.98.1.McCallum>.

McCauley, D., and R. Heffron. 2018. "Just Transition: Integrating Climate, Energy and Environmental Justice." *Energy Policy* 119. <doi.org/10.1016/j.enpol.2018.04.014>.

McKeon, N. 2015. *Food Security Governance: Empowering Communities, Regulating Corporations.* Routledge.

McKnight, C., F. Qiu, M. Luckert, and G. Hauer. 2021. "Prices for a Second-Generation Biofuel Industry in Canada: Market Linkages Between Canadian Wheat and US Energy and Agricultural Commodities." *Canadian Journal of Agricultural Economics* 69, 3. <doi.org/10.1111/cjag.12295>.

McLachlan, S. 2014. "'Water Is a Living Thing': Environmental and Human Health Implications of the Athabasca Oil Sands for the Mikisew Cree First Nation and Athabasca Chipewyan First Nation in Northern Alberta. Phase 2 Report." *Des Libris.* <deslibris.ca/ID/243630>.

McLaughlin, J.E. 2008. "Gender, Health and Mobility: Health Concerns of Women Migrant Farm Workers in Canada." *Health Studies* 1.

McLaughlin, J.E., and A.M. Weiler. 2016. "Migrant Agricultural Workers in Local and Global Contexts: Toward a Better Life?" *Journal of Agrarian Change* 17, 3.

McMichael, P. 2009a. "A Food Regime Genealogy." *Journal of Peasant Studies* 36, 1. <doi.org/10.1080/03066150902820354>.

____. 2009b. "A Food Regime Analysis of the 'World Food Crisis.'" *Agriculture and Human Values* 26, 4. <doi.org/10.1007/s10460-009-9218-5>.

Méndez, V.E., C.M. Bacon, and R. Cohen. 2013. "Agroecology as a Transdisciplinary, Participatory, and Action-Oriented Approach." *Agroecology and Sustainable Food Systems* 37.

Mertins-Kirkwood, H., and Z. Deshpande. 2019. *Who Is Included in a Just Transition? Considering Social Equity in Canada's Shift to a Zero-carbon Economy.* Canadian Centre for Policy Alternatives.

Migrant Rights Network. n.d. "Build a Migrant Justice Movement. We Need #StatusforAll." <migrant-rights.ca/>.

Monchalin, L. 2016. *The Colonial Problem: An Indigenous Perspective on Crime and Injustice in Canada.* Toronto: University of Toronto Press.

Morrison, D. 2011. "Indigenous Food Sovereignty: A Model for Social Learning." In H. Wittman, A. Desmarais and N. Wiebe (eds.), *Food Sovereignty in Canada: Creating Just and Sustainable Food Systems.* Halifax, NS: Fernwood Publishing.

Muscat, A., E.M. de Olde, I.J.M. de Boer and R. Ripoll-Bosch. 2020. "The Battle for Biomass: A Systematic Review of Food-feed-fuel Competition." *Global Food Security* 25, 100330. <doi.org/10.1016/j.gfs.2019.100330>.

MWAC (Migrant Workers Alliance for Change). 2020. *Unheeded Warnings: COVID-19 & Migrant Workers in Canada.* <migrantworkersalliance.org/wp-content/uploads/2020/06/Unheeded-Warnings-COVID19-and-Migrant-Workers.pdf>.

National Inquiry into Missing and Murdered Indigenous Women and Girls. 2019. *Reclaiming Power and Place: The Final Report of the National Inquiry into Missing and Murdered Indigenous Women and Girls*, Vol. 1a. <mmiwg-ffada.ca/final-report/>.

Navius Research. 2020. "Biofuels in Canada." <energybc.ca/biofuels.html#footnote-51>.

Newell, P., and D. Mulvaney. 2013. "The Political Economy of the 'Just Transition.'" *The Geographical Journal* 179, 2. <doi.org/10.1111/geoj.12008>.

NFU (National Farmers Union) and D. Qualman. 2021. *Imagine If: A Vision of a Near-Zero-Emission Farm and Food System for Canada.* Saskatoon.

OBIN (Ontario Basic Income Network). n.d. "Ontario Basic Income Network." <obin.ca>.

OFA (Ontario Federation of Agriculture) 2019. "Ontario Farmers: Take Action Now to Be Exempt from Fuel Charge." <ofa.on.ca/resources/ontario-farmers-take-action-now-to-be-exempt-from-fuel-charge/>.

Ontario. 2019. "Archived — 4.0 Feed-In Tariff Program." <ontario.ca/document/renewable-energy-de-velopment-ontario-guide-municipalities/40-feed-tariff-program>.

Otero, G., and K. Preibisch. 2015. *Citizenship and Precarious Labour in Canadian Agriculture.* Canadian Centre for Policy Alternatives. <policyalternatives.ca/sites/default/files/uploads/publications/BC%20Office/2015/11/CCPA-BC_CitizenshipPrecariousLabourCdnAgri_web.pdf>.

Polsky, J.Y., and H. Gilmour. 2020. "Food Insecurity and Mental Health during the COVID-19 Pandemic." *Statistics Canada: Health Reports* 31, 12. <doi.org/10.25318/82-003-x202001200001-eng>.

Prairie Climate Centre. 2019. "Climate Change and 70 Years of Farming." <climateatlas.ca/video/roy-mclaren>.

Province of British Columbia. n.d. "Motor Fuel Tax and Carbon Tax Exemptions." <www2.gov.bc.ca/gov/content/taxes/sales-taxes/motor-fuel-carbon-tax/business/exemptions>.

Qualman, D. 2019. *Civilization Critical: Energy, Food, Nature, and the Future.* Black Point, NS: Fernwood Publishing.

___. 2011. "Advancing Agriculture by Destroying Farms? The State of Agriculture in Canada." In Hannah Wittman, Annette Desmarais and Nettie Wiebe (eds.), *Food Sovereignty in Canada: Creating Just and Sustainable Food Systems.* Halifax, NS: Fernwood Publishing.

Qualman, D., A. Desmarais, A. Magnan and M. Wendimu. 2020. *Concentration Matters: Farmland Inequality on the Prairies.* Winnipeg: CCPA. <nfu.ca/wp-content/uploads/2020/11/Farmland-Concentration.pdf>.

Qualman, D., and NFU. 2019. *Tackling the Farm Crisis and the Climate Crisis: A Transformative Strategy for Canadian Farms and Food Systems.* Saskatoon: National Farmers Union of Canada.

Robin, T. 2019. "Our Hands at Work: Indigenous Food Sovereignty in Western Canada." *Journal of Agriculture, Food Systems, and Community Development* 9, B. <doi.org/10.5304/jafscd.2019.09B.007>.

Robin, T., M.K. Dennis and M.A. Hart. 2020. "Feeding Indigenous People in Canada." *International Social Work.* <doi.org/10.1177%2F0020872820916218>.

Rose, D.C., and J. Chilvers. 2018. "Agriculture 4.0: Broadening Responsible Innovation in an Era of Smart Farming." *Frontiers in Sustainable Food Systems* 2, 87. <doi.org/10.3389/fsufs.2018.00087>.

Rosillo-Calle, F. 2012. "Food versus Fuel: Toward a New Paradigm—The Need for a Holistic Approach." ISRN *Renewable Energy.* <doi.org/10.5402/2012/954180>.

Rosset, P.M., and M.A. Altieri. 2017. *Agroecology: Science and Politics.* Black Point, NS: Fernwood Publishing.

Rossman, P. 2013. "Food Workers' Rights as a Path to a Low-Carbon Agriculture." In N. Räthzel and D.L. Uzzell (eds.), *Trade Unions in the Green Economy: Working for the Environment.* New York: Routledge.

Sachs, C., M.E. Barbercheck, K. Brasier et al. 2016. *The Rise of Women Farmers and Sustainable Agriculture.* Iowa City: University of Iowa Press.

Silverthorn, D. 2016. "Hungry for Knowledge: Assessing the Prevalence of Student Food Insecurity on Five Canadian Campuses." Toronto: Meal Exchange. <cpcml.ca/publications2016/161027-Hungry_for_Knowledge.pdf>.

Smith, L.T. 2005. "On Tricky Ground: Researching the Native in the Age of Uncertainty." In N.K. Denzin and Y.S. Lincoln (eds.), *The Sage Handbook of Qualitative Research,* 3rd edition. Thousand Oaks, CA: Sage.

Snell, D. 2018. "'Just Transition'? Conceptual Challenges Meet Stark Reality in a 'Transitioning' Coal Region in Australia." *Globalizations* 15, 4.

Tarasuk, V., and A. Mitchell. 2020. *Household Food Insecurity in Canada, 2017–18.* Toronto: Food Insecurity Policy Research (PROOF). <proof.utoronto.ca/resources/proof-annual-reports/household-food-insecurity-in-canada-2017-2018/>.

Tuncak, B. 2020. *Visit to Canada: Report of the Special Rapporteur on the Implications for Human Rights of the Environmentally Sound Management and Disposal of Hazardous Substances and Wastes.* United Nations.

UNFCCC. 2016. *Just Transition of the Workforce, and the Creation of Decent Work and Quality Jobs.* Secretariat of the United Nations Framework on the Convention on Climate Change. <unfccc.int/resource/docs/2016/tp/07.pdf>.

Venter, O., N.N. Brodeur, L. Nemiroff et al. 2006. "Threats to Endangered Species in Canada." *BioScience* 56, 11.

Vowel, C. 2012. "Undermined at Every Turn: The Lie of the Failed Native Farm on the Prairies."

Âpihtawikosisân, May 23. <apihtawikosisan.com/2012/05/undermined-at-every-turn-the-lie-of-the-failed-native-farms-on-the-prairies/>.

Waldron, I. 2018a. "Re-Thinking Waste: Mapping Racial Geographies of Violence on the Colonial Landscape." *Environmental Sociology* 4, 1. <doi.org/10.1080/23251042.2018.1429178>.

___. 2018b. *There's Something in the Water: Environmental Racism in Indigenous & Black Communities*. Winnipeg: Fernwood Publishing.

Weiler, A.M., G. Otero and H. Wittman. 2016. "Rock Stars and Bad Apples: Moral Economies of Alternative Food Networks and Precarious Farm Work Regimes." *Antipode* 48, 4.

Weis, T. 2022. "A Political Ecology Approach to Industrial Food Production." In Mustafa Koç, Jennifer Sumner and Anthony Winson (eds.), *Critical Perspectives in Food Studies*, 3rd edition. Don Mills: Oxford University Press.

Wezel, A., S. Bellon, T. Doré et al. 2009. "Agroecology as a Science, a Movement and a Practice. A Review." *Agronomy for Sustainable Development* 29, 4.

Whyte, K.P. 2018. "Food Sovereignty, Justice and Indigenous Peoples: An Essay on Settler Colonialism and Collective Continuance." In A. Barnhill, M. Budolfson, and T. Doggett (eds.), *The Oxford Handbook of Food Ethics*. New York: Oxford University Press.

___. 2017. "Indigenous Climate Change Studies: Indigenizing Futures, Decolonizing the Anthropocene." *English Language Notes* 55, 1–2. <doi.org/10.1215/00138282-55.1-2.153>.

Wiebe, N. 2017. "Crisis in the Food System: The Farm Crisis." In Mustafa Koç, Jennifer Sumner and Anthony Winson (eds.), *Critical Perspectives in Food Studies*, 2nd edition. Don Mills: Oxford University Press.

Wolinetz, M., M. Hein and B. Moawad. 2019. "Biofuels in Canada 2019." *Navius Research*, April 25. <navius research.com/wp-content/uploads/2019/05/Biofuels-in-Canada-2019-2019-04-25-final.pdf>.

9

THE FUTURE OF WORK?
App-Based Workers and the Gig Economy

Paul Christopher Gray, Stephanie Ross and Larry Savage

YOU SHOULD KNOW THIS

- The average member of Canada's one hundred most highly paid CEOs earned as much by 11:17 a.m. on January 4, 2020, as was earned by the average Canadian full-time employee in the entire year.

- The share of unionized workers in the private sector has declined over the past few decades. Private-sector union density has fallen from 20.2 percent in 2000 to 15.9 percent in 2019.

- On May 11, 2020, Foodora exited the Canadian market after the Ontario Labour Relations Board ruled that its couriers were misclassified as independent contractors and therefore had the right to unionize. Foodora's parent company, German-based Delivery Hero, generated €1.4 billion in revenues in 2019.

- A 2017 Greater Toronto Area study, which defined gig work as platform-based work, found that among those who had done gig work, 51 percent identify as men, 48 percent as women and 1 percent as transgender. Furthermore, 54 percent are racialized and 69 percent were born in Canada. More than 70 percent are age forty-five or younger and 51 percent have children under age eighteen.

Sources: Block and Hennessy 2017, CCPA 2021, Statistics Canada 2021, O'Kane 2020.

WITH THE RISE OF COMPANIES LIKE Uber, TaskRabbit and Deliveroo, app-based gig work is transforming Canada's labour market. But does the growing gig economy offer workers and employers an innovative workforce model, or does it make work even more insecure than it already is? In this chapter, we examine the gig economy, explore both mainstream and critical perspectives on gig work, situate app-based gig work within the broader history of capitalism and review ideas and efforts to improve the terms and conditions of work in the gig economy. We argue that while aspects of gig work involve novel applications of technology, the underlying motivations and strategies of employers remain the same: to maximize profit and minimize workers' cost and power to disrupt production. Moreover, gig workers experience many of the same problems that other workers have throughout the history of capitalism, namely low wages, insecurity, alienation and a loss of control over their work lives. Indeed, these problems deserve thoughtful consideration, because the gig economy is expanding and replacing more stable, better compensated and unionized work. Though the conditions of gig worker organizing present unique challenges, they are still best served by a combination of worker collective action. The rise of the gig economy also gives us pressing reasons to rethink the design of employment law and social entitlements to better include all workers in non-standard and precarious employment.

Digital commercial platforms or apps match potential buyers to sellers and receive a percentage of the transactions. Proponents argue that platforms allow a broader range of choices, and their online transactions are faster and cheaper than in-person ones requiring travel to brick-and-mortar buildings. Compared to a traditional taxi, for example, an Uber is often easier to order, arrives quicker and costs less.

Digital platforms are the foundation of what has been called the "gig economy." Platforms facilitate two kinds of transactions — exchanges and rentals — involving two kinds of commodities — labour and non-labour. If, after using Kijiji, someone arrives at your door to pick up the old guitar you sold them, you are exchanging your non-labour commodity for their money. Or, if they arrived because you used Airbnb to sell them the temporary use of your spare room, you are renting your non-labour commodity for their money. If, however, they came to your door with the food you ordered on Uber Eats, they are exchanging their labour power, their effort to pick up and deliver your food, for money, a part of which becomes their wages.

All three of these transactions comprise the gig economy and each of them can loosely be described as a "gig" in certain contexts. However, only the third kind of transaction, the exchange of money for labour power, counts as gig work. It has also been called "platform work" or "app-based work." In this chapter, when we refer to gig work, we mean it in this sense.

There are some basic features of gig work. First, it is contingent on on-demand labour. Instead of ongoing employment based on an indefinite contract, gig workers

[handwritten note: It goes both ways — companies also suffer from the instability of workers]

are hired only when a specific service is needed. If you use Placer to pay someone to wait in a line on your behalf, once they deliver you the tickets you wanted, the relationship ends. Second, gig workers are usually paid for each product they produce, a "piece rate," not for the number of hours worked, a "time rate." The person you found on Instacart is paid for each order of grocery shopping and delivery, not the hour it took them to do it. Finally, gig workers often provide much of their own equipment. The Lyft driver supplies the car, the SkipTheDishes courier the bicycle and the ChoreRelief cleaner the mop.

There are also some important variations between different kinds of app-based gig work. Though the work is arranged through an online platform, the work itself can be done either online or offline. A common example of online gig work is "crowdsourcing," where a complex set of "microtasks," some taking a few minutes each, are presented to an undefined group of gig workers, who can be paid as little as ten cents per microtask (Kirven 2018: 258–59). These can include labelling parts of images or movies, screening online content for inappropriate material or writing product descriptions. Offline gig work is on-demand, in-person services, such as delivery, cleaning and transportation. Finally, in either kind of gig work, the customer or client can be an individual, a group or a company.

MAINSTREAM PERSPECTIVES ON APP-BASED GIG WORK

Advocates of the gig economy model argue that, in the near future, many workers will no longer be regular employees of a single company. Instead, they will be entrepreneurs who use cutting-edge technology to connect with people and move from gig to gig. Platforms allow gig workers independence and flexibility. Each gig worker, deciding when to connect and disconnect, can choose their own hours. These platforms are as mobile as the devices used to access them, so gig workers can choose where they will work. Since gig workers can register with multiple apps at once, they can decide with whom they will work. They need not deal with the bureaucracy of working for a single company, nor conform to the expectations of the regular 9-to-5 job (Sherk 2016).

> Advocates of the gig economy model argue that, in the near future, many workers will no longer be regular employees of a single company.

This positive view of gig work often appears to be shared by gig workers themselves. Although we should be wary of company surveys, which can apply selective framing and ask leading questions, Uber often refers to those it commissions, such as a 2014 survey in which 87 percent of Uber drivers said they were motivated "to be my

— millenial attitudes principle are work
— uncertainly options / not enough money / free time
care   The Future of Work? / 269

own boss and set my own schedule" (Hall and Krueger 2015: 11). Platform companies make appeals not only to workers seeking alternative forms of work, but also to
those having difficulties finding regular employment. Indeed, Airbnb has marketed
itself as "an economic lifeline for the middle class" (Heller 2017). In the Uber survey,
74 percent of respondents agreed that one of their motivations is "to help maintain
a steady income because other sources of income are unstable/unpredictable" (Hall
and Krueger 2015: 11).

How big, then, is the gig workforce? Various studies give divergent answers. In
part, this is because researchers use different definitions of the gig economy. Even
if there were common definitions, however, there is a lack of suitable data. Platform
companies are usually reluctant to release their figures. Labour market statistics are
also inadequate for capturing gig work because, for example, employment is measured in some countries only when work has occurred for at least one hour in a day or
a week (Bajwa et al. 2018). Furthermore, it is hard to estimate a total number when
people are working simultaneously for multiple companies (Forde et al. 2017; De
Stefano 2016). It is also unclear to what extent gig workers report their activities and
earnings. Finally, given the extent of digital mediation, much of the work is invisible
(Bajwa et al. 2018).

The general consensus, however, is that the gig workforce is small but significant
and growing. One study argues that, in Canada, the share of gig workers among all
workers increased from 5.5 percent in 2005 to 8.2 percent in 2016 (Jeon, Liu and
Ostrovsky 2019). Another study, which defined gig work as platform-based work,
surveyed a random sample of 2,304 residents of the Greater Toronto Area and found
that 9 percent had engaged in gig work and 38 percent had purchased services from
online platforms (Block and Hennessy 2017). These numbers undoubtedly grew
during the COVID-19 pandemic as both workers and consumers increased their engagement with digital platforms to deal with job loss and as a strategy to survive
economic lockdowns.

Studies in the US and EU have found that around one third of adults have participated in the gig economy, broadly conceived, and those who have engaged in gig
work usually range between 1 and 5 percent (Forde et al. 2017). The vast majority of
gig workers, usually more than nine out of ten, use it to supplement their earnings
from other jobs. Only a small minority are "professional" gig workers for whom it
constitutes all or most of their income. Nevertheless, as an indication of trends in
the future of work, this minority seems to be growing. In the UK, for example, the
percentage of professional gig workers grew from 5.2 percent in 2016 to 9.4 percent
in 2019 (Huws, Spencer and Coates 2019). With respect to gig work in general, one
survey of the literature asserts: "there is a broad consensus among researchers that
growth is likely; indeed, it is widely considered inevitable" (Forde et al. 2017: 38).

The likely causes for this growth are not, as it might first appear, the platform technology itself, but rather the "the prevailing regulatory environment in the national economy, and broader economic and social conditions" (Forde et al. 2017: 40). These include the influx of venture capital to platform companies, their ability to bypass many of the traditional regulations and, as part of a broader corporate trend, hiring independent contractors instead of employees, which saves money not only on labour costs but also employer contributions to things like social insurance (Forde et al. 2017). Among proponents of the gig economy, Paul Barter, a professor at the Schulich School of Business at York University, expresses a common view: "To bet against Uber is to bet against the future" (Nicoll and Armstrong 2016).

CRITICAL PERSPECTIVES ON GIG WORK

Despite widespread assertions that app-based gigs constitute "the future" of work, this perspective is not universally shared. In fact, the perceived advantages and implications of the gig economy are highly contested. Gig workers face a number of significant challenges, and some are actively resisting the growth of the gig economy model. One of the challenges is that gig workers are not deemed workers at all.

Employment Misclassification

When someone is formally hired for a job, they are usually assigned one of two legal classifications: employee or independent contractor. These classifications confer significant but distinct rights and responsibilities. They depend on the economic reality, which is determined by the extent of the payer's control over the worker; the degree to which the worker provides their own equipment and assumes financial risk; the duration of the working relationship; the extent to which the work is integral to the payer's business; and the worker's opportunity for profit (Canada n.d.; Donovan, Bradley and Shimabukuro 2017). It is more likely that a worker is an employee and the person who hires them an employer if, for example, the latter controls the manner of work and the former must get permission to work for others. Conversely, a worker is more likely to be an independent contractor if they have control over their manner of working, when they work and for whom they work.

Classification is significant because employees are legally entitled to rights that are not available to independent contractors. These include minimum standards, such as minimum wages, maximum hours, overtime and vacation pay as well as employer liability for workplace health and safety. These also include associational rights, such as the right to unionize, collectively bargain and strike. Given the character of gig work, its proper economic status is not immediately clear. Platform companies thereby "inhabit a legal 'grey zone'" (Stanford 2017: 385). They almost always misleadingly register the gig workers operating through their platforms as independent contractors, allowing platform companies to avoid the regulatory standards applicable to employers of employees, thus denying gig workers their statutory rights.

In general, the independent contractor designation transfers much of the risk to gig workers. For example, if platform companies are not liable for workplace health and safety, when bike couriers are injured on the job, they must pay the costs of their own healthcare and, if they are unable to work, bear the lost wages. Costs are also transferred to gig workers. They likely make less income than is alleged by platform companies when we account for the expenses of providing and maintaining their own equipment (Kirven 2018).

Increasingly, gig workers are challenging their misclassification as independent contractors. They contend that they are employees or, at the very least, dependent contractors. This is a hybrid classification, which means that, like independent contractors, workers are not entitled to certain regulatory standards like minimum wages but, like employees, have associational rights such as the right to unionize (Arthurs 1965–66).

These intensifying conflicts around economic classification are due, in part, to the changing character of gig work. Although many gig workers valued the independence they had when they first registered, over time, these platforms have implemented changes that have undermined this initial independence while instability persists or increases. Indeed, gig workers

> Intensifying conflicts around economic classification are due, in part, to the changing character of gig work.

point to these unilateral changes as evidence that they are not self-employed or equal partners in these platforms. Gig workers have had some success in their lawsuits against misclassification. In the following account of the arguments and counterarguments made by platform companies and gig workers, we draw extensively from a 2020 ruling by the Ontario Labour Relations Board (OLRB) in a case brought against Foodora by Toronto-based food couriers alleging misclassification (CUPW v. Foodora).

Platform companies argue that gig workers are independent contractors because they provide most, if not all, of their own equipment. Gig workers thereby generate income from this equipment as a return on their investment. In turn, platform companies are said to derive their income solely from their own investment: "Thus, in Uber and Lyft's estimation, they generate income through their software and not through the activities of the drivers" (Kirven 2018: 280).

Gig workers and their advocates offer numerous counterarguments. Although gig workers often own much of their own equipment, the most important tool is the platform itself, which they do not own. Even an investment as substantial as a car pales in importance to the platform in gig work. The platform is how customers place orders. If there is a third party, such as the restaurants participating in food delivery apps, the platform is how they receive orders. It is how customers pay and how gig workers and third parties get paid. The

> Although gig workers often own much of their own equipment, the most important tool is the platform itself, which they do not own.

platform develops lists and information of customers and participating third parties. It also develops the brand image. For all these reasons, the platform is clearly the most significant piece of equipment in gig work. If it was licensed or sold to gig workers, this might approximate the situation of independent contractors (CUPW *v. Foodora*). Otherwise, whatever else gig workers possess, they do not possess the platform.

App-based gig workers argue further that their hard work cannot be confused with entrepreneurialism if the company, through its platform, sets all the rules. Typically, gig workers must agree to the platform's terms and conditions before using it. Since there is no opportunity to negotiate,

> App-based gig workers argue further that their hard work cannot be confused with entrepreneurialism if the company, through its platform, sets all the rules.

they must either take or leave these conditions (Flanagan 2019). Usually, these terms prohibit gig workers from selling their labour directly to customers, outside of the platform (CUPW *v. Foodora*).

Further, gig workers are usually prohibited from subcontracting part or all of a job to helpers or substitutes, which is typical of independent contractors like electricians. Since the platform is registered to a personal account, the user must be the one who does the work. Users are often prohibited from swapping shifts with other gig workers and, if they cannot work, the shift goes back into the pool. Unlike independent contractors, gig workers must rely exclusively on their own labour and skill (CUPW *v. Foodora*).

Platform companies contend, however, that gig workers have the independence and flexibility typical of independent contractors because they can choose their own hours and worksites. Gig workers respond that these companies can still control shifts with respect to time, length, geographic location, number of spots and the assignment of shifts according to the company's ranking system. For example, gig workers often face significant constraints on their ability to choose their own hours. Delivery workers in particular often have to sign up for shifts on the app. This can be quite competitive, forcing many workers into less desirable shifts (Garneau 2019).

Platform companies have floated the idea that, since they do not employ managers who directly supervise and control gig workers, they are equal partners in the business. Gig workers counter that the platforms do monitor and control their work by using technology like the Global Positioning System (GPS). Platforms apply warnings and sanctions, usually called "strikes," when gig workers fail to perform work in the way determined unilaterally by the companies. In particular, they usually require workers to maintain a certain acceptance rate or customer rating, or both. Indeed, platform companies can terminate work relationships by deactivating workers' accounts, thereby preventing them from using the platform. Consequently, even if platforms do not directly supervise gig workers, they are not "uninterested middlemen" (Kirven 2018: 252).

Finally, platform companies argue that gig workers are independent contractors because they can work for multiple people or companies and can even work for multiple platforms at the same time, as long as they do not compromise service standards. Gig workers reply that economic dependence is not lessened simply because they can work for multiple companies. This is also true of employees with multiple part-time jobs. Indeed, having to work multiple jobs can be an indication of *greater* economic dependence. Moreover, even if someone works for multiple platforms, it is often the case that a single company must be given priority (Garneau 2019; CUPW v. *Foodora*).

Another way of evaluating economic dependence is "integration," the extent to which workers are integrated into a company's main activities. Integration increases the longer or more frequent their relationship and the more important each is for the compensation the other receives. Platform companies often require gig workers to work shifts with a certain amount of regularity to maintain their accounts, which entails a more continuous employment relationship than is required of independent contractors. Furthermore, on the one hand, platform companies' profits rely heavily on gig workers' efficiency and reliability and, on the other hand, gig workers depend on the platform company for their access to customers (Kirven 2018; CUPW v. *Foodora*). Some scholars argue that this mutual dependence is such that "Uber and Lyft are not 'technology companies' so much as they are transportation companies that take advantage of technology to sell labor" (Kirven 2018: 288). These arguments have resonated in some courts. For example, according to a US district court in California, Uber "does not simply sell software; it sells rides" (De Stefano 2016: 490).

For all these reasons, the OLRB ruled in February 2020 that Foodora had misclassified food couriers as independent contractors:

> There is no opportunity, nor reason, for the Foodora courier to develop any type of relationship with the customer or restaurant. In every practical sense, Foodora ensures the relationship is between itself, the customer and

the restaurant. The courier is a cog in the economic wheel — an integrated component to the financial transaction. This is a relationship that is more often seen with employees rather than independent contractors. (CUPW *v. Foodora*: para. 147)

Such legal victories, however, can be fleeting. In August 2020, when a California court ordered Uber and Lyft to comply with a new law requiring them to classify all their workers as employees, the companies threatened to suspend operations across the state. The court extended the deadline for complying with the law (Press 2020a). In the meantime, Uber, Lyft and other platform companies poured millions of dollars into a campaign supporting Proposition 22, a ballot measure that would overturn the new law requiring gig companies to classify workers as employees. These companies spent $205 million on the campaign, outspending their opponents ten to one. On November 4, 2020, 59 percent of California voters favoured the ballot measure: "Included in Proposition 22's fine print is a requirement that the measure cannot be modified with less than seven-eighths of the state legislature's approval, all but ensuring it cannot be overturned" (Press 2020b: n.p.). In Ontario, when Toronto-based food couriers won their misclassification lawsuit, Foodora promptly announced its withdrawal from all of Canada (Mojtehedzadeh 2020). Two years earlier, Foodora similarly withdrew from Australia after the initiation of a misclassification lawsuit (Chau 2018).

Such actions by these gig companies belie their claims that gig workers are equal partners. Uber and Lyft's threats to suspend the service, traditionally called a "capital strike," and Foodora's exit from Canada and Australia, referred to as "capital flight," show who owns the most important piece of equipment, who controls production, who has capital, and thus, who does not.

Gig Work, Precarious Work and the History of Capitalism

Tom Goodwin (2015: n.p.), the senior vice president of Havas Media, asserts:

> Uber, the world's largest taxi company, owns no vehicles. Facebook, the world's most popular media owner, creates no content. Alibaba, the most valuable retailer, has no inventory. And Airbnb, the world's largest accommodation provider, owns no real estate. Something interesting is happening.

Theories of digital platforms and the gig economy sometimes feature a peculiar mélange of the new and the old. On the one hand, commentators frequently deem the current technological revolutions and social transformations so unprecedented that we need entirely new concepts to explain them. On the other hand, in their search for imagery that conveys the growing dominance of platform companies, some of these very same commentators end up describing the gig economy as feudal (Weatherby 2018; De Ruyter and Brown 2019). We contend, however, that the gig economy is actually something much more familiar.

As previously described, commercial platforms take a percentage of each transaction they mediate. What we call this percentage depends on how we think of the triangular relationship between the platform owners, gig workers and customers. Some call it rent. Others call it commissions or fees. Still others call it profit. What should we call this percentage? Platforms are frequently described as marketplaces that match sellers with buyers. When the transactions involve exchanging or renting non-labour commodities, this is accurate. The percentage taken by companies like Carousell and Airbnb is payment for a service provided to the platform users who are engaging in buying, selling and renting. These platform companies have employees — say, the coder who helps to develop the software. But these employees are not necessarily the platform users. With the exchange of labour power, however, the situation is different.

Sympathetic accounts of platform companies will portray Uber, for example, as providing an opportunity for "people who have an under-used car" (Forde et al. 2017: 24–25). Nevertheless, we must note that, from Uber's perspective, the car is not a person's only underused asset. So is their labour. If an underused car can be an asset for a person, then a person's underused labour can be an asset for a company. This is because platforms are not merely a place of exchange. They can also be employers who control a place of production. An Uber rider can buy a service through the platform only because Uber, the owner of that platform, first buys and controls the labour power of the Uber driver who provides that service. The exchange of commodified labour power for wages, the contract by which the Uber driver works for Uber, is the precondition of the exchange between Uber and the Uber rider. Uber then uses a part of this latter exchange to pay the wage of the Uber driver and keeps the rest for itself. This is why the percentage they take from each exchange, the product of gig work, is most appropriately described as profit. The gig economy in general, and gig work in particular, are neither anachronistic nor futuristic. They are capitalism plain and simple.

> The gig economy in general, and gig work in particular, are neither anachronistic nor futuristic. They are capitalism plain and simple.

Each platform company attempts to not only become a market leader, but to achieve "network effects" (Flanagan 2019: 63), because "strong economies of scale and scope in networking tend to reinforce its dominance" (Stanford 2017: 384). Having a large number of users becomes the main draw for a still larger number of potential users. People choose a platform because most people already seem to be there. Nevertheless, there is another important feature of these network effects. It is how a platform becomes capital, how it becomes a privately owned, digitally based place of production (Gandini 2019).

The strategy is to grow to such a size that the platform becomes one of a few dominant companies in and across particular industries. A part of this strategy is that, when people seek a service, they increasingly turn to these platforms. But more importantly, this strategy makes it increasingly difficult to provide a service outside of these platforms. This squeezes out people who are genuinely self-employed and have control of their own labour. Formerly, the self-employed person made profit. Now, as they turn increasingly to platforms, they make wages while the platform owners make the profits.

Even when proponents of the gig economy acknowledge its capitalist character, they nonetheless emphasize its innovations, describing gig work as the future of work. But in many respects, gig work is a return to the past, when work was largely unregulated and the inequalities between employers and employees were deep. To understand why, we must situate gig work within the history of capitalism.

> In many respects, gig work is a return to the past, when work was largely unregulated and the inequalities between employers and employees were deep.

Gig work is often described, by proponents and critics alike, as "non-standard employment." This draws a contrast with the "standard employment" that prevailed in the postwar era (1945–1975). Standard employment is full-time, permanent work for a single employer. It tends to take place in a central worksite, like a factory, which is owned and supplied by the employer, as is most of the equipment (Stanford 2017).

Proponents of gig work often emphasize its independence and flexibility by focusing on the shortcomings of standard employment. They will point to workers' feelings of subordination because they work for the same boss their entire lives, or to the drudgery of mass production and the assembly line, or to the alienation provoked by corporate bureaucracy. And much of this is true. But supporters of the gig economy often neglect the advantages achieved by workers with standard employment, including stability, union representation, as well as decent pay and benefits. Indeed, one reason for the emergence of the gig economy has been the decline of the availability of standard employment and the erosion of the advantages that people with standard employment enjoy (PEPSO 2015).

This erosion is due to a series of policies and practices commonly referred to as "neoliberalism." Neoliberalism has a number of features: (1) deregulating economic activities and rolling back labour protections; (2) liberalizing trade across national borders, which intensifies global integration and competition; (3) cutting or privatizing public services in order to expand for-profit provision in the market; and (4) a more coercive turn against workers by governments and employers (Panitch and Swartz 2003). These are not merely economic policies, but a political project to reconstitute the power of employers against organized labour (Harvey 2007).

Neoliberal policies have caused the transition from standard to non-standard employment, and with it, the growth of what is called "precarious work." Precarious work is usually part-time, temporary work for low wages and meagre benefits. Precarious workers rarely have union representation and collective bargaining. If they negotiate with their employers, it is usually as individuals, which tends to mean little power to exercise the few workplace rights they do have. There is also substantial overlap between precarious work and gig work. To see how the employment instability and insecurity of precarious work is particularly pronounced for gig workers, we can look at the comments of Lukas Biewald, the co-founder and former CEO of the platform CrowdFlower: "Before the Internet, it would be really difficult to find someone, sit them down for ten minutes and get them to work for you, and then fire them after those ten minutes. But with technology, you can actually find them, pay them the tiny amount of money, and then get rid of them when you don't need them anymore" (Marvit 2014). This is why critical scholars reject platform companies' claims to be "novel" or "innovative," let alone "emancipatory." Rather, these platforms create "an extreme example of a range of forms of insecure work that have come to prominence over the last 40 years" (Flanagan 2019: 58). What is often positively depicted as independence is more realistically described as precarity.

> What is often positively depicted as independence is more realistically described as precarity.

Since gig workers are usually misclassified as independent contractors, they "end up with none of the benefits of self-employment, in terms of control, and all the problems of income insecurity" (Forde et al. 2017: 11). For example, a 2017 survey of Europe and the US found that gig workers' wages were consistently lower than minimum wages, ranging from a 3.4 percent gap in the US to a 54.1 percent gap in France (Forde et al. 2017). Gig workers also experience longer periods of unemployment than the average worker: "This might suggest that vulnerability and the amount of income insecurity inherent in unemployment renders individuals more likely to consider working through the internet as a viable option" (Piasna and Drahokoupil

2019: 40). In a comparison of European countries, there seems to be more gig work where there is more poverty (Huws, Spencer and Coates 2019).

Gig workers also face employment instability by shifting between unpredictable periods of underwork and overwork. Even when they can find a reasonable amount of work, it is often at irregular hours (Joyce et al. 2020). Despite this instability, the much-vaunted flexibility is often overstated. Gig work is regularly presented as an

> Gig workers face employment instability by shifting between unpredictable periods of underwork and overwork.

ideal opportunity for women, who, because they disproportionately have familial responsibilities, need more flexible work. Nevertheless, the forms of gig work in which women are the majority tend to offer less flexibility (Hegewisch, Childers and Hartmann 2019).

Proponents of the gig economy who describe gig work as the future of work are aided somewhat by its depiction as non-standard employment. If it is not the standard, it seems innovative. But the terms "standard" and "non-standard" employment can be misleading. Employment is "standard" if it is stable, long-term and predictable, not because this form of employment has been the standard under capitalism. Rather, standard employment has been the historical exception (De Ruyter and Brown 2019). It only became prominent in the postwar era, and even then, many were excluded on the basis of gender, racialization, immigration status and occupation (Stanford 2017). Indeed, non-standard employment, which is unstable, short-term and unpredictable, has been the historical standard in capitalism. For this reason, much of gig work is not new, but rather a return to older practices (Palmer 2014; Betti 2018).

Some aspects of gig work, such as piece rates, have existed from the earliest days of capitalism (Joyce et al. 2020). Furthermore, the casual, contingent or on-call character of gig work is not new, particularly in occupations like cleaning, childcare and delivery services (Huws, Spencer and Coates 2019; Stanford 2017). As is true of so much of the gig economy, "These practices are as old as capitalism, perhaps even older" (Stanford 2017: 383).

If this is the case, what, if anything, is new about gig work? It is neither the kind of work (e.g., cleaning services), nor the way it is organized (e.g., casual labour), but rather, that every aspect of the work process occurs through a piece of internet-connected software. It is historically unique that the worker is not only hired and paid entirely through a digital platform, but also supervised, managed and disciplined through it. Indeed, it is often the case that there is no direct human interaction between a gig worker and the company that hires them, or even between the gig workers who work for the same company, especially for those doing crowdsourcing work entirely online (Joyce et al. 2020; Huws, Spencer and Coates 2019). The sites of gig work are often quite dispersed, extending across a major metropolis and sometimes around the globe. But platform technology can allow employers to monitor and control gig workers as if they were in a more centralized workplace, like a factory or office (Joyce et al. 2020). This is worth exploring in more detail.

> It is historically unique that the worker is not only hired and paid entirely through a digital platform, but also supervised, managed and disciplined through it.

SURVEILLANCE AND CONTROL

Platforms collect massive amounts of data on gig workers' movements, which allows these companies to monitor the most minute details of their performance. For example, Uber collects information on drivers' routes, speeds and customer ratings "in a way that is integrated into its very business model: drivers must have the application switched to 'on' when they are working so that it can properly calculate the fare" (Kirven 2018: 284–85). This data is used to determine, among other things, pickup times and surge pricing, when fares are increased in periods of high demand. Therefore, "even when Uber drivers are not driving or picking up fares, they are still providing the company with valuable information. Ride-share drivers, it would seem, are always on the clock" (Huws, Spencer and Coates 2019: 19). Furthermore, platform companies are constantly refining these algorithms to produce ever more sophisticated performance indicators, incentives and penalties.

first hand account of the sene

Platform companies' reliance on customer ratings outsources managerial and supervisory activities to their customers. In the case of Uber, for example, this is the "thick surveillance" of in-car behaviours and interactions, because riders become quality assurance inspec-

> Platform companies' reliance on customer ratings outsources managerial and supervisory activities to their customers.

tors from the back seat (Jamil 2020). Gig workers depend on these ratings for continuing to attract customers on the platform. Furthermore, platform companies use these ratings to evaluate gig workers, to offer suggestions and to penalize them — and, if their ratings fall below a certain level, to deactivate their accounts (Joyce et al. 2020). It remains legally permissible to use unverified customer ratings to withhold payment from or to discharge gig workers (Stanford 2017). *now this is wrong*

When gig workers are assessed by customers instead of qualified professionals, this lowers professional standards and deskills their labour (Huws, Spencer and Coates

2019). Given the significance of online reputations for continuing to get work, as well as the inability to transfer ratings from one platform to another, gig workers are "trapped in a relationship of dependence on that platform" (Forde et al. 2017: 21). Platforms, usually lacking any process for vetting these evaluations, take them at face value (Kirven 2018). Furthermore, there is often much less recourse for gig workers to challenge and appeal these evaluations than if they had been applied by qualified professionals hired by the company. This can put immense pressure on gig workers to tolerate customers' abusive behaviour (Huws 2019:). And vice versa

This pressure is particularly acute in gig work that involves caring labour, like childcare, eldercare and housekeeping, where "the question of who does the caring is frequently as important as the caring itself" (Flanagan 2019: 60). Since customers have much more discretion in choosing who they would like to hire through the platform, unfair negative reviews have an additional layer of consequences.

Reliance on customer ratings leaves gig workers susceptible to inaccurate, arbitrary or biased evaluations (Stanford 2017). There is evidence of gender and ethnic biases in these customer ratings. Biases can be particularly acute in caring or domestic labour platforms, because customers often select from a pool of gig workers who are encouraged or required to provide extensive information about themselves. This increases the likelihood for discrimination and online harassment, especially because women disproportionately engage in caring and domestic labour. Furthermore, we must account for bias and discrimination not only in the way the technology is used, but in the technology itself (Huws, Spencer and Coates 2019). Those platforms that require workers to provide extensive personal information and engage in self-promotion can disadvantage older workers, who might be less familiar with social media, and immigrant workers for whom English is a second language (Hegewisch, Childers and Hartmann 2019).

By making the employment relationship more impersonal, platforms allow employers to evade responsibility by claiming that the algorithms make managerial decisions. Whereas workers can confront a flesh-and-blood manager, they are less able to mount challenges in a digitally mediated employment relationship. For example,

> By making the employment relationship more impersonal, platforms allow employers to evade responsibility by claiming that the algorithms make managerial decisions.

In the case of an Uber driver in Vermont, he learned that Uber had deactivated his account, an action that blocked him from working for the company, not from a person, but from a notification on his smartphone. When the driver tried to find out what happened and what he could do to reactivate his account, he discovered that he had little recourse. Instead, he confronted an impenetrable web of online forms, generic emails, and no human interaction. (Kirven 2018: 252)

This experience also belies the claim that app-based gig workers, as independent contractors, can avoid corporate bureaucracy.

Digital mediation can also increase gig workers' alienation from their jobs: "A reduction in face-to-face contact may also mean a reduction in informal on-the-job training, a lack of mentorship and a loss of opportunities for dialogue, improvement and social interaction, leading to a range of psycho-social risks that can affect the quality of service to clients as well as the wellbeing of workers" (Huws, Spencer and Coates 2019: 24). The impersonal character of these relations also tends to hide the workers "at the other side of the screen," rendering them invisible, especially for online crowdworkers (De Stefano 2016: 477). Consequently, "these activities are not even recognized as work. Indeed, they are often designated as 'gigs,' 'tasks,' 'favors,' 'services,' 'rides,' etc. The terms 'work,' 'labor,' or 'workers' are very scarcely used in this context" (De Stefano 2016: 477–78).

These increasingly sophisticated forms of surveillance can also intensify precarity. It is easier to punish and fire workers who do not meet performance targets when they are not protected by laws, regulations and unions. As performance-monitoring technology becomes increasingly cheap and intrusive, and as it becomes easier to remove contingent workers by declining to renew their contract, there is less motivation to provide positive inducements, such as higher wages or more stable jobs (Stanford 2017).

The increasing reliance on customer ratings and digital management is not unique to gig workers. In countries like France, Estonia and Slovenia, the number of non-gig workers reporting these practices actually exceeds that of gig workers (Huws, Spencer and Coates 2019). "Employers often 'sell' home-work arrangements on the basis of supposed convenience or flexibility for workers," Stanford notes, but it is "also for extending the reach of paid work time into greater portions of a worker's day" (Stanford 2017: 394). This can also extend to unpaid efforts to secure work as an integral part of that work (PEPSO 2015). Prior to the COVID-19 pandemic, workers had begun advocating for the "right to disconnect," or the "right to log off." In France, companies with fifty or more employees are now legally prohibited from emailing workers after 6 p.m. (Huws, Spencer and Coates 2019). But the expansion of unpaid work is particularly pronounced for gig workers, who "exist in a perpetual state of being 'online,' awaiting their next task from an employer" (Kirven 2018: 286–87). Since they are paid piece rates, most, if not all, of this time spent waiting is unpaid.

home arrangements ↑
and

Finally, we must note how platform companies deepen their control over gig workers by intensifying the division of labour and the deskilling of labour. Some gig work is increasingly controlled by algorithms that automatically determine various parts of the labour process. Gig workers thus have less discretion over how to perform their work and are less able to use their minds and creativity. This practice furthers the division between mental labour and manual labour. Furthermore, when tasks are broken down into their constituent parts, workers no longer require the skills necessary for conducting a number of different complex tasks. Instead, they are responsible only for one simple task, akin to a digital assembly line. This is particularly pronounced in online crowdwork, where gig workers engage in "microtasks" such as verifying which customer reviews are from real users rather than spam bot accounts. Restructuring work in this way has to do with power, in the sense of efficiency, of increasing the productive power of labour. But it also has to do with power in the other sense. By intensifying the division of labour, by deskilling labour, gig workers are made more replaceable. This reduces their leverage, thereby increasing the power of platform companies over the gig workers they employ.

HOW TO "FIX" THE GIG ECONOMY

App-based gig workers and their allies are not accepting defeat in the face of platform companies' relentless drive to restructure work in an effort to generate greater profits. In this section, we explore the actions undertaken by gig workers to fix the gig economy before discussing some of the broader policies and reforms suggested by scholars and gig workers.

GIG WORKER ORGANIZING

A 2020 global study found that there were over three hundred protests by gig workers since January 2015 (Joyce et al. 2020). These protests have increased over time. They occur most frequently among gig workers in the courier, food delivery and transportation industries. The three main forms of gig worker protest are demonstrations (27 percent), lawsuits (34 percent) and strikes (30 percent). Gig workers have also pursued corporate campaigns, which put pressure on a company by publicizing its bad practices, harming its brand image and encouraging customers and investors to side with workers or potentially end their commercial relationships.

Globally, the most common reason for gig worker protests is low wages, particularly in the US, UK, India and Pakistan. Another significant reason is working conditions, which is the primary focus in Latin America. In continental Europe, gig worker protests have been more evenly distributed between a range of grievances, including wages, working conditions, regulatory issues and their misclassification as independent contractors, which robs them of the rights of employees like minimum standards and the right to unionize. These protests take various forms, including picketing in front of company headquarters or strikes in the form of mass order refusals. The majority of gig worker protests there are led by unions of various kinds, but non-union organizations, such as informal networks and online groups, are a significant minority (Joyce et al. 2020).

Gig workers have also pursued successful lawsuits challenging their misclassification. In addition to Foodora couriers in Ontario, gig workers have achieved legal victories in France, Spain, the Netherlands and the UK. They have also used lawsuits to contest their employers' evasions of regulations, particularly in the transportation industry, likely due to "apps such as Uber having a well-known track record of attempting to circumvent transportation regulations" (Joyce et al. 2020: 5).

Gig worker organizing faces several challenges. First, app-based workers often have little institutional power. This is the power that derives from the existence of social institutions, such as unions and government regulatory agencies, that aid workers in enforcing their rights. There is a dearth of such institutions in the gig economy. Instead, they regularly depend on their structural power, which is related to their place within labour markets and workplace production processes. Workers' marketplace bargaining power gives them the ability to make demands based on the rarity of their skills, the high level of demand for the product they make or service they provide, and the low level of competition among workers amid high employment rates. Workers also have workplace bargaining power — their ability to use their position in the production and distribution process to be strategically disruptive (Vandaele 2018). Gig workers are disproportionately dependent on collective action because, as individuals, they have little marketplace or workplace bargaining power. In more centralized workplaces, like factories, "a single worker might disrupt the work of hundreds of others," which "enhances workers' capacity to demand premium pay for requisite discipline and reliability" (Stanford 2017: 393). Conversely, in a decentralized workplace, the individual's disruptive power is greatly reduced.

> Gig workers are disproportionately dependent on collective action.

Online gig workers engaging in crowdwork have little workplace bargaining power (Vandaele 2018). But those working in more public settings, such as delivery, transport and logistics, seem to be an exception. Their protests can be more disruptive because they are strategically positioned in important nodes in the relations between producers and consumers. This is increased by the network effects of these platforms, which can become near monopolies in local markets. However, as Vandaele (2018: 14) notes, "because of this disruptive capacity, it is no coincidence that digital labour platforms in the delivery and transport sector are beginning to test drone delivery systems and autonomous, self-driving vehicles; as a bonus, announcing or leaking this information can help demoralise the platform workers concerned and put a damper on any collective action." In that sense, although some gig workers have more structural power to disrupt their workplace to back demands for improvements, the challenges they face in exercising that power are still significant.

App-based workers have also made attempts to increase their institutional power. One of the major motivations for lawsuits against misclassification is to achieve the right to unionize, collectively bargain and strike. There have been several successes on this front. Danish union 3F achieved "the world's first-ever collective agreement in the platform economy," with the Danish home-cleaning platform, Hilfr.dk (Vandaele 2018: 23). German-based platform company Delivery Hero signed an agreement with a union federation, the European Federation of Food, Agriculture and Tourism Trade (EFFAT), to establish cross-border works councils, a form of workers' representation prominent in Germany. In the UK, a February 2021 Supreme Court ruling unanimously held that Uber drivers had been misclassified and should be treated as "workers," a form of employee under employment law (*Uber BV and others (Appellants) v. Aslam and others (Respondents)* 2021).

> One of the major motivations for lawsuits against misclassification is to achieve the right to unionize, collectively bargain and strike.

Gig workers face an uphill battle in the fight for unionization even if they manage to overcome a host of specific challenges in building institutional and structural power. For example, since the worksite is digitally mediated and can be incredibly dispersed, co-workers often lack the face-to-face interactions that are key to building a collective sense of purpose. When there is no "brick-and-mortar worksite" where workers begin and end their shifts, it can be difficult to know who your co-workers are (Garneau 2019).

Dispersed, digitally mediated worksites also make it difficult for workers to achieve certified unions that must be recognized by both the employer and the government. Typically, to certify a union, a significant portion of the affected workers must express support for the union through card signing or a Labour Board-supervised vote. In either case, the union must demonstrate that it has achieved the minimum threshold required by law to obtain certification or trigger a formal certification election. The exact percentage threshold required differs from jurisdiction to jurisdiction in Canada but is calculated based on a list of employees provided to the Labour Board by the employer. Employers sometimes "stack the list" by including names of people who are not actually part of this workforce in order to dilute union support. List stacking makes it more difficult for the actual workers to achieve the percentage thresholds necessary in the various phases of certification. Although Labour Board procedures allow unions to challenge specific names on the employer's list, this is much more difficult when workers do not know the identity of most of their co-workers. Consequently, the union avoidance strategy of stacking the list is much more likely to be successful in the context of the gig economy (Braley-Rattai and Savage 2020).

Gig workers are developing creative strategies for overcoming some of these challenges. For example, Foodora couriers in Toronto found that their organizing campaign was connecting with bike couriers, but not car-based couriers. Bike couriers organized free workshops on fighting parking tickets and winterizing cars, which brought many of the car-based couriers into the campaign. Foodora couriers eventually achieved 89 percent support in their union certification vote (House and Gray 2021). Gig workers are also creating "platform cooperatives" — that is, platforms that are owned and controlled jointly by the workers rather than a corporate entity. Platform cooperatives are emerging in Spain and Belgium (Vandaele 2018), and Toronto couriers have mused about pursuing such a model in the wake of Foodora's exit from the Canadian market (Hayes 2021).

BROADER POLICIES AND REFORMS

Scholars and gig workers have proposed several reforms to laws and regulations that would better account for the situation of gig workers. First, since "good policy requires good evidence," national statistical agencies should collect more and better data on gig work (Forde et al. 2017: 99). Governments should also require platform companies to provide better information about their workforces and practices.

Second, commentators argue that we need to establish minimum standards for gig work or, alternatively, introduce a universal basic income (Ford et al. 2017). We should also create minimum standards for the use of customer ratings in performance evaluations. For example, if non-payment is legally permitted, gig workers should be able to view a prospective customer's rates of non-payment. Gig workers should also be able to export and transfer their ratings and reputation history between platforms, to lower their dependence on a particular platform. Furthermore, account deactivation should require as much transparency, just cause and due process as firing an employee (Forde et al. 2017; De Stefano 2016).

Third, with respect to the legal classification of gig workers, we should reverse the burden of proof. Since companies have more wealth and power than the people who work for them, they should have to prove that those they hire are independent contractors, instead of workers having to prove they are employees. There should also be stricter enforcement and harsher penalties for companies that misclassify workers and flout previous rulings (Forde et al. 2017).

Some commentators favour creating an intermediate legal status between independent contractors and employees, which has already occurred in several countries, including Canada. This status has been called "dependent contractor" or "independent worker" (Kirven 2018: 275). Workers with this status would not have the right to things like minimum wages, but they would have the right to unionize, bargain collectively and strike.

Others contend that the existing employee classification should be expanded to include gig workers. De Stefano (2016: 495) argues that intermediate classifications will only complicate matters, "shifting the grey-zone somewhere else without removing the risk of arbitrage and significant litigation in this respect, especially if the rights afforded to workers in that category afford any meaningful protection." Furthermore, in many places where intermediate classifications already exist, workers only qualify if a significant portion of their work, often 50-80 percent, is with a particular company, a standard many gig workers cannot meet.

Fourth, we need to reform the way we access social benefits to include gig workers. Even if gig workers were classified as employees, many would still lack access to many social benefits because they were designed in a time that assumed most people were engaged in standard employment. For example, gig workers — and workers in non-standard employment more generally — cannot qualify for unemployment benefits or parental leave because they require continuous employment for a certain period of time (De Stefano 2016). National social protection systems therefore need to be adapted to include all workers in non-standard employment, including gig workers. Some argue for portable benefits and social insurance that workers can bring from job to job. The multi-employer plans in the construction industry are a potential model, where each employer makes pro-rated payments into a plan depending on the number of hours each worker has worked for them (Kirven 2018).

Fifth, some scholars (Vosko 2000; O'Grady 1992) call for sectoral bargaining as a mechanism to extend workplace protections to precariously employed workers. They point to the decree system in Quebec as a "possible starting point for conceiving of a new model, particularly for small workplaces and nonstandard workers" (Slinn 2015: 69). A decree allows government to extend certain negotiated terms and conditions of work to cover all employers and workers in a given sector (Slinn 2015). Such a system could provide all app-based gig workers in a particular jurisdiction with collective representation and bargaining rights beyond a single platform. This would ensure minimum standards across the sector.

Of course, such sweeping public policy changes are not easily implemented given the digital platforms' tenacious and well-funded opposition to regulation. However, they do demonstrate that the status quo is far from permanent and that a different set of choices could produce very different outcomes for app-based gig workers and the future of work. This issue is becoming ever more important to resolve, as growing numbers of workers come to rely on gig work, a trend that only accelerated as a result of the COVID-19 pandemic and is unlikely to be reversed.

> Sweeping public policy changes are not easily implemented given the digital platforms' tenacious and well-funded opposition to regulation.

In sum, the rise of the gig economy raises key questions about the future of work, for both gig workers and the rest of the workforce, whose labour may yet become subject to these practices. Platform-based gig work is said to provide workers with opportunities for entrepreneurship, independence, flexibility and greater control over work than is typical in standard employment. However, this lucrative business model is in fact premised on precarious employment and employee misclassification by which employers retain control but evade responsibility for those who work for them. Skirting labour and other forms of regulation are central to platform companies' profitability. However, despite significant obstacles, gig workers continue to organize, using multiple strategies to increase their institutional and structural power. Their struggles point the way to the broader reforms in labour and employment law and the social safety net that would benefit all workers, especially those in other forms of precarious employment.

DISCUSSION QUESTIONS

1. What, if anything, is fundamentally new about the gig economy?
2. Do you think gig workers should be classified as independent contractors, employees or dependent contractors? Why?
3. Is it possible to regulate the gig economy? Why have efforts to do so been so strongly resisted by commercial digital platforms?
4. How could digital platform technology be used in ways that are less harmful to gig workers?
5. Is unionization an effective way for gig workers to increase their power to shape their working conditions?
6. What is the number one policy change government could implement to improve the working conditions of app-based gig workers? Why?

GLOSSARY OF TERMS

Collective bargaining: The legal process by which unions, on behalf of a group of workers, negotiate terms and conditions of work with management.

Dependent contractor: An intermediate category of worker who is, on the one hand, more dependent on the person or company hiring them than a self-employed independent contractor and, on the other hand, has more control over their working conditions than an employee. A dependent contractor may be entitled to rights not available to independent contractors, including the right to unionize, but may not be entitled to some of the rights of employees, such as a minimum wage.

Digital platform: Internet-connected technology that links two or more parties, often for the purpose of commodity transactions. The platform receives a percentage of the transactions it mediates.

Gig economy: A broad spectrum of economic activity characterized by flexible, casual work arrangements. While gig work is not new, the term "gig economy" is generally used today to describe work arrangements that are mediated by modern technology like smartphone applications and online platforms.

Gig worker: Someone who sells their ability to work through a digital platform. This work can be done offline or online. It is typically casual, on-demand work.

Independent contractor: A category of worker that is outside the protection of employment standards and other labour laws because they are considered to be self-employed. A typical example of an independent contractor is an artist who is hired to perform a "gig" at a specific venue for a set price.

Labour union: A collective of workers legally entitled to represent a defined group of employees for the purposes of negotiating the terms and conditions of employment.

Non-standard employment: Work that is unstable, short-term and unpredictable. It is often associated with low wages, few benefits and a lack of union representation. It has increased in the neoliberal era.

Precarious employment: Employment that is characterized by erratic hours, unpredictable pay, non-permanence or a lack of benefits. Simply put, precarious employment is insecure employment.

Sectoral bargaining: A system of collective bargaining where a union or unions negotiate collective agreements with an employer or employers on a sector-wide basis rather than an employer-by-employer basis. Depending on the context, sectoral bargaining may provide workers with more leverage.

Standard employment: Full-time, permanent work for a single employer, often unionized and held over a lifetime. This form of employment became typical of industrial and other jobs in the period after the Second World War, particularly in the Global North.

RESOURCES FOR ACTIVISTS

Canadian Foundation for Labour Rights: labourrights.ca
Canadian Labour Congress: canadianlabour.ca
Canadian Law of Work Forum: lawofwork.ca
Cultural Workers Organize: culturalworkersorganize.org
Gig Workers United: gigworkersunited.ca
Hustled Podcast: thestar.com/podcasts/hustled.html
Workers Action Centre: workersactioncentre.org

REFERENCES

Arthurs, H. 1965–66. "The Dependent Contractor: A Study of the Legal Problems of Countervailing Power." *University of Toronto Law Journal* 16, 1.

Bajwa, U., L. Knorr, E. Di Ruggiero et al. 2018. *Towards an Understanding of Workers' Experiences in the Global Gig Economy.* Toronto: Global Migration & Health Initiative. <glomhi.org/uploads/7/4/4/8/74483301/workers_in_the_global_gig_economy.pdf>.

Betti, E. 2018. "Historicizing Precarious Work," *International Review of Social History* 63, 2.

Block, S., and T. Hennessy. 2017. *"Sharing Economy" or On-Demand Service Economy?* Toronto: Canadian Centre for Policy Alternatives. <policyalternatives.ca/sites/default/files/uploads/publications/Ontario%20Office/2017/04/CCPA-ON%20sharing%20economy%20in%20the%20GTA.pdf>.

Braley-Rattai, A., and L. Savage. 2020. "Despite Foodora Ruling, App-Based Workers Face Uphill Union Battle." *The Conversation,* March 15. <theconversation.com/despite-foodora-ruling-app-based-workers-face-uphill-union-battle-132744>.

Canada. n.d. "Employee or Self-Employed?" Canada Revenue Agency. <canada.ca/en/revenue-agency/services/forms-publications/publications/rc4110/employee-self-employed.html>.

Canadian Union of Postal Workers, Applicant v. Foodora Inc. d.b.a. Foodora. 2020. OLRB Case No: 1346-19-R. <canlii.org/en/on/onlrb/doc/2020/2020canlii16750/2020canlii16750.pdf>.

CCPA (Canadian Centre for Policy Alternatives). 2021. "Heading into the Pandemic, Canada's Highest Paid CEOs Made 202 Times More than Average Worker Pay in 2019." Ottawa: CCPA. <policyalternatives.ca/newsroom/news-releases/heading-pandemic-canada%E2%80%99s-highest-paid-ceos-made-202-times-more-average>.

Chau, D. 2018. "Foodora to Cease Operations in Australia Later This Month, but Lawsuits Still Ongoing" ABC *News,* August 2. <abc.net.au/news/2018-08-02/foodora-pulls-out-of-australia/10066964>.

De Ruyter, A., and M.D. Brown. 2019. *The Gig Economy.* Newcastle upon Tyne: Agenda Publishing.

De Stefano, V. 2016. "The Rise of the 'Just-in-Time Workforce': On-Demand Work, Crowdwork, and Labor Protection in the 'Gig-Economy.'" *Comparative Labor Law and Policy Journal* 37, 3.

Donovan, S.A., D.H. Bradley and J.O. Shimabukuro. 2017. *What Does the Gig Economy Mean for Workers?* Washington, DC: Congressional Research Service. <crsreports.congress.gov/product/pdf/R/R44365>.

Flanagan, F. 2019. "Theorising the Gig Economy and Home-Based Service Work." *Journal of Industrial Relations* 61, 1.

Forde, C., M. Stuart, S. Joyce et al. 2017. *The Social Protection of Workers in the Platform Economy: Study for the* EMPL *Committee.* Brussels: European Parliament Policy Department. <europarl.europa.eu/RegData/etudes/STUD/2017/614184/IPOL_STU(2017)614184_EN.pdf>.

Gandini, A. 2019. "Labour Process Theory and the Gig Economy." *Human Relations* 72, 6.

Garneau, M. 2019. "Writing the Manual on Gig Worker Organizing." *organizing.work*, September 9. <organizing.work/2019/09/writing-the-manual-on-gig-worker-organizing/>.

Goodwin, T. 2015. "The Battle Is for the Customer Interface." *techcrunch.com*, March 3. <techcrunch.com/2015/03/03/in-the-age-of-disintermediation-the-battle-is-all-for-the-customer-interface/>.

Hall, J.V., and A.B. Krueger. 2015. *An Analysis of the Labor Market for Uber's Driver-Partners in the United States.* Cambridge, MA: National Bureau of Economic Research. <nber.org/system/files/working_papers/w22843/w22843.pdf>.

Harvey, D. 2007. *A Brief History of Neoliberalism.* New York: Oxford University Press.

Hayes, R. 2021. "The Gig Is Up." *This Magazine*, January 7. <this.org/2021/01/07/the-gig-is-up/>.

Hegewisch, A., C. Childers and H. Hartmann. 2019. *Women, Automation, and the Future of Work.* Washington, DC: Institute for Women's Policy Research. <iwpr.org/wp-content/uploads/2020/08/C476_Automation-and-Future-of-Work.pdf>.

Heller, N. 2017. "Is the Gig Economy Working?" *New Yorker*, May 8.

House, J., and P.C. Gray. 2021. "Gig Workers, Unite! Inside the Foodora Union Drive." *rankandfile.ca*, January 16. <rankandfile.ca/gig-workers-unite/>.

Huws, U. 2019. "The Hassle of Housework: Digitalisation and the Commodification of Domestic Labour." *Feminist Review* 123, 1.

Huws, U., N.H. Spencer and M. Coates. 2019. *The Platformisation of Work in Europe: Highlights from Research in 13 European Countries.* Brussels: Foundation for European Progressive Studies. <feps-europe.eu/attachments/publications/platformisation%20of%20work%20report%20-%20highlights.pdf>.

Jamil, R. 2020. "Uber Work Arrangements and the Dispossession of Workers." *Global Labour Research Centre and Canadian Association of Work and Labour Studies New Voices Workshop Series*, October 15.

Jeon, S.-H., H. Liu, and Y. Ostrovsky. 2019. *Measuring the Gig Economy in Canada Using Administrative Data.* Ottawa: Statistics Canada. <www150.statcan.gc.ca/n1/en/pub/11f-0019m/11f0019m2019025-eng.pdf?st=r4pDPYUl>.

Joyce, S., D. Neumann, V. Trappmann and C. Umney. 2020. *A Global Struggle: Worker Protest in the Platform Economy.* Brussels: European Trade Union Institute. <etui.org/sites/default/files/Platform%20work%20Leeds%20Index%20Joyce%20et%20al%20Policy%20Brief%202020.02.pdf>.

Kirven, A. 2018. "Whose Gig Is It Anyway: Technological Change, Workplace Control and Supervision, and Workers' Rights in the Gig Economy." *University of Colorado Law Review* 89, 1.

Marvit, M.Z. 2014. "How Crowdworkers Became the Ghosts in the Digital Machine." *The Nation*, February 5. <thenation.com/article/how-crowdworkers-became-ghosts-digital-machine/>.

Mojtehedzadeh, S. 2020. "Inside the Battle for Foodora: 'This Is about the Whole Gig Economy.'" *Toronto Star*, May 19. <thestar.com/news/canada/2020/05/19/inside-the-battle-for-foodora-this-is-about-the-whole-gig-economy.html>.

Nicoll, E., and S. Armstrong. 2016. "Ride-Sharing: The Rise of Innovative Transportation Services." *MaRS Technology Blog*, 12 April. <marsdd.com/news/ride-sharing-the-rise-of-innovative-transportation-services/>.

O'Grady, J. 1992. "Beyond the Wagner Act, What Then?" In Daniel Drache (ed.), *Getting on Track: Social Democratic Strategies for Ontario.* Montreal: McGill-Queen's University Press.

O'Kane, J. 2020. "Foodora to Exit Canada Just Months after Workers Won the Right to Unionize." *Globe and Mail*, April 27. <theglobeandmail.com/business/article-foodora-to-exit-canada-three-months-after-workers-won-the-right-to/>.

Palmer, B. 2014. "Reconsiderations of Class: Precariousness as Proletarianization." In Leo Panitch, Greg Albo and Vivek Chibber (eds.), *Socialist Register 2014: Registering Class.* London: Merlin, 40–62.

Panitch, L., and D. Swartz. 2003. *From Consent to Coercion: The Assault on Trade Union Freedoms.* Toronto: University of Toronto Press.

PEPSO (Precarious Employment and Poverty in Southern Ontario). 2015. *The Precarity Penalty*. Hamilton/Toronto: PEPSO/United Way Toronto.

Piasna, A., and J. Drahokoupil. 2019. *Digital Labour in Central and Eastern Europe: Evidence from the ETUI Internet and Platform Work Survey*. Brussels: European Trade Union Institute. <etui.org/sites/default/files/WP%202019%2012%20%20Digital%20Labour%20Web%20version.pdf>.

Press, A.N. 2020a. "Hours Before Planned Capital Strike, Court Grants Uber and Lyft a Reprieve." *Jacobin*, August 20. <jacobinmag.com/2020/08/uber-lyft-ab5-workers-rights-capital-strike>.

____. 2020b. "With Prop 22's Passage in California, Tech Companies Are Just Writing Their Own Laws Now." *Jacobin*, November 5. <jacobinmag.com/2020/11/proposition-22-california-uber-lyft-gig-employee>.

Sherk, J. 2016. "The Rise of the 'Gig' Economy: Good for Workers and Consumers." *The Heritage Foundation: Backgrounder* 3143, October 7. <thf-reports.s3.amazonaws.com/2016/BG3143.pdf>.

Slinn, S. 2015. "Collective Bargaining." *Commissioned Reports, Studies and Public Policy Documents*. Paper 178. Toronto: Ontario Ministry of Labour.

Stanford, J. 2017. "The Resurgence of Gig Work: Historical and Theoretical Perspectives." *Economic and Labour Relations Review* 28, 3.

Statistics Canada. 2021. *Union Coverage by Industry, Annual*. Table: 14-10-0070-01. Ottawa. <www150.statcan.gc.ca/t1/tbl1/en/tv.action?pid=1410007001>.

Uber BV and others (Appellants) v. Aslam and others (Respondents). 2021. UKSC 5, On appeal from: [2018] EWCA Civ 2748 https://www.supremecourt.uk/cases/docs/uksc-2019-0029-judgment.pdf

Vandaele, K. 2018. *Will Trade Unions Survive in the Platform Economy? Emerging Patterns of Platform Workers' Collective Voice and Representation in Europe*. Brussels: European Trade Union Institute. <etui.org/sites/default/files/Working%20Paper%202018.05%20Vandaele%20Trade%20unions%20Platform%20economy%20Web.pdf>.

Vosko, L.F. 2000. *Temporary Work: The Gendered Rise of a Precarious Employment Relationship*. Toronto: University of Toronto Press.

Weatherby, L. 2018. "Delete Your Account: On the Theory of Platform Capitalism." *Los Angeles Review of Books*, April 24. <lareviewofbooks.org/article/delete-your-account-on-the-theory-of-platform-capitalism/>.

10

FIGHTING TO LOSE
Political Struggles for Climate Justice

Mark Hudson

OTHER WORLDS

I USED TO HAVE A FRIDGE magnet with the saying "There is another world, but it is in this one." The saying (one of several commonly found variants) is attributed to the French poet Paul Éluard but may have been appropriated from elsewhere (Wark 2014). In the 1990s, I found it hopeful. It held a refusal to settle for the everyday and the egregious miseries and inequalities of the world as it is and maintained that something better can be built from within it. As the evidence on climate change, and its likely consequences, started to accumulate through the early 2000s, I threw it out.

It had begun to sound less like a revolutionary rallying cry and more like an ominous warning. It makes no promises, one way or the other, about whether that other world is better or worse. My brain started to hear it in a malevolent tone, evoking scenes from Mad Max, and Cormac McCarthy's novel *The Road*. This is a chapter about whether I should fish that magnet out of the trash; whether we can restore the horizon of a better world for everyone, even as the climate destabilizes. Don't get your hopes up for an unequivocally happy answer.

In my corner here is a long tradition within Marxist theory that provides guidance for contemplating what forms of liberation might possibly be built from the disaster of an existing set of social relations (including human relations with the non-human world). Against us is the fact that, to borrow from a popular protest slogan, "there are no social relations on a dead planet." Even if that's a bit of a rhetorical overstep, the point remains

> The possibility of building just and liberatory social relations is deeply connected to the material possibilities presented by Earth's ecology.

that the possibility of building just and liberatory social relations is deeply connected to the material possibilities presented by Earth's ecology.

This chapter builds on a talk I was asked to give a couple of years ago, about building a better world in the context of the climate crisis. Both the talk and the chapter you're reading involved a lot of writing, deleting, rewriting, reading, and re-deleting, because it is exceptionally difficult to see how, given the slowly unfolding disaster of climate change, we are in a position to build a better world than we have now. That's not because the one we have now is so great. For many people, it is a world of desperate struggle, freedoms attenuated or denied, and/or a brutal daily grind for economic survival. Most of what will occur in a changing climate is going to make that worse.

That probably sounds overly fatalistic. After all, the future is not yet written, and political possibilities are a lot broader than we are usually led to believe. At the same time, the future is not completely open-ended. We are clever monkeys indeed, but we can't make anything we please at the drop of a hat, because futures are always built on pasts and presents. The shape of our pasts and presents constrain future possibilities — not only because they have literally concrete (and steel) legacies in the form of infrastructure, energy systems, transportation systems, housing and the shapes of cities, but also because they shape the ways we see the world and our roles within it. Both of these legacies — the material and the cultural/ideological — are hard to shake off. What follows is an assessment of what I think are the possible futures that might emerge from this present, an attempt to point out where I see openings — and that's all they are — for confronting not only climate change, but also other really awful aspects of current social relations.

A WORLD OF WOUNDS

I start with the warning given by Aldo Leopold, way back when he wrote the environmental classic *A Sand County Almanac* (1949) seventy years ago. "The cost of an ecological education," cautioned Leopold, "is to be alone in a world of wounds." That is, to have these kinds of conversations at this historical conjuncture is not easy, because we have to open our eyes not just to possibility, but to loss.

Don't mistake this for a conservative politics of futility. Albert Hirschman, in *Rhetoric of Reaction* (1991), argues that there are continuities in how conservatives have always attempted to shoot down progressive ideas — especially ideas that advocate using government power for progressive policy. Looking at reactionary responses to attempts from the left to expand various rights and freedoms to a broader portion of the population — from the French Revolution to the struggle for women's suffrage, to the expansion of welfare states — Hirschman distills the rhetoric employed in opposing them into three main types. One: perversity — you'll try to make the problem better, but you'll inadvertently make the problem worse. Here, you might think about conservative responses to the "Fight for $15" movement. An increase in the minimum wage such as that pushed for by Fight for $15, conservatives argued, would only serve to exacerbate poverty by forcing employers to lay off workers or would drive businesses under. Two: jeopardy—you'll make a different problem worse as you fix the first one. Here, we might think about the apparent trade-off between inflation and unemployment. If you try to use government power in the interest of full employment, conservatives argue, you'll only produce runaway inflation. Three: futility — try as you might, there's really nothing you can do about it because the problem is too deep-rooted in the essence of humanity or in the enduring structures of society. Think inequality on this one. You might also hear some of this when it comes to addressing climate change.

I am not making any of these arguments. I'm also not saying that we can't, through political struggle, achieve some justice and possibly even ameliorate some terrible outcomes of the neoliberal past — deep and increasing inequality (not just of income or wealth, but of power) primary among them. But we also have to face up to the fact that we are going to lose cherished things in the process. Here's a very small example. In October 2019, my hometown of Winnipeg, along with the rest of the southern part of Manitoba, experienced an unseasonal episode of very heavy snow early in the month. Leaves were still on the trees, and the weight of the snow wreaked havoc. Power lines came down in droves, along with about thirty thousand trees on public property. People wandered around their neighbourhoods and parks in a kind of shock, staring at the splintered remains of downed limbs and trees. Residents felt a sense of loss, reflected widely on social media and in conversations with neighbours at the time. This was very, very minor compared to the already-occurring and future-potential losses from global climate change. Rebecca Elliot, in her article on the "sociology of loss," (2018) reports on a wide array of global losses already chalked up to climate change, from whole islands to harvests. There is by now a well-rehearsed and horrifying list of damage done and damage still-to-come. People have already lost and are going to continue to lose their homes and communities and their current livelihoods. Floods will take villages, fires will torch towns and landscapes, oceans will swallow neighbourhoods and cities. Day-to-day practices of transportation are going to have to change. Our patterns of consumption of all kinds — both in kind and in quantity — are going to have to shift. Species will vanish. Practices of provisioning that have endured centuries will no longer serve. Some have lost and will lose treasured places for recreation and contemplation. As I'm writing, even more dire scientific research is rolling in. One study published in March 2021 suggests that failing the UN objective of limiting warming to 1.5 degrees Celsius, the band of Earth between twenty degrees north and twenty degrees south will surpass the wet-bulb temperature limit of human adaptation (Zhang, Held, and Fueglistaler 2021). That is, the tropics — within which 40 percent of the human population lives — might become uninhabitable. The losses we face are enormous.

So, the latter part of Leopold's warning is undeniably true, about the world of wounds. We inhabit a world that we have damaged, and the wounds are no doubt going to get worse, more visible, become more a part of our lives. The wound of climate change is not isolated, but will effect, systemically, other things we label as distinct ecological wounds — land use, water and air quality, biodiversity, deforestation, desertification, water scarcity, extreme weather, malnutrition. There is no going back to the world prior to the climate emergency, it is upon us, and no matter what we do politically and socially at this point, no matter our level of urgency, ambition, and action (and we are approaching, on a global scale, an appropriate level of ambition, but are way below where we need to be on urgency and action), we have missed our opportunity to do something adequate to stave off any effects. So, my starting premise is that we already have a different future than we thought we would have. Young people in the climate movement are looking in a clear-eyed way at this and speaking that message most clearly.

> We inhabit a world that we have damaged, and the wounds are no doubt going to get worse, more visible, become more a part of our lives.

Not only are we too far down the road to escape loss, but as many people have pointed out (for example, Klein 2014; Chernomas, Hudson and Hudson 2019), the forty years prior to 2015 or so saw the rise of a political consensus and a dominant ideological system emphasizing individualism, privatization and deregulation that cannot get us out of the climate emergency. One of its awful effects was to undermine capacities for coordination, cooperation and collective action, including those operating through the vehicle of democratic governments. These are precisely the capacities required in high quantity and quality to deal with the climate emergency. If we start from there, the questions are twofold: one is whether we can overcome being alone in of wounded world — which is the condition that neoliberal life would have us embrace — and as a start, begin talking to one another about the wounds we see and feel. The second is whether we can, through that process, generate an alternate vision of a good life and enough collective will to force a change of course away from the situation that confronts us, which is one where the wounds overcome the whole body.

By now, for many, the urgency and magnitude of the problem of climate change are well understood. There are mountains of scientific publications dealing with it, and some of it has, with uneven quality, been popularized through media. Nonetheless, it is worthwhile to go over the scale of the challenges climate change poses, the extent of our collective failure, so far, to do much about it and some of the wide range of possible consequences.

DIPLOMACY

The current international mechanism guiding governments' efforts to rein in climate change is the Paris Agreement. That agreement exists under an overarching framework convention, the United Nations Framework Convention on Climate Change, brought into being at the Rio Earth Summit in 1992. If all countries comply with the voluntary pledges and commitments they have made as part of the Paris Agreement, we are projected to have an average global temperature increase of 2.3-3.7 degrees Celsius by 2100 and continuing thereafter. Countries are not on track to meet these commitments, a fact so widely understood that it has become the frequent subject of satire (as *The Onion* [2021] put it so tragically: "World Leaders Pledge to Cut Emissions by as Much as They Can Realistically Back Out Of"). With climate policies that are actually in place (rather than simple pledges, which frequently have no policy to back them up), we are looking at an increase of between 2.4 and 4.3 degrees Celsius. The Science Advisory Group's high-level synthesis report on the latest climate science, released just before the New York climate summit in September 2019, suggests that to stay below 2 degrees, government levels of ambition have to triple. To stay below 1.5, they have to increase fivefold (World Meteorological Organization 2019). That is a tall, tall order, and it does not appear that we are rising to the challenge. A stock-taking by the United Nations of pledges made under the Paris Agreement by December 31, 2020, reported that those pledges, if met, would shave a grand total of

1 percent off of global GHG emissions by 2030. We need at least a 45 percent reduction by then. Big emitters like the United States, China and India had yet to make new pledges. The Biden presidential campaign in the United States made a lot of hay about tackling climate change, cancelled the Keystone XL pipeline's licences on day one of the presidency, and brought the US back into the Paris Agreement, but no new pledge is yet on the table. China's latest five-year economic plan suggests that its greenhouse gas emissions steps are going to be slow and short (Farand 2021).

The 2019 synthesis report referred to above charted a horrific laundry list of symptoms of climate change getting worse faster than we thought they would — sea level rise, annual declines in the extent of sea ice and ice mass, ocean acidification, intense heat waves and wildfires, tropical cyclone severity, drought and more. All this is being driven by a continued increase in global GHG emissions, at an annual rate of 1 percent over the five years preceding the report, and 2 percent in the year prior to its release. The report suggested that a peak is nowhere in sight even by 2030 based on current trends (World Meteorological Organization 2019). It is worth noting that many scientists are concerned about the highly conservative approach of the Intergovernmental Panel on Climate Change (IPCC). Their assessments and their communication to policymakers and the public, particularly concerning non-linear effects, feedback loops and the parameters of their models linking climate change to economic impacts do not reflect the intensity of the crisis (Waldman 2018; Herrando-Perez et al. 2019).

THE PANDEMIC DIP

Enter the coronavirus pandemic. GHG emissions in 2020 dropped in the context of shuttered economies and lockdown. Global economic activity slumped by an estimated 3.5 percent (IMF 2021). At the outset of the pandemic, photos showed clear waters running in the canals of Venice and wildlife reoccupying city squares left empty in the lockdown, and there were predictions of plummeting emissions. In April 2020, the International Energy Agency predicted a global emission drop of 8 percent — the largest annual decline ever. The dip was not quite that large and did not last long. Estimates of actual emissions reductions over 2020 ranged between 5.8 percent to 7 percent (Liu, Ciais, Deng et al. 2020; Tollefson 2021; Chestney 2021; Le Quéré et al. 2021) and the second half of the year was already seeing growth. In fact, China's monthly growth in CO2 emissions was already positive by April of 2020 (IEA 2021). Forecasts for 2021 suggest significant growth (IEA 2020c) — so much so that the rebound that occurred after the dip in emissions during the 2008 financial crisis is likely to be repeated (Le Quéré et al. 2021). As the authors of a recent assessment of the impact of COVID-19 on emissions suggest, "experience from several previous crises show that the underlying drivers of emissions reappear, if not immediately, then within a few years. Therefore, to change the trajectory in global CO2 emissions in the long term, the underlying drivers also need to change." Unfortunately, they also note that "most countries' COVID-19 recovery plans are in direct contradiction with countries' climate commitments" (Le Quéré et al. 2021; see also Vivid Economics 2021).

There have been many calls, including from a variety of elites and prominent individuals and organizations, to seize on the moment of the pandemic, using government recovery spending to prioritize "green" projects like building retrofits, renewable energy grids, and mass or active transportation infrastructure. Estimates on the extent of COVID recovery spending so far range from $9 trillion to $15 trillion. Of that, Bloomberg reported that as of June 2020, only 0.2 percent of the spending by the fifty biggest economies was targeted at "post carbon economic priorities" (Bloomberg 2020). The UNEP (2021) estimates a much higher but still dispiriting 18 percent of global pandemic recovery spending counts as green. Even if we look just at spending going directly to energy, the G20 has allotted slightly more of its COVID spending toward fossil fuel energy than clean energy (Energy Policy Tracker 2021). So, the pandemic, with all of its attendant disasters, provided a pause in the growth of greenhouse gases, but is so far leaving the structures for a return to that growth in place.

INVESTMENT IN RENEWABLES

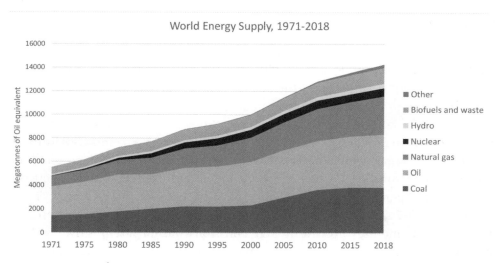

Source: IEA 2020a[1]

Prior to the pandemic, there was a lot of investment in renewables, which is a positive trend. Yet, renewables have not (York 2012), and still are not, displacing fossil fuels as the dominant mode of energy generation. Coal, oil and natural gas still make up 80 percent of the global energy mix (see above figure).

Global Investment in Clean Energy and Efficiency, and Share of Total Investment (2015-2020)

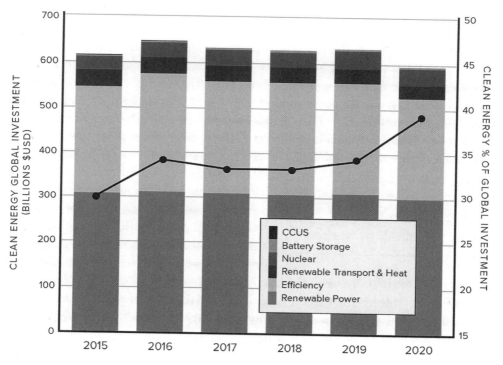

Source: IEA 2020b[2]

In fact, in 2018, the value of fossil fuel energy investment *rose* for the first time in several years, while the value of renewables investment fell. Partly this is an effect of lower costs for renewables, but these lower costs don't seem to be resulting in a wholesale abandonment of fossil fuels. The pandemic — for all the talk of green economic stimulus — has not markedly improved the picture. Investment in clean energy and efficiency took less of a hit than did investment in oil, so it made up a higher proportion of total new investment, but it actually shrunk in absolute terms (see above figure).

This overall picture of failure, combined with the science on the rate and consequences of global climate change, have prompted scholars producing and absorbing the picture to suggest that while we may not be completely screwed yet, we are well on the way (Bradshaw et al. 2021). How do we even *think* about the future in this situation, other than apocalyptically, as so many filmmakers, novelists and videogame designers have? How can we act, as members of a society that many scientists suggest is circling the drain, to move "ahead?"

WHOSE EMISSIONS?

All roads before us involve loss of some kinds. Even a successful transition to a low-carbon economy — distant as that prospect appears from where we currently stand — would produce loss and involve costs, though much less than the catastrophe of carrying on with the high-carbon economy. That means that we have to attend to how loss is going to be distributed and how that lines up with responsibility for generating the problem. Currently, the losses of climate change are, and are predicted to be, borne disproportionately by the poor. The poor are more likely to be in harm's way and less able to bear the financial costs of adaptation, defence and relocation.

> The losses of climate change are, and are predicted to be, borne disproportionately by the poor.

This pattern isn't unique to climate change; it is common to many environmental issues. Environmental hazards and burdens tend to accumulate on the low end of the income distribution, where it often intersects with race. Poorer people and racialized minorities are more likely to live with the hazardous products of industrial and extractive processes. They breathe dirtier, more toxic air and drink more contaminated water. They are more vulnerable to overheating, drought, flood and other disasters. This regressive distribution of hazard is widely recognized, though equally widely unaddressed (Salazar et al. 2019; Robertson and Westerman 2015).

Less well recognized is the equally skewed distribution of responsibility for the problem. The dominant narrative about climate change is that there is a collective "we" that is somehow indiscriminately to blame for climate change. Pushed on this, many will recognize that affluent countries bear a disproportionate historical responsibility, which is undeniable. Pushed further, some acknowledge that very, very rich individuals — clustered in the Global North, but not exclusive to it — have a grossly disproportionate effect. The total emissions of the richest 1 percent of the world population are twice those of the poorest 50 percent (UNEP 2020). An estimate of the per-capita greenhouse gas emissions of those in the top 0.1 percent of income earners on the planet suggests that they outweigh by *several hundred times* those among the bottom 50 percent (Oxfam and Stockholm Environmental Institute 2020).

But even this obscene disparity misses the mark, in some respects, as we are called to think about responsibility for climate change and about how we must reorganize in order to avoid disaster. One useful direction that the climate movement has taken more recently is to identify and call out those who have known about the dire environmental implications of burning fossil fuels, but who, because they profit handsomely from it, have worked to prevent any significant action to curtail it. This is not an easy thing for the movement to accomplish, because so many of us, including policymakers, have come to think about climate change as "everyone's" responsibility — and most significantly, as the responsibility of consumers.

This consumption-based framing ignores a key dimension of power in society — particularly how it is distributed between the vast majority of us and those who are empowered to make decisions about what gets produced and how we produce it. The story that everyone is to blame moves our gaze away from the organizations and individuals who are actually, practically responsible for both producing most of the greenhouse gases and for working very hard and very effectively for forty years to prevent us from doing anything remotely adequate to deal with the problem. These are almost exclusively corporations, both state-owned and investor-owned, and the people who own and run them. None of this means that you ought not consider the implications of buying a Lincoln Navigator if you are in the position to contemplate such a thing. But it does mean that for the vast majority of us in a capitalist society, choice is contained within a set of parameters which are largely established within corporate board rooms, with the public interest nowhere in view.

Research from the Union of Concerned Scientists in the United States shows that CO2 and methane emissions from the ninety biggest industrial carbon producers were responsible for almost half the rise in global temperature and close to a third of the sea level rise between 1880 and 2010. Research by Richard Heede (2014) and his colleagues at the Climate Accountability Institute pinpoint just twenty state- and investor-owned corporations that are responsible for 35 percent of all CO2 and methane produced since 1965. Saudi Aramco, Chevron, Gazprom, Exxon Mobil, National Iranian Oil, BP, and others appearing on the list are the most visible entities to have profited from their *fully informed* destabilization of the climate.

The year 1965 is significant because it is the point at which politicians and corporate leaders in oil and gas were unquestionably aware of the climate consequences of fossil fuel combustion, mostly thanks to the report "Restoring the Quality of our Environment," by the President's Science Advisory Committee, about which then-president Lyndon Johnson gave a speech to Congress. You might charitably say, "well, it may be that oil executives don't pay much attention to congressional reports." They do, of course, if their industry's main product is identified as responsible for future catastrophe. You would expect them to pay close attention to a task force struck by their own industry group, the American Petroleum Institute, to look into climate change. That task force heard in no uncertain terms from the pre-eminent experts on carbon dioxide and climate at the time, whom they had handpicked to speak to them, that continued burning of fossil fuels was going to lead to disaster, and that if they wanted to get off fossil fuels and onto an alternative energy source in time, they had "no leeway" to wait (Freese 2020: 232). That was 1980. If you want to give corporations and politicians a *huge* benefit of the doubt, you might push that date forward to 1988, when the first joint congressional hearings were held on climate change, which were widely covered by media, and at which scientists were even more clear and forceful on the threat. Since 1988, there has been more CO2 emitted than there was between the beginning of the Industrial Revolution and 1988.

Profiting from the road to climate disaster is not exclusive to what we commonly think of as the fossil-fuel industry. Banks and other financial corporations have poured, and continue to pour, money into fossil fuel exploration, extraction and new transportation infrastructure at a handsome return. Since the signing of the Paris Agreement, the world's sixty biggest banks have directed $3.8 trillion into fossil fuels (Rainforest Action Network 2021). Canadian banks are significant contributors. RBC is the fifth largest fossil fuel lender in the world. Canada's five major chartered banks together put $508 billion into financing oil and gas extraction during 2016–2019, with the trend line heading upward throughout the period (Rainforest Action Network 2020). While it's not a huge portion of most Canadian banks' total loans, debt financing does provide a crucial lifeblood for oil extraction (Hudson and Bowness 2021). Insurers also continue to profit by underwriting fossil fuel projects, though some have at least made commitments to stop insuring coal projects (Unfriend Coal 2019), under pressure from climate movement activists who have recently, and intelligently, been turning their attention to the financial corporations that continue to enable fossil fuel extraction.

So, from the mid-1960s onward, and accelerating through the 1990s and 2000s, when we could and should have been taking action on climate change, the corporations profiting most heavily from fossil fuel combustion were actively and effectively thwarting climate action. The same corporations that are now acknowledging climate change as a serious threat, and lining up to loudly declare their "net-zero by 2050" commitments, did their utmost, independently, through their trade associations and via front groups, think-tanks and foundations, to ensure that political action sufficient to counter the impending disaster they knew they were creating would not be forthcoming. They did so most effectively through campaigns of public misinformation about the extent and type of uncertainty within climate science (Oreskes and Conway 2010; Farrell 2016; Climate Reality Project 2019; Westervelt 2019; Freese 2020).

In short, we should give credit where credit is due: corporations have known about the problem, understood the clear connection between their profitable practices and the warming of the Earth's atmosphere and oceans, and done everything in their power to sow doubt, create uncertainty and continue on with business as usual. While it is much rarer than it was in the 1990s or early 2000s to hear outright public denial of climate change, many of the corporations in question continue to work to prevent adequate action — a phenomenon some have dubbed "the new denialism" (Klein and Daub 2016). This involves public acknowledgement of climate change, including its grave implications and public statements that a response is needed, alongside an active program of political action to thwart strong regulation or other action inimical to profitability. For example, big oil companies belonging to the Oil and Gas Climate Initiative, which purports to support action on climate change, also belong to and participate actively in trade associations like the American Petroleum Institute that lobby strenuously against climate regulation (Daub et al. 2021). So, when corporate spokespeople and politicians observe or even complain about how unrealistic the science-based GHG reduction timelines are (see, for example, the commentary by the Canadian Association of Petroleum Producers' CEO, Tim McMillan [2018], but examples from corporate bodies like CAPP or the American Petroleum Institute) — suggesting the wild unrealism of getting off fossil fuels within thirty years and cutting them in half in a decade — it is not just hollow, but despicable. They are the very reason that the timelines are now so tight and "unrealistic," and they continue to engage in business practices that they know very well will push us into a 3–5 degree warmed world. It is just as bad, if not worse, when politicians parrot this line, since unlike corporate elites, government is explicitly charged with defending the public interest.

CLIMATE CHANGE IS A CLASS CONFLICT

As a result, when we ask the question about who should be paying the financial costs for pretty much every aspect of transition, we need not look far. When we talk about accountability, we must keep our eyes firmly on those who have brought us, deliberately, to the point of emergency. There are a number of things that can and are being done to develop that accountability, primarily through mechanisms to which the industries in question are fairly amenable, such as a mild carbon tax or climate risk disclosure requirements. Conversations about expropriating the oil industry's assets, in the same way we might seize the assets of any criminal organization that produces and trades an acutely harmful substance, unfortunately do not seem to be percolating up to the levels of policy debate. However, there is climate litigation, through which citizens and some governments are attempting to hold corporations accountable for their duplicity. There are movements to shift fossil fuel subsidies toward renewables, there are divestment movements, there are international movements like BankTrack's Fossil Banks campaign, which try to render transparent the bank lending that enables climate change, and similar, national-level campaigns. Getting these corporations, and their wealthy shareholders, to pay for things like massive housing retrofit programs, public and active transport infrastructure, workforce transition, and renewable energy grids is not just possible, but appropriate and just. Where corporate malfeasance has produced these enormous costs, there is no reason whatsoever that we should be giving into the idea that somehow we "all" produced this. It is not primarily a product of individuals freely choosing to drive their cars while they happily watch the planet burn, though surely there is some oblivious behaviour of that kind. It is a question of a political economic system that precedes us, made by and for a small minority, but in which we are all embedded to varying degrees, including in its fossil-fuel based infrastructure (Hudson and Hudson 2021).

> Where corporate malfeasance has produced these enormous costs, there is no reason whatsoever that we should be giving into the idea that somehow we "all" produced this.

Hence, we have also to acknowledge that this is a class conflict. We tend to think of class conflict as something that happens on the factory floor or in the office. But of course, class interests conflict in many dimensions of our lives — through government policy, legislation, action and inaction, as well as in our day-to-day choices and the shaped practices though which we live our lives. In this case, the capitalist class has been the primary driver of greenhouse gas emissions and the main beneficiaries of the wealth created through fossil-fuelled production. They have used oceans and the atmosphere as a free dumping ground for climate-change inducing pollutants. The working classes of the world are now paying the costs. One powerful way we get distracted from the class nature of climate change, especially in the realm of international diplomacy and national government policy, is through the accounting of carbon on a national basis. We are told, for example, that for Canada or the United States to do anything serious about climate change is useless, because China or Poland will just pick up the slack as production and industry moves away from countries like Canada and the US. Indeed, some of this displacement does happen. Wealthy countries have had some success reigning in the carbon intensity (the amount of carbon it takes to produce a dollar of GDP) of their economies. But that's because they offshore a lot of their more carbon-intensive production to the Global South (UNEP 2016). We need to understand that it's frequently the same corporations doing the investing and producing, whether in Scranton, Sudbury, or Shenzhen. China is the workshop of the world, producing commodities mostly for multinational companies headquartered elsewhere, and exporting those commodities largely to "the West" in order for the profit to be realized. About 50 percent of Chinese exports are products made by foreign-owned subsidiaries or by partnerships between Chinese and foreign capitalists (Koopman, Wang and Wei 2008; Ma, Wang and Zhu 2014). Much of it is production of intermediate goods — the parts or components used in manufacturing processes — for Western multinationals. Are the resulting emissions "China's?" There has been some attempt to correct for this by attributing the emissions to the consuming, not the producing country. So, when a Canadian buys a new mobile phone sold by a Canadian or US company, no matter what basket of countries contributed to its production, the emissions count as Canadian. While this accounting shines a light on the nationality of end users, it lumps all Canadians together as somehow equally responsible for the emissions embodied in the phone. They become "Canada's" emissions. Much is obscured here, too. First of all, much of our emissions profile as "consumers" is not of our own choosing. We heat our homes, we move around, we communicate with one another through infrastructures that we have inherited or that are designed for us. In a context in which societies allocate resources on the basis of their expected return, the primary beneficiaries of these systems are corporations. So, the emissions for the cell phone more accurately belong to Apple, Samsung, or LG than they do to Canada or China.

Whatever comes next, the world will be more just if those who have profited from the perpetuation of the fossil fuel economy, even well after they knew its consequences, suffer a proportionate share of losses — in this case, by paying the lion's share of the costs of urgent transition. This means a much more aggressive redistribution than is currently contemplated. The timelines are very, very tight, and the infrastructural requirements of transition are very, very vast. They are not impossible, but as I've shown, the investment required is a lot more than we have been putting in to date, and the trend lines do not look particularly promising. The increase necessary to build the infrastructure required to keep us below 2 degrees is estimated to be in the ballpark of $300 billion per year to 2030, and over $1 trillion a year from there to 2050. That's at least 50 percent more than the projections based on current investment. The gap grows considerably, of course, if we shoot for the 1.5-degree target (McCollum et al. 2018).

So, the first way we can fight for a better world amid inevitable loss is seeking justice for harm done, and that should include a transfer from the beneficiaries of fossil fuel development to pay for the necessary transitions needed to keep us below 1.5 degrees. We could have made this easier, if we had started when we should have. But we lost the fight to get on a transition timeline that is only moderately disruptive, so major disruption is now on the agenda. There is no rewind button. Almost all of the predictions are really, really bad, though the extent of climate change, and its effects, are yet to be determined. So are the politics that flow from climate change, which will determine in conjunction with geophysical effects — what the future will look like.

CLIMATE CHANGE'S POSSIBLE FUTURES

But political possibilities — the contours of struggle — are starting to emerge. Different groups have been trying to formulate and enact their versions of the future for some time. Three such broad possibilities are becoming ever-more visible as contenders for dominance. This typology is very similar to a categorization laid out by Geoff Mann and Joel Wainwright in their book *Climate Leviathan* (2018), but they use different labels and their focus is on political formations — the kind of states that might emerge under the pressure of climate change. The following categories are less specific to the form of the state.

1. Business as Usual: This is the future of fossil-fuel driven capitalism. It is the future built into the current business plans and corporate practices of oil companies, their financial lenders, internal combustion SUV and light-truck manufacturers, urban sprawl developers, as well as states like Canada, Saudi Arabia, Russia, the US, and others, who are dependent on oil revenues. This is disaster, climatically, so the name is a bit inaccurate. A world where much of the tropics is uninhabitable and many of our resources are devoted to disaster response and adaptation will not look much like "business as usual." However, I mean it in the sense of distributions of power, wealth and income, as well as continuing reliance on fossil fuels until well after mid-century. It may not mean the end of humanity, it may not even mean the end of "civilization," but it does mean a future of much more intense suffering for a much larger portion of humanity, while the wealthy protect themselves and profit from the disruption as best they can. The wealthiest 1 percent are already planning for this. There is a brisk trade among the very rich in survival bunkers, eco-enclaves, escape to Mars, New Zealand real estate and other "bolt hole" protections from social breakdown (Osnos 2017). This is the climate future embodied in the completely insufficient policy of most governments, democratic and otherwise, in the world today.

2. Capitalist decarbonization: However, trend is not destiny, as my statistics professors liked to remind us, and there are the beginnings of technocratically and technologically driven efforts to decarbonize, driven by corporations and by states beholden to them. Effects of climate change are still bad in this future, but we start to move toward renewable forms of energy under the guidance of global treaties led by a few large, key states and capital's responses to financial climate risks. We're likely to see the use of some geoengineering, like solar radiation management (using various

means to block or diminish incoming heat from the sun), reliance on yet-unproven technologies like carbon capture use and sequestration (CCUS), and heavy reliance on carbon offsets (various means to reduce or avoid GHG emissions that would otherwise occur, in order to "cancel out" ongoing emissions), in an attempt to mitigate our failure to reduce emissions quickly or steeply enough. Much depends on the profitability of using and developing renewable energy technology, since prices still drive action. The system of high energy consumption moderated by profitable efficiencies remains in place, along with privatized control over decisions about how energy is generated and what it's used for. Workers, as in past industrial transitions, are not an active part of determining the shape and speed of transition, and as a result they are left holding the bag of energy and industrial transition. Energy workers thrown out of work are on their own to get back on their feet. Auto workers pay their mortgages or don't based on whether or not investors decide that retooling the plant to make EVs is the most profitable option. "We all" (meaning the 99 percent) pay the price of decarbonization deemed palatable,

> Workers are not an active part of determining the transition, and as a result they are left holding the bag of energy and industrial transition.

practical and profitable by capital, and it is unlikely to succeed in getting us below 1.5 to 2 degrees of warming fast enough.

3. Climate Keynesianism: This future exists more as an emerging political demand than as a current contender for dominance, though under the force of pandemic-related economic downturn, it has gained more traction. Often described as a "Green New Deal," to invoke the redistributive stimulus of the US's 1930s "New Deal," it involves mustering state resources and power to engage in a "Big Push" to overhaul energy systems, housing, public and commercial buildings and transportation in order to bring down our GHG emissions. In an effort to overcome the "jobs versus environment" conundrum, all of this is tied to large-scale employment generation. It envisions a publicly funded (either through central banks, taxation or some combination) army of solar- and wind-installers, housing retrofitters and public mass transit builders rolling out across countries. The outlines of a Green New Deal (GND) are starting to take more concrete form, mostly through lists of principles and sometimes through specific proposed and actual policies that attempt to integrate the climate emergency with questions about the distribution of costs and benefits arising from climate change and transition. In some cases, GND demands move beyond to question who the decision makers ought to be. In Canada, GND-style proposals also acknowledge the requirement of reconciliation, honouring treaties and dealing with First Nations on the basis of their sovereignty. GND proposals are targeted at multiple scales, from the neighbourhood through to the nation, and even to the level of the

globe. This final option, in terms of its ability to build a better world in the midst of loss, is no doubt a much more positive political step. Perhaps most significantly, it recognizes that the same decision-making processes that got us into our mess are unlikely to get us out of it. It also has a focus on the kind of accountability I referred to earlier, relying on transferring subsidies from fossil fuel extraction to renewables, taxing the wealthy, reinvesting in public services and providing various protections for workers whose livelihoods are jeopardized by the transition. In this sense it sounds like a social response to climate change that contributes to the building of a more just and equal (i.e., better) world. Rather than just involving policy wonks prescribing the appropriate rates of a carbon tax, the conversation about a GND involves advocates of Indigenous rights, agroecology, social housing, full employment, unionization, mass public transit, enhanced public services and durable design.

However, while there are plenty of specific proposals for a GND, there remains a lot of indeterminacy in the form it might ultimately take in policy. Will it become primarily about saving capitalism from itself, as many have claimed was the role of the first New Deal in the US? Will it be about subsidizing and de-risking investments in clean tech to make them more profitable for corporations? The most visible proposals, like that of the Biden administration in the United States, are predicated on a massive economic stimulus and a boost to growth. So will it exacerbate other environmental issues related to consumption or to mining for the raw materials necessary for green energy?

DEMOCRATIZING THE BIG DECISIONS

So, the second, and I think most promising thing, in terms of finding a better world in the wreckage of this one is bringing to light the fundamental question about who gets to determine the shape of that world. So much of our allegedly "environmental" conflict, or our "environmental" problems are actually at their root social problems about the maldistribution of decision-making power in capitalist society.

Concerns over things like forests, water, soil and air result from the fact that these things mean different things to different people. Class interests are especially important here, as capital can only ever see or understand anything in relation to that thing's role in generating or detracting from profits. Even the most ardent environmental champions from the business class would not disagree. That is why they argue that all of nature must be priced or given value through the accounting mechanism of "ecosystem services." Without those indicators of nature's relation to value, capital cannot see or acknowledge it. As James O'Connor put it, the things that are, for most of us, conditions of life (water, soil, air) are for capital conditions of production. This is a fundamental conflict over what "nature" is and over our appropriate relation to it. For the most part, we have ceded this battle, handing control over what nature is and what it is for, to corporations and investors.

An example: I recently attended a talk by a futurist who is well-plugged into high-level global bodies, advising and meeting with the UN and also with Global 500 CEOs. In this case, he was presenting to a large group of union leaders and rank-and-file members. He laid out what he saw as the future of work and energy in a carbon-constrained world, and in this vision, centre stage is given to where private investment is flowing — both in terms of the energy mix but also in terms of technological development. If you are a truck driver in the oil sands, he predicted, your days are numbered, not because we're going to act politically to stop extraction anytime soon, but because you will soon be replaced by a driverless vehicle. Decisions made by investors about productive technologies will dictate whether you continue to have a livelihood. There's nothing new about that, of course. We ceded our right to a livelihood to private capital long ago, and this futurist is relating (and naturalizing) the current reality of a system where very few people get to decide what kinds of technologies we will develop and therefore what kinds of livelihoods are available. But they are now also deciding whether we are more or less likely to have a habitable planet a century out.

Most amazingly, however, was the degree to which the workers and unionists in the room accepted at face value the idea that markets could legitimately deem their livelihoods to be extinct. If investors decide that the industry in which you work is no longer adequately profitable, or there is a more profitable way for them to organize production without you, that is "just how it is" and completely legitimate. But if *government* were to do so, by enacting, say, a cap on the amount of oil we can pull from the ground, such a decision was understood as completely illegitimate. So, it's just reality if "markets" (which are just the aggregate decisions of economic actors of varying power) decide that an industry will thrive or wither, but for a democratically elected government to do so is off limits, even if the decision is taken in an attempt to save the planet where markets are clearly failing to do so. This powerful ideological current that naturalizes markets, while disavowing the public capacity to make decisions about production, actually entails a total abdication of citizenship. Currently, our fortunes are at the disposal of a very small number of very wealthy people who decide whether, where and in what to invest. Most of us are relegated to the role of waiting to see what they decide to do, and adapting our lives to that. The mythology of venture capital (VC) firms efficiently channelling the short-term resources necessary for innovation and problem solving has seized our imaginations, bolstered by the example of software companies like Google, Facebook and other Silicon Valley folk heroes. Governments have stepped back from taking an active role in research and development. In the United States, for example, from the 1950s through the 1970s, the public sector was responsible for more than half of research and development spending, laying the groundwork for many of the technologies we now associate with private-sector innovation (MacBride 2020; Mazzucato 2013). Now about 70 percent of that spending comes from the private sector (MacBride 2020), whose preference is not for social benefit. VC funding searches for companies that can adequately monetize and reach a point where they can make an initial public offering (IPO) or get bought out by a larger, existing corporation. A great many very worthwhile, socially beneficial ideas wither and die within this privatized political economy of innovation, starved by the very narrow VC profile of a desirable company. In 2019, VC firms were managing about $444 billion in funds. In the midst of a global pandemic in which countries were scrambling for resources to develop and produce vaccines, protective equipment and a host of other desperately needed things, $121 billion of this remained uninvested, for want of the promise of sufficient returns (MacBride 2020). Private investment flows to returns, not to social need.

Government will have to be a main driver of a green new deal, and as such, if it is going to be responsive to the needs and desires of working people, we need to pick up this responsibility again. Any real GND's eventual contours will be the product of a massive fight over who governments are accountable to and who has a say in the allocation of social wealth. This is a fight that forces on the side of climate justice desperately need to renew — and must win. The stakes are now planetary and possibly "civilizational," and its timeline is urgent. We are beginning to see the stirrings of a broader confrontation over these questions, which have been muted or outside of the realm of acceptable debate for too long.

> A real GND's eventual contours will be the product of a massive fight over who governments are accountable to.

In North America, the parameters of capitalist decision making have been challenged most aggressively by Indigenous movements as part of the struggle for sovereignty over unceded land and adherence to treaties. Here, the fight to keep oil in the ground intersects with decolonial struggles. While pursuing the expansion of fossil fuel infrastructure — especially pipelines — corporations have encountered stiff resistance from the Ojibwe, the Wet'suwet'en, the Tsleil-Waututh, Beaver Lake Cree Nation, the Standing Rock Sioux and many others. Whether through courts or through active land and water defence, Indigenous communities are insisting that capital does not have free access through their territories, even when settler-colonial governments permit it. The nexus of corporate power in settler-colonial states is sharply revealed when the latter send in armed property enforcers on behalf of oil and gas companies. Through these battles, capitalist property relations — arrangements that have protected the right of capitalists to access and dispose of our conditions of life (soil, water, air, flora, a stable climate) — are publicly in question.

A TESLA IN EVERY GARAGE?
QUESTIONING THE MEANING OF THE GOOD LIFE

The third thing that I think becomes open again as a topic of conversation and debate, which has been "answered" for the last seventy years at least, is what a "good life" looks like. A strong current in the politics of the postwar era in North America has been swapping our aspirations for control over work and politics for high rates of consumption (Cross 2002; Bonneuil and Fressoz 2017; Hudson and Hudson 2021). This has in turn been premised on what Greta Thunberg called in her famous speech to the United Nations the "fairy tale" of infinite economic growth. Progress in human development has been made coterminous with economic growth. We have only dwindling alternative conceptions of what a "better world" might look like apart from endlessly expanded private production and consumption. Even as conservative policies like restraining wages and cutting public goods and services actually strangle growth, and even as they frequently sacrifice growth for upward redistribution, the vision of the better life that they extend, its rhetoric, is immersed in growth. Much of left politics is also growth-oriented, but attuned to broadly distributed growth, rather than the form of neoliberal growth we've had in which the gains are captured at the top. All three of the political possibilities emerging from climate change remain rooted in a vision of endless growth. The GND offers the possibility of a broad distribution — even a redistribution — but its forms are most often premised on an idea that we can continue to have our current lifestyle, extend that lifestyle to more people, and maintain the horizon of a yet-further improved lifestyle, all couched in veiled or explicit consumerist terms.

One of the things we know about happiness, though, is that its increase is not well served through increased consumption beyond a certain, modest level of basic consumption (Jackson 2009; Hudson and Hudson 2021). Beyond this level, objects can have meaning for us, and some of them make us better able to enjoy things that do make us happy, but in and of themselves, objects don't improve our happiness. We are enlisted, then, in a system that encourages ecologically destructive consumption, not for our own benefit, but primarily to accommodate the needs of corporate profit maximizers. A better world becomes visible and possible once we interrogate deep-seated cultural ideas like this form of "progress." We need to ask what are the hallmarks of a good society (not an ethical individual — a good society)? What do we want most to preserve or create for ourselves and for future generations? Is it more stuff? Is it cheap mobility? Is it cheap but increasingly nutritionally void food? Is it a job for a wage? Is it houses with more square footage? What does it look like beyond basic needs?

Oil, as the energetic basis of our massive but grossly unequal expansion, has played a huge role in shaping the answers to these questions for us. Our notions of progress, life quality and even freedom have been shaped by the fossil fuel economy (Huber 2013). If we want a habitable planet, it can no longer do so. There is a valid concern that the GND in some of its forms foreclose on this conversation. Indeed, opening this conversation can present opportunities to align genuine questions about the meaning of progress and a good life with political and economic strategies of austerity. It is all too true that huge swaths of the population, concentrated in but not exclusive to the Global South, struggle and often fail to make ends meet. They cannot afford education, healthcare, shelter or adequate food. Positioning climate politics as a form of denial or deeper deprivation for these people is a non-starter — both in terms of justice and in terms of practical politics. But affluence can come in different forms. Affluence can be two Teslas in the garage and a massive flat screen in every room. Or it can be convenient and comfortable mass transit, public boulevards, parks and plazas to encounter one another, libraries, shared workshops, arts and cultural spaces, and universal, high-quality education, healthcare and housing. Only one of these models can be made available to everyone along with a livable planet. Taking on this question about the good life is not necessarily to negate support for

> Only one of these models can be made available to everyone along with a livable planet.

something like a GND. As Thea Riofrancos (2019) has pointed out, in the US, there's a lot of "qualified support" for a GND that questions the central role of continued growth while embracing the political opening it provides and its calls to foreground justice for workers, for historically marginalized groups and for those on the "front lines" of climate change (a pretty broad group). Getting to a better world — one that offers a long-term sustainable model of universal affluence — through a GND involves foregrounding the question of what a political-economic system should be doing for us.

THE OPPOSITE OF PESSIMISM

So, all this chapter has offered by way of thinking about a better world on the cusp of climate crisis are a couple of openings for conversation and the possibility of repoliticizing things that have been depoliticized: the question of who gets to decide how we allocate social wealth and the question of what progress consists of. That's not much by way of a recipe for optimism. Fortunately, optimism is not a very helpful resource in this situation. There is no point in closing our eyes to the losses we will have to face, and loudly claiming in the midst of what really appears to be the already-disastrous beginnings of a catastrophe that a better world is within our grasp. The world is already worse, and as we pump more carbon dioxide into the environment, day by day, we ensure that it will be worse yet. To make such a claim would be optimism —

and entirely unfounded and unforgivable given what we face. Does that doom us to demobilizing, paralyzing pessimism? It does not.

"The opposite of pessimism," Riofrancos eloquently suggests, "isn't self-assured optimism, but rather militant commitment to collective action in the face of uncertainty and danger." It is getting on with the work that needs to be done to avoid the worst of the loss and suffering before us, even while we acknowledge and support one another through mourning what has already been lost. It is struggling to overcome the roots of the catastrophe we face, even though that might be risky personally and even though we cannot be certain of the outcome. It is about forcing into the realm of politics possibilities — of a habitable planet, of enough for everyone, of not too much for anybody, of distributed power — and then fighting for these possibilities as though you can win them.

DISCUSSION QUESTIONS

1. What are the potential drawbacks for social movements, like the climate justice movement, of acknowledging inevitable loss? Is it a bad tactic to suggest that we have already lost some aspects of a struggle?
2. What, in your view, accounts for the failure of international negotiations on climate change to accomplish any global-scale reduction in carbon dioxide emissions?
3. Do you think it is reasonable to consider nationalizing the fossil fuel industry, with the goal of phasing out oil and gas production in Canada?

GLOSSARY OF KEY TERMS

Green New Deal (GND): An umbrella term for a variety of proposals for massive public investment in decarbonizing infrastructure and economic activity. GND proposals tie investment in low-carbon technologies and infrastructure to job creation, protection for the most marginalized and redistribution of wealth.

Intergovernmental Panel on Climate Change (IPCC): The body charged by the United Nations with assessing and reporting on the science of climate change.

Net zero: A condition in which an organization, corporation or nation is absorbing, sequestering or avoiding carbon dioxide emissions equal to its production of the same. Net zero does not mean that no greenhouse gas emissions are produced, only that those emissions are being offset by some set of technologies, projects or practices. These might be internal to the organization, but might also be outside of it, as in the case of carbon offsets. Many corporations and nations, including Canada, have made net-zero commitments.

New denialism: Acknowledgement of climate change as an anthropogenic phenomenon while working to undermine effective and sufficient public action to address it.

Public affluence: A concept of welfare that emphasizes shared public goods, services and amenities, in contrast to concepts of welfare that emphasize the accumulation of private consumer goods.

United Nations Framework Convention on Climate Change: The principal international structure for climate diplomacy and the coordination of national-level reductions in GHG emissions.

Venture capital: A form of financing provided by investors to small companies and start-ups, with an eye to nurturing the company through to its purchase by a larger corporation or to an initial public offering.

Wet-bulb temperature limit: The combination of temperature and humidity at which the capacity for a body to cool itself relative to the ambient temperature via evaporation ceases to function. In humans, this occurs at a wet bulb temperature of approximately 35 degrees Celsius.

RESOURCES FOR ACTIVISTS

BankTrack: banktrack.org/

Climate Action Tracker: climateactiontracker.org/

Climate Files: climatefiles.com/

International Energy Agency, World Energy Investment Reports: iea.org/reports/world-energy-investment-2020

Labor Network for Sustainability: labor4sustainability.org/

Indigenous Environmental Network: ienearth.org/justtransition/

NOTES

1 Based on IEA data from IEA (2020a).

2 Based on IEA data from IEA (2020b).

REFERENCES

Bonneuil, C., and J.B. Fressoz. 2017. *The Shock of the Anthropocene*, trans. David Fernbach. New York: Verso.

Bloomberg Green. 2020. "How to Grow Green." Bloomberg.com. <bloomberg.com/features/2020-green-stimulus-clean-energy-future/#toaster>.

Bradshaw, C.J.A., P.R. Ehrlich, A. Beattie et al. 2021. "Underestimating the Challenges of Avoiding a Ghastly Future." *Frontiers in Conservation Science* 13.

Carter, A., and T. Dordi. 2021. *Correcting Canada's "One-Eye-Shut" Climate Policy*. Technical Paper 2021-4. Victoria: Cascade Institute. <cascadeinstitute.org/technical-paper/correcting-canadas-one-eye-shut-climate-policy/>.

Chernomas, R., I. Hudson and M. Hudson. 2019. *Neoliberal Lives: Work, Politics, Nature, and Health in the Contemporary United States*. Manchester: Manchester University Press.

Chestney, N. 2021. "IEA says Global CO2 Emissions Rising Again After Nearly 6% Fall Last Year." Reuters, March 2. <reuters.com/world/china/iea-says-global-co2-emissions-rising-again-after-nearly-6-fall-last-year-2021-03-02/>.

Climate Reality Project. 2019. "The Climate Denial Machine: How the Fossil Fuel Industry Blocks Climate Action." September 5. <climaterealityproject.org/blog/climate-denial-machine-how-fossil-fuel-industry-blocks-climate-action>.

Cross, G. 2002. *An All-Consuming Century: Why Commercialism Won in Modern America*. New York: Columbia University Press.

Daub, S., G. Blue, L. Rajewicz and Z. Yunker. 2021. "Episodes in the New Climate Denialism." In W. Carroll (ed.), *Regime of Obstruction: How Corporate Power Blocks Energy Democracy*. Edmonton: Athabasca University Press.

Elliot, R. 2018. "The Sociology of Climate Change as a Sociology of Loss." *European Journal of Sociology* 59, 3.

Energy Policy Tracker. 2021. <energypolicytracker.org/>.

Farand, C. 2021. "China Makes No Shift Away From Coal in Five-Year Plan as It 'Crawls' to Carbon Neutrality." *Climate Home News*. <climatechangenews.com/2021/03/05/china-makes-no-shift-away-coal-five-year-plan-crawls-carbon-neutrality/>.

Farrell, J. 2016. "Corporate Funding and Ideological Polarization about Climate Change." *Proceedings of the National Academy of Sciences* 113, 1.

Freese, B. 2020. *Industrial Strength Denial*. Berkeley: University of California Press.

Heede, R. 2014. "Tracing Anthropogenic Carbon Dioxide and Methane Emissions to Fossil Fuel and Cement Producers, 1854–2010." *Climatic Change* 122.

Herrando-Pérez, S., C.J.A. Bradshaw, S. Lewandowsky and D.R. Vieites. 2019. "Statistical Language Backs Conservatism in Climate-Change Assessments." *BioScience* 69, 3. <doi.org/10.1093/biosci/biz004>.

Hirschman, A.O. 1991. *The Rhetoric of Reaction: Perversity, Futility, Jeopardy*. Cambridge, MA: Belknap Press.

Huber, M. 2013. *Lifeblood: Oil, Freedom, and the Forces of Capital*. Minneapolis: University of Minnesota Press.

Hudson, I., and M. Hudson. 2021. *Consumption*. Polity Press.

Hudson, M., and E. Bowness. 2021. "Finance and Fossil Capital: A Community Divided?" *The Extractive Industries and Society* 8, 1.

IEA (International Energy Agency). 2020a. "World Total Energy Supply by Source, 1971–2018." Paris. <iea.org/data-and-statistics/charts/world-total-energy-supply-by-source-1971-2018>.

___. 2020b. "Global Investment in Clean Energy and Efficiency and Share in Total Investment, 2015–2020." Paris. <iea.org/data-and-statistics/charts/global-investment-in-clean-energy-and-efficiency-and-share-in-total-investment-2015-2020>.

___. 2020c. "Projected Global Change in CO2 Emissions, 2020 and 2021." Paris. <iea.org/data-and-statistics/charts/projected-global-change-in-co2-emissions-2020-and-2021>.

___. 2021. "Monthly Change in CO2 Emissions in China in 2020 Relative to 2019." Paris. <iea.org/data-and-statistics/charts/monthly-change-in-co2-emissions-in-china-in-2020-relative-to-2019>.

IMF (International Monetary Fund). 2021. "World Economic Outlook Update, January." <imf.org/en/Publications/WEO/Issues/2021/01/26/2021-world-economic-outlook-update>.

Jackson, T. 2009. *Prosperity Without Growth*. London: Earthscan.

Klein, N. 2014. *This Changes Everything*. New York: Alfred A. Knopf.

Klein, S., and S. Daub. 2016. "The New Climate Denialism: Time for an Intervention." <policynote.ca/the-new-climate-denialism-time-for-an-intervention/>.

Koopman, R., Z. Wang and S.-J. Wei. 2008. "How Much of Chinese Exports Is Really Made in China? Assessing Foreign and Domestic Value-Added in Gross Exports." Working Paper No. 2008-03-B. Washington, DC: *US International Trade Commission*. <usitc.gov/publications/332/ec200803b_revised.pdf>.

Le Quéré, C., G.P. Peters, P. Friedlingstein et al. 2021. "Fossil CO2 Emissions in the Post-COVID-19 Era." *Nature Climate Change* 11. <doi.org/10.1038/s41558-021-01001-0>.

Liu, Z., P. Ciais, Z. Deng, et al. 2020. "Near-Real-Time Monitoring of Global CO2 Emissions Reveals the Effects of the COVID-19 Pandemic." *Nature Communications* 11, 5172.

Ma, H., Z. Wang and K. Zhu. 2014. "Domestic content in China's exports and its distribution by firm ownership." *Journal of Comparative Economics* 43, 1.

MacBride, E. 2020. "Losing the Winner's Game." MIT *Technology Review* 123, 4.

Mann, G., and J. Wainwright. 2018. *Climate Leviathan*. New York: Verso.

Mazzucato, M. 2013. *The Entrepreneurial State*. New York: Anthem Press.

McCollum, D.L., W. Zhou, C. Bertram et al. 2018. "Energy Investment Needs for Fulfilling the Paris Agreement and Achieving the Sustainable Development Goals." *Nature Energy* 3.

McMillan, T. 2018. "With the Right Leadership, Canada Can Support World's Energy Needs." *Toronto Sun*, April 6. <torontosun.com/opinion/columnists/guest-column-with-the-right-leadership-canada-can-support-worlds-energy-needs>.

The Onion. 2021. "World Leaders Pledge to Cut Emissions by as Much as They Can Realistically Back Out Of." Instagram.

Oreskes, N., and E.M. Conway. 2010. *Merchants of Doubt*. New York: Bloomsbury.

Osnos, E. 2017. "Doomsday Prep for the Super-Rich." *New Yorker*, January 30. <newyorker.com/magazine/2017/01/30/doomsday-prep-for-the-super-rich>.

Oxfam and Stockholm Environment Institute. 2020. "The Carbon Inequality Era: An Assessment of the Global Distribution of Consumption Emissions Among Individuals from 1990 to 2015 and Beyond." <policy-practice.oxfam.org/resources/the-carbon-inequality-era-an-assessment-of-the-global-distribution-of-consumpti-621049/>.

Rainforest Action Network. 2021. *Banking on Climate Chaos: Fossil Fuel Finance Report 2021*. <ran.org/wp-content/uploads/2021/03/Banking-on-Climate-Chaos-2021.pdf>.

___. 2020. *Banking on Climate Change: Fossil Fuel Finance Report 2020*. <ran.org/wp-content/uploads/2020/03/Banking_on_Climate_Change__2020_vF.pdf>.

Riofrancos, T. 2019. "Plan, Mood, Battlefield—Reflections on a Green New Deal." *Viewpoint Magazine*, May 16. <viewpointmag.com/2019/05/16/plan-mood-battlefield-reflections-on-the-green-new-deal/>.

Robertson, C., and J. Westerman (eds.). 2015. *Working on Earth: Class and Environmental Justice*. Las Vegas: University of Nevada Press.

Salazar, D.J., S. Clauson, T. Abel and A. Clauson. 2019. "Race, Income, and Environmental Inequality in the US" *Social Science Quarterly* 100, 3.

Tollefson, J. 2021. "COVID Curbed Carbon Emissions in 2020 — But Not by Much." *Nature*, January 15. <nature.com/articles/d41586-021-00090-3#ref-CR1>.

UNEP (United Nations Environment Programme). 2021. *Are We Building Back Better? Evidence from 2020 and Pathways to Inclusive Green Economic Recovery*. Nairobi. <unep.org/resources/publication/are-we-building-back-better-evidence-2020-and-pathways-inclusive-green>.

___. 2020. *Emissions Gap Report 2020*. Nairobi. <unep.org/emissions-gap-report-2020>.

___. 2016. *Global Material Flows and Resource Productivity: Assessment Report for the UNEP International Resource Panel*. Nairobi. <resourcepanel.org/reports/global-material-flows-and-resource-productivity-database-link>.

Unfriend Coal. 2019. "Insuring Coal No More: 2019 Scorecard on Insurance, Coal, and Climate

Change." December. <insureourfuture.co/wp-content/uploads/2019/12/2019-Coal-Insurance-Scorecard-soft-version-2.pdf>.

Vivid Economics. 2021. *Greenness of Stimulus Index.* <vivideconomics.com/casestudy/green-ness-for-stimulus-index/>.

Waldman, S. 2018. "ɪᴘᴄᴄ: Was the Scary Report Too Conservative?" *E&E News,* October 11. <governor-swindenergycoalition.org/was-the-scary-ipcc-report-too-conservative/>.

Wark, M. 2014. "There Is Another World, and It Is This One." Public Seminar, January 14. <publicsem-inar.org/2014/01/there-is-another-world-and-it-is-this-one/>.

Westervelt, A. 2019. "How the Fossil Fuel Industry Got the Media to Think Climate Change Was Debatable." *Washington Post,* January 10. <washingtonpost.com/outlook/2019/01/10/how-fossil-fu-el-industry-got-media-think-climate-change-was-debatable/>.

World Meteorological Organization. 2019. *United in Science: High-Level Synthesis Report of Latest Climate Science Information Convened by the Science Advisory Group of the UN Climate Action Summit 2019.* <public.wmo.int/en/resources/united_in_science>.

York, R. 2012. "Do Alternative Energy Sources Displace Fossil Fuels?" *Nature Climate Change* 2. <doi.org/10.1038/nclimate1451>.

Zhang, Y., I. Held, and S. Fueglistaler. 2021. "Projections of Tropical Heat Stress Constrained by Atmospheric Dynamics." *Nature Geoscience* 14. <doi.org/10.1038/s41561-021-00695-3>.

11

MAKING UNIVERSITIES SAFE FOR WOMEN
Sexual Assault on Campus

Elizabeth Sheehy and Lindsay Ostridge

You Should Know This

- Annually, 460,000 Canadian women report that men have sexually assaulted them. This is a conservative estimate since it is based on self-reports by women to interviewers from Statistics Canada whom they do not know and in circumstances where the legal definition of sexual assault is not presented to them.

- A 2019 survey found that 71 percent of students had witnessed or been the victim of unwanted sexualized behaviours in a post-secondary setting.

- Among perpetrators of sexual assault, 0.3 percent are held accountable under Canadian law; 99.7 percent are not held accountable.

- Only one in three Canadians understands the criminal law of consent to sexual activity; two in three Canadians mistakenly believe that affirmative consent is not required (saying "yes," initiating or enjoying the activity) or that ongoing consent to the sexual activity is not required. One in ten does not know that consent is required between spouses, and 21 percent of those aged eighteen to thirty-four believe that when a woman sends a sexually explicit photo she is "consenting."

- The rate at which women students are sexually assaulted by men during their college years in the US sits between 15 and 34 percent.

- By June 2016, US federal authorities had opened 246 investigations of 195

---

colleges and universities for Title IX violations regarding their responses to campus sexual violence.

- Seventy-eight percent of University of Ottawa students have experienced face-to-face harassment, including 44 percent who experienced unwanted physical contact, and 67 percent had experienced online harassment.

- Women students reported 179 sexual assaults to their campus authorities in Canada in 2013, a rate that is 21 percent higher than assaults reported in 2012 and 66 percent higher than 2009.

- Only twenty-four of one hundred post-secondary institutions in Canada had, by 2016, adopted a stand-alone policy for sexual violence on campus.

Sources: Johnson 2012; Hill 2015; Burczycka 2020; Cantor et al. 2015; Krebs et al. 2007; O'Connor and Kingkade 2016; Johnson 2015b; Sawa and Ward 2015a; Kane 2016.

SEXUAL ASSAULT PERPETRATED BY MEN IN Canada constitutes a major barrier to women's freedom, security of the person and their right to equality before and under the law. Women students in post-secondary institutions are burdened by additional consequences beyond the trauma and chaos of rape: they may be unable to avoid the perpetrator if he shares a residence, classes, activities or even campus routes; their academic success will be imperilled such that they may fail courses or be forced to withdraw from programs; and they face financial penalties of wasted tuition, loss of teaching and research assistantships and the costs of counselling. Men's sexual violence thus has material consequences for women's access to educational equity.

> Men's sexual violence has material consequences for women's access to educational equity.

For these reasons, students continue to organize around sexual violence on campus, demanding that Canadian universities do more to combat this problem. Although sexual violence occurs in many social contexts and not only in the context of orientation or frosh activities, in September 2021 allegations were made on social media that up to thirty women at Western University had been drugged and raped during the first week of school. In response, approximately twelve thousand students participated in a walkout and protest at Western University to denounce rape culture and to support the four survivors of sexual violence who made formal complaints and the many more who made informal complaints via social media (Theodore and Gould 2021). Investigation continues into these allegations, and Western has instituted a new "action plan" (Nicholson and Martins 2021).

Perpetrators often target young women aged fifteen to twenty-four (Perreault and Brennan 2010), particularly those women who experience multiple oppressions like racism and disability discrimination, placing university and college students among those women most at risk. The legal system remains a hostile place for women who report sexual assault to the police, despite substantive reforms to the law intended to change both the outcomes and experiences of women who initiate criminal legal intervention. When men assault women while they are pursuing post-secondary degrees, additional issues arise that are not taken up by the criminal law — for example, the need for a safety plan for her on campus, the need to remove the perpetrator from the university community to alleviate the risk he poses to her and to other students, the need to denounce the behaviour as fundamentally inconsistent with the university's mission and the need to accommodate and support the student in her recovery and academic success. Women students are therefore demanding that their universities and colleges respond to the destructive behaviour of campus perpetrators.

This chapter will first situate campus sexual assault on the current political agenda in Canada, including the #MeToo and Black Lives Matter movements and the work of the autonomous women's movement, which supports and advocates for women who have been raped. In order to articulate the dimensions of the issue, it will also review the data on men's commission of sexual assault both off and on campus. Third, it will describe the criminal law of sexual assault and, fourth, it will outline the many obstacles women face in the legal processing of sexual assault reports when they turn to the criminal justice system.

Fifth, this chapter will examine the processes available to women on campus in Canada, including sexual harassment policies and student codes of conduct, pointing out the perils of both, before turning to consider campus sexual violence policies and new legislation in several provinces requiring universities and colleges to develop sexual violence policies and provide resources to support students who experience sexual violence. Criticisms of these policies are set out, highlighting the struggles that lie ahead. The chapter will conclude by identifying future challenges that universities and colleges face in developing and defending campus sexual violence policies: the exclusion of marginalized voices, the over-reliance on quasi-criminal models for resolving allegations of campus sexual violence and backlash from individual men and the campus anti-feminist men's rights movement.

WOMEN STUDENTS PUT CAMPUS SEXUAL ASSAULT ON THE AGENDA

Women students are demanding that their universities and colleges provide remedies for sexual violence, including alternate processes and interim measures to

allow them to continue their educational programs after men have sexually assault-
ed them. Women students' demands have a long history in campus activism (Ricci and Bergeron 2019), but the lack of data collection by post-sec-ondary institutions and the effort by some administrators to silence women who report sexual assault on campus

> Women students are demanding that their universities and colleges provide remedies for sexual violence, including alternate processes and interim measures to allow them to contin-ue their educational programs after men have sexually assaulted them.

(Laychuk 2016) has made assessment of the scope of the problem challenging. Yet frontline women's rape crisis centres have been dealing with the aftermath of cam-pus sexual assault for the decades during which they have operated across North America. By supporting these students, women's centres have contributed to the ed-ucational mission of universities, and some have also advocated on behalf of students to their universities. Women's frontline organizations thus have critical expertise in developing responses to campus sexual assault.

The evidence from the most impressive study to date, which examined seventy countries over forty years, shows that the autonomous women's movement world-wide is the single most important factor in producing positive policy change on male violence against women (Htun and Weldon 2012). Thus, it is critical to consider campus sexual assault in the wider context of the women's movement's analysis and strategies around men's violence against women, recognizing, too, that this form of sexual violence is not uniquely experienced by women students.

The contributions of #MeToo and Black Lives Matter are also foundational to student activism against campus sexual violence. These movements highlight the systemic barriers that continue to confront women who report sexual violence, and they illuminate the role of racism in generating and rationalizing vi-olence against racialized women and men.

> These movements highlight the systemic barriers that continue to confront women who report sexual violence, and they illu-minate the role of racism in generating and rationalizing violence against racial-ized women and men.

Tarana Burke, a Black feminist, survivor, activist and community organizer, start-ed the #MeToo hashtag in 2006. In an attempt to shift the legal landscape for women in the US, actress Alyssa Milano asked women in 2017 to use the hashtag #MeToo to share their experiences of sexual violence (Freeman 2019). Millions of women did, making it evident that sexual violence is a widespread societal problem embedded within our work and life cultures. #MeToo was so powerful that rates of reporting sexual violence to police increased significantly (Rotenberg and Cotter 2018). Yet many would argue that it has not done enough for survivors who also experience intersecting oppressions like racism (Freeman 2019).

The Black Lives Matter (BLM) movement demonstrates the critical role played by an intersectional, anti-racist analysis for sexual violence prevention and strategy. Started in 2013 by three American Black social activists and community organiz-ers — Alicia Garza, Patrisse Cullors and Opal Tometi — this movement lit a call to action in response to the acquittal of police officer George Zimmerman, who fatally shot Trayvon Martin (Garza 2016). Similar to #MeToo, BLM is a social movement supported by critical analysis, social media interventions and mass protest confront-ing ongoing anti-Black racism in the US and Canada. The BLM movement has chal-lenged the institutions of policing and campus security, and can offer insights into the conceptualization of sexual violence policies on campus — for example, by in-sisting that policies account for the specific forms of racist sexual violence, additional barriers to reporting and systemic remedies needed by racialized women students (Lawson 2020).

Despite the fact that men's sexual violence has long been on the feminist agenda in Canada, a series of highly publicized events at Canadian universities starting in 2013 catapulted men's sexual violence on campus into a national conversation. Rape chants by frosh students, men and women alike (CBC News 2013b), racist songs that insulted Indigenous women (Justice 2013) and a series of rapes on campus by a serial predator, all in the fall of 2013, put the University of British Columbia under intense scrutiny (Bailey 2013). A rape chant scandal also rocked Saint Mary's University (Taber 2013), while Lakehead University's failure to respond to a student's sexual assault report was exposed when she described what it was like to attend classes with her alleged perpetrator in a letter to the editor of a local paper (CBC 2013a).

Months later, a report of sexual assault by several hockey players on the University of Ottawa team was exposed at almost the same time as Facebook pages were made public in which five male student leaders at the same university denigrated sexu-ally and threatened their female student president (CBC 2014b, 2014a). Dalhousie University experienced media glare when Facebook posts of male dentistry students were shared, wherein they said they wanted to "hate fuck" their female colleagues and discussed using chloroform to drug and rape women patients (Hampson 2015). A Mount St. Vincent professor who engaged in inappropriate sexual conduct with re-spect to a female student was fired (Zaccagna 2015). A student at Brandon University was required to sign a contract, as part of the investigation of her complaint, agreeing not to discuss another student's sexual assault against her with anyone other than a counsellor, upon pain of suspension or expulsion (Laychuk 2016).

From these incidents, students have developed a powerful critique of "rape culture" on campus — a culture in which rape is encouraged, tolerated or minimized — and that provides the social context in which men who commit sexual assault are protected from repercussions. Rape culture includes a series of normative attitudes and behaviours that exist on a continuum, from the acceptance of sexism and male dominance to dating scripts, rape jokes, street harassment, body policing of women and rape proclivity (Keller, Mendes and Ringrose 2018; Strain, Hockett and Saucier 2015). Rape culture continues to be supported by television, news and music, contributing to women's ongoing sexualization, commodification and marginalization (Buchwald, Fletcher and Roth 2005; Rentschler 2014). There is also evidence that fraternities and sports teams, especially football and hockey, contribute to rape culture on campus (Martin 2016).

> Students have developed a powerful critique of "rape culture" on campus – a culture in which rape is encouraged, tolerated or minimized – and that provides the social context in which men who commit sexual assault are protected from repercussions.

Canadian students and activists have looked to the US, where a student-led movement successfully campaigned for federal intervention to ensure that post-secondary institutions either implement sexual assault policies that support women students or risk losing federal funding. Sex discrimination in education has long been prohibited under Title IX of the *Education Amendments of 1972* for institutions that receive federal financial support; students can now invoke it against universities and colleges that fail to respond appropriately to sexual harassment and sexual violence as conduct that has a discriminatory impact on them as women students (Sheehy and Gilbert 2017). Although Canada's federal government has threatened to withhold research support from universities that fail to develop sexual violence polices (Lum 2018), women students in Canada have been forced to exert pressure at the university and provincial levels because the federal government has an insignificant role in funding post-secondary institutions.

Student activism and exposés revealing that, as of 2014, only nine of eighty-seven Canadian universities even had a "sexual assault" policy (Mathieu and Poisson 2014) generated enormous political pressure for social and legal change. To understand why students are turning to their post-secondary institutions for

> Student activism and exposés revealing that, as of 2014, only nine of eighty-seven Canadian universities even had a "sexual assault" policy generated enormous political pressure for social and legal change.

responses to sexual assault, the issue must be situated in relation to the social and legal realities of sexual assault both off and on campus in Canada. Whose and which knowledge informs our understanding of this crime? What do we know about men's sexual assaults upon women students? To whom do women students turn in these circumstances?

THE SOCIAL REALITY OF SEXUAL ASSAULT IN CANADA

Sexual assault is a deeply gendered crime: 92 percent of those victimized are female (Vaillancourt 2010) and 94 percent of the perpetrators are male (Perreault 2015). Men are also the vast majority of perpetrators — 79 percent — of violent victimization against other men (Vaillancourt 2010). Sexual assault is a persistent crime. Despite the drop in all other forms of violent crime in Canada over the past decade, men's commission of sexual assault remains constant such that for the first time, women have surpassed men at the rate at which they are victimized violently (Statistics Canada 2015).

Sexual assault is also a crime that is embedded in racism, colonization and colonial practices, women's poverty and the devaluation of women with disabilities. Canada's history of slavery and the commodification of Black women's bodies (Holmes 2016), colonization, dispossession and the imposition of patriarchy on Indigenous women (Deer 2015) and the normalization of eugenics policies (Block 2000) have contributed to men's targeting of women from these groups. These intersecting oppressions also structure the forms of sexual violence that men engage in, the barriers to women's disclosure of sexual violence and the state's responses.

We do not know how many men engage in sexually assaultive behaviour. We also do not know with certainty how many women they assault each year, although we do know that it appears to be one of the most underreported of crimes. The widely cited statistic is that one in ten women who experience sexual assault report it to police. However, Statistics Canada (2015) reports that the numbers are now such that only one in twenty women report their experience of sexual assault to police.

Yet we cannot be certain that the reporting rates are not even lower. This lacuna in our knowledge is due to the reality that rape is a crime that silences women: it is inherently violent, such that the victim may not know if she will be killed, producing long-term trauma responses; it denies the personhood of the victim, rendering her an object to be used by another person and shattering her sense of safety in the world; it produces shock and disbelief, so that many women try to rationalize or normalize the perpetrator's behaviour or to lock away the memory rather than confront him or others with his acts; it commonly produces a freeze response, making women ashamed that they did not somehow "fight"; it is a crime for which many in our society blame women themselves — for their manner of dress, their consumption of alcohol, their "flirtatious" behaviour, their decisions that others perceive as "risk-taking" — leading victims to engage in self-blame and self-censorship; it is overwhelmingly committed by men known to the woman, making it very complicated for a victim to report; and it is a crime that we as a society deny, minimize and rationalize, convincing victims that they are unlikely to be believed. No wonder so few women "break the silence."

Men who rape count on the silencing effect of this crime. The social construction of knowledge about men's violence against women abets this silencing. Police data has been recognized as incomplete both because so few women choose to report to police but also because police recording practices for sexual assault are deeply problematic given the documented biases that infect them, as discussed below. Crime victimization surveys are inadequate because they are not specifically tailored to identify for women the range of behaviours that constitute "sexual assault" in legal terms, nor are the interviewers trained to gain the confidence of interviewees and respond with empathy. As Holly Johnson (2015c) argues, the low incidence rates produced by these forms of "knowledge" allowed criminologists and others to claim that women's fear of sexual violence was exaggerated and disproportionate to their documented risk.

However, the best study available of men's sexual offending against women produced startling new knowledge: men assault 39 percent of Canadian women, who experience this crime at least once over their lifetimes (Statistics Canada 1994). This 1993 Statistics Canada study, the *Violence Against Women Survey* (VAWS), as it was called, avoided many of the known problems with other efforts to survey women about sexual assault. The VAWS introduced a woman-centred survey that asked women about their experiences from the age of sixteen forward (as opposed to the past year) and specified the acts considered criminal, including sexual assaults where the woman did not resist or where she was incapable of consent — categories of criminal offending that many, including women, erroneously believe do not amount to sexual assault in law. The interviewers were trained to ensure the woman's safety needs were met and to respond to the emotional turmoil that their questions might provoke.

When we turn to sexual assault on the campus, our knowledge is even more limited, and most of it is from the US. Two recent studies place the rate at which men rape college women at between 15 and 34 percent, illustrating substantial variance in offending rates across institutions (Cantor et al. 2015; Krebs et al. 2007). Research on US campuses suggests that approximately 6 percent of male students are perpetrators, but that many of them are serial rapists, accounting for an average of six rapes each (Lisak and Miller 2002). Further, older research by Malamuth and Dean (1991) found that 16–20 percent of male students stated that they would commit rape if

326 / Power and Resistance

they thought they could get away with it; when the wording changed from "rape" to "force a woman to have sex," the numbers soared to 36–44 percent (Malamuth and Dean 1991: 234).

In Canada, DeKeseredy and Kelly (1993) surveyed students in forty-four Canadian post-secondary institutions for their experience of either perpetrating sexual assault or being perpetrated against. They found that 11 percent of males reported abusing their dating partners sexually, while 27.7 percent of females reported experiencing this behaviour. When the researchers included all forms of abuse — physical and psychological as well as sexual — their numbers rose to 19.5 percent of males self-reporting such behaviour and 45.1 percent of female students responding that they had been targeted by this behaviour (DeKeseredy and Kelly 1993). DeKeseredy, Schwartz and Tait (1993) examined sexual aggression by non-strangers and strangers against women at one Canadian university in an exploratory study and found that men had sexually assaulted 32.8 percent of the 259 women in the study in the past twelve months.

Both studies used broad definitions of sexual assault; specific questions that allowed women to measure their experience against legal understandings of sexual assault; and provided follow-up support for women surveyed. The authors concluded, however, that even these numbers were undercounts because they did not involve interviews during which women are known to make further disclosures (DeKeseredy, Schwartz and Tait 1993). Only three of the approximately 120 students who experienced sexual assault in this study said that they had reported their victimization to police — a reporting rate that sits significantly below even the rate of one in twenty women reporting to police.

More recently, journalists collected the data from Canadian universities among students who experience sexual violence to discern their reporting rates both to police and to their post-secondary institutions (Sawa and Ward 2015a). They found that, first, women students are putting pressure on their colleges and universities by reporting in increasing numbers: "In 2013, 179 assaults were reported, a 21 per cent rise over 2012 and a 66 per cent rise over the number of sexual assaults reported in 2009" (Sawa and Ward 2015a: n.p.).

Second, for some universities there is a mismatch — in fact a reversal — of women's reporting rates to their institutions as opposed to police. For example, while UBC's data shows that sixteen sexual assaults were reported to campus security for the period 2009–2013, the RCMP data shows sev-

> Many more women reported to police than to their campus authorities, suggesting that students were unaware of the university's policy.

enty sexual assaults for the same period (Sawa and Ward 2015b). Thus, many more women reported to police than to their campus authorities, suggesting that students were unaware of the university's policy.

Third, those numbers of students reporting sexual violence are only the tip of the iceberg in terms of the disconnect between what happens to women on Canadian campuses and what is reported to campus officials. Johnson (2015b) designed a campus survey for sexual violence in 2015 at the University of Ottawa. She found that 44 percent of students surveyed online reported that they had experienced some form of sexual violence while at the university. In contrast, the University of Ottawa received only ten reports of sexual violence from its students in the period 2009–2013 (Sawa and Ward 2015a).

Beyond the silencing effect of sexual assault, why do so few women students report to police or to their university? Does criminal law fairly define the wrong of sexual assault and provide appropriate legal rules for the prosecution and defence of this crime?

SEXUAL ASSAULT LAW

Canada's sexual assault law is recognized as one of the most progressive in the world for women. In 1983, in response to demands made by the women's movement in Canada, it shed many of the most sex discriminatory rules that had plagued the prosecution of rape for centuries (Boyle 1984). Criminal Code reforms made wife rape a crime for the first time; eliminated the requirement that penetration be proven; and reformed the previous evidentiary rules that had invited judges and juries to acquit on the basis of the doctrine of "recent complaint," a lack of corroborating evidence or because a woman's prior sexual experience made her not worthy of belief. More reforms followed in 1992, including the definition of legally valid "consent" and limits on the "mistaken belief in consent" defence, led by the proposals and energy of the violence against women's movement in Canada.

Between statutory definitions and judicial rulings fought for via feminist interventions in litigation (Sheehy and Tolmie 2019), Canadian law supports the following propositions: sexual contact without the "voluntary agreement" of the other person is criminal (*Criminal Code of Canada* s. 273.1); voluntary agreement is a subjective state of mind of the other person — it cannot be "implied" or presumed from the circumstances (*R v. Ewanchuk* 1999); those who are asleep, severely intoxicated (by drugs or alcohol) or passed out are legally incapable of consent (*Criminal Code of Canada* s. 273.1); voluntary agreement must be expressed by words or actions of that person, such that failure to resist or passivity does not amount to consent in law (*R v. M. (M.L.)* 1994); voluntary agreement must be obtained for "the sexual activity in question" (meaning our law does not recognize global consent); and consent can be withdrawn by words or conduct and must be contemporaneous with the sexual activity (there is no "advance consent") (*R v. J.A.* 2011).

Further, a man cannot defend himself by arguing "mistaken belief in consent" if his error arose from his intoxication or recklessness as to the woman's consent or if he failed "to take reasonable steps, in the circumstances known to him at the time, to ascertain consent" (*Criminal Code of Canada* s. 273.2(b)). Our law places limits on accused men's access to women's sexual history and their private counselling and other records, based on women's competing equality rights and the recognized need to eliminate discriminatory rape myths from criminal law (*Criminal Code of Canada* ss. 276, 278). However, women's past sexual experience and their private records can sometimes be obtained by defence lawyers, such that no woman considering reporting sexual assault can be guaranteed that the lawyer defending the accused will not be able to cross-examine her about her sexual experience or her private counselling records (Craig 2018).

THE LEGAL PROCESSING OF SEXUAL ASSAULT IN CANADA

In spite of the clear jurisprudence governing sexual assault, the law is not applied consistently by police, prosecutors and judges. Police failures include refusal to investigate women's reports or to send their rape evidence kits for forensic testing, treating women with disbelief and hostility and charging or threatening to charge women with "mischief" or "obstruction" for allegedly false reports of rape, among other responses. These failures are so pervasive and persistent that US scholar Corey Rayburn Yung argues that police are effectively "hostile gatekeepers who prevent rape complaints from progressing through the criminal justice system by fervently policing the culturally disputed concept of 'rape'" (2017: 1).

The "unfounding" rate — the rate at which police disbelieve women and decide that no crime has been committed — is higher for sexual assault than any other crime in Canada. The rate of "unfounding" on average among police departments studied is 25–43 percent, meaning that in many cities, police turn away at least one in four women who report rape, devastating the women who turned to police for aid and emboldening perpetrators (DuBois 2012: 194–95). In Ottawa between 2009 and 2013, police unfounded 38 percent of women's sexual assault complaints; by 2014, the rate had dropped to 21 percent, but at the same time the category of "founded, but unsolved" had risen from 32 to 47 percent (Johnson 2015a).

Men who rape fellow students are particularly likely to benefit from unfounding because of police adherence to rape myths that view "stranger" rape as more serious and credible than "acquaintance" rape. For example, in 2013, fifty sexual assaults were reported by UBC students to the RCMP. Of these, forty-one were unfounded — a shockingly high rate of police disregard (UBC Campus Security 2016).

Often, as Yung (2017) demonstrates with terrifying examples, police are impervious to legal reform of the definitions used to criminalize sexual violence, continuing to focus on women's behaviour, not men's, when deciding whether to investigate and lay charges. Consider, for example, the Ottawa police decision not to investigate the rape of a first-year University of Ottawa student (CBC News 2015). This student reported on September 26, 2015, to police after she had gone to the hospital and undergone a medical examination. She told them that another student had punched, strangled, raped and then spat upon her at his home the night before. Over a month later, the investigator contacted her to tell her that police had decided not to lay charges after interviewing the alleged perpetrator. Since he claimed that he thought the interaction was consensual, the officer concluded that it was a "misunderstanding" (CBC News 2015). Such an interpretation of the facts and law would see virtually all perpetrators left untouched by criminal law, if all they need do is allege "mistake." But further, given this degree of violence, "mistaken belief in consent" is arguably unavailable as a legal defence (Sheehy, Gotell, and Grant 2020).

Only after this student abandoned her right to anonymity and went public with her name and face did police reverse and claim that the investigation was "ongoing." Another two months went by before police announced that they had "laid charges," but the man had left Canada, and no arrest was made (Sibley 2016). Finally, this man was arrested in August 2016 when he attempted to re-enter Canada (Gillis 2016).

If police do lay charges, they are overwhelmingly likely to charge at the level of simple sexual assault, even in those cases where the facts support more serious charges of sexual assault causing bodily harm or using a weapon, or aggravated sexual assault, whereby the man either maims or endangers the life of the complainant (Du Mont 2003). This lower level of charge means that the degree of men's violence in many sexual assaults is rendered invisible, leaving society with a misleading statistical portrait about this crime in Canada, as well as sentences that may not fit the actual crime.

Prosecutors can be another barrier for women who report sexual assault, even if police arrest a suspect and/or recommend charges. Prosecutors may drop charges laid by police: they use a charge screening test that assesses the likelihood of conviction and the public interest in proceeding with a case, both of which may lead them to abandon prosecution. Johnson (2012) shows that about 50 percent of sexual assault charges are dropped at this stage of the legal process. For example, at the University of Victoria, police arrested a male student in relation to sexual assaults he allegedly committed against four women (Zinn 2016). However, the Crown's office refused to lay charges on the basis that the evidence did not meet their charge assessment standard, meaning that prosecutors doubted that there was a substantial likelihood of conviction (*Globe and Mail* 2016).

Crown attorneys (or Crowns) may accept a guilty plea in exchange for lesser charges of assault or a minor sentence in order to save resources and shield the complainant from the trial process. Or they may proceed to trial, but without a deep understanding or commitment to the reformed law of sexual assault (Vandervort 2012). Some Crowns hold erroneous or unchallenged beliefs about women and sexual assault, such that they may not object to defence cross-examination of the complainant that exceeds legal limits by, for example, touching on women's past sexual relationships or that relies upon racist stereotypes of Indigenous women (*R v. Barton* 2019; Lazar 2010; Vandervort 2012).

Further, the Crown represents the state, not the individual woman — meaning the Crown is not *her* lawyer — and should maintain some degree of neutrality. This is because Crown attorneys have different ethical obligations than do defence lawyers. Defence lawyers are charged with the responsibility of doing their utmost, within the limits of the law, to secure acquittal for their clients (Law Society of Ontario 2000: Chapter 5.1-1). In contrast, Crowns must act dispassionately and must not seek conviction, but rather to ensure that justice is done through a fair trial on the merits (Law Society of Ontario 2000: Chapter 5.1-3).

Unlike defence lawyers, therefore, Crowns generally do not "prepare" their witnesses for testifying, so as to avoid any suggestion that the witness's evidence has been "tainted." Crowns may also not have the budget allocation to call expert evidence to challenge erroneous beliefs about how women who experience sexual assault behave, allowing defence lawyers to impugn women's credibility by suggesting, for example, that maintaining contact with the perpetrator post-offence is inconsistent with a "real rape" having occurred.

Finally, legal aid is unavailable in most of the country for women who are sexual assault complainants, meaning that the overwhelming majority of women will testify without any legal advice or assistance. Ontario is running a pilot project in Toronto, Ottawa and Thunder Bay for sexual assault complainants to receive four hours of legal advice paid for by Legal Aid Ontario, and Newfoundland and Labrador commenced a similar project (Ceolin 2021; Roberts 2017). However, even if women have their own lawyer, with some exceptions, that lawyer does not have "standing" to intervene in the trial to supply expert evidence or to protest cross-examination by defence counsel. The more fortunate women who have support from frontline women's groups will at least have accompaniment and emotional support for the trial.

The trial, if it proceeds, will usually take place before a judge sitting alone without a jury. Women who testify can expect to undergo lengthy, repetitive, aggressive and sometimes sex discriminatory cross-examination by defence counsel in the public space of the courtroom and under the gaze of the alleged perpetrator (Craig 2018). Women's credibility will be attacked on the basis that they made bad decisions to consume alcohol, to enter a private space alone with the accused, to continue to associate with him after the assault or to wait days, months or years to report the offence to authorities.

Women's reliability as witnesses will be undermined if they did not tell the exact same account when they relay the details of the assault or if they were impaired by alcohol or drugs. As mentioned, their private counselling records and their previous sexual experiences may be used against them in cross-examination. Women's social media accounts and texts are commonly used to embarrass and discredit them when defence lawyers can access these records. A judge may put limits on abusive or discriminatory cross-examination, but judges exercise caution in appearing to favour one side or disrupting the adversarial process at the risk of their decisions being overturned (*R v. Schmaltz* 2015).

Worse, some judges share the same discriminatory beliefs as police and lawyers, as was vividly illustrated by former Justice Robin Camp's remarks in *R v. Wagar* (2015; Crawford and Tasker 2016). Camp told the complainant that if she didn't want "it" all she had to do was keep her knees together. He refused to apply the law limiting access to the complainant's prior sexual history because he did not agree with the law, and he asserted that sex and pain "sometimes go together" and that "young women want to have sex, particularly if they're drunk," among numerous other problematic comments. His fitness for judicial office was reviewed by the Canadian Judicial Council as a result of a complaint made against him; it recommended his removal from the bench (Canadian Judicial Council 2017).

Our criminal law has been particularly ineffective in grappling with men's perpetration against unconscious women, whether they are medicated, sleeping or passed out from alcohol or drug intoxication. In some cases, judges have acquitted based on men's claims that they mistakenly believed the women were awake and

> Our criminal law has been particularly ineffective in grappling with men's perpetration against unconscious women, whether they are medicated, sleeping or passed out from alcohol or drug intoxication.

indicating consent by their bodily movements (Sheehy 2012). In one particularly egregious case where the complainant fell asleep at a party fully clothed only to wake up to a complete stranger penetrating her, the Ontario Court of Appeal ruled that "it would be too onerous a test of wilful blindness to require an accused to stop the activity and, in effect, say, 'Wait a minute; do you know who I am?'" (*R v. Osvath* 1996).

As a result of these multiple challenges, sexual assault has the lowest conviction rate of any crime in Canada with the exception of attempted murder (Nicol 2013). Johnson (2012) reports that of the 2,824 sexual assaults that were prosecuted in 2006, 1,519 resulted in conviction. Her overall data, using women's self-reported sexual assaults and these outcomes, indicates that only 0.3 percent of men's sexual assaults ultimately result in criminal conviction (Johnson 2012).

The problem areas identified above — where women consumed alcohol, where they were unconscious, where women remained in social contact after the assault or where they failed to report immediately — are all situations that men can exploit on a university or college campus. For example, one study (Du Mont et al. 2009) reports that "suspected drug-facilitated sexual assault is a common problem," affecting one in five women who report to hospital-based sexual assault units in Ontario, and one third of them were students. The law's failure to respond effectively to these types of cases makes it all the more important that post-secondary institutions provide alternative processes for women students.

UNIVERSITY AND COLLEGE SEXUAL ASSAULT POLICIES

Campus sexual assault policies hold the potential to provide different kinds of support to women students. First and foremost, universities can engage in prevention and education about sexual assault by training students, faculty and staff around the legal parameters of sexual assault, offering self-defence and resistance strategies geared to women (Senn et al. 2015) and instigating bystander intervention, among other programs. Second, they can provide emergency aid and clear information when students are assaulted. Students who report must be told about the option of reporting to police, not discouraged from doing so, and supported by members of the university should the student need help going to police. Third, post-secondary institutions need to provide on-campus resources: counselling services and academic accommodation for students at the receiving end of sexual violence, regardless of whether they pursue a formal complaint against the perpetrator.

Fourth, universities should craft policies and procedures to deal with students, staff and faculty who sexually assault others in the university community. Because the mandate of a university is not to punish "crime" but rather to support its education mission through a safe environment and equitable practices, a university is free to develop alternate definitions, processes and consequences that avoid some of the problems of the criminal justice system. Therefore, universities can use broad definitions of sexual violence that might capture behaviour that is not a criminal offence — for example, cyber-sexual violence and online sexual assault (University of Ottawa 2016). Universities can place limits on what is "relevant" for the purpose of responding to a report of sexual violence, as St. Thomas University has done in its code of conduct, wherein it prohibits reliance on the manner of dress or sexual history of the complainant in determining consent (St. Thomas University 2012).

> Because the mandate of a university is not to punish "crime" but rather to support its education mission through a safe environment and equitable practices, a university is free to develop alternate definitions, processes and consequences that avoid some of the problems of the criminal justice system.

Universities can also devise less adversarial adjudicative processes and impose different consequences, all within far shorter timelines than the criminal law response. Thus, instead of the criminal law standard of "proof beyond a reasonable doubt," university policies can use a "preponderance of the evidence" standard. University processes can bar lawyers from participating and can preclude cross-examination of the parties. Universities can also administer consequences that range beyond the criminal law's sanctions of imprisonment, fine and supervision in the community. They can impose apologies, educational measures and limits on the perpetrator's movements on campus, as well as removal from residence, suspension and expulsion, among other possible responses.

But overwhelmingly, post-secondary institutions in Canada have been slow to seize this opportunity to respond to sexual violence on campus. As of 2016, 75 percent had failed to adopt stand-alone sexual assault policies (Kane 2016), leaving sexual violence to be resolved by student codes of conduct or sexual harassment policies. Yet student codes of conduct may require face-to-face confrontation between complainant and defendant or allow the two parties to directly question each other, among other practices.

Processes for sexual harassment complaints may also be inappropriate because they are predominantly focused on mediation as a method of resolution. For example, a *Globe and Mail* study found that at the high end, only two universities saw 26.67 and 22.94 percent, respectively,

> Students criticize informal processes on the bases that they may be administered in a discretionary fashion, no record may be kept, penalties are either small or non-existent and results of an investigation may be kept from the student who reported the misconduct.

resolved formally. The rest were informally resolved, whether by support to the complainant, mediation or education for the perpetrator (Chiose 2016). Data from the University of Toronto's Sexual Harassment Office shows that of the 137 complaints made over the course of 2015, not one resulted in suspension or expulsion (Negrin 2016). Students criticize informal processes on the bases that they may be administered in a discretionary fashion, no record may be kept (Chiose 2016), penalties are either small or non-existent and results of an investigation may be kept from the student who reported the misconduct (Negrin 2016).

It seems clear that harassment processes are not often perceived by students as viable options to respond to harassment, let alone sexual violence. For example, Johnson's campus climate survey at the University of Ottawa found that 78 percent of women students have experienced face-to-face harassment, including 44 percent who experienced unwanted physical contact that would arguably qualify as sexual assault (Johnson 2015b). However, only 6 percent of those harassed and 9 percent of those who said they had been sexually assaulted had sought aid from the University, including the human rights office.

Some universities launched task forces and committed to revised policies aimed at education, prevention and punishment of sexual violence on campus (UBC Point Grey Campus Safety Working Group 2015; St. Mary's President's Council 2013; University of Ottawa Task Force on Respect and Equality 2015; UBC's President's Task Force on Gender-based Violence and Aboriginal Stereotypes 2014). But even among those universities that created a stand-alone sexual violence policy, most placed it within a complex web of student codes of conduct and sexual harassment and discrimination policies. Thus, students are faced with university websites that provide conflicting information about to whom the complainant should first report and about how investigations will proceed.

For example, graduate student Mandi Gray challenged York University's claims to have remedied its sexual violence policy. She initiated and later settled a human rights complaint that painted York's policy as "smoke and mirrors": unclear in its application, un-resourced, and contradictory (Hasham 2016; Gray and Pin 2017). These vague policies have the potential to revictimize students who report by, for example, requiring that they consult with the alleged perpetrator's class schedule and figure out how to avoid accidental contact on campus, requiring students to recount their traumatic experiences to several different individuals or forcing them to participate in adjudicative processes regardless of their wishes.

Ontario women's groups and the provincial government began by providing guidance and encouragement to post-secondary institutions to develop policies and protocols for sexual violence (Ontario Women's Directorate 2013; METRAC Action on Violence 2014). Ontario then enacted legislation (Ontario 2016a) and regulations that require universities and colleges to develop policies and protocols, in cooperation and consultation with students, that address raising awareness about sexual violence, preventing and reporting sexual assault, training of students, staff and faculty, developing complaint mechanisms and response protocols and making public their activities and data. Ontario's regulations further demand that universities provide detailed information to students regarding the processes for investigation and adjudication, including the "due process" measures the institution provides, the rights to legal or other representation and the available appeal processes (Ontario 2016a).

Ontario's lead was soon followed by BC (British Columbia 2016), as well as Manitoba (Manitoba 2017), Quebec (Quebec 2017) and PEI (Prince Edward Island 2020). Other provinces like Nova Scotia and Alberta have thus far developed guidelines for the development of sexual violence policies rather than legislation (Patel and Roesch 2018).

Some of these acts have imposed additional requirements. For example, Section 3 of Quebec's law specifies that: "The policy must take into account persons at greater risk of experiencing sexual violence, such as persons from sexual or gender minorities, cultural communities or Native communities, foreign students and persons with disabilities." The laws of Manitoba and PEI both state that the policy "must be culturally sensitive and reflect the perspectives of the populations most vulnerable to sexual violence." Quebec also requires that institutions resolve sexual violence complaints within ninety days. But apart from these specifics, and requirements that support and accommodation be made available to students regardless of whether they engage a formal disciplinary process to condemn sexual violence committed against them, and prohibiting universities from requiring that victims participate in adjudicative processes, these laws have not provided detailed guidance to post-secondary institutions regarding the content of their policies.

Critics have identified many difficulties with the resulting university sexual violence policies. There are multiple inconsistencies across post-secondary institutions' policies, even within individual provinces, generating confusion among students and rendering the policies vulnerable to legal challenge (Sheehy and Gilbert 2017). Most policies have failed to grapple in any serious way with intersectionality, colonialism and anti-racism (Ostridge 2020; Bourassa et al. 2017), leaving the structural nature of sexual violence unaddressed and treating sexual violence as solely a problem of errant individuals (Gardiner et al. 2019). Further, universities have focused on increased security measures as a response to campus sexual violence, without acknowledging that "securitization" rebounds negatively on racialized students targeted for surveillance (Brockbank 2021), replicates many of the problems that drive women away from reporting to police (Brockbank 2021) and subtly shifts the responsibility to women to exercise vigilance for their own safety (Trusolino 2017; Gray and Pin 2017).

FUTURE CHALLENGES

Responses to campus sexual assault are evolving rapidly in Canada, as legislation, litigation and student activism emerge and converge. Given that some of the provincial laws require universities to consult only students — and not others, such as women's anti-violence advocates — in their development of sexual violence policies, given the vagueness of provincial laws as to the optimal model for resolving allegations of sexual violence, as well as their lack of experience in adjudicating sexual violence, and combined with the agitation of men's rights and anti-feminist groups on campuses, we can expect turmoil and uncertainty in the years to come as sexual violence policies are tested on campus, in the courts and in the media.

> We can expect turmoil and uncertainty in the years to come as sexual violence policies are tested on campus, in the courts and in the media.

First, while it is laudable that provincial governments are legislating that student voices be included in devising responses, there are serious problems with this direction. The laws give no indication as to which students or groups must have a voice or whose input should be valued, leaving universities free to consult with individual students or groups of their choosing. Some student advocacy groups like Silence is Violence have asked for meaningful and ongoing engagement from their university but have not been successful in achieving that request (Gray, Pin and Cooper 2019). Black students' organizations and those representing Indigenous students will also have valuable contributions to ensure that sexual violence policies respond to intersecting forms of oppression, but there are no formal mechanisms to ensure that universities listen. Further, even when student groups have the ear of their university, they may lack the broader or systemic understanding of men's sexual violence needed to inform policy development. They may also lack the continuity to shape university policy over the longer term given that turnover is the norm in student groups as they graduate. This gap, or legislative preference to require universities to negotiate with individual students or campus student groups rather than women's or other outside organizations, may temper the sexual violence policies that are adopted and jeopardize their potential.

To some extent, this gap has been addressed by the Canadian Federation of Students (CFS) and Students for Consent Culture (SFCC), two national student groups that advocate for improved legislation at the national and provincial level as well as conduct research and provide resources for campus-based student organizations (Canadian Federation of Students 2015; Salvino, Gilchrist and Cooligan-Pang 2017). For example, the SFCC developed a student-led action plan and scorecard system known as "Our Turn." This initiative helps student unions evaluate their university's sexual violence policy and advocate for improvements. The SFCC also provides a checklist, an open letter template and a series of advocacy best practices for student unions to follow. In addition to this project, the SFCC is conducting a mixed-methods study investigating power dynamics and coercion at universities related to the professors who perpetrate sexual violence and harassment against students (Students for Consent Culture 2021).

However, there is no guarantee that SFCC's best practices will be adopted by universities, and further, even national student groups may lack a sense of history of the women's anti-violence movement — what has been theorized from decades of experience, what has been tried and failed and where current resources and struggles are focused. Although initially universities relied on frontline rape crisis centres to assist them with sexual violence training and policy development, some institutions have now pushed the activists out, ignoring their expertise, raising the spectre of the "institutionalization" of sexual violence policies (Ricci and Bergeron 2019: 1303) and risking depoliticization of the issues and "technical professionalization" of campus sexual violence (Brockbank 2021: 9; Gardiner et al. 2019).

Second, provincial governments' decisions to leave the development of the details of sexual violence policies to individual institutions means that universities must each seek to find their own balance somewhere between quasi-criminal and restorative justice approaches, but without any guidance or model policies. As mentioned earlier, women students are already instigating complaints to provincial human rights bodies about university policy failures (Kane 2016). Women students report that campus processes too closely resemble the criminal courts, taking months and months to resolve complaints and using untrained campus security and investigators who adhere to rape myths. As one student recently reported, "I felt like my dignity was already stolen and whatever power I had left in me they took that away from me as well … I expect the university to handle these cases seriously and be able to eliminate second victimization. The process that the university has, it's basically oppressive to these individuals. It oppresses them instead of empowering them" (CBC 2021). The student sought judicial review of the University of Windsor's flawed process that resulted in her complaint being dismissed, and the court has ordered the University to proceed with adjudication (*Jane Doe v. University of Windsor* 2021).

This lean towards quasi-criminal models carries none of the benefits of a criminal process. For example, rather than providing an open and transparent process, many policies impose non-disclosure agreements that bind women to secrecy about their allegations and the outcomes. Women themselves are deprived of information about the results of investigations and the measures taken in consequence, if any. Worse still, women who report to campus authorities are vulnerable to being penalized for allegedly falsely reporting sexual violence or for alcohol and drug consumption. And finally, although these policies have imposed confidentiality obligations on women students who report based on universities' competing obligations under privacy laws (Shariff, Bellehumeur and Friesen 2020), they have done so without protecting women students from invasions of their privacy by banning reliance on women's sexual histories by men accused of sexual violence against them (Clarke 2021).

Third and finally, campus sexual assault sits within a much larger political and legal context in which men are contesting campus adjudications of responsibility by seeking judicial review and arguing that their "due process" rights have been violated. The pattern has emerged powerfully in the US, whereby universities are being sued by lawyers representing aggrieved male students who have been found responsible for sexual assault and disciplined by academic sanctions, such as through suspension or expulsion (Gutierrez 2016). These lawsuits challenge university findings on the basis of violation of fundamental fairness because, for example, they have denied the respondent student access to legal representation or to an appeal process, among other issues. This context, as well as the litigation efforts of some male students (Seymour 2015; *Allen v. Students' Society of McGill* 2021) and professors (*Brock University v. Brock University Faculty Association* 2018; *Ryerson University v. Ryerson Faculty Association* 2018) ought to caution universities and student groups to tread carefully in devising campus policies. For example, former UBC professor Steven Galloway has initiated legal action in defamation against a student who reported him for sexual violence as well as against two dozen other individuals, including two professors, for repeating her claims on social media (Quan 2021).

When university disciplinary processes are reviewed by courts, they impose generalized standards of fairness described as "justification, transparency, and intelligibility" (*AlGhaithy v. University of Ottawa* 2012). This means setting up mechanisms for the investigation of the allegation, ensuring that the investigator is not also the adjudicator, allowing both parties to provide written submissions and to see both the investigator's report and each other's submissions, providing reasons for any decision and providing avenues for appeal to both parties. In cases where consequences for students are considered "serious," such as loss of an academic year, some judges have ruled that the student is entitled to legal representation and the right to cross-examine witnesses (*Telfer v. University of Western Ontario* 2012; *Hajee v. York University* 1985).

Although the provincial laws require that sexual violence policies articulate what due process measures will be provided, universities are free to pick and choose these measures, allowing for considerable variance among universities. In turn, this variability makes it difficult to develop expertise and precedents, and it makes these policies even more vulnerable to legal challenge.

These risks — that policies will be developed without the input of those with the most expertise in women's experience of sexual violence and that universities will err on the side of choosing quasi-criminal models that fail to meet survivors' needs — are only increased by the presence of campus-based men's rights groups dedicated to "pro-redressing what they see as a gender imbalance in the current debate about equality, namely the obvious: That women are more often the victims of sexism and abuse" (McLaren 2015: n.p.). Men's rights activists have launched campaigns at the University of Alberta to remove and replace the anti-rape slogans on posters with "rape-apologist" messages (Sands 2013). One group, the Canadian Association for Equality (CAFE), claims to have set up student groups on sixteen campuses across Canada (Anderson 2016). Their activities have focused on hosting public speaking events for anti-feminists, repositioning men as the victims of women's violence and minimizing women students' sexual violence reports.

Provincial governments and post-secondary institutions in Canada have been forced, by the combined power of individual women students, women's anti-violence advocates and dogged journalism, to set upon the path of generating campus polices for sexual assault. Even as US legal developments suggest that court challenges from male students are a predictable risk of this endeavour, provincial governments are forging ahead with boilerplate legislation that leaves each university to its own designs and hence open to litigation. The lack of policy response grounded in either feminist expertise, with a broader political base to back it, or a collective commitment across and among universities to produce uniform policies and practices, means that the enforcement and defence of campus sexual assault policies will be fraught. In the long

> The lack of policy response grounded in either feminist expertise or a collective commitment across and among universities to produce uniform policies and practices means that the enforcement and defence of campus sexual assault policies will be fraught.

term, therefore, the enterprise of responding to men's violence against women in this context rests where it always has: in the hands of the autonomous women's movement in Canada.

DISCUSSION QUESTIONS

1. This chapter discusses the growing pressures on Canadian post-secondary institutions to develop and enforce policies offering preventative, remedial and disciplinary responses to sexual assaults perpetrated by men against women students. What are the risks that this focus on universities will effectively decriminalize

sexual assault and take pressure off police and the criminal justice system to respond effectively to sexual assault? Are there dangers associated with this effort to hold universities and colleges to account?

2. You may have noticed that this chapter has frequently foregrounded the agents of sexual assault — overwhelmingly men — in discussing the data and the issues. What implicit critique and messaging does the chapter convey by avoiding the passive tense, eschewing nominalization and naming the perpetrators of sexual violence? Is language power? What are the benefits and costs of so overtly naming this form of violence in law and policy?

3. This chapter discusses the roles of the autonomous women's movement, student organizations, the media and government in generating social and legal change in response to sexual violence in post-secondary institutions. What are the structural limits and the potentialities of these sites to contribute to positive change in this regard?

4. In both government policymaking and media, "gender-neutral" linguistic choices have become the norm, even when discussing social problems like men's violence against women. What are the benefits of laws and policies that focus on "gender-based violence"? What do we lose when we discuss "people" or "folks" who commit sexual assault or those who experience it?

5. In this chapter, we have discussed multiple systems of oppression. In thinking about the social structures of race, class, gender, sexuality and dis/ability, what sexual violence policy changes might women students want to request from their universities? What oppressions do you think have not been addressed in this chapter?

GLOSSARY OF KEY TERMS

Advance consent: Consent cannot be obtained when the other person is unconscious, and so in *R v. J.A.* (2011), the defence tried to argue that the complainant had given consent "in advance" of being rendered unconscious through strangulation. The Supreme Court rejected this argument and the concept of advance consent. To be valid in law, consent must be contemporaneous with the sexual activity in question so that participants remain free to change their minds and withdraw consent at any time.

Autonomous women's movement: A feminist movement dedicated to women's liberation from oppression. It is led by women and is independent of institutional support or affiliation. It prioritizes the rights and needs of women and believes in collective functioning.

Bystander intervention: Bystander training, aimed at involving men in preventing and calling out sexual violence, is in place across many campuses in Canada and the US. Bystander programs teach participants to be aware of possible risks before they occur, to challenge the normalization of sexual violence against women, to evaluate the costs and benefits of stepping in and to attempt intervention when possible.

Doctrine of recent complaint: This historical legal doctrine, also called the "hue and cry" doctrine, was premised on the (false) idea that if a woman or girl had truly been raped she would have reported the violation at the first opportunity presented to her. It has been repealed from Canadian law, but defence lawyers continue to argue that delayed disclosure of sexual violence ought to reflect poorly on the woman's credibility.

Due process rights: These are the constitutional legal rights that government must respect when invoking a legal proceeding that may result in loss of life, liberty or property. Due process rights involve certain standards of procedure — such as the individual's right to know the case against them and the right to be heard in one's own defence — that are aimed at ensuring fair treatment through the justice system.

Incapable of consent: In sexual assault law, a person is unable to consent to sexual activity, for example, when they are under the age of fourteen, between the ages of fourteen and sixteen (depending on the age of the other person) and when they are incapable of consent due to mental disability, unconsciousness or incapacitation caused by alcohol or drug intoxication.

Intersectionality: A political and analytical framework proposed by Black feminist thinkers that incorporates multiple systems of power in the analysis of oppression in social life. These systems of power include the socially constructed structures of race, class, gender, sexuality and ability (to name a few) acting as oppressions or privileges depending on social location.

Preponderance of the evidence: A legal standard of proof (also called proof on a balance of probabilities) used in civil (as opposed to criminal) proceedings. Rather than "proof beyond a reasonable doubt," which is required for the Crown to prove that the accused committed a criminal offence, this standard requires only that the pursuer prove that it is more likely than not that the prohibited act occurred.

Sexual history evidence: Evidence of the complainant's prior sexual activity, whether with the alleged perpetrator or any other person. Because lawyers can use sexual history evidence to intimidate and humiliate the woman, and because its introduction has an unreasonable and prejudicial impact upon fact-finding, it is generally prohibited under Canadian law in the absence of a compelling case for its relevance.

Standing: Only lawyers with standing can participate and advocate before a judge or a jury. In the criminal trial, only the Crown and the defence have standing, unless the defence attempts to secure access to the complainant's private records (in which case, her counsel has standing to oppose the motion) or a successful motion is made by a lawyer to the judge for standing for a particular aspect of a trial.

RESOURCES FOR ACTIVISTS

Black Lives Matter: blacklivesmatter.com
Canadian Association of Sexual Assault Centres: casac.ca
Canadian Federation of Students: cfs-fcee.ca
METRAC (Action on Violence): metrac.org
Ontario Coalition of Rape Crisis Centres: ocrcc.ca
Ontario Women's Directorate: women.gov.on.ca/english/
Silence is Violence: silenceisviolenceatyork.wordpress.com
Students for Consent Culture: sfcccanada.org
Vancouver Rape Relief and Women's Shelter: rapereliefshelter.bc.ca

REFERENCES

AlGhaithy v. University of Ottawa. 2012 ONSC 142.
Allen v. Students' Society of McGill University. 2021 QCCS 1165.
Anderson, J. 2016. "Men's Issues on Campus: Examining Men's Groups on Canadian Campuses and the Controversy Surrounding Them." *The Charlatan*, March 22. <charlatan.ca/2016/03/mens-issues-on-campus-examining-mens-groups-on-canadian-campuses-and-the-controversy-surrounding-them/>.
Bailey, I. 2013. "RCMP Hunting Serial Predator in UBC Sexual Assaults." *Globe and Mail*, October 29. <theglobeandmail.com/news/british-columbia/one-suspect-now-believed-responsible-for-six-ubc-campus-sex-assaults/article15141220/>.
Block, P. 2000. "Sexuality, Fertility and Danger: Twentieth Century Images of Women with Cognitive Disabilities." *Sexuality and Disability* 18, 4.
Bourassa, C., M. Bendig, E.J. Oleson et al. 2017. "Campus Violence, Indigenous Women, and the Policy Void." In E. Quinlan, A. Quinlan, C. Fogel et al. (eds.), *Sexual Assault on Canadian University and College Campuses*. Waterloo: Wilfrid Laurier University Press.
Boyle, C. 1984. *Sexual Assault*. Toronto: Carswell.
British Columbia. 2016. *Sexual Violence and Misconduct Policy Act*. S.B.C. Chapter 23.
Brock University v. Brock University Faculty Association. 2018 CanLII 125959.
Brockbank, M. 2021. "'Well-Intentioned in Some of the Most Dangerous Ways': Examining Bill-132 and the Subsequent Formation of Ontario University Sexual Assault Policies." *Journal for Social Thought* 5, 1.
Buchwald, E., P.R. Fletcher, and M. Roth. 2005. *Transforming a Rape Culture*, 2nd edition. Minneapolis:

Milkweed Editions.

Burczycka, M. 2020. "Students' Experiences of Unwanted Sexualized Behaviours and Sexual Assault at Postsecondary Schools in the Canadian Provinces, 2019." *Statistics Canada*, September 14. <www150.statcan.gc.ca/n1/pub/85-002-x/2020001/article/00005-eng.htm>.

Canadian Federation of Students. 2015. *Sexual Violence on Campus*. <cfs-fcee.ca/wp-content/uploads/2018/10/Sexual-Violence-on-Campus.pdf>.

Canadian Judicial Council. 2017. *Report to the Minister of Justice. Inquiry into the Conduct of the Honourable Justice Robin Camp*. <cjc-ccm.ca/cmslib/general/Camp_Docs/2017-03-08%20Report%20to%20Minister.pdf>.

Cantor, D., B. Fisher, S. Chibnall et al. 2015. *Report on the* AAU *Campus Climate Survey on Sexual Assault and Sexual Misconduct*. September 21. <aau.edu/sites/default/files/%40%20Files/Climate%20Survey/AAU_Campus_Climate_Survey_12_14_15.pdf>.

CBC. 2021. "University of Windsor Erred in Handling Student's Sexual Assault Complaint, Court Rules." May 20. <cbc.ca/news/canada/windsor/windsor-university-sexual-assault-complaint-handling-errors-court-rules-1.6031001>.

____. 2015. "Ottawa Woman Says Police Told Her Assault Was 'Misunderstanding.'" November 6. <cbc.ca/news/canada/ottawa/ottawa-woman-says-police-told-her-sexual-assault-was-misunderstanding-1.3307830>.

____. 2014a. "Allan Rock Calls University of Ottawa Incident 'Repugnant.'" March 5. <cbc.ca/news/canada/ottawa/allan-rock-calls-university-of-ottawa-incidents-repugnant-1.2561604>.

____. 2014b. "Anne-Marie Roy, UOttawa Student Leader, Subject of Explicit Online Chat." March 2. <cbc.ca/news/canada/ottawa/anne-marie-roy-uottawa-student-leader-subject-of-explicit-online-chat-1.2556948>.

____. 2013a. "Lakehead Student's Rape Allegation Prompts Task Force." October 22. <cbc.ca/m/news/canada/thunder-bay/lakehead-student-s-rape-allegation-prompts-task-force-1.2159004>.

____. 2013b. "UBC Frosh Students Sing Pro-Rape Chant." September 7. <cbc.ca/news/canada/british-columbia/ubc-investigates-frosh-students-pro-rape-chant-1.1699589>.

Ceolin, C. 2021. "How Survivors of Sexual Assault Fight the Courts to Get Justice." *CityNews*, March 9. <toronto.citynews.ca/2021/03/09/how-sexual-assault-survivors-fight-the-courts-to-get-justice/>.

Chiose, S. 2016. "Justice on Campus." *Globe and Mail*, April 1. <theglobeandmail.com/news/national/education/canadian-universities-under-pressure-to-formalize-harassment-assaultpolicies/article29499302/>.

Clarke, K. 2021. "Province Aims to Ban Universities, Colleges from Probing Survivors' Sexual Pasts." *Hamilton Spectator*, January 27. <thespec.com/news/hamilton-region/2021/01/27/province-pledges-to-strengthen-sexual-violence-policy-laws-for-universities-colleges.html>.

Craig, E. 2018. *Putting Trials on Trial: Sexual Assault and the Failure of the Legal Profession*. Montreal and Kingston: McGill-Queen's University Press.

Crawford, A., and J.P. Tasker. 2016. "Robin Camp, Federal Court Judge, Faces Inquiry after Berating Sexual Assault Complainant." CBC, January 7. <cbc.ca/news/politics/federal-court-judge-robin-camp-inquiry-1.3393539>.

Criminal Code of Canada. R.S.C. 1985, Chapter C-46.

Deer, S. 2015. *The Beginning and End of Rape: Confronting Sexual Violence in Native America*. Minneapolis: University of Minnesota Press.

DeKeseredy, W., and K. Kelly. 1993. "Woman Abuse in University and College Dating Relationships: The Contribution of the Ideology of Familial Patriarchy." *Journal of Human Justice* 4, 2.

DeKeseredy, W., M. Schwartz, and K. Tait. 1993. "Sexual Assault and Stranger Aggression on a Canadian University Campus." *Sex Roles* 28, 5.

Du Mont, J. 2003. "Charging and Sentencing in Sexual Assault Cases: An Exploratory Examination." *Canadian Journal of Women and the Law* 15, 2.

Du Mont, J., S. MacDonald, N. Rotbard et al. 2009. "Factors Associated with Suspected Drug-Facilitated Sexual Assault." *Canadian Medical Association Journal* 180, 5.

DuBois, Teresa. 2012. "Police Investigation of Sexual Assault Complaints: How Far Have We Come Since Jane Doe?" In E. Sheehy (ed.), *Sexual Assault in Canada: Law, Legal Practice and Women's Activism*. Ottawa: University of Ottawa Press.

Freeman, L. 2019. "#Metoo and Philosophy." *Newsletter on Feminism and Philosophy* 19, 1.

Gardiner, R.A., M. Shockness, J. Almquist and H. Finn. 2019. "Politics Versus Policies: Fourth Wave Feminist Critiques of Higher Education's Response to Sexual Violence." *Journal of Women and Gender in Higher Education* 12, 3.

Garza, A. 2016. "A Herstory of the #BlackLivesMatter Movement." In J. Hobson (ed.), *Are All the Women Still White? Rethinking Race, Expanding Feminisms*. Albany: SUNY Press.

Gillis, M. 2016. "Suspect Arrested at Airport in Relation to 2016 Sex-Assault Allegations." *Ottawa Citizen*, August 12. <ottawacitizen.com/news/local-news/suspect-arrested-at-airport-in-2015-sex-assault-allegations>.

Globe and Mail. 2016. "No Charges for Man Accused of Sexually Assaulting Women at UVic." April 8. <theglobeandmail.com/news/british-columbia/no-charges-for-man-accused-of-sexually-assault-ing-four-women-at-uvic/article29575761/>.

Gray, M., and L. Pin. 2017. "'I Would Like It if Some of Our Tuition Went to Providing Pepper Spray for Students': University Branding, Securitization and Campus Sexual Assault at a Canadian University." *Annual Review of Interdisciplinary Justice Research* 6.

Gray, M., L. Pin and A. Cooper. 2019. "The Illusion of Inclusion in York University's Sexual Assault Policymaking Process." In K. Malinen (ed.), *Dis/Consent: Perspectives on Sexual Consent and Sexual Violence*. Black Point, NS: Fernwood Publishing.

Gutierrez, T. 2016. "Colleges Slammed with Lawsuits from Men Accused of Sex Crimes." CBS News, March 23. <cbsnews.com/news/colleges-slammed-with-lawsuits-from-men-accused-of-sex-crimes/>.

Hajee v. York University. 1985 11 OAC 72.

Hampson, S. 2015. "How the Dentistry-School Scandal Has Let Loose a Torrent of Anger at Dalhousie." *Globe and Mail*, March 6. <theglobeandmail.com/news/national/education/how-the-dentistry-school-scandal-has-let-loose-a-torrent-of-anger-at-dalhousie/article23344495/>.

Hasham, A. 2016. "Mandi Gray Settles Human Rights Complaint with York University over Sex Assault Policies." *Toronto Star*, December 12. <thestar.com/news/gta/2016/12/12/mandi-gray-settles-hu-man-rights-complaint-with-york-university-over-sex-assault-policies.html>.

Hill, D. 2015. "Two Reasons Canadians Are Confused about Sexual Consent." *Huffington Post*, May 28. <huffpost.com/archive/ca/entry/sexual-consent-confusion_b_7453718>.

Holmes, C.M. 2016. "The Colonial Roots of the Racial Fetishization of Black Women." *Black & Gold* 2. <openworks.wooster.edu/blackandgold/vol2/iss1/2>.

Htun, M., and S.L. Weldon. 2012. "The Civic Origins of Progressive Policy Change: Combatting Violence Against Women in a Global Perspective, 1975–2005." *American Political Science Review* 106, 3.

Jane Doe v. University of Windsor. 2021 ONSC 2990.

Johnson, H. 2015a. "Improving the Police Response to Crimes of Violence Against Women: Ottawa Women Have Their Say." *Faculty of Social Sciences University of Ottawa*. <socialsciences.uottawa.ca/criminology/sites/socialsciences.uottawa.ca.criminology/files/h.johnson_research_summary.pdf>.

___. 2015b. "Campus Climate Survey." *Report of the Task Force on Respect and Equality: Ending Sexual Violence at the University of Ottawa*. <uottawa.ca/president/sites/www.uottawa.ca.president/files/report-of-the-task-force-on-respect-and-equality.pdf>.

___. 2015c. "Degendering Violence." *Social Politics* 22, 3.

___. 2012. "Limits of a Criminal Justice Response: Trends in Police and Court Processing of Sexual Assault." In E. Sheehy (ed.), *Sexual Assault in Canada: Law, Legal Practice and Women's Activism*. Ottawa: University of Ottawa Press.

Justice, D. 2013. "What's Wrong with the CUS FROSH Pocahontas Chant?" *Artswire* UBC, September 20. <wire.arts.ubc.ca/featured/whats-wrong-with-the-cus-frosh-pocahontas-chant/>.

Kane, L. 2016. "Sexual Assault Policies Lacking at Most Canadian Universities, Say Students." CBC,

March 7. <cbc.ca/news/british-columbia-universities-sex-assault-policies-1.3479314>.

Keller, J., K. Mendes and J. Ringrose. 2018. "Speaking 'Unspeakable Things': Documenting Digital Feminist Responses to Rape Culture." *Journal of Gender Studies* 27, 1.

Krebs, C.P., C.H. Lindquist, T.D. Warner et al. 2007. *The Campus Sexual Assault (CSA) Study*. Washington: National Institute of Justice. <ncjrs.gov/pdffiles1/nij/grants/221153.pdf>.

Law Society of Ontario. 2000. *Rules of Professional Conduct*. <lso.ca/about-lso/legislation-rules/rules-of-professional-conduct>.

Lawson, H. 2020. "Defunding the Police: What Will It Mean for Survivors of Sexual Violence?" *The Monitor,* June 24. <monitormag.ca/articles/defunding-the-police-what-will-it-mean-for-survivors-of-sexual-violence>.

Laychuk, R. 2016. "Brandon University Sexual Assault Victims Forced to Sign Contract that Keeps Them Silent." CBC News, April 5. <cbc.ca/news/brandon-university-behavioural-contract-1.3520568>.

Lazar, R. 2010. "Negotiating Sex: The Legal Construct of Consent in Cases of Wife Rape in Ontario, Canada." *Canadian Journal of Women and the Law* 22, 2.

Lisak, D., and P.M. Miller. 2002. "Repeat Rape and Multiple Offending Among Undetected Rapists." *Violence and Victims* 17, 1.

Lum, Z. 2018. "Canadian Universities to Face Funding Cuts if They Fail to Address Campus Sexual Assaults." *Huffington Post,* February 27. <huffpost.com/archive/ca/entry/budget-2018-universities-funding-cuts-sex-assault-campus_a_23372615>.

Malamuth, N., and K. Dean. 1991. "Attraction to Sexual Aggression." In A. Parrot and L. Bechofer (eds.), *Acquaintance Rape: The Hidden Crime*. New York: Wiley.

Manitoba. 2017. *Sexual Violence Awareness and Prevention Act*. S.M. Chapter 20.

Martin, P.Y. 2016. "The Rape Prone Culture of Academic Contexts: Fraternities and Athletics." *Gender & Society* 30, 1.

Mathieu, E., and J. Poisson. 2014. "Canadian Post-Secondary Institutions Failing Sex Assault Victims." *Toronto Star*, November 20. <thestar.com/news/2014/11/20/_postsecondary_schools_failing_sex_assault_victims.html>.

McLaren, L. 2015. "How Men's Rights Groups Are Distorting the Debate about Equality." *Globe and Mail,* March 13. <theglobeandmail.com/life/relationships/leah-mclaren-are-men-really-the-victims/article23426535/>.

METRAC (Metropolitan Action Committee) Action on Violence Against Women and Children. 2014. *Sexual Assault Policies on Campus: A Discussion Paper*. <metrac.org/resources/sexual-assault-policies-on-campus-a-discussion-paper-2014/>.

Negrin, S. 2016. "Sexual Assault Looks Different than We Think and University Policy Must Reflect That." *Ottawa Citizen,* May 11. <ottawacitizen.com/opinion/columnists/negrin-sexual-assault-looks-different-than-we-think-and-university-policy-must-reflect-that>.

Nicholson, B., and N. Martins. 2021. "Survivors of Sexual Violence at Western University Spark Nationwide Conversations." *CityNews,* September 22. <citynews.ca/2021/09/22/sexual-violence-western-university-canada/>.

Nicol, J. 2013. "Under-Reporting and Low Conviction Rates for Sexual Assault." Library of Parliament Research Publications, April 17, *HillNote* 2013-16-E.

O'Connor, L. and T. Kingkade. 2016. "If You Don't Get Why Campus Rape Is A National Problem, Read This." *Huffpost,* June 24. <huffpost.com/entry/sexual-assault-explainer_n_5759aa2fe4b0ced-23ca74f12>.

Ontario. 2016a. *Sexual Violence and Harassment Action Plan Act*. S.O. Chapter 2.

____. 2016b. Regulation 131/16. *Sexual Violence at Colleges and Universities*.

Ontario Women's Directorate. 2013. *Developing a Response to Sexual Violence: A Resource Guide for Ontario's Colleges and Universities*. <citizenship.gov.on.ca/owd/ending-violence/campus_guide.shtml>.

Ostridge, L. 2020. "Speaking Freely and Freedom of Speech: Why Is Black Feminist Thought Left Out of Ontario University Sexual Violence Policies?" *Atlantis Journal* 41, 1.

Patel, U., and R. Roesch. 2018. "Campus Sexual Assault: Examination of Policy and Research." *Journal of Aggression, Conflict and Peace Research* 10, 2.

Perreault, S. 2015. "Criminal Victimization in Canada, 2014." Statistics Canada. <www150.statcan.gc.ca/n1/pub/85-002-x/2015001/article/14241-eng.htm#archived>.

Perreault, S., and S. Brennan. 2010. "Criminal Victimization in Canada, 2009." Statistics Canada. <www150.statcan.gc.ca/n1/pub/85-002-x/2010002/article/11340-eng.htm#wb-cont>.

Prince Edward Island. 2020. *Post-Secondary Institutions Sexual Violence Policies Act.* S.P.E.I. Chapter 56.

Quan, D. 2021. "She Accused a UBC Prof of Sexual Assault. Now He's Suing for Defamation. Some Fear the 'Landmark' Case Could Have a Chilling Effect." *Toronto Star*, April 8. <thestar.com/news/2021/04/08/she-accused-a-university-prof-of-sexual-assault-now-hes-suing-for-defamation-some-fear-the-landmark-case-could-have-a-chilling-effect.html>.

Quebec. 2017. *An Act to Prevent and Fight Sexual Violence in Higher Education Institutions.* S.Q. Chapter 32.

R v. Barton, 2019 SCC 33.

R v. Ewanchuk 1999, 1 SCR 330.

R v. J.A., 2011 SCC 28.

R v. M. (M.L.), [1994] 2 SCR 3.

R v. Osvath (1996), 46 CR (4th) 124 (Ont CA).

R v. Schmaltz, 2015 ABCA 4.

R v. Wagar, 2015 ABCA 327.

Rentschler, C. 2014. "Rape Culture and the Feminist Politics of Social Media." *Girlhood Studies* 7.

Ricci, S., and M. Bergeron. 2019. "Tackling Rape Culture in Quebec Universities: A Network of Feminist Resistance." *Violence Against Women* 25, 1.

Roberts, T. 2017. "Free Legal Advice for Survivors of Sexual Assault Through NL Pilot Program." CBC News, April 25. <cbc.ca/news/newfoundland-labrador/sexual-assault-legal-advice-1.4084187>.

Rotenberg, C., and A. Cotter. 2018. "Police-Reported Sexual Assaults in Canada Before and After #MeToo, 2016 and 2017." Statistics Canada. <www150.statcan.gc.ca/n1/pub/85-002-x/2018001/article/54979-eng.htm#wb-cont>.

Ryerson University v. Ryerson Faculty Association. 2018 OLAA No. 370.

Salvino, C., K. Gilchrist, and J. Cooligan-Pang. 2017. "Our Turn: A National Action Plan to End Campus Sexual Violence." Montreal: *Student's Society of McGill University.* <ssmu.ca/wp-content/uploads/2018/03/our_turn_action_plan_final_english_web2.pdf?x26516>.

Sands, A. 2013. "'Troubling' Posters that Parody Successful 'Don't Be That Guy' Anti-Rape Campaign Appear in Edmonton." *National Post*, July 10. <nationalpost.com/news/troubling-posters-that-parody-successful-dont-be-that-guy-anti-rape-campaign-appear-in-edmonton>.

Sawa, T., and L. Ward. 2015a. "Sex Assault Reporting on Canadian Campuses Worryingly Low, Say Experts." CBC News, February 6. <cbc.ca/news/canada/sex-assault-reporting-on-canadian-campuses-worryingly-low-say-experts-1.2948321>.

____. 2015b. "UBC Sex Assault Reports Out of Sync with Police Statistics." CBC News, February 9. <cbc.ca/news/canada/ubc-sex-assault-reports-out-of-sync-with-police-statistics-1.2950264>.

Senn, C.Y., M. Eliasziw, P. Barata et al. 2015. "Efficacy of a Sexual Assault Resistance Program for University Women." *New England Journal of Medicine* 372, 24.

Seymour, A. 2015. "Hockey Players Can Sue U of O, Judge Rules." *Ottawa Citizen,* July 10. <ottawacitizen.com/news/local-news/hockey-players-can-sue-u-of-o-judge-rules>.

Shariff, S., J. Bellehumeur, and B. Friesen. 2020. "Privacy and Protection vs Accountability and Transparency." In D. Crocker, J. Minaker and A. Nelund (eds.), *Violence Interrupted: Confronting Sexual Violence on University Campuses.* Montreal: McGill-Queen's University Press.

Sheehy, E. 2012. "Judges and the Reasonable Steps Requirement: The Judicial Stance on Perpetration Against Unconscious Women." In E. Sheehy (ed.), *Sexual Assault in Canada: Law, Legal Practice and Women's Activism.* Ottawa: University of Ottawa Press.

Sheehy, E., and D. Gilbert. 2017. "Responding to Sexual Assault on Campus: What Can Canadian Universities Learn from US Law and Policy?" In E. Quinlan, A. Quinlan, C. Fogel et al. (eds.), *Sexual*

Assault on Canadian University and College Campuses. Waterloo: Wilfrid Laurier University Press.

Sheehy, E., L. Gotell and I. Grant. 2020. "The Misogyny of the So-Called Rough Sex Defence." *Policy Options,* January 31. <policyoptions.irpp.org/magazine/january-2020/the-misogyny-of-the-so-called-rough-sex-defence/>.

Sheehy, E., and J. Tolmie. 2019. "Feminist Interventions: Learning from Canada." *New Zealand Women's Law Journal* 2.

Sibley, R. 2016. "Police Lay Sexual Assault Charges in Three-Month-Old Case." *Ottawa Citizen,* January 4. <ottawacitizen.com/news/local-news/police-lay-sexual-assault-charges-in-three-month-old-case>.

St. Mary's President's Council. 2013. *Promoting a Culture of Safety, Respect and Consent at St. Mary's University and Beyond.* December 15. <smu.ca/webfiles/PresidentsCouncilReport-2013.pdf>.

St. Thomas University. 2012. "Disciplinary Processes for Cases of Social Misconduct, Appendix B, *Procedures with Respect to Sexual Assault Complaints by Students.*" December. <stu.ca/media/stu/site-content/current-students/registrarx27s-office/academic-calendar/2017-2018/2015-2016/7Regulations.pdf>.

Statistics Canada. 2015. *Self-Reported Victimization, 2014.* <www150.statcan.gc.ca/n1/daily-quotidien/151123/dq151123a-eng.htm#wb-info>.

___. 1994. *Violence Against Women Survey, 1993.* <www23.statcan.gc.ca/imdb/p2SV.pl?Function=getSurvey&SDDS=3896>.

Strain, M.L., J.M. Hockett, and D. Saucier. 2015. "Precursors to Rape: Pressuring Behaviors and Rape Proclivity." *Violence and Victims* 30, 2.

Students for Consent Culture. 2021. *Open Secrets Project, Power and Professors: A Study on Rape Culture and Accountability of Canadian Post-Secondary Institutions.* <sfcccanada.org/open-secrets-report>.

Taber, J. 2013. "Saint Mary's Student President Says Rape Chant Was 'Biggest Mistake… Probably in My Life.'" *Globe and Mail,* September 5. <theglobeandmail.com/news/national/saint-marys-student-president-says-rape-chant-was-biggest-mistake-of-my-life/article14142351>.

Telfer v. University of Western Ontario, 2012 ONSC 1287.

Theodore, H., and J. Gould. 2021. "Roughly 12,000 Attend Western Walkout Against Sexual Violence." *Interrobang,* September 24. <theinterrobang.ca/article?aID=15925>.

Trusolino, M. 2017. "'It's Not About One Bad Apple': The 2007 York University Vanier Residence Rapes." In E. Quinlan, A. Quinlan, C. Fogel et al. (eds.), *Sexual Violence at Canadian Universities.* Waterloo: Wilfrid Laurier University Press.

UBC Campus Security. 2016. "UBC Sexual Assault Statistics." <security.sites.olt.ubc.ca/ubc-sexual-assault-statistics/>.

UBC Point Grey Campus Safety Working Group. 2015. *Interim Report of the* UBC *Point Grey Campus Safety Working Group.* <bog2.sites.olt.ubc.ca/files/2014/09/2.2_2014.09_Campus-Safety-Working-Group.pdf>.

UBC's President's Task Force on Gender-based Violence and Aboriginal Stereotypes. 2014. *Transforming* UBC *and Developing a Culture of Equality and Accountability: Confronting Rape Culture and Colonialist Violence.* <equity2.sites.olt.ubc.ca/files/2014/05/Task-Force-on-IGBVAS-Final-Report-March-28-2014.pdf>.

University of Ottawa. 2016. "Sexual Violence: Support and Prevention." June. <uottawa.ca/sexual-violence-support-and-prevention/definitions>.

University of Ottawa Task Force on Respect and Equality. 2015. *Report of the Task Force on Respect and Equality: Ending Sexual Violence at the University of Ottawa.* <uottawa.ca/president/sites/www.uottawa.ca.president/files/report-of-the-task-force-on-respect-and-equality.pdf>.

Vallaincourt, R. 2010. *Gender Differences in Police-Reported Violent Crime in Canada, 2008.* Ottawa: Canadian Centre for Justice Statistics.

Vandervort, L. 2012. "Legal Subversion of the Criminal Justice Process? Judicial, Prosecutorial and Police Discretion in Edmondson, Kindrat and Brown." In E. Sheehy (ed.), *Sexual Assault in Canada: Law, Legal Practice and Women's Activism.* Ottawa: University of Ottawa Press.

Yung, C. 2017. "Rape Law Gatekeeping." *Boston College Law Review* 58, 1.

Zaccagna, R. 2015. "msvu Dismisses Instructor Who Had Sexual Relationship with Student." [Halifax] *Chronicle Herald,* January 15. <thechronicleherald.ca/metro/1263504-msvu-dismisses-instructor-who-had-sexual-relationship-with-student>.

Zinn, J. 2016. "Charges Recommended Against Uvic Student for Alleged Sexual Assaults." *Saanich News,* March 1. <saanichnews.com/news/charges-recommended-against-uvic-student-for-alleged-sexual-assaults/>.

12

RESISTING CONFORMITY
Women Talk about Their Tattoos

Jessica Antony

YOU SHOULD KNOW THIS

- Tattooing, as defined by Health Canada, is the art of depositing pigment 1–2 mm into the skin, creating a design. A tattoo gun, which is used for this practice, involves a cluster of small needles that vibrate hundreds of times per minute, puncturing the skin to deposit the ink.

- The word "tattoo" is derived from the Tahitian *tatau*, which (according to some translations) means "to mark."

- Researchers examining the mummified body of a 5,300-year-old Tyrolean man, "Otzi the Iceman," is said to have the world's oldest tattoos — sixty-one of them in total.

- In 2016, Nanaia Mahuta, a New Zealand MP (and now minister of foreign affairs), became the first woman to wear a *moko kauae*, a traditional Māori facial tattoo, in Parliament.

- In a 2018 survey of nine thousand people in eighteen countries, Italy ranked as the most tattooed country, with 48 percent of Italians having at least one tattoo. Canada ranked fifteenth, with 33 percent of Canadians having at least one tattoo.

- Employers in Canada have the right not to hire someone based on their tattoos, as long as those tattoos don't have an ethnic, religious or tribal basis.

- A 2019 Canadian survey of six hundred senior managers at companies with over twenty employees found that 15 percent of those managers felt that visible tattoos were and continue to be unacceptable, while 32 percent felt that tattoos were once problematic but are now acceptable.

Sources: Health Canada 2001; Samadelli et al. 2015; Roy 2016; Dalia Research 2018; KCY at Law 2021; Cision Canada 2019

HISTORICALLY, TATTOOS HAVE HAD A NEGATIVE image. From a Western perspective, tattooed bodies were thought to be monstrous — as examples of bodily excess, as sex objects or hypersexual beings, or as primitive, threatening or circus-like spectacles. Tattoos were associated with dangerous underclasses and sexual behaviour — a "destructive decoration that flouts the possibility of untainted flesh" (Braunberger 2000: 1; see also Hawkes, Senn and Thorn 2004). Situated within a racist ideology, tattooing and body art were interpreted not as "the rational choice of an enlightened individual, but constitute[d] instead a primitive response more usually associated with the uncivilized behaviour of savages" (Widdicombe and Wooffitt 1995: 139). Lower class, marginalized people embodied the notion of tattooing — sailor, military man, biker, gang member or prisoner — and were seen as deviant or at least countercultural.

Today, however, what was once a practice reserved for the so-called seedy underbelly of society has become, in the eyes of some, just an appropriated marketing tool. Since the early 2000s, energy drinks — like Inked, Rockstar or Wicked — have used tattoo culture as a marketing tool. Inked, in particular, is aimed at tattooed customers or "those who want to think of themselves as the tattoo type" (Associated Press/CBS News 2007). The drink's can features tribal-style designs, while the promotional posters include the outstretched, tattooed arm of a white male. This new marketing strategy, said 7-Eleven's manager of non-carbonated beverages, was created to sell a drink "that appealed to men and women, and the tattoo culture has really become popular with both genders." Tattooing can be used to sell products to the young or those who, according to 7-Eleven, "think and act young" (Associated Press 2007). In 2015, Coca-Cola released a short video as a part of their Hispanic Heritage month campaign that highlighted Hispanic families and the pride they have in their last names (Melendez 2015). As you might guess, it's not long into the video that a Coca-Cola truck pulls up and hands out cans featuring Hispanic last names. The cans in the ad also feature temporary tattoos of the last names, and in the video we see a man smiling as he adds a "Rodriguez" tattoo to his neck. While the Heritage Tattoo Cans campaign could be seen as a sign that tattoo's dubious past has disappeared, the stereotype of gang members with tattoos on their necks associated with Hispanic men was certainly not lost on critics, who noted: "this attempt to come across as culturally authentic is just cheap, insulting and yucky. (Yes, we said yucky.) It says to us that *orgullo* [pride] will always be for sale to the right bidder" (Latino Rebels 2015).

The Western history of tattooing has posed a conundrum for contemporary North American capitalist culture: in order to create a tattoo market by commodifying tattoos in the pursuit of profit, a distance from this history had to be established. While tattoos were once a form of deviance, they are now much more embedded in mainstream culture — they are made normal through reality television shows such as *Miami Ink, Ink Master* and *Tattoo Nightmares*; through marketing efforts like PETA's "Ink not Mink" campaign; through increasingly tattooed professional athletes and musicians, such as LeBron James, Post Malone and Rihanna; or even simply through the proliferation of tattoo shops and parlours throughout North America. In order to enable their capitalist commodification, tattoos and body art required a social acceptability — especially for the middle-class consumer.

One way in which social acceptability has been accomplished is through appropriating Eastern culture (DeMello 1995, 2000, 2014) — a culture in which tattoos have had considerable significance and mark a rite of passage in the achievement of personal growth. This new generation of tattooing is one that has been defined both by rejecting the traditional association to working-class and underclass meanings and history associated with the practice and by appropriating and creating new meanings, a new history and a new discourse surrounding tattooing practices. The focus of this new generation is on the tattoo as a means of personal and spiritual growth and the creation of individuality (DeMello 2000, 2014), a set of meanings that differs significantly from the working-class meanings traditionally associated with tattooing, such as masculinity and patriotism. Furthermore, the creation of an entirely new history focuses on the roots of tattooing in Japanese and Polynesian cultures, rejecting the association of tattooing with marginalized people who originally introduced the practice to Western society. As well, this new conception of tattooing borrows from the self-help discourse of the 1970s and 1980s, as tattoo enthusiasts now locate tattooing as an identity-altering practice.

Nevertheless, the remnants of Western tattoo history have not been completely erased. There is still the association of tattoos as a sign of difference and resistance. In this regard, the mainstream acceptability and popularity of tattoos have proved problematic for women who want to use tattooing as a means of expressing particular identities. The tattoo is, in this context, strange as it represents at once permanence and change. While in the physical it is permanent (tattoos are difficult and costly to remove from the skin), the meanings surrounding tattoos change over time. The problem for women, then, becomes twofold: within our capitalist and patriarchal society, how do tattooed women negotiate the tension between tattoos as a sign of conformity (to mainstream consumer culture) and one of resistance or reinvention (as a challenge to patriarchal gender roles)? Given the increasingly commodified nature of tattooing in mainstream Western culture, are women's tattoos merely a reflection of that consumerist culture? Or are women's tattoos a flouting of gender roles and resistance to a patriarchal culture that pushes women to act and carry themselves in certain,

> How do tattooed women negotiate the tension between tattoos as a sign of conformity and one of resistance or reinvention?

oppressive ways? Are so-called feminine tattoos — butterflies and flowers, for example — too "soft" to be considered a subversive resistance of patriarchy?

My interest in addressing these questions is not only as a fan of tattoos, but also as a tattooed woman myself. I got my first tattoo when I was eighteen while on a trip to Australia, shortly after I graduated from high school. Since then, I have continued to collect tattoos — including an arm sleeve and a number of large pieces on my legs and ribs. I became interested in the problems of tattoos for women as I experienced some of them myself — feeling unfeminine with such large, prominent tattoos, or thinking about my own tattoos as a commodity in comparison to those whose skin has not been marked this way.

To explore the social and individual meaning of women's tattoos, I spoke with eighteen tattooed women. These women told me the stories of their tattoos: why they got them, how they decided on them and how they feel about them. These tattoo narratives serve as a means of making connections between each tattoo project and a broader historical context, ultimately reconciling for these women the tension between conformity and resistance.

UNPACKING AUTHENTICITY AND COMMODIFICATION

Authenticity, a key theme in my analysis and the women's stories, has a number of meanings. It refers to the desire, expressed by the women I spoke with, to create a legitimate, original self-identity through their tattoo projects; a sincere, long-term commitment to a tattoo; and the sense of uniqueness that comes from being marked as different. The women didn't overtly acknowledge the nuances of authenticity but did so through the ways in which they explained and understood tattooing. Margo DeMello argues that, in appropriating the Eastern history of tattooing, contemporary North American tattoo enthusiasts have created a new tattoo "text." This new tattoo text, in presenting tattoos as a symbol of individuality, allows for tattoos to become a part of the mainstream — it allows for them to be culturally commodified.

Cultural commodification — the repackaging of once "low-class" cultural symbols and those of marginalized people into products for the consumption of the mainstream

— is what bell hooks describes as "eating the Other." She argues that through cultural commodification, the media inundate us with "messages of difference" in which our sense of self-identity can be found in the Other or, in the case of tattoos, in a practice that was once reserved for the marginalized. The Other, then, becomes a product, commodified for the mainstream, as the media tell us that "the 'real fun' is to be had by bringing to the surface all those 'nasty' unconscious fantasies and longings about contact with the Other" (hooks 1992: 21) that are entrenched in Western culture.

Commodification is integral to capitalism. As Karl Marx and Friedrich Engels (1998) argued long ago, in capitalism there is an incessant, relentless search by capitalists for new markets, for constantly pushing the market into areas of human life that have not been turned into products to buy, sell and consume. As they put it in *The Communist Manifesto* over 160 years ago, this process has "resolved personal worth into exchange value, and in place of the numberless indefeasible chartered freedoms, has set up that single, unconscionable freedom — Free Trade" (Marx and Engels 1998: 3).

There are no bounds to the desire to turn everything into products for sale. We see this in the attempts in Canada to make education and knowledge not a human right but a privilege of those able to pay for it (see, for example, Brownlee 2015). This desire to turn everything into a product takes many forms, ranging from the socialization of labour to the privatization of healthcare (see, for example, Parmet 2021). And, as David Graeber (2009: 83) argues, "If community was to be evoked, it was — as in the 'I Love New York' campaign — just another sales gimmick, since, after all, in the neoliberal universe, reality itself is simply whatever you can sell." As we will see, even self-identity is fair game in the push for commodification.

Commodification can indeed be found all around us, whether we're conscious of it or not. One example that has become more and more evident in recent years is the rise of surveillance capitalism. Ultimately an extension of the mass record-keeping we've all grown up with that, in addition to its useful social functions, allows for humans to be tracked and measured — birth certificates, real estate records, educational transcripts, social security numbers — a new kind of data mining was born with the rise of the internet, and especially social media. Whether it's your Google searches, Facebook check-ins, tweets or the hashtags you used on your last Instagram post, these platforms use the data provided by our interactions with these mostly free services to track our current behaviours — spending habits, geographical movements, political and social interests — and then predict our future behaviours, all in the name of advertising dollars. The privatization of the telecommunications industry and legislation that protects corporations like Facebook from liabilities have made it even easier for these tech giants to use our seemingly innocuous online social habits to market products to us and generate profit. Ronald Deibert — director of the award-winning Citizen Lab, an interdisciplinary body based out of the University of

Toronto that studies network surveillance, cyberespionage and internet censorship — explains that the primary customers of social media monitoring are not those of us scrolling Twitter or liking Instagram posts. "The real customers," he says, "are other businesses that are interested in predictions of human behaviour generated by the social media platforms and data analytics machinery that surrounds them. We are simply a means to a larger, commercial end. We're the livestock for their farms" (Deibert 2020: 50). That is, *we* are the product sold to advertisers, the raw data. Those advertisers then use that raw data to determine the products to market back to us and the methods by which to do so to generate profit. Social media, in effect, commodifies *us*.

This process points to the deep underlying dynamic of the commodification imperative: empty the meaning from anything and everything human and humane; reduce all to the essence of capitalism — things, people, emotions and rights are only meaningful as products to be bought and sold as the basis for profit making. Yet is this process complete and all encompassing? Does everyone go along with the commodification imperative?

The new text that is created when the practice of tattooing is appropriated from Eastern cultures is important in making sense of the ways in which the women I spoke with understand their tattoos. But to see this tattoo process as only commodification falls short because it does not recognize that the specific meanings of and narratives surrounding tattoos, political or otherwise, are constantly shifting. The ways in which we talk about tattoos has changed (as analysts like DeMello argue and as can be seen in popular and social media). And it had to for tattoos to reach their place in mainstream culture today. However, though tattoo discourse has changed as tattoos have become commodified, tattoo wearers — particularly women — are not merely marking themselves with a product devoid of any meaning except that of a popular commodity. That is, tattoos are not simply a commodification meant to represent a sense of false individuality — they are more complex than that, and they can represent genuine cultural connections made by women as they undertake their tattoo projects. More generally speaking, the sense of individuality and authenticity that tattoos represent for some women constitute one of the ways in which women negotiate conformity and resistance in a patriarchal, capitalist culture. In this sense, then, cultural commodification is nuanced and, in the case of tattoos as a form of self-identification, the struggle for self-identity is indeed one of the ways in which women confront and resist the ongoing capitalist effort to turn everything into a commodity, including permanent body modifications. The ways in which women negotiate and interpret seemingly traditionally feminine tattoo images also represents women's abilities to be agents

> Tattoos are a window into the process of commodification and the resistance to it in patriarchal capitalism.

resisting patriarchy. While tattoo culture often relegates women to being consumers of acceptably feminine tattoo designs and placements, women frequently create and negotiate their own fluid meanings for their tattoos, thus rejecting the need to conform to socially acceptable forms of expression. Tattoos and tattooing are, then, a window into this process of commodification and the resistance to it in patriarchal capitalism.

TATTOOING'S NORTH AMERICAN HISTORY

Tattooing reaches back thousands of years. It can be found in nearly all parts of the world at some time (Caplan 2000: xi). The practice was eventually appropriated by Canadian and US culture after colonial contact with cultures that revered tattooing. North American colonial tattooing is rooted in the sea voyages of early European travellers of the late eighteenth and early nineteenth centuries. Explorers to the South Pacific came into contact with the tattooed Other in Polynesia, Micronesia and Melanesia. While Europeans had experienced tattooing as early as the 1600s, it was James Cook who first documented the "pervasiveness of 'tattooing' (a derivation of the Tahitian term *ta-tu* or *tatau*) among South Pacific cultures" (Atkinson 2003: 31).

European explorers' exposure to tattooed Indigenous peoples had a profound effect — the explorers saw tattooing as a frightening foreign ritual and saw tattoos as a clear sign of their "savageness." Indigenous peoples were captured and transported back to Europe with the explorers as "living evidence of primitivism in the New World" (Atkinson 2003: 31) and then sold and paraded through European museums and sideshows. Many Indigenous people were baptized and given new, Christian names in an attempt to "liberate" them "from their 'spiritual and physical slavery'" (Oettermann 2000: 195). European sailors returned home decorated with tattoos, exposing the upper and middle classes of European society to the practice and arguably "reaffirming [their] understanding of their own cultural advancement and progress, as the outwardly uncontrolled libidinal bodies of 'backward' tribal cultures of the world articulated a brutality long overcome in Western cultures" (Atkinson 2003: 31).

The practice among South Pacific Islanders changed, too, as a result of colonizers' visits. Tattoo designs soon came to include images such as ships, flags, guns, cannons and even portraits of European royalty. Their meanings shifted, as well. For example, Hawaiian tattoos were once thought to protect the person from harm, but after the introduction of guns and other weapons, the significance of protective tattooing dwindled away. The Māori of New Zealand have traditionally tattooed their faces as a sign of status and lineage. However, after European explorers and colonizers began trading goods for the severed heads of tattooed Māori people they found so fascinating, the Maori stopped tattooing their faces in fear for their lives (Govenar 2000; Atkinson 2003).

Captain Costentenus

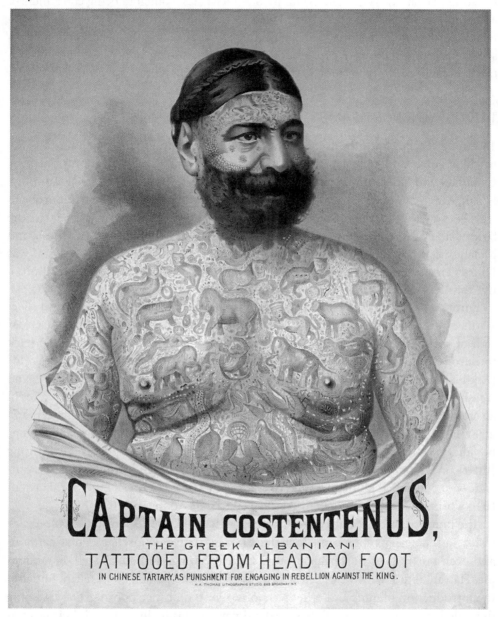

Captain Costentenus, "The Greek Albanian," was first put on display at the 1876 Centennial Exposition and later toured with P.T. Barnum's New and Greatest Show on Earth.

Source: Wikimedia Commons, commons.wikimedia.org/wiki/File:Captain_Costentenus.jpg

During this period, Europeans saw tattooing as both fascinating and deplorable — a paradox of sorts — and interpreted the tattooed body as a source of exotic entertainment. Sailors tattooed their bodies both as a keepsake of their overseas adventures and to set themselves apart from the majority in European society. With more and more sailors coming home with cultural inscriptions permanently marked on their bodies, tattooing started to creep into mainstream European culture and eventually colonial North American culture (Atkinson 2003). In 1876 at the Centennial Exposition in Philadelphia, some of the first tattooed Indigenous people were put on display for the enjoyment and wonder of the audience. Even as members of the Navy were coming home adorned with tattoos, the majority of European and North American society had little to no knowledge of the practice.

Taking their cue from the success of tattooed sideshow performers, tattooed Navy servicemen coming back from overseas started to exhibit themselves in travelling circuses and sideshows. Part of the attraction, however, was the colonial notion of a so-called savage native from a foreign land covered in frightening markings. As the Navy men were obviously of European heritage, they concocted elaborate backstories to accompany their exhibitions. Many would claim to have been captured by Indigenous tribes and tattooed against their will, thus perpetuating the notion of tattooing as the frightening ritual of an "uncivilized Other" (Atkinson 2003).

The designs that were popular largely consisted of patriotic symbols, religious imagery and erotic illustrations of women. These designs, Alan Govenar (2000: 217) argues, constituted a "folk art form" generated by word of mouth and imitation. This folk art provides, to some extent, insight into the cultural context of the time, as tattoo artists were necessarily aware of the demands of their audience. The social coercion that the designs adhered to promoted not only conformity but also tradition, thus serving as a visual representation of important symbols of the day. Primarily patriotic and religious, these designs communicated loyalty, devotion and (oddly enough) conservative morals (Govenar 2000).

By the end of the 1930s, tattoo exhibits were becoming less exciting and exotic as more and more people were becoming tattooed and exposed to tattoos. Tattooed performers then had to develop more elaborate backstories to entice their audiences — such as the "abducted farmer's daughter," who was tattooed against her will — and women, in particular, found it necessary to dress more provocatively in order to maintain the interest of the audience (Govenar 2000: 225). As tattoos became more common, sideshow audiences turned to the circus for entertainment. To attract audiences, women took centre stage as tattooed attractions — women who were often the wives and girlfriends of tattooists or were simply lured into the profession with the promise of fame and fortune (Atkinson 2003). The show then became somewhat pornographic, as women would take the stage and strip before the crowd, displaying their tattooed bodies. These shows became some of the most popular midway attractions through to the 1940s.

Maud Stevens

Maud Stevens Wagner, wife of tattooer Gus Wagner, was a circus performer and one of the first known female tattoo artists in the US.

Source: Wikimedia Commons, commons.wikimedia.org/wiki/File:Maud_Stevens_Wagner.jpeg

The introduction of tattoos into the carnival and sideshow exhibitions ultimately served as a controlled means of exploring desires and emotions that were socially repressed at the time. Tattoos were seen as a form of deviance and tattooed bodies were considered savage and frightening. The sideshows provided the means for "North Americans to experience subversive pleasures with and tortures of the flesh without sacrificing commonly held cultural understandings of corporeal respectability" (Atkinson 2003: 36). In other words, colonial North Americans were able to enjoy these pleasures from a distance, without subjecting their own bodies to the taboo of marking the skin, which was seen as lacking respectability. Indigenous women especially were seen by Europeans as the "radical self-expression, physical vanity, and exuberant sexuality they had denied themselves ... in the service of their restrictive deity" (Atkinson 2003: 31). This era firmly established the association between tattooing and social deviance, a particularly important connection to note as this association has carried through to the present. Returning home after the Second World War, servicemen found that their symbolically patriotic tattoos now held a great deal of negative social value. The significance and patriotism once associated with tattooing started to diminish, and by 1946 new recruits were no longer interested in becoming tattooed. Tattoos were even restricted in the US and Canadian military in the 1950s — if they limited the effectiveness of a man's ability to work (due to infection, for example), he would be prosecuted. In the context of the increasingly urban, family-centred nature of North American culture in the 1950s, tattoos were once again associated with disrepute and deviance. Societal values shifted toward material comfort and middle-class conformity, and tattoos were strongly identified with lower-class, criminal individuals and groups. Once a symbol of group expression and national pride, tattoos were now interpreted as a widespread sign of criminality (Govenar 2000).

THE RADICAL SHIFT TO CONTEMPORARY COMMODIFICATION

The political upheaval of the 1960s and 1970s brought with it a great many cultural shifts, including the popular conception of tattooing. Women began to question and fight normative notions of femininity and gender roles, resurrecting tattoos as a means of redefining themselves as women. Margot Mifflin explains:

> [Women] began casting off their bras as they had their corsets a half-century earlier, tattoos were rescued from ignominy and resurrected in the counter-culture by women who were rethinking womanhood. The arrival of the Pill in 1961 had given women a new sexual freedom; a little over a decade later legalized abortion secured their reproductive rights. Not surprisingly, the

breast became a popular spot for tattoos — it was here that many women inscribed symbols of their newfound sexual independence. (1997: 56)

With the swell of popularity — especially among women — in tattooing, the middle classes slowly became involved in the historically marginalized practice. As musicians, actors and other cultural icons started to embrace tattooing, it enticed young, middle-class people to follow suit. While its popularity was already entrenched among the marginalized classes, the 1960s and 1970s saw an increase in tattooing's appeal among more privileged classes, thus introducing it to the mainstream and drawing widespread attention to the practice. The designs that had held up since the early 1900s, however, were no longer of interest to young people. Not able to identify with the extremely patriotic imagery, they demanded more customized, personal images, which opened up the art to the appropriation of designs from other cultures. Tattoo artists as a whole also became a more artistically educated group in keeping with the demand for more complicated, personalized designs. Young tattoo artists began to see tattooing as a representation of identity, "treating the body as less and less of a canvass to be filled with tattoos and more as an integral part of the self, the young middle-class insurgence into the tattoo artist profession redefined many of the old ideologies held strongly in the trade" (Atkinson 2003: 45). Artists experimented with different styles and shops moved from the urban core to the youth centres of the city.

The 1970s and 1980s saw more people than ever before embrace tattooing as a form of self-expression. Michael Atkinson explains this process:

Influenced by political movements that shook conservative understandings of the body to the ground, interpretations of tattoos were more varied and subject to contextual construction. As women and more "respectable" social classes participated in tattooing it transformed into a practice of political identity construction. (2003: 46)

By the 1990s tattoos had become mainstream phenomena, with scores of tattoo shops cropping up in many major North American cities. Artists had to be able to adapt to new styles, designs and needs of their customer base. New methods of communication, and thus, marketing, brought a whole new dimension to the tattoo industry, with tattoo magazines, websites and online communities developing and flourishing, bringing artists and enthusiasts alike together "into an information-rich community of social actors" (Atkinson 2003: 48). As people are now able to learn more about the process of tattooing via online resources, as well as communicate with tattoo enthusiasts around the world, more and more people are being drawn into the practice as both tattoo artists and tattooees. The Pew Research Center, based in Washington, noted in their 2010 report that "tattoos have become something of a trademark" for Americans entering adulthood (Kwong 2012). By 2018, 33 percent of Canadians had at least one tattoo (Dalia Research 2018). In 2021, 46 percent of Americans had at least one tattoo, with the industry topping $1 billion in the US (not including tattoo removal businesses) (Ibisworld 2021).

As tattooing becomes more and more a mainstream phenomenon, the ability to decipher a tattooed body's authentic membership in a particular counterculture, while once quite apparent, is no longer so easy. Tattoos have become commodified — a trend, an immediate mark of individuality that can be bought and sold. Nevertheless, tattoos still serve as a means of communication. *What* they communicate, however, is more difficult to determine.

APPROPRIATION OR CONNECTION?

A typical non-critical commodification analysis argues that tattoos have become a false representation of self-identity — one that has been appropriated from the so-called dangerous classes and is lacking any real political meaning. Margo DeMello (2000, 2014)[1] makes just such an argument by examining the role of class hierarchy in the tattoo community, coupled with the re-inscription of the culture with the influx of middle-class wearers and artists in the so-called new generation of tattooing.

DeMello begins her investigation by outlining the history of Western tattooing and examines the state of the practice after World War II, as technological, artistic and social changes were affecting tattooing. The introduction of professionally trained tattoo artists, the use of tattooing as a countercultural symbol and the appropriation of exotic designs and images (as opposed to traditional, old-school Americana designs, which were typically highly saturated images of swallows, snakes, anchors, daggers, pin-up girls, ships and hearts, with bold outlines and a colour palette of red, yellow, black and blue) created a shift in the culture, which DeMello refers to as the "Tattoo Renaissance." As a result of this cultural transformation, tattooing began to appeal to a more middle-class clientele. Within the new tattoo generation, there is the distinction between "high" and "low" tattooing practices, which have been perpetuated and maintained within the tattoo culture through media interpretations, academic approaches and publications produced from within the community. Media accounts in particular — those produced both within and outside of the tattoo community — have had a significant effect on the polarization of tattoo culture. Mainstream media have focused on the increased popularity of tattooing among more conventional individuals, ultimately softening the public image of the practice and making it easier to digest. Tattoo publications produced within the community have focused on fine-art tattooing (or "high" tattooing), moving away from the seemingly poor-quality biker or sailor images associated with traditional ("low") tattooing. These two main sources of information dissemination have redefined the tattoo community.

The reappropriation of what was considered a low-class art form is similar to the appropriation of 1940s Hollywood glamour in gay camp: camp being the "an aesthetic in which something has appeal because of its bad taste or ironic value" (LGBT Info Wiki n.d.). Originally used to refer to garish, exaggerated or effeminate behaviour, camp "has been from the start an ironic attitude, embraced by anti-Academic theorists for its explicit defense of clearly marginalized forms" (LGBT Info Wiki n.d.). It involves the resurrection of objects and discourses of the past that are generally seen as negative and are forgotten — they are discourses that are taboo, lack respectability and are generally ignored by mainstream society. They are resurrected and reimagined for the dominant class's purposes. The problem with this strategy as it relates to middle-class tattooing practices, however, is that these seemingly "old" tattoos (the "marginalized forms") are not forgotten but are actually still used by those so-called low-class people. So, while the middle-class appropriation of tattooing may seem liberatory, it can be instead seen as an illustration of how this aesthetic has been appropriated by middle-class tattoo wearers to represent a sense of individuality. The cultural appropriation of many traditions, then, works on a pre-existing set of meanings from which new cultural symbols and meanings (or identities) can be created. However, the middle-class appropriation of tattooing doesn't really succeed here. Middle-class tattoo wearers neither possess the characteristics of the lower-class text (such as a similar socio-economic status) nor understand the meanings given to tattoos by the lower class. Thus, those previous tattoo meanings are ignored and the middle class creates new meanings out of "thin air." Put another way, the appropriation of tattoos results in tattoos' origins and history in the practices of the "deviant" and marginalized (bikers, sailors, punks) being erased because middle-class tattoo wearers have no connection to or use for that history.

Perpetuating this new cultural tattoo text is the separation of low-class from middle-class (or biker versus fine-art) tattoos. Separating the two allows middle-class tattoo wearers to reject and separate themselves from a tradition historically seen as negative but still maintain the symbolic individuality ("I'm not really trashy, I'm *unique*"). The distinction, DeMello argues, is upheld not for aesthetic reasons, but for political and social ones. Since the prior text has been rejected, and with it the prior history of tattoos (including their association with bikers, prisoners, sailors and prostitutes), a new history must be developed — one based on a "mythical, primitive past" (DeMello 1995: 13). This new, fictionalized past erases the North American tattoo tradition that was historically seen as negative. It is through middle-class tattoo magazines (like *TattooTime* or *Inked Magazine*) that this new past is perpetuated and introduced into the public discourse. *TattooTime*'s first edition (*The New Tribalism*), as well as RE/Search's *Modern Primitives,* represents this desire to return to a "primitive" past and to naturalize the practice of tattooing.

So, has tattooing's negative past been effectively eliminated? DeMello argues that it has not, the evidence being tattoo culture's increasing presence in the mainstream, especially given tattooing's roots, through both mainstream and alternative media publications. She argues that, if anything, this presence illustrates "the power of the media to effect, if not real social change … at least symbolic transformations" (DeMello 1995: 14).

While the cultural appropriation of Eastern tattooing history is important in understanding the context in which the contemporary tattoo industry resides, I found that the women I spoke with used the stories or narratives about their tattoos as a means not of appropriating something, but rather of connecting them *with* something: a history, a cultural belonging or a sense of identity. Tattoos have necessarily become commodified and bereft of meaning, partly in using narratives from Eastern culture, in order for them to be made acceptable to the mainstream and middle class. The women I spoke with, however, recognized their tattoos' commodified nature and were able to find meaning through connecting their tattoos with their sense of identity. Thus, these links are not understood by the women as cultural appropriation, but rather cultural *connection*. In these terms, we can see the nuances of appropriation and the complexity of the ways in which it permeates contemporary tattooing practices. Moreover, the ways in which the women used tattoo narratives to make connections and to give meaning is representative of the struggle and tension that they face as tattooed women and the ways they reconcile these challenges. In hearing these narratives we can see how, like cultural narratives generally, they are changing and shifting over time, from one historical era to another. That is, tattoos can be seen and interpreted as a fad or a commodity by some, but their meanings to tattoo wearers are nuanced and shifting. For the wearers, tattoos have meaning beyond their appropriation by mainstream culture as a meaningless product to be bought and sold.

> Tattoos have necessarily become commodified to be made acceptable to the mainstream.

THE FLUIDITY OF TATTOO DISCOURSE

As the meanings of tattoos change, so too does the language we use to discuss them. How do we understand them? How do we think about them? Analyses not critical of the commodification process often say that the mainstream media, academic publications and tattoo artist/enthusiast publications are responsible for shaping the way that the tattoo community is presented and understood and thus the way people, both tattooed and not, think and talk about tattoos.

The mainstream media have portrayed tattooing and tattoo culture in the past as something to fear (tattoos are for deviants, tattoos are dangerous and so forth). Media coverage now focuses on the increasing popularity of tattoos. Explaining what tattooing *used* to be and who *used* to get tattooed illustrates the practice's "seedy" roots and association with nefarious characters; now, focusing on the new generation of tattooed people — the middle class, people who exclusively seek out fine-art tattoos — effectively silences those groups of people who were traditionally associated with the practice. By selecting those who are interviewed, mainstream media sources choose who is allowed to talk and who is given a voice. Academic representations of the practice are similar in that they highlight class distinctions among tattoo users and fail to recognize the possibility of the media's role in creating these distinctions in the first place.

Those who are given a voice all seem to say the same thing and use the same discourse to talk about their tattoos. Borrowing from the self-help discourse of the 1970s and 1980s, these new-generation tattooed individuals discuss how tattoos have given them a sense of individuality, aided in their personal growth or heightened their spirituality. These motivations for becoming tattooed can be easily contrasted with the reasons people *used* to give for getting tattoos: they wanted to prove their masculinity, they were drunk and thought it would be fun, they were rejecting middle-class life and all of its meanings or they had no real reason at all. Mainstream media representations are made to be easily accessible and understandable to even non-tattooed readers:

> By first focusing their articles around a select group of middle-class individuals, most of whom have relatively small, inoffensive tattoos; by second, denying all of those who do not fit into this category the right to be represented, except as the absent unit of comparison; and third, by centering the discussion around ideas which are very popular outside of the tattoo community, the journalists are able to make the world of tattooing a safe and understandable place. (DeMello 1995: 6)

While tattoos may be seen to some as countercultural, the contemporary discourse around them is not: In combining popular self-help and personal growth discourse with so-called respectable, middle-class tattooers and tattooed people, contemporary representations of tattooing feature it as a safe and accessible phenomenon. It also helps to perpetuate the notion of tattooing as solely an identity-altering practice.

INDIVIDUALITY, SPIRITUALITY AND PERSONAL GROWTH

The self-help movement is a combination of pop psychology and self-awareness that began in the 1970s and continues today. Now a multibillion-dollar industry, the self-help or wellness movement advocates for the use of psychotherapy, webinars, twelve-step programs, books and the advice of social media influencers to "become happier and to eliminate negative behaviours or attitudes such as codependency, depression, and eating disorders, or to achieve loving relationships with others" (DeMello 2000: 144). This movement appealed to "therapeutic sensibilities" and an increasing interest in mental and emotional health and the power that is "ascribed to the individual will in achieving this." Additionally, the new-age movement, which began around the same time, saw middle-class people experimenting with and appropriating Eastern religions and "consciousness-transforming techniques" (Lasch, cited in DeMello 2000: 144), borrowing practices like Buddhism, tarot, Wicca and meditation. Within this social climate, tattoos came to be interpreted as a transformative practice, a way of getting in touch with one's spiritual essence. Many popular tattoo images and designs are derived from this appropriated new-age philosophy, such as zodiac signs, yin/yang or Sanskrit and Japanese writing. With modern Western society seen as repressive, alienating and lacking ritual, non-Western symbols and practices were adopted as they were thought to be more meaningful than those found in Western culture. It is through these narratives that people developed meaning for their tattoos, which DeMello argues are especially important "within a middle class context that traditionally has not viewed tattoos in a positive light," and that they "form the basis of the individual's personal understanding of his/her tattoo" (2000: 149).

Judy, thirty-two, has one tattoo and explained that while she is proud of it and sees it as a symbol of her strength and independence as a woman, most people are shocked to find out that she has one:

> I think sometimes it surprises people when they find out that I have a tattoo. Like, I have a fairly recent new group of friends that I've been hanging out with. I happened to mention that I had a tattoo and all of the girls were very shocked. I know this group of friends happens to be middle class to upper middle class. I think they don't really see a white, middle-class girl getting a tattoo. Those are the people that are a little more shocked and don't see it blending with my personality.

Judy's friends seem to understand tattooing as a practice that derives its meaning from the marginalized classes.

Thus, three main narratives have shaped the new generation of tattooing — its redefinition and re-inscription — and are used to describe tattoos by this new generation of tattooed individuals: individuality, spirituality and personal growth. These themes, DeMello argues, have shaped both the nature of the tattoo community and the meaning of the tattoo. The increasing middle-class participation in tattooing has resulted in a transformation of tattoo culture itself.

TATTOOS AND WOMEN'S EMPOWERMENT

While both men and women favour narratives of individuality, spirituality and personal growth, women alone also explain their tattoos in terms of control, healing and empowerment. Women were more apt to interpret their tattoos as a means of reclaiming their bodies — marking them to negate the marks of oppression and patriarchy they feel on their bodies. Foucault's notion of the body as "the object and target of power" (1975: 136) has been expanded (and criticized) by feminist scholars, who argue that women's bodies are the site "for the inscription of power and the primary site of resistance to that power" (DeMello 2000: 173; see also Butler 1999 and Grosz 1994). As Nadia Brown and Sarah Allen Gershon note:

> As active subjects, marginalized bodies can confound the dominant discourse by opposing prevailing ideologies that have marked the body with meaning. To be sure, power relations are dynamic, nuanced, and highly contextual. Power is not manifested in a static form. As such, resistance and change are incessant. Analyzing the body as a site where power is contested and negotiated [allows us] … to examine the fluidity of privilege and marginalization. (2017: 1)

While the most common narratives have been popularized and are thus more popular among the middle class, the themes of empowerment common among tattooed women do not fall within such definitive class boundaries. Economically marginalized women, DeMello notes, have had much more experience using their bodies as a site of resistance (through, for example, clothing and hairstyles) and, similarly, have been getting tattooed for much longer than middle-class women. Despite this, however, heavily tattooed women of both classes "can be said to control and subvert the ever-present 'male gaze' by forcing men (and women) to look at their bodies in a manner that exerts control" (DeMello 2000: 173). DeMello even connects this sense of control and empowerment to the "tattooed ladies" of the 1920s and 1930s circuses and sideshows — in important ways, these women were independent and decided to make a living for themselves. While women today do not get tattooed to earn a living, it can be argued that tattoos on women serve as a sign of independence. Indeed, the commodification and mainstreaming of tattoos, where meanings are fluid, has led to a "complex and nuanced cultural field" (Larsen et al. 2014: 672) — and this destabilized meaning has a more prominent effect on women, because women who choose to get tattooed are already having to navigate and reconfigure the norms and ideas around tattoos and women with tattoos in general. More broadly, the neoliberal notion of women's "choice" in how they experience and express their femininity is necessarily constrained, as "the choices that women make are already restricted to what is acceptable and oppressed within culturally restricted boundaries" (Dann and Callaghan 2019: 1). But while women's bodies — and their tattooed bodies — are read through the lens of hegemonic notions of femininity, it is through being tattooed that women can perform "multiple femininities, constructing a complex negotiation between conformity and resistance that is imbued with regulated choice" (Dann and Callaghan 2019: 1).

These anti-patriarchal discourses have, indeed, been influenced by dominant middle-class liberatory discourses, and the women (myself included) who see their tattoos as a means of securing an empowering identity connect with and infuse their own tattoo narratives with references

> Tattoo narratives, like any discourse, are fluid.

to opposing the male gaze. Nevertheless, tattoo narratives, like any discourse, are fluid. They are used to "recreate," both for the teller and the listener, the complex justifications for the tattoos — justifications that are constantly changing. As tattooing becomes mainstream, however, many tattooed people's claims that their tattoos are deeply meaningful and spiritual come into question, which suggests a class backlash: "The very same middle-class tattooists who were at the forefront of the renaissance now look nostalgically back to the old days of blue-collar values" (DeMello 2000: 191). While Judy may not necessarily subscribe to the "blue-collar values" of earlier tattoo wearers, she recognizes and notes the ways in which the mainstreaming of tattoos has left many, as some would argue, devoid of meaning:

> When I see women with flowers and Chinese characters, they don't know what they're saying. They're white like me and they have Chinese [characters] on the back of their neck or on their foot. That really irritates me. They're trying to be cool. They're trying to be something and that's not the way to do it. I don't feel tattooing is the way to make you free and strong and independent. It might be a symbol of that for some people but, just looking at other women, it really depends on the individual tattoo.

Judy interprets the preponderance of tattooing as having a negative effect on the practice as a whole, with symbols and designs permeating the industry and effectively lessening the power of some individual tattoos. The increasing popularity of tattoos creates a whitewashing effect: in order to stand out, one will have to wear increasingly more visible and subversive tattoos. Sara echoed this sentiment:

> It's become such an everyday thing that it really takes something quite extraordinary for me to be like, "Wow, that's cool." Like, if I see a woman who has a whole back piece or something insane, that's rad.... Women who aren't tattooed, I look at them and I'm like, "Wow, you're pure."

Sara's comment illustrates the changing discourse around tattooing. While at one time a tattoo can be seen as shocking — to Judy's friends, for example — in another context, tattoos become an "everyday thing" and it is instead those *without* tattoos who become shocking.

While the research on tattoo discourse is indeed helpful in understanding the ways in which the women I spoke with tell of their tattoos, much of it falls short in that there is the argument, or often just the assumption, that contemporary tattooing has lost its message or become meaningless outside of the capitalist culture of commodification and consumerism. It is here that we need to turn again to the fluidity of tattoo discourse (as with all discourse) rather than to glorify the easy-to-read tattoos of the days of sailors and bikers. While it has been argued that the traditional, working-class tattoo was characterized as "lacking in sophistication and significance and is worn by people who put very little thought into their tattoos" (DeMello 2000: 193), a number of tattoo artists today are arguing that classic Western tattooing did, in fact, have a simple, recognizable message that has been lost in contemporary fine-art tattoo imagery, tattoo trends and tattoo magazines. DeMello notes:

> The traditional American tattoo — with its easy-to-read imagery that reflected the old-fashioned values of God, mother, and country — is being displaced in favor of the contemporary tattoo, with its often unrecognizable imagery and exotic content. The contemporary tattoo is high fashion, but at the same time alienates those whose tattoos are no longer favored. (2000: 193)

These traditional tattoos are able to tell a story all by themselves while contemporary tattoos often require the wearer to construct a narrative in order to explain them. Given the discussions I had with the tattooed women, I maintain that contemporary tattoos hold just as much meaning as did the traditional designs. While traditional designs may have seemed simplistic in their message, I believe that the overarching association with deviance was perhaps the most overt message they delivered. The story they are able to tell all by themselves is one that we have come to understand through a changing discourse. Just as an eagle meant something in the early part of the century, a flower means something today. After all, not all tattoo wearers construct elaborate stories to connect their tattoos to a larger history. As with Sara, for example, some women find meaning not in the specific tattoo but in its resultant marking — that is, in the experience of being marked as tattooed.

> Some women find meaning not in the specific tattoo but in the experience of being tattooed.

FIVE TATTOOED WOMEN

Karen is a thirty-eight-year-old Mohawk mother of two. She teaches Indigenous history and works as a student advisor. She got her first tattoo, a unicorn on her arm, when she was sixteen, and since then has collected five more tattoos, the majority of which hold personal family and cultural significance for her. At nineteen, she had a dragon tattooed on her hip, "Just for fun … because dragons are cool," and a small frog and mushroom on her shoulder that she told me she would likely get covered up in the future. Years later she had the unicorn covered with a large tribal piece on her left arm and shoulder that is based on tribal designs from around the world, which is "intended to represent the concept of all [her] relations." On her right arm she has a wolf that was done in honour of her grandfather, who is a member of the Wolf Clan. On her right leg is a turtle surrounded by Celtic knot work, which she explained is in honour of her parents: "Because my father's Turtle Clan, because my grandmother's Turtle Clan, it's matrilineal, and my mom's British so I have the Celtic knot work." Most recently, she's had the confederacy wampum belt tattooed across her back. She had been intending to get this particular tattoo for the past ten years, but the time wasn't right until recently, when she completed her master's degree. "And then when I start my PhD, I'm going to get my status card tattooed on my ass," she said.

When Karen started getting tattooed as a young girl, however, tattooing wasn't the mainstream practice that it is today. "I'm old enough to remember when it was an act of rebellion, not conformity, and that's exactly what it was. I left home at a very young age, so I was a street kid, and it was part of that culture," she said. When I asked her what made her choose her first design, a unicorn, Karen told me about her experience getting that tattoo:

> I was at a big house party at a flop house, because I mean we were all street
> kids, and there was some guy who had just gotten out of Stoney [Mountain

Penitentiary] with his little homemade jail gun and was like, "Hey anybody want a tattoo?" And that was pretty much what he knew how to draw, one of the things he knew how to do. So [I said] "Okay." So that's kind of how I got that one. But, I mean, it's covered up now.

Karen describes her tattoos as an expression of her identity, of her self. For her, tattoos represent both her "ethnic and cultural identity as well as [her] spiritual beliefs." "Your body's a temple," Karen continued. "You've only got it once, you might as well paint the walls, right?" In addition to representing her cultural and spiritual identity, her tattoo projects have all been thought out and planned in consultation with her artist to balance both her body and the art. "All of my tattoos have been thought out," Karen said, "I mean, there's a reason behind them all. They either mark a point in my life or they have some sort of meaning. It's never just sort of 'Oh that looks cool, put it here,' which so many tattoos today are."

Sara is twenty-six years old and a recent graduate of a college communications program. She has three tattoos, the first of which, a line drawing of a woman that would eventually become a part of Salvador Dali's painting "The Burning Giraffe," was a gift from her parents for her twenty-first birthday. Six months after her first tattoo, she had a piece done on her calf — a collection of images from one of her favourite books, Clive Barker's *The Thief of Always*, that represent key ideas that the book portrays. "It's a tree with a treehouse in it and it's got a kite and the treehouse has a ladder going down and then there's a fish coming up on the bottom; it's all just different parts from the book," Sara tells me. A short while later, Sara had three large peonies, her favourite flower, tattooed on her right arm.

Unlike many women that I talked to, Sara doesn't associate any deep, personal significance with her tattoos: "I didn't get them because I had gone through some horrible trauma, and I didn't get them because I wanted to make a particular statement." Sara explained to me that she got her tattoos for aesthetic reasons — "Because I like them" — rather than to cover a particular body part or relay a particular message to others through her choice of design. Sara explained that she does not immediately identify as a "tattooed person" and chooses not to show them off. What is important to her, however, is that her tattoos are unique, not easily defined and not something you would see on either the wall of a tattoo shop or the arm of another tattoo enthusiast. She takes pride in her tattoos, even though, as she explained, some think of them as "weird."

Kendra emailed her responses to my questions, as she was living and teaching English in Thailand. A twenty-three-year-old, Kendra had the Chinese characters for "true love" tattooed on her left calf six years ago, at seventeen. She chose this design because, as she explained, true love is something she believes in and aspires to.

After spending some time in Paris, France, the "city of romance," ideas of love were floating around in her head: "True love represented the hope I had (and still have) for the future. I decided on Chinese because my best friend is Chinese Canadian and I always thought the language looked beautiful." Kendra's tattoo makes her feel special and hopeful, and it serves as a reminder for her never to "settle." She sees her tattoo as a legacy, a means of self-expression, "like holding the answers to a secret."

Kendra told me that once she was tattooed, she felt older, if at times a bit "cliché" given the popularity of Chinese characters as a tattoo design. At one time shy about her body, Kendra started wearing clothing in an attempt to show off her tattoo and is now really happy with her choice of location, as it is a place on her body that won't change as she ages: "At least it won't get saggy and gross like if it was on my boob or my tummy."

Kendra was initially worried about the pain and the ability to cover the tattoo, as once she finished with her time in Thailand she would be working as a teacher in Manitoba, where there were strict guidelines concerning the visibility of body modifications. She explained, "When I was in university and student teaching I heard a principal say he would 'never hire anyone with a visible tattoo.' Funny thing was the grade 1, 2, 5 and 6 teachers all had tattoos. Guess they never told him. I stuck to wearing pants."

Katie is a twenty-eight-year-old graduate student of theology. She has two tattoos, both of which were completed within a year and a half of each other: one is a simple, open-concept line drawing of a dove on her left shoulder; the other is a large "vine with Greek text as the trunk" starting at her foot and ending about five inches above her knee. The text is "Koine Greek, which is what the New Testament was written in, and it's a Bible passage, and it translates into 'Lord I believe, help my unbelief.'" Raised Mennonite and having worked as a youth pastor for four years, Katie's faith has been and still is a large part of her identity. As well, the image of peace that she has tattooed on her left shoulder is something she feels constitutes her self. While Katie is proud of her faith, she told me that people react to her differently once they find out that her leg piece holds religious connotations:

> That's probably one thing that makes me uncomfortable with my leg piece, is when people ask what the text means, all of a sudden they find out that I'm a person of faith, and they react to me differently. I don't want people to feel like I'm trying to evangelize to them because I've got this, it's my faith and it's my faith struggle and my faith journey. That's why I got it. It had nothing to do about wanting the world to know.

Despite some of the negative reactions to her tattoos that she gets from people, Katie finds the fun in it as well: "In the back of my mind I have a couple of joking translations that I would give people because who the hell's going to understand Greek? Like, if I'm out at a bar and some person is like, 'Hey what's that mean?' [I'll say] 'Look but don't touch' or 'It's all Greek to you.'"

Once she had the piece on her leg done, Katie realized she was "that girl with the huge-ass tattoo on her leg." But she doesn't mind the attention. Subverting mainstream expectations has always appealed to her, so she felt that it made sense for her to have such a visible tattoo. While being so visibly tattooed noticeably changes the interactions she has with people, Katie isn't ashamed of her artwork, but rather sees her body now as more of a potential canvas for future projects.

Lynda is fifty-four years old and has two sons, aged thirteen and twenty-nine. She got her first tattoo for her fiftieth birthday, and her eldest son went along and got one too. The tattoo, a small purple lily on her chest just under her collarbone, symbolizes a number of things for Lynda: lilies are a symbol of rebirth, which correlates to her entering a new stage in her life and celebrating moving forward; she chose purple as it is one of the highest energy centres for chakras; and purple is also a colour associated with royalty, as she explained that "anyone who knows me knows that I kind of like to be the Queen of Everything." Lynda had also given considerable thought to the placement of her tattoo. It was located on a part of her body that wouldn't change much over time and could be easily covered, and because the location was easily visible to her, the tattoo acts as a reminder that this is a good stage in her life. She researched tattoo studios in Winnipeg with her eldest son, who had already been tattooed and was quite encouraging of her decision for about two to three years before she had it done. Lynda first spoke with an artist at one studio with whom she did not feel comfortable before finally finding a place that felt right.

Lynda explained to me that fifteen years earlier, she thought of tattooing as a strange practice, but now she finds happiness in having this pretty piece of art permanently on her skin. While she told me that she has always had issues with her body image, Lynda said that her tattoo has changed how she sees herself. "Finally having something that is quite pretty that I chose leaves me more open to accepting [my body] because it's the part of me that's always going to be beautiful," she said. Being tattooed later in life has impacted her self-identity as well:

> I think it did make a difference because reaching your fifties is a difficult age. I think as women we all have those goddess archetypes in us and I know my Aphrodite had been submerged for many years and it was like a coming out, and I mean, it's very simple, it's just a little tattoo, but it really is quite powerful.

Additionally, because her generation has not subscribed to tattooing in the same way that younger generations have embraced it, she enjoys the "shock impact" when people see that she is tattooed. Working with a number of people who are younger than her, she said, "I'm the age of their mothers and their mothers aren't getting tattooed, so that obviously sort of switches things around for them, and somehow this tattoo takes a few years off, makes me more contemporary maybe?" In this regard, she has fun with her tattoo — keeping it covered most of the time at work, as it is still something that is personal for her, but showing it off in particular settings or when the topic comes up in conversation. "People don't know what to do with it sometimes, so I just have fun with it. It's just fun!"

These women use tattoo narratives to make connections to a number of things: for Karen, her tattoos connect her to her cultural heritage and to a past in which tattooing was considered an overt form of rebellion; for Sara, tattoos serve as a means of marking her as different; Kendra's tattoo connects her to culturally important notions like friendship and love; for Katie, her tattoo is a connection to and reminder of her struggles with her faith; and for Lynda, her tattoo connects her with a sense of identity. However, the connections made are done so in the context of a capitalist and patriarchal culture.

TATTOOS COMMODIFIED

While these five women all have different reasons for being tattooed and approach tattooing in different ways, they share the fact that they have become a part of a culture that has grown like wildfire. Tattooing has moved from the shadows and into the mainstream over the past few decades, helped in part by its use in advertising campaigns, product marketing or TV shows. Tattoos have saturated our culture to the point where they no longer garner the immediate shock and attention that they did many years ago. In some important ways, tattoos have become normalized.

This normalization of tattooing was not lost on the women I interviewed. During our conversations, many of the women said they regard tattoos in much the same way they do any other element of fashion. As Breccan, age twenty-seven, told me: "It's like permanently wearing a very flashy skirt or something." Katie said that she doesn't particularly feel a bond with other tattooed women, as it has become such a popular form of body modification: "It would be the same as walking down the street and seeing someone dressed in the same style that you dress." Karen associates her tattoos with fashion as well, in the sense that they are an extension of her personality, "like wearing fancy shoes or a really nice dress or something like that, except it's permanent."

Some of the women I spoke with commented that today there are so many people with tattoos, piercings and other body modifications that it is those who are "pure" —

those who are without any modifications — that may be the true rebels. That is, they see tattoos as having become "trendy." Sara noted that as tattoos have become so much a part of our culture now, when you see someone who doesn't have a tattoo, "they're almost prevailing more, and they're almost like the anti- or counterculture now."

So, knowing and given this (commodified) context in which the practice of tattooing is presently situated, is that all there is to the story? Do women simply see tattoos as fashion or do they see them more as a struggle to incorporate resistance, to invest their tattoos with some political context and meaning? The women I spoke with understand that tattoos have become commodified, rendered "normal" and fashionable, but how do they negotiate this? Given the context in which tattooing has become normalized, what, in spite of this process, makes them different? Despite the inarguably powerful effects of patriarchy and its ability to shape and influence the lives of women and how they consume popular culture (including tattoos), women remain active participants in this process. Women are, as Brenda Austin-Smith (2007: 83) argues, "capable of constructing alternative and often resistant meanings from the most conventional and conservative texts." There are a number of ways in which the women I interviewed negotiate this tension between the conformity associated with tattooing, given its mainstream popularity in Western culture, and their efforts to resist that commodification in their endeavour to construct an authentic sense of self.

> Despite the inarguably powerful effects of patriarchy and its ability to shape and influence the lives of women and how they consume popular culture (including tattoos), women remain active participants in this process.

RECONCILING TRENDINESS/MAINTAINING AUTHENTICITY

> I don't think I would relate to somebody who had a massive tribal tattoo on their arm just for the sake of getting one. I think that's part of the big issue is just, like, getting one just to say you have one. (Amber, age twenty-one, five tattoos)

Authenticity is a theme and term that is used in a variety of ways. For these women, authenticity can be an expression of long-term commitment, uniqueness and individuality, as well as a partial reaction to trendiness and fashionability, as Amber alludes to. Each woman I spoke with understood and talked about authenticity — overtly or otherwise — and desired to make connections that are shifting or to locate herself in a larger historical context. The nuances of what it means to be authentic and how one can connect in a legitimate way through her tattoos ultimately highlighted for me that appropriation is complex and certainly not a linear process. The nuances represented by the women's understandings of their tattoos also put DeMello's argument in a new and more complicated light.

The women I spoke with have agency — they aren't, and none of us are, empty vessels into which mainstream (and shifting) culture is simply poured. While they are aware that tattooing has become a trend, they are constantly both reconstructing and relocating themselves within this process of mainstreaming, of trendiness. Reconciling the desire to express themselves on their own terms and the desire to be regarded as authentic is not an easy task. Karlie, a twenty-two-year-old insurance claims adjuster with three tattoos, reflected this point:

> Well, I think there's a lot of people who, you know, critique tattoos, think that every tattoo has to be very personal, have huge deep meanings, and it can't be, like, funny or whatever. But as much as I do agree with them in some sense, that your tattoos should mean something, they don't always have to be serious. That's just me. I plan on getting some ridiculous tattoos, but other people would look at those and be like, "Well, why the hell did you get that? That's absolutely ridiculous." But I think some people take it a little bit too seriously, and sometimes I'm completely guilty of that. Even though I'm getting them, I'm judging people for them. But a lot of people just take it really seriously and they don't always need to. But on the flip side, some people don't take it seriously enough and get little fluffy unicorns on their lower back.

Karlie's comments illustrate the complexity of issues that tattooed women are faced with in their decision to get tattooed. Rejecting the need for a personal story to contextualize a tattoo design, which in its mainstream popularity has become a sign of *in*authenticity to some tattooed women, can lead to the opposite: choosing a tattoo design that is devoid of meaning, which Karlie suggests is similarly inauthentic. This seeming competition for who can be the most authentic is complex. As Gretchen Larsen and her colleagues (2014: 679) argue:

> The "stigma of the commodity" is attached to that which is impersonal, superficial, and similar, whereas the "stigma of deviance" is the stigma of the personal, individual, and otherness. Here, lack of authenticity is a major factor in the attribution of stigmatized status and individuals strive to get "closer to the self" and reject commodified styles, establishing "the imagined mainstream, as a straw man against whom one can set oneself off as more authentic."

The women I spoke with have recognized this difficult binary. Yet they have found ways in which to work around it and justify for themselves the legitimacy of their tattoo projects.

Karen has tattoos that are all strongly connected to her family and spiritual identity. However, when she started getting tattooed in the late 1980s and early 1990s, tattooing was a means of rebellion for her:

> Well, I guess there was always a push [for me] to be unique and different. I was never mainstream. You know, I was never one with the crowd and it was just one way of making myself distinct and making myself unique, right? I don't fit in and that's totally cool. So, it's just another way of expressing that, really.

Karen has also witnessed the change in the industry itself, along with the public perception of tattooing:

> Back in the day it was illegal. We just did it out the kitchen. I mean, I'm old enough to remember when getting tattoos were an act of rebellion as opposed to conformity. Which is really what all mine are, and, I mean, back in my day people would cross the street to avoid you if you had piercings and tattoos and looked like a punk rocker, with purple hair. And they did, people would look at me like, "Holy shit, you're a freak." Now people don't even blink twice, it's become mainstream. So yeah, some of my earliest tattoos were work done in the kitchen, with homemade guns and things like that, the jail house style, because, I mean, you really didn't have much of a choice back in the eighties.

Despite the development of the industry into a mainstream practice, Karen locates herself as someone who remains committed to tattooing's rebellious roots. She doesn't see herself as subscribing to trends. Rather, given her own lengthy history with the practice, tattooing constitutes for her an act of rebellion *and* a means of adornment — no matter how much more difficult it may be to define tattooing as rebellious in today's culture.

For Sara, the uniqueness of her tattoos serves as means of separating herself from the mainstream. She explained, "I never felt the need to be like, 'Oh, I think I'm so boring looking that I need to go do this or that' because I think everybody fits in their own niche. But I think my tattoos just sort of set me apart a little bit more." When she made the decision to get tattooed, Sara knew she wanted to get something that was different: "I didn't want to just go down and pick out from all the artist flash ... I didn't want to get something that everybody else would have." In this way, Sara locates herself outside of the trendiness and the mainstream because her tattoo projects are not easily defined and not something typically found on the walls of a tattoo studio. She explains her "unusual" tattoos:

> I guess you have to kind of really look at it and sort of figure out and discern what everything is.... So, I think that they make a statement that I've chosen to do something to myself to sort of differentiate myself from the masses. But in the same breath, I don't want it to seem like I felt that I was some ordinary plain Jane to begin with.

Despite her tattoos setting her apart from the mainstream, Sara recognizes that tattooing is still very much "an everyday thing," but she doesn't get wrapped up in the popularity and hype of the practice: "People make a much bigger deal out of it than I ever made out of getting them, and honestly sometimes I forget I have them." This suggests that, while her tattoos serve as a connection to a countercultural practice that is seen as somewhat deviant, Sara has chosen to reject the claims to celebrated, definitive individuality that have propelled the practice into the mainstream to begin with. It is clear that, in these terms, authenticity is a complex phenomenon.

Additionally, the women find their own meaning and context within the practice by connecting it with events in their lives, honouring their family members or honouring their faith. For Lynda, the decision to become tattooed wasn't one that was tied up in her subscription to a new trend. In fact, she admitted that in the past she found the practice strange. Instead, she sees tattooing as a permanent way to celebrate herself — as a rite of passage in turning fifty. She explained, "Well a lily is a symbol of rebirth, and I was very excited about getting it to symbolize entering a new stage in my life, becoming a crone, that whole moving forward celebration." She also expressed her understanding of tattooing as a new art form for women to explore:

> I think mostly men had owned the art, or the realm, and I think it's our new art form. Maybe we've pushed the limits more, because I don't think anyone's really encouraged us, women, to get tattooed. But I think it could have to do with it being a safe way for women to express themselves, because you can do it but not be in somebody's face about it. You don't have to talk about it. It's just a statement.

Katie sees her tattoos as a part of her identity. Her faith is a large part of her identity, and her tattoos reflect that. For her, tattooing is not about participating in a trend, but rather is about her struggle with her own faith: her leg piece reads, "Lord I believe, help my unbelief." In her words:

That's the story of my faith. I've spent a lot of years not believing and a lot of years believing but still being uncomfortable with believing. I've been a minister; I was a youth pastor for four years, full time. It was really hard. I mean this, it comes from the book of Mark, and I'm not really one of those people to sit around and quote Bible passages, but this one just stuck with me because it takes faith to say, "Lord I believe, help my unbelief." It really leaves room for questions and doubts and insecurities about it and all that kind of stuff.

It is also evident that the women are not all getting tattooed for the same reason; they have very different, often very personal, reasons for getting a tattoo. What is similar among the women, however, is the personal narrative that each constructs by way of explaining her tattoos. These narratives, like other cultural discourses, are expressed in similar, learned terms. Kendra, for example, attaches a great deal of personal meaning to her calf tattoo — the notion of "true love" is something that holds a lot of significance for her in her life. She explains:

True love is something that I believe in. True love meaning the ultimate love — something that is real, romantic, unique, extraordinary, beautiful, passionate and lifelong. I got the tattoo when I was quite young and I saw true love in everything. I was really hopeful about love, despite never having been in a relationship at that point. I saw relationships in movies, on television, in magazines and in school. The concept of true love was always floating around in my head. What sealed the deal was when Pacey on Dawson's Creek named his boat "True Love" in an episode. I could see true love everywhere and knew that it had a strong meaning for me. I wanted something as special as that in my life, I believed in it.

This idea of love is one that is learned through dominant discourse — television shows, for example — and Kendra's tattoo, as it connects her to the idea of true love, suggests an expression of emotional value. Tattoos, in this regard, can connect us with learned cultural values. For Kendra, being tattooed was a way of expressing her desire for true love and having a tattoo feels like "a legacy." Her tattoo provides her with a message of hope:

Sometimes women settle, and I wanted my tattoo to remind me to never settle. I have seen love fall apart and I have seen people fool themselves into thinking they are in love. True love is the ultimate experience in love and something that I hope to experience in my life. I think I am on my way. In fact, I know I am.

While Kendra acknowledges the "cliché" of having Chinese characters tattooed on her, she maintains her claim to authenticity — her justification for the originality of her tattoo — as she was the first of her friends, and the first of many of her classmates, to be tattooed:

> It made me feel special to have something with so much personal meaning in it. I also felt a little cliché at times. Chinese characters aren't exactly unique. I got a lot of attention for being the first kid in my class to have a tattoo. Soon after, two of my friends got one. They both got lower back tattoos and both regretted their decisions afterwards. They didn't spend a lot of time thinking about their designs. One decided in two weeks, the other in one week. But as for me, I was really proud of my tattoo and thought it was special. It made me feel special and hopeful to have the message on me.

In this way, authenticity can take on several meanings — in Kendra's case, being the first of her classmates and friends to be tattooed lent her tattoo a sense of legitimacy in its originality. The meaning of her tattoo has shifted, as she implied, as the design she chose has become quite popular — at once new and original, the symbol of the Chinese character is familiar. In fact, the appropriation and fetishization of Kanji, Hanzi and other non-English languages in white, Western tattooing practices is so prolific and, subsequently, rife with errors, that one can find blogs dedicated to the accurate translation of white people's tattoos, many of which are actually "gibberish font" (see the blog Hanzi Smatter, for example). One particularly cringey example of this is Ariana Grande's latest tattoo: what was intended as an homage to her album *7 Rings* is in fact translated in some regions to *shichirin*, a small Japanese grill (France-Presse 2019). If the fascination with Chinese characters, for example, is a result of white people longing for meaningful and authentic identity in a so-called exotic language — that they neither speak nor write — then one must question that notion of authenticity when the requisite research hasn't been done to develop a relationship to the people and culture, or even to ensure that a new tattoo indeed means "strength" and not "toilet demon" (as one post on the Hanzi Smatter blog noted) (Zuppello 2019).

> If the fascination with Chinese characters is a result of white people longing for authentic identity, then one must question that notion of authenticity when the requisite research hasn't been done to develop a relationship to the people and culture.

In the same way that the reasons for getting tattooed vary from woman to woman, the importance placed on tattoo projects by the women shifts over time, suggesting that significance is a fluid concept. Jenn, a twenty-eight-year-old legal assistant, who sports a large tribal back piece in addition to a group tattoo that she had done with her sisters, explained to me that tattooing has become less of a priority as she's grown older:

> Yes, the years I was getting my back done, it seemed like the most important thing to do. But now with a mortgage and trying to start a family it's not really something I think about. I mean, it's there and it's part of me but it's not something I think about every day — it doesn't define me anymore.

Interestingly, some of the women reject the need to attach personal significance to their tattoos, thereby resisting the self-help discourse that locates tattooing as a means of personal growth. For instance, Sara was aware that some women were motivated to get tattooed as a way of coping with difficult life experiences: "I think it's great, you know, if somebody who's had some horrible trauma done to them and this is something that they need to do to heal themselves, then right on." But this was not Sara's motivation. April, 27, who has a chrysanthemum tattooed on the side of her torso made this point more directly:

"Well, I'll just find a meaning for tattoos after I get them. Meanings of tattoos will always change too."

> I don't personally think that everyone does it to make a statement, because, like mine, a lot of people ask me if there's any meaning behind it, and I'm like "No not really" ... It shouldn't have to mean anything. If you want there to be a meaning behind it, look up the actual meaning of it, like the phoenix rising out of the fire, or the particular type of flower. There's always going to be a meaning behind something. If it's personal, for personal taste, then that's your meaning. The meaning is who you are and why you have it on you.

Similarly, Ryse, a twenty-one-year-old woman with five tattoos, told me that her notion of meaning is not static, but rather always changing: "Well, I'll just find a meaning for tattoos after I get them. Meanings of tattoos will always change too."

COMMODIFICATION OR RESISTANCE?

With the new generation of tattoo enthusiasts comes a new text through which tattooing is understood — a new history, focusing on the Japanese or Polynesian roots of tattooing, effectively distances middle-class tattoo wearers from Western tattooing's low-class, marginalized roots. In order to market tattooing as a safe, acceptable commodity by which to mark your individuality or identity, capitalist culture has framed the practice in terms of its ability to aid in personal growth, as a rite of passage or a marker of strength similar to the uses of tattooing among tribal cultures.

DeMello's theory helps to make sense of the ways in which tattoo discourse has changed over the years and the nuanced and often complex ways in which tattooing is interpreted and perceived by contemporary enthusiasts. The women I spoke with echoed the complexity of issues that arise with the decision to become tattooed and the motivations for becoming tattooed. The ways in which these women understand and talk about the meanings of their tattoos, necessarily shaped and informed by the discourse of tattooing that permeates the current social climate, reflect DeMello's argument. Personal significance and authenticity play large roles in the ways in which these women construct their tattoo projects, and the fluidity of meaning and authenticity then necessarily affects the ways in which tattoos are perceived and discussed. Their construction of tattoo narratives to tell the story of their tattoos were ways that these women felt they could make connections with, rather than, as DeMello argues, appropriate, a larger history. Similarly, the women I spoke with were acutely aware of the fact that their choices to be tattooed were inextricably linked with their gender presentation — their choice of image and placement, of whether to hide their tattoos and of the stories they told about their tattoos were informed by the ways in which gendered expectations for women are perpetuated. It is through those choices that the women I spoke with found ways to resist patriarchy — through both their tattoos and the fluid narratives around those tattoos.

Additionally, the messages relayed by the women show that the commodification argument may be too simple. Rather than see contemporary fine-art tattoos as unrecognizable, the women find meaning in their tattoos through their adaptation to the changing nature of tattoo discourse. It is through their tattoo narratives that their tattoos resist conformity and remain authentic — be that original, legitimate or sincere long-term commitments to the culture of tattooing — *despite* their commodification. This

> It is through their tattoo narratives that their tattoos resist conformity and remain authentic despite their commodification.

would suggest, more broadly speaking, that the commodification of cultural artifacts does not necessarily strip them of their political content. While cultural commodification, or "eating the Other," is a mechanism in consumerist capitalism by which the culture of marginalized people can be and is appropriated and repackaged to be sold to the mainstream — what would appear to be the process of stripping those aspects of their meaningful, non-consumption, non-market content — the political content does not, it seems, disappear entirely. While capitalist culture often neglects human rights and human-ness in the interests of marketing goods that are seen as having no meaning other than profit, rendering them devoid of real human meaning, it would appear the commodification of tattoos is not complete. It is true that tattoos have now become a means of selling products: blockbuster films often use tattoos as a way to distinguish rebellious or edgy characters; more and more popular musicians of all genres are tattooed; and ad campaigns use tattoos to sell anything from energy drinks to credit cards. They have gone from being a sign of "deviance" to a form of body modification that is acceptable by the mainstream. The difference, however, is that the tattoo is one product that cannot be bought without being intimately linked to its actual production. As Mary Kosut notes:

> As a tattooed person, you are the witness, participant, and life-long bearer of a unique production process; a process in which the producer and consumer unite in complicated exchange that is simultaneously ritualistic, economic/consumeristic, and individualistic. (2006: 1041)

Along with the actual process of getting a tattoo, the women I spoke with were able to find meaning, meaning that often shifted over time and adapted to their lives and identities, while recognizing the commodified and gendered nature of their tattoos. People want and need meaning in their lives, meaning deeper than fashion and consumerism — that is what underlies the narratives the women attached to their tattoos. Oppressive institutions like capitalism and patriarchy can be and are resisted on a number of levels. In the case of tattooing, the women I spoke with were able to access aspects of tattooing's past — despite its commodification — to find meaning and value.

DISCUSSION QUESTIONS

1. What are some cultural artifacts, other than tattooing, that have been appropriated by Western society?
2. What kinds of problems can arise when subcultures are commodified? What benefits are there?
3. What are your own impressions of the practice of tattooing? What do you think of someone when you see that they are heavily tattooed? What about someone who has *no* tattoos?
4. Were you surprised at all by the ways in which the women talked about their own tattoos?

5. How does the way in which the women in this chapter interpret their own tattoos and resist conformity reflect on the ways in which everyday people can resist capitalism and patriarchy?

GLOSSARY OF KEY TERMS

Appropriation: The ways in which cultural practices, often those of marginalized classes or peoples, are claimed by dominant society and repurposed for their own use. An example would be the ways in which Eastern tattooing practices were claimed and repurposed by Western culture in an attempt to legitimate tattooing for mainstream society.

Authenticity: The desire to create a legitimate, original self-identity through tattoo projects in the face of the commodified and gendered nature of tattoos; a sincere, long-term commitment to a tattoo; and the sense of uniqueness that comes from being marked as different.

Commodification: The inherent process in capitalism to extend the market into ever more areas of human life, rendering all things, including humans themselves, meaningful only as products to buy, sell and consume as a means to accumulate profit (Marxists.org. n.d.).

Cultural commodification: bell hooks, for example, refers to cultural commodification as "eating the Other." Cultural commodification is the practice in capitalism within which a particular cultural aspect, often of a marginalized group, is appropriated, stripped it of its original meaning and repackaged for the consumption of mainstream society.

Identity: A person's sense of self, those aspects that distinguish a person from those around them.

Old-school tattoos/tattoo designs: Images made popular with the introduction of tattooing to Western culture by sailors are referred to as old-school tattoos/tattoo designs. These images — such as flags, ships, knives, snakes, panthers, roses and erotic images of women and mermaids — invoked patriotism and masculinity.

Other: Othering refers to the way in which those not a part of the dominant class, race or gender are (mis)represented and (mis)treated by mainstream society. Marginalized classes are seen as different and inferior and treated as such. Othering is an expression of power by the dominant over the marginalized.

RESOURCES FOR ACTIVISM

Inked Magazine: inkedmag.com
Tattoo Life: tattoolife.com
Margot Mifflin: margotmifflin.com
Sailor Jerry Tattoos: sailorjerry.com/tattoos/
Tattoo Snob on Instagram: @tattoosnob
Hanzi Smatter: hanzismatter.blogspot.com/

NOTE

1 Comparatively speaking, there is little research focusing specifically on women's tattooing practices and meaning making. Margo DeMello's research is featured heavily in this chapter, as hers is one of the key texts in the academic research (along with Atkinson 2003, see also Dann and Callaghan 2019) that set the stage for the exploration into the gendered nature of tattooing.

REFERENCES

Associated Press/cbs News. 2007. "Tattoos Lose Their Cool: Want a Blasting Berry Tattoo with That Fruit Roll-Up?" December 4. <cbsnews.com/stories/2007/12/04/entertainment/main3573970.shtml>.

Atkinson, M. 2003. "Pretty in Ink: Conformity, Resistance, and Negotiation in Women's Tattooing." *Sex Roles* 47.

Austin-Smith, B. 2007. "Feeling Framed: Emotion and the Hollywood Woman's Film." In L. Samuelson and W. Antony (eds.), *Power and Resistance: Critical Thinking About Canadian Social Issues,* 4th edition. Halifax: Fernwood Publishing.

Braunberger, C. 2000. "Revolting Bodies: The Monster Beauty of Tattooed Women." nwsa *Journal* 12, 2.

Brown, N., and S.A. Gershon. 2017. "Body Politics." *Politics, Groups, and Identities* 5, 1: 1–3.

Brownlee, J. 2015. *Academia, Inc.: How Corporatization Is Transforming Canadian Universities.* Winnipeg and Black Point, NS: Fernwood Publishing.

Butler, J. 1999. *Gender Trouble: Feminism and the Subversion of Identity.* New York: Routledge.

Caplan, J. 2000. "Introduction." In J. Caplan (ed.), *Written on the Body: The Tattoo in European and American History.* London, UK: Reaktion Books.

Cision Canada. 2019. "Workplace Etiquette 2020: Survey Shows Canadian Employers Feel Foul Language, Pets Biggest Office Offenses; Non-Traditional Piercings Are A-Okay." *Cision Canada,* December 18. <newswire.ca/news-releases/workplace-etiquette-2020-survey-shows-canadian-employers-feel-foul-language-pets-biggest-office-offenses-non-traditional-piercings-are-a-okay-838-041387.html>.

Dalia Research. 2018. "Who Has the Most Tattoos? It's Not Who You'd Expect." *Medium.* <medium.com/daliaresearch/who-has-the-most-tattoos-its-not-who-you-d-expect-1d5ffff660f8>.

Dann, C., and J. Callaghan. 2019. "Meaning-Making in Women's Tattooed Bodies." *Social and Personality Psychology Compass* 13, 9.

Deibert, R. 2020. *Reset: Reclaiming the Internet for Civil Society.* Toronto: House of Anansi Press.

DeMello, M. 2014. *Body Studies: An Introduction.* New York: Routledge.

___. 2000. *Bodies of Inscription: A Cultural History of the Modern.* Durham & London: Duke University Press.

___. 1995. "Not Just for Bikers Anymore: Popular Representations of American Tattooing." *Journal of Popular Culture* 29, 3.

Foucault, M. 1975. *Discipline and Punish: The Birth of the Prison.* New York: Vintage Books.

France-Presse, A. 2019. "Ariana Grande Mocked for Japanese Tattoo Typo: 'Leave Me and My Grill Alone'" *The Guardian,* January 31. <theguardian.com/music/2019/jan/31/ariana-grande-mocked-for-japanese-tattoo-typo-leave-me-and-my-grill-alone>.

Govenar, A. 2000. "The Changing Image of Tattooing in American Culture, 1846–1966." In J. Caplan (ed.), *Written on the Body: The Tattoo in European and American History.* London, UK: Reaktion Books.

Graeber, D. 2009. "Neoliberalism, or the Bureaucratization of the World." In H. Gusterson and C. Bestsman (eds.), *The Insecure American.* Proquest Ebook Central. <davidgraeber.org/wp-content/uploads/2009-Neoliberalism-or-the-bureaucratization-of-the-world.pdf>.

Grosz, E. 1994. *Volatile Bodies: Toward a Corporeal Feminism.* Indiana: Indiana University Press.

Hawkes, D., C.Y. Senn and C. Thorn. 2004. "Factors that Influence Attitudes Toward Women with Tattoos." *Sex Roles* 50.

Health Canada. 2001. "Special Report on Youth, Piercing, Tattooing and Hepatitis C: Trendscan Findings." <phac-aspc.gc.ca/hepc/pubs/youthpt-jeunessept/>.

hooks, b. 1992. *Black Looks: Race and Representation.* Cambridge, MA: South End Press.

Ibisworld. 2021. "Tattoo Artists Industry in the US — Market Research Report." *Industry Research Report,* July 30. <ibisworld.com/united-states/market-research-reports/tattoo-artists-industry/>.

KCY at Law. 2021. "Tattoos and Piercings in the Workplace." KCY *at Law.* <kcyatlaw.ca/tattoos-piercings-workplace-canada/>.

Kosut, M. 2006. "An Ironic Fad: The Commodification and Consumption of Tattoos." *Journal of Popular Culture* 39, 6.

Kwong, M. 2012. "Tattoo Culture Making Its Mark on Millenials." CBC News Canada, September 19. <cbc.ca/news/canada/tattoo-culture-making-its-mark-on-millennials-1.1149528>.

Larsen, G., M. Patterson and L. Markham. 2014. "A Deviant Art: Tattoo-Related Stigma in an Era of Commodification." *Psychology & Marketing* 31, 8.

Latino Rebels. 2015. "Hispandering Heritage Month Begins with Coca-Cola's Ridiculous 'Heritage Tattoo Cans.'" <latinorebels.com/2015/09/05/hispandering-heritage-month-begins-with-coca-colas-ridiculous-heritage-tattoo-cans/>.

LGBT Info Wiki. n.d. "Camp (style)." LGBT *Info Wiki.* <lgbt.fandom.com/wiki/Camp_(style)>.

Marx, K., and F. Engels. 1998. *The Communist Manifesto.* Halifax: Fernwood Publishing.

Marxists.org. n.d. "Commodification." <marxists.org/glossary/terms/c/o.htm#commodification>.

Melendez, Lyanne. 2015. "Critics Call Coke's Hispanic Heritage Month Campaign 'Hispandering.'" ABC News, September 18. <abc13.com/coca-cola-hispanic-heritage-month-ad-campaigm-neck-tattoos/990371/>.

Mifflin, M. 1997. *Bodies of Subversion: A Secret History of Women and Tattoo.* New York: Juno Books.

Oetterman, S. 2000. "On Display: Tattooed Entertainers in America and Germany." In J. Caplan (ed.), *Written on the Body: The Tattoo in European and American History.* London, UK: Reaktion Books.

Parmet, W.E. 2021. "Employers' Vaccine Mandates Are Representative of America's Failed Approach to Public Health." *The Atlantic,* February 4. <theatlantic.com/ideas/archive/2021/02/privatization-public-health/617918/>.

Roy, E.A. 2016. "'This Is Who I Am,' Says First Female MP to Wear Māori Facial Tattoo in NZ Parliament." *The Guardian,* August 11. <theguardian.com/world/2016/aug/11/first-woman-mp-maori-facial-tattoo-nz-parliament-moko-kauae>.

Samadelli, M., M. Melis, M. Miccoli et al. 2015. "Complete Mapping of the Tattoos of the 5300-Year-Old Tyrolean Iceman." *Journal of Cultural Heritage* 16, 5. <sciencedirect.com/science/article/abs/pii/S1296207415000023>.

Widdicombe, S., and R. Wooffitt. 1995. *The Language of Youth Subcultures: Social Identity in Action.* New York: Prentice Hall.

Zuppello, S. 2019. "The Complicated Relationship Between Culture and Tattoos." *Inside Out,* June 11. <readinsideout.com/culture/the-complicated-relationship-between-culture-and-tattoos/>.

13

"IT SHOULDN'T BE MY OR MY PEERS' RESPONSIBILITY TO MAKE OURSELVES FEEL SAFER"

Human Rights Discourse and Gender and Sexual Minority Youth

Christopher Campbell, Tracey Peter and Catherine Taylor

You Should Know This

- 1967: Justice Minister Pierre Elliott Trudeau declares, "There's no place for the state in the bedrooms of the nation."

- 1969: Consensual sex between two adults of the same sex over the age of twenty-one is decriminalized.

- 1977: Quebec prohibits discrimination on the basis of sexual orientation.

- 1992: Justice Minister Kim Campbell ends ban on gay and lesbian people in the armed forces.

- 1995: Supreme Court rules that "sexual orientation" should be read into the list of prohibited grounds of discrimination in the *Charter of Rights and Freedoms* (in the *Constitution Act, 1982*).

- 1996: Sexual orientation is added to the *Canadian Human Rights Act*.

- 1999: Supreme Court rules in favour of same-sex couples' adoption rights.

- 2005: Canada legalizes same-sex marriage.

- 2009: Ontario Ministry of Education requires school districts to implement policies and programming to support 2SLGBTQ+-inclusive education.

- 2013: As a way to promote safe and inclusive educational practices, the Manitoba Legislature passes into law Bill 18, which, among other things, amends the *Public Schools Act* that requires educators to accommodate students who want to start 2SLGBTQ+ clubs, such as gay-straight alliances. Similar legislation is being passed or considered in other provinces/territories.

- 2017: The federal government passed Bill C-16, an amendment to the *Canadian Human Rights Act* to include "gender identity and gender expression" as protected grounds from discrimination and hate; it received royal assent in June 2017 and came into force immediately.

- 2021: The federal Liberal government passed Bill C-4, an amendment to the Criminal Code that would effectively ban the harmful and potentially damaging use of conversion therapy or reparative therapy practices, treatment or services intended to change a person's sexual orientation or gender identity.

Sources: CBC Archives n.d.; Criminal Law Amendment Act; Civil Marriage Act; Egan v. Canada; M v. H 1999; Ontario 2009

IN THE YEARS SINCE IT WAS proclaimed in 1982, the *Charter of Rights and Freedoms* has come to function as Canada's chief nation-building document in the crucial sense of providing a mechanism to protect disenfranchised citizens from forms of racism, sexism and other systems of oppression "in and before the law." Because of the Charter, lesbian, gay and bisexual (LGB) people have been able to use the court system to overturn provincial and federal laws that discriminated against them in areas such as property, hospital visitation, marriage and adoption rights. Discrimination on the grounds of gender identity or gender expression was also explicitly prohibited in the *Canadian Human Rights Act* in 2017. Because of this progress on the juridical front, it is often said that discrimination against "gay people" is a thing of the past. The Charter has been opposed all along by socially conservative groups, who regard it as left-wing social engineering: those same groups still denounce the inclusion of sexual and gender minority people in Charter protections, since they see this as caving in to the "homosexualist agenda" (see, for example, Canada Family Action Coalition n.d.). Nevertheless, while activists and social theorists alike are well aware that discrimination persists in the Charter era, and that legal equality does not necessarily translate into social justice or social equality, the Charter has tremendous symbolic value in legitimizing marginalized people, a value that goes beyond its admittedly limited spheres of legal application. Indeed, the symbolic value of the Charter has been so broadly endorsed in Canada that it is now a cornerstone of social studies curricula in which school children and youth across the land learn that Canada has a proud tradition of unerringly upholding minority rights and celebrating diversity.

Yet there is a disconnect between official Canadian human rights discourse and the experiences of sexual- and gender-minority people, who continue to suffer from discrimination in various spheres of everyday life, both public and private. For example, even the innocuous everyday practice (for cisgender heterosexual [CH] couples) of holding hands with one's partner is still unsafe for sexual minority couples in the vast majority of public places in Canada, and identifiably transgender people remain at high risk of harassment and assault in the simple act of entering a public washroom. 2SLGBTQ+ Canadians encounter discrimination and disrespect in their families (being evicted, not being allowed to be alone with family children, partners not being welcome at family gatherings); in their religious or faith communities (being shunned, expelled, required to be celibate, subjected to harmful conversion therapy practices); in employment (being denied an interview or advancement within an organization for reasons ostensibly unrelated to sexual or gender identity) and in housing (being denied rental accommodation, being ostracized or harassed by hostile neighbours). They may encounter hostility from homophobic and transphobic restaurant staff, sales clerks and healthcare providers who express their disapproval of 2SLGBTQ+ people in ways ranging from the subtle (being less respectful than with other clients) to the blatant (flat refusal of service).

Admittedly, this grim picture is not universally true of life for all 2SLGBTQ+ Canadians, nor in all places in Canada. Although most 2SLGBTQ+ Canadians are resigned to enduring the daily indignity involved in not demonstrating public affection for their partners, many live relatively openly, in stark contrast to the almost unbroken rule of self-concealment, known as being in the "closet," of a few decades ago. This is especially true of middle- or professional-class Canadians living in major urban centres who seem conventionally gendered (masculine man or feminine woman), are not members of socially conservative groups or faith traditions, are not Indigenous or people of colour and are not under the age of eighteen.

In fact, most Canadian youth spend much of their lives in a world seemingly untouched by the legal and social advances of recent decades: the world of school culture. The disconnect between human rights discourse (legal equality) and lived experience (social equality) is demonstrated acutely in the high levels of both symbolic violence and direct harassment of all kinds that 2SLGBTQ+ youth reported in the second National Climate Survey on homophobia, biphobia and transphobia in Canadian schools (Peter, Campbell and Taylor 2021). The findings of this study are referenced throughout this chapter, and student narratives from this study are included to describe the school climates that 2SLGBTQ+ youth experience.[1] Findings from several additional projects — namely, the Every Teacher Project (Taylor, Peter, Campbell et al. 2015; Taylor, Peter, Short et al. 2016), the Being Safe, Being Me 2019 survey of Canadian trans youth (Taylor, Chan, Hall et al. 2020) and a national survey of school superintendents (Taylor, Peter, Edkins et al. 2016) — are highlighted here as well. While distinct in ways suggested here, the experiences of high school students illustrate, at least in part, the contours of experience for all 2SLGBTQ+ people in Canada.

WHAT DOES 2SLGBTQ+ STAND FOR?

2SLGBTQ+ is an acronym for "Two-Spirit, lesbian, gay, bisexual, trans, queer and questioning" people and is an umbrella term for all sexual-minority (lesbian, gay, bisexual, Two-Spirit) and gender-minority (trans, which may include transgender, transsexual, Two-Spirit) people. "Gender minority" includes trans people, whose gender expression and sense of self do not match mainstream gender conventions for the sex assigned to them at birth, and non-binary people, who have a gender identity that does not fall exclusively into the man-woman gender binary. 2s stands for "Two-Spirit," which is an identity term used by some Indigenous 2SLGBTQ+ people to describe the interrelated aspects of sexuality, gender, spiritual and cultural identities, and we place it at the beginning of the acronym in recognition that Indigenous sexual- and gender-minority people were the first on Turtle Island (Canada/North America) and to commit to the goals of reconciliation. Some 2SLGBTQ+ people identify as "queer," often to signify their opposition to the normative system of sexual and gender categories that marginalize

> Some 2SLGBTQ+ people identify as "queer," often to signify their opposition to the normative system of sexual and gender categories that marginalize anyone outside the mainstream norm.

anyone outside the mainstream norm. "Q" also represents "questioning," as school-aged youth in particular are often just figuring out their own sexual and gender identities; they may feel same-sex attractions, for example, but wonder if they can be heterosexual, or they may think they are gay but come to recognize that they are trans. The plus sign at the end of the acronym is a reminder that the acronym and the various identity terms used by various sexual- and gender-minority people are constantly evolving.

WHAT IS HOMOPHOBIA?

Homophobia denotes a broad spectrum of social-climate indicators of hostility to 2SLGBTQ+ people, ranging from casual use of pejorative language to violent personal assault. Although a problematic term in some ways, "homophobia" is a much clearer term than alternatives, such as "heterosexism" and "heteronormativity," since it keeps the focus on active hostility to 2SLGBTQ+ people rather than broadening the focus to include subtler forms of discrimination (an issue that is also worthy of study and critique). The term is used here not in an etymological sense to denote an irrational fear of homosexuals, but instead to refer to a sociological concept with an established history of usage to denote hostility to 2SLGBTQ+ people. This hostility is the logical and often intended product of social institutions (such as families, places of worship and school systems) that are implicated in creating and recreating relations of inequality (see, for example, Pharr 1988; Murray 2009).

Transphobia refers to hostility towards individuals based on their expressions of gender or gender identity. Many trans people also experience homophobia, when their gender identity is conflated with homosexuality. However, the experiences of LGB people (who experience attractions to people of their own gender, and who may or may not be conventional in their gender identity and gender expression) should not be confused with those of trans people (whose gender identity or gender expression does not match societal conventions of their birth sex, and who may or may not experience same-sex attractions). Transgender identities are in contrast to cisgender ones, which denote someone whose gender identity and expression match social conventions for the sex they were assigned at birth based on the alignment of their gender identity with their body parts: the feminine person designated female at birth or the masculine person designated male at birth. To this end, cisgender heterosexual (CH) normativity represents a cultural and societal bias, often unconscious, that privileges CH identities and conventional forms of gender expression.

WHY THE FUSS?

In response to several high-profile suicides by 2SLGBTQ+ youth and the growing body of research on school climate for 2SLGBTQ+ youth, in the past decade plus there has been a greater appreciation of hostile school climates and the negative impact they have on the well-being of Canadian youth. Alongside the increasing public and media attention of these grim stories of 2SLGBTQ+ students dealing with harassment and victimization in schools, researchers have been collecting data to confirm what many 2SLGBTQ+ advocates have long known — that these are not isolated incidents that result from homophobia and transphobia in schools but the outcome of widespread negative school climates for sexual- and gender-minority youth. In order to understand the more specific contexts that put 2SLGBTQ+ youth at risk for suicide and other negative health and educational outcomes, we draw on theoretical perspectives that offer an in-depth analysis of school climate. In this regard, school culture can be examined from a poststructuralist perspective, which enables us to appreciate how school climates are characterized by CH-normative discourse practices that are hostile to 2SLGBTQ+ well-being.

POSTSTRUCTURALISM

It is crucial to social change movements to examine discourse and, in particular, language practices because they powerfully structure our sense of self and our social relations. This is the subject of poststructural analysis. Poststructuralists question the status of "common sense" and challenge mainstream assumptions (for example, that all teenagers are CH). To do this, they critique how social patterns become constituted, reproduced and contested — which is an important analytical process for resisting oppression and working for change (Ristock 2002; Weedon 1997).

Within the context of homophobia and transphobia in Canada, poststructuralism is especially useful because it offers an approach whereby dominant discourses of CH-normativity can be critically analyzed in order to understand how life experiences are influenced by various social constructions. For example, heteronormativity is widely understood as "normative sexuality," which refers to the way in which social institutions (especially familial, educational, religious and legal) overtly or covertly work to reinforce CH standards (Weiss 2001). Included within these dominant standards is the belief that all individuals fall into one of two, and only two, distinct cisgender categories: man or woman; that sexual attraction is only "normal" when it occurs between two people of binaristic man-woman genders; and that each of these genders has certain natural or essential roles and behaviours to which all individuals should conform, depending on which sex they are assigned at birth based on their body parts. Those who critique CH-normative discourse argue that it stigmatizes alternative sexualities and ways of "doing gender" that do not conform to mainstream notions of heterosexuality or masculinity/femininity. Thus, critically investigating CH-normativity enables an exploration of the ways in which homophobia and transphobia become constituted through the power of discourse and how that power can be resisted.

DISCOURSE

The study of discourse primarily stems from Michel Foucault's (1979, 1980, 1981) work. Foucault argued that, as humans, we are in a constant state of incarceration — we are imprisoned by the practices (including language practices) of modern social systems and institutions, which he calls "discourses." Foucault promoted the study of discourses (instead of focusing strictly on structural inequalities like capitalism and patriarchy) in order to analyze how "regimes of truth" are socially constructed or produced and attain the status of common sense that structures our lives. Drawing on Foucault's work, Janice Ristock (2002) maintains that critically analyzing discourses is useful because assumptions of what is normative are maintained through categories that include some (such as those who are CH) and exclude others (such as 2SLGBTQ+ people). Discourse analysis, then, can describe how who we think we are and how we act are created through an interplay of power and knowledge. As such, we can explore how the social constructions of cisgender heterosexuality form dominant discourses, which create truth claims and normalize the way all people should act and behave. Dominant discourses provide a working language in which all are expected to recognize ourselves and conform as "docile bodies" to the rules they convey, both implicitly and explicitly. Similar to the position taken by symbolic interactionists, individuals become themselves the "bearers of discourse" by thinking and acting as though they really are what discourse requires them to be; however, a Foucauldian approach differs from symbolic interactionism in that the former draws on the "microphysics of power" to explain how power is imbedded within social structures and relations, while the latter is primarily focused on the micro-level aspects of daily social interactions without a specific theory of power (Dennis and Martin 2005).

In Foucault's (1979) analysis, the social regulation of human behaviour through dominant discourses occurs through "normalized judgment." Normalized judgment refers to a desire to produce conformity through the creation of a homogenous group whereby everyone is encouraged to adopt the same behaviour and enforce it in others. There is, however, an individualizing effect because each person is measured against the dominant discursive norm. This is achieved by measuring an individual against an essential criterion (or ideal type) of appropriate behaviour and then assessing how much of a gap exists between this individual and the desired norm. For 2SLGBTQ+ people, the outcome of such discourse calculations is the effective stigmatization of their sexuality and gender expression/identity through CH-normativity.

The significance of normative discourses can be seen if we examine how social rules are often followed because of the threat of stigma on those who disregard or violate them. For instance, in order to secure normative ideals of cisgender heterosexuality, there need to be individuals who fall outside these socially constructed expectations. Creating sexual and gender outliers like 2SLGBTQ+ people as Others is one of the ways that cisgender identity and heterosexuality are normalized.

NORMALIZING GENDER

Feminist writers such as Judith Butler (1987, 1990, 1993, 1996) and Denise Riley (1988) question approaches that dichotomize man and woman. They argue that the binaries of man/woman or heterosexual/homosexual reflect universal, static and ahistorical assumptions where some individuals, such as women and homosexuals, are oppressively relegated to the subordinate end of the dichotomy. Such dualisms deal strictly with difference and opposition. The problem with the rigid dichotomy within gender is that it depends on an obviously false binary split of femininity and masculinity as opposites that are strictly attached to female and male bodies, respectively. Only through deconstructing such social constructions can the regulative and normative formations of gender identity be exposed.

Especially in the case of gender identity, feminist theory has contested the presumed fundamental assumptions of masculinity and femininity because, like heterosexism, they prohibit the possibility of alternative accounts and experiences. Linda Alcoff (1988), for instance, acknowledges that gender is not a pre-discursive entity. In other words, gender does not exist prior to the ways we think and talk about it. Rather, it is a construction that is logically formalized through a matrix of practices and customs that most people consent to perform. Likewise, for Butler (1990), identity does not precede the performance of one's gender ("doing gender"), which is instead constituted through the convergence of multiple discourses (those of family, religion, media and so on) in our lives that supply the social and language practices appropriate to our assigned sex. Over the course of countless repetitions of these performances in childhood and adolescence, assigned gender comes to feel natural to many people, as though it arises directly from one's birth sex. "Doing gender," then, encompasses how males and females "perform" different roles in society, as though it is natural that they do so. But if gender is performative rather than a natural function of birth sex, why should all young people be expected to "perform" the feminine woman/girl or the masculine man/boy and be stigmatized when they do not?

Within a performative framework, the ideals inherent in dominant discourses of masculinity and femininity are not suitable to all men and women. Although it could be argued that most people are more or less comfortable with playing their parts as laid out in CH-normative discourse, many are not, and the existence of people living as 2SLGBTQ+ shows that it is possible to resist discursively dictated norms of masculinity and femininity and to create alternative or resistant identities that perform subcultural variations of gender roles or identities. We may be "incarcerat-ed" in profound ways by normative discourses, but we are clearly not doomed to live as "docile bodies."

NORMALIZING HETEROSEXUALITY

In *The History of Sexuality*, Foucault (1981) explores the "truth effects" of sex rather than its "origins." This is a crucial distinction, as the study of truth effects is much more interested in the consequences of beliefs being accepted as true than in whether they do in fact correspond to some objective reality. Because sexuality, as we experience it, is so powerfully structured by discourse, it cannot be specifically located or contained within an individual's body, nor is it a natural phenomenon. Rather, sexuality is formed within and informed by social forces. Sexuality, then, is something that is culturally constructed, sustained and reproduced through a collection of socially prescribed norms. That does not mean that without discourse there would be no sexual desire (or death, or sunrises, or trees); it means, rather, that our experience of sexuality is inseparable from the discourses about sexuality in which our lives are lived and that the feeling of "naturalness" is itself a product of discourse.

Foucault explains the inseparability of sexuality from discourse by arguing that the Victorian era (mid- to late nineteenth century) saw a "proliferation of discourse" around sex in which sexual relations were strictly regulated in order to produce and reproduce docile bodies in family units that served the interests of the new industrial economy and social order. Sexuality was no longer seen as the property of just a body. Instead, it became the quintessential representation of self, which influenced the way people talked about sex. This "deployment of sexuality" operated through normalizing techniques, and created — via social discourse — "compulsory heterosexuality" (Rich 1980), which continues to be socially enforced.

As mentioned earlier, even today, years after the repeal of most discriminatory laws against 2SLGBTQ+ people, cis-normative, heteronormative categories resonate in various communities. Implicit in CH assumptions are normalcy and naturalness, which thereby construct all other sexualities as abnormal and unnatural. Same-sex attractions and/or transgender identities continue to be stigmatized as deviant, and cisgender heterosexuality

> Same-sex attractions and/or transgender identities continue to be stigmatized as deviant, and cisgender heterosexuality continues to be maintained in part through the social penalties for failing to conform, which range from fairly minor to brutal.

continues to be maintained in part through the social penalties for failing to conform, which range from fairly minor to brutal (an example of such brutality is Scott Jones of Nova Scotia, who was left a paraplegic in 2013 from being stabbed in the neck and the back because he is gay — see CBC News 2013). Cisgender heterosexuality, then, becomes regulated and is regarded as not just the normalized but the *normal* form of sexuality and gender identity.

POWER/KNOWLEDGE/RESISTANCE

Also central to a poststructuralist framework are the interrelated concepts of power, knowledge and resistance. Specifically, Foucault (1979, 1980) maintains that a conventional model of power focuses on the repressive state apparatus of law enforcement, overlooking the complex and multifaceted existence of domination via the knowledge-producing institutions of society — institutions such as religion, psychiatry and education — which produce knowledge that comes to be accepted as the truth. Foucault (1980) contends that power and knowledge are so implicated in each other that the two are inseparable; hence his use of the term "*pouvoir/savoir*" or "power/knowledge." Producing knowledge is seen as having powerful effects on people — a very different idea from the truism that (acquiring) knowledge results in one having power. However, Foucault was not interested in the exercise of juridical power through incarceration or corporal punishment, where there is little or no possibility of resistance, but rather in the kinds of power that are exercised throughout our social relations and that exist without the use of brute force. For him, therefore, "where there is power, there is resistance" (1979: 95). Resistance is like power in that it has no life outside the relationship in which it is occurring; as a result, power and resistance can be examined only in particular contexts and thus not by using generalities. Finally, resistance manifests itself in multiple ways because it is not a homogeneous, fixed phenomenon.

Such theorizing enables the examination of situations where someone, for example, may feel powerless in one instance (for example, students among teachers and school administrators) but powerful in another (for example, the same students participating in homophobic and transphobic bullying). The interrelatedness of power and powerlessness also allows us to conceptualize how people can be in a privileged and an oppressed situation at the same time.

2SLGBTQ+ and CH people alike are bound to dominant sexual discourses that locate them in very different positions in the social-sexual hierarchy — a hierarchy that subordinates 2SLGBTQ+ individuals. Nevertheless, it is possible to disrupt this control of sexuality by engaging in counter-discourses, such as those for 2SLGBTQ+ rights, that challenge what is accepted as "real" or "natural." This allows space for "agency," or living out alternatives, where individuals do not behave like docile bodies; they thereby jeopardize the "naturalness" of everyday sexual knowledge and custom, exposing it as a set of oppressive fictions and thus opening spaces for others to act in ways that dominant discourses otherwise foreclose.

LANGUAGE

Knowledge is embedded in language, which does not always reflect "reality." Instead, language reproduces a world that is constantly in transition and is never definitive. Language, then, organizes experience and is not an expression of unique individuality; put another way, we are "born into language" and its representations of ourselves and our world. Its social influence in the construction of an individual's subjectivity is enormous. However, that process is neither fixed nor stable. We can conceive of language as a system of "signs." Embedded in each sign is a "signifier" (a sound, text or image) and a "signified" (the meaning of the signifier). For instance, there is nothing inherent to the term "faggot" — rather, the meaning of faggot is produced in relation to other signifiers of sexuality, such as "straight," to which meaning is attached, and vice versa (Weedon 1997: 23). Language, then, is a powerful tool of oppressive discourses; in the spheres of gender and sexuality, language classifies and orders experiences by signifying cisgender heterosexuality as normal and any other ways of doing gender and sexuality as abnormal.

The best way to understand the effects of language is to analyze the discourse systems in which it is used. For example, language like "that's so gay" is pretty much an everyday occurrence that both draws on and reinforces homophobic and transphobic discourses. When such language is used, normalized discourses of femininity and masculinity as well as compulsory heterosexuality are reinforced because statements like "that's so gay" are usually used as analogous to "that's so absurd" or as being somehow disagreeable, and in so doing these statements reinforce heterosexuality as sensible or "correct."

These processes of discourse and language play out in everyday life, not only enforcing CH-normativity, but also producing the counter-discourses of diverse sexuality and gender identities. Examining the discourses around gender and sexuality show that the "promise" of the *Charter of Rights and Freedoms* is far from having been achieved when it comes to gender and sexuality.

EXPERIENCES OF 2SLGBTQ+ YOUTH

The case of homophobia and transphobia in high schools illustrates these general processes of CH-normativity, and resistance to it, in Canadian society. To give empirical substance to the general and theoretical discussions above, we discuss the results of a major study of homophobia and transphobia among students and young people in Canada below (Peter, Campbell and Taylor 2021).

A School Climate Survey and Its Participants

A high school student survey was conducted between April 2019 and May 2020, conceived as a follow-up to the first National Climate Survey on homophobia, biphobia and transphobia in Canadian schools administered a decade previously. The survey asked participants a series of questions on their school climate in the past year, with a particular focus on experiences of hostility, targeted harassment, impacts and interventions. In total, 3,558 individuals answered the questionnaire. Their social characteristics are broad, representing much of Canada:

- Nearly two thirds (62 percent) identified as straight/heterosexual. Thirty-eight percent identified as 2SLGBTQ+.

- Over half (57 percent) identified as woman/girl, 36 percent identified as man/boy, 6 percent identified as non-binary, 4 percent as trans and 9 percent as additional/alternative gender minority identity terms such as Two-Spirit, genderqueer, transmasculine, transfeminine, agender and genderfluid (note: given the fluidity of gender, overall percentages exceed 100 percent because participants could select more than one gender identity). Seven percent selected more than one gender identity from the multiple options provided.

- Participants were distributed across the regions of Canada, with higher numbers from the Atlantic provinces where two school systems agreed to introduce the survey throughout the province in whole-school settings.

- Seventy-eight percent of participants identified as white, 8 percent as Indigenous, 8 percent as Asian, 2 percent as Black and 3 percent as another racialized identity, including those with multiple racialized identities.

- Participants were fairly evenly distributed across grades, with 16 percent in Grade 8, 25 percent in Grade 9, 22 percent in Grade 10, 17 percent in Grade 11 and 17 percent in Grade 12.

- The average age of respondents was 15.9 years, with a median age of 16 years.

Hostile Discourse within Canadian Schools

While there have been some improvements between what students reported experiencing in the first Climate Survey and what they reported in the second, it would appear that, despite any popular conceptions to the contrary, Canadian schools are, like Canadian society generally is, still hostile for 2SLGBTQ+ students. There is a good deal of symbolic violence in schools and elsewhere — 2SLGBTQ+ people hear lots of homophobic comments, either directed at them or just voiced generally, all the time. Almost two thirds (64 percent) of the surveyed students, for example, reported hearing expressions like "that's so gay" daily or weekly in school, and only 10 percent commented that they never heard such remarks in school. In addition, almost half (48 percent) of the students reported hearing remarks such as "faggot," "queer," "lezbo" or "dyke" daily or weekly in school, while 19 percent commented that they never heard such remarks in school.

> Almost two thirds (64 percent) of the surveyed students reported hearing expressions like "that's so gay" daily or weekly in school, and only 10 percent commented that they never heard such remarks in school.

The Every Teacher Project (Peter, Campbell and Taylor 2015), conducted in 2013, confirms the widespread use of homonegative language in Canadian schools. Of the 3,319 educators surveyed across Canada, nearly half (49 percent) reported hearing comments like "that's so gay" at least weekly in their school, and only 12 percent indicated that they had never heard such comments. Over one quarter (27 percent) of educators reported hearing homophobic comments such as "faggot" or "dyke" at least weekly at their school. The lower numbers from the Every Teacher Project are to be expected given that such language is often used when teachers are not present (in hallways, washrooms and changerooms, for example). Homonegative language ("that's so gay"), however, is so societally pervasive that even teachers reported hearing it from their peers (22 percent), with 20 percent indicating that it was only in the staff room (and other non-student places) and 4 percent reporting that such language was used in the presence of students.

Even though the signifier "that's so gay" does not directly mean "homosexual," its signified message is that something is absurd, strange or worthless. As one student from the first Climate Survey so succinctly describes, "The expression 'that's so gay' is extremely commonly used but I've found that, more often than not, people don't use it as a way to verbally bash gay people, just simply as a synonym for [...] 'weird' and don't actually have the anti-gay beliefs behind the phrase." For 2SLGBTQ+ students, however, the expression "that's so gay" is only the tip of the iceberg when it comes to hearing derogatory language that goes to the core of their identity, as the following comments illustrate:

> I hear so, so many times "that's so gay" or "F*ggot" from people I call my friends and though I continually tell them that it's not ok they say it was a joke.

> A lot of students, cis male mostly, say derogatory slurs about LGBT daily and it makes me and my LGBT friends feel not safe.

As in all contexts, language is relational and a powerful tool of oppression because it structures experience by signifying what is normal and what is not. Since the majority of students in the majority of schools across Canada regularly are subjected to hearing "that's so gay" in their school, the implicit message is that homosexuality is absurd and worthless and that heterosexuality, conversely, is cool and valuable. Such homophobic language practices draw on and reinforce heteronormative discourse in which 2SLGBTQ+ identities are not recognized as acceptable or natural.

Negative gender-related or transphobic comments are very common in our society, and potentially increasing as trans visibility increases. For instance, men and boys who display feminine qualities are often chastised for acting like a woman/girl. Schools clearly illustrate this kind of discursive oppression. "Don't be a girl" is a common phrase directed at boys in high schools. Sexual- and gender-minority students were somewhat more likely to note the use of transphobic language and language that negatively targets gender. For instance, 29 percent of trans participants reported hearing explicitly transphobic language daily or weekly, compared to 19 percent of participants in general. Thirty-eight percent of trans participants reported hearing comments about "girls not acting feminine enough" daily or weekly, followed by 29 percent of LGBQ girls, 24 percent of CH boys, 23 percent of CH girls and 21 percent of GBQ boys. Seventy-eight percent of trans youth and 78 percent of cisgender LGBQ girls reported hearing negative remarks about girls daily or weekly in school, compared to 68 percent of CH girls, 58 percent of cisgender GBQ boys, and 56 percent of CH boys. It is not surprising that trans students reported hearing transphobic comments more frequently than CH students, given that they would be the most aware about the rules of CH-normative discourse and the penalties for departing from them. In addition to trans students being more acutely aware of these remarks, it is also likely that such remarks are deliberately made in their presence.

CONSEQUENCES OF VIOLATING DOMINANT DISCOURSE

There are significant consequences for individuals, whether 2SLGBTQ+ or CH, who violate the CH-normative rules of dominant sexuality and gender discourse. The contours and variations of these negative consequences are well illustrated by life in high schools. For students, this process occurred in three contexts: unsafe spaces, more directed forms of violence (that is, verbal and physical harassment as well as other forms of victimization) and the impact of such CH-normative violations.

Unsafe Spaces

There are a variety of spaces in everyday life that are not safe for 2SLGBTQ+ people; spaces that CH people take for granted as non-threatening — some highly visible and public, some more hidden from view — ranging from restaurants to workplace hallways to elevators and stairwells. We gave students a list of places involved in everyday life at school (hallways, the cafeteria, classrooms, the library, stairwells/under stairs, the gymnasium, physical education changerooms, the school grounds, washrooms, school buses and spaces occupied while travelling to and from school) and asked them to identify any that they thought would be unsafe for 2SLGBTQ+ students. Fifty-seven percent of CH students and 71 percent of 2SLGBTQ+ students identified at least one area at school that was unsafe for 2SLGBTQ+ individuals. Not surprisingly, there was a positive relationship between sexual orientation/gender identity and how unsafe high school seems for 2SLGBTQ+ students, with the students most stigmatized in CH-normative discourse being most likely to see school as unsafe for 2SLGBTQ+ students. For example, 90 percent of transgender, 73 percent of cisgender LGBQ girls and 64 percent of cisgender GBQ boys acknowledged at least one area of their school as being unsafe for 2SLGBTQ+ students, compared to 57 percent of CH students. Moreover, compared to non-2SLGBTQ+ students, 2SLGBTQ+ youth were significantly more likely to see washrooms (56 versus 34 percent), changerooms (53 versus 27 percent) and hallways (43 versus 34 percent) as unsafe, which is relatively consistent with GLSEN's US-based study (Kosciw et al. 2020) and the Canadian trans youth survey, where 55 percent of trans youth reported avoiding school locker rooms and 55 percent school washrooms for safety reasons (Taylor, Chan, Hall et al. 2020). It is interesting to note that two of these spaces are private areas (physical education changerooms and washrooms), while the third (hallways) is a public place. However, these three spaces are largely unsupervised, which makes them easy sites for student-to-student harassment.

The prevalence of homophobic harassment was highlighted by several students:

I hate how when I'm taunted and insulted and yelled at constantly it's considered as everyday regular bullying when the difference is because I'm queer and I stand up for my fellow queer students. I was given death threats and nothing was done besides giving a "slap of the hand" to my bully. It needs to be understood that the suffering of queer students in school is different to those of straight people.

Safety is not just physical, but also emotional. No one would've been beaten at my school for being gay or trans, but social exclusion, whispers, rumours, verbal bullying and such were prominent.

I had a classmate of mine at [school] say he wants to burn the gays, and if his brother was gay he threatened to kill him. I told my principal that and he didn't do anything.

As is evident in these narratives, prejudice is more likely to occur in some places than others, depending on factors such as opportunity, exposure, presence of potential witnesses and the type of activity associated with the place (for example, showering and contact sports).

Directed Violence

The perceived safety of a space is largely determined by the likelihood, or the perception of the likelihood, of encountering some kind of violence. 2SLGBTQ+ people find many "normally" safe places to be ones in which they often encounter violent behaviour — verbal and physical — directed at them by others. This represents another, more direct way that CH-normativity is enforced. Three out of five (57 percent) transgender students, 42 percent of cisgender LGBQ girls, 38 percent of cisgender GBQ boys, 15 percent of CH girls and 12 percent of CH boys reported having been the target of mean rumours or lies during the last twelve months. Over half (53 percent) of trans students and 37 percent of cisgender LGBQ students were verbally harassed about their sexual orientation at school, compared to only 8 percent of CH students. In addition, 63 percent of trans, 40 percent of cisgender LGBQ, and 15 percent of CH respondents reported being the targets of verbal harassment because of their gender expression. It is also important to point out that anywhere between 5 percent and 15 percent of CH-identified students reported experiencing verbal harassment due to their gender expression or perceived sexual orientation. In a school of one thousand students, where up to, say, 90 percent are CH, this translates to approximately ninety CH youth who are verbally harassed because they don't live up to the dominant discourses of gender within a school culture (that is, girls who are not feminine enough or boys who are not masculine enough). Similar results were found in the Every Teacher Project (Taylor, Peter, Campbell et al. 2015). For example, 67 percent of teachers were aware of verbal harassment of at least one 2SLGBTQ+ student in the past year, 55 percent knew of incidents where rumours or lies were spread about a student's sexual orientation (or perceived sexual orientation) or their gender identity and one-third (33 percent) were aware of physical harassment.

> In a school of one thousand students, where up to, say, 90 percent are CH, this translates to approximately ninety CH youth who are verbally harassed because they don't live up to the dominant discourses of gender within a school culture.

These are not just statistics. They are real people suffering the real humiliation of a high level of directed violence, as the following comments from 2SLGBTQ+ students describe:

I got chased out of school for being gay but I had a boyfriend [who] also got kicked by 12 girls in a parking lot.

I got things like food thrown at me from the bus, while they yell tranny or fag at me.

I'm a joke to everyone, I am harassed for being trans almost everyday.

I'm frequently cyberbullied for being LGBTQ.

I just want people to accept LGBTQ+ in my school. I tell my principal and vice principal that I'm being bullied for my gender/sexual orientation but they don't do anything about it.

My committee once held a booth to inform others about LGBTQ facts and history. About ten guys came up and started saying really nasty things like "Gays should die," "If I saw two dudes kissing, I would beat them up," and "Gays are disgusting."

There are groups of boys who will sexually harass or assault students that are perceived as female. They ignore it when they are told to stop and will even get physical without consent. On several occasions I have been catcalled or felt up while trying to get home. Many students fear these boys due to how they don't hesitate to become violent.

Clearly, there is a high level of victimization due to sexual- and gender-related harassment (as well as the depression, anxiety and fear associated with it) endured by 2SLGBTQ+ students and CH students in Canadian schools.

2SLGBTQ+ people experience many forms of physical violence, up to and including murder. Certainly the tragic killing of forty-nine individuals at a gay nightclub in Orlando, Florida, by a lone gunman in June 2016 provides a frightening reminder of the real-life "truth effects" of some people's acceptance of homophobic discourse (see Alvarez and Pérez-Peña 2016). While such brute force is at the extreme end of homophobic discourse and unlikely to occur in a school setting, educational institutions are not immune to horrible forms of violence, as we have seen in the multiple mass murders that have taken place in schools. However, homophobic brute force in schools most often takes the form of bullying because of one's sexual orientation and shows clearly that gender makes a significant difference to the quality of the lives of sexual-minority students.

Impacts

Not surprisingly, these levels of violence and abuse have dire consequences for 2SLGBTQ+ people. Harassment, violence and verbal abuse can only add to the stress levels in their lives. They feel emotional anguish as well as alienation from the communities in which they live. These stresses can lead to serious health consequences and are repeatedly regarded as factors leading individuals toward emotional distress or suicidal feelings that are often still acute in adulthood (Peter, Taylor and Campbell 2016; Peter and Taylor 2014; Taylor, Chan, Hall et al. 2020). For instance, comparing students' feelings of safety with their experiences of physical harassment, it is not surprising to see that those who have experienced physical harassment perceive their school as being less safe. Eight-nine percent of 2SLGBTQ+ students who experienced physical harassment indicated that they felt unsafe in their school (compared with 56 percent of 2SLGBTQ+ students who had not been physically harassed), while 43 percent of CH students who had been harassed reported feeling unsafe (compared to only 8 percent of those CH students who had not been harassed). Several 2SLGBTQ+ students describe the impacts of not feeling safe:

> I feel unsafe all the time, I just choose to very rarely skip because I risk my safety for my grades.

> Some trans students have been forced to participate in physical education classes while grouped with their assigned birth sex...

> Just the general feeling unsafe to come out/dress the way I want to because of students using LGBT terms negatively.

> I watched a transgender girl completely de-transition out of fear after receiving death threats that nobody did anything about.

The connections between homophobia/transphobia and acute mental distress are stark. For instance, over half (55 percent) of educators in our Every Teacher Project were aware of LGBTQ students who had self-harmed due to experiencing homophobic or transphobic harassment, and 47 percent knew of a LGBTQ student who considered suicide. In terms of emotional distress, in our student climate survey we found that over half (57 percent) of trans students and 47 percent of cisgender LGBQ students were "extremely upset" by homophobic comments. Thirty-seven percent of trans students and 26 percent of cisgender LGBQ respondents indicated that sometimes they felt depressed about school, compared to 16 percent of CH students, and 30 percent of trans and 17 percent of cisgender LGBQ students indicated that they didn't feel they belonged at their school, compared to 10 percent of CH students. Three students describe how difficult it is to be a sexual or gender minority (or to be perceived as one) in Canadian schools and its impact on their identity:

> One of my friends was outed and she doesn't feel safe in her class anymore. Transphobia is absolutely rampant, and lots of people make rape or sexual assault jokes.

> I feel like school in general is safer for stealth trans kids and people who can more hide their queerness. But for those of us who are very apparently LGBTQ+ it can get scary sometimes. I used to skip classes because I had homophobic and transphobic teachers who made me feel unsafe and unwelcome in the classroom.

> Because I am not out yet and/or I don't act feminine, I feel safe. Which I usually act feminine but preferred not to do in school because didn't wanted to people publicly find out I'm gay. (Which I don't care about people in school to find out, I'm scared that my parents [will] find out.)

> Bathrooms and changerooms feels unsafe at times. Scared I'll be called out

for not being feminine enough to use the girls bathroom/changeroom or that people will be suspicious of my intentions in either places.

I'm pretty solidly closeted so that acts like a barrier to any harm that may come by me. I'm not extremely concerned about direct violence, but transphobia and homophobia are definitely present in the school atmosphere and very concerning to me...

Skipping school is one way to deal with feeling unsafe either at school or on the way to school. Thirty-seven percent of 2SLGBTQ+ students, compared to 18 percent of CH respondents, reported skipping because they felt unsafe at school or on the way to school. Transgender students were even more likely to miss school because they felt unsafe (48 versus 32 percent for cisgender LGBQ respondents). GLSEN

> Transgender students were even more likely to miss school because they felt unsafe.

(Kosciw et al. 2020) reports similarly: 33 percent of LGBTQ students reported missing at least one day of school in the past month because they felt unsafe or uncomfortable, with those who had experienced some form of harassment or discrimination being more likely to skip school (e.g., 44 percent of those who had experienced LGBTQ-related discrimination in their school reported they had missed school in the past month compared to 16 percent of those who had not experienced discrimination).

Homophobic and transphobic bullying also leads students to feel less attached to their school communities. For instance, almost three quarters (74 percent) of trans and 57 percent of LGBQ participants strongly agreed or somewhat agreed with the statement "It is hard for me to feel accepted at my school," compared to 37 percent of CH students. Trans students were also less likely (11 percent) to agree with the statement, "I feel like a real part of my school," compared to 20 percent of cisgender LGBQ and 24 percent of CH students.

These statistics are important, not only because of what they reveal about the degree of fear sexual- and gender-minority students experience on a regular basis, but also because of the potential impact missing classes can have on the academic achievement for these students. In short, the experiences of these students do seem to suggest that being on the outside of CH-normative discourse in a school setting where sexuality and gender norms are strictly regulated makes it much harder for 2SLGBTQ+ students to engage with school life, either socially or academically.

CONFLICTING DISCOURSES:
HUMAN RIGHTS VERSUS HALLWAY PEDAGOGY

> Most of the gay community in my school are bullied. We all stick together, but that doesn't always help. Many gays are depressed because of this, and teachers and adults need to help and stand up for our community. We are not aliens, we're people, and we have rights.

Time spent in high school is very tumultuous for most students. However, as this comment from a student who participated in the first National Climate Survey suggests, for 2SLGBTQ+ students, high school represents not only a hostile experience, but also one that occurs in a deeply contradictory discourse context. On the one hand, schools promise safety and respect for all students. For example, students learn in social studies that Canada defends everyone's human rights and celebrates diversity/multiculturalism. On the other hand, however, students witness the disrespect of 2SLGBTQ+ students every day, and they often see their teachers look the other way. The combined pedagogical effect of these conflicting discourses is the message that the *Charter of Rights and Freedoms* applies to everyone but gay people — if it applied to them, more teachers would be saying something about all the abuse they take. It is no different for 2SLGBTQ+ people in general — we live in a society that constantly proclaims the great freedoms we all enjoy. Yet the promises of "life, liberty, and security of person" (as outlined in Section 7 of the Charter) conflict with the lived experiences of 2SLGBTQ+ people.

Many school systems have begun to implement interventions that are designed to send the message that 2SLGBTQ+ people are indeed entitled to the same rights as everyone else and that 2SLGBTQ+ students are fully welcome in the school community. These interventions, such as gay-straight alliance/gender and sexuality alliance clubs (GSAs), 2SLGBTQ+-inclusive curricula and anti-homophobia and anti-transphobia harassment policies, can be thought of as counter-discourse and resistance strategies. In a 2014 survey, superintendents across Canada representing 141 school districts (36 percent of all districts in Canada) reported on the forms and extent of school system interventions made in support of the well-being of 2SLGBTQ+ students and staff in school districts (Taylor, Peter, Edkins et al. 2016). Over one third (38 percent) reported that their district has a policy that specifically addresses 2SLGBTQ+-inclusive education, which most often covered issues pertaining to harassment. But what is the students' knowledge of, and experiences with, anti-homophobia policies as well as GSAS?

GSAS

GSAS are official student clubs with 2SLGBTQ+ and CH student membership and typically one or two teachers who serve as faculty advisors. In our Every Teacher Project, over half of high school teachers indicated that their school had a GSA (Taylor, Peter, Campbell et al. 2015). Superintendents report that 51 percent of their districts had at least one GSA or some other LGBTQ-specific club (Taylor, Peter, Edkins et al. 2016).

The purpose of GSAS is to provide a much-needed safe space in which 2SLGBTQ+ students and allies can work together on making their schools more welcoming for sexual- and gender-minority students. GSAS have been shown to have many benefits (Saewyc et al. 2014), one of which is greater awareness for the school community as a whole. One student described their school's inclusive efforts as extending beyond the GSA club:

> My school's super inclusive. We have several LGBT friendly and encouraging events, such as fundraisers, a drag race, two GSA clubs, and a rainbow painting (representing the gay straight alliance) right outside the school....

One teacher from our Every Teacher Project commented:

> Individual teachers are improving with regards to addressing homophobic and transphobic harassment issues. We have an active GSA in the school and they work on educating both staff and students through school activities. (Taylor, Peter, Campbell et al. 2015: 36)

This educator's experience has occurred elsewhere. Our study found a positive correlation between the presence of a GSA and participation in LGBTQ-awareness days (for example, 2SLGBTQ+ pride events, LGBT history month and so on). Educators from schools with a GSA are more likely to acknowledge the helpfulness of such clubs in creating safer schools for LGBTQ students (79 percent versus 58 percent for those from high schools without a GSA). 2SLGBTQ+ students from schools in districts that publicly endorse GSA clubs were more likely (63 percent) to see their school administrators (i.e., principal or vice-principal) as being supportive of their school's club than those from districts that did not encourage GSAS (20 percent) or those who did not know whether their district supported GSAS (44 percent). Further, 2SLGBTQ+ students who indicated their administrators were very supportive (75 percent) or somewhat supportive (61 percent) were more likely to feel like a real part of their school, compared to those who saw them as being either unsupportive or neither supportive nor unsupportive (34 percent). This also had impacts for 2SLGBTQ+ students' feelings of safety, with those from schools with very supportive administrators (38 percent) and somewhat supportive administrators (52 percent) less likely to report feeling unsafe than those from schools either unsupportive or neutral administrators.

As a staple of recent Canadian legislation (as seen in Ontario, Manitoba and Alberta) and one of the simplest interventions to implement, GSAs function as effective protective factors for 2SLGBTQ+ youth. It is important to note, however, that not all GSAS are the same. For instance, Fetner and colleagues (2012) contend that even though generally GSAs serve a positive function, each club creates its own character based on its school and community context, the openness around membership and the group's commitment to activity or activism within their school or wider community (see also Poteat et al. 2015). It is also worth acknowledging that these positive outcomes are not guaranteed and require the investment of the school community to support potentially transforming GSA clubs. For instance, two 2SLGBTQ+ students expressed frustration with the limitations of GSAs in the broader school:

> LGBT people are silenced and GSA is useless because you're still keeping it a group, not the entire school.

> We tried to make an LGBT club last year, but we kind of all stopped going…. Our principal is not a fan of the community, though, and he said that the rainbow flag was not a real flag.

Too often, a "one and done" mentality exists, whereby school administrators permit (or are forced to permit by provincial legislation) a GSA but fail to encourage capacity building or provide adequate resources, supports and/or funding for ongoing programming (Russell 2011; Taylor, Peter, Edkins et al. 2016).

INSTITUTIONAL RESPONSES

Sexual- and gender-minority students in schools with comprehensive anti-harassment policies that clearly included sexual orientation and gender identity/expression report lower levels of harassment, fewer homophobic and transphobic comments and more staff intervention when such comments are made (Kosciw et al. 2020). Moreover, in the US, generic safe-school policies that do not include specific measures on homophobia are ineffective in improving the school climate for LGBTQ students. We asked Canadian students whether their schools had anti-homophobia policies or procedures as a context for their reporting about their lives at school. Asking students about policy, of course, does not indicate whether or not schools actually have policies, only whether or not students think that they do. It is likely that some students were wrong about their schools or school divisions not having policies. However, students reporting either that anti-homophobia policies do not exist when in fact they do, or that they do not even know whether or not their schools or school boards have such policies, suggests that schools need to make further efforts to publicly implement their policies among their student bodies: a procedure for reporting homophobic incidents that youth do not know about is not effective.

2SLGBTQ+ students who reported that their schools had anti-homophobia or anti-transphobia policies or procedures were significantly more likely to feel that their school community was supportive of 2SLGBTQ+ individuals (44 versus 9 percent); to report that teachers or other staff intervened more effectively in incidents of homophobia (34 versus 7 percent); and to feel more comfortable at their school (for instance, 64 percent of students from schools with policies or procedures for reporting incidents of homophobia or transphobia agreed that they could be themselves at school, compared to 42 percent of those from schools without policies or procedures).

What about educators and institutional/school policies? In the Every Teacher Project, the presence of a policy aids in administrators' commitment to provide resources for LGBTQ issues. For instance, two thirds (67 percent) of educators from schools with an anti-homophobic harassment policy and almost three quarters (74 percent) of those from schools with an anti-transphobic harassment policy reported having a resource person specializing in LGBTQ issues, versus 32 percent of those from schools without an anti-homophobic policy and 34 percent without an anti-transphobic harassment policy. For teachers who indicated that their school had progressive policies, those educators who responded that they had not received sufficient training or had not been trained at all were significantly more likely to report being aware of verbal harassment (80 percent) than those who felt that they were very well or adequately prepared (60 percent). As one teacher comments:

> I feel sometimes teachers choose to ignore a comment so they don't have to deal with it. There is no direction on who to give the problem to or what the follow up would be. We have an equity binder but were told to read it on our own with no direction. So basically it will be shelved and not looked at.

Thus, while anti-homophobic and/or anti-transphobic harassment policies on their own are not enough to lower the incidence of harassment, a policy effectively implemented by incorporating staff training can.

Little is known about the outcomes of 2SLGBTQ+-inclusive curriculum (because there has been very little of it in existence that has been comprehensively and consistently implemented). It is an established principle of inclusive education that it is important for marginalized students to see their identity group represented in the curriculum to counter the impacts of stigmatization they experience elsewhere (much like seeing racialized individuals in mainstream television commercials). We found, for example, and that students who viewed their schools as being supportive of 2SLGBTQ+ people, which includes curricular inclusion, having supportive teachers, 2SLGBTQ+ events and GSAS, were more likely to have better mental health, more likely to feel like they belonged at their school and less likely to skip school. Elsewhere, 2SLGBTQ+-inclusive curricula are correlated with students feeling safer at school, experiencing less harassment, having better academic outcomes and higher academic aspirations (Kosciw et al. 2020). Even though widespread inclusion of 2SLGBTQ+ curriculum is rare, the majority of Canadian educators (78 percent) report having included 2SLGBTQ+ content in some way in their classroom, ranging from one-off references to repeated occasions and multiple methods (Taylor, Peter, Campbell et al. 2015). However, while these attempts at 2SLGBTQ+ inclusion are increasingly common, the need for greater resources and professional development is still needed, as one in five educators reported not knowing of any 2SLGBTQ+ education resources, including inclusive curriculum guides.

REASON FOR HOPE

As the experiences of students and educators show, the bad news is that both homophobia and transphobia are widespread in Canadian schools, thereby casting doubts that 2SLGBTQ+ people have achieved social equality within the Canadian landscape. The good news, however, is that in schools where even small efforts have been made, students and teachers report better climates, thereby providing support for the importance of legal rights for 2SLGBTQ+ people. The substantial improvements in school culture associated with even modest interventions such as minor curricular inclusion suggest that even though homophobia and transphobia may be pervasive in Canadian schools, they are perhaps not very deeply rooted. In this regard, much like the "legal equality" guaranteed through official legislation as well as the Charter, institutional legislation within schools does provide students with some safety.

And yet there is even better news. Fifty-nine percent of CH-identified students, or roughly 1,280 of the 2,170 straight students, found it upsetting to hear homophobic remarks. There are many reasons why so many CH students would be upset by homophobic and transphobic bigotry. Some of these CH students are perceived to be 2SLGBTQ+ themselves and targeted accordingly, or they are targeted just to damage their social standing. Other students are upset by homophobia/transphobia because

they have an 2SLGBTQ+ parent or sibling, or they have a 2SLGBTQ+ friend. Still other students are simply kind
and feel empathy for their
peers who are being grossly
mistreated. And then there
are those who are ashamed

> Fifty-nine percent of CH-identified students found it upsetting to hear homophobic remarks.

of themselves for participating in bullying or for remaining silent when it was going
on. Finally, some simply find the presence of homophobia/transphobia depressing to
the human spirit and are disheartened to be a part of a school community that continually abuses people. This 59 percent suggests that there is a great deal of untapped
solidarity for their 2SLGBTQ+ peers among CH students and that the majority of students, both 2SLGBTQ+ and CH alike, would welcome some help from the adult world
in shifting their school culture towards a social justice approach. The Every Teacher
Project suggests that help could be on its way. In fact, the vast majority of educators
surveyed (85 percent) reported that they approve of LGBTQ+-inclusive education,
and almost all (96 percent) see 2SLGBTQ+ rights as human rights.

If so many students are upset by such degradation and so many teachers are supportive of 2SLGBTQ+ rights, why do so few intervene when homophobic/transpho-
bic comments are made or they witness homophobic/transphobic harassment and
abuse? Many students are afraid to act because they are well aware that challenging
CH-normative discourse puts them in danger of being perceived as 2SLGBTQ+ and becoming the targets of name-calling and violence. For them, the costs of speaking up
outweigh the benefits. We must never forget that high school is a time in the human
lifecourse when fitting in is one of the most important elements of well-being and
survival. Teenagers fall into line with using language like "that's so gay" or "faggot"
without fully understanding the painful bite of these words for 2SLGBTQ+ people,
who are well aware of their lowly positions in CH-normative discourse. Students using such language may not like these phrases, but the thought of leaving the "group"
and finding themselves in the uninhabitable zone of schoolyard discourse is also
agonizing. This is not to suggest that students are docile bodies with no agency or
ability to engage in transformative social change on issues pertaining to social justice or human rights; indeed, in some schools, students have led the way on this and
other social justice issues, lobbying the school administration to implement GSAs,
organizing 2SLGBTQ+-inclusive events, participating in 2SLGBTQ+ pride marches and
speaking up in class to critique homophobia or to address the absence of 2SLGBTQ+
content. It is simply to remind us that young people learn life lessons not only when
adults demonstrate apparent hypocrisy, but also when they demonstrate the courage
of their convictions. As one 2SLGBTQ+ student writes:

> I usually feel pretty safe at school, but sometimes I wish the adults would make more of an effort with correcting derogatory behaviour. It shouldn't be my or my peers' responsibility to make ourselves feel safer.

It is entirely unrealistic to always expect students to carry the heavy intervention load when incidents of homophobia/transphobia take place in school culture, which then leaves teachers and other educational personnel to step up. The Every Teacher Project asked educators who reported hearing homonegative ("that's so gay") and homophobic comments ("faggot" or "dyke") from students whether they had intervened. Nearly two thirds (64 percent) indicated that they always intervened when they heard homonegative comments, and 70 percent always intervened when they heard homophobic comments. Moreover, only 30 percent of teachers felt that their schools responded effectively to incidents of LGBTQ harassment; these numbers were slightly higher for educators from schools with anti-harassment policies, with, for instance, 44 percent of educators from schools with anti-transphobia policies indicating their school responded effectively compared to only 14 percent in schools without a policy (Taylor et al. 2015). As one teacher comments,

> I believe that my school is poorly equipped/prepared to deal with such incidents. They would rather pretend that these students do not exist. Nobody wants to talk about it. I know LGBT students who are getting bullied and I don't think anything is done.

The Every Teacher Project illustrates that while some educators are stepping up and intervening when they witness incidents of LGBTQ bullying, far too many still do not. The silence from these teachers helps to not only validate homophobia and transphobia, but it also ensures the recirculation of fear by teaching young people that they are on their own on this issue and that adults will not help them. Sadly, some school authorities and some parents tacitly approve of homophobia as an efficient strategy for enforcing compulsory heterosexuality. Unfortunately, some parents are so terrified of their children turning out gay that they would rather see them unhappy than see them un-heterosexual. Yet if all teachers, administrators and school boards started to speak respectfully of 2SLGBTQ+ people (literally and through specific interventions at the school and district levels), the silent majority of students — both 2SLGBTQ+ students and the 59 percent of CH students who report finding hom-

> Sadly, some school authorities and some parents tacitly approve of homophobia as an efficient strategy for enforcing compulsory heterosexuality.

ophobia distressing — would have more reason for courage. Young people may learn new ways to say "that's foolish" without insulting categories of people, and they may come to understand that most of their peers are not committed to homophobic behaviours either. 2SLGBTQ+ youth and the 59 percent of young CH people who quietly wish for something better would have a solid group of allies, backed by ample human rights legislation, that could alter the discourse systems of students across Canada.

RESISTANCE AND COUNTER-DISCOURSES

Given the hostile school climates that many 2SLGBTQ+ students face daily, it is apparent that there is a clear disconnect between Canada's official human rights discourse, which is endorsed broadly in society and specifically in classrooms, and the homophobic and transphobic discourse of Canadian schools. The end result is that schools are too often failing the children and youth they should be protecting and respecting, and as a result too many 2SLGBTQ+ students are going through school being harassed and disrespected. The hopeful findings — that the majority of CH students are distressed by homophobia and transphobia in schools and that most teachers are supportive of 2SLGBTQ+-inclusive education — highlight this gap even more clearly. The question is: where do we go from here to change the homophobic and transphobic landscape across Canadian schools and in society generally?

The first National Climate Survey (Taylor and Peter 2011) succeeded in providing statistically rigorous evidence that schools were hostile places for many 2SLGBTQ+ students, and in the intervening ten-plus years, many school systems have introduced anti-homophobia and anti-transphobia polices; further to this, GSAs have become much more commonplace in schools, providing students with much-needed social supports and safer places. These are good first steps, but they have not eradicated homophobia or transphobia in schools, and much of the hostile discourse marginalizing sexual and gender diversity has persisted, as the second Climate Survey findings demonstrate. However, what we also see is that when 2SLGBTQ+ students perceive their school community to be supportive, there are profound benefits. For instance, compared to 2SLGBTQ+ students who saw their school community as being unsupportive of 2SLGBTQ+ students, those who saw their school community as being

> When 2SLGBTQ+ students perceive their school community to be supportive, there are profound benefits.

very supportive were more likely to have positive mental health (32 percent from supportive schools versus 6 percent from unsupportive ones), to feel like they belonged at their school (85 percent versus 25 percent) and to feel safer at school (69 percent versus 16 percent). Supportive schools are ones that have made comprehensive interventions that clearly demonstrate 2SLGBTQ+ students are welcome and valued in their schools, and they explicitly work to challenge homophobia, transphobia and erasure. These supports go beyond simply having a related harassment policy or allowing a GSA to meet on school property at the end of the day. They include clear declarations of support for 2SLGBTQ+ people; full implementation of policies that explicitly name 2SLGBTQ+ identities as protected from harassment; professional development for teachers on implementing these policies; effectively intervening in instances of harassment; developing 2SLGBTQ+-inclusive teaching practices and content; and providing students not only with support but with adequate resources to form thriving GSAS and to enjoy 2SLGBTQ+-positive events and activities throughout their schools.

A serious critique of supportive or "inclusive" education is that it does not radically transform dominant discourse, only adjusts it to make room for formerly marginalized people. While this makes for lifesaving improvements in the quality of life for those people, it stops short of challenging the system of categorizing people by their sexualities and gender identifications that has been deployed as an effective system of social regulation and oppression in the first place. As Henry Louis Gates (1993) wrote with reference to multiculturalism as an inclusive response to anti-Black racism, "if I can be denigrated as an X, I can be affirmed as an X," but that leaves the "race" discourse that invites racism intact in the first place, making multiculturalism a rather feeble defence against future flair-ups of racism. Similarly, sex categorization invites sexism, and so on. Foucault styled this sort of affirmation-based approach an example of "reverse discourse."

However, what reverse discourses such as inclusion can do is subdue the most extreme techniques of marginalization that help to keep docile bodies in line by reminding us of the penalty for falling outside the category of cisgender heterosexuality: these techniques vigorously and often aggressively work to reinforce dominant discourses that are built on categorizing types of people, and they typically include violence, rejection, ostracization, bullying and ridicule. Insofar as schools are "total institutions" (as sociologist Irving Goffman termed prisons because they govern every aspect of life), those schools that consistently reinforce support for 2SLGBTQ+ people rather than hostility towards them can open up space for what Foucault called a genuine "counter-discourse" to emerge.

Queer discourse has emerged over the last twenty years as just such a counter-discourse. Queering is an approach to refusing to identify with the classification system of dominant gender and sexuality discourse; hence the mantra "We're here, we're queer, get used to it" (in other words, "Back off! I'm not going to oblige by categorizing myself within a discourse system that oppresses me"). Many education scholars have taken a queer approach to understanding the problem of homophobic and transphobic hostility in schools by introducing students to queer concepts and analytical techniques as a way of helping young people refuse classification of themselves through dominant discourse to become more self-governing. (This refusal would not necessarily mean fewer "boys" will be attracted to "girls," or fewer "girls" will prefer a feminine style; it would mean that they would recognize the huge discourse system of cultural pressures and rewards that lead to them thinking of cisgender heterosexuality as the best form of gender and sexuality, exclusively natural, normal and even admirable.) The RISE Project on 2SLGBTQ+-expansive teacher education (uwinnipeg. ca/rise) has worked to develop guidelines for education professors on how to prepare teachers not only to support and include 2SLGBTQ+ students in untransformed schools, but to employ queer pedagogy to transform their schools as well. Education scholar Alex Wilson, who has written extensively on Indigenous concepts of gender and sexuality, argues that what is needed is not just inclusion, but a whole paradigm shift. Throughout her work, Wilson offers an entirely different discourse system that centres Indigenous knowledges and worldviews and enacts queering approaches to challenge the interlocking, mutually reinforcing dominant discourses of settler-colonialism and cisgender heterosexuality (Wilson 2015; Wilson and Laing 2018). Accordingly, gender expression and sexual orientation are not reflections of an inner reality that require "coming out" but ways of being that are relationally based and reflect connection to Indigenous culture, land, community and spirituality that reflect "coming in." What is key for our purposes in this chapter, though, is not so much the specific contours of this discourse, but its example of counter-discourse — one that sets out to replace rather than to reform our current discourse.

As we described throughout this chapter, homophobia and transphobia are powerful discourse systems in schools and in Canadian society more generally. The social constructions of cisgender heterosexuality form strongly normative discourses that produce constructions of gender as a binary concept or sexuality as "normally" heterosexual. However, as we have seen, these discourses have negative impacts for 2SLGBTQ+ people, and indeed for everyone, and contribute to hostile and disrespectful social conditions such as those experienced in schools. Exposing the materiality of cis-normative, heteronormative discourse through critical examination of how it was invented and how the interplay of power and knowledge ultimately sanctions homophobic and transphobic climates helps us to understand the importance of refusing incarceration as docile bodies. To truly support 2SLGBTQ+ students and counter heteronormative and gender-normative discourses in schools, we need nothing less than transformed understandings of gender and sexuality. Protecting, consoling, including, welcoming and appreciating 2SLGBTQ+ students are important actions, too, but they are not enough to create truly equitable conditions. This is no small task, certainly, but as sites of learning and knowledge development, educational institutions such as schools are situated precisely where this change needs to occur.

DISCUSSION QUESTIONS

1. Thinking back to when you were in high school, would you agree that there was a disconnect (that is, a contradictory experience) between human rights discourse and the discourse of your school environment (high levels of homophobia and transphobia)? How widespread were homophobic and transphobic language and harassment in your school?

2. Why do you think narratives like "that's so gay" are used so frequently in high school and among young people?

3. In your high school, was there a GSA club? Were there specific anti-homophobic policies and procedures for reporting incidents of abuse and harassment? If yes, do you think it made your school community a more welcoming environment? If no, do you think your school community would have benefited from being a more accepting place for 2SLGBTQ+ youth?

4. Discuss the aggressive gender policing that youth participate in with reference to Foucault's concept of docile bodies and the constitutive effects of dominant discourse. What practices are involved in gender policing? What might happen if students stopped acting as agents of CH-normative discourse in school culture?

5. Some people prefer "queer" to "LGBT" because it signifies a rejection of the CH-normative system of sexuality and gender categories. If that system has always oppressed sexual- and gender-minority people, why would some still prefer the identity terms "lesbian," "gay," "bisexual," "trans" or "Two-Spirit" over the term "queer"? Account for this using some of the discourse concepts discussed in this chapter. What difference might it make if 2SLGBTQ+ people and their allies stopped referring to themselves as 2SLGBTQ+ or "straight," and instead started using "queer" this way?

6. It is often said that homophobia is a "natural" response to "unnatural" sexual practices and gender expression. However, now that dominant discourses such as those emanating from healthcare, law and the media have become more 2SLGBTQ+-inclusive, polls show that far fewer Canadians are homophobic. This suggests that homophobia is not natural but discursively constructed. If homophobia is not natural, and seems to be on the decline, why might some discourse communities be so adamantly opposed to 2SLGBTQ+-inclusive education? In other words, who benefits from the maintenance of homophobia and transphobia? What is all this discrimination for? In your answer, think about how homophobia and transphobia might function to serve the interests of dominant culture by maintaining socially conservative family and economic arrangements.

GLOSSARY OF KEY TERMS

Bisexual: A term used to describe a person who is attracted physically and emotionally to people of their own gender and people of a gender different from their own. Pansexual is sometimes used alternately for people who are attracted to multiple gender identities or expressions.

Cisgender: Often abbreviated to "cis," describes a person whose gender identity aligns with conventional social expectations for the sex assigned to them at birth (e.g., a cisgender woman is someone who identifies as a woman and who was assigned female sex at birth).

Gay: A term used to describe a person who is physically and emotionally attracted to someone of the same gender. Gay can include both men and women, or refer to men only.

Gender expression: The way a person publicly shows their gender identity in social contexts through clothing, speech, body language, wearing of makeup and/or accessories and other forms of displaying masculinity or femininity.

Gender identity: A person's internal and individual experience of their gender as being man, woman, non-binary or another gender. Gender expression relates to how a person presents their sense of gender to the larger society. Gender identity and gender expression are often closely linked with the term "transgender."

Gender minority: A more general description of transgender, transsexual, Two-Spirit or non-binary people.

Homosexual: In contrast to "heterosexual," the word "homosexual" is deeply connected with pathologizing and oppressive meanings from legal, religious and medical institutions and thus is not commonly used in the 2SLGBTQ+ community.

Lesbian: A woman who is attracted physically and emotionally to other women.

Perceived sexual orientation: The perception of someone's sexual orientation based on gender expressions, mannerisms or behaviours that presumes someone is either heterosexual or lesbian, gay or bisexual without knowing what their true sexual orientation really is.

Queer: Historically, a negative term for homosexuality, but more recently reclaimed by the LGBT movement to refer to itself and celebrate non-normative identities. Increasingly, the word "queer" is popularly used by LGBT youth to refer positively to themselves and as a form of resistance to conventional social, cultural and political norms.

Questioning: A term used to describe a person who is in the process of understanding their sexual orientation or gender identity.

Sexual minority: A more general description of people whose sexual orientation is not completely or exclusively heterosexual.

Sexual identity/orientation: A person's deep-seated feelings of sexual, romantic and emotional attraction to another person. This may be with people of the same gender (lesbian or gay), the conventionally "opposite" gender (heterosexual/straight) or different genders (bisexual or pansexual).

Straight/heterosexual: A person who is sexually and emotionally attracted to someone of the "opposite" sex. Some trans and non-binary people may also identify as heterosexual.

Trans or transgender: A term used to describe a person whose gender identity, outward appearance, expression and/or body does not fit into conventional expectations of male or female. Often used as an umbrella term to represent a wide range of nonconforming gender identities and behaviours, including non-binary and transsexual people.

Two-Spirit: Some Indigenous people identify themselves as Two-Spirit rather than as lesbian, gay, bisexual or trans, and the term can refer to sexual orientation or gender identity. Two-Spirit is an English-language, pan-Indigenous term that is used to represent the various words in different Indigenous languages to affirm the interrelatedness of multiple aspects of identity, including gender identity and expression, sexuality, community, culture, relationship to land and spirituality.

RESOURCES FOR ACTIVISM

Egale (Equality for Gays and Lesbians Everywhere) Canada: egale.ca
Gay, Lesbian, Straight Education Network (GLSEN): glsen.org
Institute for Sexual Minority Studies and Services (ISMSS): ismss.ualberta.ca
McCreary Centre Society: mcs.bc.ca
RISE Research Program: uwinnipeg.ca/rise
Stonewall: stonewall.org/uk

NOTE

1   All student narratives and comments in this chapter are from the second National Climate Survey, unless otherwise noted. Minimal editing was done to these quotations, except to ensure clarity. For

details on the methodology, ethics approvals and the complete findings, see the final report on the second National Climate Survey (Peter, Campbell and Taylor 2021).

REFERENCES

Alcoff, L. 1988. "Cultural Feminism versus Post-Structuralism: The Identity Crisis in Feminist Theory." SIGNS: *Journal of Women in Culture and Society* 13, 3.

Alvarez, L., and R. Pérez-Peña. 2016. "Orlando Gunman Attacks Gay Nightclub, Leaving 50 Dead." *New York Times*, June 12. <nytimes.com/2016/06/13/us/orlando-nightclub-shooting.html?_r=0>.

Butler, J. 1996. "Sexual Inversions." In S. Hekman (ed.), *Feminist Interpretations of Michel Foucault*. University Park: Pennsylvania State University Press.

____. 1993. *Bodies that Matter: On the Discursive Limits of "Sex."* New York: Routledge.

____. 1990. *Gender Trouble: Feminism and the Subversion of Identity*. New York: Routledge.

____. 1987. "Variations on Sex and Gender: Beauvoir, Wittig, and Foucault." In S. Benhabib and D. Cornell (eds.), *Feminism as Critique*. Minneapolis: University of Minnesota Press.

Canada Family Action Coalition. n.d. <familyaction.org>.

CBC Archives. n.d. "Trudeau: 'There's No Place for the State in the Bedrooms of the Nation.'" <cbc.ca/archives/entry/omnibus-bill-theres-no-place-for-the-state-in-the-bedrooms-of-the-nation>.

CBC News. 2013. "Scott Jones Says He Was Attacked for Being Gay." December 11. <cbc.ca/news/canada/nova-scotia/scott-jones-says-he-was-attacked-for-being-gay-1.2459289>.

Civil Marriage Act, 2005, SC 2005, c 33.

Criminal Law Amendment Act, 2001, SC 2002, c 13.

Dennis, A., and P.J. Martin. 2005. "Symbolic Interactionism and the Concept of Power." *The British Journal of Sociology* 56, 2.

Egan v. Canada [1995] 2 SCR 513.

Fetner, T., A. Elafros, S. Bortolin and C. Drechsler. 2012. "Safe Spaces: Gay-Straight Alliances in High Schools." *Canadian Review of Sociology* 49, 2.

Foucault, M. 1981. *The History of Sexuality: An Introduction,* translated by R. Hurley. Harmondsworth: Penguin.

____. 1980. *Power/Knowledge: Selected Interviews and Other Writings*, translated by C. Gordon. New York: Pantheon Books.

____. 1979. *Discipline and Punish: The Birth of the Prison*, translated by A. Sheridan. New York: Vintage Books.

Gates, H.L. 1993. "Beyond the Culture Wars: Identities in Dialogue." *Profession*. <jstor.org/stable/25595500>.

Kosciw, J.G., C.M. Clark, N.L. Truong, and A.D. Zongrone. 2020. *The 2019 National School Climate Survey: The Experiences of Lesbian, Gay, Bisexual, Transgender, and Queer Youth in Our Nation's Schools*. GLSEN. <glsen.org/sites/default/files/2020-10/NSCS-2019-Full-Report_0.pdf >.

Murray, D. (ed.). 2009. *Homophobias: Lust and Loathing Across Time and Space*. Durham: Duke University Press.

M v. H [1999] 2 S.C.R. 3.

Ontario. 2009. "Equity and Inclusive Education in Ontario Schools: Guidelines for Policy Development and Implementation." <itstartswithyou.ca/emodules/osstf/presentation_content/external_files/Ontario%20Guidelines%20for%20Policy%20Development%20and%20Implementation.pdf>.

Peter, T., C. Campbell and C. Taylor. 2021. *Still in Every Class in Every School: Final Report on the Second Climate Survey on Homophobia, Biphobia, and Transphobia in Canadian Schools*. Toronto, ON: Egale Canada Human Rights Trust.

Peter, T., and C. Taylor. 2014. "Buried Above Ground: A University-Based Study of Risk/Protective Factors for Suicidality among Sexual Minority Youth." *Journal of* LGBT *Youth* 11, 2.

Peter, T., C. Taylor and C. Campbell. 2016. "'You Can't Break ... When You're Already Broken': The

Importance of School Climate When Examining LGBTQ Youths' Experiences with Suicide and Suicide Behaviour." *Journal of Gay and Lesbian Mental Health* 20, 3.

Pharr, S. 1988. *Homophobia: A Weapon of Sexism*. Inverness: Chardon Press.

Poteat, V.P., H. Yoshikawa, J.P. Calzo et al. 2015. "Contextualizing Gay-Straight Alliances: Student, Advisor, and Structural Factors Related to Positive Youth Development among Members." *Child Development* 86, 1.

Rich, A. 1980. "Compulsory Heterosexuality and Lesbian Existence." SIGNS: *Journal of Women in Culture and Society* 5, 4.

Riley, D. 1988. *"Am I That Name?" Feminism and the Category of 'Women' in History*. Minneapolis: University of Minnesota Press.

Ristock, J.L. 2002. *No More Secrets: Violence in Lesbian Relationships*. New York: Routledge.

Russell, S.T. 2011. "Challenging Homophobia in Schools: Policies and Programs for Safe School Climate." *Educa em Revista, Curitiba, Brasil* 39.

Saewyc, E., C. Konishi, H.A. Rose and Y. Homma. 2014. "School Based Strategies to Reduce Suicidal Ideation, Suicide Attempts, and Discrimination among Sexual Minority and Heterosexual Adolescents in Western Canada." *International Journal of Child, Youth and Family Studies* 5, 1: 89–112.

Taylor, A.B., A. Chan, S.L. Hall et al. 2020. *Being Safe, Being Me 2019: Results of the Canadian Trans and Non-Binary Youth Health Survey*. Vancouver, Canada: Stigma and Resilience Among Vulnerable Youth Centre, University of British Columbia.

Taylor, C., and T. Peter. 2011. *Every Class in Every School: The First National Climate Survey on Homophobia, Biphobia, and Transphobia in Canadian Schools. Executive Summary*. Egale, Toronto. <egale.ca/awareness/every-class/>.

Taylor, C., T. Peter, C. Campbell et al. 2015. *The Every Teacher Project on LGBTQ-Inclusive Education in Canada's K–12 Schools: Final Report*. Winnipeg, MB: Manitoba Teacher's Society.

Taylor, C., T. Peter, T. Edkins et al. 2016. *Final Report of the National Inventory of School District Interventions in Support of LGBTQ Student Wellbeing*. Vancouver, BC: Stigma and Resilience Among Vulnerable Youth Centre, School of Nursing, University of British Columbia.

Taylor, C., T. Peter, D. Short et al. 2016. "Gaps between Beliefs, Perceptions, and Practices: Findings from the Every Teacher Project on LGBTQ-Inclusive Education in Canadian Schools." *Journal of LGBT Youth* 13, 1–2.

Weedon, C. 1997. *Feminist Practice and Poststructuralist Theory*, second edition. Cambridge: Blackwell.

Weiss, J.T. 2001. "The Gender Caste System: Identity, Privacy, and Heteronormativity." *Law and Sexuality* 10.

Wilson, A. 2015. "Our Coming In Stories: Cree Identity, Body Sovereignty and Gender Self-Determination." *Journal of Global Indigeneity* 1, 1. <ro.uow.edu.au/jgi/vol1/iss1/4>.

Wilson, A., and M. Laing. 2018. "Queering Indigenous Education." In L. Tuhiwai Smith, E. Tuck, and K.W. Yang (eds.), *Indigenous and Decolonizing Studies in Education: Mapping the Long View*. Taylor & Francis.

14

CRIME AS A SOCIAL PROBLEM
Social Inequality and Justice

James F. Popham, Anna Johnson and Les Samuelson

YOU SHOULD KNOW THIS

- In 2017, fifty thousand people faced charges related to possession of cannabis, despite the federal government indicating that the substance would be legalized by year's end.

- During the initial wave of COVID-19 in early 2020, an estimated 3,700 elderly Canadians died of the virus while in long-term care facilities (LTCF). Despite clear evidence of negligence, no charges have been brought against the operators of these LTCFs.

- Approximately 30 percent of Indigenous persons in Canada, 16 percent of women and 20 percent of racialized persons live below the poverty line.

- As of 2020, nearly one in three incarcerated persons in Canada was Indigenous, compared to being 5 percent of the population; Indigenous women account for 40 percent of the incarcerated female population, more than doubling in number since 2004.

- The National Inquiry into Missing and Murdered Indigenous Women and Girls issued 231 Calls for Justice. As of 2021, the Canadian government has made limited effort to address these calls, although a National Action Plan was released in June of that year.

Sources: Canada 2021a; Ontario 2021; Canada 2019 Canada, Office of the Correctional Investigator 2020; Canada 2020; MMIWG 2019

THE RULE OF LAW AND OUR DEFINITIONS OF CRIME

CRIME PLAYS AN INTEGRAL ROLE IN shaping your understanding of the world around you and often dictates the way you operate within it. You are, for instance, bound to certain actions on the road by codified traffic laws. You know which side of the road to drive on, what to do at a stop light and when to use your turn indicators (we hope!). These expectations instill a sense of confidence when operating a vehicle or conveyance on public roads, with the implicit understanding that to break these laws is to commit a crime warranting a range of sanctions and punishments, something no motorist wants. By that same measure, you've probably also witnessed people violating these laws from time to time, which reifies your sense of who the bad person — the criminal — really is.

These ideas are backed by the concept of the "rule of law," which is the idea that all people, regardless of their position in life, are equally subject to the codified rules and obligations that govern our behaviours. The rule of law lays the foundation for our *Charter of Rights and Freedoms* (Canada 1982), holding that a person's personal circumstance, including their wealth, gender, sexual orientation, religion, skin colour, occupation or ethnicity, among other factors, should have no bearing on how they are treated by the law and the type of justice they receive. Of course, this principle is much easier to define than it is to enforce, and these challenges often carry over to dialogue about crime and criminality. The public's interpretation of wrongfulness is often influenced by a number of exigent factors that aren't related to a literal reading of the law. Consider times where you've broken rules or even laws: do *you* consider yourself to be a criminal? Bearing your answer in mind, take a moment to consider three more questions:

What is a crime?

Who is a criminal?

What is justice?

At first the answers to these questions might seem straightforward enough. In its simplest form, a crime occurs when legal sanctions (for example, the *Criminal Code of Canada*) are violated; a criminal is the person or persons commit these acts; and justice occurs when the state takes action to mend or redress criminalized actions (Tappan 1947). Indeed, this is the approach that many people who study crime take. William O'Grady (2018), a professor of criminology at the University of Guelph, explains that this "objectivist-legalistic" standpoint assumes that our Criminal Code provides a "factual and precise" definition of crime that represents the values or moralities of the people it governs. The objectivist-legalistic view also assumes that legal codes are "normative" — it assumes most people generally agree with the codified rules and prohibitions we find in the *Criminal Code* and that these rules provide an instruction manual for *good* behaviour within society. Much of our Criminal Code, law enforcement, justice system and many academic practitioners subscribe to this belief (O'Grady 2018: 1).

Perhaps you might perceive some of the problems that come from normative assumptions about law. Canada is an enormous nation with a diverse population, and each person residing in Canada may have their own interpretation of what right and wrong can mean. These differences of beliefs can be a function of parenting, family, neighbourhood, geography, culture, finances, gender and sexual identity, education and a range of many other often subtle influences (Eisenberg 2019). Given the diversity of Canada — or, for that matter, any large group of people — it becomes very difficult to imagine millions of people could possibly agree on anything, let alone a set of rules intended to control their lives!

A contextual consideration for this discussion comes from the legalization of cannabis in October of 2018, concluding nearly a century of legal prohibition in Canada. The *Cannabis Act* (Bill C-45), which legalized recreational use of cannabis and set out a framework for its retail sale, was highly contested among Canadian lawmakers and was indicative of the nations' myriad perspectives on right and wrong (Cox 2018). For instance, former prime minister Stephen Harper, speaking just three years before C-45 passed, vehemently argued that "marijuana is infinitely worse [than tobacco] and it's something that we do not want to encourage" (Watters 2015). His comments, issued as our nation's leader,

> Stephen Harper vehemently argued that "Marijuana is infinitely worse [than tobacco] and it's something that we do not want to encourage."

suggested that his Conservative government would maintain tough anti-drug laws in line with what he felt the people of Canada wanted. Indeed, when it came time for the Canadian Parliament to vote, all Conservative politicians present — whose job is to represent the interests of individuals living in their geographical riding — voted against legalizing cannabis (Tasker 2017). While cannabis retail stores are now common throughout the country, many Canadians spoke out against its legalization by proxy through their elected representatives.

These debates help to illustrate the social nature of crime in Canada. The legalization of cannabis came after hundreds of thousands of individuals received criminal records during the years that possession and use of the substance was illegal. In fact, nearly fifty thousand cannabis-related drug offences were reported by Canadian police services in 2017, meaning that many people faced charges *after* the Canadian government indicated that it would be legalizing the substance within a year (Canada 2021a). This returns us to our questions about crime: What differences lay between the person who used cannabis before October 2018 and the person who used it afterward? The legalization of cannabis is not a unique situation — in many cases formerly criminalized acts have been removed from the Criminal Code, ranging from duelling to same-sex marriage (Hennigar 2007). If the law is normative, how do we explain the public's changing opinions on right and wrong?

Crime Pyramid

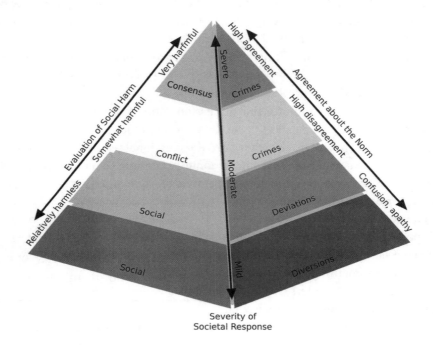

Severity of
Societal Response

Adapted by James Popham from Hagan (1991: 13).

John Hagan (1991) attempted to articulate the changing nature of crime in Canada using the pyramid diagram depicted in the figure above. He indicates that there are four levels of deviance: "social diversions," "social deviations," "conflict crimes" and "consensus crimes." The level of deviance attributed to a given act can be calculated by estimating public perception about its social harm, agreement about its wrongfulness and the type of punishment most people believe to be suitable for the act. For example, Hagan (1991) points to tattoos as something that might occur in the social diversions category, as most people are often apathetic about body art; societal response is often limited to rebuke by grandparents; and having a tattoo is relatively harmless to society. On the other hand, severe crimes like homicide and sexual assault would be what Hagan (1991) calls consensus crimes as it's highly likely that the public agrees about their unlawfulness, harm and the severity of warranted responses.

Of note, Hagan (1991) points out that most criminalized acts in Canada would fall somewhere in the "conflict crimes" section of his diagram. These are acts that are often contested within society and thus unevenly enforced in various jurisdictions. Returning to our discussion about traffic laws, you might consider how motorists who speed on major highways are often tolerated by the police whereas those who speed in school zones are more likely to face significant penalties. Hagan (1991) demonstrates these fluidities by pointing to practical differences between the rule of law rule and law enforcement. He argues that the public rarely reaches a consensus when defining deviance except in the most heinous of situations; rather, most acts of deviance are at best social diversions that have been criminalized due to uneven social and political pressures.

Missing from Hagan's (1991) pyramid (although he does discuss it later on within his book) are the additional influences of identity and power on the criminalization of certain acts and individuals. Many nations, Canada included, have long histories of applying the law differentially, often along socially constructed categories like racial and ethnic heritage, gender and class. This differential treatment has become the dominant approach of criminological study over the past half century, which has shifted toward critical analysis of the underlying implications of legal regulation. To this end, O'Grady (2018) argues that a substantial proportion of rules that we take for granted as law are actually attempts at moral regulation reflecting the interests and beliefs of a relatively small portion of the population. These pressures are often referred to as "legal moralisms," which assumes that "a legitimate function of law in a civil society [is] to prohibit and sanction behaviors that are commonly regarded as 'immoral,' even if these

> A substantial proportion of rules that we take for granted as law are actually attempts at moral regulation reflecting the interests and beliefs of a relatively small portion of the population.

activities do not appear to cause harm" (Hannem and Bruckert 2014: 324).

The ambiguous line between moral and immoral behaviour is often influenced by dominant social groups' normative expectations of how people *ought* to act (Valverde 2009). Thus, in the Canadian context, our criminal justice system includes a number of contemporary and historic sanctions intended to shape or limit the ways individuals might lead their lives, including union busting, criminalizing sex work, enforcing religious education and regulating access to mind-altering substances (Strange and Loo 1997). Setting aside the unlikelihood that people wholly agree with the meaning of morality, the legal moralism that we encounter in the Canadian justice system often has roots in maintaining power — and thus *control* — over the population rather than protecting society (Hannem and Bruckert 2014; Valverde 2009; Strange and Loo 1997).

These processes closely align with the forces underlying the Potlach ban of 1885 embedded within the *Indian Act* of Canada. "Potlatches" are culturally and spiritually important events for many Pacific Northwest First Nations. They feature gift-giving feasts to celebrate births, deaths, adoptions, weddings and other rite-of-passage events, and they often aided the redistribution of wealth by sharing luxury and common goods between communities. The Potlatch also played an integral role in passing down the oral histories and values of nations (Edwards 2020; Joseph 2018). The ceremony, which contravened the religious and individualistic work ethics of European colonists, was criminalized by the government with the express intention of fostering assimilation. Lawmakers, including Sir John A. MacDonald (Canada's first prime minister), believed that gutting the culture of Indigenous communities would create a social vacuum that could then be filled with "Canadian" values (Edwards 2020; Joseph 2018; LaViolette 1973). The nefarious intent of these actions is captured in sociologist Forrest E. LaViolette's (1973: 44) writing: "None the less such a law would help, it was felt, in achieving a Canadian standard of self-support and of citizenship for the Northwest Coast Indians."

Systemic and intentionally discriminatory regulations like the Potlatch ban are endemic to Western justice philosophies, which are often structured along economic lines (Reiman and Leighton 2013). These fractures provide shelter and immunity from justice to those in dominant cultural groups while also working to enforce their norms onto other, less powerful people, labelling the poorest members of society as "typical" criminals and exaggerating harms from their actions. Such labelling often occurs subtly, at the overlap of social, mediated and political forces to shape public opinions about criminality and embed these biases as legal moralism. In other words, our perceptions about crime are manipulated, sometimes intentionally, to reproduce commonsensical knowledge about "good guys and bad guys."

> Our perceptions about crime are manipulated, sometimes intentionally, to reproduce commonsensical knowledge about good guys and bad guys.

The objectivist-legalist interpretation of crime and wrongdoing, which mirrors the common-sense approach (Reiman and Leighton 2013), is pervasive and embedded in Canada's justice system. Scholars across the globe have identified the role of economic power in justice matters at all levels. Moreover, critical criminologists have repeatedly emphasized that our society is also characterized by other inequalities of power based upon class, race and gender (O'Grady 2018). A range of these analyses have focused on how socio-legal practices reinforce class-based inequalities, the patriarchal subjugation of women, and injustice against Indigenous peoples. These inequalities generate differences of involvement and treatment within our criminal justice system, from the definition of crime to the responses of criminal justice personnel, to notions of offenders and victims. Each of these social categories intersects with differential treatment in the criminal justice system. Certain individuals and groups are not born more "criminal" than any others, but moralistic influences on justice shape their life conditions. The remainder of this chapter will unpack how these differences influence the way various social groups are received and treated in Canada's criminal justice system, focusing on the influences of class, gender identity and Indigeneity.

CLASS AND CRIME

The relative "class" of individuals and organizations, measured by factors like access to resources and social esteem (Cohen et al. 2017), plays a significant role in determining their experiences with the criminal justice system. On the one hand, the structure of the law is often formed around the types of acts that are most commonly attributed to certain classes of society — for example, the so-called "street crimes" — which are typically attributed to economically and socially marginalized groups and include interpersonal acts threatening personal health, life, sexual freedom or property, as well as drug use (Beckett 1994) — make up the majority of Canada's Criminal Code. On the other hand, "suite crimes," which consist of illegal or unethical acts committed through legitimate business activities for the purpose of personal or organizational gain by individuals of social esteem (Piquero et al. 2008; Pontell 2016) are far less likely to be criminalized and can often be understood as part of doing business (Reiman and Leighton 2013).

Application of the law by members of the criminal justice system and the public as a whole is dramatically affected by class. To illustrate, the most recent court data provided by the Canadian Centre for Justice Statistics (Malakieh 2020) indicates that just five street crimes (theft, impaired driving, failure to comply with an order, common assault and breach of probation) accounted for nearly 50 percent of all adult criminal cases in 2016–2017. Similarly, Piquero et al. (2008) found that in all but a few cases, the public will perceive street crimes to be more serious than suite crimes regardless of the potential harm or number of people affected. These arguments parallel the contradictions of the rule of law discussed earlier — the expectation that all people are considered equal under the law is often not the case.

While not necessarily always acting in unison, powerful members of society are often able to influence political and legal processes so that both the structure of the law and the administration of justice overlook the social, economic and physical harms inflicted upon society by them and the corporations they control. Put bluntly:

> Corporate actors regularly and repeatedly violate … standards of moral and legal behaviour, do much more physical and economic harm than any other violators of these standards, and continue to be treated as upright members of our society, giving meaning to Clarence Darrow's aphorism that most people classified as criminals are "persons with predatory instincts without sufficient capital to form a corporation." (Glasbeek 2002: 118)

For instance, representatives of the tobacco industry have long been known to fund lobbying groups who attempt to disrupt legislation intended to control the industry by refuting scientific evidence and threatening job losses (Hastie and Kothari 2009).

The tragic events that occurred in Lac-Mégantic, Quebec, are a culmination of these effects. In the early hours of July 16, 2013, a train of seventy-two oil tankers, operated by the Montreal, Maine, and Atlantic Railway Ltd. (MMA) and carrying 7.7

> The tobacco industry [has] long been known to fund lobbying groups who attempt to disrupt legislation intended to control the industry by refuting scientific evidence and threatening job losses.

million litres of crude oil, derailed in Lac-Mégantic's central business district. Many of the tank cars ruptured, flooding the streets with a highly flammable type of oil that ignited and exploded almost immediately. The catastrophic chain of events killed forty-seven people and destroyed an entire community (Giovannetti 2013: 2).

The negligence that caused these events prompted national scrutiny, including a railway investigation report by the Canadian Transportation and Safety Board (TSB). The TSB identified eighteen causes and contributing factors to the derailment and explosion, as well as sixteen findings as to risk. Many of these factors and risks resulted from intentional decisions and attributable actions at MMA's executive level, including "[a] weak safety culture," "not having emergency assistance plans," and "ineffective training and oversight on train securement" (TSB 2014: 10). Despite these damning criticisms, no criminal charges were laid against MMA or its executives. When criminal charges were finally reported months after the explosion, they were directed at junior employees of MMA and the sole crew member operating the doomed train, leaving many observers frustrated with justice processes that did not penalize the responsible corporation (Snider 2015).

Lac-Mégantic Derailment and Explosion, July 6, 2013

Lac-Mégantic, the morning after the derailment and explosion of a Montreal, Maine, and Atlantic Railway Ltd. train killed forty-seven people.

Photo by Sûreté du Québec. Reprinted under Creative Commons License, CC BY-SA 1.0, Wikimedia Commons.

Sadly, Canada has endured a legacy of tragic events brought on by corporate misdeeds, which often affect the most vulnerable members of our society. As with Lac-Mégantic, the ramifications of prioritizing profit over people were brought into sharp relief during the early months of the COVID-19 pandemic when Brigadier General C.J.J. Mialkowski (2020) issued a report on Operation LASER undertaken by Canadian Armed Forces' (CAF) Joint Task Force Central. LASER is the CAF's ongoing response to the pandemic, and in early 2020 its actions included the provision of medical resources to aid healthcare provision at privately operated long-term care facilities (LTCF) in Quebec and Ontario. Mialkowski's (2020) report focused on the operations in Ontario LTCFs and described the appalling conditions that service members encountered, many of which could have been easily remediated to reduce the spread of the virus. The LASER report observed LTC support staff rotating between different facilities, vulnerable individuals being left unattended for days and the sharing of medical supplies between COVID positive and negative patients, along with a host of other harmful acts.

In many cases, the mistreatment was connected with inadequate staffing and/or managerial decisions intended to reduce the operating costs of the facility. Consider this observation, taken at the Eatonville Care Centre in Etobicoke, Ontario:

> Extra soaker pad: Residents who routinely soil their bed despite incontinence products are not permitted to have an extra soaker pad or towel in bed to help protect sheets and blankets from soiling. (PSWs *[personal support workers] are afraid for their jobs on this issue*). (Mialkowski 2020: A-1/3, emphasis added)

These inhumane conditions at privately operated long-term care facilities in Ontario were reported less than a year after the conclusion of a public inquiry into the safety and security of their residents. The inquiry was initiated following revelations that Elizabeth Wettlaufer, a former nurse who confessed to murdering at least eight LTCF residents, was able to commit her crimes due to systemic vulnerabilities in the industry (Gillese 2019). Several of the report's recommendations focused on improving training at no cost to employees and improving hiring practices with the goal of developing a "just culture" that avoids worker burnout and ensures better-than-adequate treatment of elderly Canadians. It now appears that many of these recommendations — whose ramifications could have helped to address the COVID-19 crisis head-on — were not implemented in a timely manner by the operators of LTCFs in Canada. As with the Lac-Mégantic tragedy, no criminal charges have yet been laid against the operators of these facilities despite an estimated 3,793 deaths (Ontario 2021).

> In many cases, the mistreatment was connected with inadequate staffing and/or managerial decisions intended to reduce the operating costs of the facility.

A defining feature in these incidents is the role of those with economic power in determining who will and will not be held accountable for the damages and loss of life experienced. A systematic pattern of downloading responsibility is apparent: guilt is passed down the chain of command until reaching an individual or entity who does not have the economic capacity to fund their legal defence. This pattern mirrors the notion of "governmentality" proposed by social theorist Michel Foucault (1991), who suggested that the organization of society exists because we recreate it through our actions towards, and

> Guilt is passed down the chain of command.

judgments of, others. In this process, the public takes on a greater role in identifying risky people (criminals, for example) but does not create new categories — rather, we amplify those that have been presented to us as the *bad* elements of society. These amplifications lead into a disproportionate focus on street crimes despite the similar or greater effect of suite crimes (Pontell 2016).

End Profit for Long-Term Care

A lawn sign produced by UNIFOR *in their campaign to raise awareness about the harms occurring at private, for-profit long-term care homes in Ontario.*

Photo by Leslie Popham. Reprinted with Permission.

Canadian legal experts Dorothy Chunn and Shelley Gavigan (2004) argue that governmentality is intrinsically linked with legal moralism, leading to public and state preoccupation on street-level acts that appear to harm us through our pocketbooks and linking acts like welfare use to criminality. "To be poor" Chunn and Gavigan

(2004: 220) write, "[is] to be culpable, or at least vulnerable to culpability." Glasbeek (2002) observes that 80 percent of welfare fraud convictions lead to imprisonment, compared to just 4 percent of tax evasion cases, even though the tax fraudsters caused far greater financial harms to Canadian governments (and, thus, to Canadians in lost government revenue that others have to make up). Corporations, even government corporations, and the privileged can apparently kill, maim and rob with relative impunity while the poor get prison.

One of the underlying elements of this bias is the fact that many corporate harms — even when they are ordered or enacted by a single individual within the corporate structure — are often not defined as criminal. In Canada, the Crown must successfully establish the "blameworthiness" of a defendant before securing conviction against them, which includes establishing *mens rea*, a "guilty mind" (Verdun-Jones 2007: 66). This principle imposes significant difficulties when pursuing criminal cases against corporations, as their complex structure tends to obfuscate internal lines of communication, ultimately making it unclear who possesses the organization's "mind" (Canada, Department of Justice 2015). It therefore becomes exceedingly difficult to prosecute individuals acting on behalf of the corporation unless their actions directly cause a harm. In addition to the problem of *mens rea*, corporations have been almost exclusively prosecuted for regulatory violations — such as those governing health and safety — and not for the consequences of those violations regardless of criminality (Reasons, Ross and Patterson 1986; McMullan 1992; Coleman 2002). This approach is an outcome of corporate lobbyists taking leadership roles in the development of governance and regulations under the guise being enlisted to cooperate in creating "workable laws." In these areas, corporations are not viewed as conscious (let alone conscientious) entities.

When critically interpreted, the tragic events discussed above reveal a trend of *in*justice in the Canadian criminal justice system that places the interests of the economic elite above all others. This point is emphasized by the lack of action in response to numerous tragedies, despite clear linkages between corporate intentions and outcomes. Rather than taking decisive action, the collective patchwork of provincial and federal legislation designed to govern Canadian workplaces has been rendered toothless through revision, loopholes and inaction (Hastie and Kothari 2009). The economically bifurcated nature of the justice system is further retrenched by drawing comparisons between legal responses to corporate wrongdoing and the wrongdoing of the individual. It seems very likely, for example, that the public would interpret an intentional omission of safety protocols leading to workplace accidents and deaths as a "consensus crime" on Hagan's (1991) pyramid (Piquero et al. 2008); however, the complicated form of modern corporations has effectively obfuscated the possibility of a corporate guilty mind. Maddeningly, society remains as a whole unconcerned with corporate criminality, choosing instead to focus on the wrongs of our neighbours.

INDIGENOUS PEOPLES AND THE CRIMINAL (IN)JUSTICE SYSTEM

Legal moralism extends beyond economic indicators, leading to systems of laws that directly and indirectly target those whose cultures and moralities do not align with the beliefs of dominant groups. Such beliefs are grounded in colonial beliefs that centre on individualism and assume that other ideals, like those of reciprocity, are unnatural (Coulthard 2010). In Canada, as well as other common-law nations like the United States, Australia and New Zealand, these normative beliefs and the enforcement thereof have contributed to the overrepresentation of First Nations, Inuit, Métis and Black peoples, as well as other people of colour and marginalized groups, in the criminal justice system (Jeffries and Stenning 2014; Tauri 2009; Marchetti and Downie 2014). As is explored below, overrepresentation in the Canadian context means that the proportion

> The overrepresentation of Indigenous peoples in the justice system stems from colonization and its processes.

of non-white people present in our criminal justice system far outpaces their proportion of the general population.

This overrepresentation, particularly of Indigenous peoples, stems from colonization and its processes, including displacement, residential schools, racism, systemic discrimination, cultural assimilation and the erosion of their political and cultural systems (Green 1998; *R. v. Gladue* 1999; Adjin-Tetty 2007; Murdocca 2013). The final report of the Truth and Reconciliation Commission (TRC) (2015a: 5) highlights Canada's history of colonization:

> For over a century, the central goals of Canada's Aboriginal policy were to eliminate Aboriginal governments; ignore Aboriginal rights; terminate the Treaties; and, through a process of assimilation, cause Aboriginal peoples to cease to exist as distinct legal, social, cultural, religious, and racial entities in Canada. The establishment and operation of residential schools were a central element of this policy, which can best be described as "cultural genocide." Physical genocide is the mass killing of the members of a targeted group, and biological genocide is the destruction of the group's reproductive capacity. Cultural genocide is the destruction of those structures and practices that allow the group to continue as a group.

In addition to residential schools, the *Indian Act* of 1876, displacement and Artic relocation policies were all used to violently oppress and eliminate First Nations, Inuit and Métis peoples' identities and their ties to their land and culture. The law often justified these actions, as was explored earlier in our discussion of the Potlatch ban.

Enforcement of these regulations gave way to a system of law enforcement that continues to be deeply prejudiced against Indigenous peoples. The police played a significant role in enforcing moralistic laws in the emerging nation of Canada, including the regulations imposed under the *Indian Act*, as well as the forced attendance at residential schools. As Sherene Razack (2015) explains, policing has long been used by colonial powers like Canada to maintain territorial claims by actively displacing Indigenous bodies. These enforcement regimes catalyzed a legacy of harmful policing practices that continue today (Alberton et al. 2019). For instance, in Saskatoon, Saskatchewan, a series of inquiries over the past two decades have identified a policing practice known as "starlight tours." In these incidents, Indigenous peoples were taken into custody by police officers and dropped off at the city limits during frigid winter months. At least three Indigenous men died from this practice.

Similarly, a 2016 report titled *Broken Trust: Indigenous People and the Thunder Bay Police Service* (OIPRD 2018) pointed out the many ways in which police mistreatment and inaction contributed toward more than thirty suspicious deaths of Indigenous peoples in northern Ontario's largest city.

In its report, the Office of the Independent Police Review Director (OIPRD: 9) concluded that the police service had "failed on an unacceptably high number of occasions to treat or protect the deceased and his or her family equally and without discrimination"; that officers engaged in racial stereotyping by making generalized assumptions about Indigenous peoples; and that systemic racism occurs

> The [Thunder Bay Police Service] "failed on an unacceptably high number of occasions to treat or protect the deceased and his or her family equally and without discrimination."

within the police service at all levels. The investigator made forty-four recommendations to address the systemic and institutionalized racism inherent in the TBPS (OIPRD 2018).

In addition to the harmful practices described above, the over-policing of Indigenous peoples has also contributed toward disproportionate rates of incarceration. A recent study commissioned by the Department of Justice Canada (Clark 2019) found that Indigenous peoples account for 28 percent of all inmates in Canada, despite representing only 4.1 percent of the general population. These rates are notably higher for Indigenous women, who account for 40 percent of incarcerated women, and for youth, with Indigenous girls accounting for 60 percent of correctional admissions and men accounting for 47 percent.

St. Anne's Indian Residential School

Indigenous children at St. Anne's Indian Residential School in Fort Albany, Ontario, circa 1945. Children were forcibly removed from their families under punishment of law. The TRC identified 3,200 children who died while attending residential schools; however, this number is known to be a very low estimate (Truth and Reconciliation Commission 2015b).

Edmund Metatawabin collection, University of Algoma. Reprinted under Public Domain.

While these figures have attracted the attention of public officials, it appears that their concerns have not translated into effective policy or procedural changes as the relative proportion of incarcerated Indigenous peoples has continued to grow year over year for at least the last decade (Clark 2019). Notably, thirteen different provincial and federal commissions and inquiries between 1989 and 2019 have examined the impact of discrimination and colonization on the overrepresentation of Indigenous peoples in the criminal justice system, highlighting the differential treatment of Indigenous peoples by criminal justice agents from arrest to conviction (Rudin 2019). As a whole, these reports made 690 recommendations for improving and addressing the overrepresentation; however, the majority of these recommendations remain unaddressed (Rudin 2019).

Perhaps one of the most significant government attempts to address Indigenous overrepresentation in prisons came in 1996 when the federal government amended the Criminal Code judicial sentencing instructions for the prosecution of Indigenous people as a policy strategy to curb their overrepresentation in provincial and federal prisons (Murdocca 2013). The provision encourages judges to consider unique alternatives to incarceration when sentencing Indigenous offenders. The Canadian government claimed that this reform would better align the mainstream justice system with principles of traditional Indigenous justice (Balfour 2013). The sentencing section, s.718.2(e) of the Criminal Code, states:

> all available sanctions, other than imprisonment, that are reasonable in the circumstances and consistent with the harm done to victims or to the community should be considered for all offenders, with particular attention to the circumstances of Aboriginal offenders. (*Criminal Code of Canada* 1985)

In 1999, the Supreme Court affirmed the purpose of attempting to reduce the high rate of Indigenous incarceration in *R v. Gladue* and acknowledged the need to address the overrepresentation of Indigenous peoples in Canadian prisons. The court instructed that when determining an appropriate sentence for Indigenous offenders, sentencing judges must consider the systemic elements that affect Indigenous peoples, including intergenerational trauma stemming from residential schools and the Sixties Scoop. Moreover, judges must apply the provision for all Indigenous peoples regardless of whether or not the offender lives on reserve. These elements became commonly known as "Gladue factors" (Rudin 2019).

Unfortunately, the overrepresentation continues to grow despite the implementation s.718.2(e) more than twenty years ago. Additionally, the Gladue provision has faced criticism for failing to consult with Indigenous communities, misinterpreting and conflating principles of Indigenous justice and assuming a singular definition thereof (LaRocque 1997; Comack and Balfour 2004; Adjin-Tetty 2007; Murdocca 2013). Moreover, the power to consider alternatives to imprisonment and the unique circumstances of Indigenous peoples is left in the

Gladue has faced criticism for failing to consult with Indigenous communities, misinterpreting and conflating principles of Indigenous justice.

hands of judges who are, for the most part, white men from middle/professional-class backgrounds (Proulx 2000; Wihak 2008). Many scholars find that judges may have a limited understanding of both Indigenous cultures and the ongoing impact of colonization on Indigenous peoples, which can result in them relying on stereotypical characterizations of Indigenous offenders, leading to muted impacts on Indigenous incarceration rates (Comack and Balfour 2004; Savarse 2005; Hurlbert 2008; Murdocca 2013). These factors may play a role in the legislation's lack of impact on Indigenous incarceration rates (Welsh and Ogloff 2008; Balfour 2013; Murdocca 2013).

For several decades, inquiries and governmental reports have recommended incorporating Indigenous practices into corrections to provide culturally appropriate programing both in prisons and in community sanctions (Aboriginal Justice Inquiry of Manitoba 1991; Commission on First Nation and Metis People 2004; Truth and Reconciliation Commission 2015a). Despite the availability of Indigenous programing at certain Correctional Services of Canada run facilities, they often lack of resources or funding and have strict requirements to qualify for programs. Moreover, many such programs tend to homogenize the identity and cultures of Indigenous peoples, ignoring recommendations that they must be culturally appropriate, Elder-run and fit the different needs and cultures of offenders (Martel and Brassard 2008; Martel, Brassard and Jaccoud 2011).

These examples of the treatment of Indigenous peoples from all criminal justice agencies demonstrate the colonial and violent nature of Canada's criminal justice system. In addition to economic divisions, our system also incorporates laws and regulations that reflect the European, colonial nature of Canada, demonstrating a continuation of the imposition of colonial conduct ideology through the forceful removal of Indigenous cultures.

GENDER AND CRIME

Crime is also a gendered phenomenon. In 2018/2019, men accounted for 85 percent of adults admitted to provincial/territorial custody and 93 percent of adults admitted to federal custody, despite accounting for 49 percent of the Canadian population (Malakieh 2020). As with economic/class position and racial identity, a number of gendered legal moralisms complicate public views about crime. The experiences of men and women as both perpetrators and victims of crime are different and unique in a number of ways. However, the criminal justice system often fails to account for these differences when arresting, sentencing and punishing people labelled "criminal."[1]

Consider that one in four people *accused* of a criminal offence in 2017 was identified a woman or girl (Savage 2019). While the objectivist-legalistic approach has led many of our criminal justice institutions to view all people who violate rules as simply criminal, critical criminological inquiry has demonstrated that the profile of women involved with the criminal justice system is different than men who commit crime in many ways. For example, women who encounter the justice system are more likely than men to have been involved in non-violent crimes — and in cases where a violent crime has been recorded, it is typically simple assault (Jeanis and Smith 2020). Notably, when violent offences are perpetrated by women, approximately nine in ten victims are acquaintances, intimate partners, current/former spouses and other family members rather than strangers, and the violent act often occurs in response to physical, sexual or emotional violence (Hotton, Jacob and Hobson 2017; Jeanis and Smith 2020). Risk factors for women encountering the justice system may include previous and early victimization, homelessness, poverty and negative familial and intimate relationships that often involve physical and/or sexual violence (Jeanis and Smith 2020).

Despite gender differences, criminological theories have focused only on explaining and responding to crimes perpetrated by men and applied these theories universally without acknowledging the variation among and characteristics of women involved with the criminal justice system. Many of these theories attributed criminal behaviour committed by women to excess masculinity or lack of civilization, implying that female criminality results from being incompatible with legal moralism that expects women to be quiet, subservient accessories to men (Hannem and Bruckert 2014; Gundy and Baumann-Grau 2013).

The failure to consider the unique experiences of criminalized women by classical criminological theorists has contributed to the formation of criminal justice policies that neglect their needs and unique experiences. Feminist criminologists provide an alternative framework that considers the criminal behaviour — *and victimization* — of women in the context of the overlapping influences of a patriarchal society and its casting of race, class, age and gender. They offer a premise of "gender-specificity" that considers how the "historical, social, emotional, and biological/physical needs of women" have been ignored in criminal justice systems, leading to ineffective treatment or rehabilitation options (Gundy and Baumann-Grau 2013: 6).

"Intersectionality," first articulated by Kimberlé Crenshaw in 1991, identifies the significance of "account[ing] for multiple grounds of identity when considering how the social world is constructed" (Crenshaw 1991: 1245). Crenshaw (1991, 2005) critiques the law's failure to consider the intersection of Black women in both gender and race-based oppression. Her approach also explains how the Canadian criminal justice system fails to consider the intersectional location of Indigenous women when they present as both perpetrators and victims of crime. Carastathis (2016) applies Crenshaw's (2005: 60) argument to explain how law serves to reproduce deeply entrenched social hierarchies: by offering remedy for discrimination only where claims are non-intersectional, that is, where plaintiffs can demonstrate — through their hold on whiteness or maleness, or, indeed, both — that their experiences of discrimination are legible through one, and only one, category of discrimination.

The criminal justice system's neglect of the unique positions of women — particularly Black, Indigenous, and women of colour — is evident in their treatment in the same system, even in policies that are intended to be beneficial.

In 1990, the Task Force on Federally Sentenced Women, whose report is titled *Creating Choices*, reviewed the mistreatment of federally sentenced women and identified the systemic discrimination women, and Indigenous women in particular, faced, along with the lack of programming available to address their needs (Canada, Correctional Service 1990). The report advanced a federal corrections model to address these specific needs of incarcerated women and put forward several recommendations to address the needs of federally sentenced women. In response, Prison for Women (P4W) was closed. P4W opened in 1934 and was, for many years, the only prison for women in Canada. Its conditions were very harsh, paternalistic and far inferior to prisons for men. P4W was replaced with five regional prisons across Canada, including a healing lodge for Indigenous women.

> The criminal justice system's neglect of the unique positions of women — particularly Black, Indigenous, and women of colour — is evident in their treatment in the same system.

Despite the closure of P4W and the recommendations made in *Creating Choices*, women in both federal and provincial institutions continue to face violence, additional punishment and institutional charges, mental health concerns, self-injury, segregation and physical restraints (Chartrand 2015). For example, a 2013 coroner's inquest into the death of Ashley Smith, a young woman who was asphyxiated while in custody at a federal institution, identified a series of failures regarding the treatment of women by Correctional Service Canada (Canada, Correctional Service 2013).

> Incarcerated women face violence, additional institutional charges, mental health concerns, self-injury, segregation and physical restraints.

Prison for Women, Kingston, Ontario

The Prison for Women in Kingston under demolition. Despite renovation plans, the building is currently stewarded by Queen's University and stands largely unused. There are several controversial tours of the nearby Kingston Penitentiary.

Photo by Actionhamster. Reprinted under creative commons license, Wikimedia Commons.

Failures like those described above are amplified for Indigenous women: in addition to their high representation in the prison system, Indigenous women are also more likely than non-Indigenous women to be classified as maximum security, more likely to be considered high risk, and more likely to be incarcerated for minor drug offences (Baigent 2020). To fully understand Indigenous women's over-involvement in the justice system, and their (discriminatory) high-risk classifications, we must consider the kinds of lives that they often experience. Consider the following "life profile" of a federally sentenced Indigenous woman:

> She may work the streets because she needs money to live on and she does not have the education, skills and training to get a job. She may be subjected to racism, stereotyping and discrimination because of her race and colour. However, her experience on the streets becomes violent as she continues to

experience sexual, emotional, and physical abuse. She is likely to become involved in an abusive relationship. There are usually children born from this relationship and the social, emotional and economic struggle continues. The cycle of an unhealthy family continues. (Green 2000)

Each of these barriers falls into place one by one to shuffle women of economic and social disadvantage into prison, where they face further discrimination through classification (Chartrand 2015). This can be described as a victimization-criminalization continuum, wherein the adverse effects of trauma experienced by women are overlooked within the criminal justice system, leading to missing or limited restorative services and support (Baigent 2020: 4). These trends persist in twenty-first-century Canada.

Women who have been victims of crime face similarly gendered forms of mistreatment in all parts of the justice system. The main areas of concern have been the system's biases, injustices and ineffectiveness in dealing with women who are victims of intimate partner violence and sexual assault (Comack and Balfour 2004). Consider institutionalized responses to sexual assault in Canada. Bill C-127, a 1983 reform to the Criminal Code, abolished the legal charge of "rape" as well as the separate charges of indecent assault on a male and indecent assault on a female, and it removed spousal immunity for sexual assault. In its place, the federal government amended the definition of assault to include sexual assault measured at three different levels. The intent was to increase the reporting of rape by victims by reducing associated stigma. The legislative change was also to emphasize, as many academics and feminists had strenuously contended, that sexual assault/rape is primarily a violent act of male domination in sexual form.

Still, much skepticism remained over the extent to which these changes would produce any significant increase in the reporting of sexual assault by women or would alter the judicial stereotyping and traumatization of sexually assaulted women. Women's advocates argued that the legislation merely paid lip service to the advancement of equality and would fail to produce societal changes (Balfour and Du Mont 2012). Many of these fears were realized when, in 1992, "rape shield" provisions designed to protect victims from having to recount their previous sexual history during trials were repealed by the Supreme Court of Canada, leaving lawmakers scrambling to define the meaning of "no means no" (Tang 1998).

Moreover, the actual effectiveness of the sexual offences law has long been questioned. For example, less than 1 percent of sexual assaults that occur in Canada result in conviction, largely because these crimes go unreported. Indeed, one analysis of Canadian data estimated that just five percent of sexual

> Less than 1 percent of sexual assaults that occur in Canada result in conviction.

assaults are ever reported to police services (Johnson 2017). Rather, women who have experienced sexual assault distrust the criminal justice system — they fear its processes, being blamed, being retraumatized by the police, lawyers, Crown attorneys and judges, and they fear retaliation by their abusers (Craig 2018; Johnson 2017). These fears are commonly reported *despite* the provisions outlined in the Criminal Code.

Similar concerns about the capacity to protect women from other crimes, including murder, have been made by advocacy groups. For instance, the Canadian Femicide Observatory for Justice and Accountability (CFOJA) uses the term "femicide" to "underscore that women and girls are often killed *because* they are women and girls — because of their sex or gender, because of hatred towards women and girls." The CFOJA argues that misogynistic beliefs are embedded in Canada's legal moralism, "minimizing and/or normalizing the killing of women and girls in our society" (Dawson et al. 2020: 10). They identify that despite more education about and awareness of male-perpetrated violence against women, there remains significant gaps between the actual and officially recorded rates of violence perpetrated against women, limiting the government and non-profit groups' capacity to champion better prevention initiatives.

These concerns have long been raised by victims, their families and the advocacy groups that represent them. For example, the mandate of the National Inquiry into Missing and Murdered Indigenous Women and Girls, which arose through long-term advocacy by a number of grassroots organizations and movements, was "to inquire into and report on the systemic causes of all forms of violence — including sexual violence — against Indigenous women and girls"(MMIWG 2019: 11). Charlotte Baigent (2020: 6) highlights some of the unique risks Indigenous women face as victims of violence and femicide:

> Compared to non-Indigenous women, Indigenous women are nearly three times more likely to be killed by a stranger, to be sexually assaulted, and/or to become victims of intimate partner violence. Compared to Indigenous men, Indigenous women are also more likely to suffer physical or sexual assault as minors. Despite these conditions of endangerment, Indigenous women are over-policed and under-protected.

In other words, police often ignore Indigenous women on reserve who call for help but are more likely to charge and criminalize Indigenous women with violence or other crimes when they do respond to police calls (Baigent 2020).

The mistreatment of women in all aspects of the criminal justice process is once again symptomatic of a divisive system that aims to preserve the colonial and patriarchal moralism within Canadian legal systems. Failure to consider the intersecting oppressions women face will lead to the criminal justice system perpetuating the historical discrimination of women as both perpetrators and victims.

CHANGING SOCIETY, NOT FIGHTING CRIME

The injustices in the criminal justice system, catalyzed as they are by normative assumptions embedded within various legal codes and justice institutions, do no not occur without resistance. Entire networks of politicians, advocates, scholars and publics are constantly working to change Canada's criminal justice system and our understandings of crime and criminality. While advancements come in fits and starts — usually in response to tragic events emerging from disparity — they nonetheless introduce a modicum of social justice into Canadian systems.

For example, the past decade has borne witness to greater and greater scrutiny of unjust policing practices across Canada. Issues of over- and under-policing of racialized communities, undue scrutiny and racial profiling are more and more denounced (OHRC 2019). Major demonstrations and movements like Idle No More and Black Lives Matter have garnered public attention and have effectively used alternative media formats to share their messaging. A major contribution was Desmond Cole's 2015 article "The Skin I'm In," published in *Toronto Life* magazine.[2] In this telling narrative, he details many encounters with the police as a black man residing in Toronto. Cole (2015) recounted how he was often subject to "carding" during which police officers stop individuals and request identification documents while filling out information sheets. Those who are stopped need not be suspected of any wrongdoing. Rather, the Toronto Police Service's carding policy allowed for officers to stop anyone they wish to ask for information. Desmond Cole's experience highlights that those who were stopped were predominantly people of colour — an experience shared by many other Black, Indigenous, and people of colour.

Greater social awareness of these activities, spurred on by actors like Cole (2015), have driven the courts and policymakers to scrutinize and condemn carding. A recent Ontario Court of Appeal decision (*R v. Omar* 2018 ONCA 975; Izadi 2019) made clear that the arbitrary detention of people of colour, made on the basis of their appearance alone, constituted a breach of Charter rights. While this decision was ultimately overturned by the Supreme Court of Canada, it resonates with growing criticism of racialized police practices in Canada (OHRC 2019), as well as provincial laws regulating carding. Notably, in 2017, the Honourable Michael H. Tulloch was appointed by the Government of Ontario to lead an independent review of Ontario's carding regulation. In his final report, Tulloch (2018: 83) recommended that "the regulation should expressly state that no officer should arbitrarily or randomly stop individuals to request their identifying information." There are still significant barriers and systemic forms of racism affecting the equitable treatment of Black, Indigenous and people of colour by the police in Canada (inquiries into the mistreatment of Indigenous peoples by police services in Saskatoon and Thunder Bay, described earlier, are testament to this point), but the rise of social media as a primary mode of communication has borne new public scrutiny about this mistreatment and may yet contribute to structural change.

Recent political changes have also shifted perspectives and action directed toward equality in justice for women. On November 4, 2015, Prime Minister Justin Trudeau introduced a cabinet that was, for the first time in Canadian history, gender balanced. Moreover, the prime minister instructed Patty Hajdu, then minister of status of women, to "work with experts and advocates to develop and implement a comprehensive federal gender violence strategy and action plan, aligned with existing provincial strategies" (Canada 2017). Trudeau said Hajdu would "be supported by the Minister of Justice to make any necessary *Criminal Code* changes and by the President of the Treasury Board who will develop strategies to combat sexual harassment in federal public institution."

Significant inroads are yet required — for example, it has taken the government more than two years to officially respond to the final report issued by the National Inquiry into Missing and Murdered Indigenous Women and Girls. The 2019 document, *Reclaiming Power and Place*, provides 231 Calls for Justice to address the victimization and genocide of First Nations, Inuit and Métis women, girls and 2SLG-BTQI+ people (MMIWG 2019). In its 2021 response to the calls, *Federal Pathway to Address Missing and Murdered Indigenous Women, Girls and 2SLGBTQQIA+ People*, the Government of Canada committed to ending violence through cultural, health and wellness, human safety and security, and justice themes. Of relevance to this chapter, the federal government (2021b: 15) acknowledged that there is a national need to

> address racism and discrimination throughout the policing and justice systems and improve access to justice to provide a fairer, stronger, more inclusive and representative justice system that respects the rights of Indigenous Peoples, and protects Indigenous women, girls and 2SLGBTQQIA+ people.

To move beyond piecemeal and partial socio-legal reforms in criminal and social justice, we need to develop more comprehensive theoretical, analytical and policy-based critiques of our society. Yet these kinds of initiatives will only partially confront the status quo. To reduce the prevailing inequities, we need to focus on society's structural and cultural conditions and its distribution of power, the elements that are at the centre of the problem. At this level, basic changes are difficult to achieve because they confront the underlying, socially entrenched inequalities of life conditions and power relations. Justice must be accessible to *all* people before a real "society" can exist. Our criminal justice system must take seriously a rule of law that does not favour one social group over another, nor prioritize the interests of the wealthy, colonizers or cisgender men.

The past several years have demonstrated that this social awakening can occur: enormous public support for the Black Lives Matter movement; the lampooning of billionaires like Jeff Bezos, whose wealth is borne of exploitative labour; and social media-driven crusades for women's sexual rights are all resplendent examples of social movements seeking equity under the law. If these transformative movements are to persist, they must continue to come from within. Harry Glasbeek puts this very well at the conclusion of his book *Wealth by Stealth* (2002: 283), writing that societies must "engage in their struggles to bring together people and power, break down the corporate shield, and lay the groundwork for a humanizing transformation of our polity."

DISCUSSION QUESTIONS

1. Identify an act or action that might be considered a "conflict crime." Are the legal responses to this act justifiable? How could they be changed?
2. Identify a common rule or social norm that is "common sense" to you. How do you think someone from another culture or background might interpret your morality?
3. Critically evaluate the truth of the statement that "criminal law and the justice system protect us from serious economic and physical harm."
4. Is it possible to hold corporations to justice when there is no clear *mens rea* (guilty mind) who is responsible for a harmful action?
5. How might the criminal justice system be adapted to better serve the unique needs of women? What about other intersectional considerations?
6. What would you do to address inequalities in Canada's criminal justice system?

GLOSSARY OF KEY TERMS

Carding: Alternately called street checks, community contacts, contact interviews or information checks by Canadian police forces and the media, carding occurs when police officers arbitrarily stop individuals and request their identification as well as other information, such as purpose or destination. Despite public outcry, carding still occurs in many of Canada's largest cities.

Charter of Rights and Freedoms, **Sections 7 and 1(d)**: Prior to 1941, corporations were immune to any criminal liability because *mens rea*, "guilty mind," could not corporately exist. Section 7 and Section 1(d) of the Charter have been used to argue against this rigid *mens rea* requirement in prosecution of corporate crime.

Conflict crimes: Defined by criminologist John Hagan (1991), these are criminalized acts that have a high degree of public disagreement about the behaviour, its harmfulness to society and the type of punishment administered when individuals commit this act.

Corporate crime/suite crime: Harmful economic, human and environmental acts committed by corporate agents in the pursuit of organizational goals, usually profit, and which generally go unpunished by the state.

Criminal Code s.718.2(e): A provision in the *Criminal Code of Canada* added in 1996 that directs sentencing judges to consider alternatives to incarceration when sentencing Indigenous peoples.

Critical criminology: Grounded in the Marxist concepts of social class conflict and advocacy of significant social change, this theory sees crime and criminal justice as reflecting and reproducing inequalities in society. As well, it is an activist perspective in that the point of critical analysis is not just to study society, but to eliminate unjust social acts and inequalities.

European colonialism: The takeover by white settlers of land belonging to Indigenous peoples, resulting in their nearly complete genocide, both physically and culturally.

Femicide: The killing of women and girls, often because of their gender alone.

Gladue factors: unique circumstances stemming from colonization that may play a role in bringing an Indigenous person before the court, including racism, displacement, Indian residential schools, the Sixties Scoop and the child welfare system.

Governmentality: French philosopher Michel Foucault suggested that people are governed by the organized collection of behaviours that we take for granted as part of day-to-day life, and these behaviours tend to reinforce the ideologies of dominant classes. An example would be the routinization of work schedules very early on in life.

Ideology: The starting point for justice in many societies is their collective understanding of right and wrong, which constitutes a guiding ideology. Ideologies are generally malleable and are often shaped by the most powerful members of society rather than through democratic processes.

Legal moralism: Our legal system operates under the assumption that laws are reflective of a general societal sense of right and wrong. These morals are then used to justify criminalizing acts or behaviours; however, there are often conflicting moralities that are ignored.

Objectivist-legalistic framework: An assumption that the law reflects what most people in a society believe to be just or good behaviour. By extension, the law is understood to be a guideline for a good and moral life.

Over-incarceration of Indigenous peoples: In Western Canada since the Second World War, Indigenous peoples have been incarcerated both provincially and federally far in excess of their percentage of the general population.

Prison for Women (P4W): A federal prison that opened in 1934 to house federally sentenced women. Conditions were very harsh, paternalistic and far inferior to prisons for men. Inmate despair and suicide were thus major problems. The prison was closed in July 2000.

Rule of law: A conceptualization of the law that views it as the ultimate authority in society, and therefore expects all people to be held accountable to the law regardless of their background.

Rape shield law: In sexual assault trials, limits the introduction of evidence or cross-examination of the past sexual behaviour of complainants.

Sexual assault: The intentional use of force or threat thereof to engage in sexual behaviours without consent. Recent data from Statistics Canada suggests that approximately one in four women have experienced sexual assault and that only one in twenty sexual assaults are reported to police.

Starlight tours: When police arrest Indigenous peoples and drive them to the outskirts of town and leave them to walk back, often in the winter. This practice has led to some individuals freezing to death. These actions have been attributed to the Saskatoon Police Service.

RESOURCES FOR ACTIVISTS

Safe passage: safe-passage.ca/
Stolen Sisters: cbc.ca/news2/interactives/stolen-sisters/
Crude #5 — A Town, Annihilated: canadaland.com/podcast/crude-5-why-lac-meg-antic-could-happen-again/
P4W Memorial Collective: p4wmemorialcollectivedotcom.wordpress.com/
John Howard Society of Canada: johnhoward.ca/

NOTES

1   It is important to acknowledge that gender is complex and constructed through socialization and the embodiment of gender identities (Scarborough 2018). This section focuses specifically on female-born persons who identify as women. While not the focus of this section, it is important to be mindful that members of the 2SLGBTQI+ community also face violence and heterosexism from police, the courts and in corrections (Nadal 2020).

2   In 2020, Cole published a book, *The Skin We're In*, which expanded on a year of anti-Black sentiment and racism occurring in Canada and globally during 2017.

REFERENCES

Aboriginal Justice Inquiry of Manitoba. 1991. *Report of the Aboriginal justice inquiry of Manitoba. Vol. 1: The Justice System and Aboriginal People.* Manitoba: Queen's Printer.

Adjin-Tettey, E. 2007. "Sentencing Aboriginal Offenders: Balancing Offenders' Needs, the Interests of Victims and Society, and the Decolonization of Aboriginal Peoples." *Canadian Journal of Women and Law* 19.

Alberton, A.M., K.M. Gorey, G.B. Angell and H.A. McCue. 2019. "Intersection of Indigenous Peoples and Police: Questions About Contact and Confidence." *Canadian Journal of Criminology and Criminal Justice* 61, 4.

Baigent, C. 2020. "Why Gladue Needs an Intersectional Lens: The Silencing of Sex in Indigenous Women's Sentencing Decisions." *Canadian Journal of Women and the Law* 32, 1.

Balfour, G. 2013. "Do Law Reforms Matter? Exploring the Victimization–Criminalization Continuum in the Sentencing of Aboriginal Women in Canada." *International Review of Victimology* 19, 1.

Balfour, G., and J. Du Mont. 2012. "Confronting Restorative Justice in Neo-Liberal Times: Legal and Rape Narratives in Conditional Sentencing." *Sexual Assault in Canada: Law, Legal Practice And Women's Activism.* Black Point, NS: Fernwood Publishing.

Beckett, K. 1994. "Setting the Public Agenda: 'Street Crime' and Drug Use in American Politics." *Social Problems* 41, 3.

Canada. 2021a. *Cannabis Legalization and Regulation.*

____. 2021b. *Federal Pathway to Address Missing and Murdered Indigenous Women, Girls and 2SLG-BTQQIA+ People.* <rcaanc-cirnac.gc.ca/DAM/DAM-CIRNAC-RCAANC/DAM-RECN/STAGING/texte-text/fed_patway_mmiwg_2slgbtqqia_1622728066545_eng.pdf>.

____. 1982. *Canadian Charter of Rights and Freedoms*, Part 1 of the Constitution Act, 1982, being Schedule B to the Canada Act 1982 (UK), 1982, c 11.

Canada, Correctional Service. 2013. *Coroner's Inquest Touching the Death of Ashley Smith.*

____. 1990. *Creating Choices: The Report of the Task Force on Federally Sentenced Women.* <csc-scc.gc.ca/women/092/002002-0001-en.pdf>.

Canada, Department of Justice. 2020. *Overrepresentation of Indigenous People in the Canadian Criminal Justice System: Causes and Responses.* Department of Justice. <justice.gc.ca/eng/rp-pr/jr/oip-cjs/toc-tdm.html>.

____. 2015. *Government Response to the Fifteenth Report of the Standing Committee on Justice and Human Rights.* <justice.gc.ca/eng/rp-pr/other-autre/jhr-jdp/corp-pers.html>.

Canada, Office of the Correctional Investigator. 2020. "Indigenous People in Federal Custody Surpasses 30%: Correctional Investigator Issues Statement and Challenge" [press release].

Canada, Office of the Prime Minister of Canada. 2017. Minister of Status of Women Mandate Letter. <pm.gc.ca/eng/minister-status-women-mandate-letter>.

Carasthatis, A. 2016. *Intersectionality: Origins, Contestations, Horizons.* University of Nebraska Press.

Chartrand, V. 2015. "Landscapes of Violence: Women and Canadian Prisons." *Champ Pénal Penal Field* XII.

Clark, S. 2019. *Overrepresentation of Indigenous People in the Canadian Criminal Justice System: Causes and Responses*. Department of Justice. <justice.gc.ca/eng/rp-pr/jr/oip-cjs/oip-cjs-en.pdf>.

Chunn, D.E., and S. Gavigan. 2004. "Welfare Law, Welfare Fraud, and the Moral Regulation of the 'Never Deserving' Poor." *Social & Legal Studies* 13, 2.

Cohen, D., F. Shin, X. Liu et al. 2017. "Defining Social Class Across Time and Between Groups." *Personality and Social Psychology Bulletin* 43, 11.

Cole, D. 2015. "The Skin I'm In: I've Been Interrogated by Police More Than 50 Times — All Because I'm Black." *Toronto Life*, April 21.

Coleman, J.W. 2002. *Criminal Elite: Understanding White-Collar Crime*. New York: Worth Publishers.

Comack, E., and G. Balfour. 2004. *The Power to Criminalize: Violence, Inequality, and the Law*. Black Point, NS: Fernwood Publishing.

Commission on First Nations and Métis People. 2004. *Legacy of Hope: An Agenda for Change*. Final Report, Volume 1.

Coulthard, G. 2010. "Place Against Empire: Understanding Indigenous Anti-Colonialism." *Affinities: A Journal of Radical Theory, Culture, and Action* 4, 2.

Cox, C. 2018. "The Canadian Cannabis Act Legalizes and Regulates Recreational Cannabis Use in 2018." *Health Policy* 122, 3.

Craig, E. 2018. *Putting Trials on Trial: Sexual Assault and The Failure of the Legal Profession*. Montreal: McGill-Queen's University Press.

Crenshaw, K. 2005. "A Black Feminist Critique of Antidiscrimination Law." In D.M. Adams (ed.), *Philosophical Problems in the Law*. Belmont, CA: Thomson Wadsworth.

___. 1991. "Mapping the Margins: Intersectionality, Identity Politics, and Violence against Women of Color." *Stanford Law Review* 43, 6.

Dawson, M., D. Sutton, A. Zecha et al. 2020. *#Callitfemicide: Understanding Sex/Gender-Related Killings of Women and Girls in Canada, 2020*. Centre for the Study of Social and Legal Responses to Violence.

Edwards, A. 2020. "When Knowledge Goes Underground: Cultural Information Poverty, and Canada's Indian Act." *Pathfinder: A Canadian Journal for Information Science Students and Early Career Professionals* 1, 2.

Eisenberg, A. 2019. "Multiculturalism in a Context of Minority Nationalism and Indigenous Rights: The Canadian Case." In R. Ashcroft and M. Bevir (eds.), *Multiculturalism in the British Commonwealth: Comparative Perspectives on Theory and Practice*. Berkeley: UC Press Luminos.

Foucault, M. 1991. "Governmentality." In G. Burchell, C. Gordon and P. Miller (eds.), *The Foucault Effect: Studies in Governmentality*. Chicago: University of Chicago Press.

Gillese, E.E. 2019. *Public Inquiry into the Safety and Security of Residents in the Long-Term Care Homes System. Vol. 2: A Systematic Inquiry into the Offences*. Toronto: Queen's Printer for Ontario.

Giovannetti, J. 2013. "Last Moments of Lac Mégantic: Survivors Share their Stories." *Globe and Mail*, November 28.

Glasbeek, H. 2002. *Wealth by Stealth: Corporate Crime, Corporate Law and the Perversion of Democracy*. Toronto: Between the Lines.

Green, N. 2000. *Profile of an Aboriginal Woman Serving Time in a Federal Institution*. <csc-scc.gc.ca/aboriginal/002003-1009-eng.shtml>.

Green, R.G. 1998. *Justice in Aboriginal Communities*. Saskatoon: Purich Publishing.

Gundy, A.V., and A. Baumann-Grau. 2013, *Women, Incarceration, and Human Rights Violations: Feminist Criminology and Corrections*. New York: Taylor & Francis Group.

Hagan, J. 1991. *The Disreputable Pleasures: Crime and Deviance in Canada*. Toronto: McGraw-Hill Ryerson Ltd.

Hannem, S., and C. Bruckert. 2014. "Legal Moralism, Feminist Rhetoric, and the Criminalization of Consensual Sex in Canada." In J. Kilty (ed.), *Within the Confines: Women and the Law in Canada*. Toronto: Women's Press.

Hastie, R.E., and A.R. Kothari. 2009. "Tobacco Control Interest Groups and Their Influence on Parliamentary Committees in Canada." *Canadian Journal of Public Health* 100, 5.

Hennigar, M. 2007. "The Unlikely Union of Same-Sex Marriage, Polygamy and the Charter in Court." *Constitutional Forum Constitutionnel* 16, 2.

Hotton, T., J. Jacob, and H. Hobson. 2017. *Women and the Criminal Justice System*. Statistics Canada.

Hurlbert, M. 2008. "R. v. Moccasin and Struggles for Fairness in Aboriginal Sentencing." *Saskatchewan Law Review* 71, 1.

Indian Act, Revised Statues of Canada (1985, c.I-5).

Izadi, M. 2019. "To Stop or Not to Stop? Police Carding Practices." *Law Now* 43, 5.

Jeanis, M.N., and S.A. Smith. 2020. "Female Perpetrators: Risks, Needs, and Pathways to Offending." In J. Hector (ed.), *Women and Prison*. London: Springer International Publishing.

Jeffries, S., and P. Stenning. 2014. "Sentencing Aboriginal Offenders: Law, Policy, and Practice in Three Countries." *Canadian Journal of Criminology and Criminal Justice* 56, 4.

Johnson, H. 2017. "Why Doesn't She Just Report It? Apprehensions and Contradictions for Women Who Report Sexual Violence to the Police." *Canadian Journal of Women and the Law* 29, 1.

Joseph, B. 2018. *21 Things You May Not Know About the Indian Act*. Indigenous Relations Press.

LaRocque, E. 1997. "Re-Examining Culturally Appropriate Models in Criminal Justice Application." In M. Asch (ed.), *Aboriginal and Treaty Rights in Canada*. Vancouver: UBC Press.

LaViolette, F.E. 1973. *The Struggle for Survival: Indian Cultures and the Protestant Ethic in British Columbia*. Toronto: University of Toronto Press.

Malakieh, J. 2020. *Adult and Youth Correctional Statistics in Canada 2018/2019*. Statistics Canada.

Marchetti, E., and R. Downie. 2014. "Indigenous People and Sentencing Courts in Australia, New Zealand, and Canada." In Sandra M. Bucerius and Michael Tonry (eds.), *The Oxford Handbook of Ethnicity, Crime, and Immigration*. Oxford: Oxford University Press.

Martel, J., and R. Brassard. 2008. "Painting the Prison 'Red': Constructing and Experiencing Aboriginal Identities in Prison." *British Journal of Social Work* 38, 1.

Martel, J., R. Brassard, and M. Jaccoud. 2011. "When Two Worlds Collide: Aboriginal Risk Management in Canadian Corrections." *British Journal of Criminology* 51.

McMullan, J. 1992. *Beyond the Limits of the Law*. Black Point, NS: Fernwood Publishing.

Mialkowski, C.J.J. 2020. OP LASER — JTFC *Observations in Long Term Care Facilities in Ontario*. *MacLean's*. <macleans.ca/wp-content/uploads/2020/05/JTFC-Observations-in-LTCF-in-ON.pdf>.

MMIWG (National Inquiry into Missing and Murdered Indigenous Women and Girls). 2019. *Reclaiming Power and Place: The Final Report of the National Inquiry into Missing and Murdered Indigenous Women and Girls*.

Murdocca, C. 2013. *To Right Historical Wrongs: Race, Gender and Sentencing in Canada*. Vancouver: UBC Press.

Nadal, K., J. 2020. *Queering Law and Order: LGBTQ Communities and the Criminal Justice System*. Lanham, MD: Lexington Books

O'Grady, W. 2018. *Crime in a Canadian Context: Debates and Controversies*, 4th edition. Toronto: Oxford University Press Canada.

OHRC (Ontario Human Rights Council). 2019. *Policy: Eliminating Racial Profiling in Law Enforcement*. Government of Ontario. June 20. <www3.ohrc.on.ca/sites/default/files/RACIAL%20PROFILING%20Policy%20FINAL%20for%20Remediation.pdf>.

OIPRD (Office of the Independent Police Review Director). 2018. *Broken Trust. Indigenous People and the Thunder Bay Police Service*. <oiprd.on.ca/wp-content/uploads/OIPRD-BrokenTrust-Final-Accessible-E.pdf>.

Ontario. 2021. *COVID-19 Data: Long-Term Care Homes*. <data.ontario.ca/dataset/long-term-care-home-covid-19-data>.

Piquero, A.R., N.L. Piquero, K.J. Terry et al. 2008. "Uncollaring the Criminal: Understanding Criminal Careers of Criminal Clerics." *Criminal Justice and Behavior* 35, 5.

Pontell, H. 2016. "Theoretical, Empirical, and Policy Implications of Alternative Definitions of 'White-Collar Crime': 'Trivializing the Lunatic Crime Rate.'" In S. Van Slyke, M. Benson, and F. Cullen (eds.), *The Oxford Handbook of White-Collar Crime*. Oxford: Oxford University Press.

Proulx, C. 2000. "Current Directions in Aboriginal Law/Justice in Canada." *Canadian Journal of Native Studies* 20, 2.

R v. Gladue, [1999] 1. S.C.R. 688.

R v. Omar [2018] ONCA 975.

Razack, S. 2015. *Dying from Improvement: Inquests and Inquiries into Indigenous Deaths in Custody.* Toronto: University of Toronto Press.

Reasons, C., L. Ross and C. Patterson. 1986. "Your Money or Your Life: Workers' Health in Canada." In S. Brickey and E. Comack (eds.), *The Social Basis of Law.* Toronto: Garamond.

Reiman, J., and P. Leighton. 2013. *The Rich Get Richer and the Poor Get Prison.* New York: Allyn and Bacon.

Rudin, J. 2019. *Indigenous People and the Criminal Justice System: A Practitioner's Handbook.* Toronto: Emond Publishing.

Savage, L. 2019. *Female Offenders in Canada, 2017.* Canadian Centre of Justice Statistics, Statistics Canada.

Savarse, J. 2005. "Gladue Was a Woman: The Importance of Gender in Restorative-Based Sentencing." In R.M. Gordon and E. Elliot (eds.), *New Directions in Restorative Justice.* Cullompton: Willan Publishing.

Scarborough, W.J. 2018. "Introduction: New Developments in Gender Research: Multidimensional Frameworks, Intersectionality, and Thinking Beyond the Binary." In B. Risman, C. Froyum and W. Scarborough (eds.), *Handbook of the Sociology of Gender,* 2nd edition. London: Springer International Publishing.

Snider, L. 2015. *About Canada: Corporate Crime.* Black Point, NS: Fernwood Publishing.

Strange, C., and T.M. Loo. 1997. *Making Good: Law and Moral Regulation in Canada, 1867–1939.* Toronto: University of Toronto Press.

Tang, K.L., 1998. "Rape Law Reform in Canada: The Success and Limits of Legislation." *International Journal of Offender Therapy and Comparative Criminology* 42, 2.

Tappan, P.W. 1947. "Who Is the Criminal?" *American Sociological Review* 12. 1.

Tasker, P.J. 2017. "Federal Marijuana Legislation Clears House of Commons, Headed for the Senate." CBC News, November 27. <cbc.ca/news/politics/cannabis-legalization-legislation-1.4421910>.

Tauri, J. 2009. "An Indigenous Perspective on the Standardisation of Restorative Justice in New Zealand and Canada." *Indigenous Policy Journal* 20, 3.

TSB (Transportation Safety Board of Canada). 2014. *Lac-Mégantic Runaway Train and Derailment Investigation Summary.* Queen's Printer (Catalogue no. R13D0054).

Truth and Reconciliation Commission of Canada. 2015a. *Truth and Reconciliation Commission of Canada: Calls to Action.*

___. 2015b. *Canada's Residential Schools: Missing Children and Unmarked Burials.*

Tulloch, M. 2018. *Report of the Independent Street Checks Review.* Queen's Printer for Ontario.

Valverde, M. 2009. *Law's Dream of a Common Knowledge.* Princeton: Princeton University Press.

Verdun-Jones, S. 2007. *Criminal Law in Canada.* Toronto: Thomson-Nelson.

Watters, H. 2015. "Stephen Harper Calls Marijuana 'Infinitely Worse' than Tobacco." CBC News, October 3. <cbc.ca/news/politics/stephen-harper-pot-marijuana-1.3255727>.

Welsh, A., and J. Ogloff. 2008. "Progressive Reforms or Maintaining the Status Quo? An Empirical Evaluation of the Judicial Consideration of Aboriginal Status in Sentencing Decisions." *Canadian Journal of Criminology and Criminal Justice* 50, 4.

Wihak, L. 2008. "Quiet Contributions: Re-Examining the Benefits of a Restorative Approach to the Aboriginal Context." *Windsor Yearbook of Access to Justice* 26, 1.

15

EMBODIED OPPRESSION
The Social, Ecological and Structural Determinants of Health

Elizabeth McGibbon

YOU SHOULD KNOW THIS

- The richest 20 percent of Canadians own nearly 70 percent of the wealth. The bottom 20 percent own almost nothing (less than 1 percent).

- The top 10 percent of Canadian families own 60 percent of financial assets — including stocks and bonds — more than the bottom 90 percent combined.

- Canada's CEOs make 206 times the salary of their average worker, one of the worst wage gaps of any advanced country.

- Globally, the world's ten richest men have seen their combined wealth increase by half a trillion dollars since the pandemic began — more than enough to pay for a COVID-19 vaccine for everyone and to ensure no one is pushed into poverty by the pandemic.

- Uncollected corporate taxes amount to $88 billion a year, which corporations and wealthy individuals are estimated to divert to overseas tax havens every year. According to a 2019 Canada Revenue Agency report, Canadian corporations dodged up to $11billion in taxes in a year.

- From 2000 to 2010, studies comparing lung, breast, prostate and colorectal cancer mortality rates and mortality trends for Blacks and whites in the US showed that survival rates are consistently lower in Black people that in white people.

The breast cancer mortality disparity ratio between Black and white women increased from 30.3 to 41.8 percent.

- Among patients fifty years or older in Canada, women are less likely than men to be admitted to an ICU and to receive selected life-supporting treatments, and they are more likely than men to die after a critical illness. Older lesbians often experience triple discrimination because of their status as women, older adults and lesbians, while ethnic minority LGBT older adults face a "quadruple whammy."

- Excess hospitalization rates associated with low socio-economic status account for an estimated 33 to 40 percent of hospitalizations in Canada. In fifteen metropolitan areas in Canada, the total yearly estimated excess costs were $123 million for males and $125 million for females. National costs are therefore likely in the multibillion-dollar range.

- At least 200,000 Canadians experience homelessness in any given year. At least thirty thousand Canadians are homeless on any given night. At least fifty thousand Canadians are part of the "hidden homeless" on any given night, staying with friends or relatives on a temporary basis because they have nowhere else to go.

- In 2010, Canada dropped from sixth to twenty-fourth on international infant mortality indicators, just above Hungary and Poland. The main causes cited by researchers are poverty, isolation and premature births.

Sources: OXFAM 2021; Evans 2019; O'Keefe, Meltzer and Bethea 2015; Fowler, Sabur, Li et al. 2007; Clay 2014; CIHI 2010a, 2012; Priest 2010)

WHEN ONE INDIVIDUAL INFLICTS BODILY INJURY upon another such that death results, we call the deed manslaughter; when the assailant knew in advance that the injury would be fatal, we call this deed murder. But when society places hundreds of proletarians in such a position that they inevitably meet a too early and an unnatural death, one which is quite as much a death by violence as a sword or bullet; when it deprives thousands of the necessities of life, places them under conditions which they cannot live — forces them through the strong arm of the law, to remain in such conditions until that death ensues, which is the inevitable consequence — knows that these thousands of victims must perish, yet permits these conditions to remain, its deed is murder just as surely as the deed of the single individual; disguised malicious murder, murder against which none can defend himself, which does not seem what it is, because no man sees the murderer, because the death of the victim seems a natural one, since the offense is more one of omission than commission, but murder it remains. (Engels [1845] 2009: 152)

Human health is intimately tethered to its social, political, economic, historical and cultural contexts. In all countries, whether low, middle or high income, there are wide disparities in the health status of different social groups. The lower an individual's socio-economic position, the higher their risk of ill health. Isms such as classism, genderism, racism and sexism further compound the likelihood of ill health. We live and die according to our food and housing security, the neighbourhoods we live in, our access to health and social care and education, and other forces and systems shaping the conditions of daily life. These forces and systems include dominant economic policies, development agendas, social norms, social policies and political systems (WHO 2011). Oppression is a process that involves all of these institutionalized procedures and practices of domination, power and control that create and sustain injustice. The specifics of people's health, and how disease and illness are inscribed on the body, are all central aspects of understanding how oppression is embodied, on the ground, in people's everyday struggles across the lifecourse. Oppression is also embodied in our planet — the living, breathing ecological context for all our lives.

The primary factors that shape the health of Canadians are not medical treatments or lifestyle choices, but rather the living conditions they experience — the social determinants of health (SDH). They include disability, early child development, education, employment and working conditions, income and income distribution, unemployment and job security, food and housing insecurity, globalization, health services, immigration, Indigenous ancestry, social exclusion and social safety nets (Raphael et al. 2020). Despite substantial evidence that these social determinants are the strongest determinants of health, an individualistic, largely apolitical stance about health and illness persists. Notable exceptions include innovations in public health, community health and in Indigenous (First Nations, Métis, Inuit) health systems. Health inequities — the systematic differences in the health status across different population groups — have significant social and economic costs to individuals and societies. There is an urgent need for a sustained and critical counter-narrative to create an intellectual and ethical space where we care about each other and the planet and where we understand that human suffering and ecological degradation have political origins that *we can challenge and change.*

> Health inequities – the systematic differences in the health status across different population groups – have significant social and economic costs.

The goal of this chapter is to describe how oppression becomes embodied across the lifecourse — how health and illness are persistently and disproportionately distributed across the isms and how ecological and structural contexts are intimately connected to the SDH. I begin with an explanation of critical perspectives on health to lay the foundation for the chapter's framework: the social, ecological and structural determinants of health. Each of these determinants, although described somewhat separately for clarity, operate in synergy with each other for individuals, families, communities, nations and the planet. I examine a case of environmental racism in the Alberta oil sands to illustrate how the determinants of health come together. The chapter concludes with personal and collective imperatives and pathways for action.

PERSPECTIVES ON HEALTH AND ILLNESS

The notion of health is deeply embedded in cultural, economic, social and political conversations, law and policymaking, institutional structures and in our everyday lives. In a Western, Eurocentric worldview (which is by far the dominant view in Canadian institutions and systems) health is defined relatively narrowly, despite increasing use of language that seems to imply a more enlightened or progressive approach, such as "holistic health," "comprehensive health systems," "diverse populations" and so on. In contrast, critical perspectives on health focus on naming and tackling the root causes (the causes-of-the-causes) of worsening health outcomes for more and more Canadians.

Critical Perspectives on Health

One of the distinct features of critical perspectives on health is that they integrate a lifecourse perspective rather than the commonly used lifespan perspective. The lifespan perspective views ages and stages as largely discrete periods of analysis in human life: infancy, childhood, young adulthood, adulthood, middle age and old age. In contrast, a lifecourse perspective reflects evidence that health status at any given age reflects not only current conditions, but also prior living circumstances *in utero* onwards (Kuh and Ben-Shalmo 1997). For example, the lifecourse perspective underscores intergenerational impacts of poverty, or near poverty, for the working poor. The cumulative embodiment of colonialism for Indigenous peoples becomes more clearly visible, particularly the intergenerationally traumatic impacts of colonial oppression and genocide. A lifecourse perspective also helps us deliberatively identify the cumulative bodily impacts of commonly used environmental toxins such as pesticides and herbicides. For example, we know that along the lifecourse, chronic exposure to farming pesticides eventually produces higher rates of breast and prostate cancer (Patel and Sangeeta 2019). Lifelong exposure to vehicular exhaust and industrial air pollutants produces higher rates of asthma among children who live near factories or highways (Barret 2012). It turns out that many of these increased health threats fall along income, social class, racial and geographic lines. Low-income housing is most prominent near factories or major motorways, and rural people are more likely to be exposed to industrial farming toxins. In this way, the lifecourse perspective also underscores the synergies among the ecological determinants of health ("ecodeterminants") and human and planetary health.

Critical Perspectives and Critical Health Studies

There are many ways to define critical perspectives on health. The following clusters provide many of the core ideas, where power/powerlessness, privilege/disadvantage, justice/injustice are explicitly articulated to root or structural causes. These clusters are also the particular foci of social justice–oriented critical health studies.

Explicitly and deliberatively analyzing:

- root or structural causes of threats to human and planetary health and well-being

- the nature and extent of the beneficiaries of sustained oppression (e.g., directors and shareholders of transnational corporations; hyper-rich individuals)

- structural violence (sv): social murder (early death), slow violence (ecosystem destruction), as well as paths to identify and confront sv, such as trauma- and violence-informed public policymaking

- cultural, political, economic power: spaces of power (local, national, global); places of power (closed, invited, claimed); and forms of power (visible, hidden, invisible) (Gaventa 2006)

- language: the discourses of critical health studies and critical social justice are themselves pivotal sites of power, where language can both constrain or liberate social justice action.

Explicitly and deliberatively integrating:

- narrations of justice/injustice: First-voice, quantitative and numerical research, storytelling. Everyone is entitled to their own opinion, but everyone is not entitled to their own facts

- synergies of the structural determinants of health, the SDH, and the ecodeterminants of health

- already well-developed critical perspectives (e.g., critical feminist policy studies, post-colonial perspectives, anti-racist perspectives, queer theory, transgender theory, feminist intersectionality theory and critical disability studies)

- historical trajectories (past, present, future) that help to map the genesis and maintenance of oppressive health-damaging regimes over time (e.g., colonialism, neoliberalism, pan-capitalism).

Creating and sustaining disruption and resistance:

- public truth telling (public forums, gatherings; the written and spoken word in the form of posters, blogs, research articles, teachings and so on)

- cultivating and enacting critical perspectives: taking sides, acting in solidarity, taking risks, developing political literacy, working at the grassroots, listening to dissenting voices, educating for social change

Source: McGibbon 2021

Critical perspectives about health and wellness expose the root causes of health inequities and identify some of their unjust structural, public policy-created origins. A central aspect of the critical perspective's counter-narrative is a deliberative and detailed critique of current health paradigms, particularly Western, biomedical, Eurocentric impacts that remain so dominant and intransigent. Skipping this analytical step makes it difficult to sustain action to destabilize the dominance of biomedical thinking and its influence on the ways that health is framed.

> Critical perspectives expose the root causes of health inequities and identify their unjust structural, public policy-created origins.

Biomedical Dominance in Health Thinking and Policymaking

A biomedical focus or worldview plays a central role in how we think about health. Although there are many assumptions underlying a biomedical worldview, important foundations include: (1) beliefs of individualism (a micro-level focus on individuals, their behaviours and pathophysiologies in the absence of integrating root causes of ill health, such as social, political, cultural and economic forces); (2) positivist beliefs of the possibility and desirability of "objectivity" and "neutrality" (beliefs about the apolitical nature of knowledge, including the possibility of being "neutral" and eliminating bias); and (3) foundations in Western, Eurocentric ways of knowing, with the near exclusion of areas such as Indigenous and Africentric knowledge systems.

It has been proven time and time again that one of the most accurate predictors of health outcomes is socio-economic status (SES) — the more money a person, family or community has, the better their health will be across the lifecourse (Raphael 2019). Although "lifestyle" factors, such as losing weight, quitting smoking and getting more exercise have been shown to improve health for some, these are not the root causes of ill health. For example, Indigenous peoples and Canadians of African descent have much worse heart health outcomes when compared to the general Canadian population (McGibbon and Etowa 2009; Schultz et al. 2020). Yes, improving lifestyles is likely to improve health, especially for those who can afford health enhancers such as healthy food and secure shelter. However, it will not tackle the root or macro causes of persistently compromised health outcomes—intergenerational impacts and traumas of colonialism, slavery, land dispossession and genocide.

Biomedical neutrality has played, and continues to play, a central role in social control. If we can keep citizens and public policymakers boxed into an apolitical body-part-focused framing of human health, then there is little room for questioning the politics and economics of health and well-being. Although the dominance of biomedicine has been critiqued extensively (see Breggin 2008, 1991; Breggin and Ginger 1998; Caplan 1996; Illich 1976; Zola 1978), it still has a profound and persistent influence on the ways that policymakers, health practitioners and most of us understand health. When we think about health, many of us are already thinking from a biomedical perspective. We are all familiar with this framing of health because health knowledge continues to be grounded in biomedical ways of thinking and doing things. We grew up with it. Feminist sociologist Judy Lorber (1994) famously stated that asking people to notice gender is like asking fish to notice water. In the health world, asking people to notice the dominance of biomedicine is also akin to asking fish to notice water.

Despite the language of "holism" in public policy related to health and in clinical practice, the biomedical model continues to be based on the belief that the whole can be reduced to the sum of its parts, as if families, communities or nations exist in these discrete, disconnected apolitical forms. If we have any doubt that this is still the case, we need only think about our health systems encounters. If we have a problem with one of our bones, we go to, or are referred to, the bone specialist (orthopod); if we have a problem with our skin, we go to the skin specialist (dermatologist); if we have a problem with our ovaries we go to the ovary specialist (the gynecologist); if we have a problem with depression we go to the depression specialist (psychiatrist) and so on. Eurocentric thinking about health is so grounded in a focus on body parts that it is very difficult to even envision a reconfigured perspective on health, although Indigenous and Africentric ways of knowing continue to be a cornerstone of leadership in shifting Canadian ways of thinking about health towards a more intellectually and culturally sophisticated worldview about health.

Another cornerstone of the biomedical model is empiricism — the claim that facts and truths exist *a priori* and that knowledge of these facts or truths may only be developed from that which is directly observable (Cruickshank 2012). The unobservable is thus suspect. Important examples include mental health struggles such as post-traumatic stress, where there is no "test" or quantitative measure to verify its existence. For example, combat soldiers have been met with decades of denial of the impact of war experiences on military personnel. Directly observable medical measures of traumatic stress are not possible in the same way that, say, medical problems such as diabetes and infection can be detected through laboratory tests. In the context of the biomedical model, soldiers were therefore simply not believed, a practice that persists to this day as veterans continue to be placed in the position of lobbying for their rights to crucial counselling supports.

The biomedical version of empiricism is especially problematic because choices about where and how to even look for "facts and truths" are filtered through the lens of isms such as ableism, ageism, classism, colonialism, ethnocentrism, heterosexism, racism, sexism and genderism. This is one reason it has taken health knowledge so long to integrate ideas from the social sciences and humanities. The relatively recent rhetoric of evidence-based practice, grounded in empiricism, also becomes open to scrutiny — evidence according to whose worldview, whose voice and whose ways of knowing? Empiricism supports the invisibility of practices such as colonialism and post-colonialism, where truth and reconciliation have taken centuries for settlers to begin to acknowledge. A central pathway for the biomedical reinforcing of oppressions such as colonialism is through assessments and interventions that are focused almost exclusively on the individual. This micro focus locates the problem and accountability for solutions within the individual, while at the same time reinforcing the powerful message that micro-analyses are sufficient and desirable.

The biomedical model is a well-established and significant barrier to opening up our minds and hearts to "other" ways of knowing and public policymaking. Biomedically infused thinking permeates our own worldviews and the worldviews of system decision makers in health, justice, education and so on. The key idea here is that the power and influence of these societal structures are largely invisible. Although they shape and control our ways of thinking, societal processes and structures operate mostly without our direct observation or any sort of explicit critique.

The Social, Ecological and Structural Determinants of Health

The Structural Determinants of Health

(e.g., neoliberal public policy, governance; colonialism, white privilege; the isms; patriarchy; pan-capitalism; dominance of manufactured & financial capital; social murder, slow violence...)

The Ecological Determinants of Health

(e.g., pollution, ecotoxicity, resource, and ozone layer depletion, ocean acidification, desertification, deforestation, soil erosion, species extinction, biodiversity loss...)

The Social Determinants of Health

SDH (e.g., housing, health care services food security; living wage, education...)
Isms as SDH (e.g., ageism, classism, heterosexism, racism, sexism...),
Geographies as SDH (e.g., built environment, segregation, ghettoization, toxic dumping...)

As feminist sociologist Dorothy Smith (1987) pointed out, in order to make sense of how we are part of these larger processes, including the dominance of biomedicine, it is important to identify how they are connected to our everyday lives. Smith calls these processes "ruling relations" and describes them as a complex of organized practices, including government, law, business and financial management, professional organizations and educational institutions as well as the discourses and texts that interpenetrate these sites of power.

A SOCIAL, ECOLOGICAL AND STRUCTURAL DETERMINANTS OF HEALTH FRAMEWORK

Knowledge about the determinants of health continues to evolve, integrating overarching processes that impact human health and the health of all living things, including planet Earth. A social, ecological and structural determinants framework explains how all these processes come together. Beginning with a description of the SDH, I explore what is meant by "structural determinants of health" and how the eco-determinants play an important part in establishing health outcomes.

THE SOCIAL DETERMINANTS OF HEALTH

Definitions of the SDH range from conventional, biomedically oriented perspectives to critical perspectives. Conventional perspectives go something like this: societal contexts such as how much education and income we have, whether or not we have adequate food, housing and so on, have been shown to determine our health outcomes. When individuals, families and communities have more formal education, they are more likely to secure full-time, meaningful employment with employer-provided health and social benefits and are thus more likely to have the financial capacity to have safe, adequate housing, fresh, nutritious food and access to healthcare. Our health is a result of these SDH as well as our lifestyles and motivation to exercise and eat healthy diets. If we have more of these health-enhancing determinants, we and our families will be healthier. We, as a society, need to make sure that people have an equal share of these determinants. Health and social care practitioners need to help individuals and families in their quest to attain these determinants through healthy lifestyles.

However, these conventional perspectives keep the conversation squarely focused on the individual and sometimes the family. Responsibility for the solution therefore rests in the microcosm of the individual-family realm. Conventional perspectives identify individual behaviours as key influences on health, yet they fail to identify how the SDH come to be unequally distributed (Raphael 2021). That is, conventional perspectives recognize the social nature of health and illness, but they do not question how and why inequities in social determinants exist. These perspectives imply some sort of nebulous force that can be held accountable to "make sure" that people do not fall through the cracks, or suffer, or die due to inequities in the SDH.

For example, let's say you receive $900 per month from social assistance. Your $700 rent is automatically redirected to your landlord. Your home is a 12 x 12 room with a bathroom available in a common hallway. You are caring for your adult son, who has a chronic psychotic illness. He would be homeless if he was not living with you. The social assistance rules in your province dictate that your son cannot apply for assistance because he is living with you, his mother. He has little to no coverage for his medications and you are in a chronic state of outright crisis or semi-crisis because you are a loving, competent mother who wants to provide the very best of a decent life for your children, regardless of their age. Conventional approaches to the SDH are of little relevance for you and your son. Who, actually, is "making sure" that you have an "equal share"? Or, more importantly, who is failing to make sure? No amount of lifestyle coaching, anti-smoking conversations and comprehensive tips about thrifty shopping will be of any value whatsoever to you in your day-to-day struggle to stay alive. In fact, suggesting that these are solutions is morally reprehensible.

Critical perspectives on the SDH go something like this: societal power and inequality structures most potently determine where we are situated in terms of the SDH. These structures and processes are dominated by a very few people who have economic and political power. The SDH and their distribution are the results of the power and influence of those who create and benefit from social, and thus health, inequities (Raphael 2021). Vast wealth accumulation for the very few means proportional deprivation at the bottom, where this family is located. The richest 20 percent of Canadians own nearly 70 percent of the wealth. The bottom 20 percent own almost nothing (less than 1 percent). The richest eighty-six families own more than the bottom 11 million people combined. If we consider financial assets such as stocks and bonds, the top 10 percent own 60 percent of financial assets — more than the bottom 90 percent combined. Canada's CEOs make 206 times the salary of their average worker, one of the worst wage gaps of any advanced country (Broadbent Institute 2014). Globally, "the world's ten richest men have seen their combined wealth increase by half a trillion dollars since the COVID-19 pandemic began — more than enough to pay for a vaccine for everyone and to ensure no one is pushed into poverty by the pandemic" (Oxfam 2021).

So, from a critical perspective, tackling root causes of inequities in the SDH, such as the growing income gap, will have a far more long-term impact on this family's chances of escaping poverty and improving their health. Yes, they need help in their day-to-day struggles, a burden that is increasingly being borne by food banks, shelters and soup kitchens in Canada. But what longer-term root structures and processes are at play here? Although the answer is complex, a critical perspective sheds light on the root causes of wealth inequality. For example, support for the social safety net, an ethical imperative in social democratic countries, has traditionally come from the taxation base — our taxes are used to support social expenditures, such as financial support of education, health and social care, child care, transportation and housing. However, social support expenditure in Canada has steadily decreased since the 1980s (Broadbent Institute 2014). The erosion of the social safety net has taken place during a time when uncollected corporate taxes amount to $88 billion a year, which corporations and wealthy individuals are estimated to divert to overseas tax havens every year (Finn 2012). According to a Canada Revenue Agency report, Canadian corporations recently dodged up to $11 billion in taxes in a year (Evans 2019).

The creation and maintenance of a strong social safety net in Canada is a matter of choice and preference, not a matter of available money. Most of the countries in Europe, many with less income than we potentially have at our disposal, have been able to establish a wide range of social programs that far surpass ours in quality and accessibility. (Finn 2012: 1)

Critical perspectives on the SDH integrate the root causes of ill health: economic oppression and unequal distribution of wealth that lead to disenfranchisement, human and treaty rights violations and social exclusion. A related aspect of critical perspectives on the SDH is the insistence on spotlighting the beneficiaries of persistent inequity. When societal deprivations increase for some people, there is a corresponding increase in the wealth and power of that small group of economically privileged people — those who successfully lobby for tax structures that favour the corporate sector and the wealthy, for reductions in public expenditures, wages and worker benefits and decreasing worker rights and protection (Raphael 2021). Furthermore, this situation is morally indictable. Specifically:

> When societal deprivations increase for some people, there is a corresponding increase in the wealth and power of that small group of people.

- Individuals experiencing adverse-quality SDH do so because others experience excessively favourable SDH;

- Individuals experiencing adverse-quality SDH — low income; insecure employment, food and housing; lack of health and social services; and social exclusion — have very limited means of having policy-makers address their situations; and

- These processes are clearly unjust and unfair. (Raphael 2021: 46)

Critical perspectives reject acontextual, individualistic understandings of the SDH. Instead, they focus on the root causes of health inequity. There is an intentional use of "equity" rather than "equality." Equality is when everyone is treated equally — that is, in the same way. Equity is when we address unfairness and policy-created unequal distribution of the material goods necessary to sustain a decent and productive quality of life for Canadians. For example, asthma rates are higher in children whose families live in poverty. This is because they are more likely to live in damp, mouldy housing or near a major road or factory. The physical cause of increased asthma is damp housing, but it is poverty that causes people to live in damp housing. These political, economic and social root causes of ill health, such as poverty and racism, are also referred to as social pathogens. These pathogens do not have the same visibility of well-known physiological pathogens such as cancer, bacteria and so on. In the area of human and ecological health, the origins of social pathogens remain largely hidden. One of the main ways that this invisibility is created and perpetuated in the health fields and in health-related public policymaking is through the often-used discourse of "vulnerability" as well as the discourse of "at-risk" people, populations and species. Instead of vulnerable and at risk, the term "under threat" is more likely to hold perpetrators, such as the beneficiaries of unjust public and institutional policy, accountable.

> "Social pathogens" are the political, economic and social root causes of ill health.

The vulnerability discourse (using the word "vulnerable" when describing people or ecosystems with compromised health) implies that a person, ecosystem, plant or animal, for example, is somehow more prone to experiencing health inequities in much the same way as one might be more prone to catching a cold. These discourses imply an unknown force that is somehow causing the same people, over and over, to have chronic diseases and serious health difficulties. Similarly, in the ecological context, plant and animal species are said to be at risk due to the degradation of their environments. This cause is most often taken for granted, rather than linked to capitalism and weak or non-existent environmental protection legislation. The at-risk discourse (using the words "at risk" when describing people or ecosystems with compromised health) effectively hides the structural, root causes of ill health and suffering by limiting the analysis to the micro context. Yes, there are risk factors, such as watershed pollution in the case of endangered waterfowl and poverty in the case of human families, but what is causing these risks in the first place? What and who are creating these risks for at-risk people, species and biospheres?

INTERSECTIONS OF THE SOCIAL DETERMINANTS OF HEALTH

One of the most interesting aspects of the SDH is that they do not happen in isolation of each other. The concept of intersectionality highlights the pointy edges of injustice — the places and spaces where unfair distribution of wealth plays out on the ground in the social determinants of people's everyday lives. Let's consider Shafik, a twelve-year-old boy who lives in Montreal. If Shafik has no access to open play spaces, it is likely that his parents do not have adequate income for safe, affordable housing. Since the best predictor of income is formal education, it is also likely that his parents have not had the opportunity to achieve adequate education to ensure employment security in a meaningful well-paying job with employer-provided health and social care benefits. All these SDH (access to play space, adequate income, affordable housing, formal education) combine or intersect to deepen disadvantage, and the result is not four times the disadvantage for Shafik and his family. Rather, there is a health-damaging, intergenerational synergy among these SDH as they interact and intersect to persistently and negatively impact psychological, spiritual and physical health outcomes across the lifecourse.

Intersections of the Social Determinants of Health

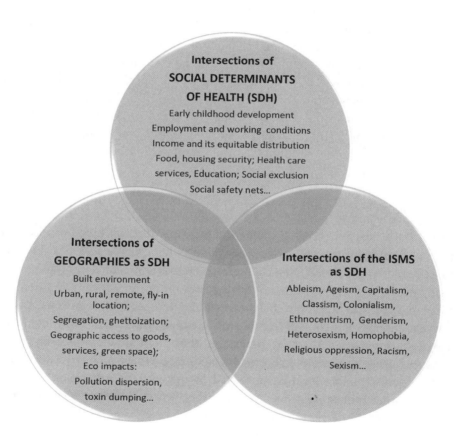

Intersections of
**SOCIAL DETERMINANTS
OF HEALTH (SDH)**
Early childhood development
Employment and working conditions
Income and its equitable distribution
Food, housing security; Health care
services, Education; Social exclusion
Social safety nets...

Intersections of
GEOGRAPHIES as SDH
Built environment
Urban, rural, remote, fly-in
location;
Segregation, ghettoization;
Geographic access to goods,
services, green space);
Eco impacts:
Pollution dispersion,
toxin dumping...

**Intersections of the ISMS
as SDH**
Ableism, Ageism, Capitalism,
Classism, Colonialism,
Ethnocentrism, Genderism,
Heterosexism, Homophobia,
Religious oppression, Racism,
Sexism...

Intersectionality provides important insights about the complexities of the SDH.[1] Collins (1990) describes how oppressions in society do not operate independently;

rather, they intersect in complex patterns. Perspectives that view each oppression as additive, rather than interlocking, fail to stress the centrality of power and privilege. The oppressions of sexism, racism, heterosexism and ageism, for example, can and do happen together to create a synergy of social and

> The oppressions of sexism, racism, heterosexism and ageism, for example, can and do happen together to create a synergy of social and material disadvantage.

material disadvantage, the parts of which interact to form a complex whole that cannot be disentangled into any single phenomenon (McGibbon and McPherson 2012).

The mental and physical health impacts of the intersections of racism, classism, genderism and ethnocentrism have been known for decades. However, SDH-specific intersectionality applications are relatively new (Hankivsky and Christoffersen 2008). Health-related intersections of the SDH, the ISMS as SDH and geographies as SDH were first described in 2007 (McGibbon 2007). Specifically, health inequities were described as intersections of three spaces of inequities: the SDH, the ISMS as SDH and the geographic or spatial contexts of oppression as SDH. An intersectionality lens has also informed policy to improve the social determinants of child mental health, where factors such as early childhood education often intersect with housing security, racism and ghettoization (McPherson and McGibbon 2014).

On the Ground: Healthcare Access and Intersections of the SDH

Access to healthcare involves complex interactions of many kinds of discrimination. For example, in the point-of-care context (when people seek healthcare), the personal experience of racial discrimination, such as clinician stereotyping and expressing prejudice in the healthcare setting, can reduce patients' use of healthcare services and their inclination to follow up on medical recommendations, as well as negatively impacting their satisfaction with medical treatments (Mody et al. 2012). These practices may be overt or covert, and they can happen whether or not clinicians are aware of their discriminatory actions or inactions. Discrimination at this individual clinician level is supported by systemic or institutional racism in health and other societal systems. "Systemic racism," or "institutional racism," refers to "how ideas of white superiority are captured in everyday thinking at a systems level: taking in the big picture of how society operates" (O'Dowd 2020) and looking at how it impacts one-on-one interactions.

It has also been shown that racialized peoples experience inequities in effective acute cardiac care therapies and life-saving heart health interventions (Brewer and Cooper 2014). For example, among US patients who arrive in the emergency department with a heart attack, Black people are less likely to be admitted to medical facilities with cardiac treatment capabilities and high-quality cardiac outcomes (Mody et al. 2012). Studies in the US have also found evidence of racism in areas such as clinicians failing to prescribe correct or sufficient medications, provide increased necessary treatment and provide needed surgical intervention, even after controlling for clinical and socio-economic factors. In Canada, Indigenous individuals are diagnosed with heart disease at an increasingly younger age, have greater severity at diagnosis, develop higher rates of complications and experience poorer treatment outcomes (Crowshoe et al. 2018).

Moreover, women of colour are under threat of double jeopardy as sexism intersects with racism to prevent timely access to healthcare (McGibbon, Waldron and Jackson 2013). In the US, pregnant Black women are three to four times more likely to die from pregnancy-related complications than white women (CDC 2019). Furthermore, intersecting racism and sexism in pregnancy outcomes have led to "disbelieving Black women to death" (St. Claire 2020). In a study by Quach et al. (2012), breast cancer patients reported experiencing different forms of medical discrimination related to social class, race and language. These discriminations included clinicians making assumptions about race, ethnicity and education that compromised quality of care (Quach et al. 2012). African American women are roughly two times more likely to die of breast cancer than white women, according to the National Cancer Institute (Yedjou et al. 2019). In a US study, health systems' institutional racism was associated with increased odds of Black women being diagnosed with breast cancer due to lack of access to preventive care (Beyer, Young and Bemanian 2019).

Other significant racial disparities have been documented for melanoma, stomach cancer, colorectal cancer, prostate cancer and cervical cancer, among others (Nelson 2020). A 2000–2010 review compared lung, breast, prostate and colorectal cancer mortality rates and mortality trends for Blacks and whites in the US (O'Keefe, Meltzer and Bethea 2015). Across all four cancers, survival rates were consistently lower in Black people than in white people. The causes of these premature deaths are far-reaching; however, cancer and other health disparities have been consistently linked with health systems' institutional racism (see Krieger 2003, 2014). Breast cancer statistics in the review were particularly troubling. The authors found that the gap in breast cancer mortality between Black and white women is increasing and, between 2000 and 2010, the breast cancer mortality disparity ratio increased from 30.3 percent to 41.8 percent. In Canada, there is limited evidence about inequities in breast cancer detection and treatment, although there are some important initial studies (Yavari et al. 2010).

Genderism, including sexism, is a seemingly intransigent barrier in access to health and social care. Structural sexism refers to the "systematic gender inequality in power and resources" (Homan 2019: 490). In Homan's analysis, structural sexism occurs at every level of the gender system: institutional (gendered inequality in economic, legal, political and cultural institutions), interactional or relational (patterns of behaviour, organizational practices, gendered power and resource inequality in interactional settings such as at point of care) and individual (gendered selves and internalized gender ideologies, such as sexism and gender binary dominance, that reinforce gendered power and resource inequalities). These three areas of the gender system come together in specific and measurable ways in healthcare access.

A Canadian study of almost half a million critical care patients' charts found that women, particularly those over fifty years of age, were less likely than men to receive care in an intensive care unit (ICU) (Fowler et al. 2007). These outcomes persisted even when women and men had the same severity of problems and therefore required comparable treatment. After adjusting for illness severity, older women were also less likely to receive life-saving interventions such as mechanical ventilation (assisted breathing) or pulmonary artery catheterization (a common procedure that aids in the diagnosis and management of numerous cardiovascular illnesses) and they were more likely than men to die after a critical illness (Fowler et al. 2007). These statistics point to the spectre of ageism in women's access to acute care. Although there are few studies about how ageism intersects with heterosexism and racism in healthcare access, Clay (2014) discusses how older lesbians experience multiple discriminations: "Older lesbians often experience triple discrimination because of their status as women, older adults and lesbians, while ethnic minority LGBT older adults face a quadruple whammy" (46).

2SLGBTQ+ peoples consistently experience discrimination and oppression in healthcare systems and services. They are invisible at both point-of-care and policy levels due to their invisibility in federal health policy (Mulé and Smith 2014). There is a lack of education of heath care professionals about 2SLGBTQ+ health and well-being (Dudar, Ghaderi, Gallant et al. 2018) and there is healthcare provider discrimination when 2SLGBTQ+ people disclose their gender identity (Rossman, Salamanca and Macapagal 2017). Using the 2015 US Transgender Survey, Kcomt et al. (2020) analyzed data from almost twenty thousand transgender people (adults aged twenty-five to sixty-four). Almost one-quarter (22.8 percent) avoided healthcare due to anticipated discrimination. Living in poverty or a rural area as well as visual nonconformity were significant risk factors for transgender people experiencing discrimination in healthcare encounters. These examples illustrate how the SDH overlap and intersect to deepen disadvantage, and, on the other side of the coin, to increase privilege. Healthcare access directly mirrors where one finds oneself along the SDH spectrum of advantage and disadvantage.

THE ECOLOGICAL DETERMINANTS OF HEALTH ✳✳✳

The ecological determinants of health ("ecodeterminants") include human health and the health of the whole natural world on Earth, including resource and ozone layer depletion, ocean acidification, desertification, deforestation, species extinction and biodiversity loss and rapidly increasing land, water and air pollution and eco-toxicity. "There is a growing recognition that the Earth is itself a living system and that the ultimate determinant of human health (and that of all other species) is the health of the Earth's life-supporting systems" (CPHA 2015: 1). Earth systems encompass all ecological systems, including the atmosphere (the set of layers of gasses/air surrounding the planet), the geosphere (solid parts of the earth — "the earth beneath our feet"), the hydrosphere (watersheds, oceans, ice caps) and the biosphere (all global ecosystems of life on Earth) (McGibbon 2021). Attention to the ecological determinants of health dates at least back to the Industrial Revolution in Europe, where it became clear that industrialization resulted in health harms due to many causes, including air pollution and working in toxic factory environments. Capitalism's modern impacts have vastly accelerated the environmental and human harms of global climate damage, recently made more publicly visible through Edward Burtinsky's haunting and exquisite photography of the Anthropocene (Burtynsky, Baichwal and de Pencier 2018).

The term "Anthropocene epoch," first described by Paul Crutzen (2006) as the current geological age, refers to complex and even irreversible changes in Earth's natural systems. It is characterized by the dominance of humans over the global environment. The on-the-ground meaning of the Anthropocene involves synergistic impacts on Earth systems, including climate and atmospheric crises, global plastic pollution and nuclear testing. "Since we depend on [Earth] systems for the most fundamental determinants of our health, these human-induced changes present a profound threat to the health of the world's population in the 21st century" (Hancock 2011). Evidence has shown that toxic geographies of the Anthropocene brutally play themselves out in cells, tissues, immune systems and even epigenetic makeup (Gillings and Paulsen 2014). In humans, increased temperatures associated with climate change have been shown to increase cardiovascular and respiratory hospital admissions (Peters and Schneider 2021), deaths due to asthma and to heat exhaustion (Introcaso 2018) and deaths due to zoonoses such as COVID-19 (WHO 2020).

Not surprisingly, these Anthropocene-induced illnesses and deaths are disproportionately distributed according to the isms. For example, environmental pollutants and particulate matter associated with increased COVID-19 mortality are significantly more prevalent in oppressed communities (Wu et al. 2020). Ecosystem harms disproportionately impact marginalized and racialized geographies, not only in urban areas in Western countries, but especially in areas such as India and Southeast Asia (Wu et al. 2020). Impacts of the Anthropocene epoch are rooted in globe-wide legacies of patriarchy and colonialism, challenging us to see the Anthropocene's broader context, history and necropolitics — the control of who lives and who dies. In her book *A Billion Black Anthropocenes*, Kathryn Yussof (2019: 29) analyzes colonial imperialism in the language of the Anthropocene:

> [The Anthropocene] has been taken up in the world, purposed, and put to work as a conceptual grab, materialist history, and cautionary tale of planetary predicament. Equally, this planetary analytic has failed to do the work to properly identify its own histories of colonial earth-writing, to name the masters of broken earths, and to redress the legacy of racialized subjects that geology leaves in its wake.

The ecological determinants of health are intimately connected with the structural determinants of health. For example, Yussof further explains how descriptions of the Anthropocene have failed to grapple with the inheritance of violent dispossession of Indigenous land and the use of dominant colonial narratives to justify ongoing displacement of Indigenous peoples for the purpose of resource extraction and corporate profit. Embodied oppression cannot fully be analyzed or understood without tackling intersecting health impacts across the social, ecological and structural determinants of health.

THE STRUCTURAL DETERMINANTS OF HEALTH

Structural analyses point to the largely hidden role of the economic organization of society in the production and distribution of disease and burden of illness, as well as the ways that disease and illness are framed and treated (McGibbon 2017). Structural determinants are the root causes of inequities in health and well-being— "they are part of the political, economic, and social structure of society and of the culture that informs them" (Navarro 2007: 2). They include neoliberal public policy and governance; colonialism, white privilege; the isms; patriarchy; pan-capitalism; the dominance of manufactured and financial capital; social murder and slow violence. The word "structural" is used because its origins are explicitly traceable to societal structures and ruling relations such as government, law, business and financial management, professional organizations and educational institutions. The following discussion describes how oppression becomes embodied (finds its way into our bodies).

THE POLITICAL ECONOMY OF EMBODIED OPPRESSION

> Health is a political choice, and politics is a continuous struggle for power among competing interests. Looking at health through the lens of political determinants means analyzing how different power constellations, institutions, processes, interests, and ideological positions affect health.... The key political debates in public health revolve around the primacy of economic over social policies (often referred to as neoliberalism), charity versus entitlements, and concepts of liberty. (Kickbusch 2015)

"Epidemiology" is the study of patterns, causes and effects of disease and illness across defined populations or groups of people. Some branches of epidemiological science have evolved over time to encompass the social, political and economic root causes of illness and suffering — as covered, for example, in *The Widening Gap: Health Inequalities and Policy in Britain* (Shaw et al. 1999). The authors combined mortality and morbidity statistics across the lifecourse, linking them to poverty, housing insecurity and public policy. This integration of social science and epidemiology, called "social epidemiology" was first used in an article in the *American Sociological Review* in 1950: "The relationship of fetal and infant mortality to residential segregation: An inquiry into social epidemiology" (Krieger 2001). This topic is as timely now as it was in 1950, and the need to fully integrate social and biological origins of disease continues to be centrally relevant:

> Grappling with notions of causation, in turn, raises not only complex philosophical issues but also, in the case of social epidemiology, issues of accountability and agency: simply invoking abstract notions of "society" and disembodied "genes" will not suffice. Instead, the central question becomes: Who and what is responsible for population patterns of disease and wellbeing, as manifested in present, past and changing social inequalities in health. (Krieger 2001: 688)

Social epidemiology provides the theoretical context for us to understand why patterns of health and illness mirror inequitable distributions of deprivation and privilege across the SDH. As described earlier, these inequities are the result of political decision making and public policies that favour wealth concentration among relatively few individuals, a trend that is growing.

The recognition that politics and health are intertwined is surprisingly old. Almost two hundred years ago, in 1842, Rudolf Virchow (1821–1902), a Polish anthropologist and physician, noted that all diseases have two causes: one pathological, the other political. More recently, Vincente Navarro, stressing the importance of the relationship between social class and health, called for a "materialist epidemiology," one that integrates the ways that the societal hierarchy of class relations "conditions most potently how other variables affect the population's health" (2002: 21). Navarro (2002, 2004) and Esping-Anderson (2002), for example, outline a political economy approach about how we can tackle health inequities and their genesis in material and social deprivation. A political economy approach interrogates economic doctrines to disclose their sociological and political premises: "In sum, [it] regards economic ideas and behavior not as frameworks for analysis, but as beliefs and actions that must themselves be explained" (Mayer 1987: 3). The political economy of health refers to a close examination of how economic doctrines most powerfully determine the health of citizens over time.

Marx ([1845] 1977) was the first to describe a methodological approach to understanding the linkages among society, economics and history. Rather than viewing the field of economics as consisting of objective and quantifiable sets of measurements and models, he explored how the politics of a nation very much influenced the direction and outcomes of its economic policy. Marx explained that in order to survive and exist over generations, it is necessary for human beings to produce and reproduce the material requirements of life. Materialist approaches are based in his assertion that economic factors — the way people produce these necessities of life — determine the kind of politics and ideology a society can have. A political economy lens is central to modern efforts to understand and tackle the root causes of social problems, including growing inequities in health outcomes.

These structural determinants of health, although rarely listed in most national health plans, are the most important policies in determining a population's health outcomes (Navarro 2007). However, political will, and hence capacity to address inequities in the SDH, varies from state to state according to prevailing political ideologies. Inequities in the SDH are particularly evident in neoliberal political economies, where the prevailing ideology is that individuals have the right and responsibility to look after themselves and that the state should only intervene when people are already destitute. Economic policies are market driven, and corporate profit is viewed as an essential aspect of a robust economy. In contrast, social democratic political economies are grounded on the ideological inspiration of reducing poverty, inequality and unemployment. The organizing principles are universalism (for example, universal access to education and health and social care) and the socialist ideals of equality, the social rights of all citizens, justice, freedom and solidarity (Bryant 2009; Esping-Anderson 2002). Social democratic policies lead to better health outcomes across all social classes, races, ethnicities and ages (Raphael 2016). A cycle of oppression underscores the social, political and economic chain of causation that creates and sustains the systemic causes of ill health. Oppression is deeply embedded in systemic ruling relations, resulting in persistent and toxic consequences for the mental, physical and spiritual health of oppressed peoples.

THE CYCLE OF OPPRESSION

Cycle of Oppression:
Everyday Mechanisms of Structural Violence

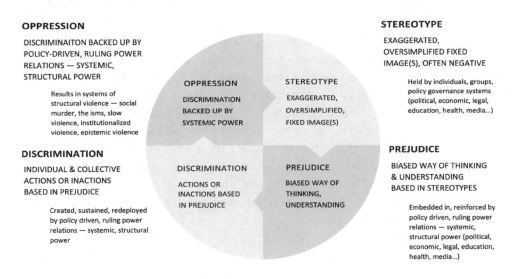

OPPRESSION

DISCRIMINAITON BACKED UP BY POLICY-DRIVEN, RULING POWER RELATIONS — SYSTEMIC, STRUCTURAL POWER

> Results in systems of structural violence — social murder, the isms, slow violence, institutionalized violence, epistemic violence

STEREOTYPE

EXAGGERATED, OVERSIMPLIFIED FIXED IMAGE(S), OFTEN NEGATIVE

> Held by individuals, groups, policy governance systems (political, economic, legal, education, health, media...)

DISCRIMINATION

INDIVIDUAL & COLLECTIVE ACTIONS OR INACTIONS BASED IN PREJUDICE

> Created, sustained, redeployed by policy driven, ruling power relations — systemic, structural power

PREJUDICE

BIASED WAY OF THINKING & UNDERSTANDING BASED IN STEREOTYPES

> Embedded in, reinforced by policy driven, ruling power relations — systemic, structural power (political, economic, legal, education, health, media...)

(Central figure labels:) OPPRESSION — DISCRIMINATION BACKED UP BY SYSTEMIC POWER; STEREOTYPE — EXAGGERATED, OVERSIMPLIFIED, FIXED IMAGE(S); DISCRIMINATION — ACTIONS OR INACTIONS BASED IN PREJUDICE; PREJUDICE — BIASED WAY OF THINKING, UNDERSTANDING

Oppression is a cyclic process that involves the thinking, actions and inactions of people in their everyday lives and the ways that this thinking originates and is reinforced by systemic, structural power. The following on-the-ground examples illustrate how the cycle of oppression (including stereotyping, prejudice, discrimination, systemic oppression) operates to create, reinforce, sustain and constantly redeploy the systemic causes of health and social inequities. The cycle of oppression ultimately results in "structural violence," first described by Johan Galtung (1969). It is distinguished from personal or direct violence, where the actor(s) may be directly identified, such as damage or death by fist, gun or knife; whereas in structural violence (built into, embedded in societal structures), there is no such actor (McGibbon 2021). As the Cycle of Oppression (above figure) illustrates, structural violence includes the violent impacts of systemically produced, sustained and avoidable damage to human and ecological health. Structural action or lack of action is violent because it results in suffering, death and ecosystem damage. Oppression also leads to what is known as oppression stress. Our body's adrenal system adjusts itself to give us the energy and concentration to handle everyday ups and downs of stress and even crises. However, when individuals and families live in a chronic state of stress due to oppressions such as racism, sexism or heterosexism, or a chronic day-to-day money crisis, then the adrenal system becomes fatigued, which contributes to immunosuppression, diabetes, heart disease and depression.

On the Ground: Racism as a Social Pathogen

The case of Mr. Brian Sinclair illustrates how the Cycle of Oppression operates in the everyday, ultimately resulting in systemic or structural violence. Research has shown that when Indigenous peoples in Canada seek healthcare, stereotyping, prejudice, discrimination and racism are common at point of care (Cameron et al. 2014). Racism was certainly evident in the death of Mr. Sinclair, a forty-five-year-old Indigenous man who was also a double amputee. He was referred by a community physician to Winnipeg's Health Sciences Centre in 2008, complaining of abdominal pain and a catheter problem. The inquest into Mr. Sinclair's death reported that he was ignored by staff and that other emergency room visitors repeatedly asked the nurses and the security staff to attend to him. The inquest also reported that some staff stereotyped Mr. Sinclair as "a drunk" and a homeless person.

Stereotyping led to prejudice — preconceived opinions and ways of thinking about Mr. Sinclair as he waited for care and treatment. Prejudice led to discrimination — in this case, lack of action. Mr. Sinclair was left in distress and without emergency care for thirty-four hours. He died in the emergency department and was then left unattended for several more hours until rigor mortis occurred. Discrimination was backed up by institutional power — in this case, a healthcare system with embedded allowances for clinical treatment based on discrimination, as well as a legal system that hid racism under the guise of "access block" and "patient flow problems" (Zbogar 2014). Since legal and health systems are supported at the systemic or structural level, the events leading to Mr. Sinclair's death are called structural violence.

> The Sinclair family, their legal counsel, and local Indigenous leaders asked the provincial inquest into the matter to strongly consider the ways in which Mr. Sinclair's race, disability (Mr. Sinclair was a double amputee and had suffered some cognitive impairment), and social class resulted in his lack of treatment. (Leyland et al. 2016: 4)

Oppression is also reflected in the racism-caused death of Joyce Echaquan, a thirty-seven-year-old Atikamekw (Ati-kamek) mother of seven from Manawan, an

Indigenous community 250 kilometres north of Montreal. She died on September 28, 2020, in the Centre Hospitalier de Lanaudière in Joliette, Quebec, where she had entered with stomach pains likely related to a pre-existing heart condition. Starla Myers (2020), who reported about Ms. Echaquan, described some of these stereotypes and prejudices that contributed to her death:

> The thought that Indigenous people are benefiting from "free handouts" is a direct result of Canada's colonial foundations. Such thinking suggests that the original people could not care for themselves and subsequently, that the "savages" required state-sponsored rescuing.... While in the hospital, Echaquan made a Facebook livestream video of her treatment. As Echaquan writhed in pain, the hospital staff could be heard saying in French ... "You're stupid as hell..." "You made some bad choices, my dear," while another staff says, "What are your children going to think, seeing you like this?

Ms. Echaquan had similar experiences in her previous encounters with this hospital. After one of her hospital stays, she even said to her family "One of these days, they're going to kill me" (Myers 2020). Perhaps oppression happened here when staff, their supervisors and hospital administrators looked the other way. Oppression definitely happened with administrative negligence regarding systematic and mandatory cultural safety training requirements for themselves and for all staff.

The 2016 death of Mr. Hugh Papik, a sixty-seven-year-old Elder from the Northwest Territories is another of the many deplorable and preventable tragedies caused by racism in healthcare systems. Staff at his care home called his daughter and told her to pick him up because he was drunk. Mr. Papik had a history of heart problems but none with drinking. Despite these facts, staff at the local health center did not perform a physical exam. By the time his niece persuaded medical staff to fly Mr. Papik to a hospital in Yellowknife, he was declared brain dead and removed from life support. In the investigation into Mr. Papik's death, territorial health minister Glen Abernethy stated that recommendations from the investigation will help to address systemic racism in health delivery (Weber 2016). These narratives are examples of how the cycle of oppression can operate in the healthcare system, even without clinicians noticing or being able to identify their related thoughts, behaviours and racial profiling.

On the Ground: Wealth, SES and Hospitalization Rates

There are numerous stereotypes about people, families and communities who have low or no income. Prejudicial thinking assumes that poverty is the result of lack of moral fortitude and laziness. Discrimination involves countless micro and macro aggressions against people who live in poverty, from the demeaning bureaucratic hurdles that families must overcome to prove that they are worthy of social assistance to the legislative organization of the remarkable income gap in Canada. During the COVID-19 pandemic, hospitalization rates closely mirrored SES — the lower the SES, the higher the rate of hospitalization (Canadian Press 2021). There were nearly fourteen thousand hospital stays for patients diagnosed with COVID-19 in Canada between January and November of 2020, along with more than 85,400 emergency department visits for COVID-19. The Canadian Institutes for Health Information (CIHI) found that 30.2 percent of all COVID-19 hospitalizations came from Canada's lowest income neighbourhoods, compared to 12.1 percent from the highest income areas. The COVID-19 pandemic provides a worldwide natural experiment about marginalization and racialization that was well in place long before the pandemic. Here, it is important to note that over a decade ago, CIHI published information directly linking excess hospitalization rates with SES. "Excess rates" refers to rates that are above the average Canadian hospitalization rates. The rapidly increasing income gap is writ large in the hospitals of the country. For males and females, excess rates associated with socio-economic status account for an estimated 33 to 40 percent of hospitalizations (CIHI 2010b).

In other words, if you are poor, you are 33 to 40 percent more likely to be hospitalized than the average Canadian. In the US, findings from a country-wide statistical analysis indicated that the rate of hospital stays among patients between the ages of forty-five and sixty-four was nearly 50 percent higher for people in the lowest-income communities (Wier, Merrill and Elixhauser 2009). Excess hospitalization rates reflect compromised SDH outcomes related to food and housing insecurity, racism and inequities in early childhood education, to name a few. The root causes of increasing poverty rates in Canada include key public policy issues such as inequitable income distribution and historical erosion of a public network of health and social services (Raphael 2019). The economic burden is substantial. In a CIHI (2020b) study of only fifteen metropolitan areas in Canada, the total yearly estimated costs of excess hospitalization were $123 million for males and $125 million for females. National costs are therefore likely in the multibillion-dollar range. Since up to 40 percent of hospitalizations are related to having a lower SES, it is no leap of logic that healthcare cost increases are heavily bound to social injustice in Canada.

On the Ground:
Social Murder and Deaths due to Poverty and Racism

Social murder is a form of structural violence that results in early death (Chernomas and Hudson 2009). Use of the term social murder was galvanized by Chernomas and Hudson (2007), who analyzed how public policies are designed to maximize the accumulation of profit while socializing the associated risks and costs. Excess deaths related to poverty and racism cannot, then, be just taken as "the way things are." They are, in a sense, unnaturally caused deaths captured in the concepts of structural violence and social murder. Engels' [1845] 2009 treatise on social murder over a century and a half ago remains urgently relevant today. Engels explained that when society deprives thousands of the necessities of life so that they die an early death, this is social murder. Such death is caused by societal conditions rather than a gun or a knife, but it is murder nonetheless. The perpetrators are therefore not easily identifiable. Engels' words of 1845 were eerily prophetic: the measure of a society is its willingness to provide for the collective well-being of all citizens, especially those who are most under threat of social and material deprivation. Countries such as Sweden have demonstrated that social democratic public policy supports health for all, along with a strong, fiscally responsible economy. These facts demonstrate that ill health is tied to a nation's political will to make (or not to make) socially just public policy decisions over time. One of the most documented examples of social murder involves the death of infants and newborns.

Infant mortality is a well-known global benchmark for measuring equity across the lifecourse. A 2010 Organisation for Economic Co-operation and Development (OECD) report stated that Canada had dropped significantly on infant mortality indicators. Once able to boast about its high world ranking for low infant mortality, Canada dropped from sixth to twenty-fourth place as of 2010 (Priest 2010), and it is in twenty-ninth place as of 2020 (OECD 2020). The main causes cited by researchers are poverty, isolation and premature births (Priest 2010). Yet in 2010, the response from the Society of Obstetricians and Gynaecologists of Canada was to propose a national birthing plan that would focus on accurate data gathering, maternity patient safety and the creation of a model of sustainable maternity and newborn care. In 2015, the Public Health Agency of Canada (PHAC 2015) listed similar interventions, such as incentives to promote breastfeeding, dietary interventions and postnatal education and health promotion. These are no doubt reasonable suggestions. However, they fail to reflect (and hence fail to address) evidence about the root causes of infant mortality:

- racism-related stress and socio-economic hardship (Bishop-Royse et al. 2021)

- the high prevalence of low-income among women who experience serious hardships during pregnancy (Braveman et al. 2010)

- high poverty rates and lack of access to a socialized healthcare system, as in the US (Tillett 2010)

- significant correlation of high poverty rates with infant mortality rates among minority and white mothers in the US (Fishman et al. 2021)

- significant correlation among poverty level, geographic areas and infant mortality rates (Mohamoud, Kirby and Ehrenthal 2019)

- high correlation of inequality and child relative poverty with infant mortality rates in rich societies (Pickett and Wilkinson 2007)

Current data does not allow for nationwide statistical analyses of newborn death rates in industrialized countries along socio-economic or racial lines; however, it is known that one of the main causes of newborn death is prematurity. The US has one of the highest preterm birth rates (one in eight) in the industrialized world and a correspondingly high newborn death rate. Most preterm births occur when the mother is an adolescent, and the US also has the highest adolescent pregnancy rate in the industrialized world. Evidence also shows that newborn and infant mortality are often higher among poor and racial and ethnic minority mothers. Poor and minority groups also suffer higher burdens of prematurity and low birth weights (Save the Children 2013). Root causes are persistent racism and the long-term erosion of social safety nets in Canada and other rich countries in the industrialized world.

ENVIRONMENTAL RACISM: HOW THE SOCIAL, ECOLOGICAL AND STRUCTURAL DETERMINANTS OF HEALTH COME TOGETHER

Structural violence can take many forms, one of which is social murder. "Slow violence" is another form of structural violence. It refers to long-term assaults on planetary life and ecosystems and a broad range of environmental and structural damage, such as toxic dumping, greenhouse gas production, desertification and the climate crisis. These violences produce cataclysmic changes that are felt over time, for generations, hence the term "slow." In all forms of structural violence, the perpetrators are very difficult to hold accountable, but death and destruction persist on a grand scale nonetheless. Slow violence has far-reaching impacts on how people experience the SDH.

> To confront what I am calling slow violence requires that we attempt to give symbolic shape and plot to formless threats whose fatal repercussions are

dispersed across space and time. Politically and emotionally, different kinds of disasters possess unequal heft. Falling bodies, burning towers, exploding heads have a visceral, page-turning potency that tales of slow violence cannot match. Stories of toxic buildup, massing greenhouse gases, or desertification may be cataclysmic, but they're scientifically convoluted cataclysms in which casualties are deferred, often for generations. In the gap between acts of slow violence and their delayed effects, both memory and causation readily fade from view and the casualties thus incurred pass untallied. (Nixon 2007: 14)

The Syncrude and Suncor oil sands in Alberta are an urgent and clear example of how the social and ecological determinants of health are nested within the structural (political and public policy) determinants of health. The tar sands are a case of environmental racism because Indigenous peoples and treaty lands are significantly and disproportionally impacted.

A BRIEF PUBLIC POLICY HISTORY OF TAR SANDS

Oil sands, also known as tar sands, are large deposits of a type of oil called bitumen, which is extremely heavy crude oil. Bitumen extraction in tar sands mining operations produces a toxic brew of petrochemical waste products called "tailings," which are a mixture of water, sand, fine silts, clay, residual bitumen and lighter hydrocarbons, inorganic salts and water-soluble organic compounds and include other compounds such as naphthenic acids, cyanide, phenols, arsenic, cadmium, chromium, copper, lead and zinc. In 2016, Alberta produced about 81 percent of Canada's crude oil (CEC 2020). For over fifty years, the tar sands industry in Alberta has stored these wastes in enormous lakes that the industry refers to as tailings ponds. These toxic lakes are the largest human-made structure in the world and can be seen from space — they are bigger than England and are two and a half times the size of Nova Scotia (Sierra Club 2021). As of 2017, these ponds held one trillion litres of sludge that is unlike any other industrial by-product in the world. They contain a unique cocktail of toxic chemicals and hydrocarbons that will remain in molasses-like suspension for centuries if left alone (Berman 2017). Tar sands are the emblematic form of extreme oil, and their continued extraction is the "end game" for the planet's climate. They are "extreme" because climate science has shown us that most of the hydrocarbons buried under the northwestern boreal forest must stay in the ground if we do not want the planet's temperature to rise more than 1.5 degrees Celsius above pre-industrial levels (Berman 2017).

Following a years-long international investigation backed by the Canadian, US and Mexican governments, the 2020 Commission for Environmental Cooperation report confirmed that Syncrude and Suncor tailings ponds are leaking toxic fluids into groundwater and the tributaries of the Athabasca River (CEC 2020). Scientific reports have found that the chemicals that leak from tailings ponds sicken local communities, poison wildlife, and pose the ever-growing threat of contaminating the region's water resources. They pose a growing threat to First Nations communities, the boreal forest and aquatic ecosystems in Canada, especially in Alberta (NRDC 2020). The cost of clean-up, as predicted by the NRDC (2020), is upwards of $58 billion, leaving Albertans wondering who is going to take responsibility for this aspect of the tailings ponds (NRDC 2020).

In response to the serious health situation in Alberta, the Canadian minister of environment and climate change, Jonathan Wilkinson, asserted: "We will ensure enforcement officers will be given the tools they need to ensure polluters are held to account when environmental laws are broken" (Government of Canada 2021). Indigenous leaders have repeatedly called for health studies and noted that the expansion of the tars sands is violating their treaty rights. Yet the federal government has not taken a stand to punish oil sands companies for leaking tailings ponds (Government of Canada 2021). As a result, Canada's political economy has been reshaped by extractivist forces based in the western tar sands (Pineault 2018). In 2015, a directive was put into place to require companies to reduce tailings. Not a single company complied. Rather than fining the companies or refusing permits, the federal government simply removed the directive. Although Suncor's mine is scheduled to close in 2033, they have been granted until after 2100 (into the next century) to figure out how to clean up their tailings and reclaim the land. They will be "treating" their tailings by dumping them into pits and covering them with freshwater to form a permanent "lake." Despite the fact that the auditor general estimated that tailings liabilities now surpass $20 billion (Berman 2017), oil corporations aren't being held accountable. This capitalist pressure to extract is causing an ecological crisis marked by the principles of accumulation of corporate capital for the very few (Pineault 2018). Extreme oil has flourished in the face of decades of evidence about extreme and publicly known health and environmental impacts.

HUMAN AND ENVIRONMENTAL HEALTH IMPACTS OF TAR SANDS

Tailings ponds are known to contain lead, which can permanently impair children's brain and nervous system development; mercury, which can have damaging impacts on the nervous, immune and digestive systems and harm children's development; and arsenic and benzene, which are well-established carcinogens (NRDC 2020). People who live near tar sands strip-mining, drilling and processing operations in Canada face health risks from additional air and water pollution, and there are reports of an increased incidence of cancer (NRDC 2014). Snow and water in an area extending outward thirty miles from upgrading facilities at Fort McMurray contained high concentrations of pollutants associated with fossil fuels (Kelly et al. 2009). These chemicals often present serious risks to human health — some are known to damage DNA, others are carcinogens, and many have negative developmental impacts (NRDC 2014). Elevated rates of leukemia and other cancers of the lymph and blood-forming systems exist in areas surrounding upgrading and petrochemical manufacturing facilities just north of Edmonton. Experts have found similar elevated risks in other populations living downwind of industrial facilities with similar emissions, which have also been linked to increased rates of leukemia and childhood lymphohematopoietic cancers (Simpson et al. 2013).

Public hearings began in early 2014 following complaints that the tar sands operations have caused nausea, headaches, skin rashes, memory loss, joint pain, exhaustion and respiratory problems, forcing several families to leave the area (NRDC 2014). Scientists noted that cancer diagnoses in 1996–2006 were 30 percent higher for residents of Fort Chipewyan (located where the Athabasca River empties into Lake Athabasca) than what would be expected. Biliary tract cancers, blood and lymphatic cancers, lung cancers in women and soft tissue cancers all occurred at rates higher than expected (Alberta Cancer Board 2009). Smog and soot-forming pollutants from the use of heaters, boilers and hydro-treating have been tied to increased cancer risks, increased respiratory issues including asthma, cardiovascular illness, developmental delays and other negative health effects (NRDC 2014). The metal-laden dust that blows off petroleum coke piles can contaminate nearby homes and yards, where it can accumulate, and children can be exposed. This dust is a pollutant recognized as contributing to heart attacks, asthma, decreased lung function and even premature death (NRDC 2014). Yet this evidence continues to be largely ignored by both provincial and federal governance bodies as well as Big Oil transnational corporations, who are the primary beneficiaries.

IMPERATIVES AND PATHWAYS FOR SOCIAL JUSTICE ACTION

Embodied oppression occurs when the structural, systemic and institutionalized root causes of ill health produce illness and suffering across the lifecourse. The interplay of politics, economics and policy, referred to as the political economy of health, is an important aspect of this process. Oppression becomes inscribed on the body, in-

> Embodied oppression occurs when the structural, systemic, institutionalized root causes of ill health produce illness and suffering across the lifecourse.

side and outside. The body becomes the terrain where oppression plays itself out, from social murder as a result of racism in healthcare systems to the myriad diagnoses of low- or no-income people, who fill hospital beds at a disproportionate rate. This collective, oppression-caused suffering is a wake-up call for all of us and an indictment of a public system that is failing millions of Canadians as well as failing to protect the Earth's life support systems.

Social pathogens, such as structural violence, slow violence and social murder, are very difficult to expose. When we hear of or see these pathogens, our first task is to grieve and then to continually move to a different moral terrain where our own humanity is implicated in each and every transgression. Lila Watson, an Australian Indigenous woman, responded to mission workers by saying, "If you have come to help me, you are wasting your time. But if you have come because your liberation is bound up with mine, then let us walk together." Acting for change is about realizing that our own liberation is connected to the liberation of all people. Depending on the social or ethical issue at hand, we may find ourselves in various stages in our commitment to taking action and our ability to see how our own social justice actions are part of a larger justice movement that impacts all of us and the planet. Perhaps we see tackling health inequities as someone else's responsibility. We may have significant barriers to action because we are experiencing oppression in our own lives. Social justice action is difficult because it challenges oppressive structures that are deeply embedded in social, cultural, political and economic processes and decision making over time.

Personal action for social change is perhaps the most difficult place to start because it is often easier to think about what other people, politicians and "the government" can do. Personal action is an integral part of collective or social action. Capacity for personal action happens on a continuum, from supporting oppression on one end to confronting oppression on the other end (see figure below). Wijeyesinghe, Griffin and Love (1997) provided a detailed description of the stages that we can consider in acting for change. It is important to note that the continuum applies to our own personal action for justice as well as collective, public action — locally, regionally, nationally and internationally. On one end of the continuum, we actively participate in oppression. When we support oppression, our actions maintain oppressive social structures and ruling relations. It is crucial to note that we can support oppression *without actually realizing or noticing* that we are doing so. For example, this process is frequently a conundrum for white people, since the prevailing thinking is that we must actually be able to identify our white privilege before it can be said to exist.

Knowing about our own unearned privileges is a foundational process in confronting oppression. For example, white privilege (see DiAngelo 2018), heterosexual privilege (see Vaccaro and Koob 2019), male privilege and class privilege (see

Liu 2017) are invisible, often lifelong advantages. These privileges exist regardless of whether or not the bearers are aware of their privilege. One of the most important starting points in working for social change is to embrace the fact that oppressions often flourish without the oppressors being willing or able to name their participation. We support oppression when we actively participate in oppression, deny or ignore oppression or recognize oppression but take no action. For example, it is known that toxic waste dumps and landfills are consistently located near communities of colour the world over, including many of our own communities. When we know this fact, yet take no notice of where our own garbage is going when it leaves our curb, then we are participating in oppression. When we fail to educate ourselves about the long-term consequences of conservative economic policy, then we are participating in oppression.

Acting for Social Justice

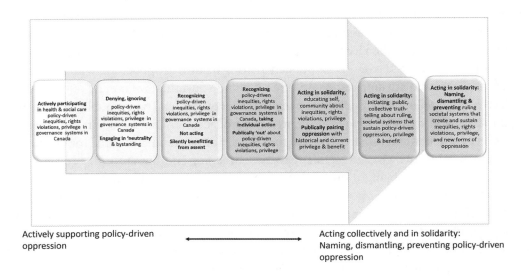

Actively supporting policy-driven oppression

Acting collectively and in solidarity: Naming, dismantling, preventing policy-driven oppression

Noticing or witnessing oppression and taking the stance that it is none of our business, or that it is someone else's responsibility to speak up, is the same as not doing anything in the face of need. Reverend Martin Niemöller's famous story reminds us that claiming neutrality, or standing by, has ethical consequences:

> In Germany they first came for the Communists, and I didn't speak up because I wasn't a Communist. Then they came for the Jews, and I didn't speak up because I wasn't a Jew. Then they came for the trade unionists, and I didn't

speak up because I wasn't a trade unionist. Then they came for the Catholics, and I didn't speak up because I was a Protestant. Then they came for me and by that time no one was left to speak up.

It is very difficult to understand how silence is assent because it is an absence of action. Silence is often disguised as neutrality. We may decline to join conversations about pressing social justice concerns, such as the missing and murdered Indigenous girls and women in Canada or the unmarked graves (nearly two thousand as of July 2021) of Indigenous children who were murdered in Indian residential schools. Our silence is likely to be interpreted as neutrality, implying that we do not have an opinion about, say, the connections between colonialism, residential schools and the disproportionately high rate of murders of Indigenous girls and women in Canada. However, silence is assent.

When we move along the continuum, we consciously become more aware of the injustices around us. We often feel guilt once we see the enormity of the problems and instances of our own complicit behaviour. We recognize specific injustices and begin to take individual action. We are "publicly out" about injustice. Individual or personal action can then lead to acting collectively and in solidarity as we participate in educating others. Here, we are publicly pairing historical oppression with its related privileges and advantages. As we move beyond educating, we initiate public, collective truth telling about oppression and support others who take a public stance. In the structural area of the continuum, we act in collective solidarity to name, dismantle and prevent oppression. We tackle the social, political and economic root causes. Here, social justice change often supports democracy and human rights related to health, such as lobbying municipal (for example, for non-racist landfill locations), provincial or territorial governments (such as community-driven food collectives and community gardens) and federal governments (for example, halting the privatization of healthcare) for socially just public policy. In collective action for social justice and health, there is no streamlined separation among the levels of governmental and regional policymaking bodies. For instance, when lobbying for community-driven health and social care, discussions and action will need to happen within the local or district health and social services jurisdictions as well as provincial and federal jurisdictions. Ideas for change often emanate from anger or outrage about erosion of existing justice-based policies or services. Action for social justice and health tackles these root causes of embodied oppression, and even in democracies such as Canada, there are significant barriers to action. The challenge is to continually find our own entry points in a global movement that is increasingly being framed in the context of an ethical commitment to tackle social injustices and climate crises.

DISCUSSION QUESTIONS

1. What are some of the differences between a "lifestyle" approach to understanding health problems and a structural perspective? Why and how does the lifestyle approach persist? Who benefits and who is disadvantaged by the persistence of a lifestyle approach?
2. What are some of the ways that the biomedical model continues to block progress on tackling inequities in the social determinants of health?
3. What are some case study examples of how inequities in the three areas of the SDH (SDH as laid out by Raphael et al. (2020), the isms as SDH and geographies as SDH) operate on the ground in people's everyday lives? Use the SDH intersectionality figure to guide your discussion.
4. Debate the following statements: (1) People can choose to be healthy if they really want to; (2) women can leave an abusive relationship if they really want to; and (3) in countries such as Canada, people can achieve pretty much anything they want to if they try hard enough.
5. Why are the structural determinants of health largely hidden?
6. What are some of the ecological issues that you are most concerned about? List and then discuss (1) some of the specific ways that this slow violence impacts human health across the lifecourse, and (2) your points of entry for social change (local, regional, global).
7. What are some of the social justice and health issues that you are most passionate about? Locate yourselves (individually and/or in groups) on the social justice continuum, then talk about what actions you can take to move to the next stage on the continuum.

GLOSSARY OF KEY TERMS

Critical health studies: A relatively new field of knowledge that synthesizes critical perspectives in the social sciences and humanities with deliberative examination of the mechanisms that impact human and ecological health across the lifecourse.

Ecological determinants of health (ecodeterminants): The ecological determinants of health include human health and the health of the whole natural world on Earth, including resource and ozone layer depletion, ocean acidification, desertification, deforestation, species extinction and biodiversity loss, rapidly increasing land, water and air pollution and ecotoxicity.

Embodied oppression: Occurs when the structural, systemic, institutionalized root causes of ill health produce illness and suffering across the lifecourse. Oppression is inscribed on the bodies, minds and spirits of oppressed groups and peoples.

Health inequities: Systemic differences in the health status of different population groups. Social factors, including education, employment status, income level, gender and ethnicity have a marked influence on health and illness. The lower an individual's socio-economic position, for example, the higher their risk of poor health across the lifecourse.

Intersectionality: The ways oppressions intersect. Sexism, racism, heterosexism and ageism, to name a few, can and do happen together to produce a complex synergy of material and social disadvantage. These oppressions work together, fusing into a complex whole that cannot be disentangled into any single phenomenon.

Oppression: A cyclical process involving institutionalized procedures and practices of domination and control that create and sustain injustice. Stereotyping leads to prejudicial thinking, which leads to discriminatory action or inaction. Discrimination is backed up by institutional power, the organizational structures in society (law, healthcare, education, political economies, corporate power).

Oppression stress: Our body's adrenal system adjusts itself to give us the energy and concentration to handle everyday ups and downs of stress and even crises. However, when individuals and families live in a state of chronic stress due to oppressions such as racism, sexism or heterosexism, or a chronic day-to-day money crisis, then the adrenal system becomes fatigued, which contributes to immunosuppression, diabetes, heart disease and depression.

Political economy of health: Political economy interrogates economic doctrines and structures to discern their sociological and political premises. The political economy of health refers to a close examination of how economic doctrines most powerfully determine the health of citizens.

Slow violence: A form of structural violence referring to long-term assaults on planetary life and ecosystems and a broad range of environmental and structural damage to the planet. Some examples are toxic build-up, massing greenhouse gases, desertification and climate change. These casualties produce cataclysmic changes that are felt over time, for generations.

Social murder: A form of structural violence. When public policy decision making and social structures deprive thousands of the necessities of life and force them to remain in such conditions so that they die an early death, this is social murder — death that is caused by societal conditions rather than a gun or a knife, but is murder nonetheless.

Structural determinants of health: Structural determinants are root causes — the causes-of-the-causes — of inequities in health and well-being and they are part of the political, economic and social structures of society and of the culture that informs them. Structural determinants include neoliberal public policy and governance; colonialism; white privilege; the isms; patriarchy; pan-capitalism; the dominance of capitalists; social murder; and slow violence.

Structural violence: The violent impacts of systemically produced, sustained and avoidable damage to human and ecological health. The origins are explicitly traceable to societal structures or ruling relations. Slow violence and social murder are examples of structural violence.

RESOURCES FOR ACTIVISTS

Anti-oppression resources and exercises: organizingforpower.org/anti-oppression-resources-exercises/
The ENRICH Project: enrichproject.org/
Canadian Centre for Policy Alternatives: policyalternatives.ca/
Global Citizen: globalcitizen.org/en/
Canadian Anti-Racism Network: stopracism.ca
The Socialist Project: socialistproject.ca/leftstreamed/

NOTE

1 Intersectionality theory has its origins in critical feminist perspectives, most notably introduced by Black feminist scholars such as Kimberlé Crenshaw (1989), bell hooks (1990), Patricia Hill Collins (1990, 2002, 2005) and Agnes Calliste (2000).

REFERENCES

Alberta Cancer Board. 2009. *Cancer Incidence in Fort Chipewyan, Alberta 1995–2006.* Edmonton: Alberta Cancer Board Division of Population Health and Information Surveillance.

Barret, J.R. 2012. "Proximity Plus Pollution: Understanding Factors in Asthma Among Children Living Near Major Roadways." *Environmental Health Perspectives* 120, 11.

Berman, T. 2017. "Canada's Most Shameful Environmental Secret Must Not Remain Hidden." *The Guardian,* November 14.

Beyer, K.M., S. Young and A. Bemanian. 2019. "Persistent Racial Disparities in Breast Cancer Mortality Between Black and White Women: What Is the Role for Structural Racism?" *Geospatial Approaches to Energy Balance and Breast Cancer.* New York: Springer Link Publishing.

Bishop-Royse, J., B. Lange-Maia, L. Murray, et al. 2021. "Structural Racism, Socio-Economic Marginalization, and Infant Mortality." *Public Health* 190.

Braveman, P., K. Marchi, S. Egerter et al. 2010. "Poverty, Near Poverty, and Hardship Around the Time of Pregnancy." *Maternal and Child Health Journal* 14, 1.

Breggin, P.R. 2008. *Brain-Disabling Treatments in Psychiatry: Drugs, Electroshock and the Psychopharmaceutical Complex*, 2nd edition. New York: Springer Publishing.

___. 1991. *Toxic Psychiatry: Why Therapy, Empathy and Love Must Replace the Drugs, Electroshock, and Biochemical Theories of the New Psychiatry*. New York: St. Martin's Press.

Breggin, P.R., and G.R. Ginger. 1998. *The War Against Children of Color. Psychiatry Targets Inner City Youth*. Monroe, ME: Common Courage Press.

Brewer, L.C., and L.A. Cooper. 2014. "Race, Discrimination, and Cardiovascular Disease." *American Medical Association Journal of Ethics* 16, 6.

Broadbent Institute. 2014. *The Wealth Gap: Perceptions and Misconceptions in Canada*. Ottawa: Broadbent Institute.

Bryant, T. 2009. *An Introduction to Health Policy*. Toronto: Canadian Scholars' Press.

Burtynsky, E., J. Baichwal, and M. de Pencier. 2018. *Anthropocene*. Göttingen, Germany: *Steidl*.

Calliste, A. 2000. *Anti-Racist Feminism: Critical Race and Gender Studies*. Halifax: Fernwood Publishing.

Cameron, B., M.D. Carmargo Plazas, A.S. Salas et al. 2014. "Understanding Inequalities in Access to Health Care Services for Aboriginal People: A Call for Nursing Action." *Advances in Nursing Science* 37, 3.

Canadian Press. 2021. "COVID Hospitalization Costs $23,000 per Stay, Four Times as Much as Average: CIHI." Canadian Press, March 25. <ctvnews.ca/health/coronavirus/covid-hospitalization-costs-23-000-per-stay-four-times-as-much-as-average-cihi-1.5361631>.

Caplan, P. 1996. "They Say You're Crazy: How the World's Most Powerful Psychiatrists Decide Who's Normal." New York: Perseus Books.

CDC (Centers for Disease Control and Prevention). 2019. *Pregnancy-Related Deaths*. February 26.

CEC (Commission for Environmental Cooperation). 2020. "Alberta Tailings Ponds II: Factual Record Regarding Submission SEM-17-001." Montreal, Canada. <cec.org/wp-content/uploads/wpallim-port/files/17-1-ffr_en.pdf>.

Chernomas, R., and I. Hudson. 2009. "Social Murder: The Long Term Effects of Conservative Economic Policy." *International Journal of Health Services* 39, 1.

___. 2007. *Social Murder and Other Shortcomings of Conservative Economics*. Winnipeg: ARP Books.

CIHI (Canadian Institute for Health Information). 2010a. "*National Health Expenditure Trends, 1975–2010.*" Toronto.

___. 2010b. *Hospitalization Disparities by Socio-economic Status for Males and Females*. Catalogue Number: H117-5/20-2010E-PDF. Ottawa: CIHI. <publications.gc.ca/site/eng/441512/publication.html>.

Clay, R.A. 2014. "Double-Whammy Discrimination: Health Care Providers' Biases and Misunderstandings Are Keeping Some Older LGBT Patients from Getting the Care They Need." *Monitor on Psychology* 45, 10.

Collins, P.H. 2005. *Black Sexual Politics: African Americans, Gender, and the New Racism*. New York: Routledge.

___. 2002. "The Politics of Black Feminist Thought." In C.R. McCann and S. Kim (eds.), *Feminist Theory Reader: Local & Global Perspectives*. London: Routledge.

___. 1990. *Black Feminist Thought: Knowledge, Consciousness and the Politics of Empowerment*. Boston: Unwin Hyman.

CPHA (Canadian Public Health Association). 2015. Global Change and Public Health: Addressing the Ecological Determinants of Health. Ottawa.

Crenshaw, K. 1989. "Demarginalizing the Intersection of Race and Sex: A Black Feminist Critique of Antidiscrimination Doctrine, Feminist Theory, and Anti-Racist Politics." *University of Chicago Legal Forum* 14.

Crowshoe, L., D. Dannenbaum, M. Green et al. 2018. "Type 2 Diabetes and Indigenous Peoples." *Canadian Journal of Diabetes* 42.

Cruickshank J. 2012. "Positioning Positivism, Critical Realism and Social Constructionism in the Health Sciences: A Philosophical Orientation." *Nursing Inquiry* 19.

Crutzen, P. 2006. "The Anthropocene." In E. Ehlers and T. Krafft (eds.), *Earth System Science in the*

Anthropocene. Berlin: Springer.

DiAngelo, R. 2018. "White Fragility." Video: *Seattle Channel*, July 3. <youtube.com/watch?v=45ey-4jgoxeU>.

Engels, F. [1845] 2009. *The Condition of the Working Class in England*. New York: Penguin Classics.

Esping-Anderson, G. 2002. *Why We Need a New Welfare State*. Oxford: Oxford University Press.

Evans, P. 2019. "Canadian Corporations Dodged up to $11B in Taxes in a Year, CRA Report Finds." CBC News, Jun 18. <cbc.ca/news/business/cra-corporate-taxes-1.5179489>.

Finn, E. 2012. "Government's Forgone Income: Huge Tax Cuts, Uncollected Taxes Starve Our Social Programs." *The Monitor*, July 12. Ottawa: Canadian Center for Policy Alternatives.

Fishman, S.H., R.A. Hummer, G. Sierra et al. 2021. "Race/Ethnicity, Maternal Educational Attainment, and Infant Mortality in the United States." *Biodemography and Social Biology* 66.

Fowler, R.A., N.S. Sabur, P. Li, et al. 2007. "Sex- and Age-Based Differences in the Delivery and Outcomes of Critical Care." *Canadian Medical Association Journal* 177, 12.

Galtung, J. 1969. "Violence, Peace, and Peace Research. *Journal of Peace Research* 6, 3.

Gaventa, J. 2006. *Exploring Power for Change (The Power Cube)*. Brighton, UK: University of Sussex, Institute for Development Studies.

Gillings, J., and T. Paulsen. 2014. "Microbiology of the Anthropocene." *Anthropocene* 5.

Government of Canada. 2021. "Government of Canada Legislates Climate Accountability with First Net-zero Emissions Law." News release, June 30. Ottawa: Government of Canada.

Hancock, T. 2011. "It's the Environment Stupid! Declining Ecosystem Health is THE Threat to Health in the 21st Century." *Health Promotion International* 26.

Hankivsky, O., and A. Christoffersen. 2008. "Intersectionality and the Determinants of Health: A Canadian Perspective." *Critical Public Health* 18, 3.

Homan, P. 2019. "Structural Sexism and Health in the United States: A New Perspective on Health Inequality and the Gender." *American Sociological Review* 84, 3.

hooks, b. 1990. "*Yearning: Race, Gender & Cultural Politics*." Toronto: Between the Lines.

Illich, I. 1976. *Limits to Medicine: Medical Nemesis. The Expropriation of Health*. Middlesex, UK: Penguin.

Introcaso, D. 2018. "Climate Change Is the Greatest Threat to Human Health in History." *Health Affairs*, December 19.

Kcomt, L., K.M. Goreyb, B.J. Barrett and S. Esteban McCabe. 2020. "Healthcare Avoidance Due to Anticipated Discrimination Among Transgender People: A Call to Create Trans-affirmative Environments." *SSM — Population Health* 11, 100608.

Kelly, E.N., J.W Short, D.W. Schindler et al. 2009. "Oil Sands Development Contributes Polycyclic Aromatic Compounds to the Athabasca River and its Tributaries." *Proceedings of the National Academy of Sciences* 106, 52.

Kickbusch, I. 2015. "The Political Determinants of Health — 10 Years On." *British Medical Journal* 331.

Krieger N. 2014. "Discrimination and Health Inequities." *International Journal of Health Services* 44.

____. 2003. "Does Racism Harm Health? Did Child Abuse Exist Before 1962? On Explicit Questions, Critical Science, and Current Controversies: An Ecosocial Perspective." *American Journal of Public Health* 93, 2.

____. 2001. "Theories for Social Epidemiology: An Ecosocial Perspective." *International Journal of Epidemiology* 30.

Kuh, D., and Y. Ben-Shalmo. 1997. *A Lifecourse Approach to Chronic Disease Epidemiology*. Oxford: Oxford University Press.

Leyland, A., J. Smylie, M. Cole et al. 2016. "Health and Health Care Implications of Systemic Racism on Indigenous Peoples in Canada: Indigenous Health Working Group [Fact Sheet]." *College of Family Physicians of Canada*.

Liu, W.M. 2017. "White Male Power and Privilege: The Relationship Between White Supremacy and Social Class. *Journal of Counseling Psychology* 64, 4.

Lorber, J. 1994. *Paradoxes of Gender*. New Haven, CT: Yale University Press.

Marx, K. [1845] 1977. "*A Contribution to the Critique of Political Economy*." Moscow: Progress Publishers.

Mayer. C.S. 1987. *In Search of Stability: Explorations in Historical Political Economy*. Cambridge: Cambridge University Press.

McGibbon, E. 2021. "People Under Threat: Social, Ecological and Structural Determinants of Health." In E. McGibbon (ed.), *Oppression: A Social Determinant of Health*. Halifax: Fernwood Publishing.

___. 2017. "The Social Determinants of Health: Embodied Oppression Across the Lifecourse." In W. Antony and J. Antony (eds.), *Power and Resistance: Critical Thinking about Canadian Social Issues*, 6th edition. Halifax: Fernwood Publishing.

___. 2007. "Health Inequities and the Social Determinants of Health: The Spatial Contexts of Oppression." Invited keynote presentation, Health Geomatics Conference, Nova Scotia Health Research Foundation, Halifax, NS, October.

McGibbon, E., and J. Etowa. 2009. *Anti-Racist Health Care Practice*. Toronto: Canadian Scholars Press.

McGibbon, E., and C. McPherson. 2012. "Applying Intersectionality and Complexity Theory to Address the Social Determinants of Women's Health." *Women's Health and Urban Life: An International Journal* 10, 1.

McGibbon, E., I. Waldron and J. Jackson. 2013. "The Social Determinants of Cardiovascular Health: Time for a Focus on Racism." Guest editorial. *Diversity and Equality in Health and Care: An International Journal* 10.

McPherson, C., and E. McGibbon. 2014. "Intersecting Contexts of Oppression Within Complex Public Systems." In A. Pycroft and C. Bartollas (eds.), *Applying Complexity Theory: A Whole Systems Approaches to Criminal Justice and Social Work*. Bristol: Policy Press.

Mody, P., A. Gupta, B. Bikdeli et al. 2012. "Most Important Articles on Cardiovascular Disease Among Racial and Ethnic Minorities." *Circulation: Cardiovascular Quality and Outcomes* 5, 4.

Mohamoud, Y.A., R.S. Kirby and D.B. Ehrenthal. 2019. "Poverty, Urban-Rural Classification and Term Infant Mortality: A Population-based Multilevel Analysis." BMC *Pregnancy Childbirth* 19, 40.

Mulé, N.J., and M. Smith. 2014. "Invisible Populations: LGBTQ People and Federal Health Policy in Canada." *Canadian Public Administration* 57, 2 (June).

Myers, S. 2020. "'One Day They Are Going to Kill Me': Joyce Echaquan Killed by Canada's Racist Healthcare System." *Real People's Media*, October 3. <realpeoples.media/one-day-they-are-going-to-kill-me-joyce-echaquan-killed-by-canadas-racist-healthcare-system/>.

Navarro, V. 2007. "What Is National Health Policy?" *International Journal of Health Services* 37, 1.

___. 2004. *The Political and Social Contexts of Health*. New York: Baywood Publishing.

___. 2002. "A Historical Review (1965–1997) of Studies on Class, Health & Quality of Life: A Personal Account." In V. Navarro (ed.), *The Political Economy of Social Inequalities: Consequences for Health and Quality of Life*. New York: Baywood Publishing.

Nelson, B. 2020. "How Structural Racism Can Kill Cancer Patients." *Cancer Cytopathology* 83–84.

Nixon, R. 2007. "Slow Violence, Gender, and the Environmentalism of the Poor." *Journal of Commonwealth and Postcolonial Studies* 13.

NRDC (Natural Resources Defense Council). 2020. *Report: Alberta's Tailings Ponds*. <environmentaldefence.ca/report/albertas-tailings-ponds/>.

___. 2014. "Tar Sands Crude Oil: Health Effects of a Dirty and Destructive Fuel." <nrdc.org/sites/default/files/tar-sands-health-effects-IB.pdf>.

O'Dowd, M.F. 2020. "Explainer: What Is Systemic Racism and Institutional Racism?" *The Conversation*, February 4. <theconversation.com/explainer-what-is-systemic-racism-and-institutional-racism-131152>.

O'Keefe, E.B., J.T. Meltzer and B.N. Bethea. 2015. "Health Disparities and Cancer: Racial Disparities in Cancer Mortality in the United States, 2000–2010." *Frontiers in Public Health* 3, 51.

OECD (Organisation for Economic Co-operation and Development). 2020. *Health at a Glance: OECD Indicators*. Paris.

Oxfam. 2021. "Mega-Rich Recoup COVID-Losses in Record-Time Yet Billions Will Live in Poverty for at Least a Decade." Oxfam press release, January 25. <oxfam.org/en/press-releases/mega-rich-recoup-covid-losses-record-time-yet-billions-will-live-poverty-least>.

Patel, S., and S. Sangeeta. 2019. "Pesticides as the Drivers of Neuropsychotic Diseases, Cancers, and Teratogenicity Among Agro-workers as Well as General Public." *Environmental Science Pollution Research* 26.

Peters, A., and A. Schneider. 2021. "Cardiovascular Risks of Climate Change." *Nature Reviews Cardiology* 18, 1–2.

PHAC (Public Health Agency of Canada). 2015. "Maternal Infant Health (0-2years)." Ottawa.<cbpp-pcpe.phac-aspc.gc.ca/public-health-topics/maternal-infant-health/>.

Pickett, K.E., and R.G. Wilkinson. 2007. "Child Wellbeing and Income Inequality in Rich Societies: Ecological Cross Sectional Study." *British Medical Journal Online* 24, 335. <doi.org/10.1136/bmj.39377.580162.55>.

Pineault, E. 2018. "The Capitalist Pressure to Extract: The Ecological and Political Economy of Extreme Oil in Canada." *Studies in Political Economy* 99, 2.

Priest, L. 2010. "Why Are Our Babies Dying?" *Globe and Mail*, May 22.

Quach, T., A. Nuru-Jeter, P. Morris et al. 2012. "Experiences and Perceptions of Medical Discrimination Among a Multiethnic Sample of Breast Cancer Patients in the Greater San Francisco Bay Area, California." *American Journal of Public Health* 102, 5.

Raphael, D. 2021. "Critical Perspectives on the Social Determinants of Health." In E. McGibbon (ed.) *Oppression: A Social Determinant of Health*. Halifax: Fernwood Publishing.

____. 2019. *Poverty and Policy in Canada*. Toronto: Canadian Scholars Press.

____. 2016. Critical Perspectives on the Social Determinants of Health. Toronto: Canadian Scholars' Press.

Raphael, D., T. Bryant, J. Mikkonen and A. Raphael. 2020. *Social Determinants of Health: The Canadian Facts*. Oshawa: Ontario Tech University Faculty of Health Sciences and Toronto: York University School of Health Policy and Management.

Rossman, K., P. Salamanca and K. Macapagal. 2017. "A Qualitative Study Examining Young Adults' Experiences of Disclosure and Nondisclosure of LGBTQ Identity to Health Care Providers." *Journal of Homosexuality* 64, 10.

Save the Children. 2013. *Surviving the First Day: State of the World's Mothers, 2013*. London.

Schultz, A., L. Dahl, E. McGibbon et al. 2020. "Differences in Coronary Artery Disease Complexity and Associations with Mortality and Hospital Admissions Among First Nations and Non-First Nations Patients Undergoing Angiography: A Comparative Retrospective Matched-Cohort Study." *Canadian Medical Association Journal Open* 8, 4. <doi.org/10.9778/cmajo.20190171>.

Shaw, M., D. Dorling, D. Gordon and G.D. Smith. 1999. *The Widening Gap: Health Inequalities and Policy in Britain*. Bristol: Policy Press.

Sierra Club. 2021. "Tar Sands." Ottawa. <sierraclub.ca/en/tar-sands>.

Simpson, I.J., J.E. Marrero, S. Batterman et al. 2013. "Air Quality in the Industrial Heartland of Alberta, Canada and Potential Impacts on Human Health." *Atmospheric Environment* 81.

Smith, D. 1987. *The Everyday World as Problematic: A Feminist Sociology*. Toronto: University of Toronto Press.

St. Clair. 2020. "'Disbelieving Black Women to Death,' the Double Jeopardy: Racism and Sexism Affects Black Women's Access to and Quality of Care During Pregnancy, Birth, and Postpartum." Unpublished honours thesis, Omaha: University of Nebraska.

Tillett, J. 2010. "Global Health and Infant Mortality: Can We Learn from Other Systems?" *Journal of Perinatal and Neonatal Nursing* 24, 2.

Vaccaro, A., and R.M. Koob. 2019. "A Critical Understanding of LGBTQ Microaggressions: Toward a More Comprehensive Understanding." *Journal of Homosexuality* 66, 10.

Virchow, R. 1842. *Report to Her Majesty's Principal Secretary of State for the Home Department, from the Poor Law Commissioners on an Inquiry into the Sanitary Condition of the Labouring Population of Great Britain*. London: W. Clowes and Sons, for HMSO.

Weber, B. 2016. "Northwest Territories Report into Elder's Death Will Help Address Systemic Racism in Health Care." Canadian Press, March 1.

WHO (World Health Organization). 2020. "Director-General's Statement on IHR Emergency Committee on Novel Coronavirus (2019-nCoV)." Geneva.

___. 2011. "Ten Facts on Health Inequities and Their Causes." *Fact Files*, October.

Wier, L.M., C.T. Merrill, and A. Elixhauser. 2009. "Hospital Stays Among People Living in the Poorest Communities, 2006." *Health Care Cost and Utilization Project*, May.

Wijeyesinghe, C.L., P. Griffin, and B. Love. 1997. "Racism: Curriculum Design." In M. Adams, L. Bell and P. Griffin (eds.), *Teaching for Diversity and Social Justice: A Sourcebook*. New York: Routledge.

Wu, R.C., R.C. Nethery, B. Sabath et al. 2020. *Exposure to Air Pollution and COVID-19 Mortality in the United States*. Boston: Department of Biostatistics, Harvard T.H. Chan School of Public Health.

Yavari, P., M.C. Barroetavena, T.G. Hislop and C.D. Bajdik. 2010. "Breast Cancer Treatment and Ethnicity in British Columbia, Canada." *BioMedCentral Cancer* 10.

Yedjou, C.G., J.N Sims, L. Miele et al. 2019. "Health and Racial Disparity in Breast Cancer." *Advances in Experimental Medical Biology* 1152.

Yusoff, K. 2019. *A Billion Black Anthropocenes*. Minneapolis, MN: University of Minnesota Press.

Zbogar, V. 2014. "Brian Sinclair's Death Was a Homicide: But Call It Whatever You Want, Just Address the Discrimination." *Winnipeg Free Press,* June 16.

Zola, I.K. 1978. "Medicine as an Institution of Social Control." In J. Ehrenreich (ed.), *The Cultural Crisis of Modern Medicine*. New York: Monthly Review Press.

ABOUT THE AUTHORS

Jeffrey Ansloos (he/him) is the Canada Research Chair in Critical Studies in Indigenous Health and Social Action on Suicide and an assistant professor of Indigenous health and social policy at the University of Toronto. His work focuses on social and environmental dimensions of Indigenous health, Indigenous cultural, social and political theory, and ethics. He is nehiyaw (Cree) and English and is a member of Ochekwi-Sipi (Fisher River Cree Nation).

Jessica Antony (she/her) is a writer, editor and communication specialist. She has a master's degree in Media Studies from Concordia University and was co-editor of the sixth edition of *Power and Resistance: Critical Thinking About Canadian Social Issues* (2017). In addition to her writing and editing practice, she trains people in collaborative communication and teaches in the Department of Rhetoric at the University of Winnipeg.

Wayne Antony (he/him) is a co-publisher at Fernwood Publishing. He is also a founding member of the Canadian Centre for Policy Alternatives-Manitoba (CCPA-MB) and has been on the steering committee since its inception in 1996; he is also on the board of the Riverview Garden Society. Prior to the CCPA, he was active in Winnipeg with the Socialist Education Centre and Thin Ice. Wayne also taught as a sessional at the University of Winnipeg for eighteen years. He is co-author of three reports on the state of public services in Manitoba (for CCPA–MB), co-editor (with Dave Broad) of *Citizens or Consumers? Social Policy in a Market Society* (1999) and *Capitalism Rebooted: Work and Welfare in the New Economy* (2006) and co-editor (with Julie Guard) of *Bankruptcies and Bailouts* (2009).

Evan Bowness (he/him) is a postdoctoral researcher at the University of the Fraser Valley, located on the unceded territory of the Stó:lō peoples. He has a PhD from the Institute for Resources, Environment and Sustainability at the University of British Columbia and studies emerging agricultural technologies, urban food systems and food sovereignty. Evan is co-author (with Dana James) of *Growing and Eating Sustainably: Agroecology in Action* (2021).

Christopher Campbell (he/him) is a PhD candidate in education at the University of Manitoba focusing on 2SLGBTQ+-inclusive policy. He has worked as the research coordinator for the Every Teacher Project and on the RISE Project on 2SLGBTQ+-expansive teacher education, and he was a co-investigator on the second National Climate Survey on homophobia, biphobia, and transphobia in Canadian schools.

Wendy Chan (she/her) is a professor of sociology in the Department of Sociology and Anthropology at Simon Fraser University. Her research examines the intersections of race, racism, gender, immigration, crime and criminal justice. She has published six books, including *Hiding in Plain Sight: Immigrant Women and Domestic Violence* (2020), *Racialization, Crime and Criminal Justice in Canada* (2014), *Criminalizing Race, Criminalizing Poverty: Welfare Fraud Enforcement in Canada* (2007), and *Women, Murder and Justice* (2003).

Bryan Dale (he/him) is an assistant professor in the Department of Environment and Geography at Bishop's University in Sherbrooke, Quebec — the unceded territory of the Abenaki people. His research explores food sovereignty and agroecology in the Canadian context as well as the connections between these concepts and climate change mitigation efforts.

Karl Gardner (he/him) is an organizer, educator and a post-doctoral fellow in the Department of Political Science at University of Toronto. His activism focuses on migrant justice and Indigenous solidarity. His scholarship focuses on the politics of social movements, citizenship, migration, and municipal politics in Canada.

Paul Christopher Gray (he/him) is an assistant professor in the Department of Labour Studies at Brock University. His recent work has focused on public sector workers and precarious workers in the airline industry. He is currently writing an essay about the Foodsters United Campaign, a union drive by Toronto-based food couriers working in the gig economy.

Mark Hudson (he/him) is an associate professor in the Sociology and Criminology Department, and Coordinator of the Global Political Economy Program, at the University of Manitoba. He is most recently co-author of the books *Consumption* (2020) and *Neoliberal Lives: Work, Nature, Politics, and Health in the Contemporary United States* (2019). His current research is on fossil fuel and financial capital in Canada, as well as on unions in climate politics.

Dana James (she/her) is a PhD candidate and Vanier Scholar in the Institute for Resources, Environment and Sustainability at the University of British Columbia. As a settler scholar-activist of German, British and Dutch descent, her research explores agroecology, food sovereignty, and land and climate justice in settler-colonial contexts across North America (Turtle Island) and Latin America. Dana is co-author (with Evan Bowness) of *Growing and Eating Sustainably: Agroecology in Action* (2021).

Anna Johnson (she/her) is a PhD candidate in the Department of Sociology and Anthropology at the University of Guelph. She is deeply committed to indigenization and decolonization of the academy. Anna has two main areas of research: Indigenous justice and criminal justice responses to filicide and child homicide.

Murray Knuttila is professor emeritus at Brock University and the University of Regina. He is co-author (with Wendee Kubik) of three editions of *State Theories* (2000) and the author of *Paying for Masculinity: Boys, Men and the Patriarchal Dividend* (2016).

Robyn Maynard (she/her) is a writer and scholar based in Toronto. She is the award-winning and bestselling author of *Policing Black Lives: State Violence in Canada from Slavery to the Present* (2018) and the co-author of *Rehearsals for Living* (forthcoming, June 2022). Her work can be found at www.robynmaynard.com and she tweets at @PolicingBlack.

Elizabeth McGibbon (she/her) is a professor at St. Francis Xavier University. Her focus is on how public policy-created oppression "gets under the skin" to deepen disadvantage and create intergenerational health damage while enhancing privilege and wealth for some. Elizabeth is author of two editions of *Oppression: A Social Determinant of Health* (2021) and co-author (with Josephine Etowa) of *Anti-Racist Health Care Practice* (2009). Her current research includes a SSHRC-funded study applying institutional ethnography to study how Canadian public policy discourses stall progress in health equity.

Lindsay Ostridge (she/her) is a PhD candidate at the Institute of Feminist and Gender Studies, University of Ottawa. Her research focuses on analyzing current sexual violence prevention campaigns and policies. She has published in *Atlantis: Critical Studies in Gender, Culture & Social Justice* and the *Canadian Journal of Family and Youth*. She is supported in part by funding from the Social Sciences and Humanities Research Council.

Pamela Palmater is a Mi'kmaw lawyer, professor and Chair in Indigenous Governance at Ryerson University. She is the author of numerous articles as well as three books: *Beyond Blood* (2009); *Indigenous Nationhood* (2015); and *Warrior Life* (2020). Pam worked as a lawyer at the federal government for ten years in issues of treaties, claims, self-government, land and registration. She is a frequent contributor to the various media in Canada, as well as producing her blog, *Indigenous Nationhood*, the podcast *Warrior Life* and her YouTube channel, *Education for the Resistance*.

Tracey Peter (she/her) is a professor of sociology and criminology and the academic director of the Centre of Social Science Research and Policy at the University of Manitoba. She has been involved in numerous large-scale national studies involving youth and other marginalized populations (including as the principal investigator on the second National Climate Survey in Canadian schools). Her general research and publication interests include issues of homophobia, biphobia and transphobia/2SLGBTQI+-inclusive and expansive education; mental health and well-being; education and work; and research methods/social statistics.

James F. Popham (he/him) is an assistant professor with the department of criminology at Wilfrid Laurier University's Brantford Campus. James has a history of working with communities and their representatives to include their voices in policy decisions. His family is central in his purpose, and he hopes that his children will foster positive change wherever life takes them. James also researches the role digital technologies play in shaping individuals' sense of right and wrong, which influenced his contributions as a co-editor for the recent book *Critical Perspectives on Social Control and Social Regulation in Canada* (2020).

Tabitha Robin (she/her) is a mixed-ancestry Swampy Cree researcher, educator and writer. She is a PhD candidate at the University of Manitoba, studying Indigenous food sovereignty in the Faculty of Social Work and the Department of Native Studies. She spends much of her time on the land, working with her people, and learning traditional Cree food practices.

Stephanie Ross (she/her) is an associate professor and the director of the School of Labour Studies at McMaster University. Her research and teaching focuses on union politics, structure and strategy, public sector unions, unions' use of social movement-style campaigns and labour movement renewal. With Larry Savage, she has published five books, including *Building a Better World: An Introduction to the Labour Movement in Canada* (2015). She is the founding president of the Canadian Association for Work and Labour Studies.

Sarah-Louise Ruder (she/her) is a PhD student at the University of British Columbia's Institute for Resources, Environment and Sustainability. She lives and works on the traditional, ancestral, and unceded territories of the Musqueam, Squamish, and Tsleil-Waututh Nations. Her interdisciplinary research explores transitions to more sustainable, food-secure and equitable food systems and the politics of novel agrifood technologies.

Les Samuelson (he/him) is a retired associate professor of sociology at the University of Saskatchewan. His research interests were criminology and delinquency, Aboriginal justice, law and society and criminal justice policing.

Larry Savage (he/him) is a professor and Chair of the Department of Labour Studies at Brock University. His teaching and research are focused on collective bargaining, union strategy and labour politics. Savage has published seven books on the Canadian labour movement, including his latest co-edited book with Stephanie Ross, *Rethinking the Politics of Labour in Canada, 2nd edition* (2021).

Elizabeth Sheehy, LL.B, LL.M., LL.D. (honoris causa), O. Ont., F.R.S.C. and recipient of the Person's Award from the Governor General of Canada, is a professor emerita at the University of Ottawa, where she taught criminal law and sexual assault law over thirty-four years. She has acted as co-counsel for the Women's Legal Education and Action Fund (LEAF) and has participated in the legal work for many ground-breaking cases and criminal law reforms. Her books include an edited collection, *Sexual Assault in Canada: Law, Legal Practice and Women's Activism* (2012), and *Defending Battered Women on Trial: Lessons from the Transcripts* (2013). Her most recent article analyzes the sexual assault acquittal of an Ottawa police officer who illegally strip-searched a young Black Canadian woman, S.B.

Catherine Taylor (she/her) is the director of the RISE research program on 2SLGBTQI+-expansive education (uwinnipeg.ca/rise) and a senior scholar at the University of Winnipeg. As the lead researcher for RISE, she has led several large-scale research projects on 2SLGBTQI+-expansive education, including the first National Climate Survey, the Every Teacher Project, and the RISE Project, and she was a co-investigator on the second National Climate Survey.

A.J. Withers (they/them) is a long-time anti-poverty and disability justice organizer in Toronto. They hold a PhD from the School of Social Work at York University, where they are also adjunct faculty in Critical Disability Studies. A.J. is the author of *Fight to Win: Inside Poor People's Organizing* (2021), co-author (with Chris Chapman) of *A Violent History of Benevolence: Interlocking Oppression in the Moral Economies of Social Working* (2019) and author of *Disability Politics and Theory* (2012). Their doctoral research examines how governments work from the standpoint of homelessness activists in the Ontario Coalition Against Poverty.

ACKNOWLEDGEMENTS

Thanks to everyone who has been involved in this, the seventh, edition of *Power and Resistance*. To all the authors, those who are new to the project and those who revised chapters for this edition, our thanks for your insights, your hard work and your commitment to social justice in Canada. Our thanks as always to the team at Fernwood Publishing — making books is impossible without you: to Jess Herdman, Bev Rach and Debbie Mathers for production, to Jenn Harris for copy editing, and to Evan Marnoch for designing the cover. Finally, to everyone who struggles for social justice in Canada: without your dedication and selfless-ness this place would be worse off and it is your strength and commitment that inspires this book and us. We hope this book will play some small part in creating a society where everyone is valued and respected.

— Jessica Antony, Wayne Antony and Les Samuelson

INDEX